CLASSICS UK

THE TRANS FORMERS

VOLUME THREE

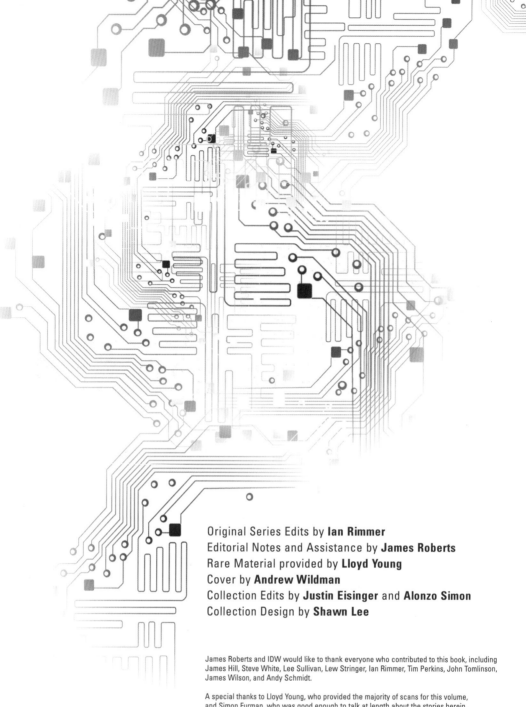

Original Series Edits by **Ian Rimmer**
Editorial Notes and Assistance by **James Roberts**
Rare Material provided by **Lloyd Young**
Cover by **Andrew Wildman**
Collection Edits by **Justin Eisinger** and **Alonzo Simon**
Collection Design by **Shawn Lee**

James Roberts and IDW would like to thank everyone who contributed to this book, including James Hill, Steve White, Lee Sullivan, Lew Stringer, Ian Rimmer, Tim Perkins, John Tomlinson, James Wilson, and Andy Schmidt.

A special thanks to Lloyd Young, who provided the majority of scans for this volume, and Simon Furman, who was good enough to talk at length about the stories herein.

Special thanks to Hasbro's Aaron Archer, Jerry Jivoin, Michael Verret, Ed Lane, Joe Furfaro, Jos Huxley, Andy Schmidt, Heather Hopkins, and Michael Kelly for their invaluable assistance.

IDW founded by Ted Adams, Alex Garner, Kris Oprisko, and Robbie Robbins | International Rights Representative, Christine Meyer: christine@gfloystudio.com

ISBN: 978-1-61377-231-7   15 14 13 12   1 2 3 4

Licensed By:

Ted Adams, CEO & Publisher
Greg Goldstein, President & COO
Robbie Robbins, EVP/Sr. Graphic Artist
Chris Ryall, Chief Creative Officer/Editor-in-Chief
Matthew Ruzicka, CPA, Chief Financial Officer
Alan Payne, VP of Sales

Become our fan on Facebook **facebook.com/idwpublishing**
Follow us on Twitter **@idwpublishing**
Check us out on YouTube **youtube.com/idwpublishing**
www.IDWPUBLISHING.com

Originally published by Marvel UK as THE TRANSFORMERS Issues #78–112.

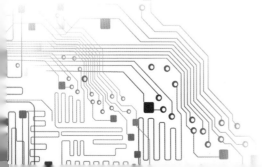

ep·ic (pk)
adj.
1. Of, constituting, having to do with, or suggestive of a literary epic
2. Surpassing the usual or ordinary, particularly in scope or size
3. Heroic and impressive in quality
4. A story in *Transformers* (UK), at least six issues in length, usually involving Galvatron and/or time travel

I have *Transformers UK* to thank for enriching my vocabulary. Before Simon Furman's erudite scripts and breathless editorial copy, I was unfamiliar with words such as "milestone," "inimitable," "penultimate," and "progenitor." At first I didn't know what it meant to "rend" something "asunder," nor did I appreciate fully the significance of delivering a "coup de grace." When something happened "in one fell swoop," I had to work out what exactly that entailed. To this day I remain unsure precisely what's involved when one "reaps the whirlwind."

Strange as it may seem, I don't recall having come across the word "epic" before; or if I had, it hadn't been used as a word used to describe an extra long, extra exciting Transformers story.

Before we go further, let's distinguish a *TFUK* epic from a mere *TFUK* story arc. The former tended to be a multi-part story with a single title, whereas the latter was a series of loosely interconnected stories with multiple titles. There are exceptions to the rule: "Wanted: Galvatron, Dead or Alive" is considered an old school epic even though the story unfolds as a series of two-parters, while the determinedly epic "Matrix Quest," although promoted (on the covers of the US comic at least) under a banner title, is episodic in nature and feels more like a story arc. Confused yet?

Let's go back to the beginning for some clarity. "Target: 2006" (*TFUK* issues #78–88) isn't just the first epic; it's the epic against which all subsequent epics were measured. The four-part "Dinobot Hunt" (issues #47–50) and "In The National Interest" (issues #74–77) both approached epic status, but lacked the scope and sheer size to qualify. With "Target," Furman perfected the formula: high page-count, large cast, a few deaths or apparent deaths, shocking

revelations, and events that would reverberate across later issues.

I started reading *TFUK* with issue #113, which just so happened to coincide with the start of the aforementioned "Wanted" saga. A few issues in and Autobots were travelling back in time, a robotic bounty hunter named Death's Head was blowing Bumblebee to smithereens, and Ultra Magnus was tearing into Galvatron while an entire forest blazed around them— and I thought all that was the norm; I thought all *TFUK* stories were like that. This changed with issue #121, which reprinted a US story about a car thief who uses a giant alien spanner to extort money.

"The Legacy of Unicron" (issues #146–151) was the first story since "Target: 2006" to use the same title for more than two issues; it also kick-started the *TFUK* tradition of beginning the New Year with a British story set 20 years ahead of the present day (encouraging the editorial team to coin a new term: "future epics"). "Legacy" was shorter, tighter, and more focused than "Wanted," but— paradoxically—much larger in scope: for arguably the first time (in the comic, at least), the lives of all the Autobots and Decepticons were threatened.

"Space Pirates" followed (issues #183–188), seemingly cementing the "six issue epic" format and again dealing with a threat to the entire Cybertronian race (this time from the Quintessons). By now, 70 issues in, I was intimately familiar with the language of *TFUK*—not just the words used in the scripts, but the editorial style and tone of the comic itself. I knew what constituted an epic; and I knew that their impending arrival was usually trailed on the letters page, then on the "TransFormation" page.

A simple fact: I have never, *ever* been more excited about a story— any story, in any medium—than I have about "Time Wars" (issues #199–205). Not only was this a seven-part story, not only did it encompass issue #200, but it promised to conclude The Galvatron Saga—the overarching UK storyline that had begun two and a half years earlier, before I was a Transformers fan. I think time itself actually slowed down between issues #198 and 199.

"Time Wars" marked the end of the "Target: 2006" style *TFUK* mega-story. With issue #213, in the face of falling sales, the comic switched

format: the 11-page lead strip was split in two, with original British material running to only five (black and white) pages.

Furman's immediate response was to write the first epic of the black and white era. "Aspects of Evil" ran for five issues and focused on Megatron, Shockwave, Galvatron, Scorponok, and finally Unicron. But while "Aspects" strove valiantly to make the most of the new five-page format, the story's climax served to reinforce its limitations: squeezing "the third coming of Unicron" into five pages made this reader realize that the era of old-school *TFUK* epics was over.

Furman wrote two more black and white epics: "Perchance to Dream" (issues #255–260) and the so-called Dark Rodimus Saga (#251–254). The latter is actually two stories, "The Void" and "White Fire," and I class it as an epic in the knowledge that I'm undermining my earlier definition; but by being the last *TFUK* story to feature the future cast, it seems to bring down the curtain on the run of UK stories begun by "Target: 2006," way back in issue #78.

When I look back over my experiences as a *TFUK* reader, the big story moments—the moments that ensured *TFUK* was the last thing I read at night and the first thing I read in the morning—all happened during epics: Death's Head crushing Shockwave's brain module; the first telling of the origin of the Transformers; the arrival of Metroplex; Galvatron's eyeball being sucked from its socket by a space/time rift (yeah, you read that right). Okay, so Megatron crushing Nightstick to death and decapitating Cyclonus happened in a one-issue story, but that event precipitated "Time Wars," so there.

In the final analysis, the *TFUK* epics were the lifeblood of the title. They weren't necessarily the best stories, but they were the ones you remembered, and the ones you looked forward to the most. They adrenalized *TFUK* and reminded readers of the scope and grandeur of the Transformers Universe. Let's face it—it's probably because of "Target: 2006" or "The Legacy of Unicron" or "Time Wars" that you're still here, reading this foreword, reading this book, 21 years after *TFUK* ended. How's that for reaping the whirlwind?

James Roberts
May 2012

TRANSFORMERS UK–THE BASICS

Between September 1984 and January 1992, Marvel UK published 332 issues of *Transformers.* The large format comic magazine launched as a part-color, part-black and white biweekly before becoming a full-color weekly with issue #27. With issue #309 it reverted to biweekly.

Every issue ran to 24 pages, with the exception of issues #1–26, which were 32 pages, and the occasional bumper-sized 28-page issue.

The comic typically contained 11 pages of *Transformers* comic strip, consisting of either an American reprint or all-new British material. From issue #213 until issue #289 the comic printed a six-page U.S. strip and a five-page UK strip side by side. The last 40 or so issues contained 10 or 11 pages of American strip.

Bulking out each issue was a five- or six-page back-up strip, sourced from Marvel US and usually featuring either robotic characters such as Machine Man or Iron Man, or another toy tie-in such as G.I. JOE (initially marketed as Action Force in the UK) or Visionaries. Early issues featured extra comic strips and features, the latter invariably robot-related. Humor strips featured throughout the title's run, most of them created by artist and writer Lew Stringer.

Although the comic was simply called *Transformers,* to avoid confusion with its American equivalent the articles that follow refer to it as either *Transformers UK* or *TFUK.*

A COMPLETE HISTORY OF *TRANSFORMERS UK*

PART 3: ENTER GALVATRON

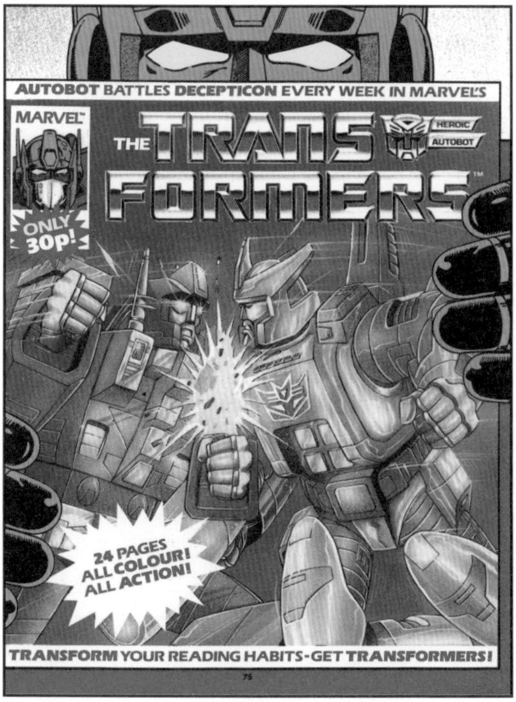
AUTOBOT BATTLES DECEPTICON EVERY WEEK IN MARVEL'S
MARVEL
THE TRANSFORMERS
HEROIC AUTOBOT
ONLY 30P!
24 PAGES ALL COLOUR! ALL ACTION!
TRANSFORM YOUR READING HABITS-GET TRANSFORMERS!

This advert appeared only once, in the *Transformers: The Movie* winter special.

This volume covers issues #78–112 of the British *Transformers* comic—a relatively brief period in the seven-year lifespan of *TFUK,* but one that is significant for several reasons. Over the course of these 35 issues, longstanding editor Ian Rimmer left (to be replaced by writer and former assistant editor Simon Furman), *Transformers: The Movie* was released in British cinemas, and hand-painted artwork was dropped in favor of "mechanical" coloring.

Meanwhile, in the stories themselves, readers were introduced to the New Leaders (Galvatron and Ultra Magnus), as well as the Wreckers and a host of other soon-to-be-iconic characters such as Hot Rod, Kup, and Cyclonus. Anything else? Oh yes, Optimus Prime and Megatron died.

BEYOND YOUR WILDEST IMAGINATION

Rimmer, Furman, and art director John Tomlinson—the comic's core editorial team—first heard about *Transformers: The Movie* early in 1986, when Hasbro UK gave them a sneak preview of the script (back when the film was still set in 2006, not 2005). Given that Transformers was, by then, a *bona fide* pop culture phenomenon, it's not surprising that the *TFUK* team thought the film would do well at the box office.

"We had high hopes for the Movie," Furman confirms. "We just thought it was going to be number one in cinemas. I was always too old to really appreciate the animated series—I liked it, I thought it was fine, but it felt very kiddie and ridiculous in places. But the animated Movie was spectacular. It was before I'd been exposed to manga or anything like that, and I think we were all of us just blown away by it. We thought 'this is it—it's arrived—we're gonna have a big blockbuster film.'"

TFUK was already selling phenomenally well on the back of the stories and the toys; had the Movie performed as well as expected, one can only imagine how many more tens of thousands of copies it would have sold. "Well we gained readers anyway," Furman points out. "The fact that the Movie came and went without a ripple was a surprise to us—I really don't know why it bombed—but I think those who did see it absolutely loved it; and back in those days [the idea that young cinemagoers would be inspired to buy tie-in comics] actually worked: the kids who liked the film bought *TFUK* especially because we

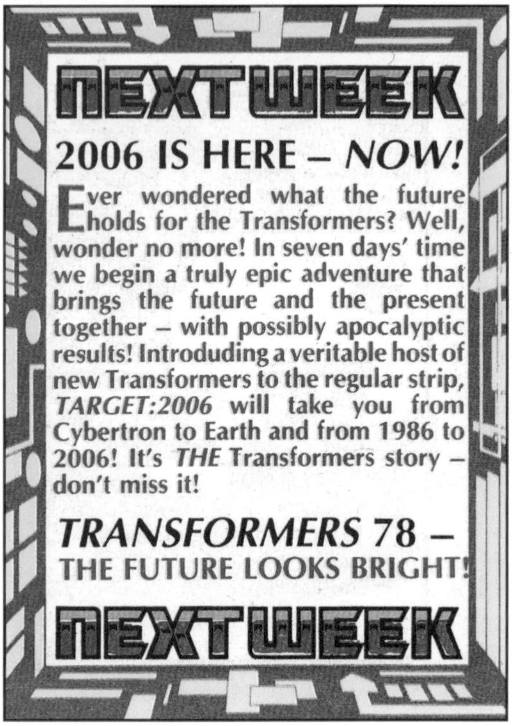

NEXT WEEK

2006 IS HERE – *NOW!*

Ever wondered what the future holds for the Transformers? Well, wonder no more! In seven days' time we begin a truly epic adventure that brings the future and the present together – with possibly apocalyptic results! Introduding a veritable host of new Transformers to the regular strip, *TARGET:2006* will take you from Cybertron to Earth and from 1986 to 2006! It's *THE* Transformers story – don't miss it!

TRANSFORMERS 78 –
THE FUTURE LOOKS BRIGHT!

NEXT WEEK

This "Next Week" box appeared in issue #77.

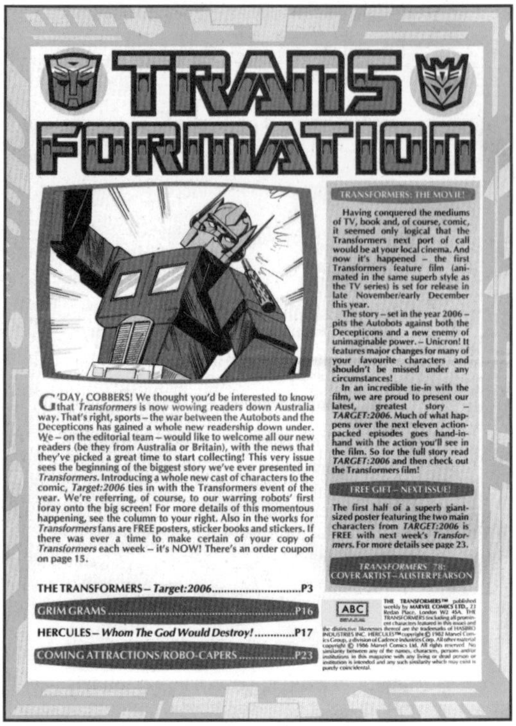

TRANS FORMATION

G'DAY, COBBERS! We thought you'd be interested to know that *Transformers* is now wowing readers down Australia way. That's right, sports – the war between the Autobots and the Decepticons has gained a whole new readership down under. We – on the editorial team – would like to welcome all our new readers (be they from Australia or Britain), with the news that they've picked a great time to start collecting! This very issue sees the beginning of the biggest story we've ever presented in *Transformers*. Introducing a whole new cast of characters to the comic, *Target:2006* ties in with the Transformers event of the year. We're referring, of course, to our warring robots' first foray onto the big screen! For more details of this momentous happening, see the column to your right. Also in the works for *Transformers* fans are FREE posters, sticker books and stickers. If there was ever a time to make certain of your copy of *Transformers* each week – it's NOW! There's an order coupon on page 15.

THE TRANSFORMERS – *Target:2006*............P3
GRIM GRAMS............P16
HERCULES – *Whom The God Would Destroy!*............P17
COMING ATTRACTIONS/ROBO-CAPERS............P23

TRANSFORMERS: THE MOVIE!

Having conquered the mediums of TV, book and, of course, comic, it seemed only logical that the Transformers next port of call would be at your local cinema. And now it's happened – the first Transformers feature film (animated in the same superb style as the TV series) is set for release in late November/early December this year.

The story – set in the year 2006 – pits the Autobots against both the Decepticons and a new enemy of unimaginable power. – Unicron! It features major changes for many of your favourite characters and shouldn't be missed under any circumstances!

In an incredible tie-in with the film, we are proud to present our latest, greatest story – *TARGET:2006*. Much of what happens over the next eleven action-packed episodes goes hand-in-hand with the action you'll see in the film. So for the full story read *TARGET:2006* and then check out the Transformers film!

FREE GIFT – NEXT ISSUE!

The first half of a superb giant-sized poster featuring the two main characters from *TARGET:2006* is FREE with next week's *Transformers*. For more details see page 23.

TRANSFORMERS 78:
COVER ARTIST – ALISTER PEARSON

ABC

THE TRANSFORMERS™ published weekly by MARVEL COMICS LTD., 23 Redan Place, London W2 4SA. THE TRANSFORMERS (including all prominent characters featured in this issue) and the distinctive likenesses thereof are the trademarks of HASBRO INDUSTRIES INC. HERCULES™ copyright © 1982 Marvel Comics Group, a division of Cadence Industries Corp. All other material copyright © 1986 Marvel Comics Ltd. All rights reserved. No similarity between any of the names, characters, persons and/or institutions in this magazine with any living or dead person or institution is intended and any such similarity which may exist is purely coincidental.

The "TransFormation" page from issue #78.

were featuring Movie characters, and that was one reason for bringing back Galvatron [in early 1987]."

Irrespective of its merits as entertainment, the Movie was effectively a multi-million dollar advert for both the toys and, by extension, the comic—and from Marvel UK's perspective it made sense to promote it heavily within the pages of *TFUK* via the editorial pages and the strips themselves. The sidebar in issue #71's "TransFormation" page hinted at things to come: "We're working right now on what is quite simply the biggest Transformers story ever! We'll just mention—for the moment—that it features a character called Ultra Magnus, another called Galvatron, and ties in with a certain feature film that'll be in your local cinema in the not too distant *future*!"

"Target: 2006" kicked off in issue #78 and ran for an unprecedented 11 weeks, reaching its conclusion in mid-November, when the Movie was originally expected to premiere in the UK (it was put back to December 12th—closer to school holidays).

"We wanted to run a long UK story to build up a backlog of US material," says Rimmer when asked why "Target: 2006" was so very long. "I think we got to a stage when we were using US material almost as soon as it had been printed in the States, so we needed additional breathing space. Also, we might have been trying to manipulate things so that certain US stories appeared in certain UK issues, even to the extent of trying to know what would be available to us for issue #100."

As Furman explains elsewhere in this volume, the purpose of "Target: 2006" was to introduce the New Leaders first and promote the Movie second. Realizing they were about to print the greatest Transformers story to date, and with the Movie just around the corner, *TFUK* organized a run of free gifts and special features: issues #79 and #80 each came with half of a huge Magnus/Galvatron poster painted by Robin Smith, and UK-exclusive fact files on both characters were published in issues #81 and #87. Issue #81 came bagged with a *Secret Wars* sticker book from Panini (a packet of stickers followed in issue #82). Best of all—from a fan's perspective—was issue #83's "The Middle Years," a full-page text piece by Furman that explained what had happened on Cybertron in the four million years since the departure of the Ark. As with the Autobot, Decepticon, and human "Who's Whos" and the three "Robot War" features, "The Middle Years" was proof that *TFUK* cared about the stories it was telling. It was, by all accounts, a great time to be both a fan and a creator of *Transformers* comics.

"Yeah," says Furman. "I think everybody [in the editorial team] at this stage was just enjoying it. Just gradually over the previous story arc we were starting to think a little grander: from 'Dinobot Hunt' to the interconnected 'Devastation Derby/Special Teams' storyline, it was like we were finding our feet and our confidence and thinking we can do these bigger storylines. And the stories themselves seemed to have a life of their own: we never had to think particularly hard about the next batch because we were on a roll. We were feeling much more unshackled at this point; we knew we kept having to go back [to the US reprints] but we weren't as awed by it anymore. We just thought 'let's do our own thing and we'll put the pieces where they need to be and we'll find out what Bob's gonna do next.' And [being asked to introduce the New Leaders] felt like the biggest invitation to do our own big storyline because we were going to use characters without having to

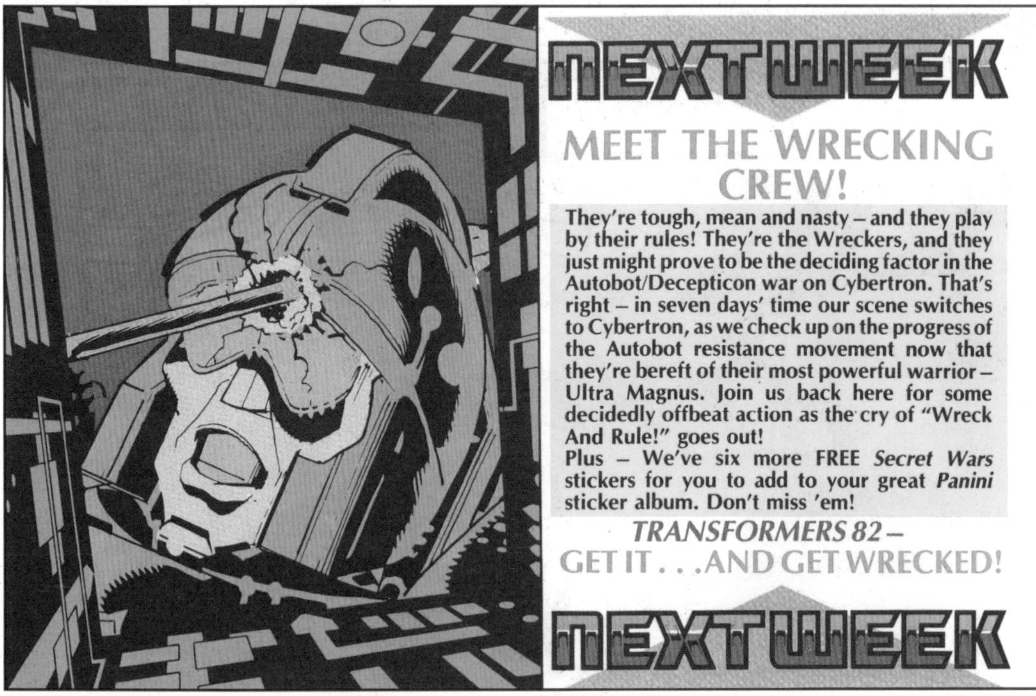
NEXT WEEK
MEET THE WRECKING CREW!
They're tough, mean and nasty – and they play by their rules! They're the Wreckers, and they just might prove to be the deciding factor in the Autobot/Decepticon war on Cybertron. That's right – in seven days' time our scene switches to Cybertron, as we check up on the progress of the Autobot resistance movement now that they're bereft of their most powerful warrior – Ultra Magnus. Join us back here for some decidedly offbeat action as the cry of "Wreck And Rule!" goes out!
Plus – We've six more FREE Secret Wars stickers for you to add to your great Panini sticker album. Don't miss 'em!
TRANSFORMERS 82 –
GET IT . . . AND GET WRECKED!
NEXT WEEK

Issue #81's "Next Week" feature marks the first mention of The Wreckers.

worry about what the Americans were going to do with them.

"And when you read the stories from this era you can see we were full of ideas: we were young and bright and we wanted just to throw everything at it. So yeah, I think we were having a good time, and I think it translated to the audience as well."

Indeed, the comic was so popular that Furman was invited to appear on the first series of *Get Fresh*, a Saturday and Sunday morning kids' TV show set on a spaceship and broadcast over the summer months. He made his TV debut on a Sunday in early October 1986.

"They dragged me off to Carlisle in Cumbria to go on Border TV. Geoff [Senior] lived in Thursby [in south Carlisle] so I stayed with him and then we went on to the studio the next day. They possibly asked for Ian and he just said 'I don't want to do this!' Does footage of the interview exist? Yes, I have it on video... somewhere."

"All I can suggest," says Rimmer when asked why Furman appeared on TV and not him, "is that perhaps the TV people wanted to talk about future storylines, and I figured Simon would be a better bet than me for that. Also, he's a lot more 'tele-genic' than me..!"

Issue #84's "TransFormation" page announced the release of the comic adaptation of *Transformers: The Movie*, a reprint of the US mini-series. The 76-page winter special would cost a whopping £1.45, nearly five times the cost of the weekly comic and twice the price of the last *Collected Comics*. Also promised for late November was the first of the two *Transformers Universe* specials, which together would feature "fact files on just about every Transformer you've come across (and a few besides!)." Five weeks later, issue #89's "TransFormation" page blamed "unforeseen circumstances" for the cancellation of said specials; instead, the profiles would be serialized in *TFUK* "in weekly segments (as space permits)" called *Transformers A to Z*. Profiles on Air Raid and Astrotrain appeared in issue #89, while Wildrider and Windcharger–the last in the series–would appear four years later, in issue #290.

COLOR SEPARATION

Issue #88 brought the curtain down on "Target: 2006" but also signaled another ending: it was the last *Transformers* strip to be hand-painted. The decision to dispense with the services of the likes of Gina Hart, Steve Whitaker, John Burns, and Tony Jozwiak was taken by Marvel UK managing director Robert Sutherland on the simple grounds that the alternative–color separation–was cheaper.

The decision was greeted with dismay by the *TFUK* editorial team, particularly Rimmer: "Whenever they can, management will try to find some way to cut costs, so eventually it was insisted upon that all original material was going to be colored mechanically [i.e. color-separated]. I was always a champion of the full color artwork—those early issues of *TFUK* had some fantastic color work—and we resisted the change as long as we could. It was Robert's decision to switch that ultimately led to a big dispute between us. He may also have had some pressure from Marvel US, because I got the impression they weren't keen on our painted strips. When we had [one time editor-in-chief] Tom DeFalco stationed at Marvel UK for a period, he received a package from Marvel US one day. I happened to be close by when he opened it—and a bunch of coloured wax crayons fell out, along with a note to the effect that he might need those while he was with us..."

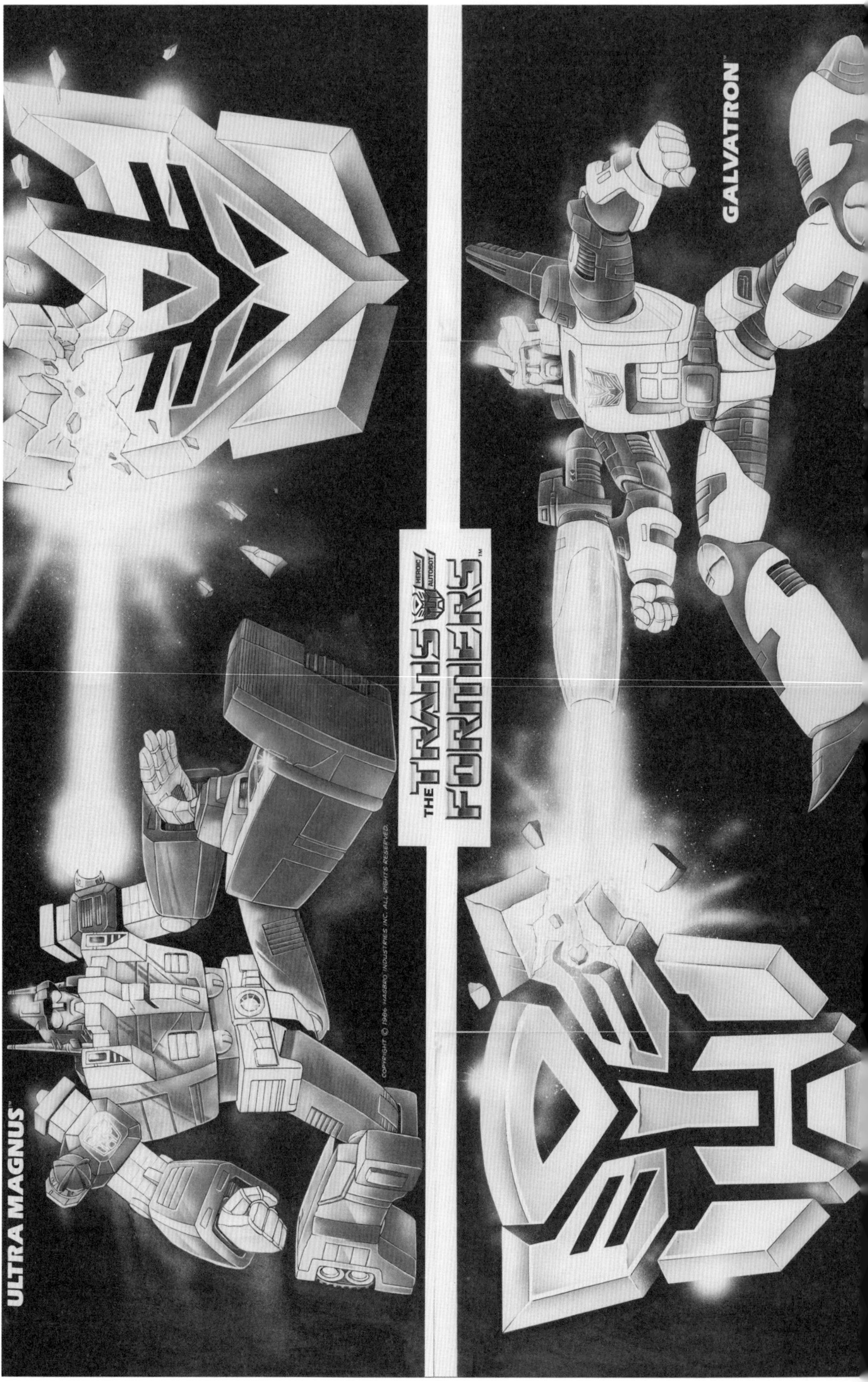
ULTRA MAGNUS™
GALVATRON™
THE TRANSFORMERS™
HEROIC AUTOBOT
COPYRIGHT © 1986 HASBRO INDUSTRIES INC. ALL RIGHTS RESERVED.

Robin Smith's hand-painted two-part New Leaders poster was given away in issues #79–80.

"I remember we were incredibly disappointed when 'color-sepping' took over from the hand-painted strips," agrees Tomlinson. "It was purely a cost-cutting measure. At the time we felt we were somehow lowering the quality of the strips and cheapening the comic, but in the hands of certain colorists, particularly Steve White and Nick Abadzis, color-sepping soon became an art form in itself and they achieved some quite spectacular results. We certainly didn't lose any readers in the switch."

The cover artwork continued to be hand-painted for the time being—even the reprinted US covers were spruced up in this fashion, with Robin Bouttell doing the honors. "Enlarging the US covers might well have given rise to the coloring looking unsatisfactory," says Rimmer when asked why the artwork was touched up. "And the cover image is, after all, an advert for the title in the shops, so it's got to be as good as you can make it. Hope my memory isn't playing tricks, but I think John [Tomlinson] was pushing for us to try something different with the covers, so it was probably his idea to use the black and white image from the US cover, resize that, then have it colored separately. It may well have been initially just an experiment, but Robin turned in such good work that we continued with it when we could justify it."

Although they were recolored, the US covers tended to be re-used no matter what. "Yeah, we occasionally dropped a US cover if we didn't like it and felt we could produce something better, but using them was the norm, and expected."

WHITE, KING OF COLORS

In the post-hand-painted era, self-described "lowly color separator" Steve White was king: he colored virtually every British TFUK strip from "The Gift" in issue #93 to "The Fall and Rise of the Decepticon Empire" in issues #213 and #214, and was even responsible for adding color to the late-period black and white strips such as "Way of the Wolf!" when they were reprinted in the 1991 Transformers Annual. His bold, clean, striking colors gave each strip added punch and made him a household name among TFUK readers.

White began working for Marvel UK "accidentally… it was a case of right place, right time. A school friend of mine, Gary "Glib" Gilbert [one-time TFUK designer and letterer] landed a job at Marvel UK in February 1986. We had been in the same art class and had drawn comics together. One Saturday I asked him if there were any jobs going and he called me on the Monday night to say there was indeed a vacancy. So I called up on the Tuesday, was offered an interview the following day, ran around assembling a portfolio that night and was offered the job on the Wednesday."

As a child growing up in '70s Britain, White was a fan of the extremely violent weekly anthology comic, Action. "Around this time I began to take note of artists I liked. Then Star Wars arrived and I began drawing lots of spaceships and aliens. 2000 AD came out shortly after although I picked it up largely

because of Flesh—a dinosaur comic strip! It was heaven! I began copying Ramon Sola's style but was also taken with Dave Gibbons, Mike McMahon, Brian Bolland, and especially Kev O'Neill. His style blew me away."

Besides coloring, White turned his hand to editing, writing, and illustrating. "I was never a very confident artist so I never expected to amount to anything. Editing seemed to be a compromise, really, and that only came about because of the job at Marvel UK. I landed an assistant editor job in the Junior Department working on comics like Acorn Green and started to do a bit of freelance coloring on Care Bears and similar kids' titles. Then one day I was summoned to the Boys Action Department and was asked about coloring Transformers as it was switching from hand-painted to mechanical colors. It was the last holdout for hand coloring—pretty much everything else was being mechanically colored by that point."

White became renowned for his use of rich tones and contrast. "I think John Higgins enters the picture here," he says. "He did amazing things with mechanical colors on Watchmen and I had gotten to know him because of his work on Transformers. He was very encouraging and helped me push the envelope; trying to go for metallic effects on the robots, that sort of thing. I used to love using 'double attack' lighting—using two different light sources to create interesting lighting effects. I also fell under the spell of European coloring."

But before White made his debut in issue #93 it was time for TFUK to catch up on the American storyline. Issues #89–92 reprinted "Aerialbots Over America!" and "Heavy Traffic!" Some six months after they'd appeared in a dream sequence in the UK story "Second Generation!", the Special Teams were finally appearing "in the flesh."

EXIT FURMAN

In November 1986 assistant editor Simon Furman left TFUK to become editor of the upcoming ThunderCats comic. Although he continued to write scripts for TFUK in a freelance capacity, he no longer wrote the editorial copy or answered letters. "Around the time 'Target: 2006' wrapped up I wasn't in the Transformers office that much," he recalls. "I don't think I was replaced [as assistant editor]. My memory may be faulty, but I think Ian just was editor. I guess he was Grimlock for a while."

Editorial upheavals or not, there was a still a weekly comic to put out. Issue #89's "TransFormation" page plugged the "giant-sized story scheduled for our landmark issue #100," hinting that it would explain where Optimus, Ratchet, and Prowl disappeared to during "Target: 2006." The story received another plug in a "Grim Grams" that was bursting with teasers about the future: Grimlock opines that the Autobots are too dependent on Optimus (foreshadowing "Prey!"), hints that he may return to Cybertron (as happens in "…The Harder They Die!") and even suggests that he could succeed Prime as leader (which he would do six months hence, in issue #112's US reprint "King of the Hill!"). Indeed, the story hints are so plentiful one is tempted to

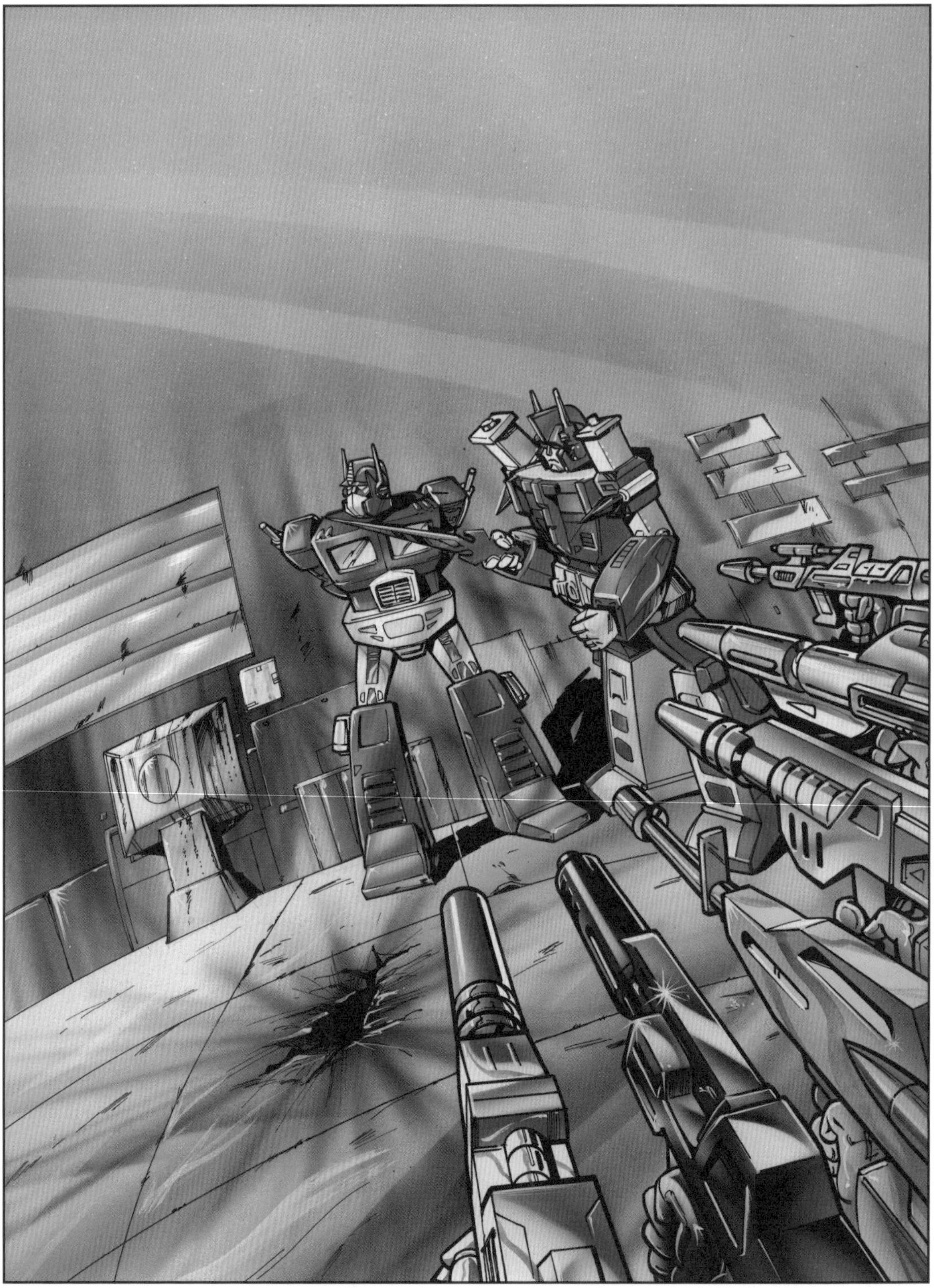

Lee Sullivan's cover for issue #99, presented without text for the first time.

think that Furman was still Grimlock at this stage. Perhaps it was his farewell issue…

The next few issues, published in the lead up to the release of *Transformers: The Movie*, featured an array of *Movie*-related competitions, adverts and features: issue #90 offered readers a chance to win 20 giant-sized *Movie* posters; issue #91 featured a review of the *Movie* by Grimlock (who unsurprisingly concluded that the film was "utterly, utterly brilliant!"); and issue #92 featured adverts for the *Movie* poster magazine and the *Movie* soundtrack. The other notable aspect of issue #92 was the cover, which was drawn by newcomer Lee Sullivan. Sullivan would go on to become one of the most popular *Transformers* artists, rivaling Geoff Senior and Andy Wildman.

COVER STAR

Sullivan's big break had come about via his friendship with sometime *TFUK* artist John Higgins. "I met John in 1985, through my local art retailer," he recalls. "He was looking for someone to letter or color a strip he was producing for a music magazine. I did some coloring for him and he kindly let me tag along with him on a visit to Marvel UK, where he was dropping off some work. Ian and Simon took a look at my stuff and Ian gave me a color cover [issue #92] to work on. It was a bit too dark and doomy for the production team!"

Sullivan had always wanted to work in comics, having been an avid collector of *TV Comic, Eagle, TV21,* and *Countdown,* plus Marvel US reprint titles and *Doctor Who Weekly/Monthly.* "But I had no idea how to break into comics so I [enrolled in] a technical and wildlife illustration course. I got a job as a designer/illustrator for British Aerospace Guided Weapons division, then freelanced in advertising illustration. When *Doctor Who Weekly* arrived on the scene I started producing samples for it, but when I found out what the page rate was (from David Lloyd, whom I met at a Who convention) I realized I wasn't quick enough at that stage to earn a living from comics. So I forgot about comics for a while…"

Lee Sullivan's cover for issue #111, presented without text for the first time.

Sullivan admits that when he was offered issue #92 he was unfamiliar with the toys or the comic. "I'd never heard of Transformers! I was in my late twenties and Transformers was a phenomenon for young kids at the time. I also couldn't understand them at all—how they changed sizes, why they transformed. But the toys were marvelous—I bought one, Hot Rod, and really admired the construction of them."

Sullivan's covers were so bright and shiny they practically gleamed; for someone who was new to the game, he seemed eager to push the envelope. "Both Ian and Simon were very easy editors to work for," he says when asked whether he was encouraged to experiment. "They were confident enough to let artists get on with it, but clear about what wasn't working when they saw it. I was a specialist in line and airbrush before going into comics, and the disciplines combined fairly naturally for the cover work. I think I was only reined in once, on issue #111, and that was

Lee Sullivan's first cover for *TFUK* (issue #92), presented without text for the first time.

because I'd picked up on John Higgins' technique of using airbrush or toothbrush spatter to quickly texture a piece. That didn't find favor, probably because of the inadequacies of color printing at the time. I perfected a smooth, bold style which was definitely my own. I've never had a subtle color palette!"

As for art references, Lee relied on "lots of photocopies of box art and the Hasbro style guides for the animation versions, particularly from the Movie, which came out around then. Those style guides were later adapted and incorporated into the *Transformers Universe* book. I also collected store catalogs that featured the toys and ripped out the pages and bundled all of that reference into one file. It was just impossible to work out what any given character looked like though, because all the sources were so different. The animated versions were mostly what we used, and for shorthand I basically looked at—and ripped off—everything everyone else was drawing."

APPROACHING 100

The US reprints took a break in issue #93, making way for a special Christmas story, "The Gift," by James Hill (script), Martin Griffiths (pencils), and Tim Perkins (inks). 12 months earlier, with issue #41, *TFUK* had undergone a festive redesign, with snow and holly added to the editorial pages; the editorial team evidently thought they could do better, because issue #93's "TransFormation" page, complete with the Transformers logo as a giant Christmas pudding, was probably the single most Christmassy page ever printed anywhere.

Issue #94 was the New Year issue, kicking off 1987 with a reprint of the US story "Decepticon Graffiti!" For the first time the cover box gave the comic's price in US and Canadian dollars, reflecting the fact that

TFUK was now being distributed in comic shops on the other side of the Atlantic.

"A lot of Marvel UK titles were already distributed in Australia," recalls Rimmer. "But it was a different story with distribution to the States. There was a tremendous demand for Transformers material out there following *The Movie*, and the powers that be wanted to try and tap into that market. Any decisions about international distribution, though, were not editorial ones." The comic was on sale in the US and Canada for $1.25 and $1.75 respectively, but after six weeks dropped to $1.00 and $1.50—the same as most newsstand comics.

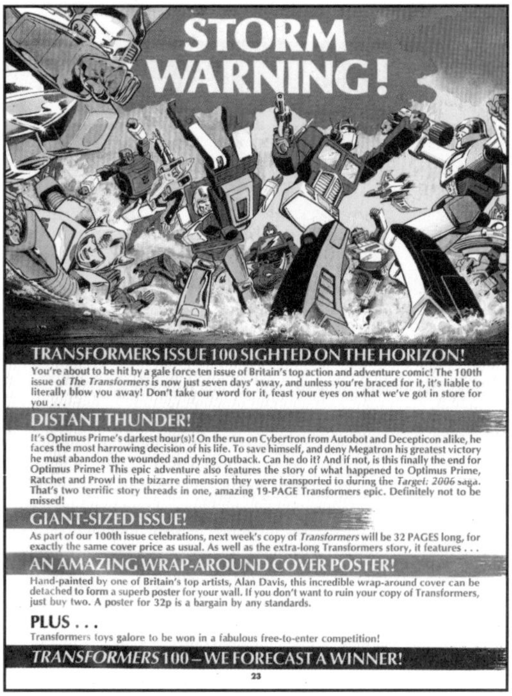
STORM WARNING!

TRANSFORMERS ISSUE 100 SIGHTED ON THE HORIZON!

You're about to be hit by a gale force ten issue of Britain's top action and adventure comic! The 100th issue of *The Transformers* is now just seven days' away, and unless you're braced for it, it's liable to literally blow you away! Don't take our word for it, feast your eyes on what we've got in store for you . . .

DISTANT THUNDER!

It's Optimus Prime's darkest hour(s)! On the run on Cybertron from Autobot and Decepticon alike, he faces the most harrowing decision of his life. To save himself, and deny Megatron his greatest victory he must abandon the wounded and dying Outback. Can he do it? And if not, is this finally the end for Optimus Prime? This epic adventure also features the story of what happened to Optimus Prime, Ratchet and Prowl in the bizarre dimension they were transported to during the *Target: 2006* saga. That's two terrific story threads in one, amazing 19-PAGE Transformers epic. Definitely not to be missed!

GIANT-SIZED ISSUE!

As part of our 100th issue celebrations, next week's copy of *Transformers* will be 32 PAGES long, for exactly the same cover price as usual. As well as the extra-long Transformers story, it features . . .

AN AMAZING WRAP-AROUND COVER POSTER!

Hand-painted by one of Britain's top artists, Alan Davis, this incredible wrap-around cover can be detached to form a superb poster for your wall. If you don't want to ruin your copy of Transformers, just buy two. A poster for 32p is a bargain by any standards.

PLUS . . .

Transformers toys galore to be won in a fabulous free-to-enter competition!

TRANSFORMERS 100 – WE FORECAST A WINNER!

23

Issue #99's special "Next Week" feature.

After "Decepticon Graffiti!" came the next batch of British stories: issue #96 kicked off a nine-issue "Return to Cybertron" arc for Optimus Prime and Megatron—a last hurrah for the two iconic characters before they were (sort of) killed off. With issue #97 the cover price increased from 30p to 32p: the first price hike since the comic had gone weekly with issue #27. The "TransFormation" page blamed "rising production costs," and by way of consolation readers were given Ultra Magnus and Galvatron sticker badges with issues #98–99.

TFUK had by now taken to describing itself as "Britain's top action and adventure comic"—so how did such a comic celebrate its 100th issue? With a bumper, 32-page issue containing 19 pages of Brit-strip and a wraparound, hand-painted cover by none other than Alan 'Excalibur' Davis!

"All of us had worked with Alan on Marvel UK's *Captain Britain* title," says Rimmer. "When the planning for issue #100 came up, we wanted something special for the cover, and I think by then Alan was working for Marvel US with Chris Claremont on *Excalibur* and *Uncanny X-Men*. So we jokingly said, 'Let's ask Alan if he'll do 100,' never for one second thinking that he'd be interested. Yet, probably because of the *Captain Britain* connection, and like the classy guy he is, he helped us out and said yes." "Alan's son was a Transformers fan," adds Furman (perhaps accounting for the "Alan and Thomas Davis" credit on the cover).

TFUK barreled into its next century with the return of Galvatron and the Dinobots, although the reappearance of the latter was deliberately withheld from readers so as to give Part 1 of "Fallen Angel" a killer cliffhanger. The Next Week box for issue #102 ranked the impending Galvatron vs Dinobots smack-down alongside other famous *TFUK* scraps: "Remember Megatron's dust up with Shockwave way back in issue #25? What about Prime's tussle with Shockwave again, from *Transformers* #40? And who could forget Ultra Magnus and Galvatron slugging each other to a standstill in issue #86?"

NOT A DREAM, NOT AN IMAGINARY TALE...

By the time the latest run of UK stories climaxed in issue #104, both Magnus and Galvatron were back on present day Earth and the scene was set for eight issues of US reprints (the backlog of American material was perhaps unsurprising given that *TFUK* had featured just six issues' worth of *TFUS* since the redesign/revamp in issue #74).

Reprinted in issues #105 and 106 was the controversial "Afterdeath!", wherein Optimus Prime effectively commits suicide after endangering the lives of characters in a computer game. Megatron would take similarly drastic action in the next story, "Gone But Not Forgotten!" It goes without saying that Optimus Prime and Megatron were the two most recognizable (and in Prime's case, one of the most popular) Transformers. In story terms, killing them off was absolutely massive: the biggest, boldest and most shocking event in *TFUK* history. *TFUK* had a gift for teasing readers with hints about upcoming stories–the hyperbole surrounding the arrival of the Special Teams started some three months before they made their debut, and the New Leaders were trailed well in advance. One wonders why was there no equivalent promotional campaign ahead of the deaths of the Autobot and Decepticon leaders? Where were the hints on the "TransFormation" page of "massive shocks in store"? Where were the full-page "Death of Optimus Prime" ads in other Marvel UK titles? Why was everything so... downplayed?

There are three possible reasons for *TFUK*'s uncharacteristically subdued approach: one, the deaths were considered by the editorial team to be insufficiently dramatic or memorable (in other words, the stories weren't that good); two, readers would be confused by Prime dying in 1987 when, according to *Transformers: The Movie*, he wasn't due to meet his end until the year 2005/6; and three, there was a concern that removing these two popular characters from the picture would actually harm sales. "Initially I was very surprised that Prime was to be killed off," recalls Rimmer, "but less so Megatron. Bumping off a lead villain is one thing, but doing that to your lead hero struck me as perplexing. And yes, we were definitely underwhelmed with the way Prime was killed—if you are going to go down that route, I'd at least have had him bow out in a blaze of glory."

"Clearly Hasbro US must have said something along the lines of 'they must be phased out,'" says Furman. "But replacing them with Grimlock and Ratchet always struck me as a very strange decision."

Issues #109–112 reprinted *TFUS* #26 and 27. Issue #111, in which the leaderless Autobots look for someone to replace Optimus Prime, was published at the same time as the UK General Election—"Vote for me!" says Grimlock on the cover. Issue #112 featured two letters concerning Prime's death, the first from a reader questioning how he could die when he appears in *The Movie*, the second from the mother of a young boy who was in tears at the death of his hero. "These are just two of the many letters I've

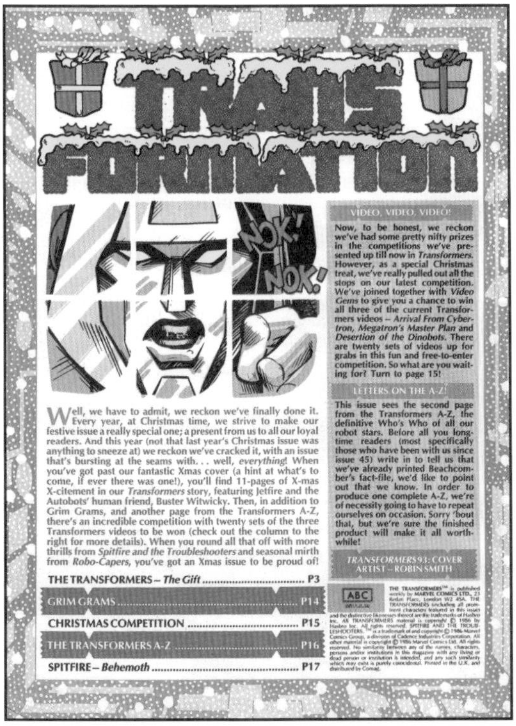

TRANSFORMATION

VIDEO, VIDEO, VIDEO!

Now, to be honest, we reckon we've had some pretty nifty prizes in the competitions we've presented up till now in *Transformers*. However, as a special Christmas treat, we've really pulled out all the stops on our latest competition. We've joined together with *Video Gems* to give you a chance to win all three of the current Transformers videos – *Arrival From Cybertron, Megatron's Master Plan* and *Desertion of the Dinobots*. There are twenty sets of videos up for grabs in this fun and free-to-enter competition. So what are you waiting for? Turn to page 15!

LETTERS ON THE A-Z!

This issue sees the second page from the Transformers A-Z, the definitive Who's Who of all our robot stars. Before all you long-time readers (most specifically those who have been with us since issue 45) write in to tell us that we've already printed Beachcomber's fact-file, we'd like to point out that we know. In order to produce one complete A-Z, we're of necessity going to have to repeat ourselves on occasion. Sorry 'bout that, but we're sure the finished product will make it all worthwhile!

Well, we have to admit, we reckon we've finally done it. Every year, at Christmas time, we strive to make our festive issue a really special one; a present from us to all our loyal readers. And this year (not that last year's Christmas issue was anything to sneeze at) we reckon we've cracked it, with an issue that's bursting at the seams with. . . well, *everything*! When you've got past our fantastic Xmas cover (a hint at what's to come, if ever there was one!), you'll find 11-pages of X-mas X-citement in our *Transformers* story, featuring Jetfire and the Autobots' human friend, Buster Witwicky. Then, in addition to Grim Grams, and another page from the Transformers A-Z, there's an incredible competition with twenty sets of the three Transformers videos to be won (check out the column to the right for more details). When you round all that off with more thrills from *Spitfire and the Troubleshooters* and seasonal mirth from *Robo-Capers*, you've got an Xmas issue to be proud of!

TRANSFORMERS 93: COVER ARTIST – ROBIN SMITH

ABC

Issue #93's "TransFormation" page.

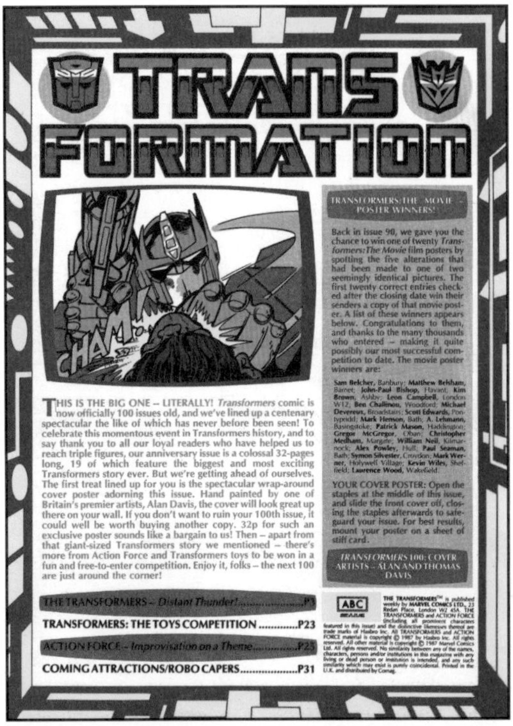

TRANSFORMATION

THIS IS THE BIG ONE – LITERALLY! *Transformers* comic is now officially 100 issues old, and we've lined up a centenary spectacular the like of which has never before been seen! To celebrate this momentous event in Transformers history, and to say thank you to all our loyal readers who have helped us to reach triple figures, our anniversary issue is a colossal 32-pages long, 19 of which feature the biggest and most exciting Transformers story ever. But we're getting ahead of ourselves. The first treat lined up for you is the spectacular wrap-around cover poster adorning this issue. Hand painted by one of Britain's premier artists, Alan Davis, the cover will look great up there on your wall. If you don't want to ruin your 100th issue, it could well be worth buying another copy. 32p for such an exclusive poster sounds like a bargain to us! Then – apart from that giant-sized Transformers story we mentioned – there's more from Action Force and Transformers toys to be won in a fun and free-to-enter competition. Enjoy it, folks – the next 100 are just around the corner!

TRANSFORMERS: THE MOVIE – POSTER WINNERS!

Back in issue 90, we gave you the chance to win one of twenty *Transformers: The Movie* film posters by spotting the five alterations that had been made to one of two seemingly identical pictures. The first twenty correct entries checked after the closing date win their senders a copy of that movie poster. A list of these winners appears below. Congratulations to them, and thanks to the many thousands who entered – making it quite possibly our most successful competition to date. The movie poster winners are:

Sam Belcher, Banbury; **Matthew Belsham**, Barnet; **John-Paul Bishop**, Havant; **Kim Brown**, Ashby; **Leon Campbell**, London W12; **Ben Challinou**, Woodford; **Michael Devereux**, Broadstairs; **Scott Edwards**, Pontypridd; **Mark Henson**, Bath; **A. Lehmann**, Basingstoke; **Patrick Mason**, Haddington; **Gregor McGregor**, Oban; **Christopher Medham**, Margate; **William Neil**, Kilmarnock; **Alex Powley**, Hull; **Paul Seaman**, Bath; **Symon Silvester**, Croydon; **Mark Werner**, Holywell Village; **Kevin Wiles**, Sheffield; **Laurence Wood**, Wakefield.

YOUR COVER POSTER: Open the staples at the middle of this issue, and slide the front cover off, closing the staples afterwards to safeguard your issue. For best results, mount your poster on a sheet of stiff card.

TRANSFORMERS 100: COVER ARTISTS – ALAN AND THOMAS DAVIS

ABC

Issue #100's "TransFormation" page.

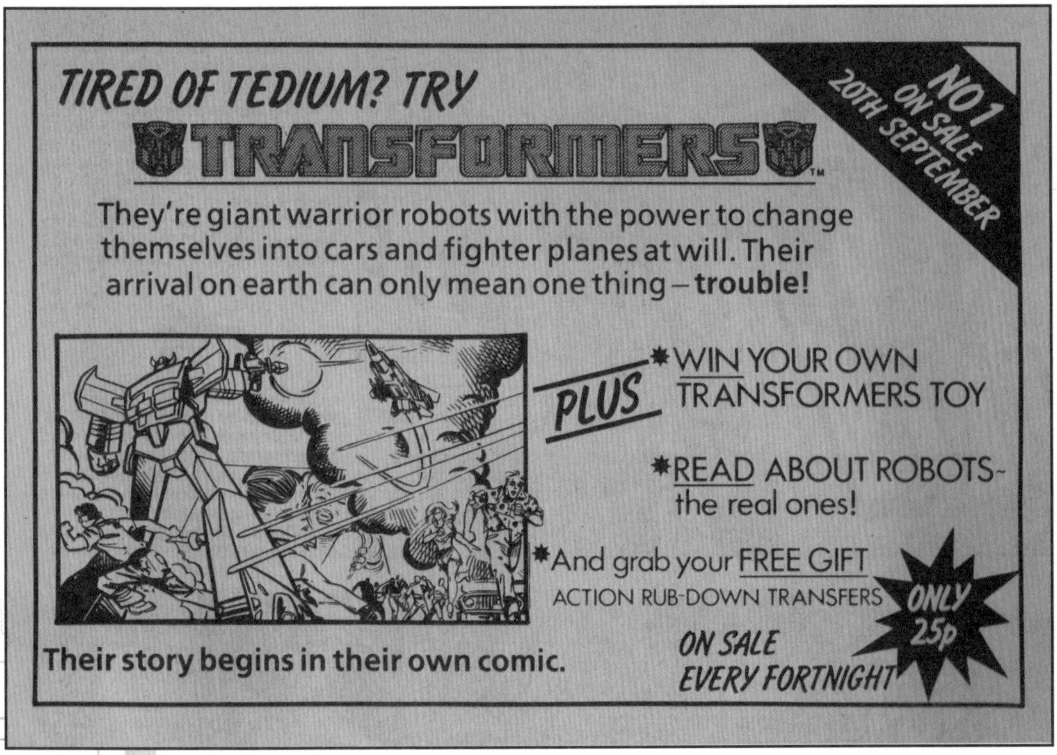

TIRED OF TEDIUM? TRY
TRANSFORMERS™
NO 1 ON SALE 20TH SEPTEMBER
They're giant warrior robots with the power to change themselves into cars and fighter planes at will. Their arrival on earth can only mean one thing – trouble!
PLUS
*WIN YOUR OWN TRANSFORMERS TOY
*READ ABOUT ROBOTS – the real ones!
*And grab your FREE GIFT ACTION RUB-DOWN TRANSFERS
ONLY 25p
Their story begins in their own comic.
ON SALE EVERY FORTNIGHT

In late summer 1984 this advert appeared in *Mighty World of Marvel*.

GRIM GRAMS

GRIM GRAMS, Marvel Comics,
23 Redan Place,
Bayswater,
LONDON W2 4SA.

All readers who have a letter (sorry, not 'Your Choice' or Stock Exchange) or drawing printed in Grim Grams will receive a mini-Autobot toy.

Dear Grimlock,
I am writing to you with a question about issue 106 of Transformers. You showed Optimus Prime being destroyed at the end of the computer game he played alongside his Protectobots against Megatron and the Combaticons in Multi-World. This cannot be true, because Optimus Prime doesn't die until the year 2006 (as seen in Transformers: The Movie). Is the explanation that this was another facsimile construct of Prime. I doubt it, as Prime acted and spoke just as he would normally. Please explain this for me. By the way, why was Grim Grams not featured in issues 102 – 105? It's one of my favourite features! And keep the Transformers A – Z going – it's brill!
Thomas Hughes,
Chester.

Dear Grimlock,
I'm writing on behalf of my four year old son, Daniel (and myself as a harrassed parent!). He thinks – Ethan Zachary

is a "really stupid person" to have blown up Optimus Prime. He's in tears because we have been searching the shops since before Christmas to find an Optimus Prime toy, and now it seems that there's no chance of finding one. Can you help?
Mum Talbot & Daniel,
Guildford.

Hmm – I thought Optimus Prime's explosive demise would provoke quite a bit of comment (these are just two of the many letters I've received on the subject.) The most common complaint/observation is that Prime cannot be dead as he appears in Transformers: The Movie (which is set in the future). Perhaps this just means that the saga of Optimus Prime is not quite as over as it seems. Megatron certainly didn't think he'd seen the last of Prime (in issue 108), so you never know! The Optimus Prime toy is now officially NOT in the Hasbro toy range, so we really don't know where to suggest you try. Maybe the toy will make a comeback as well. I'll let you know if it does. And anyway, what's all this sadness for? So what if Prime's gone! As you can clearly see from this issue's story, his replacement more than makes up for whatever loss you may be feeling (smirk, smirk!).
15

Dear Grimlock,
I have been collecting Transformers comic from the very beginning (around the end of 1984), and now have 38 of the toys. There are some questions I'd like to ask you. 1) In issues 98 and 101 you mentioned a Transformers TV series that picks up from where the movie left off. When will it be on? 2) In Transformers: The Movie Galvatron shoots and destroys Starscream with his proton cannon. How come he didn't destroy the mini-Autobots in issue 101, when he shot them with the same weapon? 3) There used to be a comic called Scream that finished in 1984. In it there was a story called The Dracula File, written by Simon Furman. Is this the same Simon Furman that writes Transformers?
Cameron Egerton,
Callander.

Aha – a long-time Transformers reader, eh? Okay, kid – here we go with some answers: 1) The TV series is still in production, so we've no date for its release in the U.S. let alone over here. However, we pick up from the end of the Transformers movie right here in issue 113. Not to be missed. 2) In Transformers: The Movie Galvatron drew his firepower from Unicron himself, so his proton cannon was more powerful then than it is now. 3) I've talked to stubble Furman and he admits that it was indeed he at the typewriter for The Dracula File and sundry other Scream stories. He assures me that this was when he was young and confused!

STOCK EXCHANGE

Wanted: Ultra Magnus (all weapons and in good condition). Swap: Brawl, Vortex, and Air Raid (all weapons and in good condition). Contact: Lawrence Nuttall, 1 Denmark Square, Northtown, Aldershot, Hants. GU12 4TN.

Letters page from issue #112.

received on this subject," says Grimlock, adding, "Perhaps [the events in the Movie] just mean that the saga of Optimus Prime is not quite as over as it seems."

But while readers were reeling from the death of Optimus Prime, Marvel UK was coming to terms with Rimmer's decision to step down as TFUK editor after two years and nearly ninety issues.

"Why did I leave? Well, it kind of goes back to the arguments I mentioned earlier about mechanical color— that was one of the disputes I was having with senior

management. We weren't on the same page about what Marvel UK should be doing in the future. And the longer I stayed in an editorial position at Marvel, the less chance I'd have to do the thing that I'd grown to really want to do in comics, which was write. I just thought it was time to stop and become freelance. And I still am!"

Over the course of two years, with the help of Furman and Tomlinson, Rimmer had turned TFUK from an entertaining but somewhat ungainly robot-focused fortnightly into a bright, dynamic Transformers-focused weekly. His contribution to the success of the title cannot be overestimated. Looking back, he says there is very little he would have done differently, and attributes much of the incredible success of the title to outside forces.

"I think we were fortunate in the sense that we had a lot of support from Hasbro with the TV adverts. And we got lucky with the idea that we could produce a weekly full-color comic—that came about at the right time. And of course the actual toys did very well. Transformers was the sell-out toy one Christmas, and people were phoning up the office and asking whether we could supply them with Optimus Prime! It was a case of, 'Sorry, we haven't got any either!' But yeah, with Transformers I think it was just the right time—the right era. Everything fell into place."

He recalls the "TFUK era" with fondness. "I've always looked back on that as a very fun time. Working with Simon, John, Richard [Starkings], and then a little later Steve Robinson—that was particularly nice. I enjoyed working with those guys. We each had different talents, we each brought something different to [TFUK], but it worked well—it benefited the comic."

NEXT WEEK

IT'S BACK TO THE FUTURE...
AND HOW!

If you think our recent Transformers stories have been exciting, wait'll you see the epic adventure that begins next issue! In response to the many questions and requests from people wanting to know what happened after the end of Transformers: The Movie, in seven days' time we go back to the future – to the year 2007 – to see exactly how Rodimus Prime, Wreck-Gar and the other Autobots are coping after their apocalyptic battle with Unicron. You might have thought that with the planet-eater destroyed and Galvatron here on present-day Earth, Rodimus Prime would be able to take it easy. But, as you'll begin to see next issue, Prime's troubles are only just beginning! And don't miss the meanest, nastiest character we've ever introduced. He's a bounty-hunter by the name of Death's Head, and he hunts Transformers! Don't dare miss next issue!

TRANSFORMERS 113 – OUT OF
THIS WORLD... AND TIME!

NEXT WEEK

Issue #112's "Next Week" feature.

ALL CHANGE, YES?

TFUK was about to enter the post-*Movie*, post-Prime era, with Furman replacing Rimmer as editor. Within weeks of his appointment, a certain freelance peacekeeping agent would make his debut appearance and Marvel UK would stage its first and only crossover event: the *Transformers/Action Force* epic, "Ancient Relics!"

In cinematic terms, *The Movie* had sunk without a trace, but its impact on *TFUK* would prove to be significant and long lasting. The next 100 issues would see Galvatron, Ultra Magnus, and/or Rodimus Prime appear in virtually every British strip. From now on the UK and US stories would essentially run in parallel, each telling their own epic tales rather than weaving in and out of each other. Will Simpson would leave and Geoff Senior would soon be taking a sabbatical, but new artists like Dan Reed and Lee Sullivan would take their place.

The toys themselves, while no longer quite the phenomenon thay had been in 1984 and 1985, were still selling well, and in the autumn of 1987 Hasbro would tell *TFUK* to pull out the stops and promote a major new toy release: after the Special Teams and the New Leaders, it was now time for the Headmasters.

Volume 4 of *Transformers Classics UK* will cover issues #113–145 and include the 1987 *Transformers Annual* and the *Transformers/Action Force* crossover, "Ancient Relics!"

COLORING: A BEGINNER'S GUIDE

Colorist Steve White offers a layperson's guide to the lost art of color separation, or "sepping."

I'VE BEEN MISSING SOMETHING IN MY LIFE...
...COLOR!

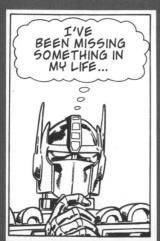

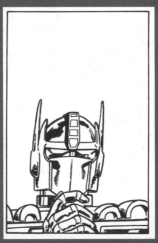

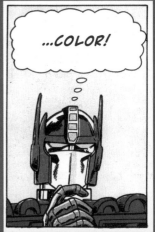

The color separation process—what we called the "nine-sheet method"—used three percentages (25%, 50%, and 100%) of three colors (cyan, magenta, and yellow) to make the colors. It was three times three, hence the nine sheets. To make brown, for instance, you had 25%C 50%M 100%Y. I think you had about 80 different possibilities.

+
+
=

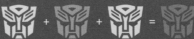

The colorist would do a color rough of the black and white page—essentially just coloring in a photocopy—then mark up the page with the various percentages you wanted. We used a set of markers that were as near as dammit to the 80-odd variations, so the rough was more or less a facsimile of the final page.

The page was then given to the separator, who would wax a black and white version of the page to a sheet of acetate, mount it on a drawing board, put another sheet of acetate over the top, and use these opaque red-ink pens to fill all the bits of 25% cyan, then another sheet for the 50% cyan, and on and on until you had the nine sheets.

Sepping was a lowly job that people did freelance as well as in-house. We had various strange types doing it for the money and some were better than others. Some were just plain awful. You had to make sure the ink coverage was complete and that it went up to the line, while also making sure no sections of a particular color had been missed so that a brown didn't end up a green if you missed the 50% red. It was laborious and tedious, while the ink fumes tended to make you pretty befuddled on occasion.

We did do some clever things. You couldn't blend colors as such, but if we had, for instance, an explosion, you could feather the edge of a color with a scalpel to create a more interesting effect. It all seems like using charcoal on a cave wall now...

Below:
Issue #78 (September 13th, 1986) • Cover by Alister Pearson • "Target: 2006" Prologue • First appearance of Galvatron, Cyclonus, Scourge, Impactor, Roadbuster, and Skater • "Hercules" back-up strip

Right:
Issue #79 (September 20th, 1986) • Cover by John Higgins • "Target: 2006" Part 1 • First appearance of Ultra Magnus • Free gift: the Ultra Magnus half of a New Leaders poster painted by Robin Smith

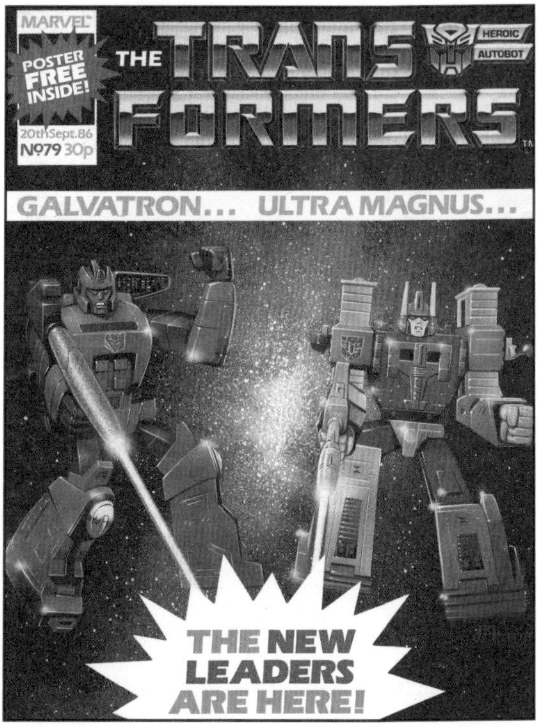

MARVEL
POSTER FREE INSIDE!
THE TRANSFORMERS
HEROIC AUTOBOT
20th Sept.86
Nº79 30p
GALVATRON... ULTRA MAGNUS...
THE NEW LEADERS ARE HERE!

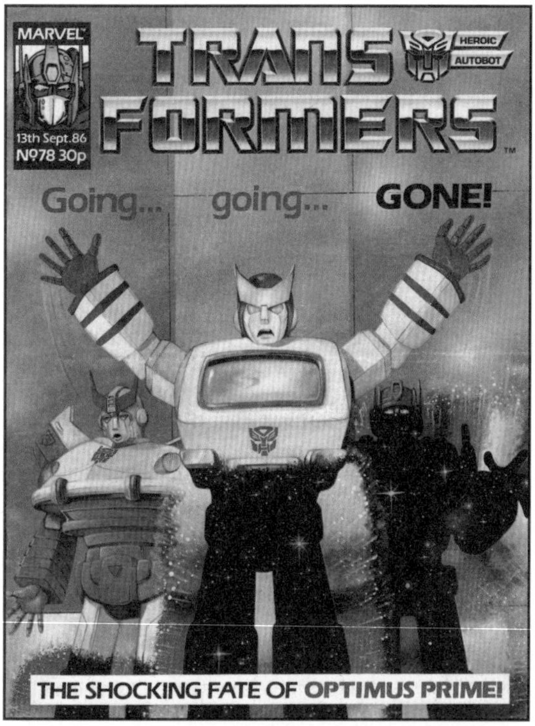

MARVEL
TRANSFORMERS
HEROIC AUTOBOT
13th Sept.86
Nº78 30p
Going... going... GONE!
THE SHOCKING FATE OF OPTIMUS PRIME!

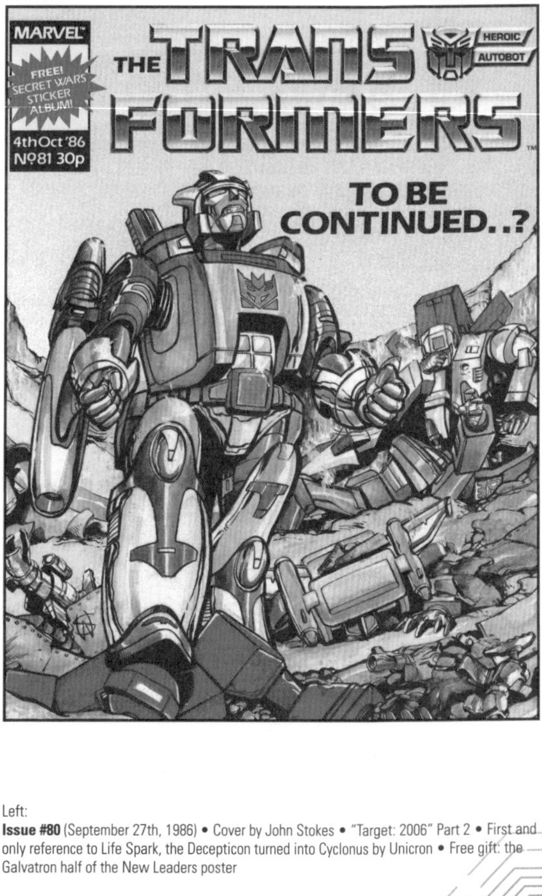

MARVEL
FREE! SECRET WARS STICKER ALBUM!
THE TRANSFORMERS
HEROIC AUTOBOT
4th Oct '86
Nº81 30p
TO BE CONTINUED..?

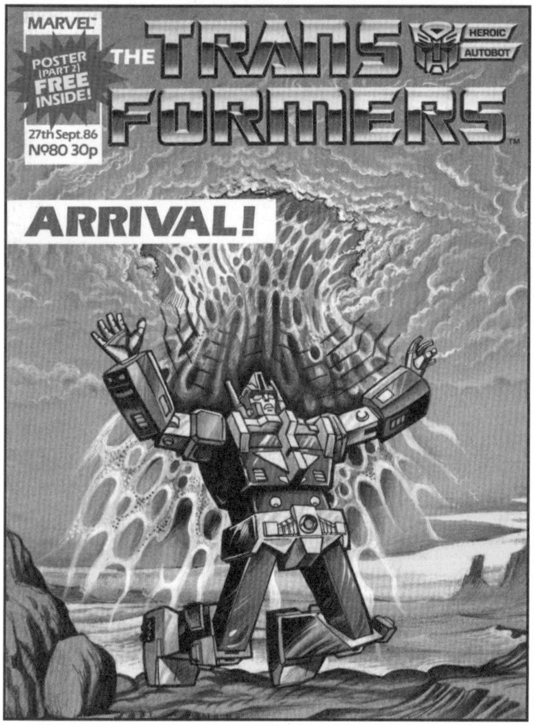

MARVEL
POSTER (PART 2) FREE INSIDE!
THE TRANSFORMERS
HEROIC AUTOBOT
27th Sept.86
Nº80 30p
ARRIVAL!

Left:
Issue #80 (September 27th, 1986) • Cover by John Stokes • "Target: 2006" Part 2 • First and only reference to Life Spark, the Decepticon turned into Cyclonus by Unicron • Free gift: the Galvatron half of the New Leaders poster

Above:
Issue #81 (October 4th, 1986) • Cover by Will Simpson • "Target: 2006" Part 3 • Free gift: Panini Secret Wars sticker album and stickers • New Leaders fact file: Ultra Magnus (reprinted in this volume)

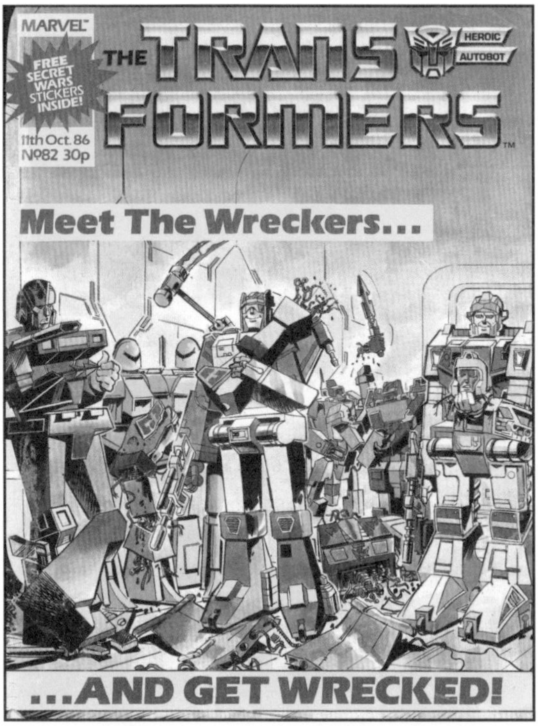
MARVEL
THE TRANSFORMERS
HEROIC AUTOBOT
FREE SECRET WARS STICKERS INSIDE!
11th Oct. 86
Nº82 30p
Meet The Wreckers...
...AND GET WRECKED!

Left:
Issue #82 (October 11th, 1986) • Cover by Phil Gascoine • "Target: 2006" Part 4 • Free gift: Secret Wars stickers • First appearance of Rack 'n Ruin, Whirl, Fang, and (as facsimile constructs) Octane, Blitzwing, Thrust, Dirge, and Ramjet

Below:
Issue #83 (October 18th 1986) • Cover by Robin Smith • "Target: 2006" Part 5 • Feature: *Cybertron—The Middle Years* (by Simon Furman)

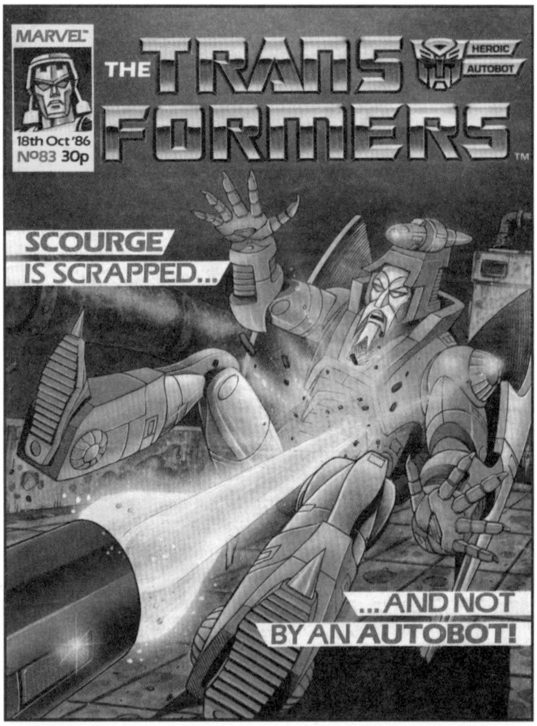
MARVEL
THE TRANSFORMERS
HEROIC AUTOBOT
18th Oct '86
Nº83 30p
SCOURGE IS SCRAPPED...
...AND NOT BY AN AUTOBOT!

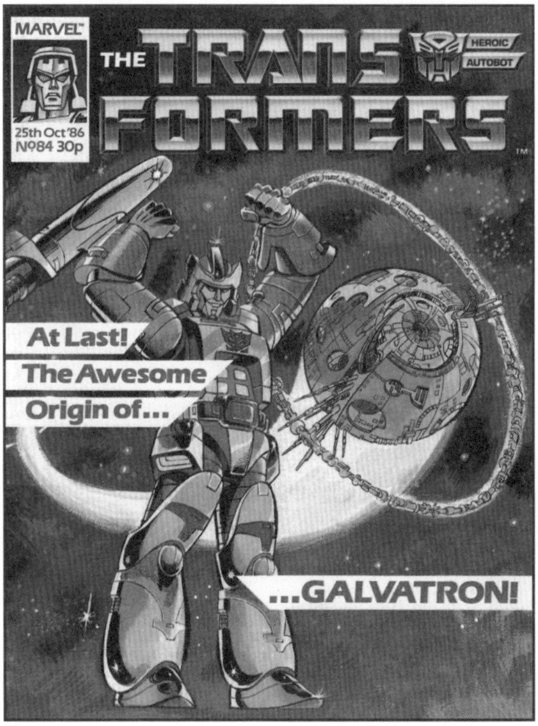
MARVEL
THE TRANSFORMERS
HEROIC AUTOBOT
25th Oct '86
Nº84 30p
At Last!
The Awesome
Origin of...
...GALVATRON!

Above:
Issue #84 (October 25th, 1986) • Cover by Phil Gascoine • "Target: 2006" Part 6 • First appearance of Springer, Broadside, Sandstorm, Hot Rod, Kup, Blurr, and Unicron

Right:
Issue #85 (November 1st, 1986) • Cover by Robin Smith • "Target: 2006" Part 7 • "Hercules" back-up strip ends

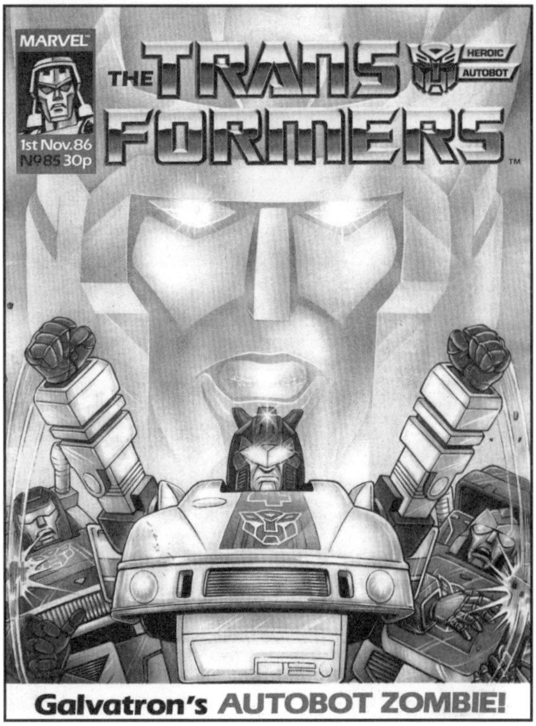
MARVEL
THE TRANSFORMERS
HEROIC AUTOBOT
1st Nov. 86
Nº85 30p
Galvatron's AUTOBOT ZOMBIE!

Below:
Issue #86 (November 8th, 1986) • Cover by Robin Smith • "Target: 2006" Part 8 • New back-up strip: "Spitfire and the Troubleshooters"

Right:
Issue #87 (November 15th, 1986) • Cover by Phil Gascoine • "Target: 2006" Part 9

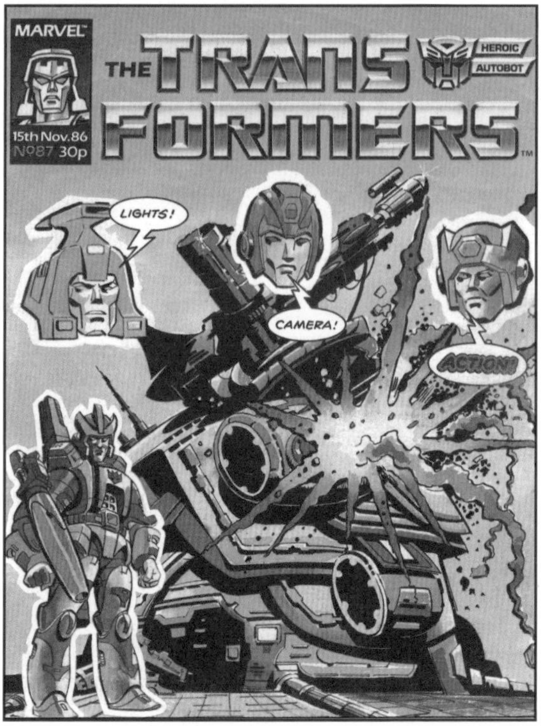
MARVEL
15th Nov. 86
Nº87 30p
THE TRANSFORMERS
HEROIC AUTOBOT
LIGHTS!
CAMERA!
ACTION!

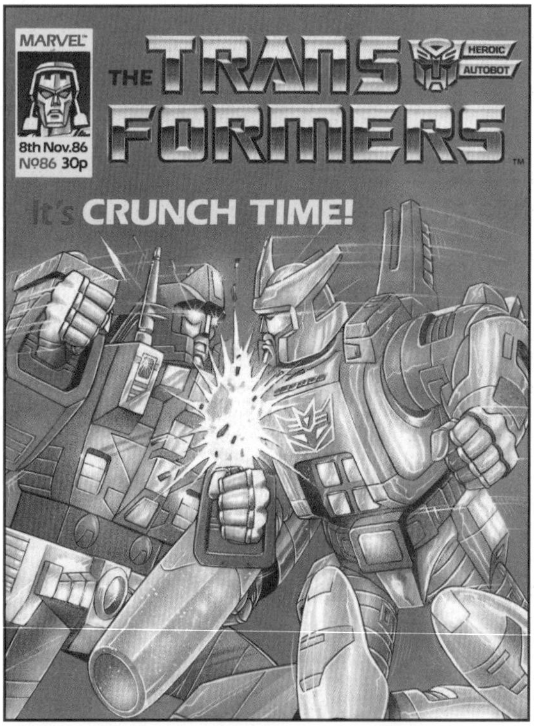
MARVEL
8th Nov. 86
Nº86 30p
THE TRANSFORMERS
HEROIC AUTOBOT
It's CRUNCH TIME!

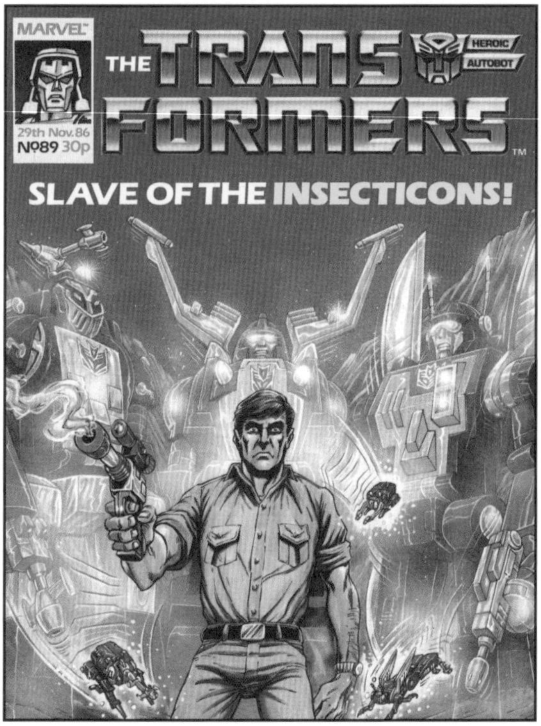
MARVEL
29th Nov. 86
Nº89 30p
THE TRANSFORMERS
HEROIC AUTOBOT
SLAVE OF THE INSECTICONS!

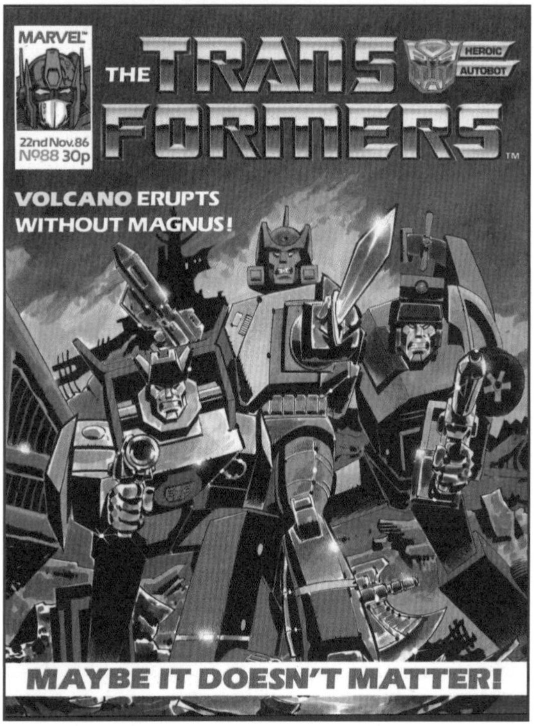
MARVEL
22nd Nov. 86
Nº88 30p
THE TRANSFORMERS
HEROIC AUTOBOT
VOLCANO ERUPTS WITHOUT MAGNUS!
MAYBE IT DOESN'T MATTER!

Left:
Issue #88 (November 22nd, 1986) • Cover by Geoff Senior • "Target: 2006" Epilogue • Last painted strip • First appearance of Macabre • Death of Impactor • New Leaders fact file: Galvatron (reprinted in this volume)

Above:
Issue #89 (November 29th, 1986) • Cover by Robin Smith • Reprints pages 1–11 of "Aerialbots Over America!" (*TFUS* issue #21) • The Aerialbots are created • The Transformers "A to Z" (featuring Air Raid and Astrotrain) replaces the "Interface" fact files

TARGET: 2006

Originally printed in issues #78–88
Published September 13–November 22, 1986
Prologue and Parts 1 and 2 reprinted as *Collected Comics* #15 (February 1990), re-using cover to issue #79
Reprinted by Titan Books (softback and hardback editions) in 2002
Reprinted by IDW in 2007 with new covers by Nick Roche (art), Liam Shalloo, and Josh Burcham (colors)

"No, Jazz… Not **like** Megatron—I **AM** Megatron!"

"Target: 2006" is the biggest *TFUK* story, the most famous *TFUK* story, and the story half-remembered by British thirtysomethings whose love of Transformers petered out in the late '80s. It's the story that contains one iconic image after another (Optimus, Prowl, and Ratchet fading away to nothing; Ironhide digging Megatron and Soundwave from the rubble; Galvatron riding on top of Ultra Magnus' cab and, later, dragging said Autobot, dazed and defeated, from a raging conflagration). And it's the story that many fans hold up as evidence that *TFUK* gave its readers the definitive account of the Transformers' war.

"Target: 2006" is to *TFUK* what the "Dark Phoenix" saga is to the *Uncanny X-Men*, or "Year One" is to *Batman*. It is the quintessential *TFUK* epic.

Given the nature of the story in question it is perhaps appropriate that (from the perspective of this fan, at least) the circumstances leading to its creation are only fully appreciated some 25 years after it was printed. "Target: 2006" has always been synonymous with creative freedom: by introducing a cast of characters who hailed from the future, Simon Furman was able to step away from US continuity and do his own thing. Without "Target: 2006" there would have been no Death's Head, no "Legacy of Unicron," no Quintesson invasion, no "Time Wars."

And yet the genesis of this groundbreaking story is characterised by severe creative constraints and limitations. Usually, all Furman had to worry

about when writing British strips was making sure that they slotted neatly into pre-existing US material; by and large, he had the freedom to decide which characters to use. With "Target: 2006," he was effectively ordered by Hasbro UK to write a story focusing on Galvatron and Ultra Magnus—two characters who (for reasons that remain unclear to this day) were not going to feature in *Transformers* US at all. Furthermore, Galvatron would not exist, in terms of story chronology, until 2005 or 2006. Complicating matters still further was the need for *TFUK* to run a story that promoted, and ideally tied in with, the Christmas release of *Transformers: The Movie*, but without giving away the ending or indeed too many of the major plot points in the film. Furman was somehow able to turn all of the above to his advantage.

"Target: 2006" was not written to promote the arrival in cinemas of *Transformers: The Movie* (the animated film which would premiere in the UK in December 1986), but the arrival in toy shops of Ultra Magnus and Galvatron, a.k.a. The New Leaders. Magnus and Galvatron were here to usurp Optimus and Megatron, and as far as Hasbro UK was concerned it was the job of *TFUK* to introduce the new characters in style.

"We heard about the Movie in early 1986, through Hasbro UK," recalls Furman. "I remember all of the editorial team sitting down and reading an early draft of the script. Hasbro basically said we needed to have Galvatron and Magnus in a story because they were planning a big marketing push on the toys and billing it as The New Leaders and everything. It was

Covers for issues #1–2 of IDW's "Target: 2006" reprint.

definitely a case of, 'They're going to be featured on the cover, they're going to be promoted as a toy and you're going to get your TV advertising,' and so we needed a story to match the promotional push. But as Magnus and Galvatron weren't going to be in the US story we had to find a way to bring them into the UK strip.

"The trouble was, we couldn't set 'The New Leaders' story *after* the Movie because we knew the strip was going to run before the December premiere and we didn't want to give away the ending of the film.

"We toyed with the idea of making it a prequel, but then realized that Megatron isn't Galvatron until midway through the Movie—and that pointed us to the fact that if we wanted to feature Galvatron in our story we had to set it after the point Megatron is transformed, but not go so far as to have Hot Rod become Rodimus Prime."

Boxed into a narrative corner by circumstances outside his control, Furman reached for a classic science fiction plot device that had yet to be used in a *Transformers* comic: time travel.

"I was reared on time travel stories, so it didn't feel like a huge stretch [to use it as a plot device]. Then I thought, 'If we're going to take characters back in time we need a story that gives some nods to the Movie without giving the whole game away.'"

In issue #96, two readers who have read the comic adaptation of *The Movie* ask Grimlock how it is possible, given the non-stop action, for Galvatron, Cyclonus, and Scourge to travel back in time to 1986. Grimlock explains that when Galvatron announces "Decepticons—to Earth!" he is actually referring to the Earth of 1986. "I can't remember when I decided that it was that line [which linked the Movie and "Target: 2006"]," admits Furman. "It's quite possible that I didn't decide until asked the question."

Writing an 11-part story gave Furman the opportunity to create multiple plots that would run in parallel. In fact, "Target: 2006" essentially tells three stories: Galvatron's arrival from the future; Ultra Magnus' investigation into the disappearance of Optimus and Co.; and Emirate Xaaron's plan to launch *Operation: Volcano* and strike out against the Decepticons on Cybertron.

"It didn't work for us to have two time travellers," says Furman, explaining how the three storylines came about. "I mean, I know there are a lot of time travellers in it, but it didn't

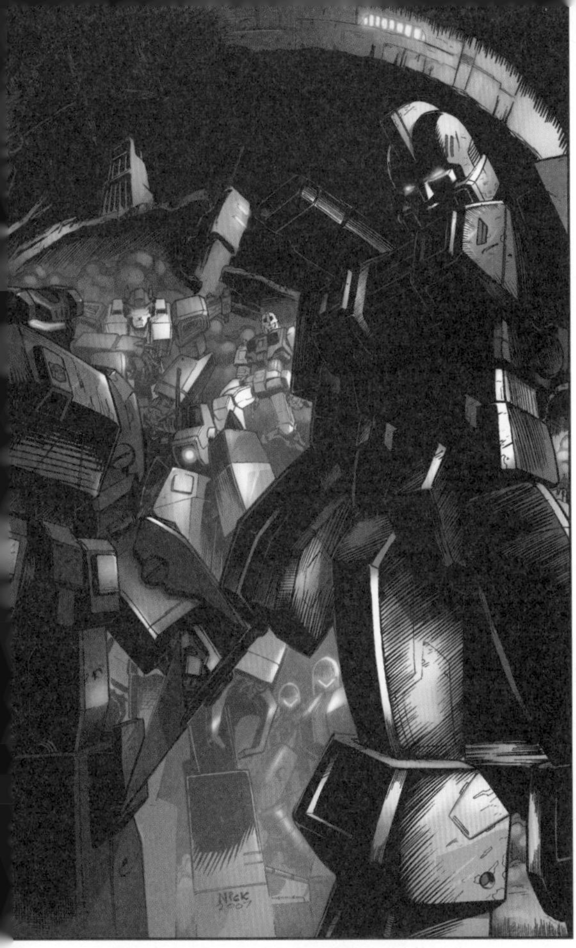

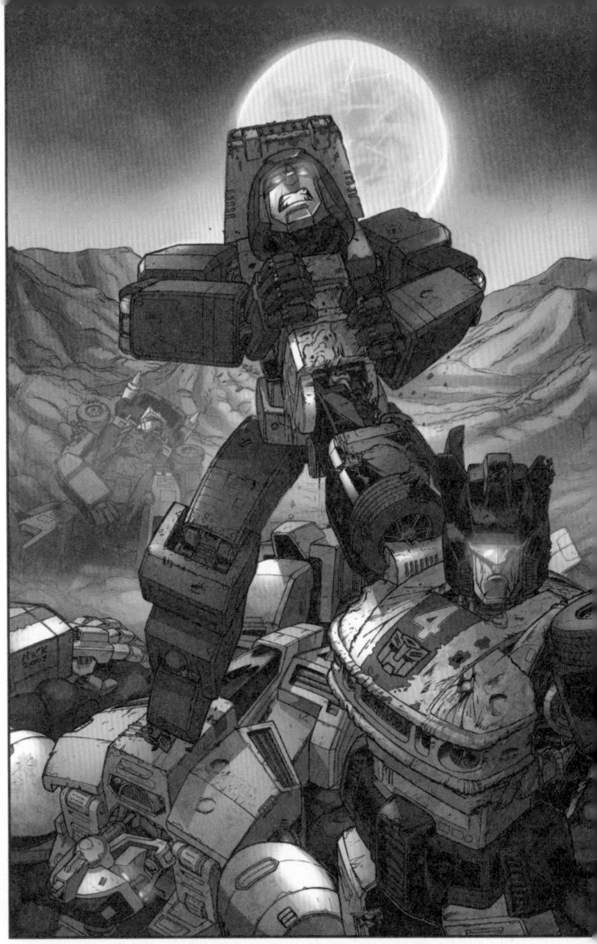

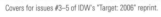

Covers for issues #3–5 of IDW's "Target: 2006" reprint.

work to bring Ultra Magnus back as a time traveller, so that kind of necessitated him being on Cybertron—and there, suddenly, was the Cybertron storyline."

Taken as a whole, "Target: 2006" reads as a proud summation of almost everything that's come before it—in both UK *and* US stories. From the destruction of the Decepticons' space ship to the appearance of practically every character in the series (and name-checks for everyone from Omega Supreme to obscure generics like Spanner), it's as if Furman is taking every opportunity to remind readers of the breadth and depth of the TF Universe.

"We were always, *always* trying to tie the bigger storyline together," he says, "particularly because the American stories looked so different. Whenever we did UK stories we tried to name-check characters from those stories. And our readers weren't stupid—they must've seen the difference visually—so we'd try and keep it all one seamless whole. Ian was big on that. He'd say, 'Let's make sure that this doesn't look like our stuff, their stuff.'"

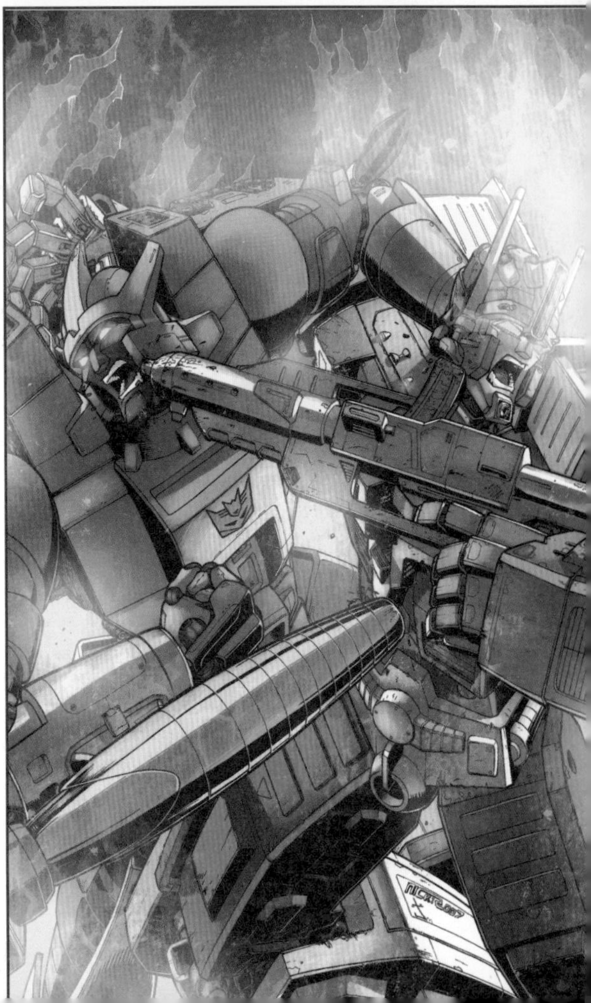

But it's not just the set-up or the new characters or the sheer length that makes "Target: 2006" so exciting; it's the way in which the story is told. There are relatively few instances of one installment flowing directly into the next; instead, each 11-page episode is practically a self-contained story—one that is usually told in flashback or bookended by certain phrases or events. Rather than move from A to B to C and so on, "Target: 2006" jumps about from character to character, subplot to subplot, teasing and foreshadowing, honing in on key moments and then winding back the clock to explain what precipitated them. It even follows one of the greatest cliffhangers of all time—Ironhide disinterring Megatron and Soundwave—with an 11-page interval (albeit an 11-page interval that introduces the Wreckers).

Furman agrees that the story was ambitious in structure as well as scope. "It evolved as it went along, but it definitely marked the point where I got experimental in how I told stories. There are almost no linear episodes. I mean, 'Wreck and Rule!' sits on its own and plays out in a fairly linear fashion, but even that has its bookends. Virtually every episode has a kind of 'we're going to play around with structure here,' whether it's flashback or the fact that we're seeing things from different perspectives or there's someone telling a story. Even the big battle between Ultra Magnus and Galvatron plays out mostly in flashback. You could see we were getting more confident because we were trying different things all the time."

It's not just the writing that pushes the boundaries; the artists and inkers and colorists rose to the occasion too. The sense of visual experimentation is most apparent in Geoff Senior's art: in his three issues (#83, #84, and #86) he deploys a huge variety of overlapping images, insets, borderless panels, and off-page bleeds. One suspects that Marvel UK senior management told Geoff and others to "rein it in," for subsequent stories were markedly more traditional in terms of panel layout.

"I think the three Geoff episodes are kind of the pinnacle of his time on *Transformers*," says Furman. "He went on to do many more strips in the UK and the US and in *Generation 2*, but to me, this was when he was at his best—precisely because he was allowed to be a little more experimental and dynamic with his storytelling."

Furman had no influence over which artists drew which parts of the story. "That was all Ian—he was the one who got Ron Smith to do the Wreckers issue. I know Ian really rated Geoff's work, so he may well have arranged for him to draw issue #86 [Magnus versus Galvatron], it being a kinetic action issue. I know that Geoff's panels at the time were extremely violent, like the bit [in issue #83] when the sheet metal is thrown into Grapple's chest."

Senior himself admits he can't recall many of the *TFUK* strips he worked on, but issue #86 stands out: "When I think of *Transformers*, the one story I always think of is the one where Galvatron is riding on the back of Ultra Magnus—the one with the big explosion at the end. That's the one that sticks in my head. I enjoyed that one–it was an interesting challenge; the storytelling was interesting. Gina Hart colored it and did a really good job."

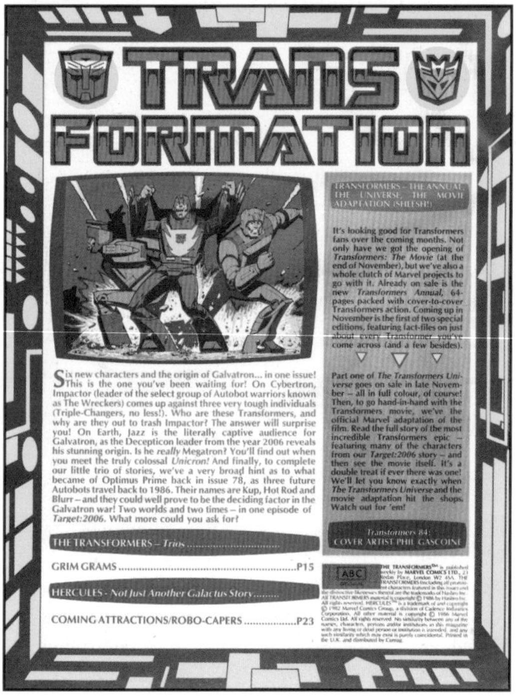
TRANS FORMATION

TRANSFORMERS – THE ANNUAL, THE UNIVERSE, THE MOVIE ADAPTATION (SHEESH!)

Six new characters and the origin of Galvatron... in one issue! This is the one you've been waiting for! On Cybertron, Impactor (leader of the select group of Autobot warriors known as The Wreckers) comes up against three very tough individuals (Triple-Changers, no less!). Who are these Transformers, and why are they out to trash Impactor? The answer will surprise you! On Earth, Jazz is the literally captive audience for Galvatron, as the Decepticon leader from the year 2006 reveals his stunning origin. Is he *really* Megatron? You'll find out when you meet the truly colossal *Unicron!* And finally, to complete our little trio of stories, we've a very broad hint as to what became of Optimus Prime back in issue 78, as three future Autobots travel back to 1986. Their names are Kup, Hot Rod and Blurr – and they could well prove to be the deciding factor in the Galvatron war! Two worlds and two times – in one episode of *Target:2006*. What more could you ask for?

It's looking good for Transformers fans over the coming months. Not only have we got the opening of *Transformers: The Movie* (at the end of November), but we've also a whole clutch of Marvel projects to go with it. Already on sale is the new *Transformers Annual*, 64-pages packed with cover-to-cover Transformers action. Coming up in November is the first of two special editions, featuring fact-files on just about every Transformer you've come across (and a few besides).

Part one of *The Transformers Universe* goes on sale in late November – all in full colour, of course! Then, to go hand-in-hand with the Transformers movie, we've the official Marvel adaptation of the film. Read the full story of the most incredible Transformers epic – featuring many of the characters from our *Target:2006* story – and then see the movie itself. It's a double treat if ever there was one! We'll let you know exactly when *The Transformers Universe* and the movie adaptation hit the shops. Watch out for 'em!

Transformers 84:
COVER ARTIST PHIL GASCOINE

THE TRANSFORMERS – *Trios* ....

GRIM GRAMS P15

HERCULES - *Not Just Another Galactus Story* ....

COMING ATTRACTIONS/ROBO-CAPERS P23

ABC

THE TRANSFORMERS™ is published weekly by MARVEL COMICS LTD., 23 Redan Place, London W2 4SA. [illegible]

Issue #84's "TransFormation" page.

"There are panels drawn by other artists that stick in my mind," says Furman, "like the last page of the prologue [drawn by Jeff Anderson], where Galvatron, Cyclonus, and Scourge are revealed in the storm—that's a particular favorite. The Wreckers splash page [by Ron Smith] I love. But possibly the one I still look at and think 'that's amazing' is the conclusion of the Ultra Magnus/Galvatron fight... It just looks so fantastically *huge*: the explosions, the fire, everything. Gina did an amazing job. And I'm loathe to praise my own writing, but I love that last page with the art and the dialog: 'There's a winner—and it's Galvatron.' It's my favorite page for lots of reasons.

"The other thing that I think particularly helps [to make 'Target: 2006' stand out]—and this is no offence to the letterers who went before—but Richard Starkings' sound effects and lettering just kind of seemed to add to it as well. That was the first time I think we had amazing sound effects. I wrote them, but the realization of them… I do think that Richard really brought some extra oomph."

"Target: 2006" had been preceded by another British strip, the four-part "In the National Interest," meaning that readers were treated to an unmatched 15-week run of UK stories. Until that point, the UK "fill ins" had run to 10 issues at most, which would have made "Target" a six-part story similar to "The Legacy of Unicron" and "Space Pirates." One wonders whether "Target" was always intended to be as long as it was. "I asked myself that question," laughs Furman. "I don't know whether it just grew organically until it reached 11 parts, or whether we knew we had to fill 11 issues before American material would be ready. I'm sure we just thought it was a big event so we could do one big story."

Something "Target: 2006" does effortlessly, and with considerable panache, is introduce new toy-based characters. Aside from The New Leaders, Hot Rod, Kup, Blurr, Cyclonus, and Scourge all make their first appearance and yet none of them feel crowbarred into the story. Springer, Broadside, and Sandstorm crop up too, bringing the tally of new characters to ten. And then, just for good measure, Furman decides to introduce the Wreckers: Impactor and Rack 'n Ruin were entirely new, comic-only characters; Roadbuster and Whirl were available as toys, but only in the US; and Twin Twist and Top Spin–the Jumpstarters—had made only one previous appearance in an out-of-continuity text story published in the first *Transformers Annual*. Did Furman not feel he had enough characters to deal with already?

"My attitude was always to make the new characters feel like they were integral to the story. I don't think we short changed characters overly much—some Wreckers got more of a look in than others, but... we tried to give them all an outing, at least.

"I mean with Impactor, in terms of story, I always knew he was going to die. But actually creating a new Transformer was new for us. I think we were possibly aware that we couldn't keep him around at the end of the story because it may have led to questions like, 'Why can't I have an Impactor toy?'

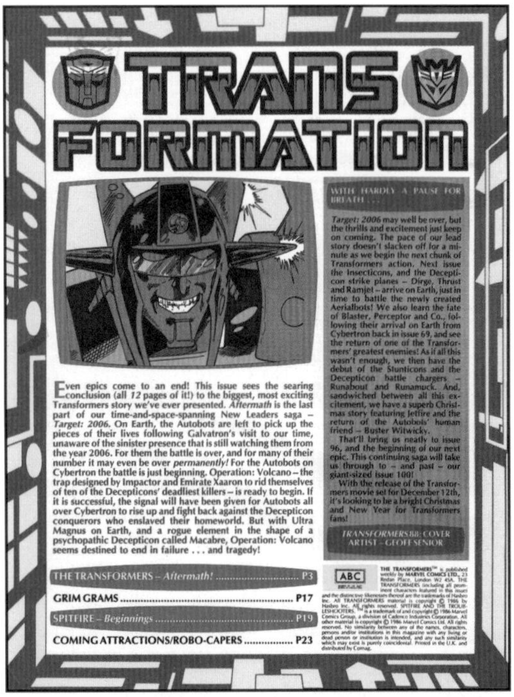
TRANSFORMATION

WITH HARDLY A PAUSE FOR BREATH . . .

Target: 2006 may well be over, but the thrills and excitement just keep on coming. The pace of our lead story doesn't slacken off for a minute as we begin the next chunk of Transformers action. Next issue the Insecticons, and the Decepticon strike planes – Dirge, Thrust and Ramjet – arrive on Earth, just in time to battle the newly created Aerialbots! We also learn the fate of Blaster, Perceptor and Co., following their arrival on Earth from Cybertron back in issue 69, and see the return of one of the Transformers' greatest enemies! As if all this wasn't enough, we then have the debut of the Stunticons and the Decepticon battle chargers – Runabout and Runamuck. And, sandwiched between all this excitement, we have a superb Christmas story featuring Jetfire and the return of the Autobots' human friend – Buster Witwicky.

That'll bring us neatly to issue 96, and the beginning of our next epic. This continuing saga will take us through to – and past – our giant-sized issue 100!

With the release of the Transformers movie set for December 12th, it's looking to be a bright Christmas and New Year for Transformers fans!

TRANSFORMERS 88: COVER ARTIST – GEOFF SENIOR

Even epics come to an end! This issue sees the searing conclusion (all *12* pages of it!) to the biggest, most exciting Transformers story we've ever presented. *Aftermath* is the last part of our time-and-space-spanning New Leaders saga – *Target: 2006*. On Earth, the Autobots are left to pick up the pieces of their lives following Galvatron's visit to our time, unaware of the sinister presence that is still watching them from the year 2006. For them the battle is over, and for many of their number it may even be over *permanently!* For the Autobots on Cybertron the battle is just beginning. Operation: Volcano – the trap designed by Impactor and Emirate Xaaron to rid themselves of ten of the Decepticons' deadliest killers – is ready to begin. If it is successful, the signal will have been given for Autobots all over Cybertron to rise up and fight back against the Decepticon conquerors who enslaved their homeworld. But with Ultra Magnus on Earth, and a rogue element in the shape of a psychopathic Decepticon called Macabre, Operation: Volcano seems destined to end in failure . . . and tragedy!

THE TRANSFORMERS – *Aftermath!* P3
GRIM GRAMS P17
SPITFIRE – *Beginnings* P19
COMING ATTRACTIONS/ROBO-CAPERS P23

ABC

THE TRANSFORMERS™ is published weekly by MARVEL COMICS LTD., 23 Redan Place, London W2 4SA. THE TRANSFORMERS (including all prominent characters featured in this issue) and the distinctive likenesses thereof are the trademarks of Hasbro Inc. All TRANSFORMERS material is copyright © 1986 by Hasbro Inc. All rights reserved. SPITFIRE AND THE TROUBLESHOOTERS.™ is a trademark of and copyright © 1986 Marvel Comics Group, a division of Cadence Industries Corporation. All other material is copyright © 1986 Marvel Comics Ltd. All rights reserved. No similarity between any of the names, characters, persons and/or institutions in this magazine with any living or dead person or institution is intended, and any such similarity which may exist is purely coincidental. Printed in the U.K. and distributed by Comag.

Issue #88's "TransFormation" page.

"So yes, we thought we'd made Impactor a Nick Fury-Howling Commando-type of leader. He was just an archetype really, but we had a bit of fun with him. Rack 'n Ruin–I don't know *where* he came from. I have a feeling it was probably the name first and I went from there, with Ron drawing him."

In issue #92, a reader asks Grimlock why Impactor had two hands on Page 13 of issue #79. Grimlock explains that Impactor's right arm was interchangeable, "allowing him to have a variety of weapon arms or a normal arm." The robotic bounty hunter Death's Head, famous for his interchangeable wrist attachments, would make his debut in issue #113. Does Grimlock's reply, written by Furman, mark the beginning of the character? "I think quite possibly yes. We never used the interchangeable arm in 'Target,' but yes, that's probably a seed of what became Death's Head in the end."

One pre-existing character, Omega Supreme, is notable by his absence. In issue #79 Smokescreen suggests that they set Omega on Galvatron and the other Decepticons, but nothing comes of it. "He'd have been one character too many in the mix," says Furman, explaining why Omega is mentioned but never seen. "And the trouble with Omega Supreme is that he is such a powerful character that it would have felt like you were subordinating Ultra Magnus. If you have Omega, then Magnus doesn't become as important and necessary. So he was off stage for the duration."

At the heart of "Target: 2006," of course, is Galvatron. Never before in *TFUK* had there been a character as powerful. His invulnerability becomes a subplot in its own right, with readers anticipating a supremely satisfying moment when Magnus confronts and defeats the Decepticon. Instead, it is Magnus who is defeated.

Galvatron was never going to be beaten in a straight fight, says Furman. "It was very much a case of 'we can't have him beaten because he goes straight back into the Movie and he still has to be the unbeaten Galvatron.' But we also wanted a villain who was incredibly powerful. Megatron always underperformed in the stories and the cartoons. Galvatron was supposed to be the ultimate Megatron and therefore someone who your average Autobot just could not beat. I'm a big fan of Alan Moore's run on *Captain Britain*, and you had this fantastic villain called The Fury, and he just couldn't be stopped. Nobody beat him—even at the end it takes everything everybody's got to kill him. So we wanted to do a really bad bad guy."

So how do you defeat a villain who cannot be beaten physically? Simple: you trick him. "Target: 2006" has epic fight scenes, time travel, and fistfuls of new characters; it features glimpses of Unicron, the final battle between Megatron and Optimus Prime, and the death of Starscream; and if all that wasn't enough, it also has a devilishly clever and original climax. Galvatron is defeated not by a special weapon, or by everyone else teaming up to fight him, but by trickery: he's led to believe that he's time-jumped into a parallel universe—a parallel past, specifically—where his actions will have no bearing on his future: a remarkably sophisticated dénouement for a comic that was aimed at 8 to 12 year olds.

Furman says that, unlike the usual two- and four-part stories, the conclusion of "Target: 2006" was only sketched out when the first episodes went to print. "Ian and I would go through all the stories, all the scripts, and often we would write the story in outline first and then break it down into episodes. So when we were planning a big storyline we would kind of address it up front and think 'this is what we want to do and this is where we want it to go.' But I can't hand on my heart swear that when we started Part 1 of 'Target: 2006' we knew exactly how we were going to get Galvatron out of there in the end."

And while the "parallel universe ploy" was the answer, Furman still had to find a dramatic and convincing way to make Galvatron leap to the wrong conclusion. In the end, Hot Rod, Blurr, and Kup disguise an offline Skywarp as Starscream, who then proceeds (by means of a fake pre-recorded message) to goad Galvatron into destroying him 20 years too soon. It's barmy but brilliant, not least because it hinges on something that is unique to Transformers: the ability to disguise one Decepticon jet as another by spray-painting them. Furman himself, however, would not necessarily agree with such a positive critical analysis.

"The trick at the end—Ian and I were worried about it at the time. We wondered whether we were jumping the shark with this whole idea. We asked ourselves, 'is this a stretch even for our audience?' In retrospect it plays OK, but it's like, 'they've got to repaint Skywarp, they've got to kind of do a recording of Starscream's voice, and Galvatron's not got to notice any of this.' And at the time I'm afraid we did think 'are we pushing this too far?' And we tried to set it up as well as possible—the whole thing's supposed to happen in a split second: he loses his temper and blows 'Starscream' to hell. We were aware that it was possibly a bit contrived. But I guess it doesn't play too badly in the end.

"There was never really a Plan B as far as the ending was concerned. I think we'd have had to have some more direct interference from Unicron, because we always had it that Unicron was pulling the strings of Hot Rod and Kup and the others. And so we'd probably have had them come back with some kind of super-weapon that could restrain him and take him back—restrained rather than defeated. But I don't think we got that far at the time!"

"Target: 2006" finished in November 1986, a month or so before the release in UK cinemas of *Transformers: The Movie*. As a teaser for the film, the story worked a treat: by issue #88, *TFUK* readers knew that in the Movie, Optimus Prime and Megatron would clash for the last time; Starscream would die; and a mysterious and phenomenally powerful being called Unicron would attempt to destroy Cybertron. Perhaps even more exciting, they would get to see the likes of Galvatron, Ultra Magnus, Hot Rod *et al* on the big screen. And given that "Target: 2006" had established Galvatron as virtually omnipotent, how on earth would the Autobots of 2006 defeat him?

Furman says that he tried to avoid putting spoilers in "Target: 2006", but that certain things—the fact that Megatron became Galvatron; the fate of Starscream—were unavoidable. "With Starscream's death it was neither integral enough to the Movie to be a problem or [even] such a big event—because at the time, Starscream, while he was a good, strong character, wasn't a main character in the way that he would go on to become."

"Target: 2006" was notable for something else too: in the eyes of die-hard *TFUK* fans, it legitimized The Movie. Aside from the first season, the animated series was rarely seen on British TV, and was always treated by *TFUK* as a rogue continuity, easily ignored in favor of the "proper" storyline being played out in the comic. But "Target: 2006" had made it very clear that for the first (and, as it would turn out, only) time, the cartoon–in Movie form–was part of that "proper" storyline. *TFUK* readers could therefore go to the cinema knowing that events on screen were happening to "their" characters in "their" comic.

Over a quarter of a century later, "Target: 2006" still stands up as one of—if not the—best *Transformers* stories ever. Furman says he remains proud of the story, even if he doesn't consider it perfect. "If I had to rewrite it I think I'd make more of Operation: Volcano. It felt a bit rushed and a bit anticlimactic. It just got squeezed out with everything else and I don't feel it lived up to its hype, given that it was supposedly this big event."

And yet there are very few Transformers fans who could find significant fault in a story that introduced Galvatron, Ultra Magnus, and the Wreckers to the *TFUK* Universe, and that told the world—well, UK comic fans, at least—that *TFUK* wasn't the biggest-selling comic just because it featured cool toys, but because it told thrilling, 122-page action adventure stories on a par with anything the likes of *2000AD* was putting out. It's fair to assume that "Target: 2006" transformed a fair few casual readers into the type of diehard *TFUK* loyalists that kept the title going for another five years.

Continuity

As Furman says, "Target: 2006" was designed to slot in between US stories, specifically "Showdown!" (from *TFUS* #20, reprinted in *TFUK* #72–73) and "Aerialbots Over America!" (*TFUS* #21, reprinted in *TFUK* #89–90). If you were an American reader, you'd have assumed that the injury that Optimus Prime is recovering from in "Aerialbots Over America!" was the one he sustained whilst saving Skids' life in issue *TFUS* #19. As a UK reader, you'd have noticed that Prime no longer had the injury at the start of "Target: 2006" (issue #78), and therefore have assumed that it'd been patched up. In literally

the last panel of "Target: 2006" (issue #88) Prime sports an identical injury, and it's not until issue #100's "Distant Thunder!" that we learn that it was sustained during his adventures in Limbo. See, it all makes perfect sense!

The sheer size and scope and, well, epicness of "Target: 2006" makes the sudden lurch back to the comparitively small-scale US stories seem particularly jarring. And whilst Rimmer and Furman did their best to smooth all the stories into one cohesive whole, it is strange to hear Optimus Prime remark in issue #89's reprint of "Aerialbots Over America!" that the arrival of so-called Cybertronian Seven (Blaster, Perceptor *et al*) constitutes "the most serious turn of events since we arrived on this planet four million years ago."

Furman's first opportunity to contextualize "Target: 2006" came with issue #96's "Prey," which kicked off the next batch of UK stories. The first page has Optimus watching a bank of monitor screens that show scenes from both US and UK stories: the Decepticon jets arriving over the space bridge (from "Aerialbots Over America!") and Scourge throwing a slab of metal (from part five of "Target: 2006").

"We were at pains always to tell readers that this was all still one big story," says Furman. "Whenever we finished something big like 'Target: 2006' there was never very much of a lead back in to the US reprints. I think there's one panel at the end of 'Target' that vaguely feeds back into the 'Aerialbots' story. But until 'Prey' there's no fall out from 'Target'—it's a little bit like, 'Finally Optimus acknowledges that all this has gone on in his absence.'"

Reprint editions

Marvel UK planned to reprint "Target: 2006" across four issues of the *Collected Comics* series, starting with issue #15, but as the "TransFormation" page in issue #276 made clear, these plans were abandoned after the original prints of Parts 3–5 went missing in transit. Somewhat confusingly, the cover to *Collected Comics* #16 is a reprint of issue #84.

Galvatron and Ultra Magnus stick-on badges given away free with issues #98–99.

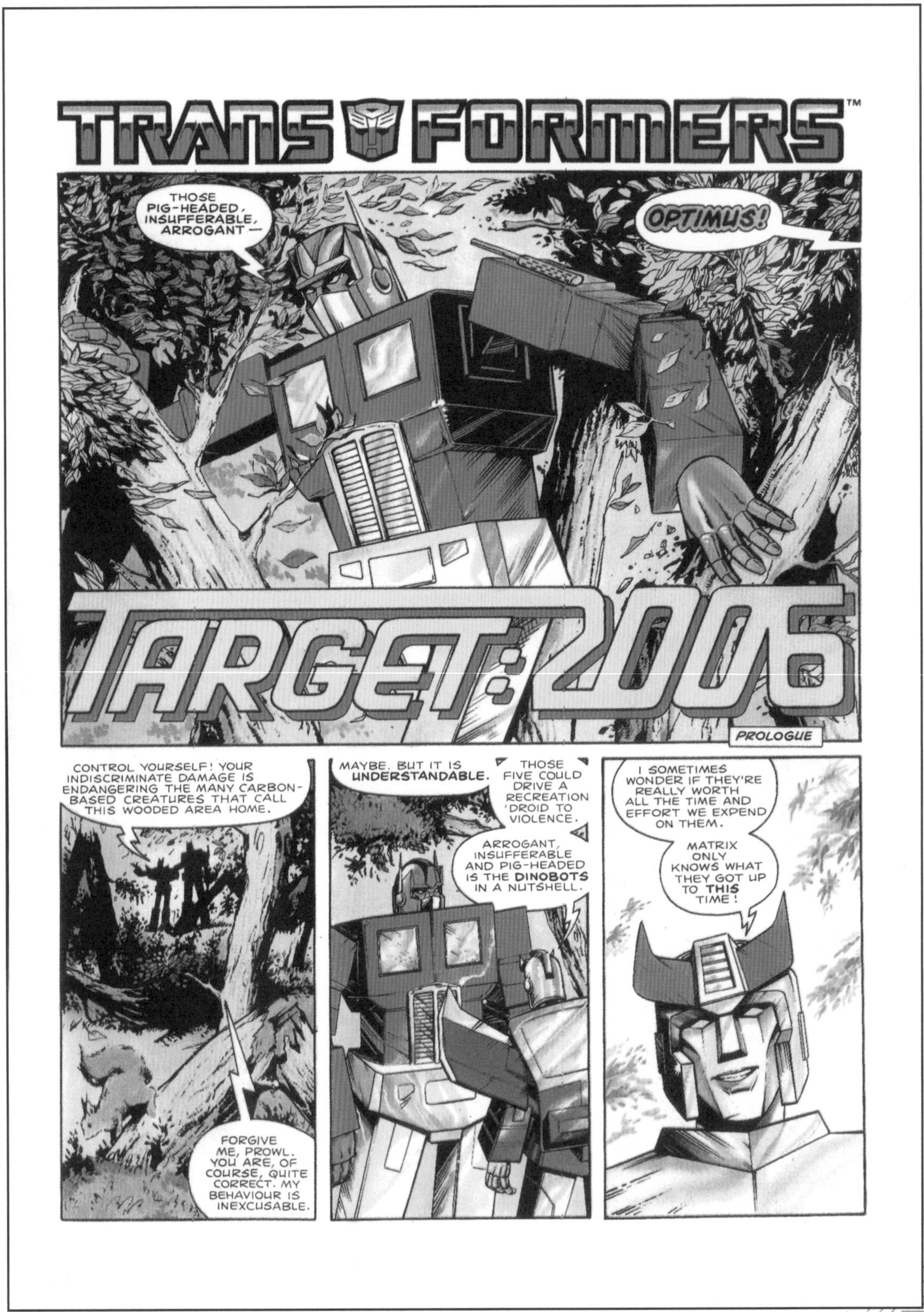
TRANSFORMERS
THOSE PIG-HEADED, INSUFFERABLE, ARROGANT —
OPTIMUS!
TARGET: 2006
PROLOGUE
CONTROL YOURSELF! YOUR INDISCRIMINATE DAMAGE IS ENDANGERING THE MANY CARBON-BASED CREATURES THAT CALL THIS WOODED AREA HOME.
FORGIVE ME, PROWL. YOU ARE, OF COURSE, QUITE CORRECT. MY BEHAVIOUR IS INEXCUSABLE.
MAYBE. BUT IT IS UNDERSTANDABLE.
THOSE FIVE COULD DRIVE A RECREATION 'DROID TO VIOLENCE.
ARROGANT, INSUFFERABLE AND PIG-HEADED IS THE DINOBOTS IN A NUTSHELL.
I SOMETIMES WONDER IF THEY'RE REALLY WORTH ALL THE TIME AND EFFORT WE EXPEND ON THEM.
MATRIX ONLY KNOWS WHAT THEY GOT UP TO THIS TIME!

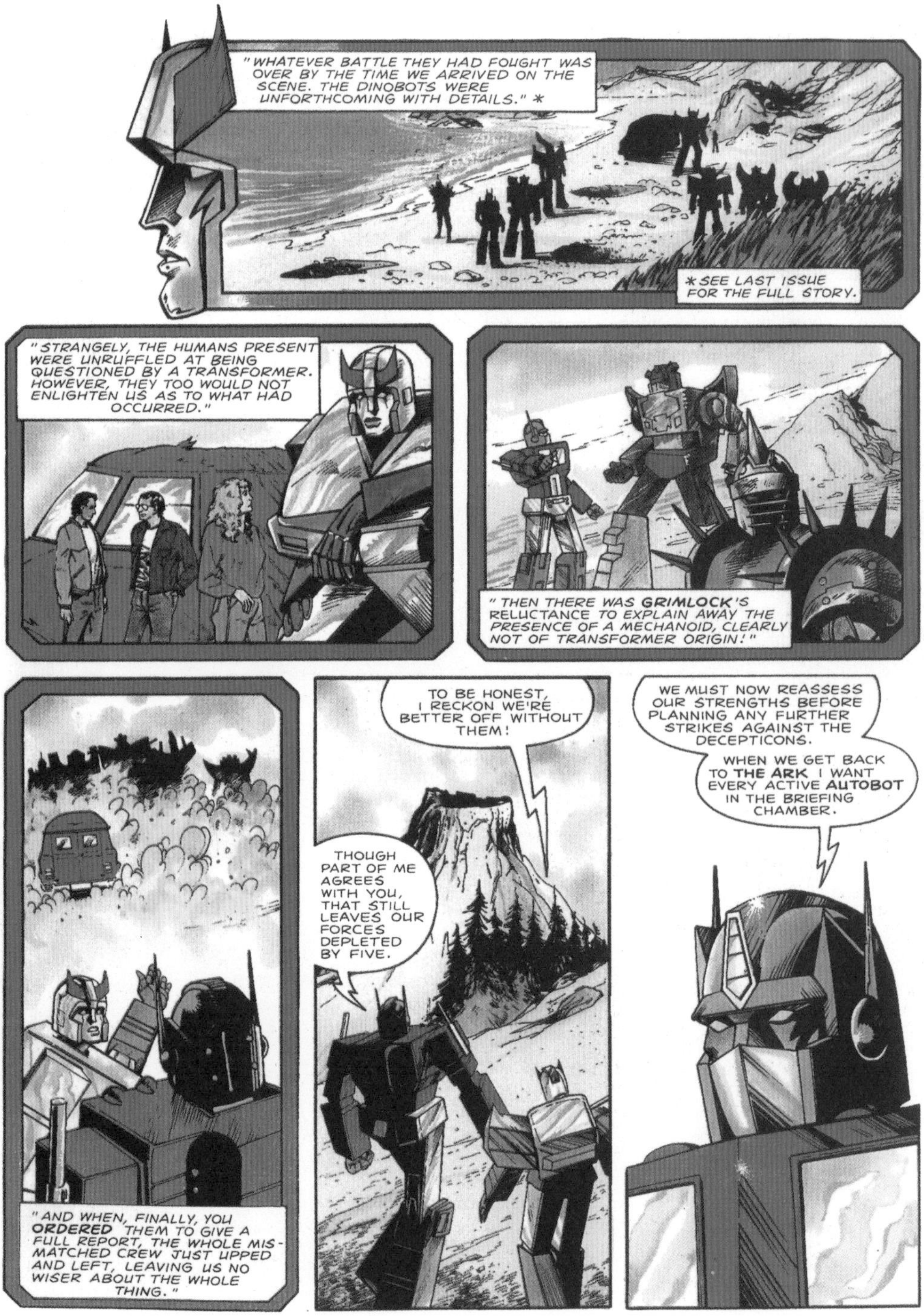

"WHATEVER BATTLE THEY HAD FOUGHT WAS OVER BY THE TIME WE ARRIVED ON THE SCENE. THE DINOBOTS WERE UNFORTHCOMING WITH DETAILS." *
* SEE LAST ISSUE FOR THE FULL STORY.
"STRANGELY, THE HUMANS PRESENT WERE UNRUFFLED AT BEING QUESTIONED BY A TRANSFORMER. HOWEVER, THEY TOO WOULD NOT ENLIGHTEN US AS TO WHAT HAD OCCURRED."
"THEN THERE WAS GRIMLOCK'S RELUCTANCE TO EXPLAIN AWAY THE PRESENCE OF A MECHANOID, CLEARLY NOT OF TRANSFORMER ORIGIN!"
"AND WHEN, FINALLY, YOU ORDERED THEM TO GIVE A FULL REPORT, THE WHOLE MIS-MATCHED CREW JUST UPPED AND LEFT, LEAVING US NO WISER ABOUT THE WHOLE THING."
TO BE HONEST, I RECKON WE'RE BETTER OFF WITHOUT THEM!
THOUGH PART OF ME AGREES WITH YOU, THAT STILL LEAVES OUR FORCES DEPLETED BY FIVE.
WE MUST NOW REASSESS OUR STRENGTHS BEFORE PLANNING ANY FURTHER STRIKES AGAINST THE DECEPTICONS.
WHEN WE GET BACK TO THE ARK I WANT EVERY ACTIVE AUTOBOT IN THE BRIEFING CHAMBER.

CYBERTRON.

THIS IS IACON. ONCE THE GLEAMING JEWEL IN CYBERTRON'S CROWN, THE **AUTOBOTS'** CAPITAL CITY IS NOW A DESERTED, SMOULDERING RUIN.

BUT, OF LATE – UNKNOWN TO THE DECEPTICONS – IACON HAS ONCE MORE BECOME PIVOTAL IN THE LIVES OF THE REMAINING AUTOBOTS.

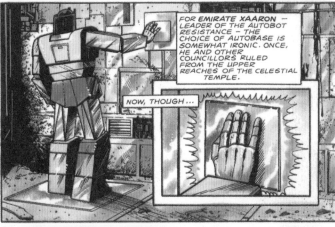

FOR EMIRATE XAARON – LEADER OF THE AUTOBOT RESISTANCE – THE CHOICE OF AUTOBASE IS SOMEWHAT IRONIC. ONCE, HE AND OTHER COUNCILLORS RULED FROM THE UPPER REACHES OF THE CELESTIAL TEMPLE.

NOW, THOUGH ...

THE AUTOBOT HIGH COMMAND HAVE HAD TO MOVE, QUITE LITERALLY...

UNDERGROUND!

EMIRATE, WE WERE WORRIED.

YOUR CONCERN IS APPRECIATED, SKATER.

HOWEVER, I MERELY RAN INTO A DECEPTICON COMMANDO STRIKE SQUAD AND WAS FORCED TO LAY LOW FOR A WHILE.

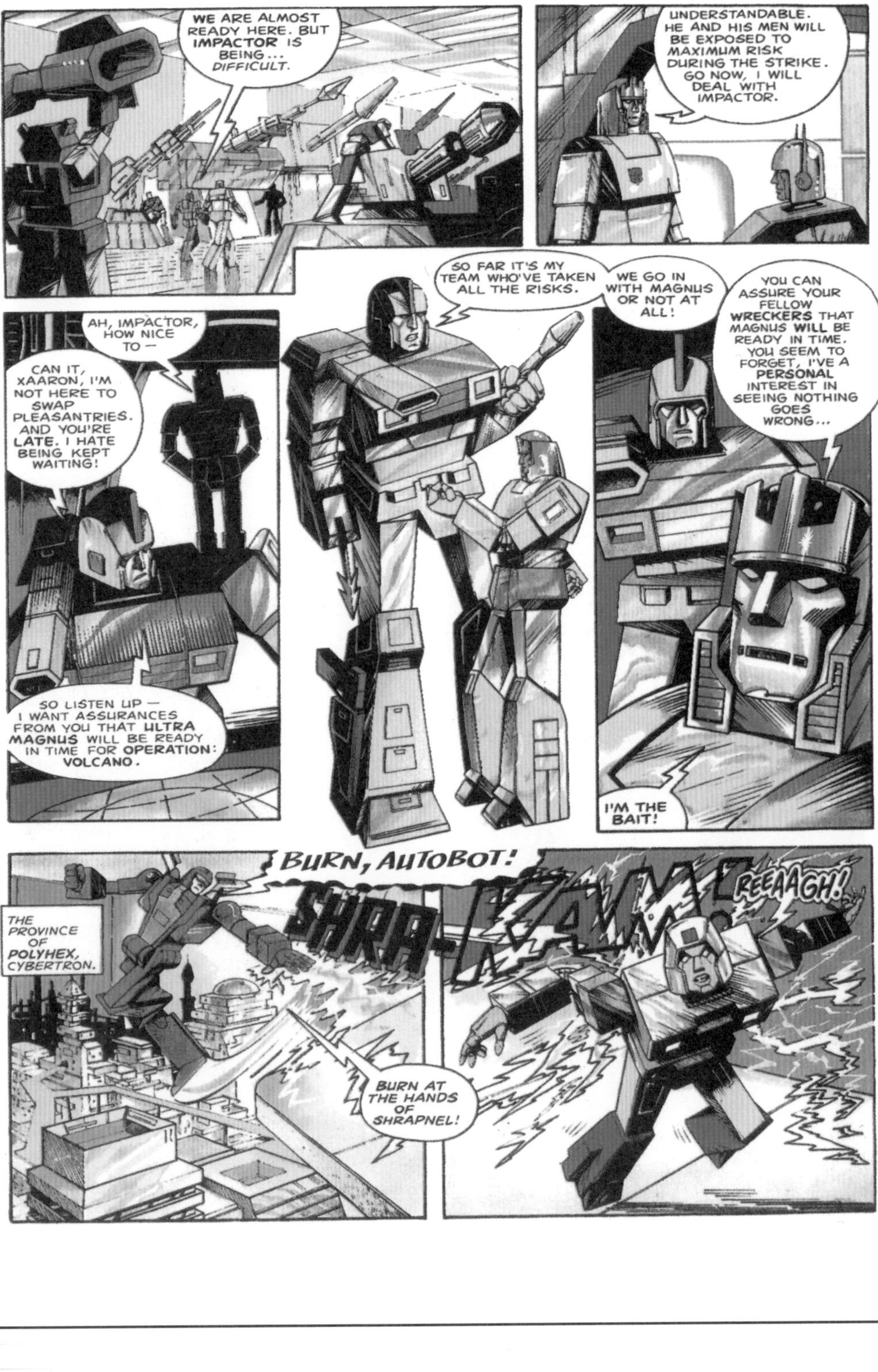
WE ARE ALMOST READY HERE. BUT IMPACTOR IS BEING... DIFFICULT.
UNDERSTANDABLE. HE AND HIS MEN WILL BE EXPOSED TO MAXIMUM RISK DURING THE STRIKE. GO NOW, I WILL DEAL WITH IMPACTOR.
AH, IMPACTOR, HOW NICE TO —
CAN IT, XAARON, I'M NOT HERE TO SWAP PLEASANTRIES. AND YOU'RE LATE. I HATE BEING KEPT WAITING!
SO LISTEN UP — I WANT ASSURANCES FROM YOU THAT ULTRA MAGNUS WILL BE READY IN TIME FOR OPERATION: VOLCANO.
SO FAR IT'S MY TEAM WHO'VE TAKEN ALL THE RISKS.
WE GO IN WITH MAGNUS OR NOT AT ALL!
YOU CAN ASSURE YOUR FELLOW WRECKERS THAT MAGNUS WILL BE READY IN TIME. YOU SEEM TO FORGET, I'VE A PERSONAL INTEREST IN SEEING NOTHING GOES WRONG...
I'M THE BAIT!
THE PROVINCE OF POLYHEX, CYBERTRON.
BURN, AUTOBOT!
SHRA-KZAM!
REEAAGH!
BURN AT THE HANDS OF SHRAPNEL!

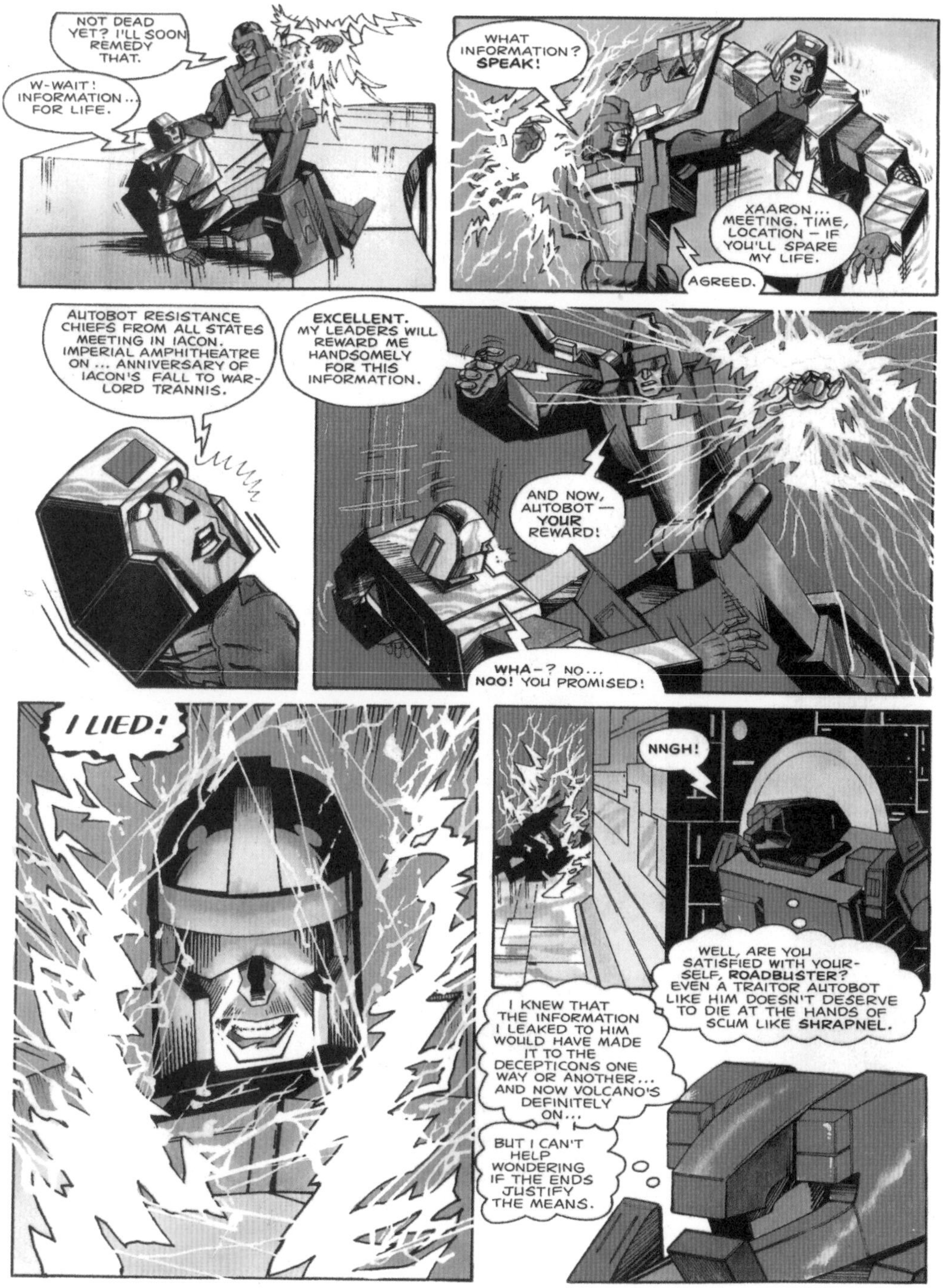

NOT DEAD YET? I'LL SOON REMEDY THAT.
W-WAIT! INFORMATION... FOR LIFE.
WHAT INFORMATION? SPEAK!
XAARON... MEETING. TIME, LOCATION — IF YOU'LL SPARE MY LIFE.
AGREED.
AUTOBOT RESISTANCE CHIEFS FROM ALL STATES MEETING IN IACON. IMPERIAL AMPHITHEATRE ON ... ANNIVERSARY OF IACON'S FALL TO WAR-LORD TRANNIS.
EXCELLENT. MY LEADERS WILL REWARD ME HANDSOMELY FOR THIS INFORMATION.
AND NOW, AUTOBOT — YOUR REWARD!
WHA-? NO... NOO! YOU PROMISED!
I LIED!
NNGH!
WELL, ARE YOU SATISFIED WITH YOUR-SELF, ROADBUSTER? EVEN A TRAITOR AUTOBOT LIKE HIM DOESN'T DESERVE TO DIE AT THE HANDS OF SCUM LIKE SHRAPNEL.
I KNEW THAT THE INFORMATION I LEAKED TO HIM WOULD HAVE MADE IT TO THE DECEPTICONS ONE WAY OR ANOTHER... AND NOW VOLCANO'S DEFINITELY ON...
BUT I CAN'T HELP WONDERING IF THE ENDS JUSTIFY THE MEANS.

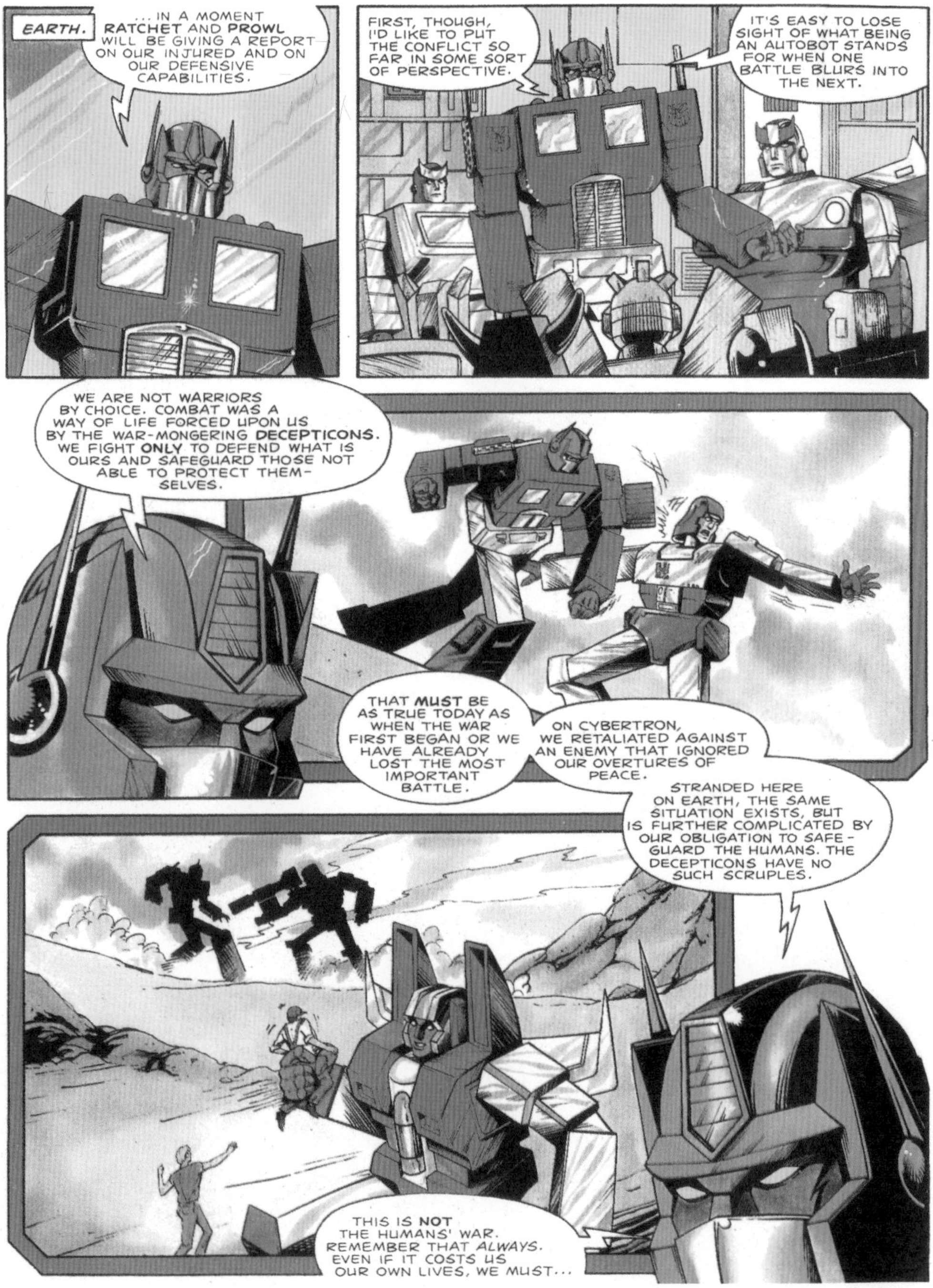
EARTH.
...IN A MOMENT RATCHET AND PROWL WILL BE GIVING A REPORT ON OUR INJURED AND ON OUR DEFENSIVE CAPABILITIES.
FIRST, THOUGH, I'D LIKE TO PUT THE CONFLICT SO FAR IN SOME SORT OF PERSPECTIVE.
IT'S EASY TO LOSE SIGHT OF WHAT BEING AN AUTOBOT STANDS FOR WHEN ONE BATTLE BLURS INTO THE NEXT.
WE ARE NOT WARRIORS BY CHOICE. COMBAT WAS A WAY OF LIFE FORCED UPON US BY THE WAR-MONGERING DECEPTICONS. WE FIGHT ONLY TO DEFEND WHAT IS OURS AND SAFEGUARD THOSE NOT ABLE TO PROTECT THEM-SELVES.
THAT MUST BE AS TRUE TODAY AS WHEN THE WAR FIRST BEGAN OR WE HAVE ALREADY LOST THE MOST IMPORTANT BATTLE.
ON CYBERTRON, WE RETALIATED AGAINST AN ENEMY THAT IGNORED OUR OVERTURES OF PEACE.
STRANDED HERE ON EARTH, THE SAME SITUATION EXISTS, BUT IS FURTHER COMPLICATED BY OUR OBLIGATION TO SAFE-GUARD THE HUMANS. THE DECEPTICONS HAVE NO SUCH SCRUPLES.
THIS IS NOT THE HUMANS' WAR. REMEMBER THAT ALWAYS. EVEN IF IT COSTS US OUR OWN LIVES, WE MUST...

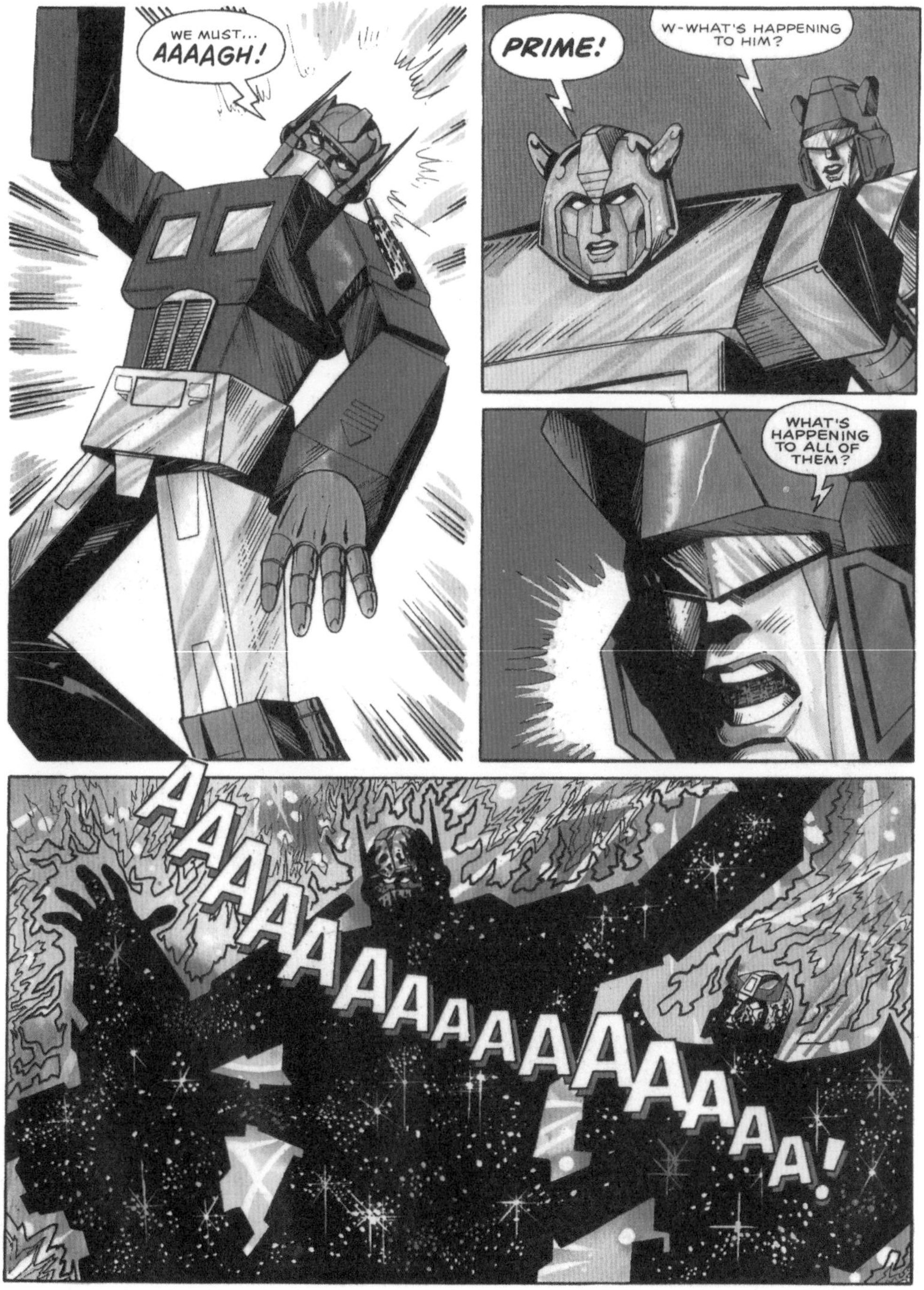

WE MUST... AAAAGH!
PRIME!
W-WHAT'S HAPPENING TO HIM?
WHAT'S HAPPENING TO ALL OF THEM?
AAAAAAAAAAAAAAAAAA!

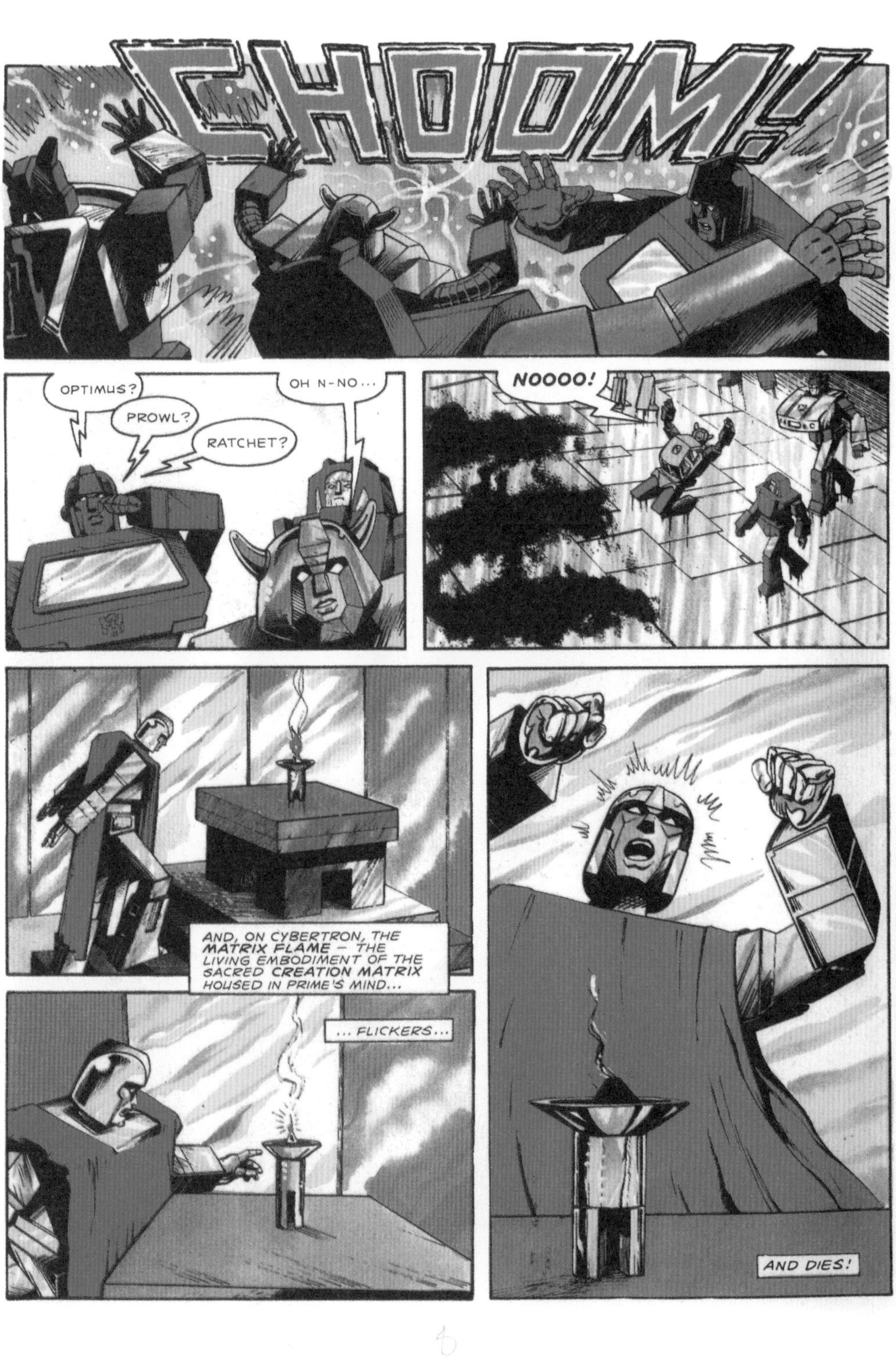
CHOOM!
OPTIMUS?
PROWL?
RATCHET?
OH N-NO...
NOOOO!
AND, ON CYBERTRON, THE MATRIX FLAME – THE LIVING EMBODIMENT OF THE SACRED CREATION MATRIX HOUSED IN PRIME'S MIND...
...FLICKERS...
AND DIES!

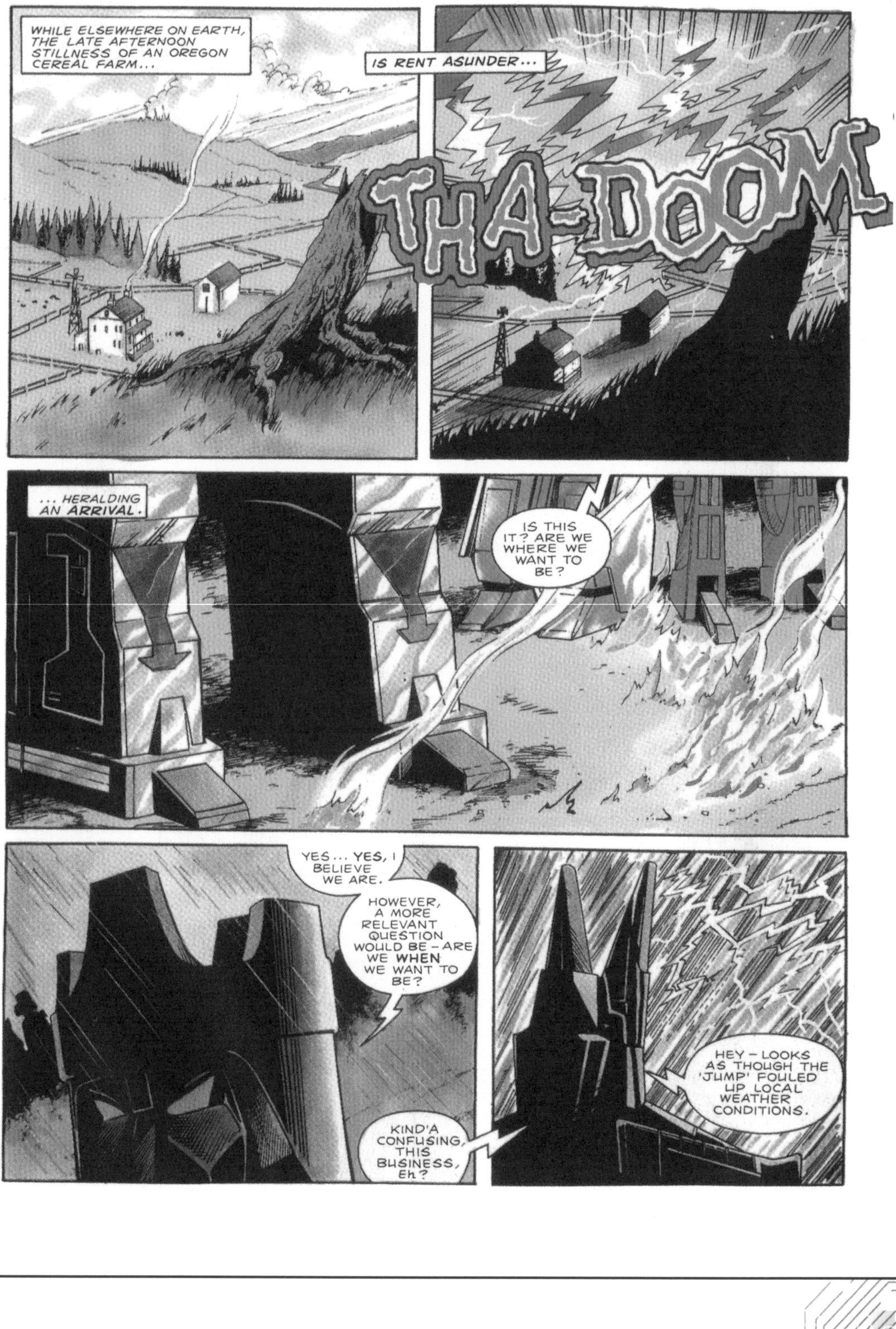
WHILE ELSEWHERE ON EARTH, THE LATE AFTERNOON STILLNESS OF AN OREGON CEREAL FARM...
IS RENT ASUNDER...
THA-DOOM
... HERALDING AN ARRIVAL.
IS THIS IT? ARE WE WHERE WE WANT TO BE?
YES... YES, I BELIEVE WE ARE.
HOWEVER, A MORE RELEVANT QUESTION WOULD BE - ARE WE WHEN WE WANT TO BE?
KIND'A CONFUSING, THIS BUSINESS, EH?
HEY - LOOKS AS THOUGH THE 'JUMP' FOULED UP LOCAL WEATHER CONDITIONS.

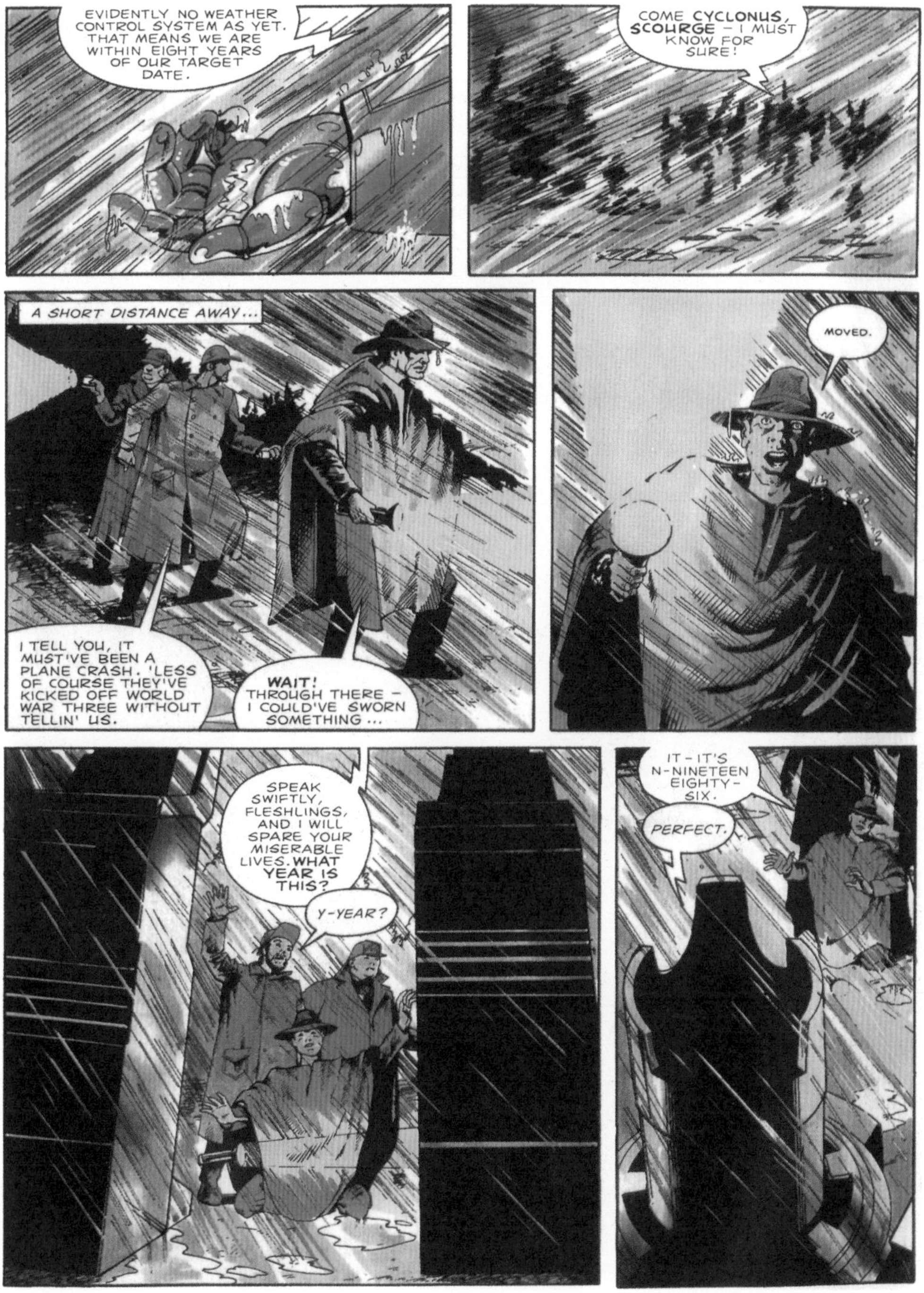
EVIDENTLY NO WEATHER CONTROL SYSTEM AS YET. THAT MEANS WE ARE WITHIN EIGHT YEARS OF OUR TARGET DATE.
COME CYCLONUS, SCOURGE – I MUST KNOW FOR SURE!
A SHORT DISTANCE AWAY...
I TELL YOU, IT MUST'VE BEEN A PLANE CRASH. 'LESS OF COURSE THEY'VE KICKED OFF WORLD WAR THREE WITHOUT TELLIN' US.
WAIT! THROUGH THERE – I COULD'VE SWORN SOMETHING ...
MOVED.
SPEAK SWIFTLY, FLESHLINGS, AND I WILL SPARE YOUR MISERABLE LIVES. WHAT YEAR IS THIS?
Y-YEAR?
IT-IT'S N-NINETEEN EIGHTY-SIX.
PERFECT.

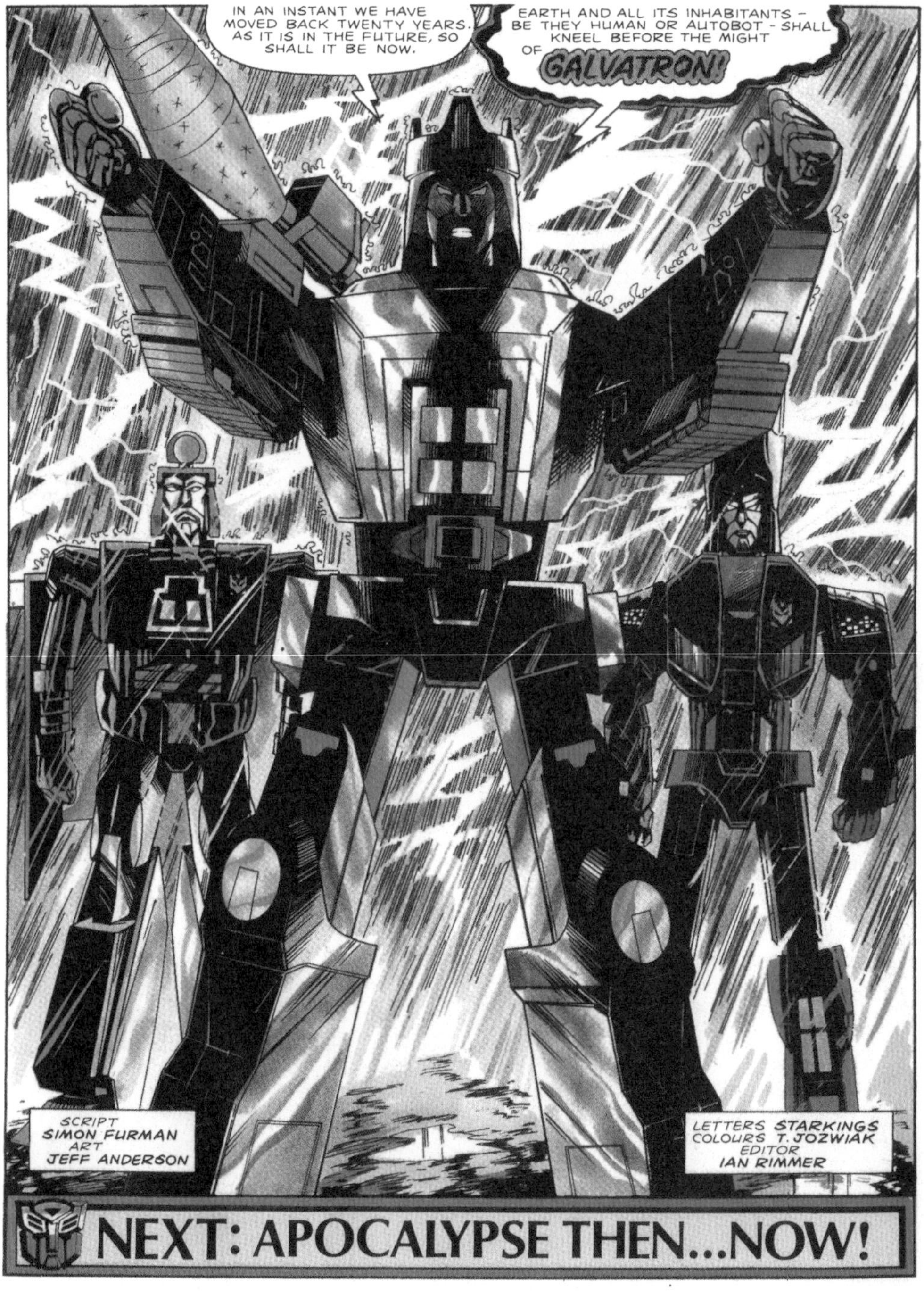
IN AN INSTANT WE HAVE MOVED BACK TWENTY YEARS. AS IT IS IN THE FUTURE, SO SHALL IT BE NOW.
EARTH AND ALL ITS INHABITANTS – BE THEY HUMAN OR AUTOBOT – SHALL KNEEL BEFORE THE MIGHT OF GALVATRON!
SCRIPT SIMON FURMAN ART JEFF ANDERSON
LETTERS STARKINGS COLOURS T. JOZWIAK EDITOR IAN RIMMER
NEXT: APOCALYPSE THEN...NOW!

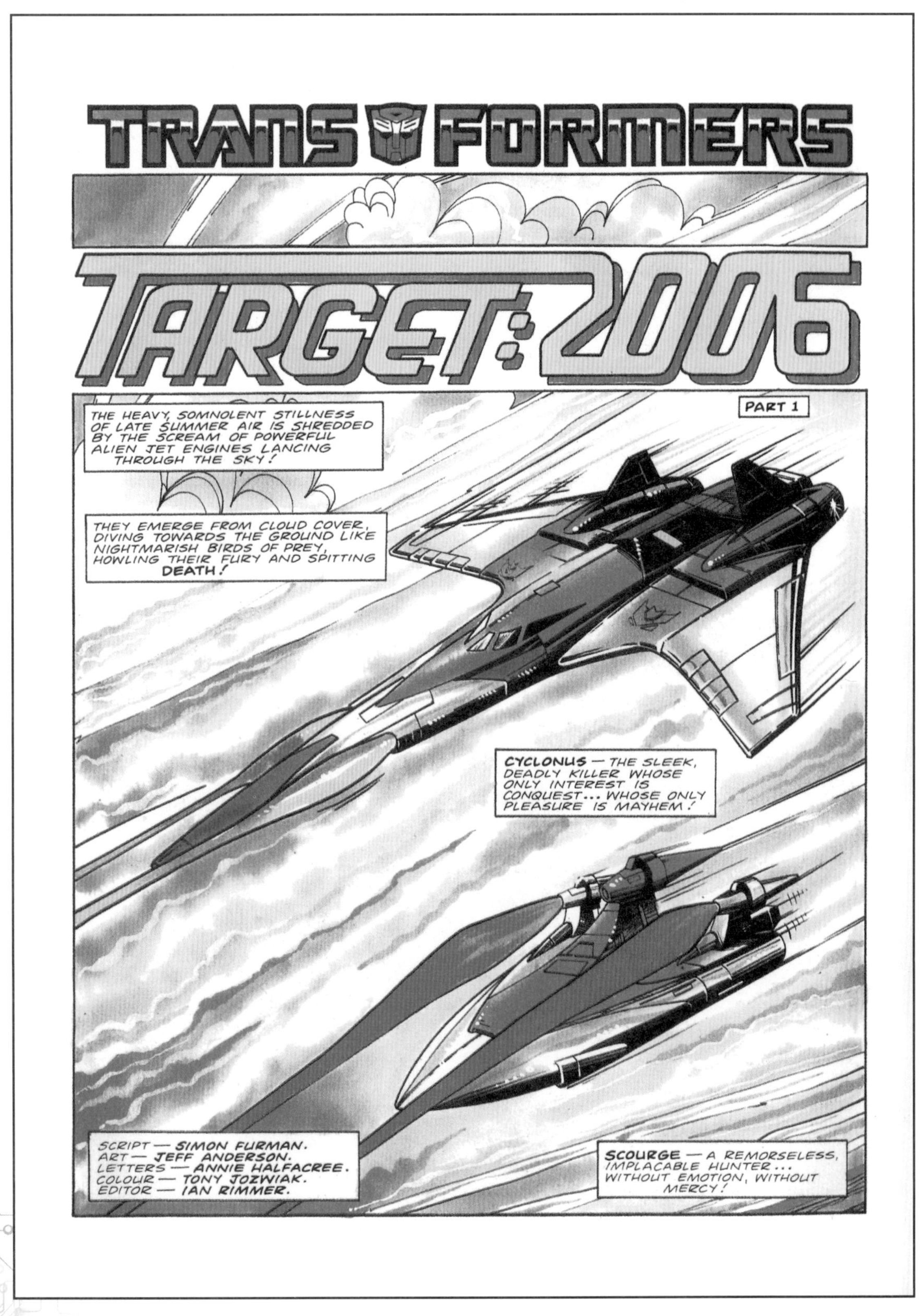
TRANSFORMERS
TARGET: 2006
PART 1
THE HEAVY, SOMNOLENT STILLNESS OF LATE SUMMER AIR IS SHREDDED BY THE SCREAM OF POWERFUL ALIEN JET ENGINES LANCING THROUGH THE SKY!
THEY EMERGE FROM CLOUD COVER, DIVING TOWARDS THE GROUND LIKE NIGHTMARISH BIRDS OF PREY, HOWLING THEIR FURY AND SPITTING DEATH!
CYCLONUS — THE SLEEK, DEADLY KILLER WHOSE ONLY INTEREST IS CONQUEST... WHOSE ONLY PLEASURE IS MAYHEM!
SCRIPT — SIMON FURMAN. ART — JEFF ANDERSON. LETTERS — ANNIE HALFACREE. COLOUR — TONY JOZWIAK. EDITOR — IAN RIMMER.
SCOURGE — A REMORSELESS, IMPLACABLE HUNTER... WITHOUT EMOTION, WITHOUT MERCY!

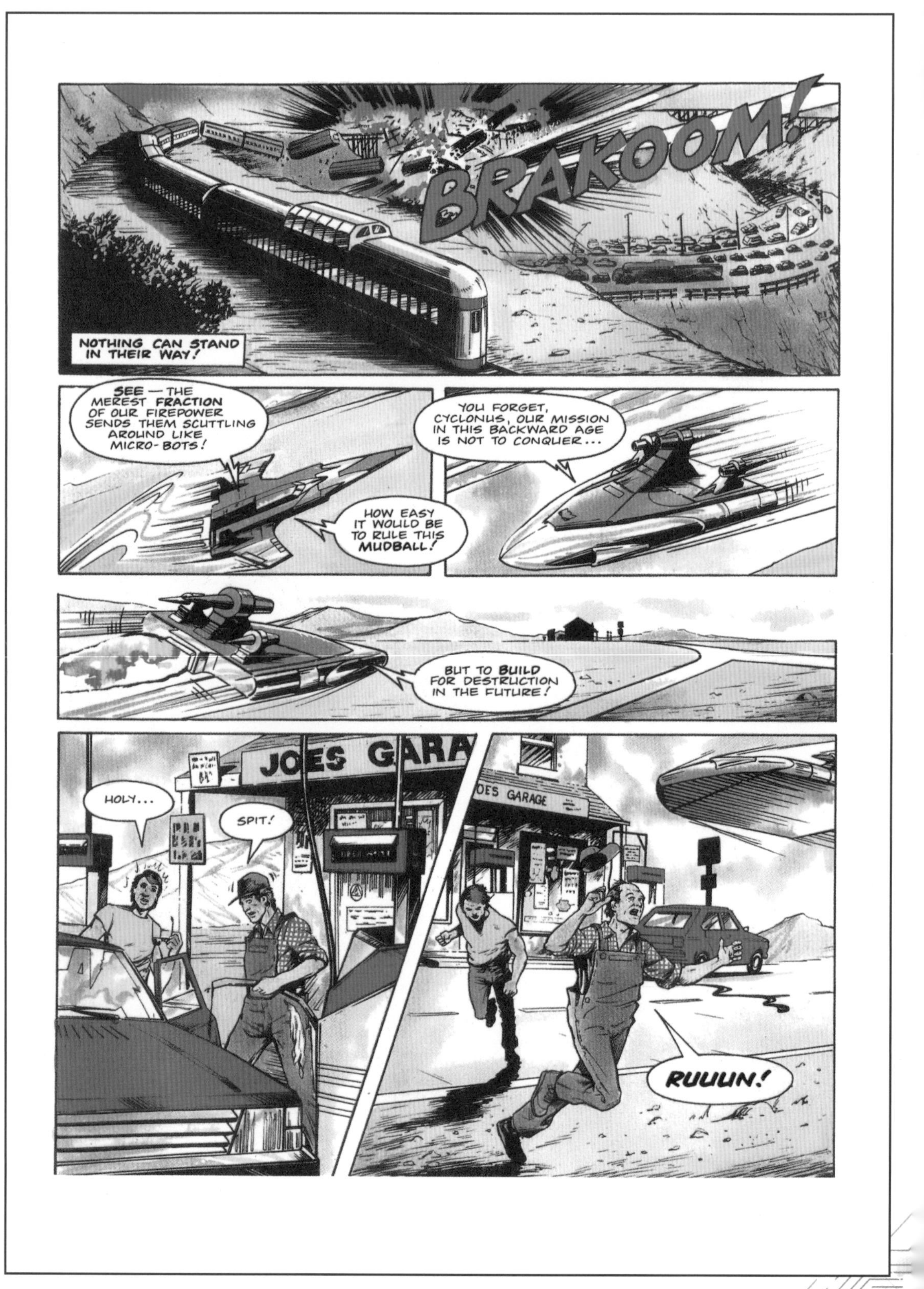
BRAKOOM!
NOTHING CAN STAND IN THEIR WAY!
SEE — THE MEREST FRACTION OF OUR FIREPOWER SENDS THEM SCUTTLING AROUND LIKE MICRO-BOTS!
HOW EASY IT WOULD BE TO RULE THIS MUDBALL!
YOU FORGET, CYCLONUS, OUR MISSION IN THIS BACKWARD AGE IS NOT TO CONQUER...
BUT TO BUILD FOR DESTRUCTION IN THE FUTURE!
JOES GARA
HOLY...
SPIT!
JOE'S GARAGE
RUUUN!

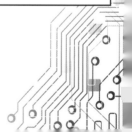

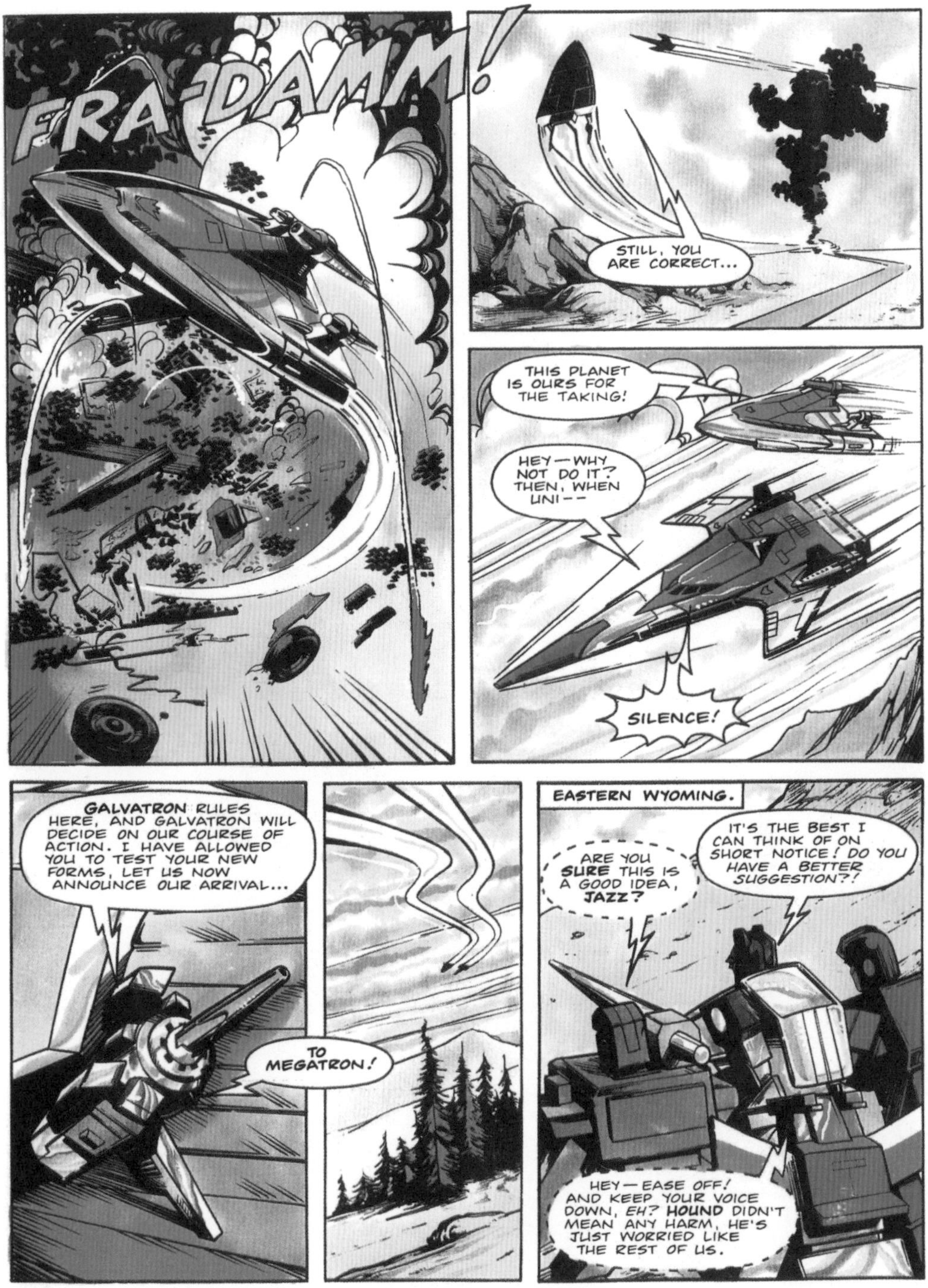
FRA-DAMM!
STILL, YOU ARE CORRECT...
THIS PLANET IS OURS FOR THE TAKING!
HEY—WHY NOT DO IT? THEN, WHEN UNI--
SILENCE!
GALVATRON RULES HERE, AND GALVATRON WILL DECIDE ON OUR COURSE OF ACTION. I HAVE ALLOWED YOU TO TEST YOUR NEW FORMS, LET US NOW ANNOUNCE OUR ARRIVAL...
TO MEGATRON!
EASTERN WYOMING.
ARE YOU SURE THIS IS A GOOD IDEA, JAZZ?
IT'S THE BEST I CAN THINK OF ON SHORT NOTICE! DO YOU HAVE A BETTER SUGGESTION?!
HEY—EASE OFF! AND KEEP YOUR VOICE DOWN, EH? HOUND DIDN'T MEAN ANY HARM, HE'S JUST WORRIED LIKE THE REST OF US.

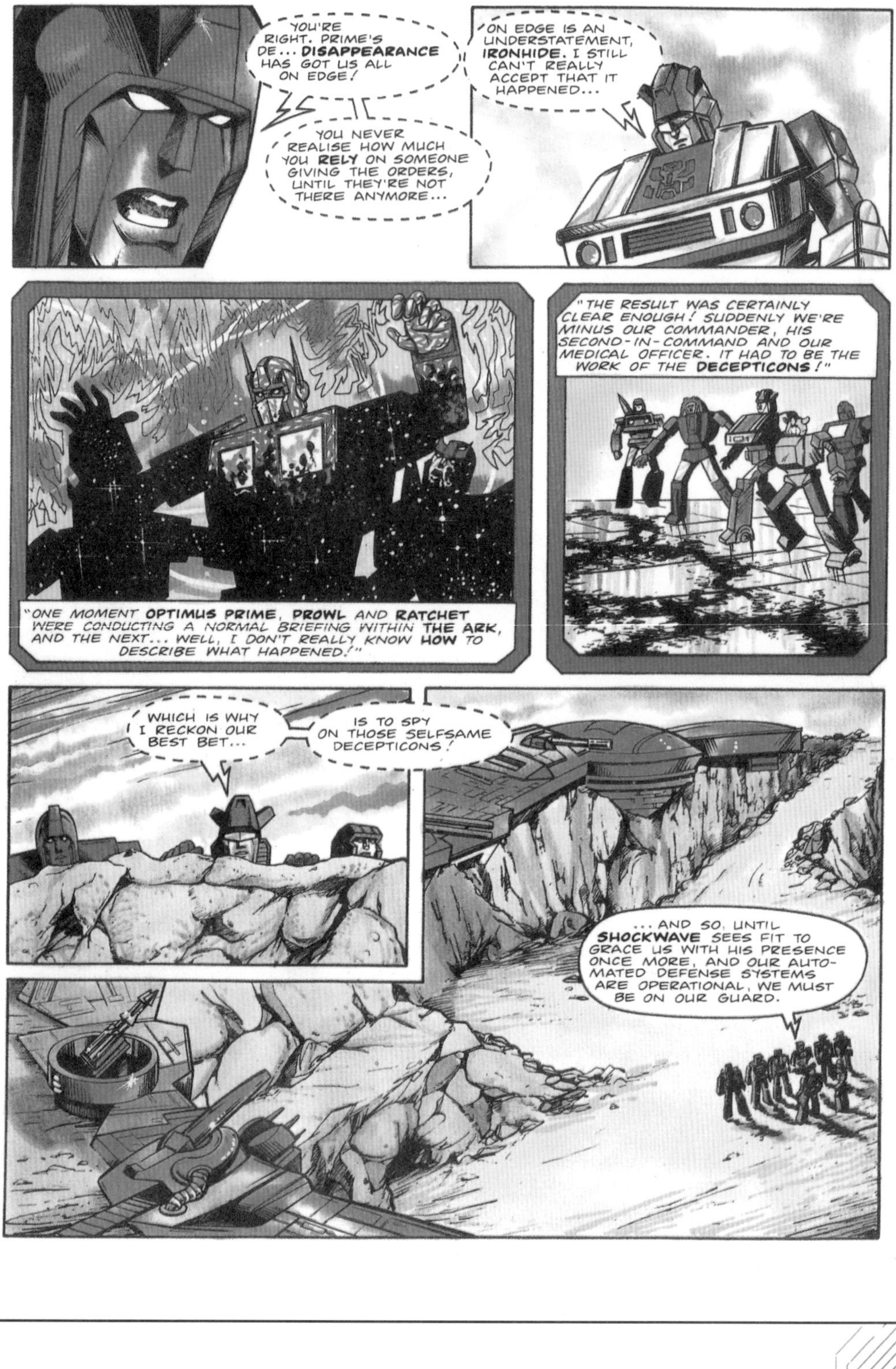
YOU'RE RIGHT. PRIME'S DE... **DISAPPEARANCE** HAS GOT US ALL ON EDGE!
YOU NEVER REALISE HOW MUCH YOU **RELY** ON SOMEONE GIVING THE ORDERS, UNTIL THEY'RE NOT THERE ANYMORE...
ON EDGE IS AN UNDERSTATEMENT, **IRONHIDE.** I STILL CAN'T REALLY ACCEPT THAT IT HAPPENED...
"ONE MOMENT **OPTIMUS PRIME**, **PROWL** AND **RATCHET** WERE CONDUCTING A NORMAL BRIEFING WITHIN **THE ARK**, AND THE NEXT... WELL, I DON'T REALLY KNOW **HOW** TO DESCRIBE WHAT HAPPENED!"
"THE RESULT WAS CERTAINLY CLEAR ENOUGH! SUDDENLY WE'RE MINUS OUR COMMANDER, HIS SECOND-IN-COMMAND AND OUR MEDICAL OFFICER. IT HAD TO BE THE WORK OF THE **DECEPTICONS**!"
WHICH IS WHY I RECKON OUR BEST BET...
IS TO SPY ON THOSE SELFSAME DECEPTICONS!
...AND SO, UNTIL **SHOCKWAVE** SEES FIT TO GRACE US WITH HIS PRESENCE ONCE MORE, AND OUR AUTO-MATED DEFENSE SYSTEMS ARE OPERATIONAL, WE MUST BE ON OUR GUARD.

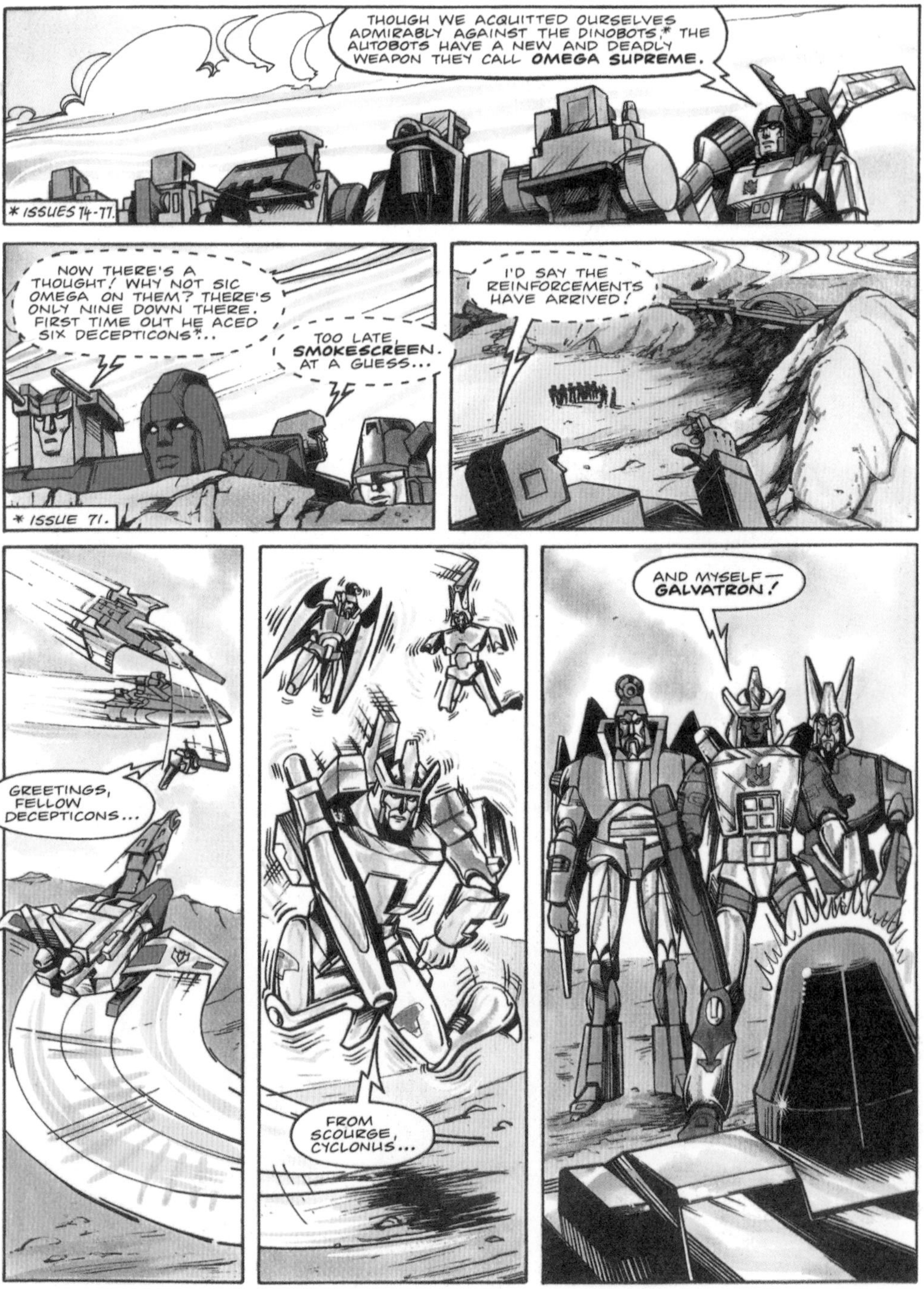

THOUGH WE ACQUITTED OURSELVES ADMIRABLY AGAINST THE DINOBOTS,* THE AUTOBOTS HAVE A NEW AND DEADLY WEAPON THEY CALL OMEGA SUPREME.
* ISSUES 74-77.
NOW THERE'S A THOUGHT! WHY NOT SIC OMEGA ON THEM? THERE'S ONLY NINE DOWN THERE. FIRST TIME OUT HE ACED SIX DECEPTICONS*...
TOO LATE, SMOKESCREEN. AT A GUESS...
* ISSUE 71.
I'D SAY THE REINFORCEMENTS HAVE ARRIVED!
GREETINGS, FELLOW DECEPTICONS...
FROM SCOURGE, CYCLONUS...
AND MYSELF— GALVATRON!

SOUNDWAVE?

SCANNING, COMMANDER **MEGATRON**.

HMMM, THOUGH THEIR NAMES AND FORMS ARE UNFAMILIAR TO ME, A SURFACE SCAN OF THEIR MINDS VALIDATES THEIR CLAIM.

JUST ONE OF THE MANY IMPROVEMENTS MADE BY **UNICRON**. A PITY SUCH A POWERFUL AND RESOURCEFUL BEING MUST --

HOWEVER, SOME FORCE PREVENTS MY PROBING ANY FURTHER.

ENOUGH! WHO EXACTLY ARE YOU, GALVATRON? DID **STRAXUS** SEND YOU ACROSS THE SPACE BRIDGE FROM **CYBERTRON**?

STRAXUS? OH YES, I REMEMBER HIM. **NO**... I AM NO MERE LACKEY AT THE BECK AND CALL OF AN UNIMAGINATIVE TYRANT LIKE STRAXUS!

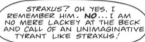

I AM THE **ULTIMATE DECEPTICON**. MORE POWERFUL THAN ANY THAT HAVE EVER EXISTED. IN MY TIME I RULE SUPREME!

YOU SEE, MEGATRON — I COME FROM **THE FUTURE**! FROM A CYBERTRON, AN EARTH, TWENTY YEARS HENCE. **I AM DECEPTICON LEADER IN THE YEAR 2006!**

WHAT?!

SUSPEND YOUR DISBELIEF FOR A MOMENT.

SUFFICE IT TO SAY THAT CERTAIN... AH, CONDITIONS IN 2006 MADE IT ESSENTIAL FOR US TO TIME-JUMP. EVEN IF YOU CANNOT ACCEPT THIS FACT, YOU KNOW WE **ARE** DECEPTICONS.

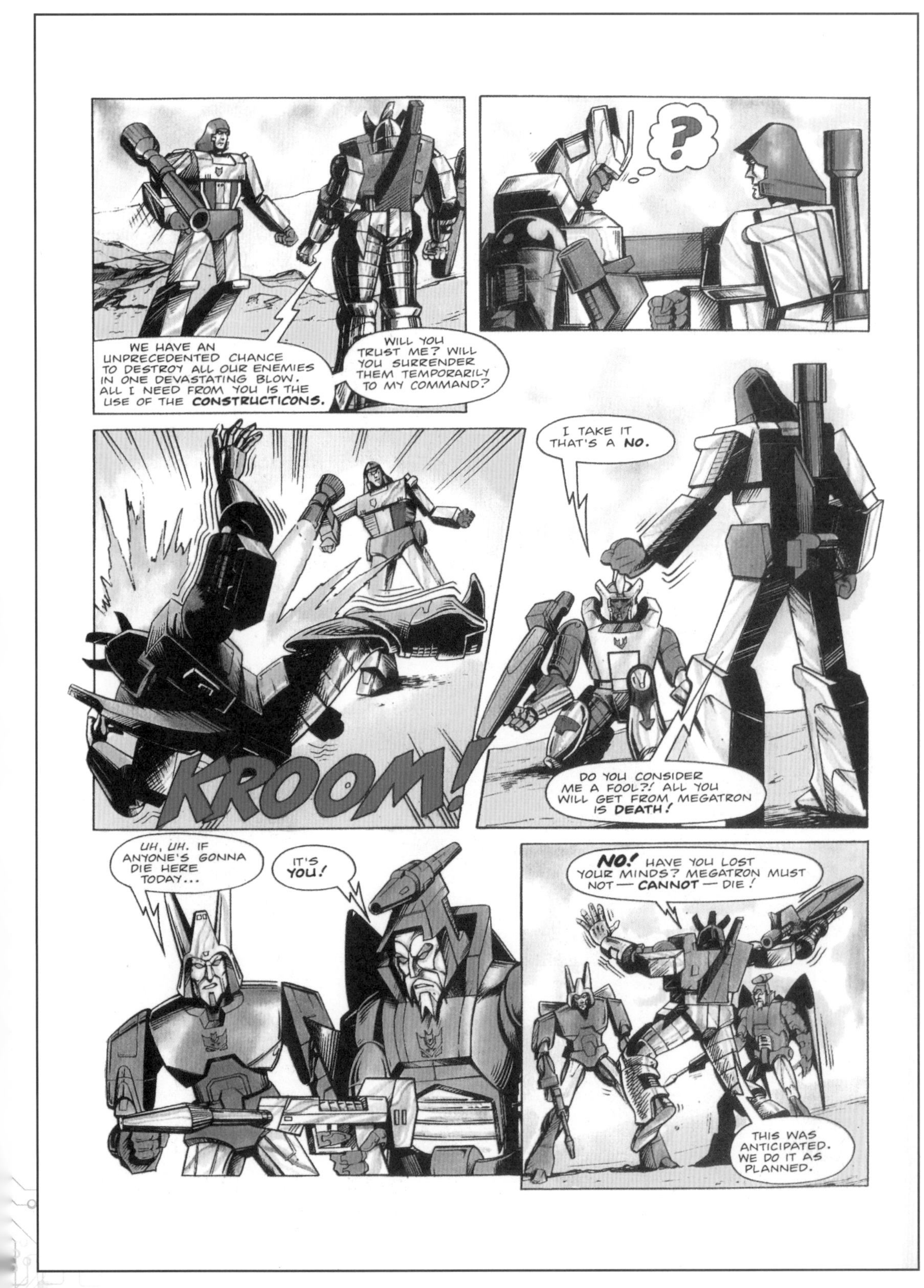
WE HAVE AN UNPRECEDENTED CHANCE TO DESTROY ALL OUR ENEMIES IN ONE DEVASTATING BLOW. ALL I NEED FROM YOU IS THE USE OF THE CONSTRUCTICONS.
WILL YOU TRUST ME? WILL YOU SURRENDER THEM TEMPORARILY TO MY COMMAND?
?
KROOM!
I TAKE IT THAT'S A NO.
DO YOU CONSIDER ME A FOOL?! ALL YOU WILL GET FROM MEGATRON IS DEATH!
UH, UH. IF ANYONE'S GONNA DIE HERE TODAY...
IT'S YOU!
NO! HAVE YOU LOST YOUR MINDS? MEGATRON MUST NOT—CANNOT—DIE!
THIS WAS ANTICIPATED. WE DO IT AS PLANNED.

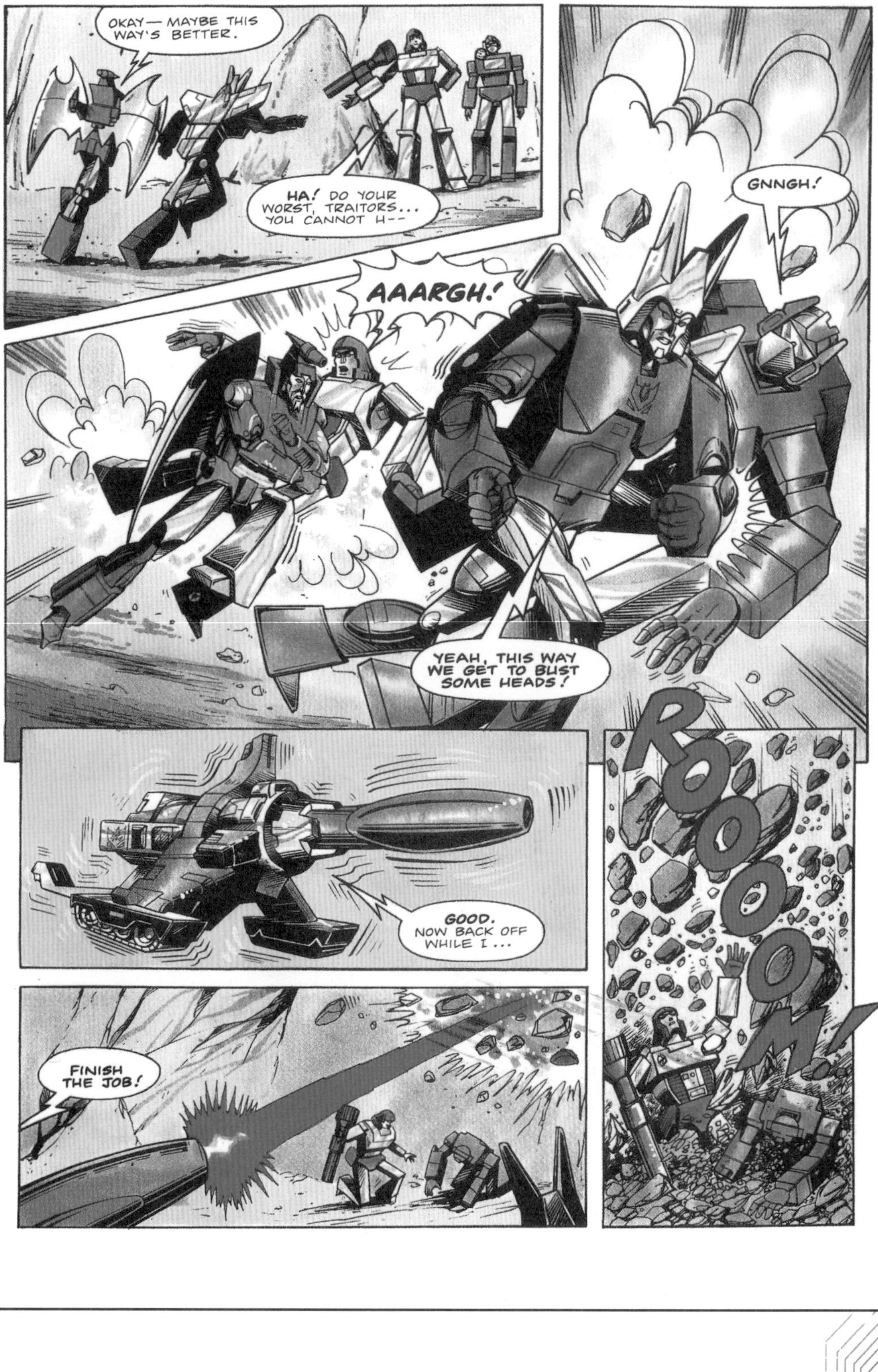

OKAY— MAYBE THIS WAY'S BETTER.
HA! DO YOUR WORST, TRAITORS... YOU CANNOT H--
GNNGH!
AAARGH!
YEAH, THIS WAY WE GET TO BUST SOME HEADS!
GOOD. NOW BACK OFF WHILE I...
FINISH THE JOB!
ROOOOM!

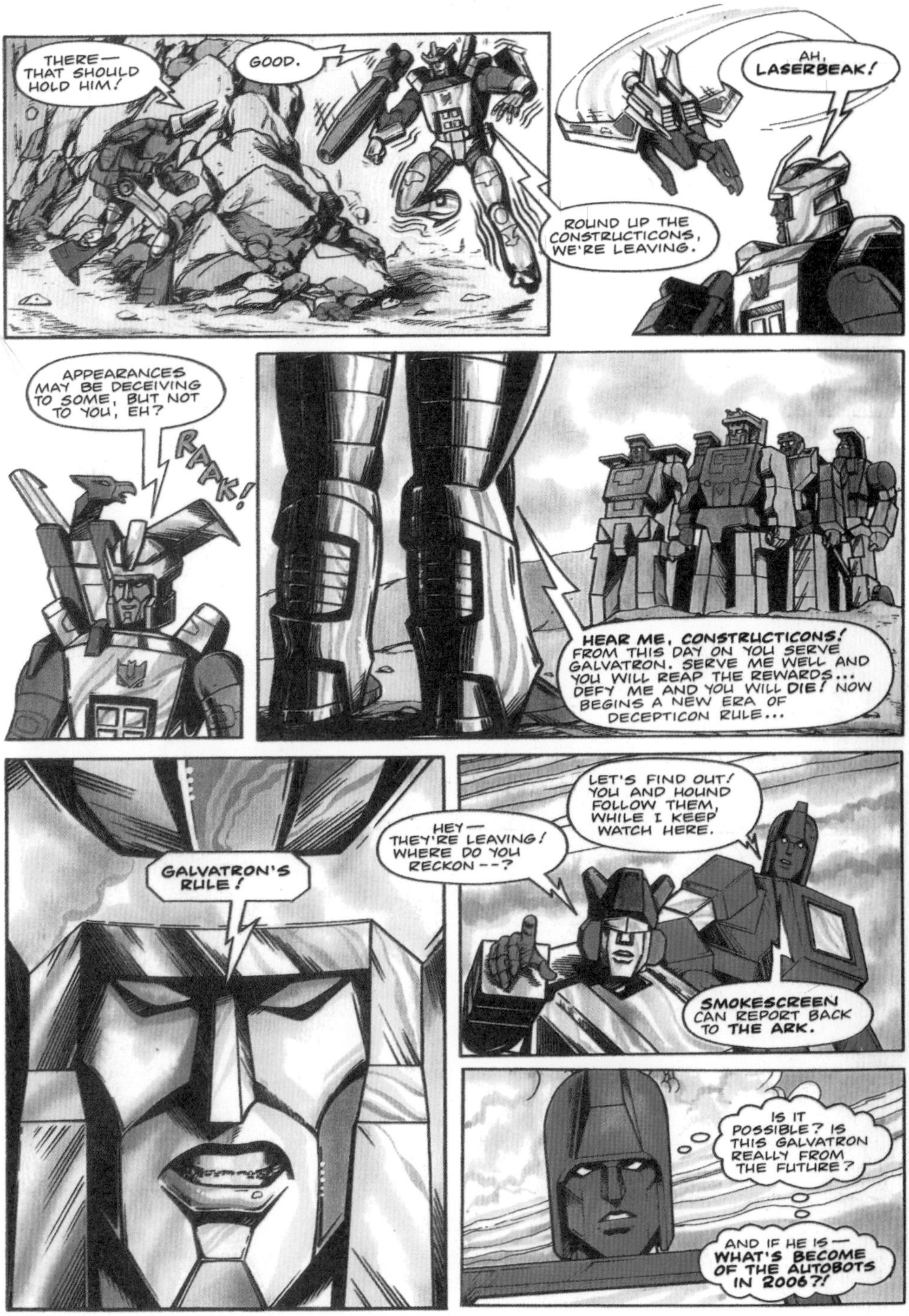
THERE— THAT SHOULD HOLD HIM!
GOOD.
AH, LASERBEAK!
ROUND UP THE CONSTRUCTICONS, WE'RE LEAVING.
APPEARANCES MAY BE DECEIVING TO SOME, BUT NOT TO YOU, EH?
RAAK!
HEAR ME, CONSTRUCTICONS! FROM THIS DAY ON YOU SERVE GALVATRON. SERVE ME WELL AND YOU WILL REAP THE REWARDS... DEFY ME AND YOU WILL DIE! NOW BEGINS A NEW ERA OF DECEPTICON RULE...
GALVATRON'S RULE!
HEY— THEY'RE LEAVING! WHERE DO YOU RECKON--?
LET'S FIND OUT! YOU AND HOUND FOLLOW THEM, WHILE I KEEP WATCH HERE.
SMOKESCREEN CAN REPORT BACK TO THE ARK.
IS IT POSSIBLE? IS THIS GALVATRON REALLY FROM THE FUTURE?
AND IF HE IS— WHAT'S BECOME OF THE AUTOBOTS IN 2006?!

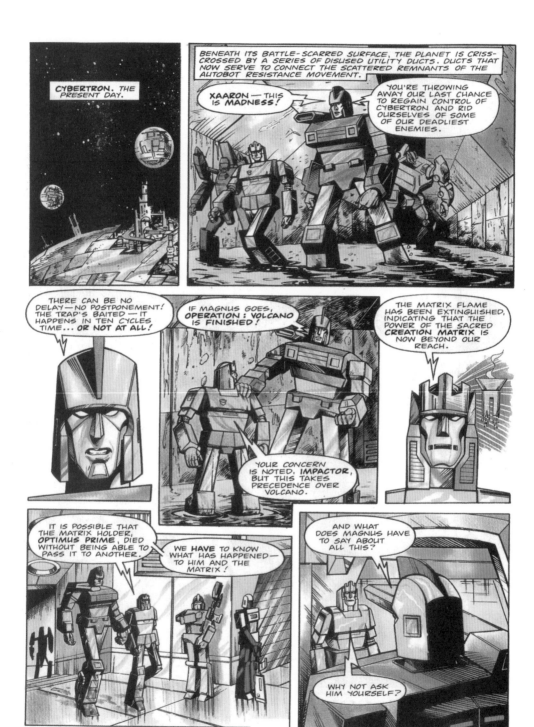

CYBERTRON. THE PRESENT DAY.

BENEATH ITS BATTLE-SCARRED SURFACE, THE PLANET IS CRISS-CROSSED BY A SERIES OF DISUSED UTILITY DUCTS. DUCTS THAT NOW SERVE TO CONNECT THE SCATTERED REMNANTS OF THE AUTOBOT RESISTANCE MOVEMENT.

XAARON — THIS IS MADNESS!

YOU'RE THROWING AWAY OUR LAST CHANCE TO REGAIN CONTROL OF CYBERTRON AND RID OURSELVES OF SOME OF OUR DEADLIEST ENEMIES.

THERE CAN BE NO DELAY — NO POSTPONEMENT! THE TRAP'S BAITED — IT HAPPENS IN TEN CYCLES TIME... OR NOT AT ALL!

IF MAGNUS GOES, OPERATION: VOLCANO IS FINISHED!

THE MATRIX FLAME HAS BEEN EXTINGUISHED, INDICATING THAT THE POWER OF THE SACRED CREATION MATRIX IS NOW BEYOND OUR REACH.

YOUR CONCERN IS NOTED, IMPACTOR, BUT THIS TAKES PRECEDENCE OVER VOLCANO.

IT IS POSSIBLE THAT THE MATRIX HOLDER, OPTIMUS PRIME, DIED WITHOUT BEING ABLE TO PASS IT TO ANOTHER.

WE HAVE TO KNOW WHAT HAS HAPPENED — TO HIM AND THE MATRIX!

AND WHAT DOES MAGNUS HAVE TO SAY ABOUT ALL THIS?

WHY NOT ASK HIM YOURSELF?

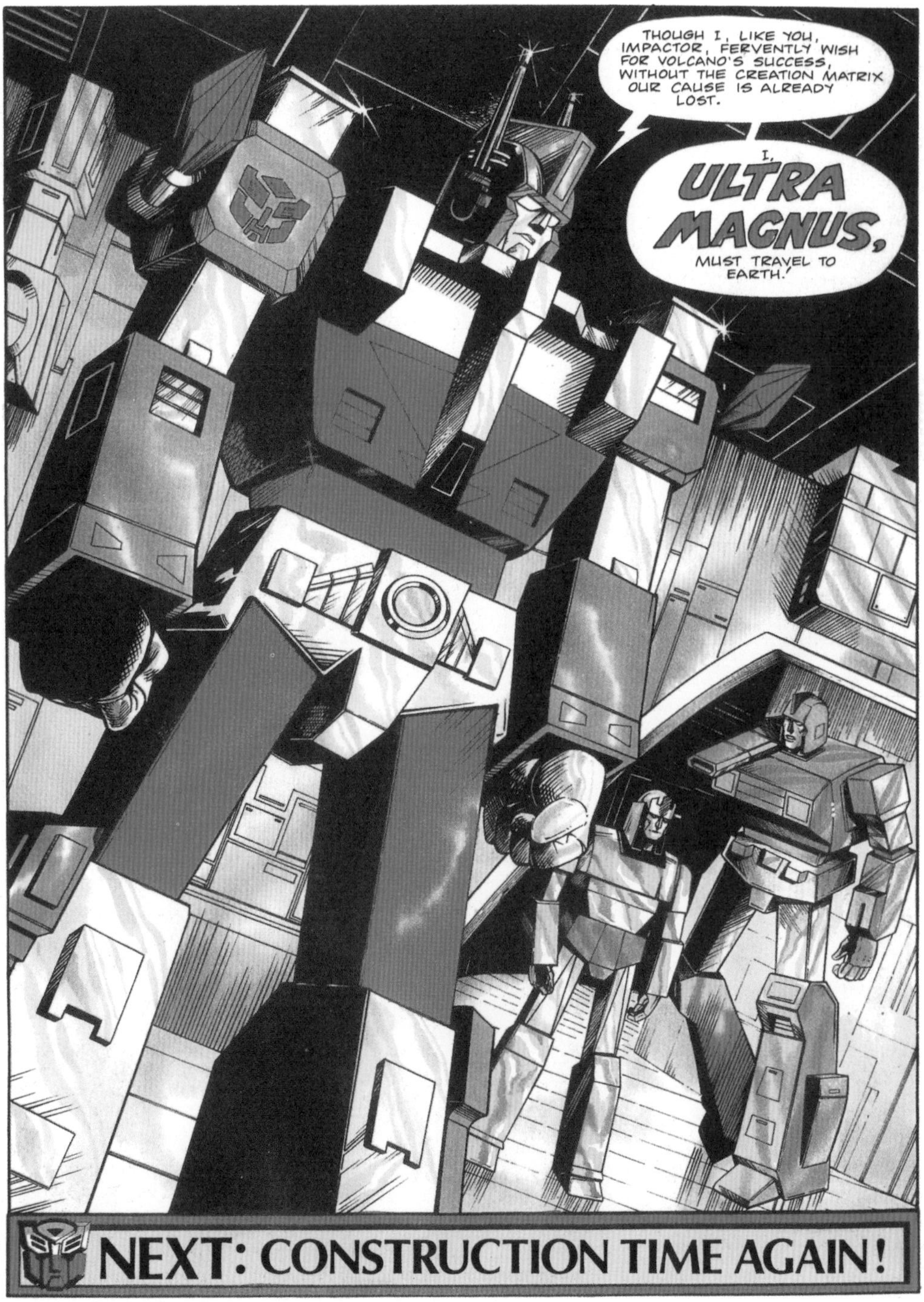

THOUGH I, LIKE YOU, IMPACTOR, FERVENTLY WISH FOR VOLCANO'S SUCCESS, WITHOUT THE CREATION MATRIX OUR CAUSE IS ALREADY LOST.
I, ULTRA MAGNUS, MUST TRAVEL TO EARTH!
NEXT: CONSTRUCTION TIME AGAIN!

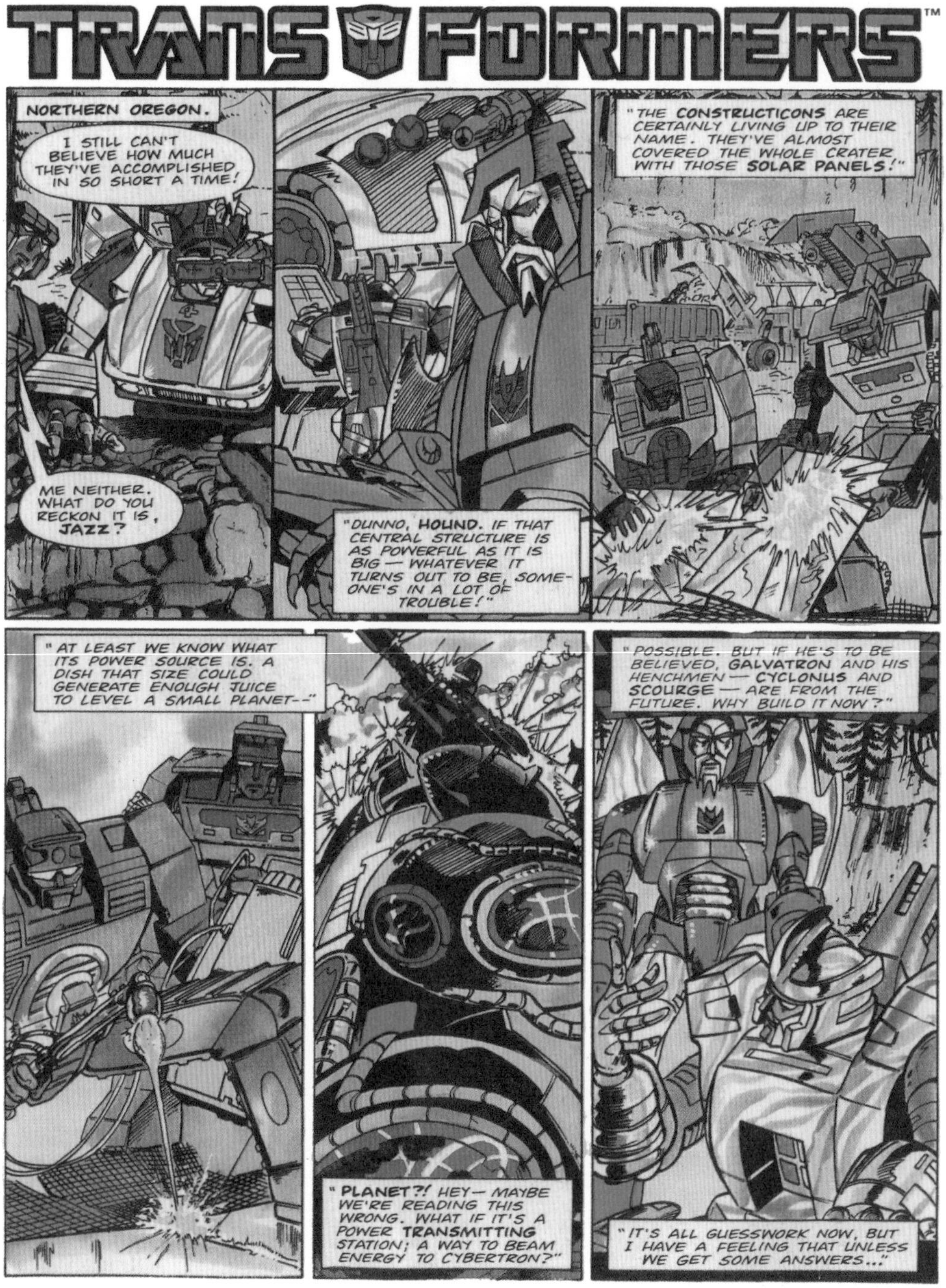
TRANSFORMERS
NORTHERN OREGON.
I STILL CAN'T BELIEVE HOW MUCH THEY'VE ACCOMPLISHED IN SO SHORT A TIME!
ME NEITHER. WHAT DO YOU RECKON IT IS, JAZZ?
"DUNNO, HOUND. IF THAT CENTRAL STRUCTURE IS AS POWERFUL AS IT IS BIG — WHATEVER IT TURNS OUT TO BE, SOME-ONE'S IN A LOT OF TROUBLE!"
"THE CONSTRUCTICONS ARE CERTAINLY LIVING UP TO THEIR NAME. THEY'VE ALMOST COVERED THE WHOLE CRATER WITH THOSE SOLAR PANELS!"
"AT LEAST WE KNOW WHAT ITS POWER SOURCE IS. A DISH THAT SIZE COULD GENERATE ENOUGH JUICE TO LEVEL A SMALL PLANET--"
"PLANET?! HEY— MAYBE WE'RE READING THIS WRONG. WHAT IF IT'S A POWER TRANSMITTING STATION; A WAY TO BEAM ENERGY TO CYBERTRON?"
"POSSIBLE. BUT IF HE'S TO BE BELIEVED, GALVATRON AND HIS HENCHMEN — CYCLONUS AND SCOURGE — ARE FROM THE FUTURE. WHY BUILD IT NOW?"
"IT'S ALL GUESSWORK NOW, BUT I HAVE A FEELING THAT UNLESS WE GET SOME ANSWERS..."

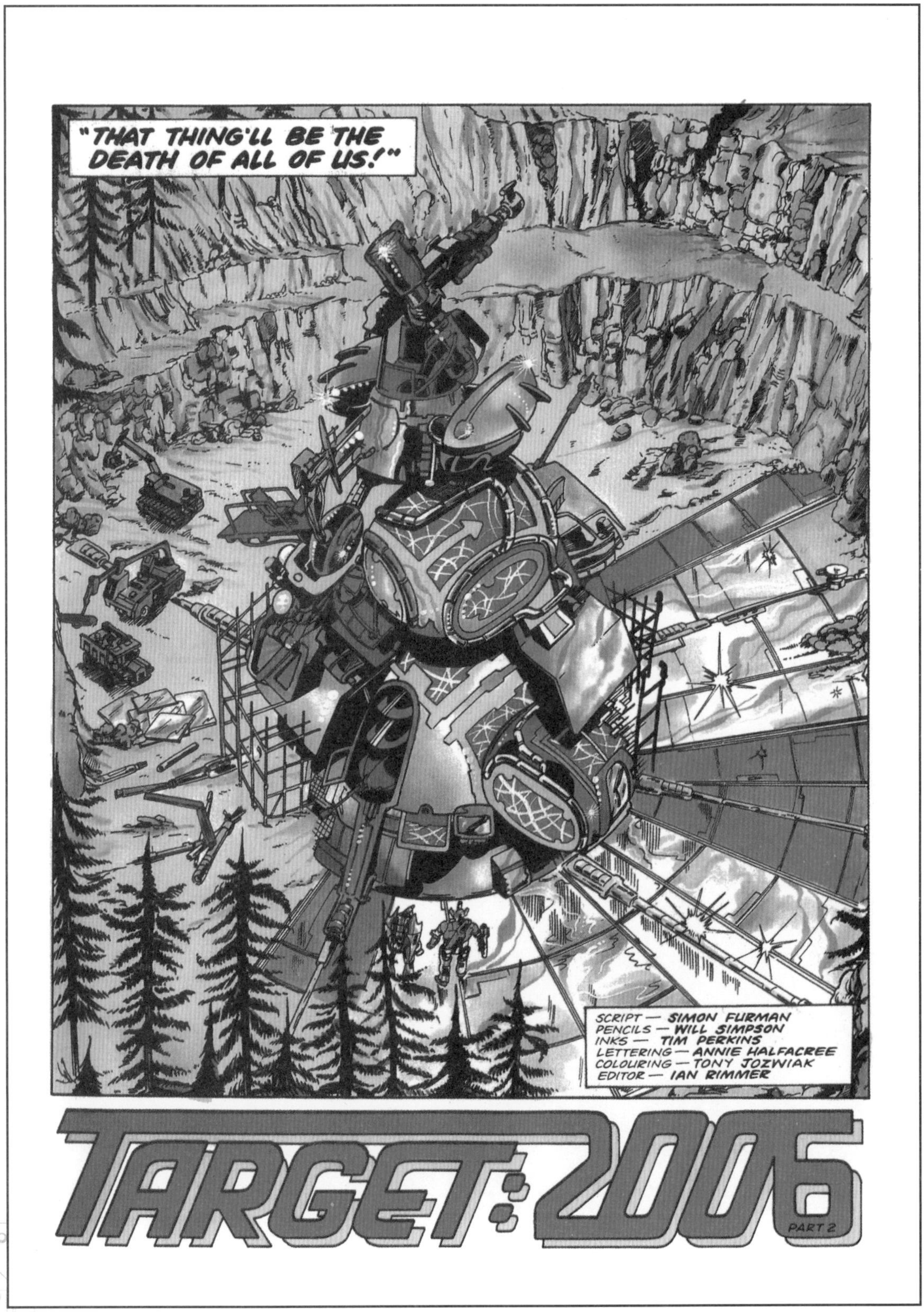
"THAT THING'LL BE THE DEATH OF ALL OF US!"
SCRIPT — SIMON FURMAN
PENCILS — WILL SIMPSON
INKS — TIM PERKINS
LETTERING — ANNIE HALFACREE
COLOURING — TONY JOZWIAK
EDITOR — IAN RIMMER
TARGET: 2006
PART 2

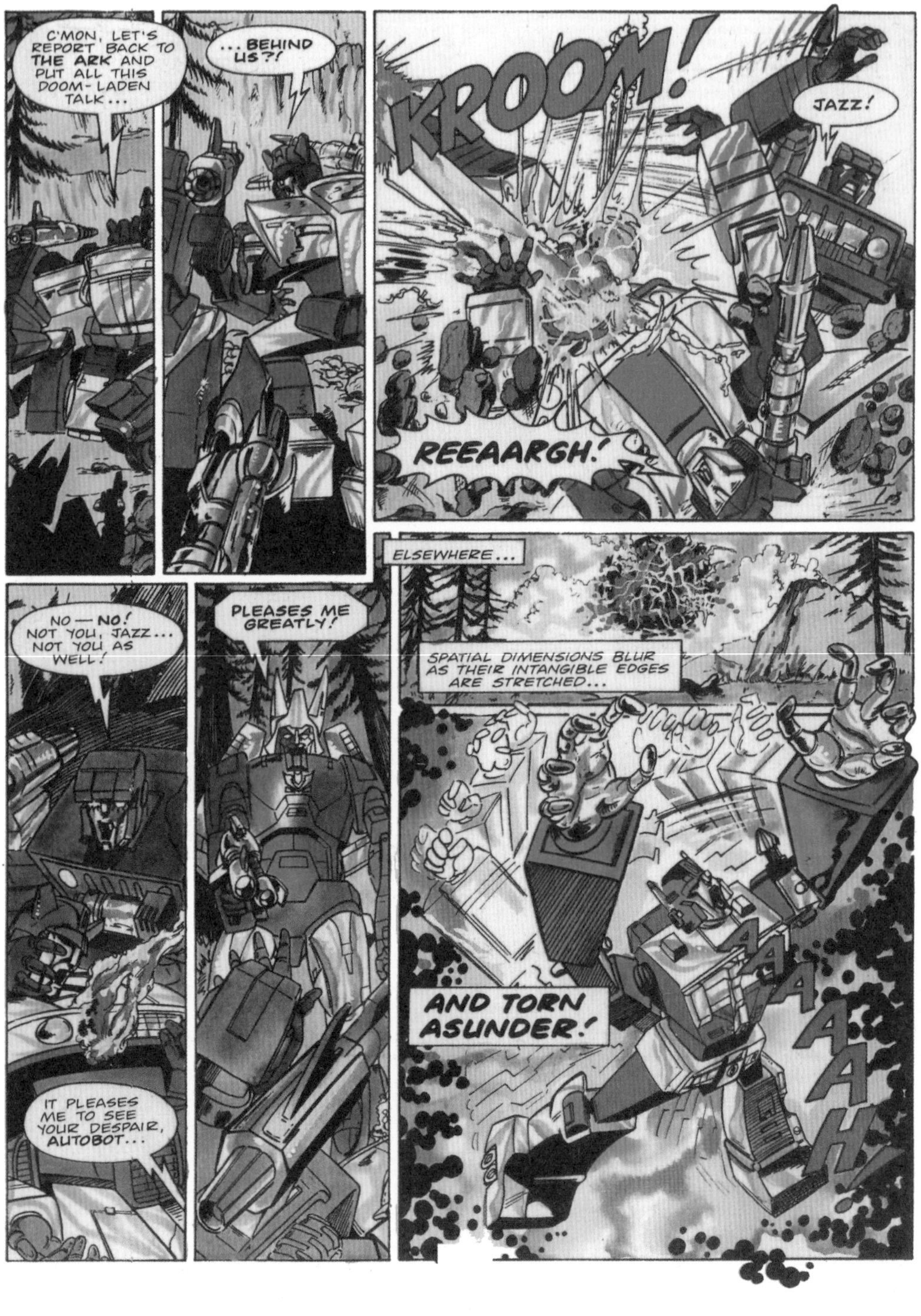

C'MON, LET'S REPORT BACK TO THE ARK AND PUT ALL THIS DOOM-LADEN TALK...
...BEHIND US?!
KROOM!
JAZZ!
REEAARGH!
NO—NO! NOT YOU, JAZZ... NOT YOU AS WELL!
IT PLEASES ME TO SEE YOUR DESPAIR, AUTOBOT...
PLEASES ME GREATLY!
ELSEWHERE...
SPATIAL DIMENSIONS BLUR AS THEIR INTANGIBLE EDGES ARE STRETCHED...
AND TORN ASUNDER!
AAAAAH!

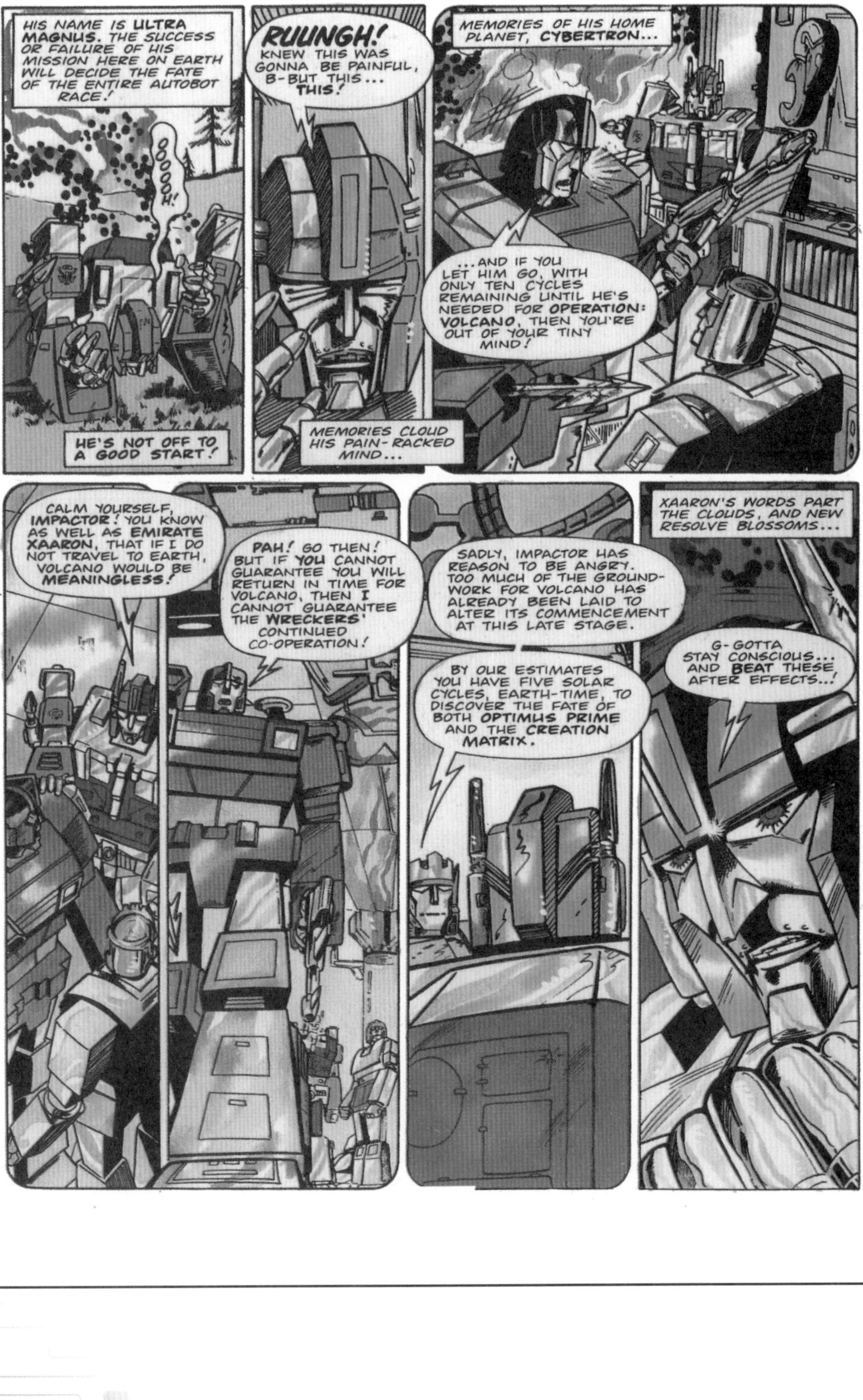
HIS NAME IS ULTRA MAGNUS. THE SUCCESS OR FAILURE OF HIS MISSION HERE ON EARTH WILL DECIDE THE FATE OF THE ENTIRE AUTOBOT RACE!
OOOOOH!
HE'S NOT OFF TO A GOOD START!
RUUNGH! KNEW THIS WAS GONNA BE PAINFUL, B-BUT THIS... THIS!
MEMORIES CLOUD HIS PAIN-RACKED MIND...
MEMORIES OF HIS HOME PLANET, CYBERTRON...
...AND IF YOU LET HIM GO, WITH ONLY TEN CYCLES REMAINING UNTIL HE'S NEEDED FOR OPERATION: VOLCANO, THEN YOU'RE OUT OF YOUR TINY MIND!
CALM YOURSELF, IMPACTOR! YOU KNOW AS WELL AS EMIRATE XAARON, THAT IF I DO NOT TRAVEL TO EARTH, VOLCANO WOULD BE MEANINGLESS!
PAH! GO THEN! BUT IF YOU CANNOT GUARANTEE YOU WILL RETURN IN TIME FOR VOLCANO, THEN I CANNOT GUARANTEE THE WRECKERS' CONTINUED CO-OPERATION!
SADLY, IMPACTOR HAS REASON TO BE ANGRY. TOO MUCH OF THE GROUND-WORK FOR VOLCANO HAS ALREADY BEEN LAID TO ALTER ITS COMMENCEMENT AT THIS LATE STAGE.
BY OUR ESTIMATES YOU HAVE FIVE SOLAR CYCLES, EARTH-TIME, TO DISCOVER THE FATE OF BOTH OPTIMUS PRIME AND THE CREATION MATRIX.
XAARON'S WORDS PART THE CLOUDS, AND NEW RESOLVE BLOSSOMS...
G-GOTTA STAY CONSCIOUS... AND BEAT THESE AFTER EFFECTS...!

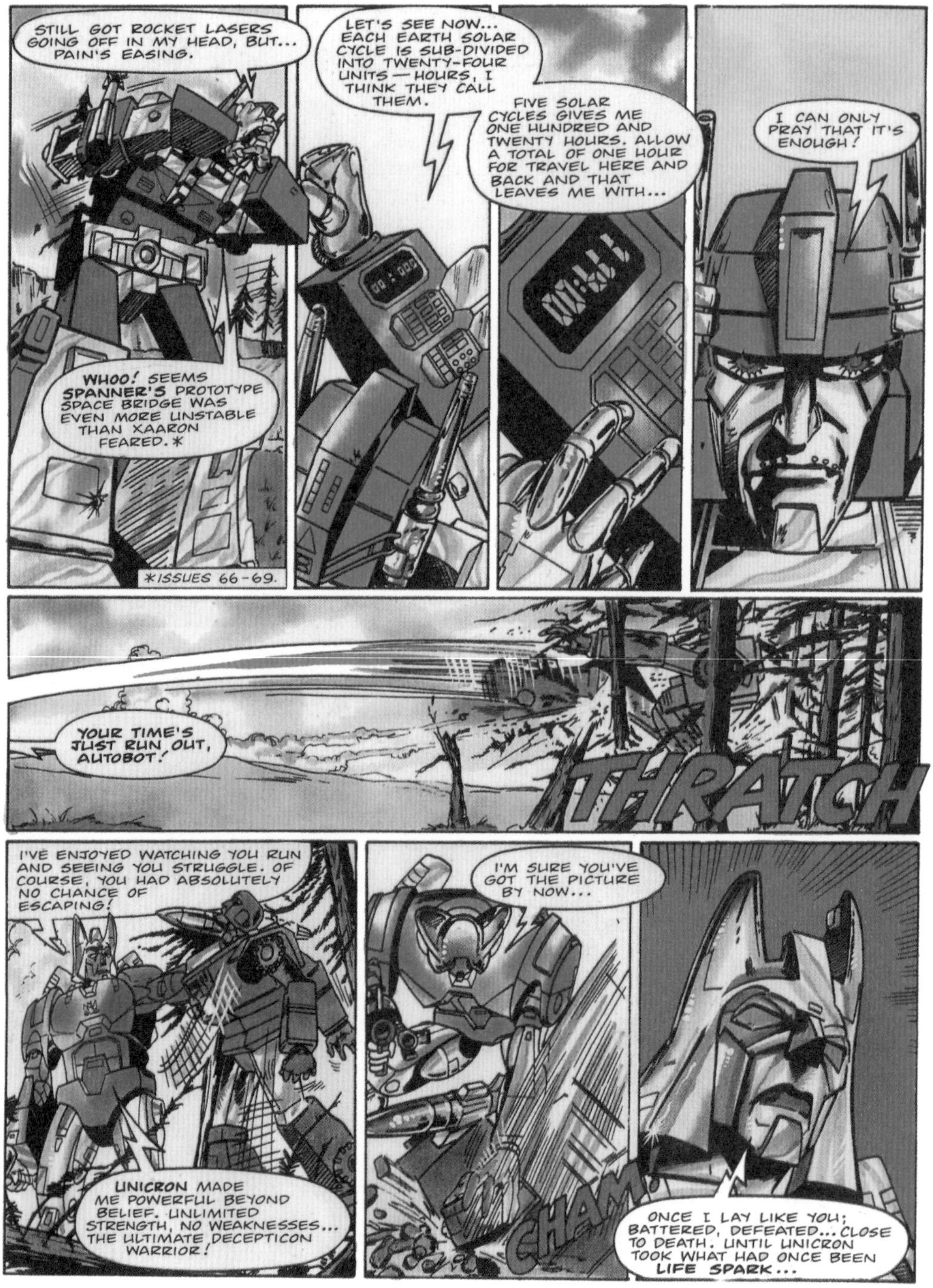

STILL GOT ROCKET LASERS GOING OFF IN MY HEAD, BUT... PAIN'S EASING.
WHOO! SEEMS SPANNER'S PROTOTYPE SPACE BRIDGE WAS EVEN MORE UNSTABLE THAN XAARON FEARED.*
*ISSUES 66-69.
LET'S SEE NOW... EACH EARTH SOLAR CYCLE IS SUB-DIVIDED INTO TWENTY-FOUR UNITS — HOURS, I THINK THEY CALL THEM.
FIVE SOLAR CYCLES GIVES ME ONE HUNDRED AND TWENTY HOURS. ALLOW A TOTAL OF ONE HOUR FOR TRAVEL HERE AND BACK AND THAT LEAVES ME WITH...
I CAN ONLY PRAY THAT IT'S ENOUGH!
YOUR TIME'S JUST RUN OUT, AUTOBOT!
THRATCH
I'VE ENJOYED WATCHING YOU RUN AND SEEING YOU STRUGGLE. OF COURSE, YOU HAD ABSOLUTELY NO CHANCE OF ESCAPING!
UNICRON MADE ME POWERFUL BEYOND BELIEF. UNLIMITED STRENGTH, NO WEAKNESSES... THE ULTIMATE DECEPTICON WARRIOR!
I'M SURE YOU'VE GOT THE PICTURE BY NOW...
CHAM
ONCE I LAY LIKE YOU; BATTERED, DEFEATED... CLOSE TO DEATH. UNTIL UNICRON TOOK WHAT HAD ONCE BEEN LIFE SPARK...

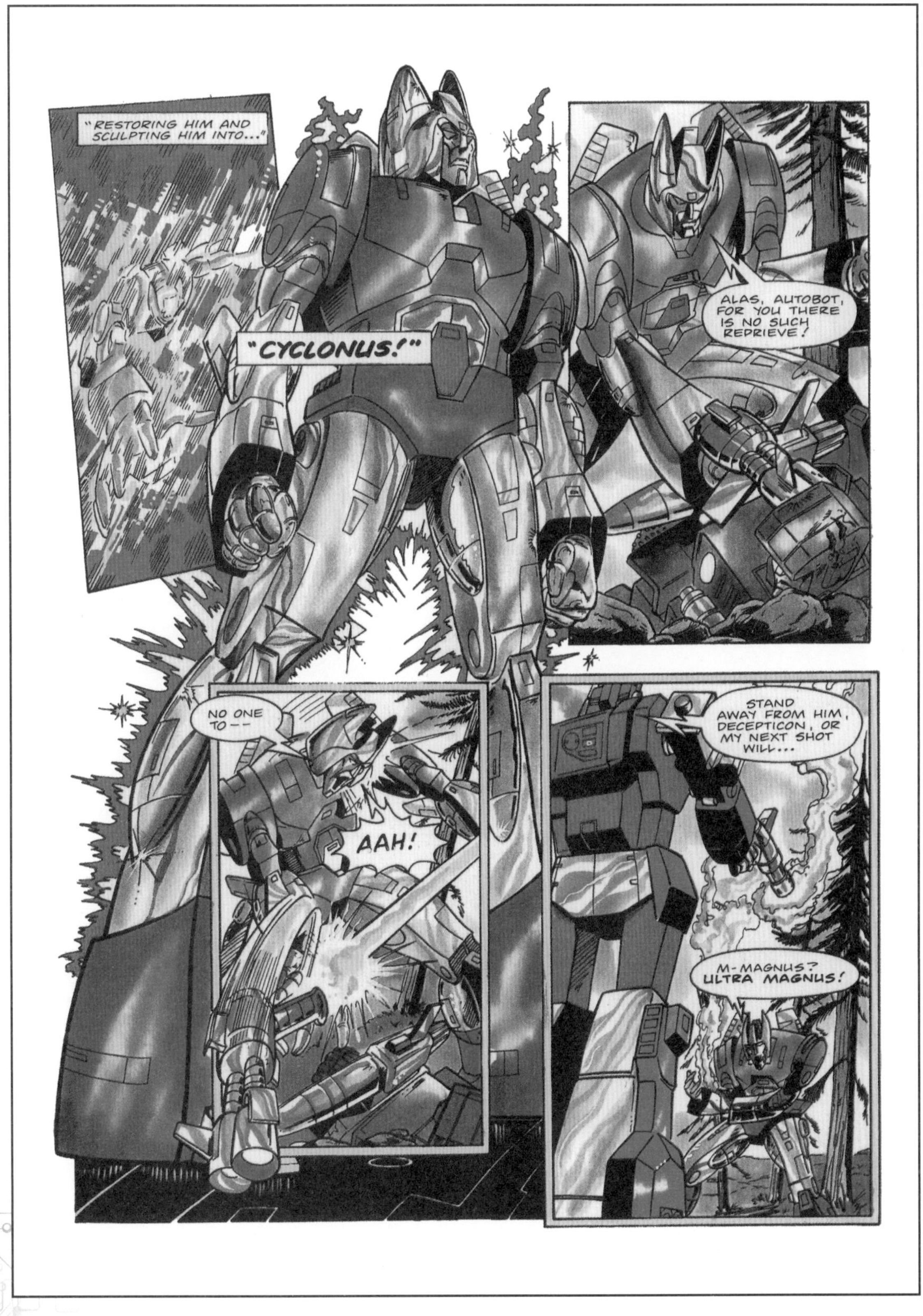

"RESTORING HIM AND SCULPTING HIM INTO..."
"CYCLONUS!"
ALAS, AUTOBOT, FOR YOU THERE IS NO SUCH REPRIEVE!
NO ONE TO--
AAH!
STAND AWAY FROM HIM, DECEPTICON, OR MY NEXT SHOT WILL...
M-MAGNUS? ULTRA MAGNUS!

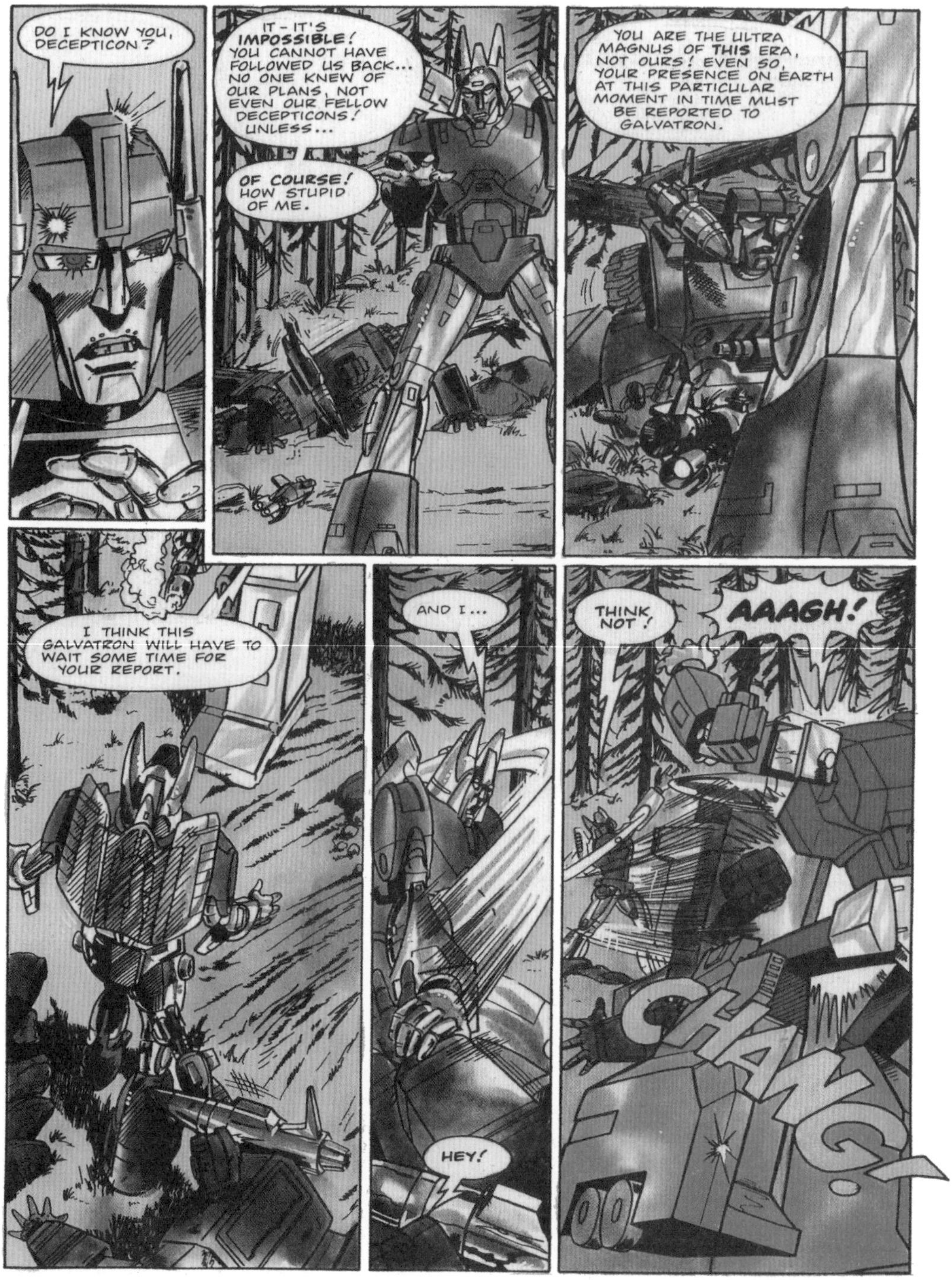

DO I KNOW YOU, DECEPTICON?
IT - IT'S **IMPOSSIBLE!** YOU CANNOT HAVE FOLLOWED US BACK... NO ONE KNEW OF OUR PLANS, NOT EVEN OUR FELLOW DECEPTICONS! UNLESS...
OF COURSE! HOW STUPID OF ME.
YOU ARE THE ULTRA MAGNUS OF **THIS** ERA, NOT OURS! EVEN SO, YOUR PRESENCE ON EARTH AT THIS PARTICULAR MOMENT IN TIME MUST BE REPORTED TO GALVATRON.
I THINK THIS GALVATRON WILL HAVE TO WAIT SOME TIME FOR YOUR REPORT.
AND I...
HEY!
THINK NOT!
AAAGH!
CHANG!

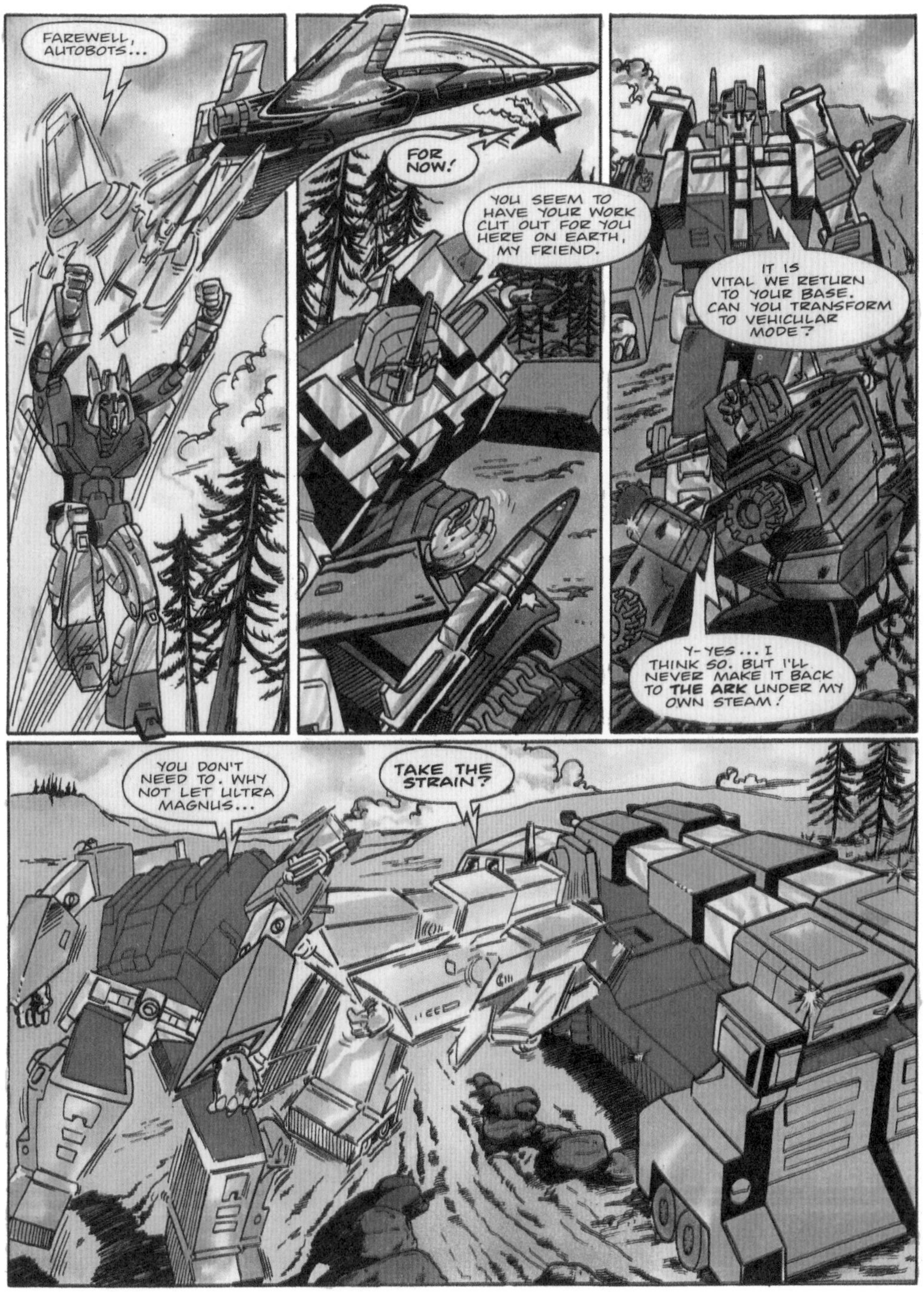
FAREWELL, AUTOBOTS...
FOR NOW!
YOU SEEM TO HAVE YOUR WORK CUT OUT FOR YOU HERE ON EARTH, MY FRIEND.
IT IS VITAL WE RETURN TO YOUR BASE. CAN YOU TRANSFORM TO VEHICULAR MODE?
Y-YES... I THINK SO. BUT I'LL NEVER MAKE IT BACK TO **THE ARK** UNDER MY OWN STEAM!
YOU DON'T NEED TO. WHY NOT LET ULTRA MAGNUS...
TAKE THE STRAIN?

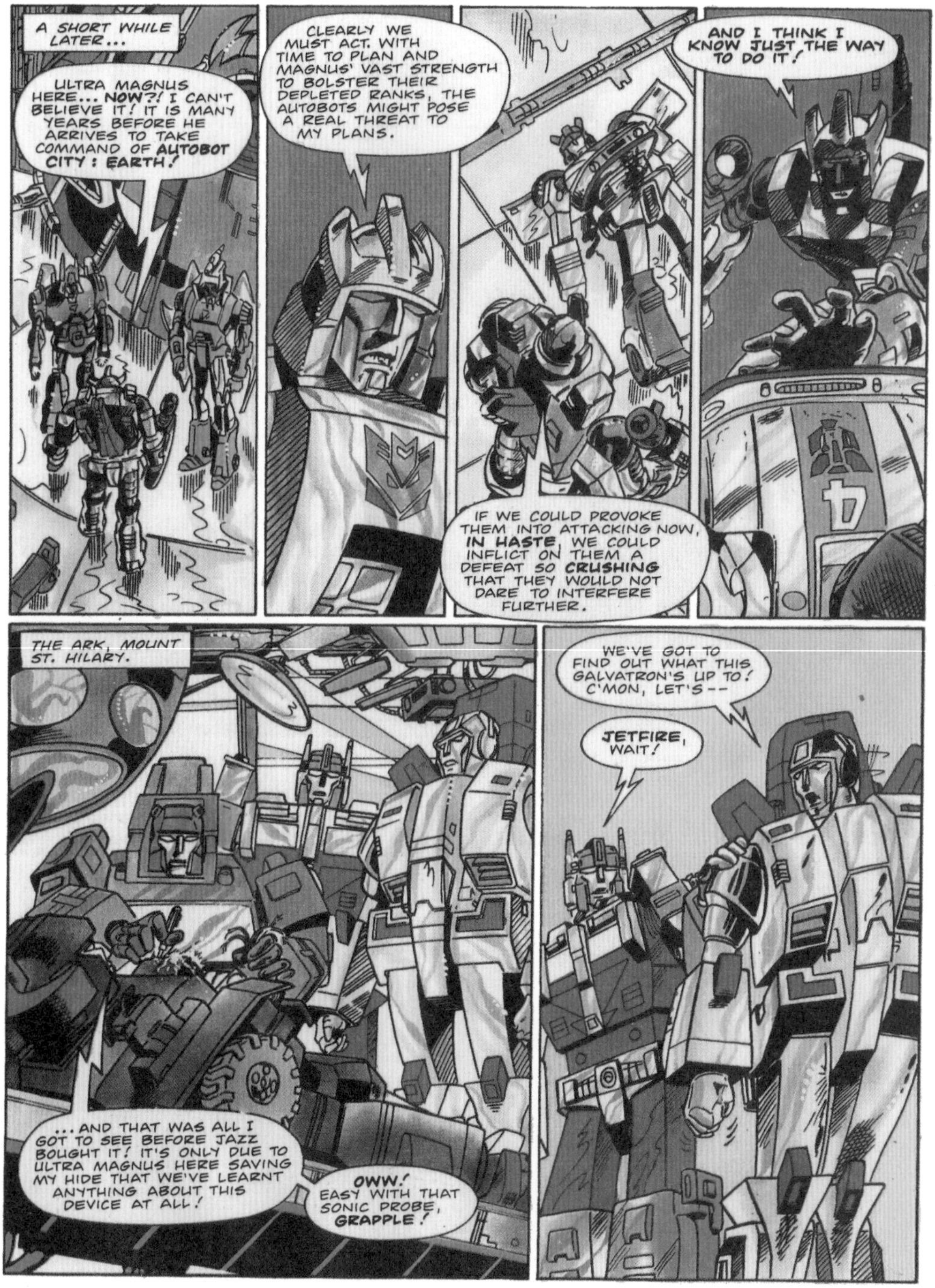
A SHORT WHILE LATER...
ULTRA MAGNUS HERE... NOW?! I CAN'T BELIEVE IT! IT IS MANY YEARS BEFORE HE ARRIVES TO TAKE COMMAND OF AUTOBOT CITY : EARTH!
CLEARLY WE MUST ACT. WITH TIME TO PLAN AND MAGNUS' VAST STRENGTH TO BOLSTER THEIR DEPLETED RANKS, THE AUTOBOTS MIGHT POSE A REAL THREAT TO MY PLANS.
IF WE COULD PROVOKE THEM INTO ATTACKING NOW, IN HASTE, WE COULD INFLICT ON THEM A DEFEAT SO CRUSHING THAT THEY WOULD NOT DARE TO INTERFERE FURTHER.
AND I THINK I KNOW JUST THE WAY TO DO IT!
THE ARK, MOUNT ST. HILARY.
...AND THAT WAS ALL I GOT TO SEE BEFORE JAZZ BOUGHT IT! IT'S ONLY DUE TO ULTRA MAGNUS HERE SAVING MY HIDE THAT WE'VE LEARNT ANYTHING ABOUT THIS DEVICE AT ALL!
OWW! EASY WITH THAT SONIC PROBE, GRAPPLE!
WE'VE GOT TO FIND OUT WHAT THIS GALVATRON'S UP TO! C'MON, LET'S--
JETFIRE, WAIT!

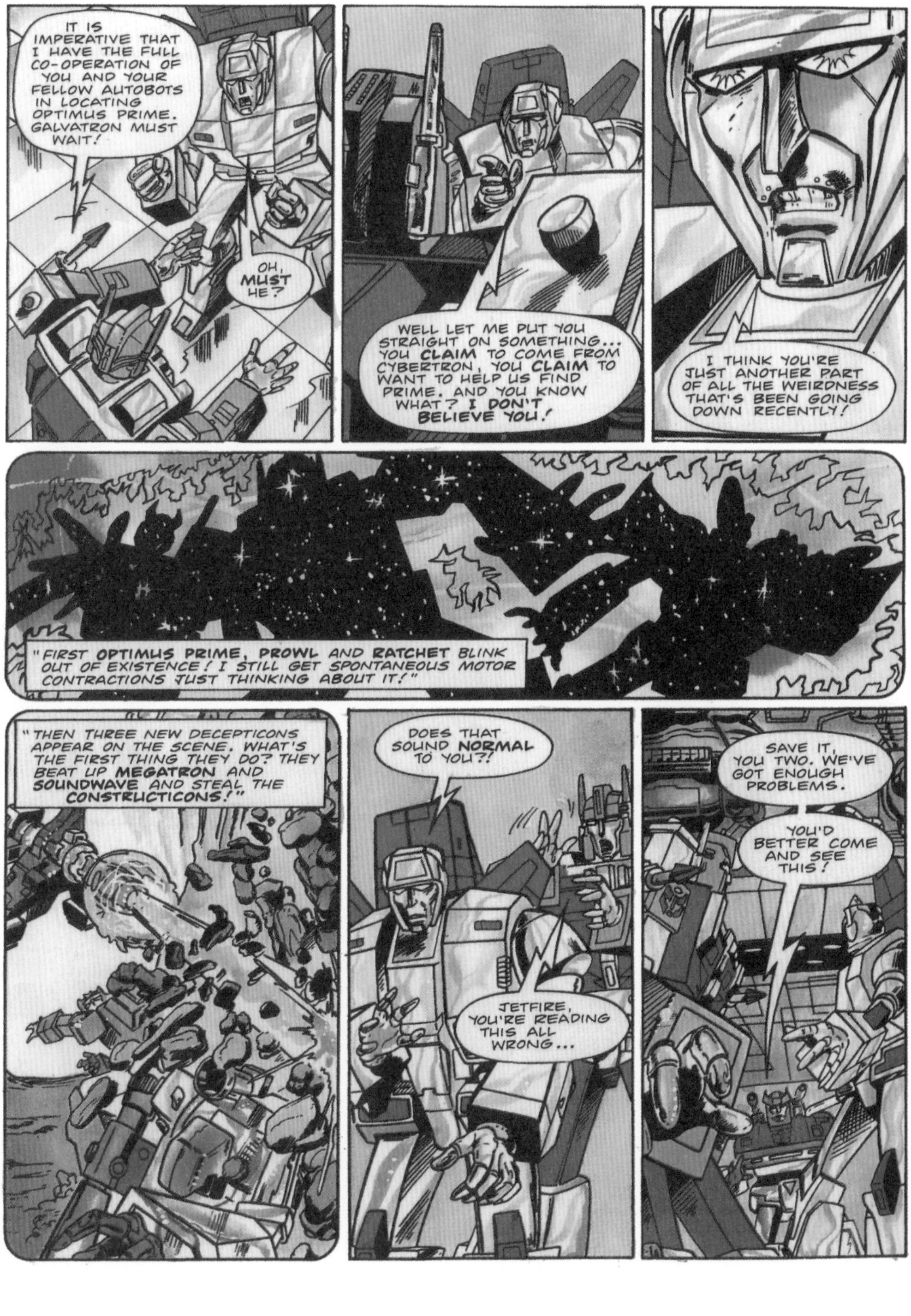
IT IS IMPERATIVE THAT I HAVE THE FULL CO-OPERATION OF YOU AND YOUR FELLOW AUTOBOTS IN LOCATING OPTIMUS PRIME. GALVATRON MUST WAIT!
OH, MUST HE?
WELL LET ME PUT YOU STRAIGHT ON SOMETHING... YOU CLAIM TO COME FROM CYBERTRON, YOU CLAIM TO WANT TO HELP US FIND PRIME. AND YOU KNOW WHAT? I DON'T BELIEVE YOU!
I THINK YOU'RE JUST ANOTHER PART OF ALL THE WEIRDNESS THAT'S BEEN GOING DOWN RECENTLY!
"FIRST OPTIMUS PRIME, PROWL AND RATCHET BLINK OUT OF EXISTENCE! I STILL GET SPONTANEOUS MOTOR CONTRACTIONS JUST THINKING ABOUT IT!"
"THEN THREE NEW DECEPTICONS APPEAR ON THE SCENE. WHAT'S THE FIRST THING THEY DO? THEY BEAT UP MEGATRON AND SOUNDWAVE AND STEAL THE CONSTRUCTICONS!"
DOES THAT SOUND NORMAL TO YOU?!
JETFIRE, YOU'RE READING THIS ALL WRONG...
SAVE IT, YOU TWO. WE'VE GOT ENOUGH PROBLEMS.
YOU'D BETTER COME AND SEE THIS!

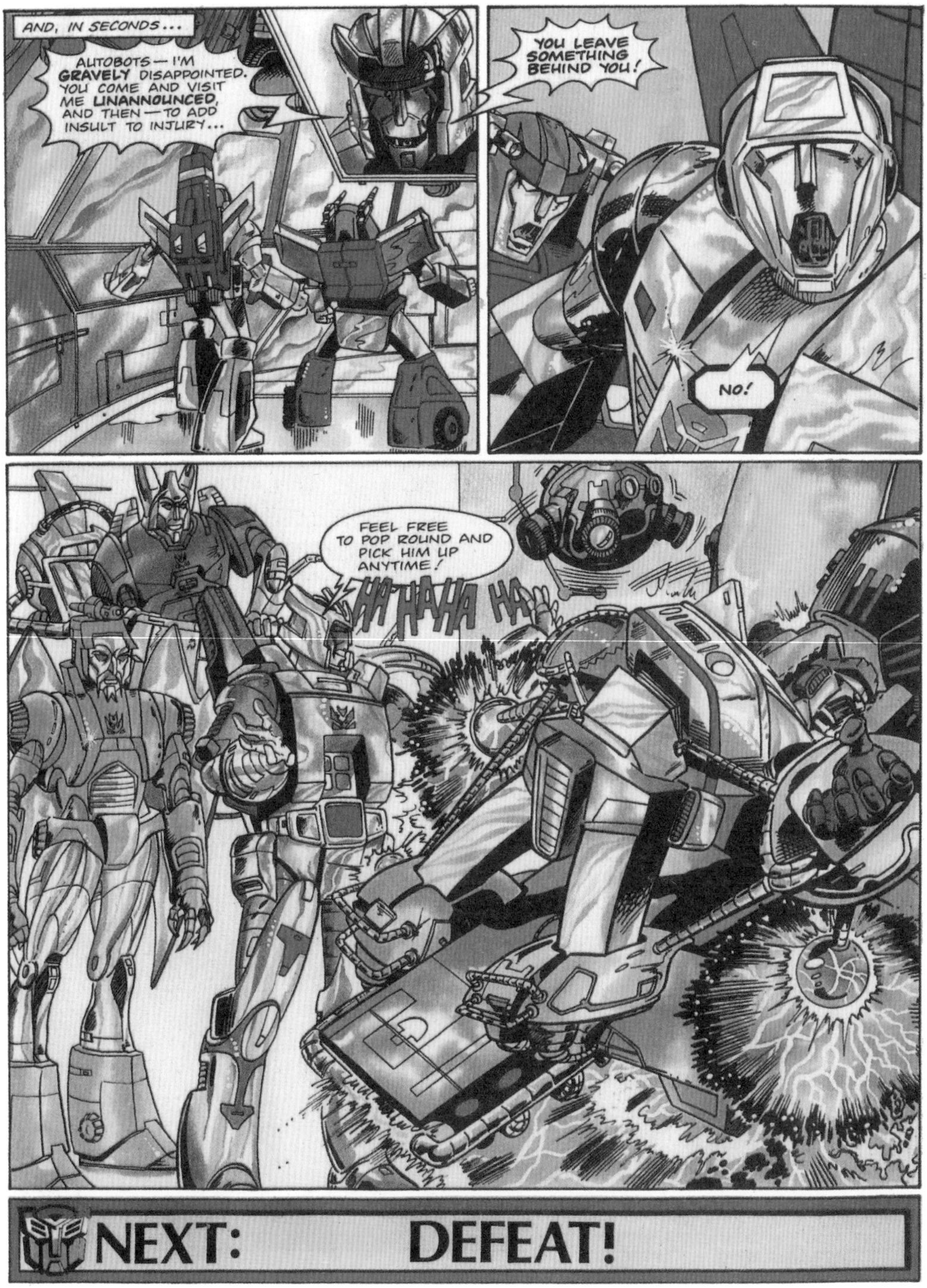
AND, IN SECONDS...
AUTOBOTS— I'M GRAVELY DISAPPOINTED. YOU COME AND VISIT ME UNANNOUNCED, AND THEN—TO ADD INSULT TO INJURY...
YOU LEAVE SOMETHING BEHIND YOU!
NO!
FEEL FREE TO POP ROUND AND PICK HIM UP ANYTIME!
HA HAHA HA HA
NEXT: DEFEAT!

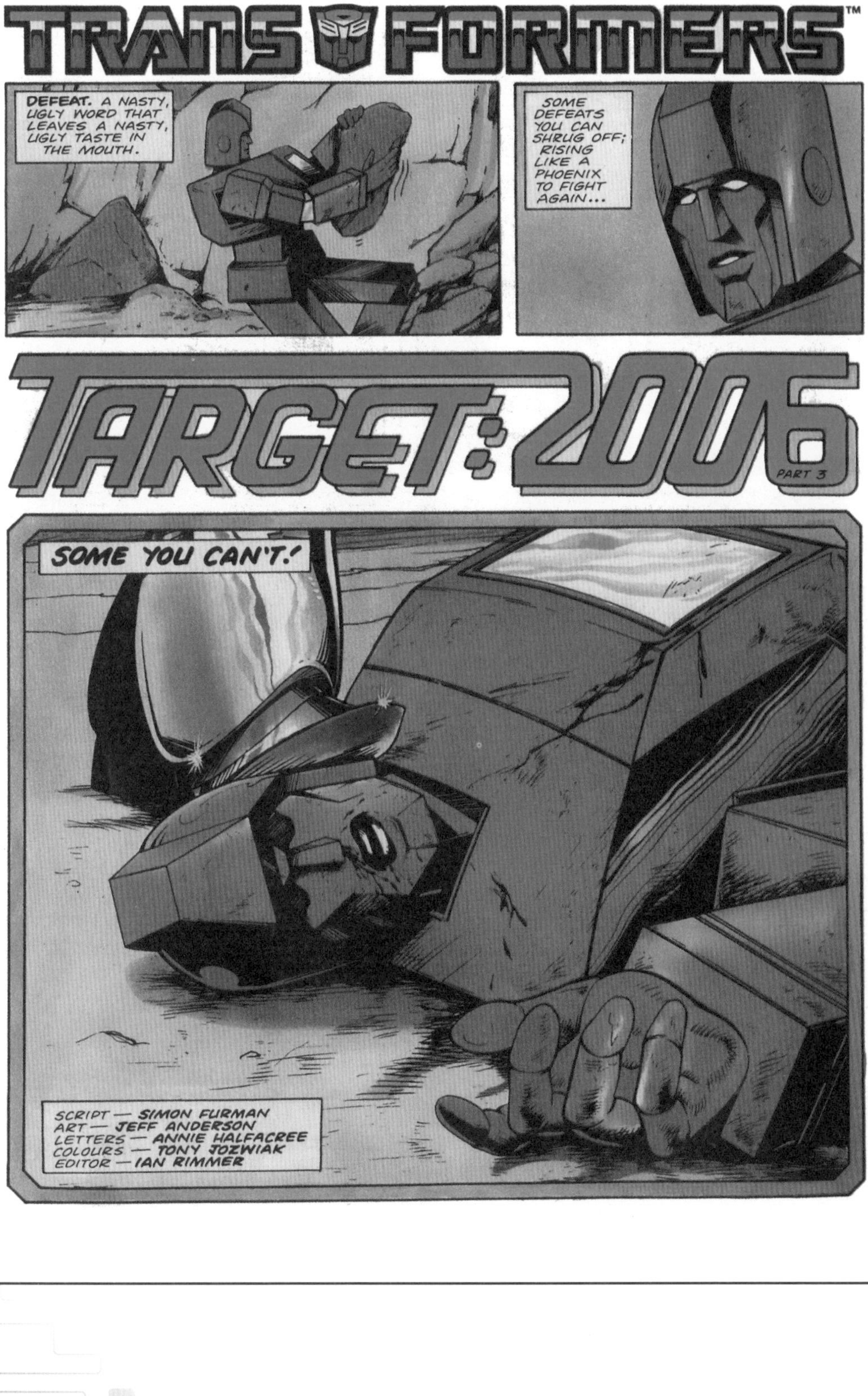
TRANSFORMERS
DEFEAT. A NASTY, UGLY WORD THAT LEAVES A NASTY, UGLY TASTE IN THE MOUTH.
SOME DEFEATS YOU CAN SHRUG OFF; RISING LIKE A PHOENIX TO FIGHT AGAIN...
TARGET: 2006
PART 3
SOME YOU CAN'T!
SCRIPT — SIMON FURMAN
ART — JEFF ANDERSON
LETTERS — ANNIE HALFACREE
COLOURS — TONY JOZWIAK
EDITOR — IAN RIMMER

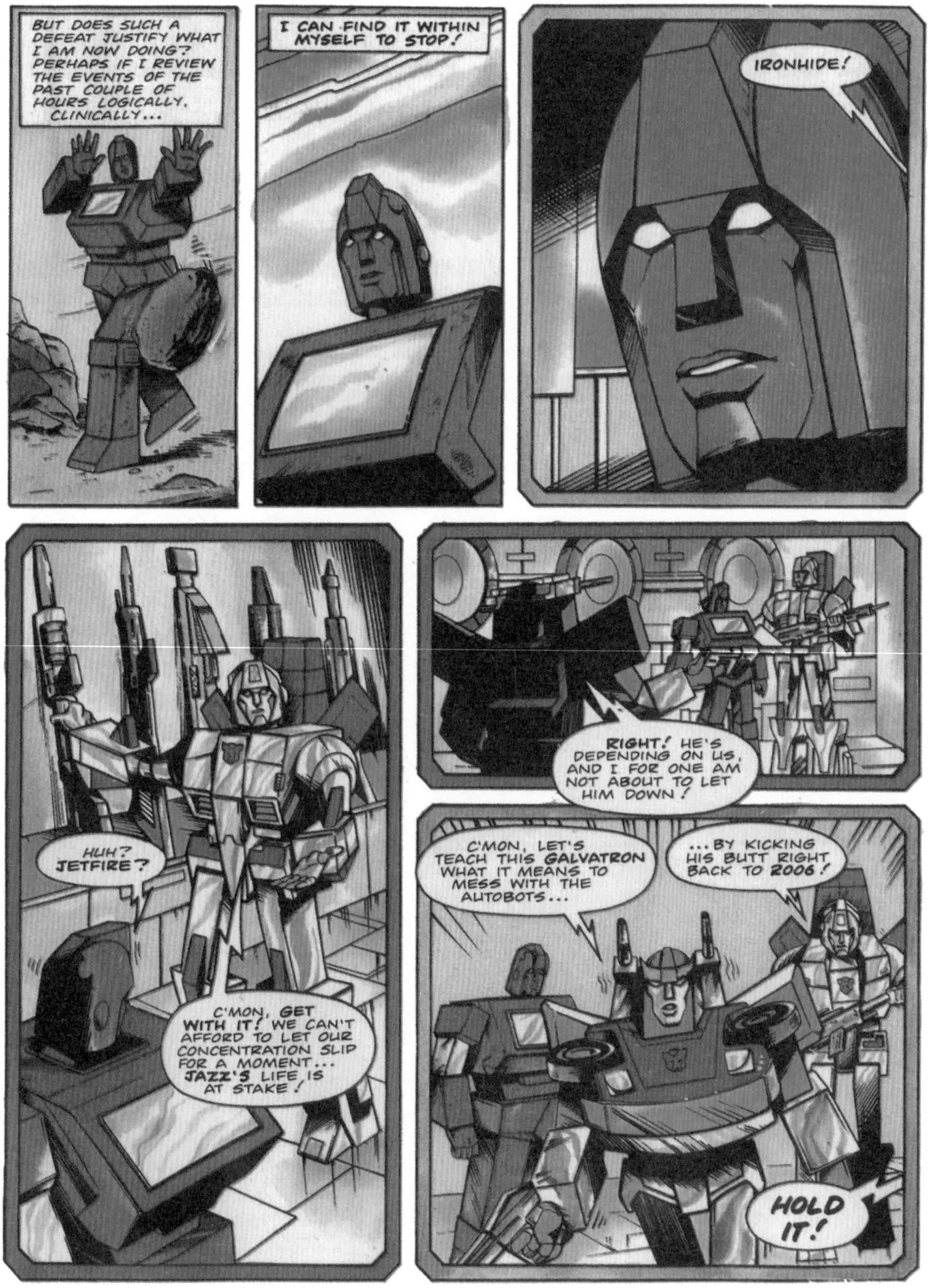
BUT DOES SUCH A DEFEAT JUSTIFY WHAT I AM NOW DOING? PERHAPS IF I REVIEW THE EVENTS OF THE PAST COUPLE OF HOURS LOGICALLY. CLINICALLY...
I CAN FIND IT WITHIN MYSELF TO STOP!
IRONHIDE!
HUH? JETFIRE?
C'MON, GET WITH IT! WE CAN'T AFFORD TO LET OUR CONCENTRATION SLIP FOR A MOMENT... JAZZ'S LIFE IS AT STAKE!
RIGHT! HE'S DEPENDING ON US, AND I FOR ONE AM NOT ABOUT TO LET HIM DOWN!
C'MON, LET'S TEACH THIS GALVATRON WHAT IT MEANS TO MESS WITH THE AUTOBOTS...
...BY KICKING HIS BUTT RIGHT BACK TO 2006!
HOLD IT!

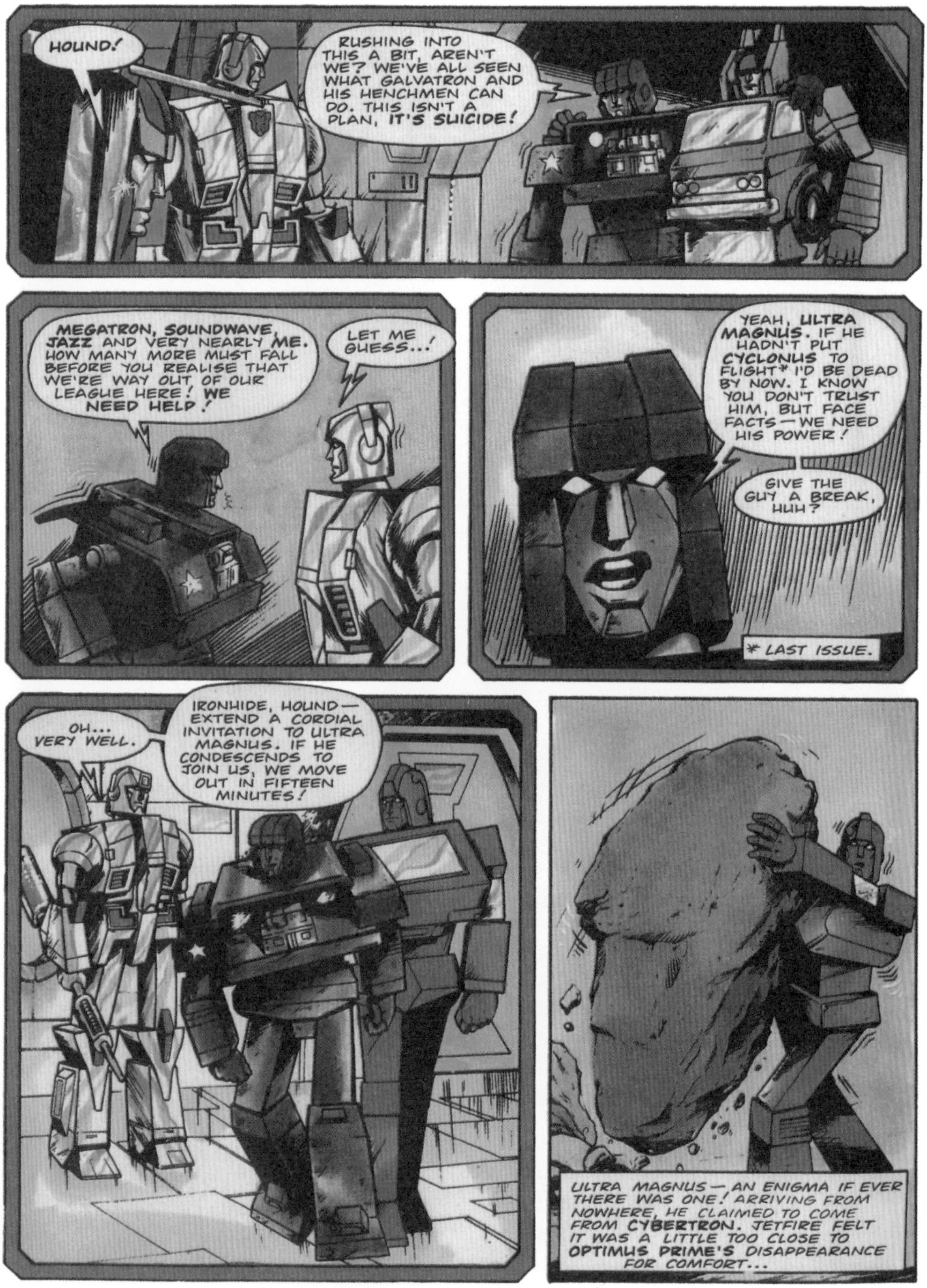
HOUND!
RUSHING INTO THIS A BIT, AREN'T WE? WE'VE ALL SEEN WHAT GALVATRON AND HIS HENCHMEN CAN DO. THIS ISN'T A PLAN, IT'S SUICIDE!
MEGATRON, SOUNDWAVE, JAZZ AND VERY NEARLY ME. HOW MANY MORE MUST FALL BEFORE YOU REALISE THAT WE'RE WAY OUT OF OUR LEAGUE HERE! WE NEED HELP!
LET ME GUESS...!
YEAH, ULTRA MAGNUS. IF HE HADN'T PUT CYCLONUS TO FLIGHT* I'D BE DEAD BY NOW. I KNOW YOU DON'T TRUST HIM, BUT FACE FACTS — WE NEED HIS POWER!
GIVE THE GUY A BREAK, HUH?
* LAST ISSUE.
OH... VERY WELL.
IRONHIDE, HOUND — EXTEND A CORDIAL INVITATION TO ULTRA MAGNUS. IF HE CONDESCENDS TO JOIN US, WE MOVE OUT IN FIFTEEN MINUTES!
ULTRA MAGNUS — AN ENIGMA IF EVER THERE WAS ONE! ARRIVING FROM NOWHERE, HE CLAIMED TO COME FROM CYBERTRON. JETFIRE FELT IT WAS A LITTLE TOO CLOSE TO OPTIMUS PRIME'S DISAPPEARANCE FOR COMFORT...

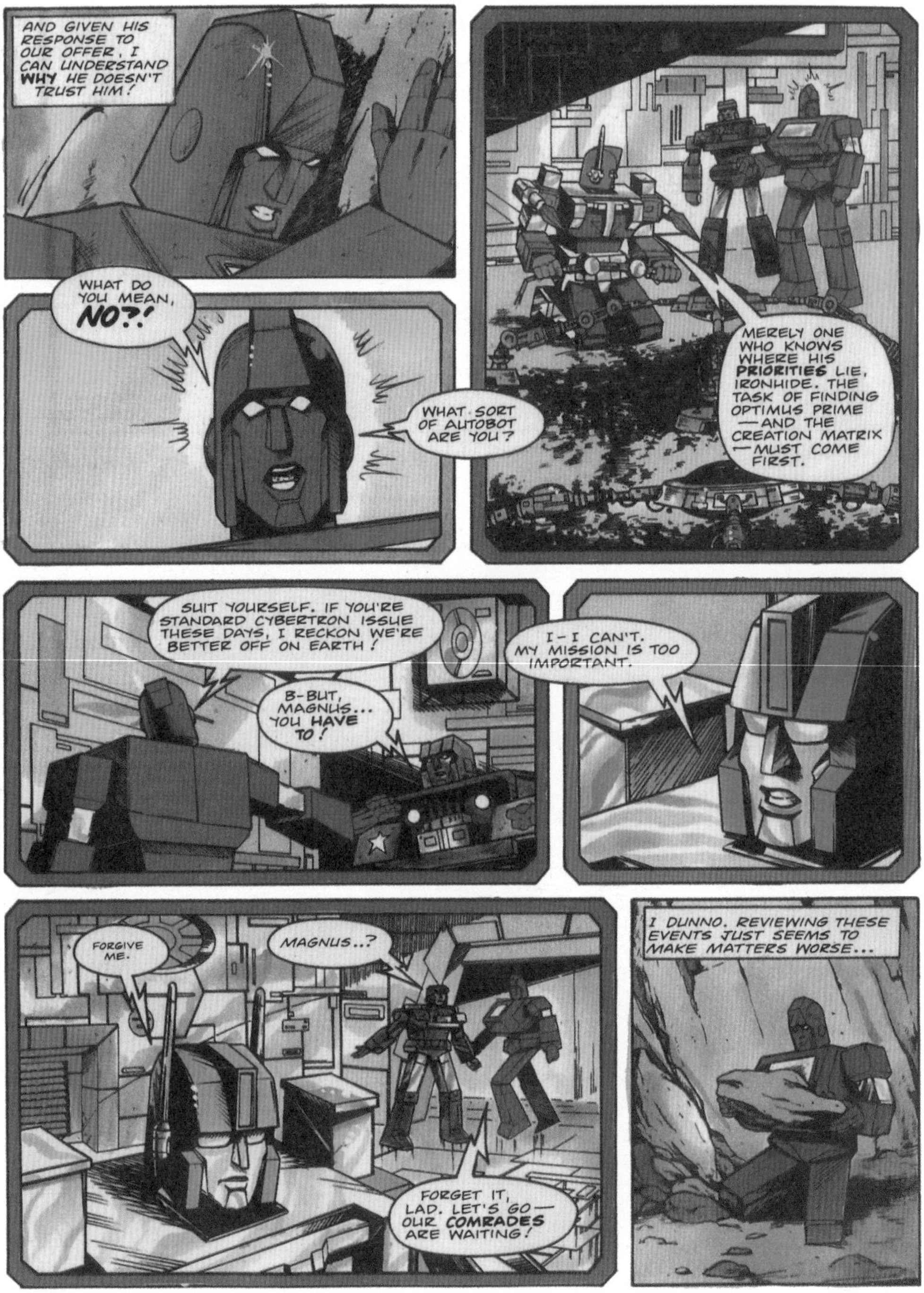
AND GIVEN HIS RESPONSE TO OUR OFFER, I CAN UNDERSTAND WHY HE DOESN'T TRUST HIM!
WHAT DO YOU MEAN, NO?!
WHAT SORT OF AUTOBOT ARE YOU?
MERELY ONE WHO KNOWS WHERE HIS PRIORITIES LIE, IRONHIDE. THE TASK OF FINDING OPTIMUS PRIME —AND THE CREATION MATRIX —MUST COME FIRST.
SUIT YOURSELF. IF YOU'RE STANDARD CYBERTRON ISSUE THESE DAYS, I RECKON WE'RE BETTER OFF ON EARTH!
B-BUT, MAGNUS... YOU HAVE TO!
I-I CAN'T. MY MISSION IS TOO IMPORTANT.
FORGIVE ME.
MAGNUS..?
FORGET IT, LAD. LET'S GO— OUR COMRADES ARE WAITING!
I DUNNO. REVIEWING THESE EVENTS JUST SEEMS TO MAKE MATTERS WORSE...

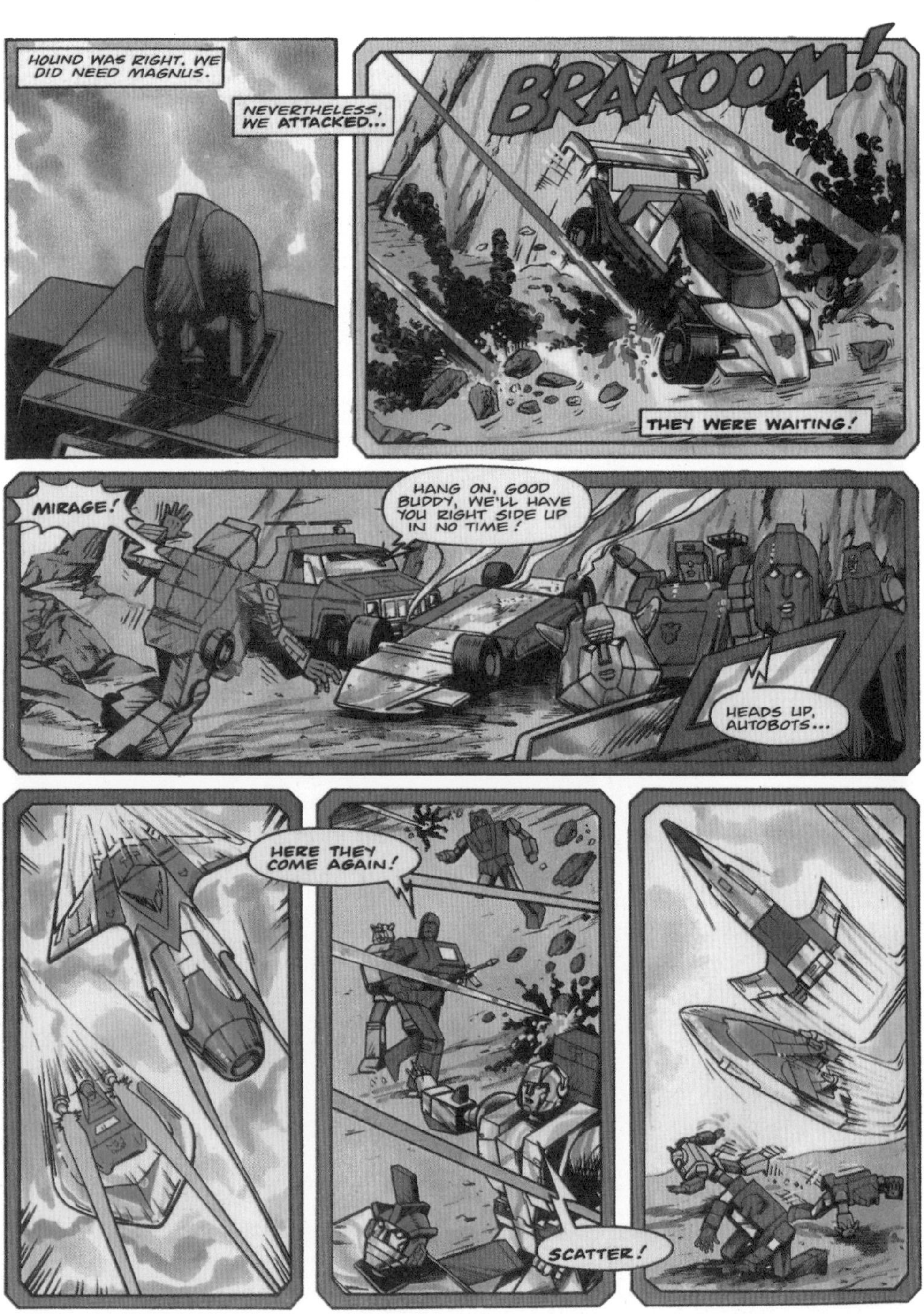
HOUND WAS RIGHT. WE DID NEED MAGNUS.
NEVERTHELESS, WE ATTACKED...
BRAKOOM!
THEY WERE WAITING!
MIRAGE!
HANG ON, GOOD BUDDY, WE'LL HAVE YOU RIGHT SIDE UP IN NO TIME!
HEADS UP, AUTOBOTS...
HERE THEY COME AGAIN!
SCATTER!

THEY'RE TURNING FOR ANOTHER RUN! AUTOBOTS — GIVE ME COVERING FIRE...

LET'S TAKE THE FIGHT TO THEM!

HE'S ON HIS WAY ...JUST AS GALVATRON PREDICTED!

IT'S YOUR SHOW NOW, CYCLONUS. MAKE IT LOOK GOOD, EH?

THAT'S GONNA' BE DIFFICULT...

AGAINST SUCH FEEBLE OPPOSITION!

SHRANG!

WHA— AARGH!

HE'S IN TROUBLE! PICK YOUR TARGETS CAREFULLY... READY...

FIRE!

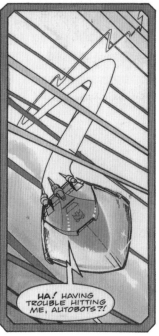

HA! HAVING TROUBLE HITTING ME, AUTOBOTS?!

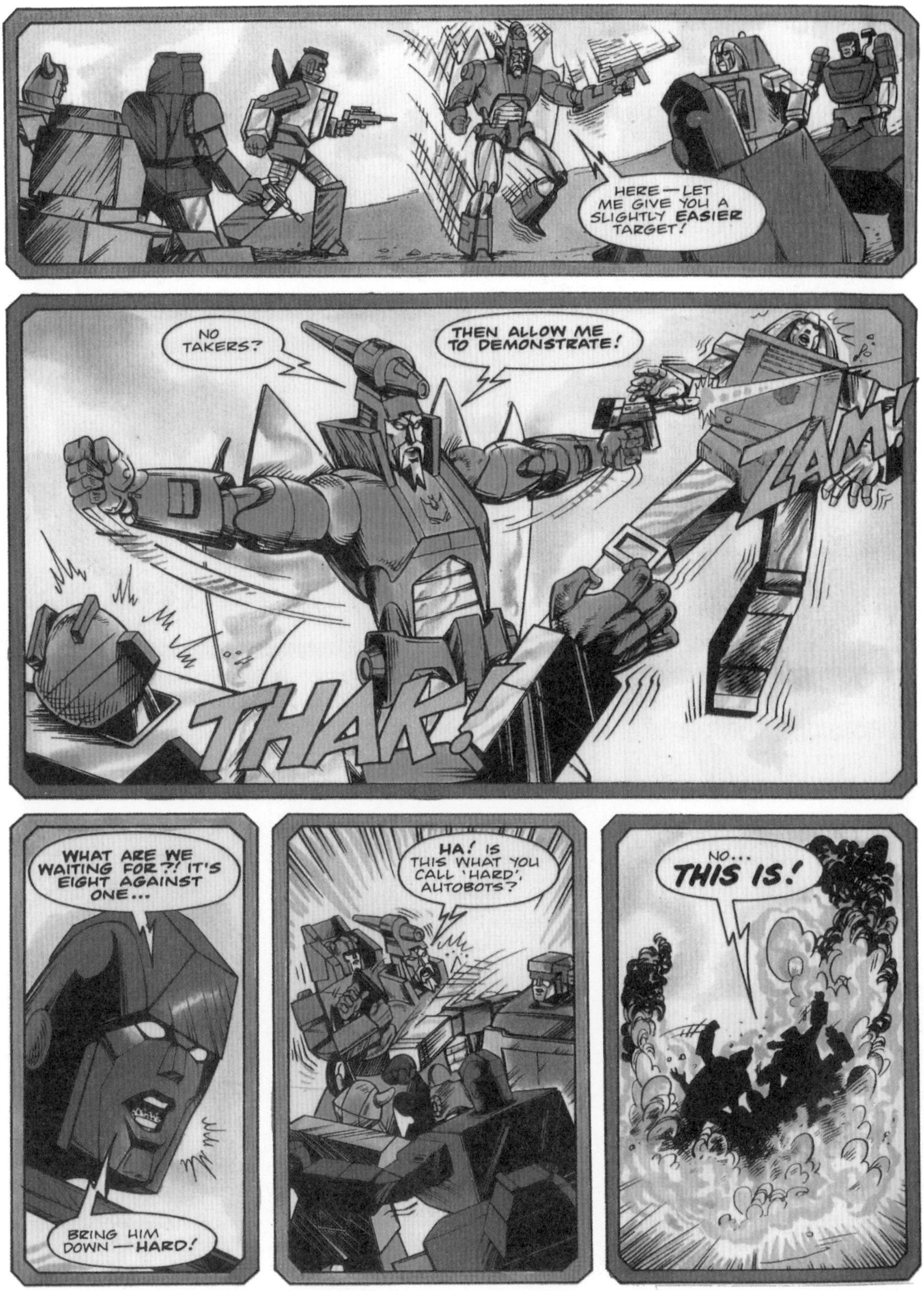
HERE—LET ME GIVE YOU A SLIGHTLY EASIER TARGET!
NO TAKERS?
THEN ALLOW ME TO DEMONSTRATE!
ZAM!
THAK!
WHAT ARE WE WAITING FOR?! IT'S EIGHT AGAINST ONE...
BRING HIM DOWN—HARD!
HA! IS THIS WHAT YOU CALL 'HARD', AUTOBOTS?
NO... THIS IS!

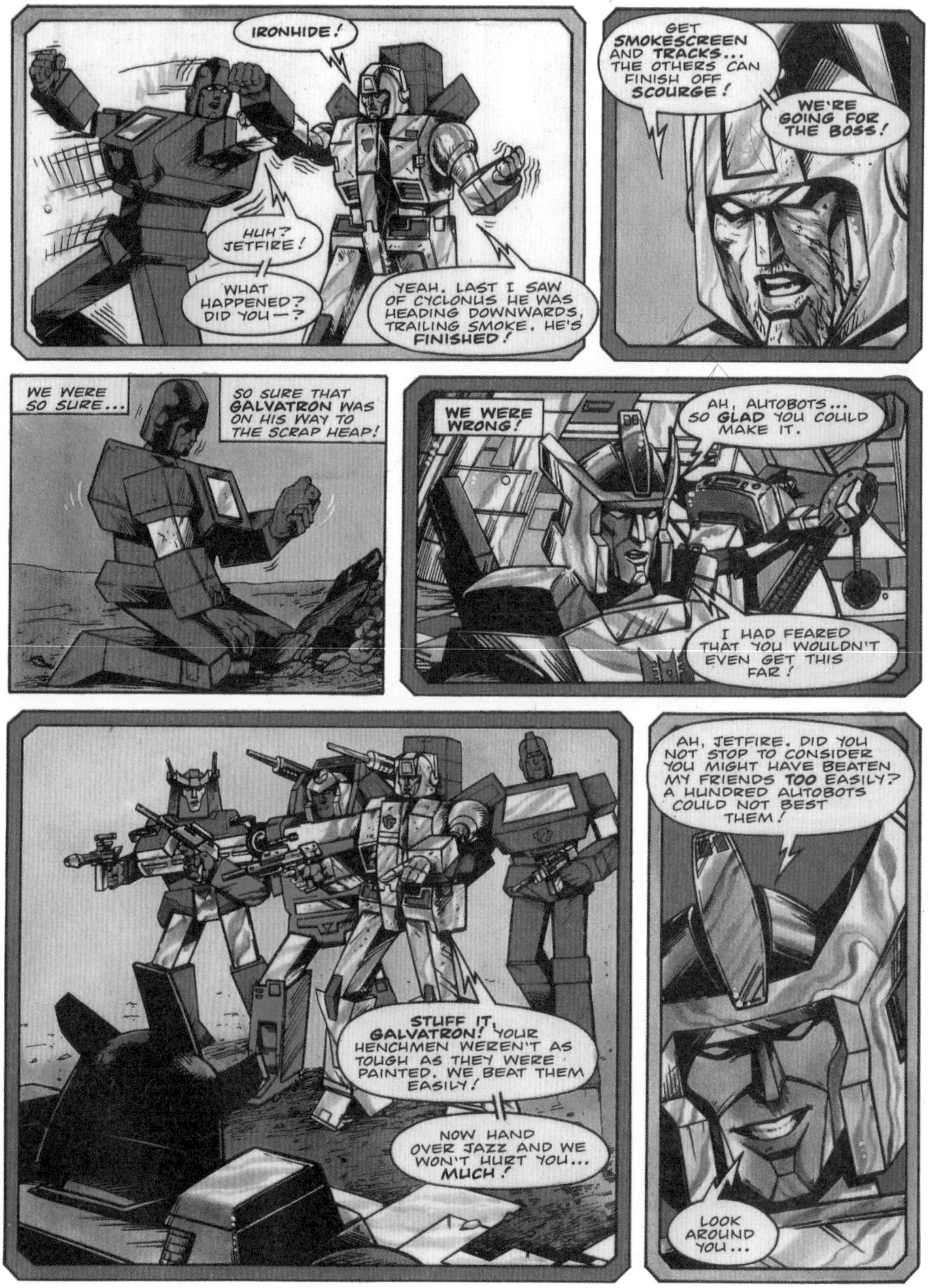
IRONHIDE!
HUH? JETFIRE!
WHAT HAPPENED? DID YOU—?
YEAH. LAST I SAW OF CYCLONUS HE WAS HEADING DOWNWARDS, TRAILING SMOKE. HE'S FINISHED!
GET SMOKESCREEN AND TRACKS... THE OTHERS CAN FINISH OFF SCOURGE!
WE'RE GOING FOR THE BOSS!
WE WERE SO SURE...
SO SURE THAT GALVATRON WAS ON HIS WAY TO THE SCRAP HEAP!
WE WERE WRONG!
AH, AUTOBOTS... SO GLAD YOU COULD MAKE IT.
I HAD FEARED THAT YOU WOULDN'T EVEN GET THIS FAR!
STUFF IT, GALVATRON! YOUR HENCHMEN WEREN'T AS TOUGH AS THEY WERE PAINTED. WE BEAT THEM EASILY!
NOW HAND OVER JAZZ AND WE WON'T HURT YOU... MUCH!
AH, JETFIRE. DID YOU NOT STOP TO CONSIDER YOU MIGHT HAVE BEATEN MY FRIENDS TOO EASILY? A HUNDRED AUTOBOTS COULD NOT BEST THEM!
LOOK AROUND YOU...

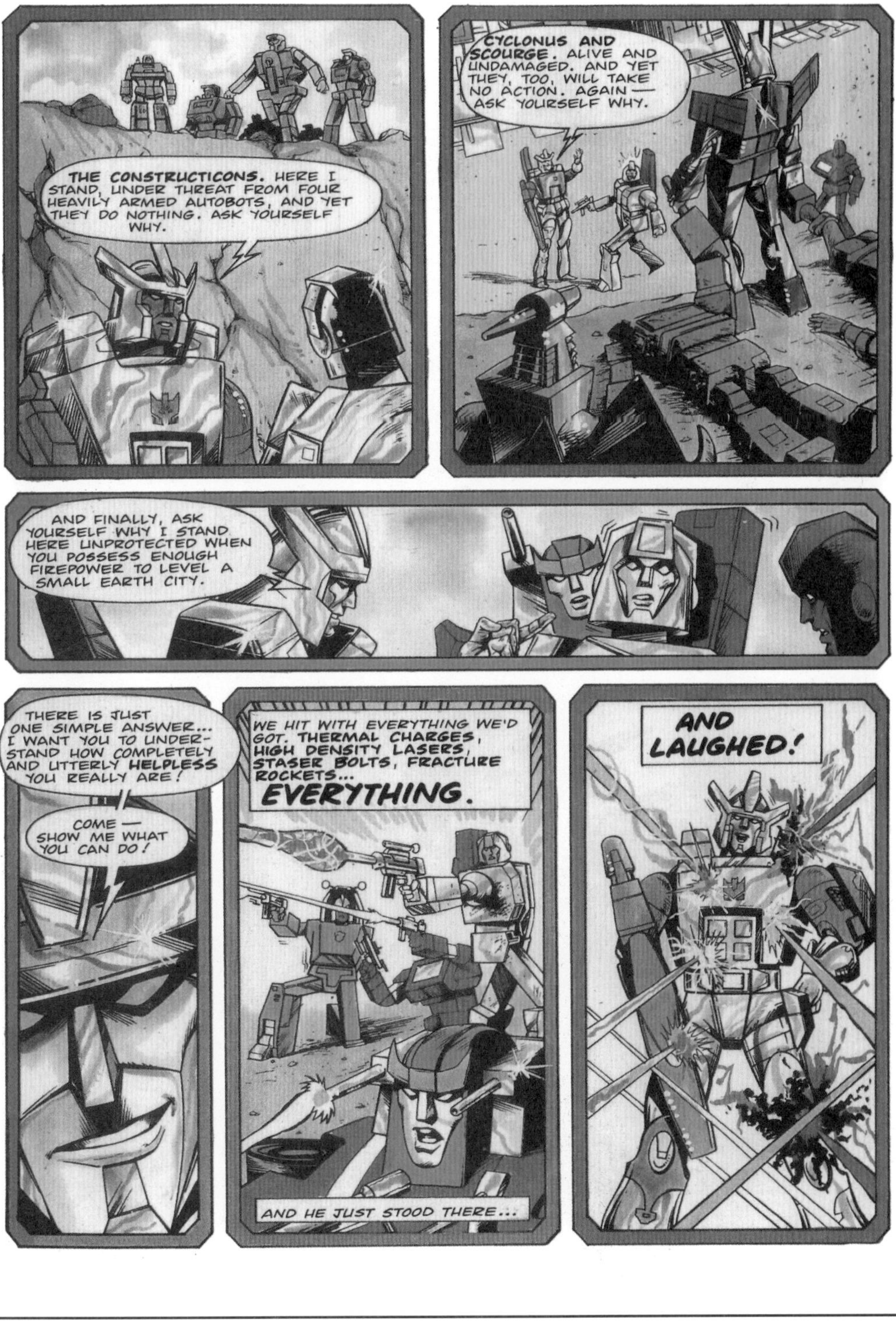
THE CONSTRUCTICONS. HERE I STAND, UNDER THREAT FROM FOUR HEAVILY ARMED AUTOBOTS, AND YET THEY DO NOTHING. ASK YOURSELF WHY.
CYCLONUS AND SCOURGE. ALIVE AND UNDAMAGED. AND YET THEY, TOO, WILL TAKE NO ACTION. AGAIN — ASK YOURSELF WHY.
AND FINALLY, ASK YOURSELF WHY I STAND HERE UNPROTECTED WHEN YOU POSSESS ENOUGH FIREPOWER TO LEVEL A SMALL EARTH CITY.
THERE IS JUST ONE SIMPLE ANSWER... I WANT YOU TO UNDERSTAND HOW COMPLETELY AND UTTERLY HELPLESS YOU REALLY ARE!
COME — SHOW ME WHAT YOU CAN DO!
WE HIT WITH EVERYTHING WE'D GOT. THERMAL CHARGES, HIGH DENSITY LASERS, STASER BOLTS, FRACTURE ROCKETS... EVERYTHING.
AND HE JUST STOOD THERE...
AND LAUGHED!

HE BEAT THE FUEL OUT OF US FOR GOOD MEASURE! IT WASN'T NECESSARY, WE WERE ALREADY DEFEATED.

HE KNEW THAT AND RELISHED EVERY MOMENT!

YOU'RE NOT EVEN WORTH KILLING! A MORE WORTHY FOE MIGHT DESERVE THAT HONOUR, BUT NOT YOU!

CRAWL BACK TO WHATEVER HOLE YOU CAME FROM, AUTOBOTS, AND PRAY THAT OUR PATHS DO NOT CROSS AGAIN!

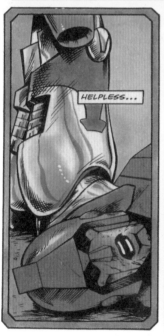

HELPLESS...

QUITE HELPLESS. WITHOUT OPTIMUS PRIME TO LEAD US... WITHOUT SOMEONE TO LEAD US, WE'RE FINISHED. SOMEONE HAS TO TAKE CHARGE...

WHICH IS WHY I'M DIGGING...

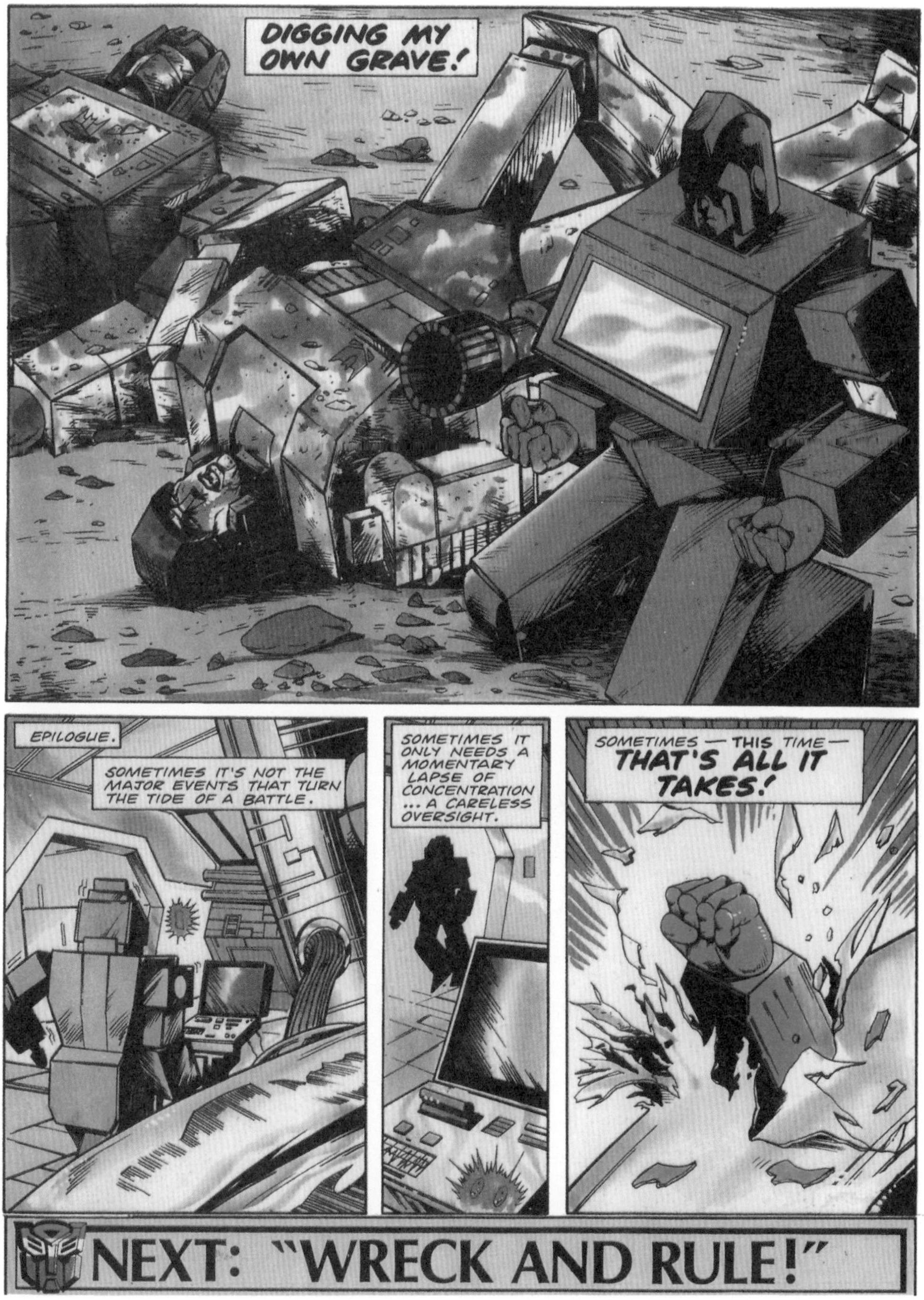

DIGGING MY OWN GRAVE!
EPILOGUE.
SOMETIMES IT'S NOT THE MAJOR EVENTS THAT TURN THE TIDE OF A BATTLE.
SOMETIMES IT ONLY NEEDS A MOMENTARY LAPSE OF CONCENTRATION ... A CARELESS OVERSIGHT.
SOMETIMES — THIS TIME — THAT'S ALL IT TAKES!
NEXT: "WRECK AND RULE!"

INTRODUCING THE NEW LEADERS!

ULTRA MAGNUS

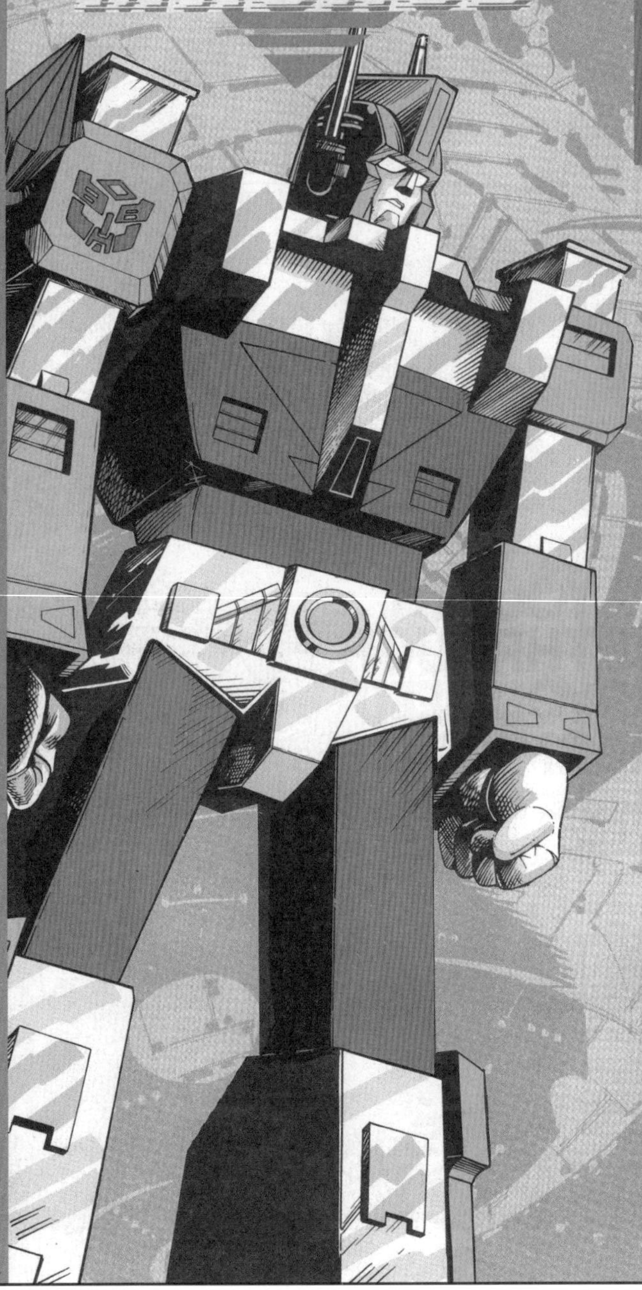

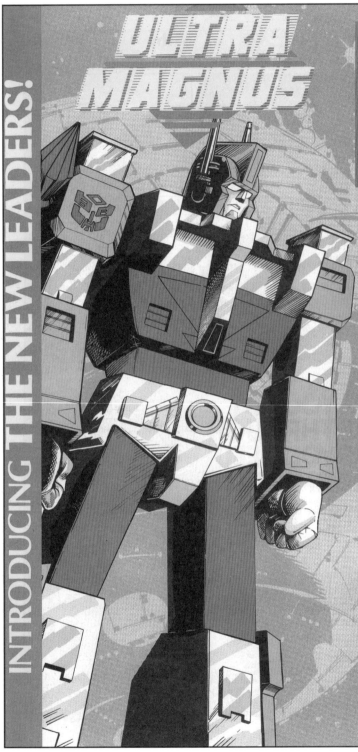

The biggest event to occur in recent Transformers history is the introduction of Ultra Magnus and Galvatron – the New Leaders. They will feature prominently as the saga of *Target:2006* unfolds over the coming weeks, and by the time the story reaches its searing climax in issue 88, you'll be ready for some big-screen action starring them both in *Transformers: The Movie!* For the moment, join us for an in-depth insight into the first of our New Leaders. . .

ORIGIN: With the Autobot resistance movement on Cybertron at a low ebb, the remaining Autobot elders decided that they needed a new warrior; a figurehead to inspire their troops. Many years were spent designing and building that warrior – a warrior that would become known as Ultra Magnus. When at last he was finished, the Elders tapped the power of Creation Matrix, embodied on Cybertron by the Matrix Flame, to instil him with life. With Ultra Magnus now functional, the Autobot resistance was at last able to prepare for a mass uprising. That uprising would be heralded by the destruction of some of the Decepticons' deadliest killers. It was dubbed *Operation:Volcano,* and would be spearheaded by Ultra Magnus himself.

PROFILE: Ultra Magnus is all soldier – with magnificent fighting skills, courage, and a rare gift for battlefield improvisation. He is resolute, fair and courageous beyond reproach – ever ready to sacrifice himself for the good of his troops and his mission. However, he is uncomfortable when the mantle of leadership is placed on his shoulders. He is happiest when he's carrying out orders, rather than giving them. He sees himself as a follower, not a commander, yet if forced by circumstance, he would willingly accept the responsibility. Magnus' only failing is that once he has accepted a certain task, his single-minded purpose sometimes blinds him to other things that should demand his attention.

ABILITIES: He is incredibly powerful, with a vast capacity for close combat. In both robot and car-carrier modes he carries neutron missile launchers, capable of firing up to a range of thirty miles. Powerful head mounted message receiving antennae enable Magnus to keep in constant touch with his fellow Autobots. In car-carrier mode, Ultra Magnus can carry other vehicle Autobots aboard him.

Originally printed in *Transformers UK* issue #81.

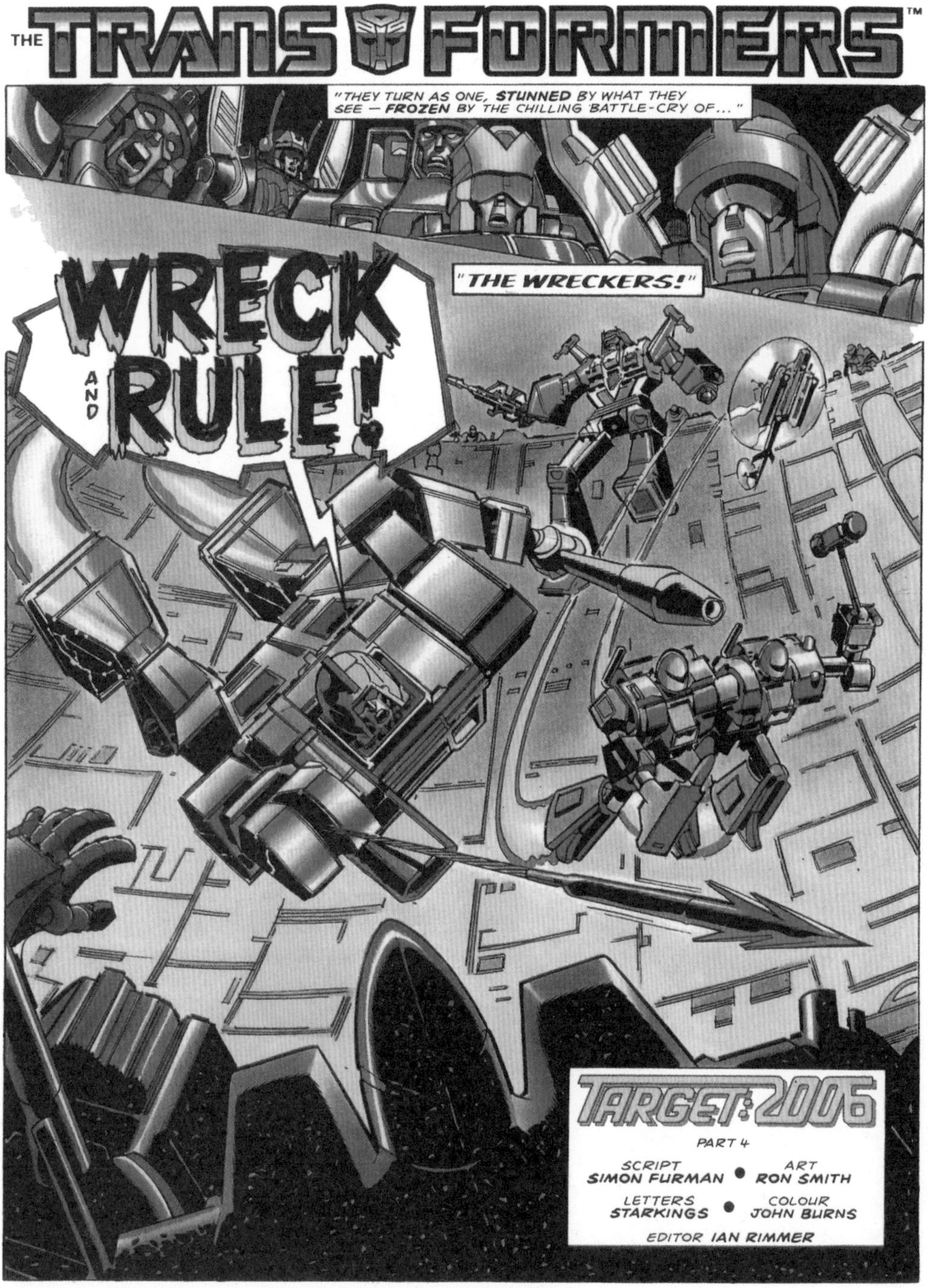
THE TRANSFORMERS
"THEY TURN AS ONE, STUNNED BY WHAT THEY SEE — FROZEN BY THE CHILLING BATTLE-CRY OF..."
"THE WRECKERS!"
WRECK AND RULE!
TARGET: 2006
PART 4
SCRIPT SIMON FURMAN • ART RON SMITH
LETTERS STARKINGS • COLOUR JOHN BURNS
EDITOR IAN RIMMER

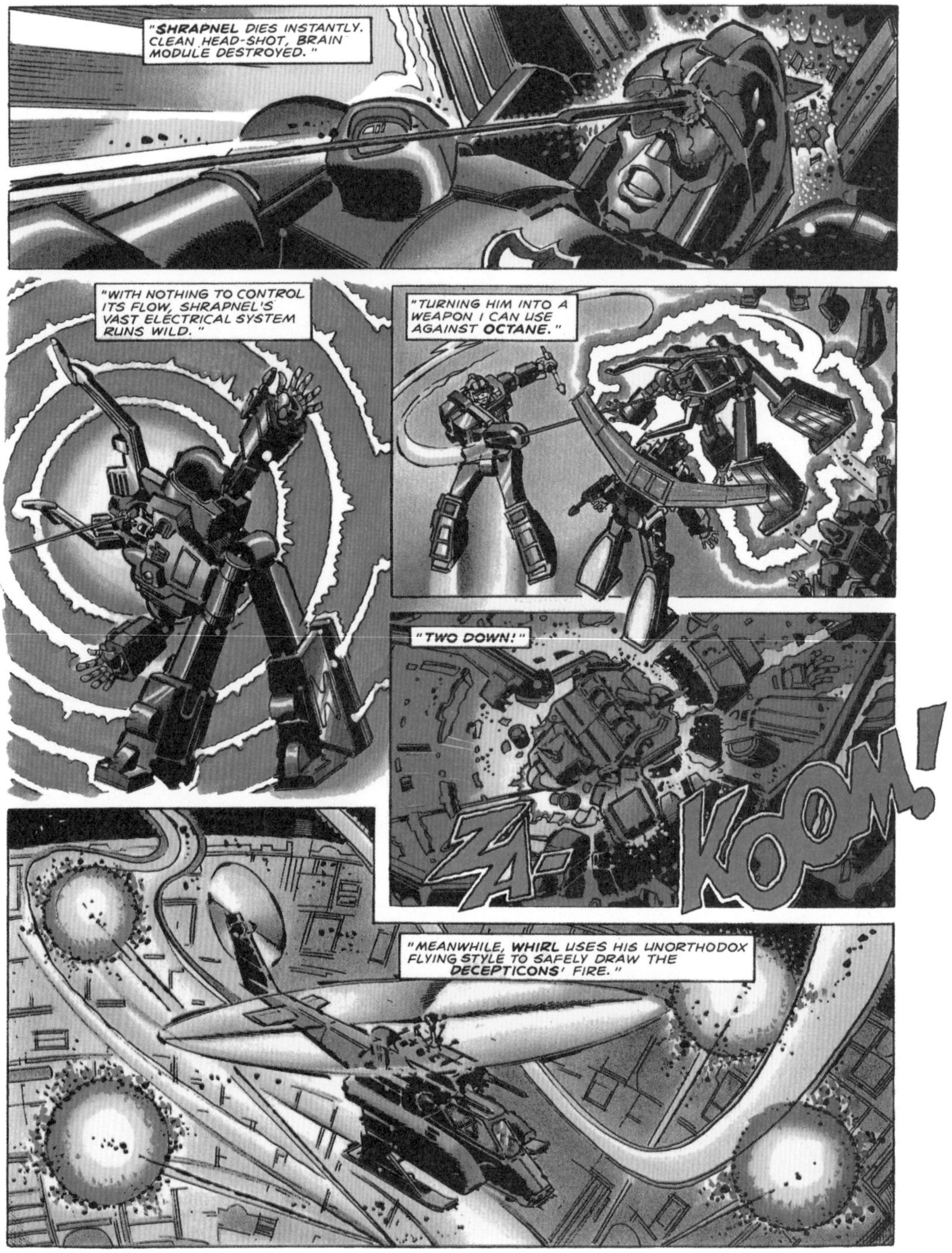
"SHRAPNEL DIES INSTANTLY. CLEAN HEAD-SHOT, BRAIN MODULE DESTROYED."
"WITH NOTHING TO CONTROL ITS FLOW, SHRAPNEL'S VAST ELECTRICAL SYSTEM RUNS WILD."
"TURNING HIM INTO A WEAPON I CAN USE AGAINST OCTANE."
"TWO DOWN!"
ZA-KOOM!
"MEANWHILE, WHIRL USES HIS UNORTHODOX FLYING STYLE TO SAFELY DRAW THE DECEPTICONS' FIRE."

"ALLOWING *RACK* AND *RUIN* TO GET IN CLOSE ENOUGH ON *THRUST*..."

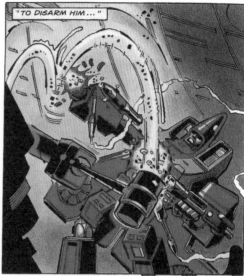

"TO DISARM HIM..."

"AND DEMONSTRATE THEIR UNIQUE STYLE..."

"OF HAND-TO-HAND COMBAT!"

"AS PER USUAL, OUR RESIDENT GLORY-HOG, *TOPSPIN*, TAKES ON TOO MANY FOES."

"*BOMBSHELL* AND *BLITZWING* HE CAN HANDLE, BUT *DIRGE* AND *RAMJET* AS WELL — NO WAY!"

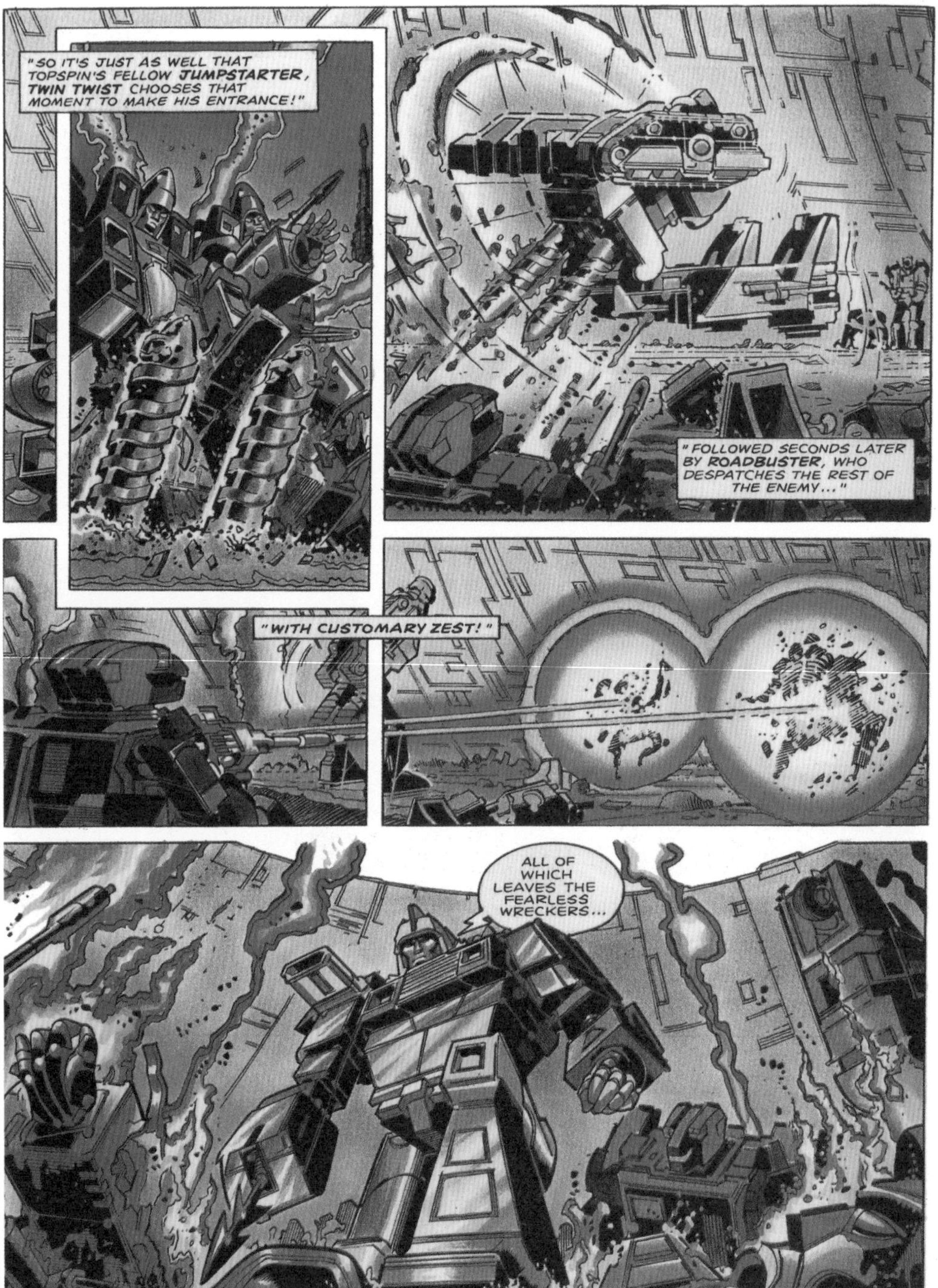
"SO IT'S JUST AS WELL THAT TOPSPIN'S FELLOW JUMPSTARTER, TWIN TWIST CHOOSES THAT MOMENT TO MAKE HIS ENTRANCE!"
"FOLLOWED SECONDS LATER BY ROADBUSTER, WHO DESPATCHES THE REST OF THE ENEMY..."
"WITH CUSTOMARY ZEST!"
ALL OF WHICH LEAVES THE FEARLESS WRECKERS...

...TO BE **ANNIHILATED** BY THE **DECEPTICON** REINFORCEMENTS THAT'LL BE POURING THROUGH THAT ARCH!

THAT'S ABOUT THE SIZE OF IT. WITHOUT **ULTRA MAGNUS** THERE TO HOLD THEM OFF, WE'LL BE DEAD IN LESS TIME THAN IT TAKES TO TELL.

TO THINK WE WERE SO CLOSE TO PULLING OFF **OPERATION: VOLCANO** WITHOUT A HITCH...

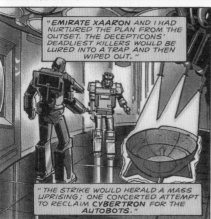

"**EMIRATE XAARON** AND I HAD NURTURED THE PLAN FROM THE OUTSET. THE **DECEPTICONS'** DEADLIEST KILLERS WOULD BE LURED INTO A TRAP AND THEN WIPED OUT."

"THE STRIKE WOULD HERALD A MASS UPRISING; ONE CONCERTED ATTEMPT TO RECLAIM **CYBERTRON** FOR THE **AUTOBOTS**."

"THE TRAP HAD BEEN BAITED."

AUTOBOT RESISTANCE CHIEFS FROM ALL STATES MEETING IN IACON. IMPERIAL AMPHITHEATRE ON ... ANNIVERSARY OF IACON'S FALL TO WARLORD TRANNIS.

"THE BAIT TAKEN!"

"WITH ONLY TEN CYCLES LEFT TILL 'VOLCANO', THE MATRIX FLAME WAS EXTINGUISHED, INDICATING THAT THE SACRED **CREATION MATRIX** WAS IN DIRE JEOPARDY."

"UNFORTUNATELY, THE MATRIX IS — OR **WAS** — HOUSED IN THE MIND OF **OPTIMUS PRIME**, ON A DISTANT PLANET CALLED EARTH."

"SO THE MOST IMPORTANT ELEMENT OF **OPERATION: VOLCANO** — MAGNUS HIMSELF — HEADS FOR EARTH IN SEARCH OF PRIME, TRAVELLING VIA AN UNSTABLE PROTOTYPE **SPACE BRIDGE**, BUILT BY THE NEUTRALIST SCIENTIST, SPANNER."

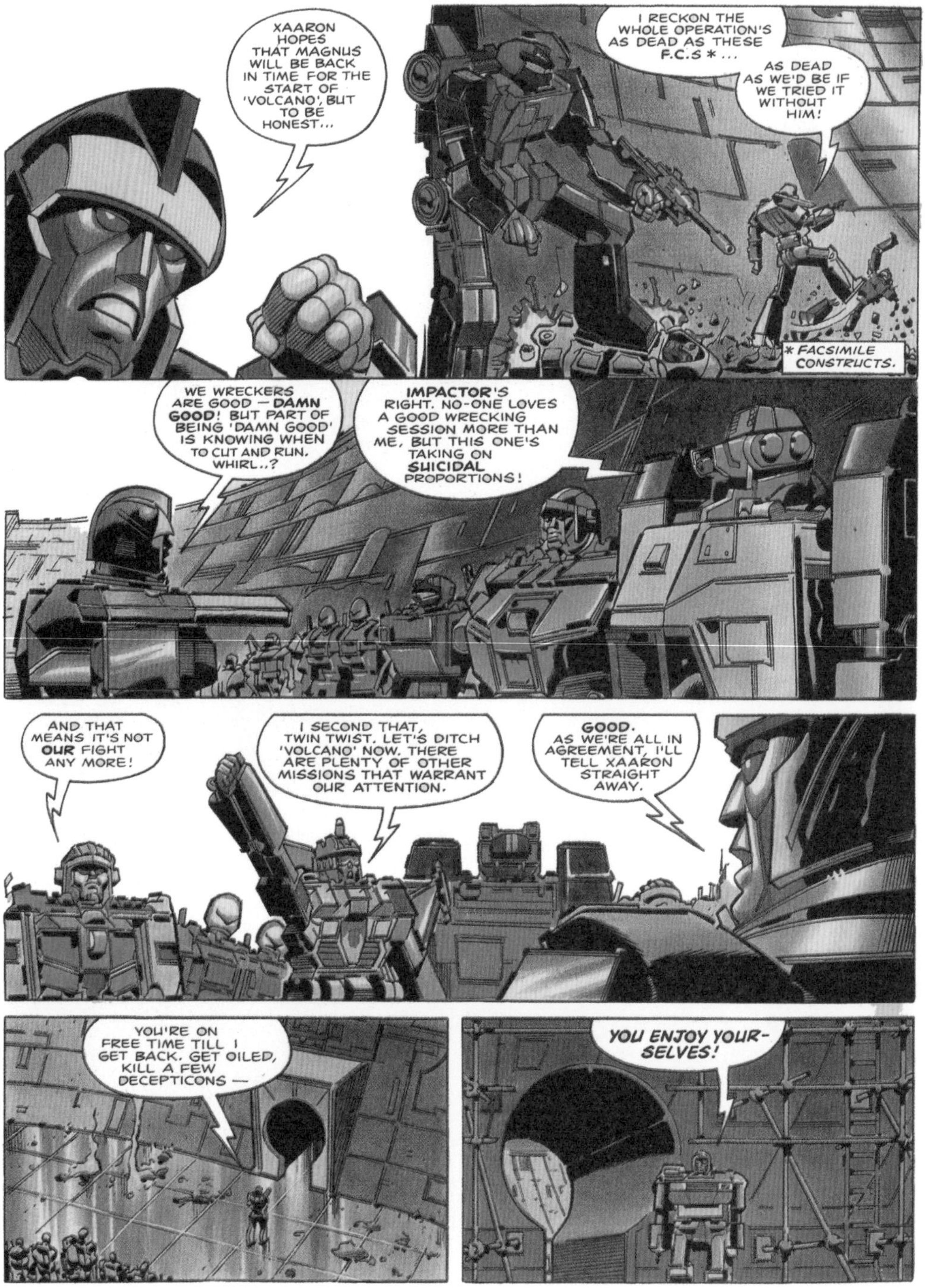

XAARON HOPES THAT MAGNUS WILL BE BACK IN TIME FOR THE START OF 'VOLCANO', BUT TO BE HONEST...
I RECKON THE WHOLE OPERATION'S AS DEAD AS THESE F.C.S *...
AS DEAD AS WE'D BE IF WE TRIED IT WITHOUT HIM!
* FACSIMILE CONSTRUCTS.
WE WRECKERS ARE GOOD — DAMN GOOD! BUT PART OF BEING 'DAMN GOOD' IS KNOWING WHEN TO CUT AND RUN. WHIRL..?
IMPACTOR'S RIGHT. NO-ONE LOVES A GOOD WRECKING SESSION MORE THAN ME, BUT THIS ONE'S TAKING ON SUICIDAL PROPORTIONS!
AND THAT MEANS IT'S NOT OUR FIGHT ANY MORE!
I SECOND THAT, TWIN TWIST. LET'S DITCH 'VOLCANO' NOW. THERE ARE PLENTY OF OTHER MISSIONS THAT WARRANT OUR ATTENTION.
GOOD. AS WE'RE ALL IN AGREEMENT, I'LL TELL XAARON STRAIGHT AWAY.
YOU'RE ON FREE TIME TILL I GET BACK. GET OILED, KILL A FEW DECEPTICONS —
YOU ENJOY YOURSELVES!

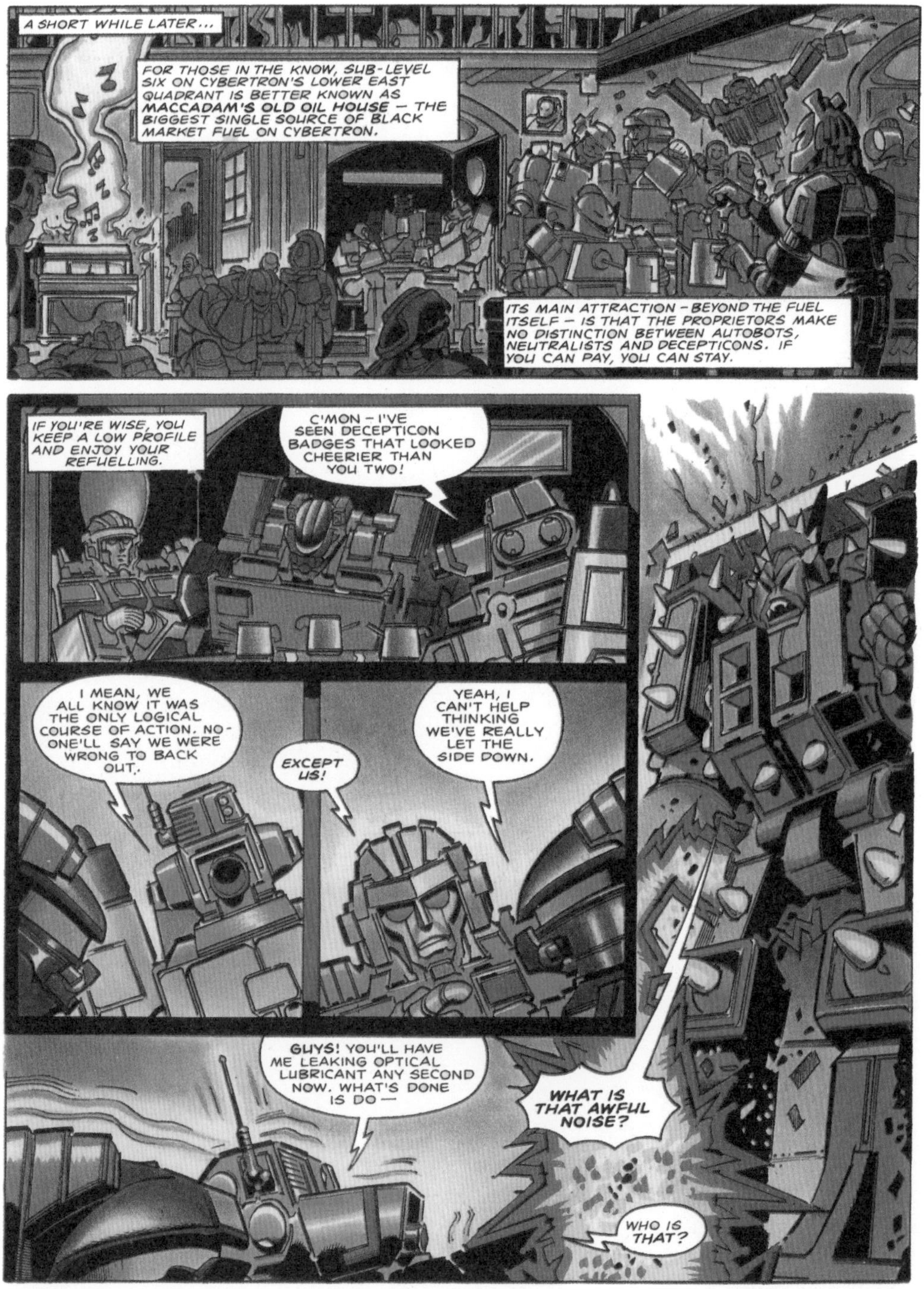
A SHORT WHILE LATER...
FOR THOSE IN THE KNOW, SUB-LEVEL SIX ON CYBERTRON'S LOWER EAST QUADRANT IS BETTER KNOWN AS **MACCADAM'S OLD OIL HOUSE** — THE BIGGEST SINGLE SOURCE OF BLACK MARKET FUEL ON CYBERTRON.
ITS MAIN ATTRACTION — BEYOND THE FUEL ITSELF — IS THAT THE PROPRIETORS MAKE NO DISTINCTION BETWEEN AUTOBOTS, NEUTRALISTS AND DECEPTICONS. IF YOU CAN PAY, YOU CAN STAY.
IF YOU'RE WISE, YOU KEEP A LOW PROFILE AND ENJOY YOUR REFUELLING.
C'MON — I'VE SEEN DECEPTICON BADGES THAT LOOKED CHEERIER THAN YOU TWO!
I MEAN, WE ALL KNOW IT WAS THE ONLY LOGICAL COURSE OF ACTION. NO-ONE'LL SAY WE WERE WRONG TO BACK OUT.
EXCEPT US!
YEAH, I CAN'T HELP THINKING WE'VE REALLY LET THE SIDE DOWN.
GUYS! YOU'LL HAVE ME LEAKING OPTICAL LUBRICANT ANY SECOND NOW. WHAT'S DONE IS DO —
WHAT IS THAT AWFUL NOISE?
WHO IS THAT?

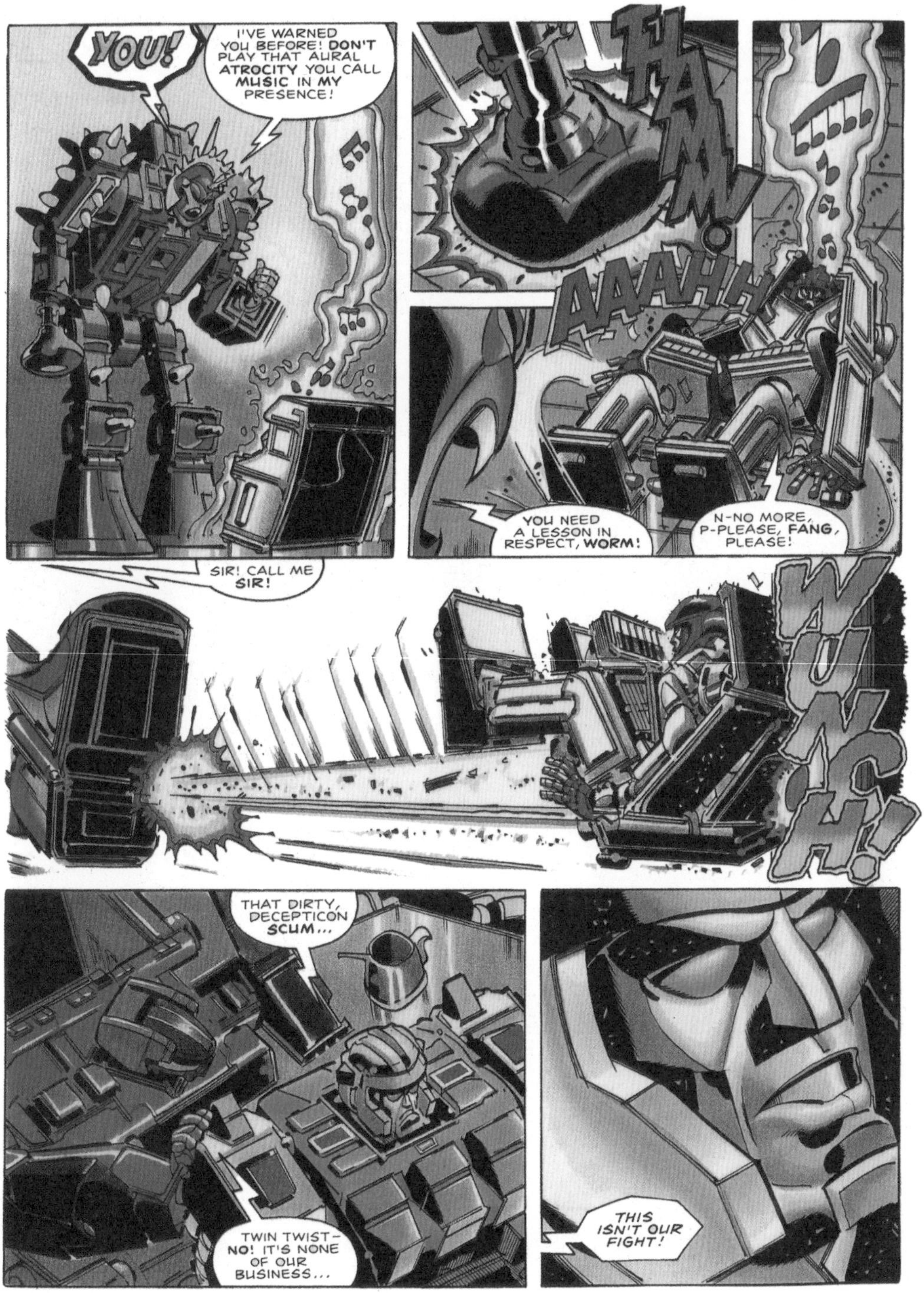
YOU!
I'VE WARNED YOU BEFORE! DON'T PLAY THAT AURAL ATROCITY YOU CALL MUSIC IN MY PRESENCE!
THAM!
AAAHH!
YOU NEED A LESSON IN RESPECT, WORM!
N-NO MORE, P-PLEASE, FANG, PLEASE!
SIR! CALL ME SIR!
WUNCH!
THAT DIRTY, DECEPTICON SCUM...
TWIN TWIST-- NO! IT'S NONE OF OUR BUSINESS...
THIS ISN'T OUR FIGHT!

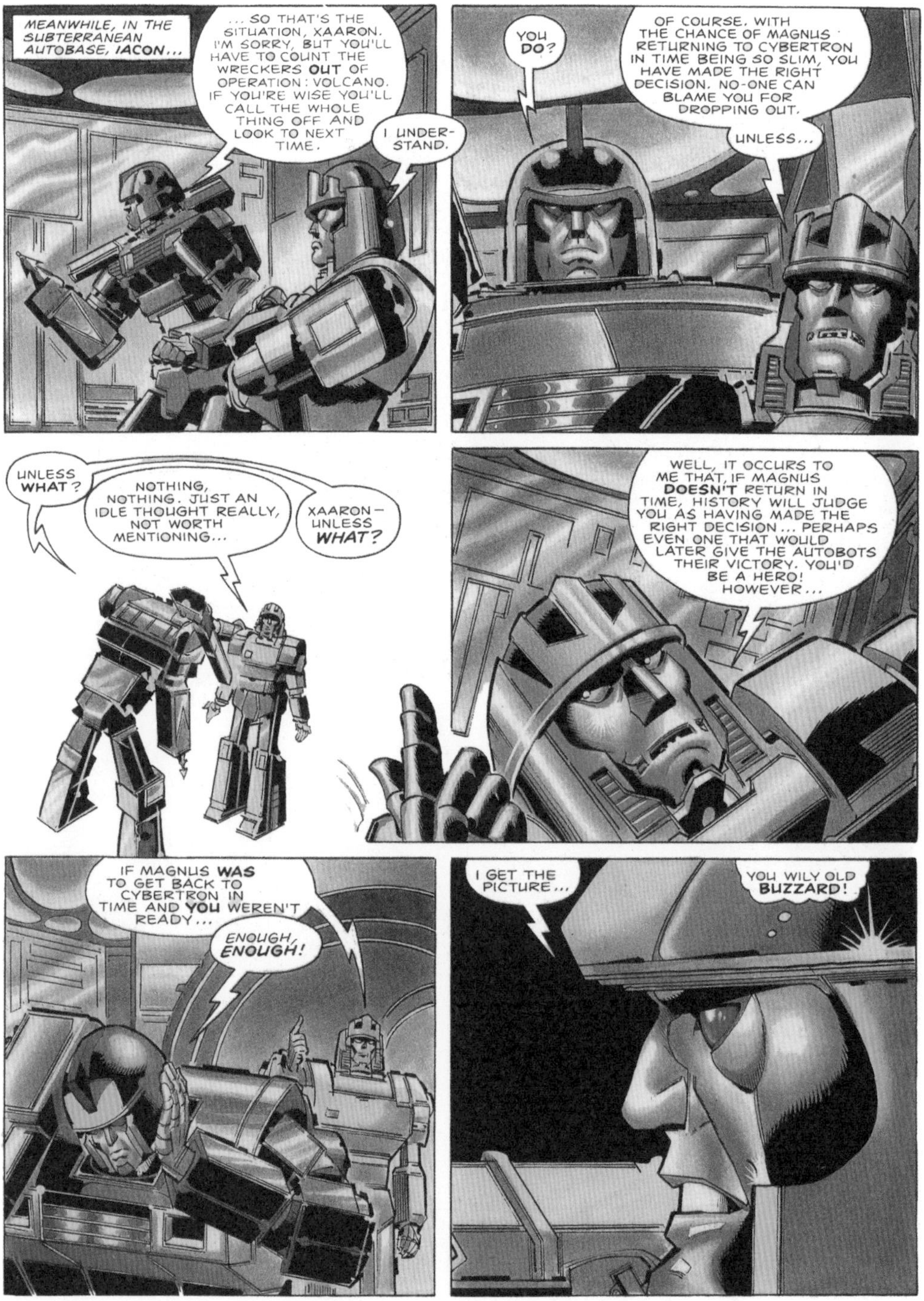
MEANWHILE, IN THE SUBTERRANEAN AUTOBASE, IACON...
... SO THAT'S THE SITUATION, XAARON. I'M SORRY, BUT YOU'LL HAVE TO COUNT THE WRECKERS OUT OF OPERATION: VOLCANO. IF YOU'RE WISE YOU'LL CALL THE WHOLE THING OFF AND LOOK TO NEXT TIME.
I UNDERSTAND.
YOU DO?
OF COURSE. WITH THE CHANCE OF MAGNUS RETURNING TO CYBERTRON IN TIME BEING SO SLIM, YOU HAVE MADE THE RIGHT DECISION. NO-ONE CAN BLAME YOU FOR DROPPING OUT.
UNLESS...
UNLESS WHAT?
NOTHING, NOTHING. JUST AN IDLE THOUGHT REALLY, NOT WORTH MENTIONING...
XAARON— UNLESS WHAT?
WELL, IT OCCURS TO ME THAT, IF MAGNUS DOESN'T RETURN IN TIME, HISTORY WILL JUDGE YOU AS HAVING MADE THE RIGHT DECISION... PERHAPS EVEN ONE THAT WOULD LATER GIVE THE AUTOBOTS THEIR VICTORY. YOU'D BE A HERO! HOWEVER...
IF MAGNUS WAS TO GET BACK TO CYBERTRON IN TIME AND YOU WEREN'T READY...
ENOUGH, ENOUGH!
I GET THE PICTURE...
YOU WILY OLD BUZZARD!

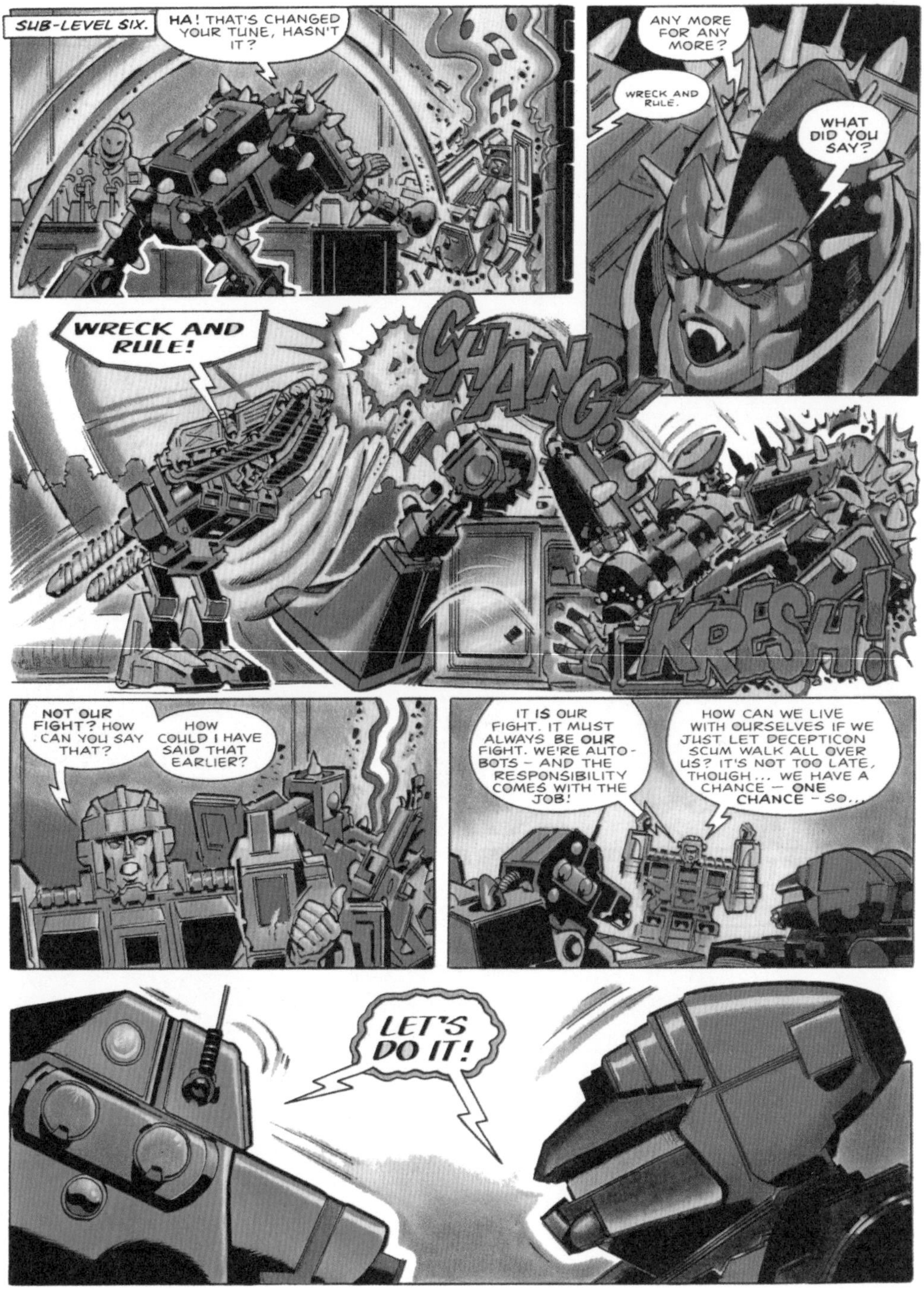
SUB-LEVEL SIX.
HA! THAT'S CHANGED YOUR TUNE, HASN'T IT?
ANY MORE FOR ANY MORE?
WRECK AND RULE.
WHAT DID YOU SAY?
WRECK AND RULE!
CHANG!
KRESH!
NOT OUR FIGHT? HOW CAN YOU SAY THAT?
HOW COULD I HAVE SAID THAT EARLIER?
IT IS OUR FIGHT. IT MUST ALWAYS BE OUR FIGHT. WE'RE AUTO-BOTS — AND THE RESPONSIBILITY COMES WITH THE JOB!
HOW CAN WE LIVE WITH OURSELVES IF WE JUST LET DECEPTICON SCUM WALK ALL OVER US? IT'S NOT TOO LATE, THOUGH... WE HAVE A CHANCE — ONE CHANCE — SO...
LET'S DO IT!

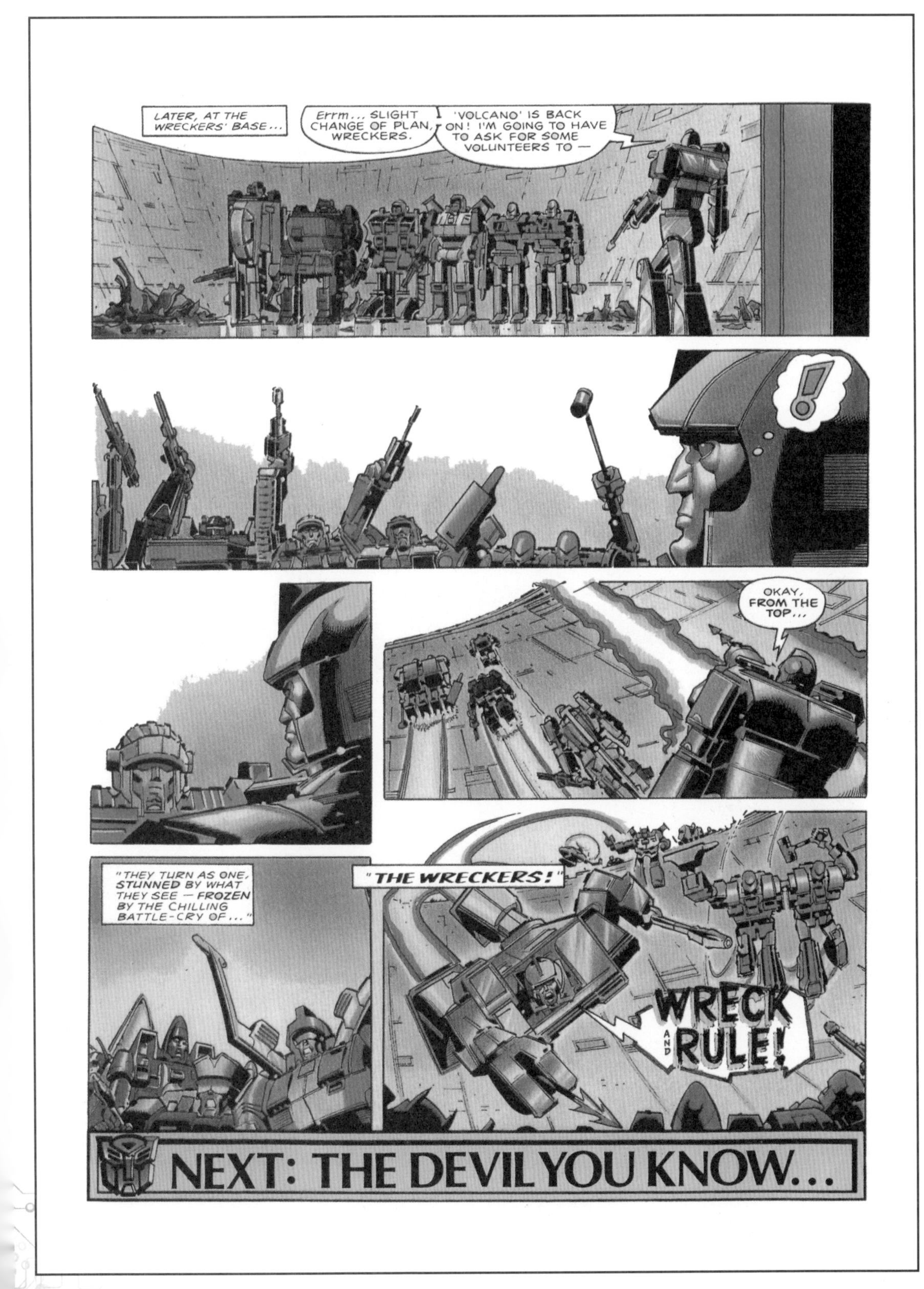
LATER, AT THE WRECKERS' BASE...
Errm... SLIGHT CHANGE OF PLAN, WRECKERS.
'VOLCANO' IS BACK ON! I'M GOING TO HAVE TO ASK FOR SOME VOLUNTEERS TO —
!
OKAY, FROM THE TOP...
"THEY TURN AS ONE, STUNNED BY WHAT THEY SEE — FROZEN BY THE CHILLING BATTLE-CRY OF..."
"THE WRECKERS!"
WRECK AND RULE!
NEXT: THE DEVIL YOU KNOW...

TRANS ⬡ FORMERS

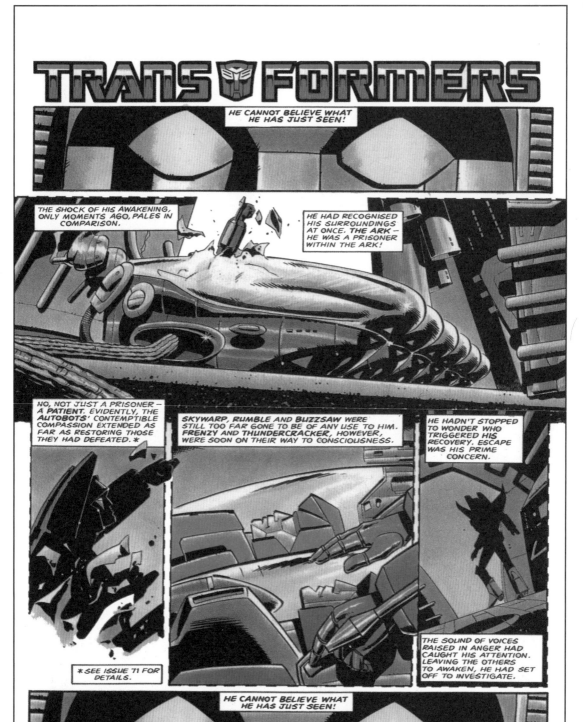

HE CANNOT BELIEVE WHAT HE HAS JUST SEEN!

THE SHOCK OF HIS AWAKENING, ONLY MOMENTS AGO, PALES IN COMPARISON.

HE HAD RECOGNISED HIS SURROUNDINGS AT ONCE. *THE ARK* — HE WAS A PRISONER WITHIN THE ARK!

NO, NOT JUST A PRISONER — A *PATIENT*. EVIDENTLY, THE *AUTOBOTS'* CONTEMPTIBLE COMPASSION EXTENDED AS FAR AS RESTORING THOSE THEY HAD DEFEATED. *

SKYWARP, RUMBLE AND *BUZZSAW* WERE STILL TOO FAR GONE TO BE OF ANY USE TO HIM. *FRENZY* AND *THUNDERCRACKER*, HOWEVER, WERE SOON ON THEIR WAY TO CONSCIOUSNESS.

HE HADN'T STOPPED TO WONDER WHO TRIGGERED HIS RECOVERY. ESCAPE WAS HIS PRIME CONCERN.

*SEE ISSUE 71 FOR DETAILS.

THE SOUND OF VOICES RAISED IN ANGER HAD CAUGHT HIS ATTENTION. LEAVING THE OTHERS TO AWAKEN, HE HAD SET OFF TO INVESTIGATE.

HE CANNOT BELIEVE WHAT HE HAS JUST SEEN!

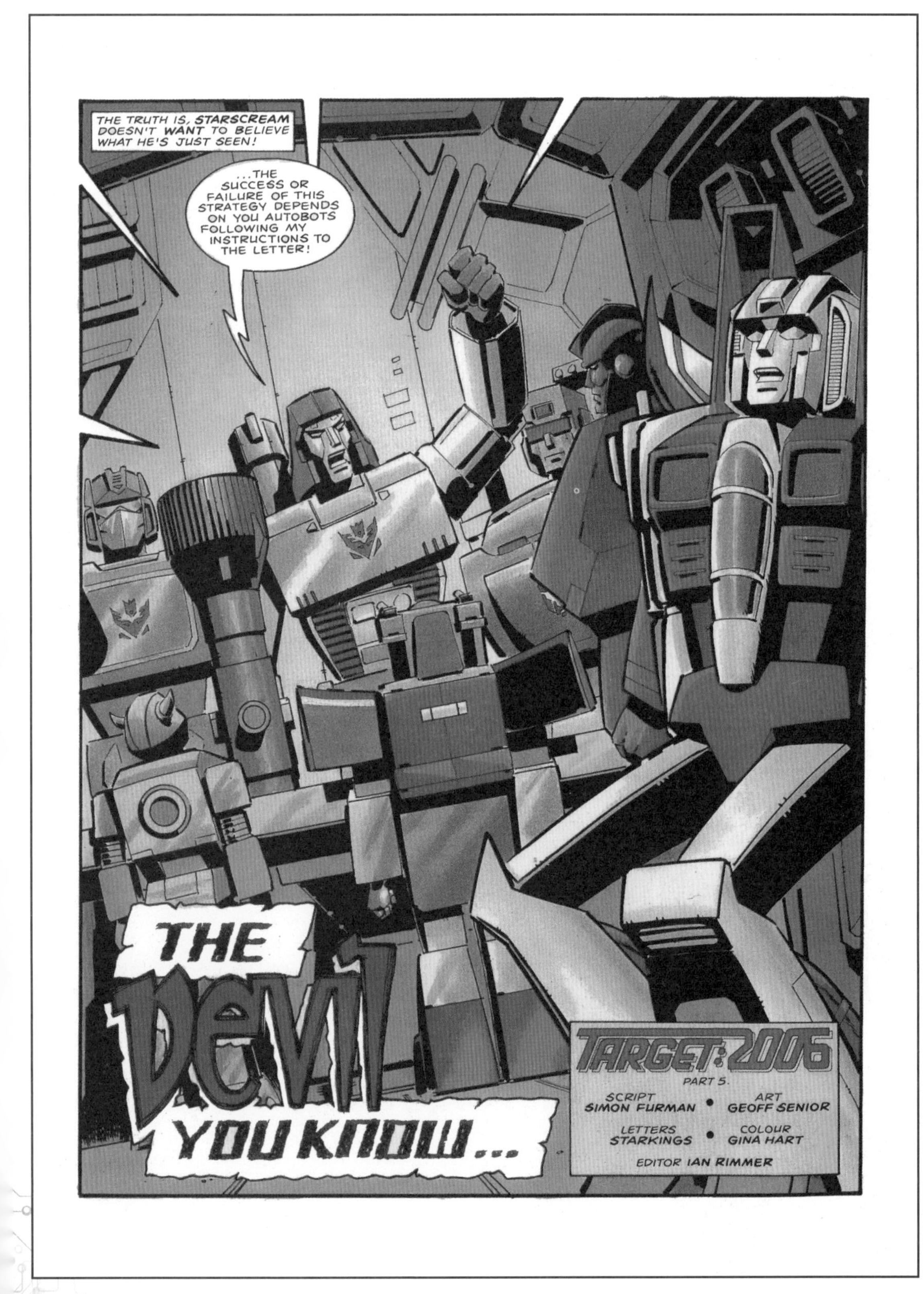
THE TRUTH IS, STARSCREAM DOESN'T WANT TO BELIEVE WHAT HE'S JUST SEEN!
...THE SUCCESS OR FAILURE OF THIS STRATEGY DEPENDS ON YOU AUTOBOTS FOLLOWING MY INSTRUCTIONS TO THE LETTER!
THE DEVIL YOU KNOW...
TARGET: 2006
PART 5.
SCRIPT SIMON FURMAN • ART GEOFF SENIOR
LETTERS STARKINGS • COLOUR GINA HART
EDITOR IAN RIMMER

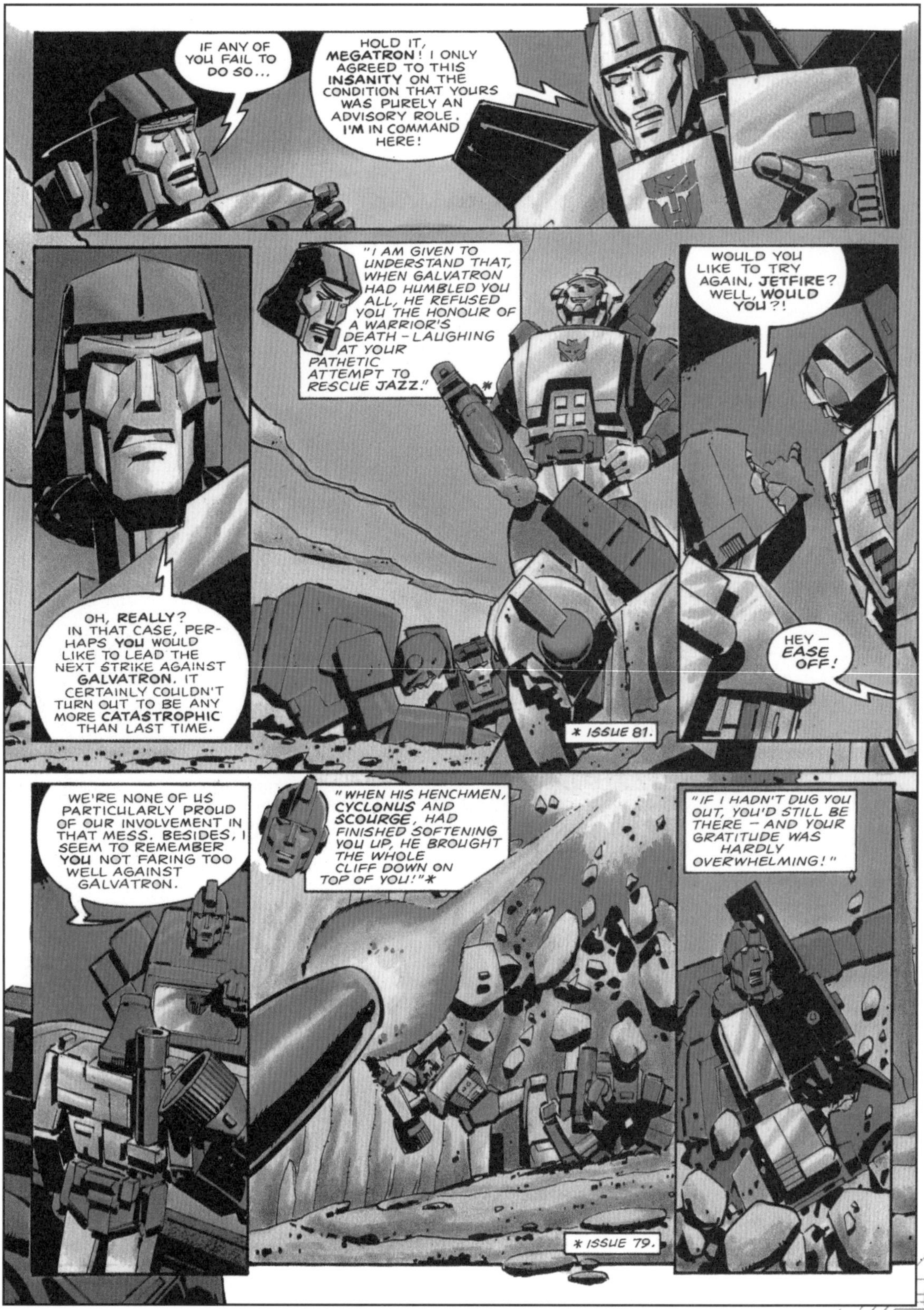
IF ANY OF YOU FAIL TO DO SO...
HOLD IT, MEGATRON! I ONLY AGREED TO THIS INSANITY ON THE CONDITION THAT YOURS WAS PURELY AN ADVISORY ROLE. I'M IN COMMAND HERE!
OH, REALLY? IN THAT CASE, PERHAPS YOU WOULD LIKE TO LEAD THE NEXT STRIKE AGAINST GALVATRON. IT CERTAINLY COULDN'T TURN OUT TO BE ANY MORE CATASTROPHIC THAN LAST TIME.
"I AM GIVEN TO UNDERSTAND THAT, WHEN GALVATRON HAD HUMBLED YOU ALL, HE REFUSED YOU THE HONOUR OF A WARRIOR'S DEATH - LAUGHING AT YOUR PATHETIC ATTEMPT TO RESCUE JAZZ."*
* ISSUE 81.
WOULD YOU LIKE TO TRY AGAIN, JETFIRE? WELL, WOULD YOU?!
HEY - EASE OFF!
WE'RE NONE OF US PARTICULARLY PROUD OF OUR INVOLVEMENT IN THAT MESS. BESIDES, I SEEM TO REMEMBER YOU NOT FARING TOO WELL AGAINST GALVATRON.
"WHEN HIS HENCHMEN, CYCLONUS AND SCOURGE, HAD FINISHED SOFTENING YOU UP, HE BROUGHT THE WHOLE CLIFF DOWN ON TOP OF YOU!"*
* ISSUE 79.
"IF I HADN'T DUG YOU OUT, YOU'D STILL BE THERE - AND YOUR GRATITUDE WAS HARDLY OVERWHELMING!"

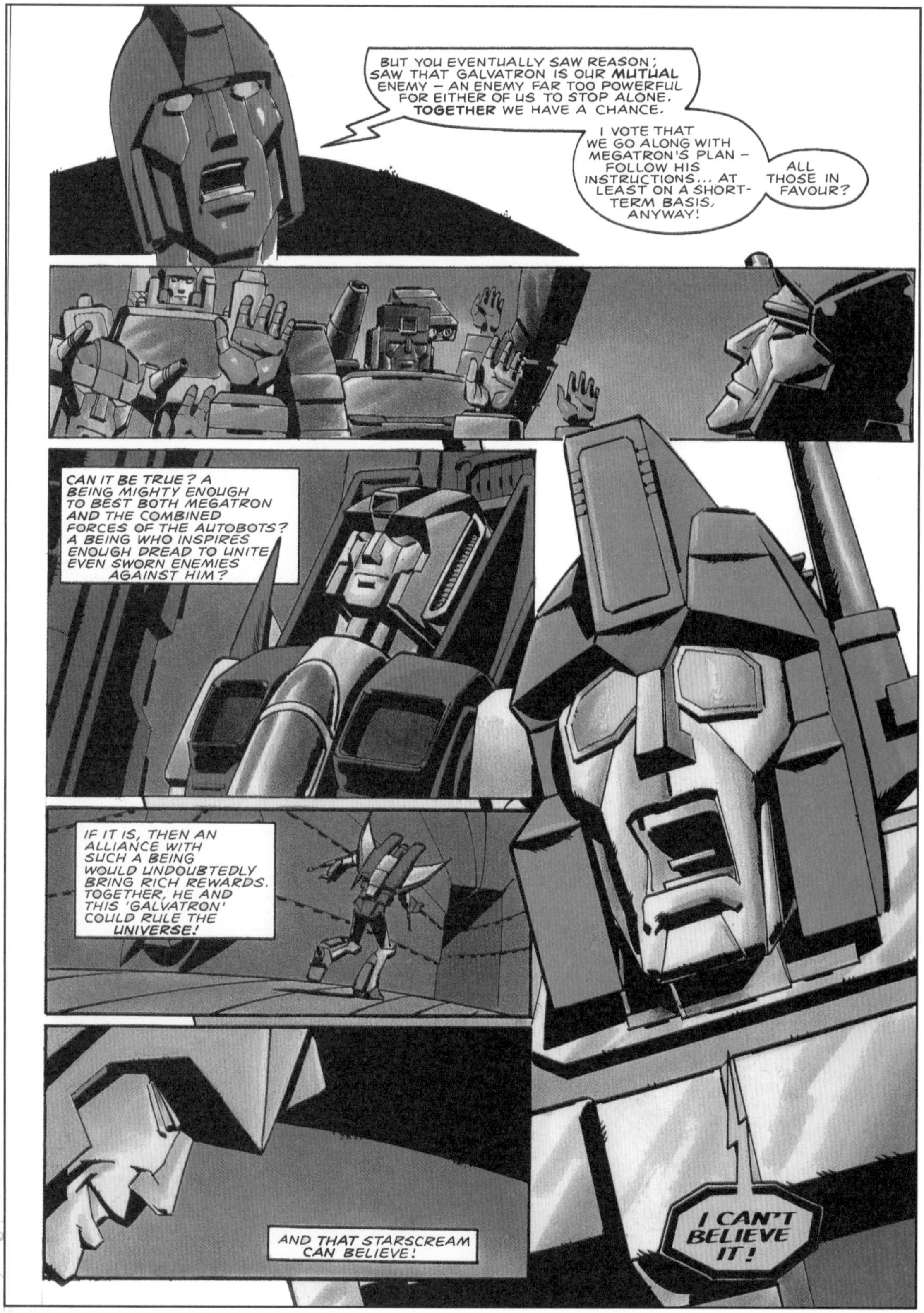
BUT YOU EVENTUALLY SAW REASON; SAW THAT GALVATRON IS OUR MUTUAL ENEMY – AN ENEMY FAR TOO POWERFUL FOR EITHER OF US TO STOP ALONE. TOGETHER WE HAVE A CHANCE.
I VOTE THAT WE GO ALONG WITH MEGATRON'S PLAN – FOLLOW HIS INSTRUCTIONS... AT LEAST ON A SHORT-TERM BASIS, ANYWAY!
ALL THOSE IN FAVOUR?
CAN IT BE TRUE? A BEING MIGHTY ENOUGH TO BEST BOTH MEGATRON AND THE COMBINED FORCES OF THE AUTOBOTS? A BEING WHO INSPIRES ENOUGH DREAD TO UNITE EVEN SWORN ENEMIES AGAINST HIM?
IF IT IS, THEN AN ALLIANCE WITH SUCH A BEING WOULD UNDOUBTEDLY BRING RICH REWARDS. TOGETHER, HE AND THIS 'GALVATRON' COULD RULE THE UNIVERSE!
I CAN'T BELIEVE IT!
AND THAT STARSCREAM CAN BELIEVE!

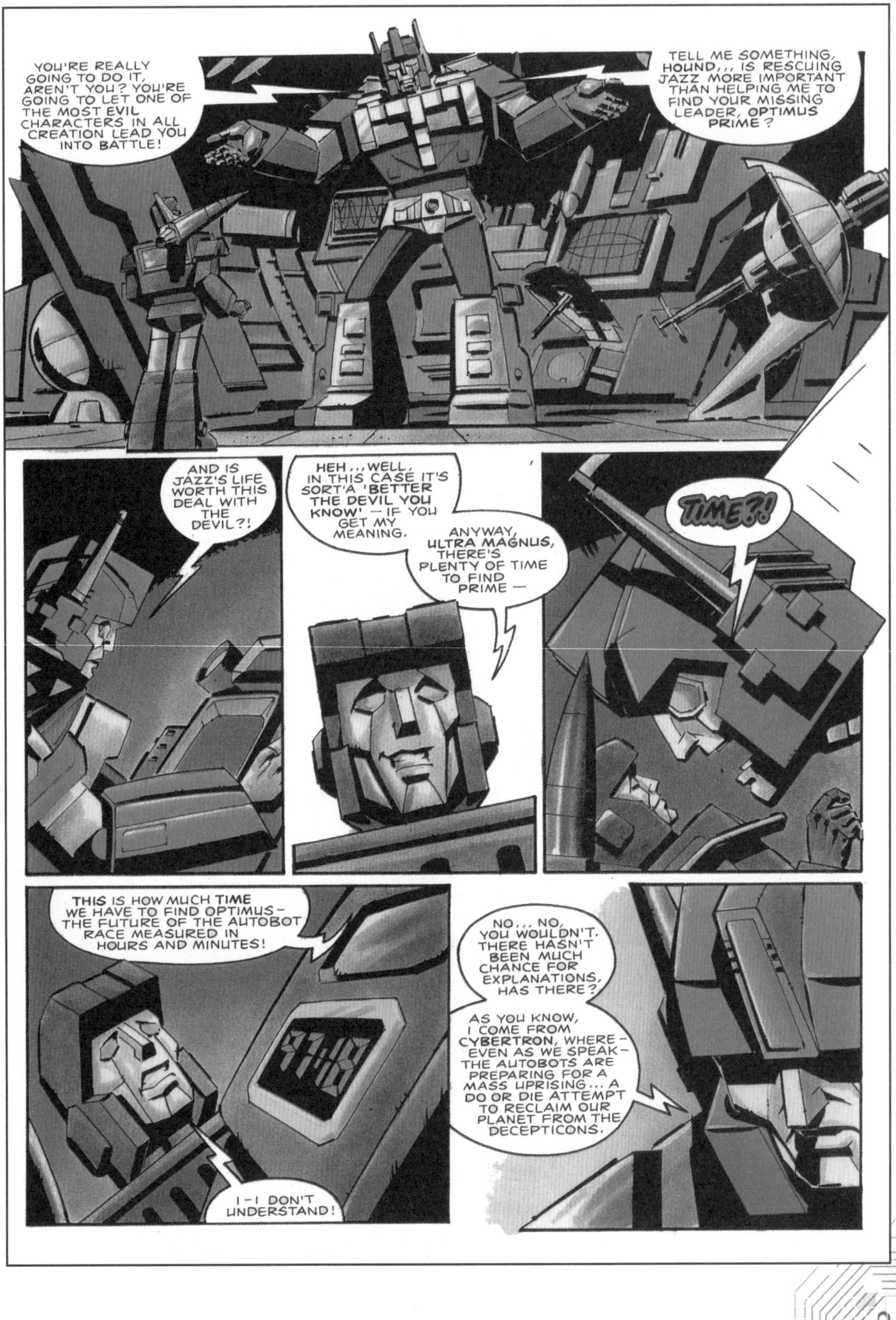
YOU'RE REALLY GOING TO DO IT, AREN'T YOU? YOU'RE GOING TO LET ONE OF THE MOST EVIL CHARACTERS IN ALL CREATION LEAD YOU INTO BATTLE!
TELL ME SOMETHING, HOUND,.. IS RESCUING JAZZ MORE IMPORTANT THAN HELPING ME TO FIND YOUR MISSING LEADER, OPTIMUS PRIME?
AND IS JAZZ'S LIFE WORTH THIS DEAL WITH THE DEVIL?!
HEH.., WELL, IN THIS CASE IT'S SORT'A 'BETTER THE DEVIL YOU KNOW' — IF YOU GET MY MEANING.
ANYWAY, ULTRA MAGNUS, THERE'S PLENTY OF TIME TO FIND PRIME —
TIME?!
THIS IS HOW MUCH TIME WE HAVE TO FIND OPTIMUS — THE FUTURE OF THE AUTOBOT RACE MEASURED IN HOURS AND MINUTES!
I-I DON'T UNDERSTAND!
NO.., NO, YOU WOULDN'T. THERE HASN'T BEEN MUCH CHANCE FOR EXPLANATIONS, HAS THERE?
AS YOU KNOW, I COME FROM CYBERTRON, WHERE — EVEN AS WE SPEAK — THE AUTOBOTS ARE PREPARING FOR A MASS UPRISING... A DO OR DIE ATTEMPT TO RECLAIM OUR PLANET FROM THE DECEPTICONS.

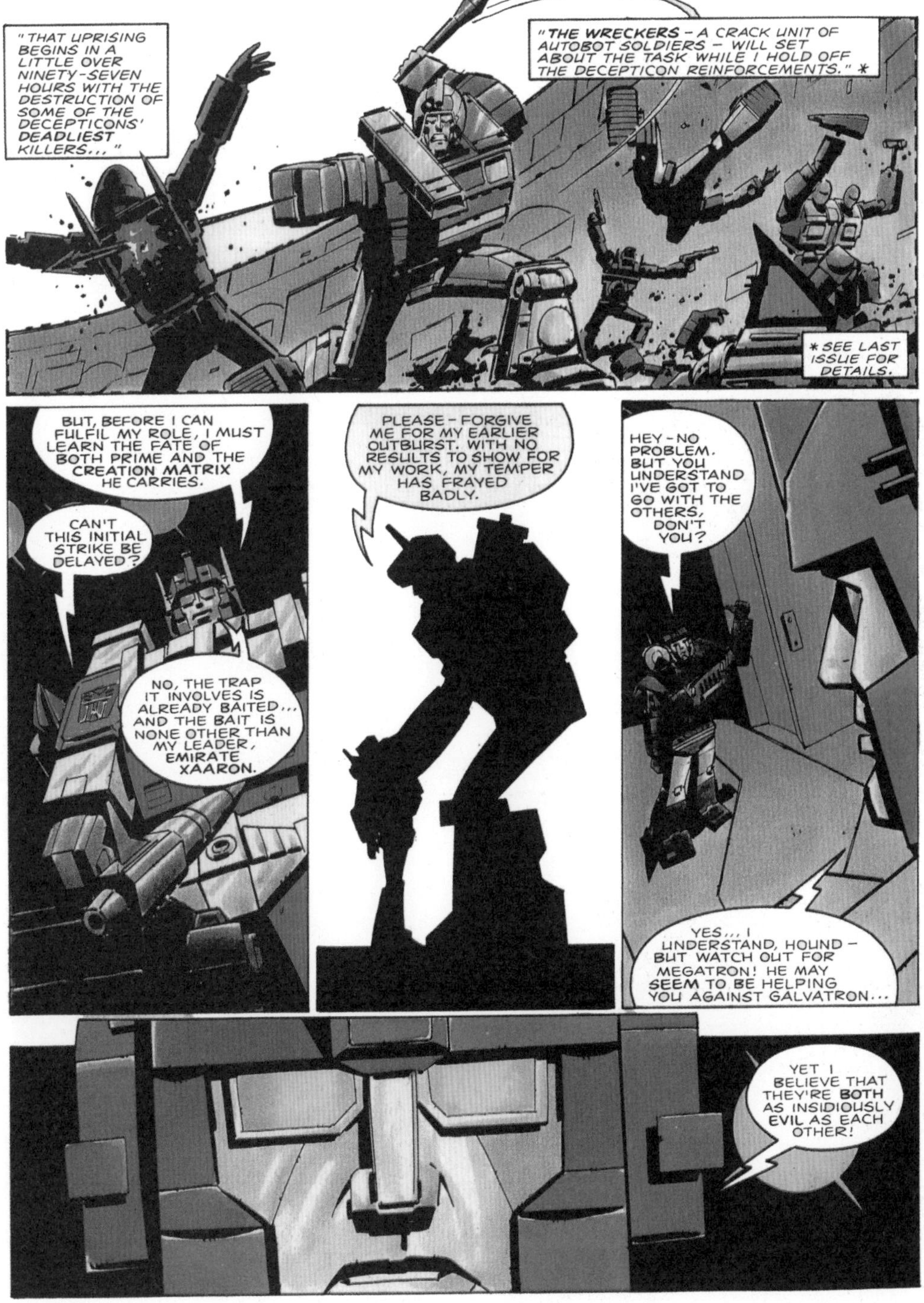
"THAT UPRISING BEGINS IN A LITTLE OVER NINETY-SEVEN HOURS WITH THE DESTRUCTION OF SOME OF THE DECEPTICONS' DEADLIEST KILLERS..."
"THE WRECKERS - A CRACK UNIT OF AUTOBOT SOLDIERS - WILL SET ABOUT THE TASK WHILE I HOLD OFF THE DECEPTICON REINFORCEMENTS." *
* SEE LAST ISSUE FOR DETAILS.
BUT, BEFORE I CAN FULFIL MY ROLE, I MUST LEARN THE FATE OF BOTH PRIME AND THE CREATION MATRIX HE CARRIES.
CAN'T THIS INITIAL STRIKE BE DELAYED?
NO, THE TRAP IT INVOLVES IS ALREADY BAITED... AND THE BAIT IS NONE OTHER THAN MY LEADER, EMIRATE XAARON.
PLEASE - FORGIVE ME FOR MY EARLIER OUTBURST. WITH NO RESULTS TO SHOW FOR MY WORK, MY TEMPER HAS FRAYED BADLY.
HEY - NO PROBLEM. BUT YOU UNDERSTAND I'VE GOT TO GO WITH THE OTHERS, DON'T YOU?
YES... I UNDERSTAND, HOUND - BUT WATCH OUT FOR MEGATRON! HE MAY SEEM TO BE HELPING YOU AGAINST GALVATRON...
YET I BELIEVE THAT THEY'RE BOTH AS INSIDIOUSLY EVIL AS EACH OTHER!

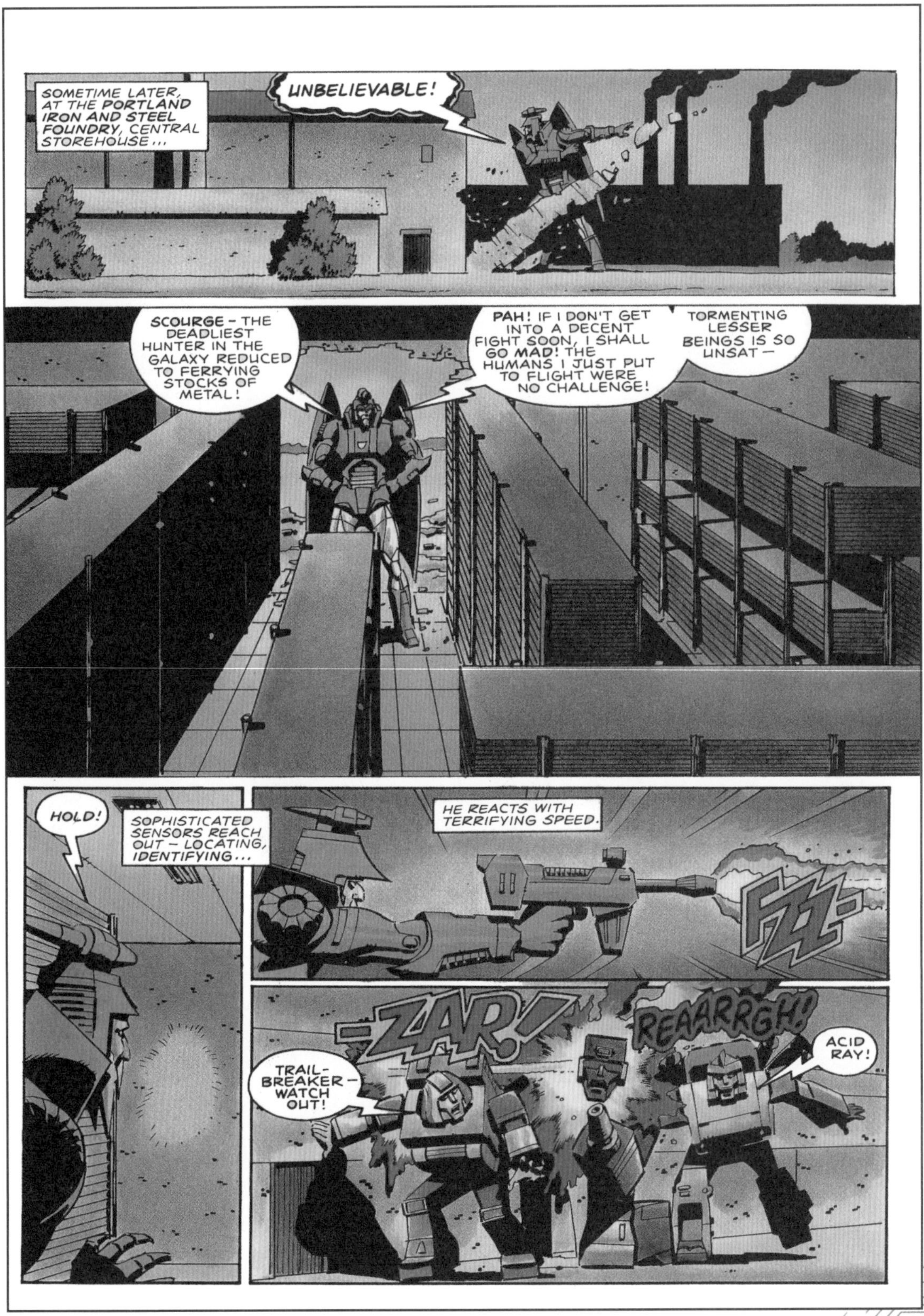
SOMETIME LATER, AT THE PORTLAND IRON AND STEEL FOUNDRY, CENTRAL STOREHOUSE...
UNBELIEVABLE!
SCOURGE - THE DEADLIEST HUNTER IN THE GALAXY REDUCED TO FERRYING STOCKS OF METAL!
PAH! IF I DON'T GET INTO A DECENT FIGHT SOON, I SHALL GO MAD! THE HUMANS I JUST PUT TO FLIGHT WERE NO CHALLENGE!
TORMENTING LESSER BEINGS IS SO UNSAT—
HOLD!
SOPHISTICATED SENSORS REACH OUT – LOCATING, IDENTIFYING...
HE REACTS WITH TERRIFYING SPEED.
FZZ-
-ZAR!
REAARRGH!
ACID RAY!
TRAIL-BREAKER-WATCH OUT!

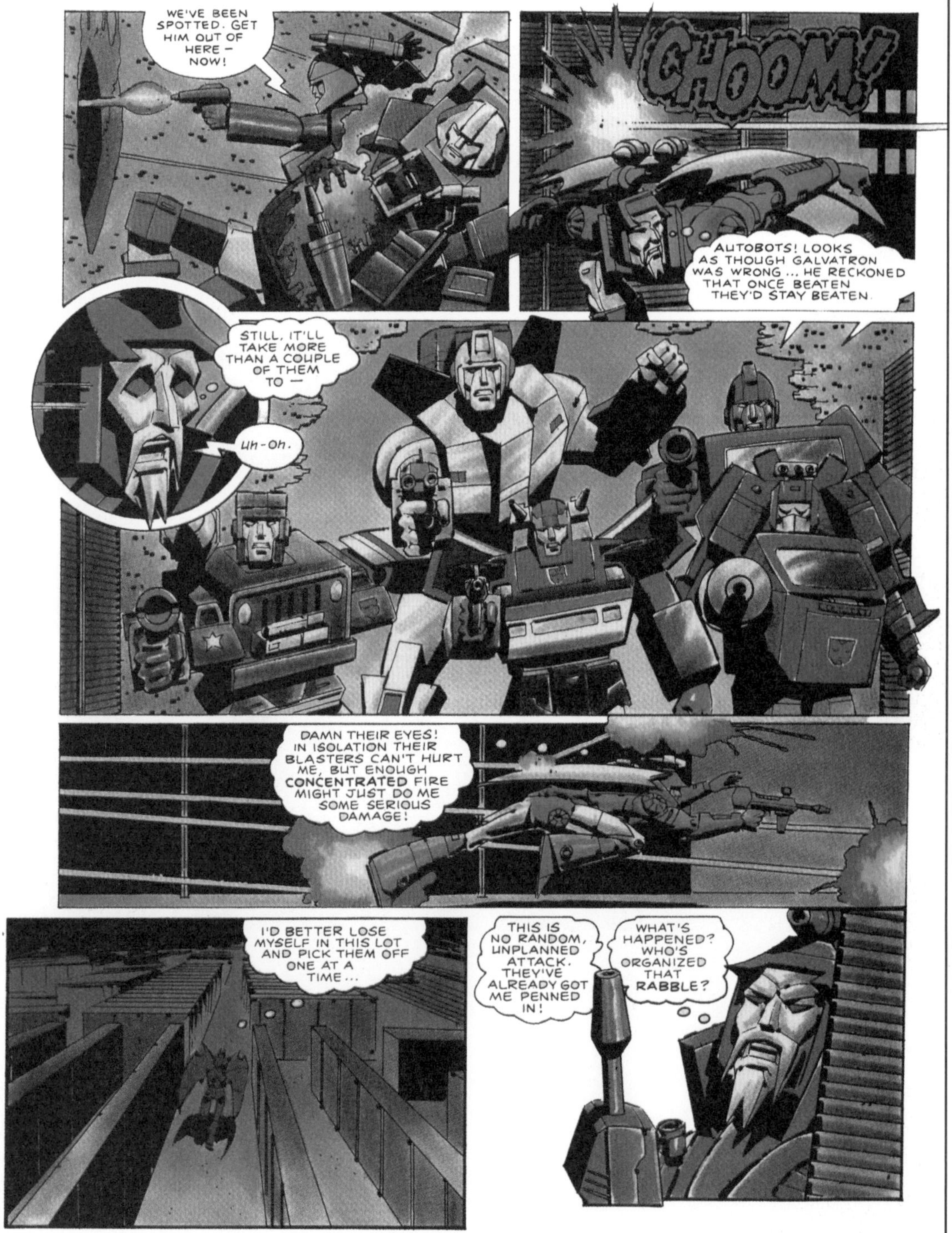
WE'VE BEEN SPOTTED. GET HIM OUT OF HERE — NOW!
CHOOM!
AUTOBOTS! LOOKS AS THOUGH GALVATRON WAS WRONG ... HE RECKONED THAT ONCE BEATEN THEY'D STAY BEATEN.
STILL, IT'LL TAKE MORE THAN A COUPLE OF THEM TO —
uh-oh.
DAMN THEIR EYES! IN ISOLATION THEIR BLASTERS CAN'T HURT ME, BUT ENOUGH CONCENTRATED FIRE MIGHT JUST DO ME SOME SERIOUS DAMAGE!
I'D BETTER LOSE MYSELF IN THIS LOT AND PICK THEM OFF ONE AT A TIME...
THIS IS NO RANDOM, UNPLANNED ATTACK. THEY'VE ALREADY GOT ME PENNED IN!
WHAT'S HAPPENED? WHO'S ORGANIZED THAT RABBLE?

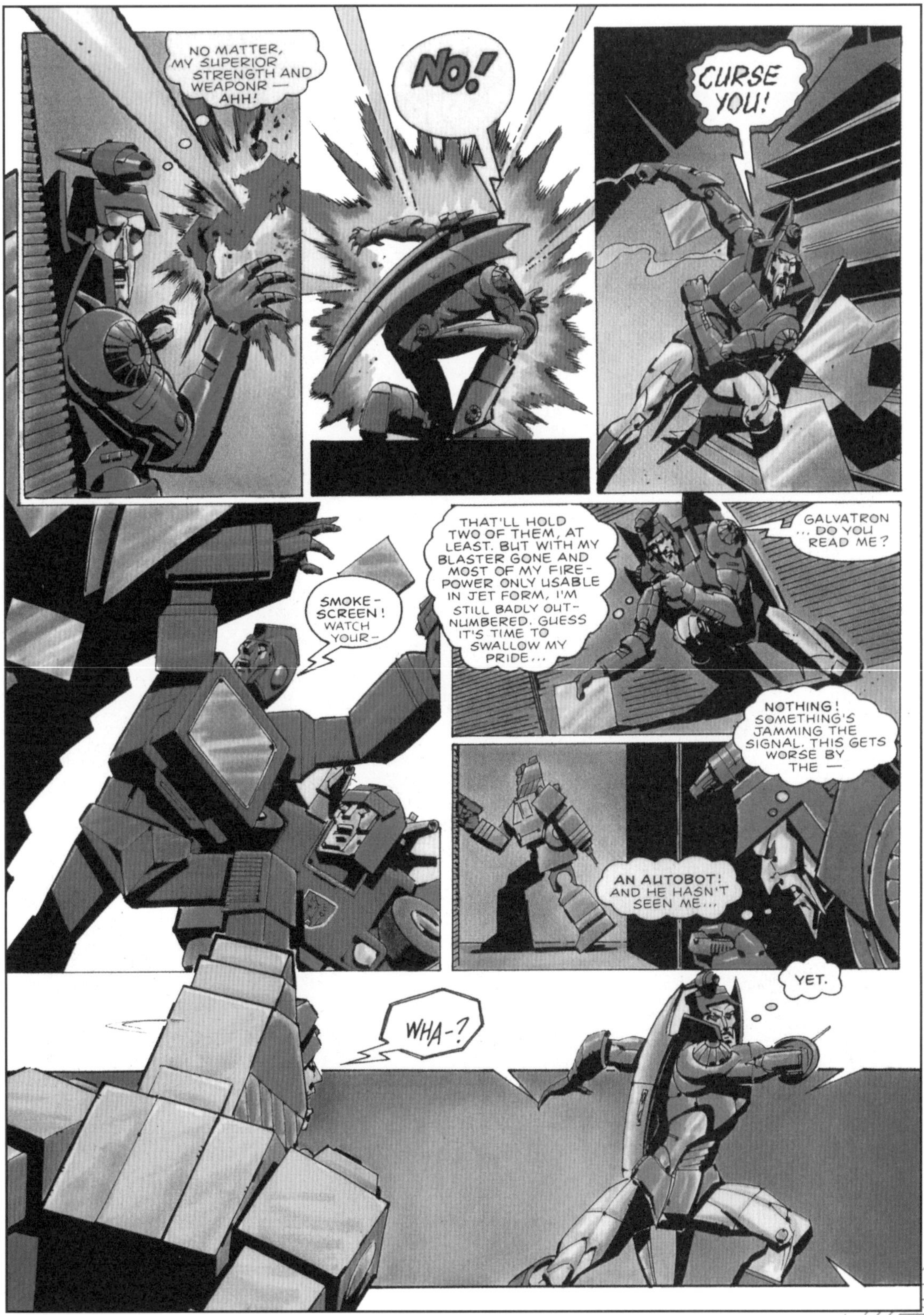
NO MATTER, MY SUPERIOR STRENGTH AND WEAPONR — AHH!
NO!
CURSE YOU!
SMOKE-SCREEN! WATCH YOUR-
THAT'LL HOLD TWO OF THEM, AT LEAST. BUT WITH MY BLASTER GONE AND MOST OF MY FIRE-POWER ONLY USABLE IN JET FORM, I'M STILL BADLY OUT-NUMBERED. GUESS IT'S TIME TO SWALLOW MY PRIDE...
GALVATRON ... DO YOU READ ME?
NOTHING! SOMETHING'S JAMMING THE SIGNAL. THIS GETS WORSE BY THE —
AN AUTOBOT! AND HE HASN'T SEEN ME...
YET.
WHA-?

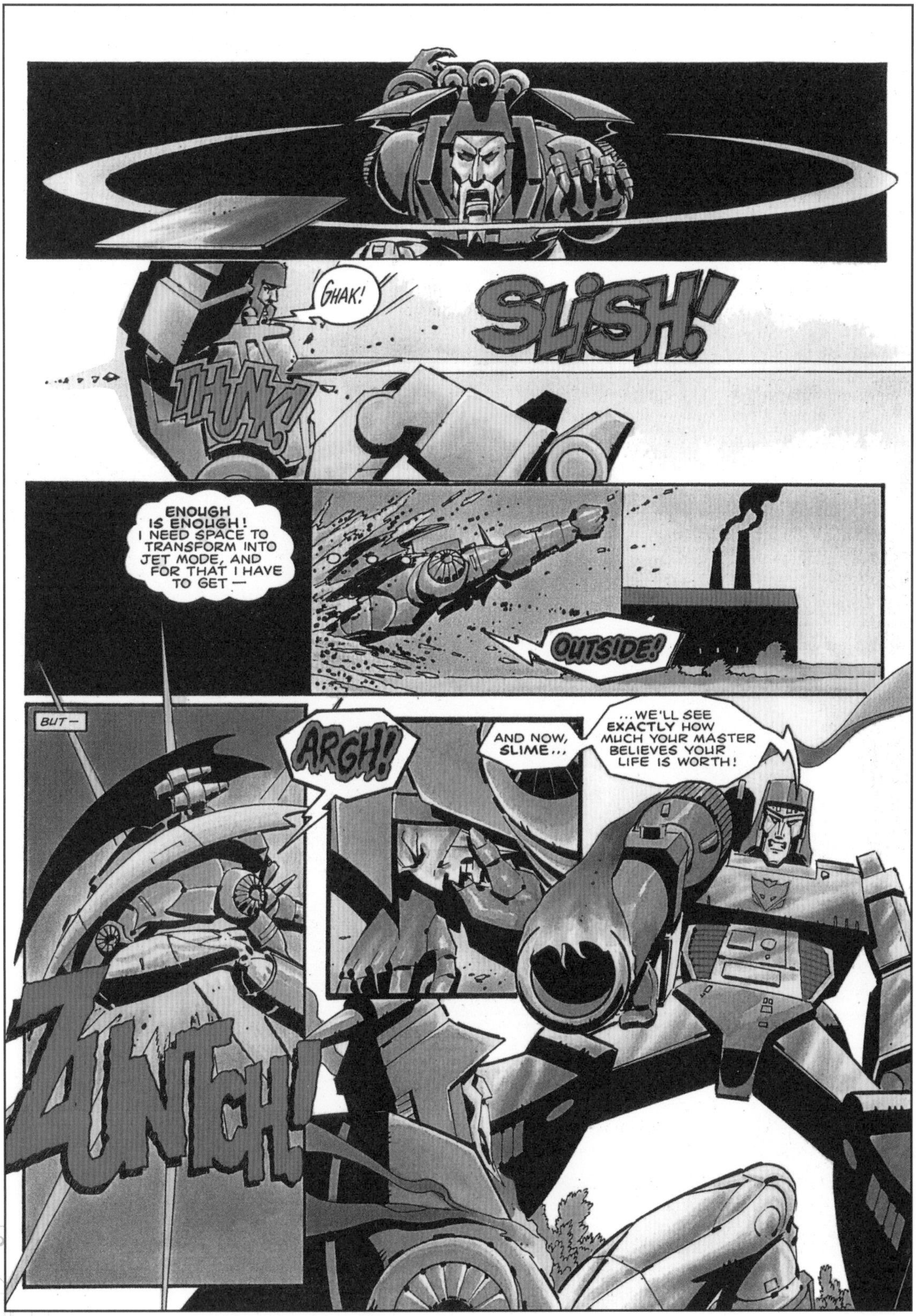
GHAK!
SLISH!
THUNK!
ENOUGH IS ENOUGH! I NEED SPACE TO TRANSFORM INTO JET MODE, AND FOR THAT I HAVE TO GET —
OUTSIDE!
BUT —
ARGH!
AND NOW, SLIME...
...WE'LL SEE EXACTLY HOW MUCH YOUR MASTER BELIEVES YOUR LIFE IS WORTH!
ZUNTCH!

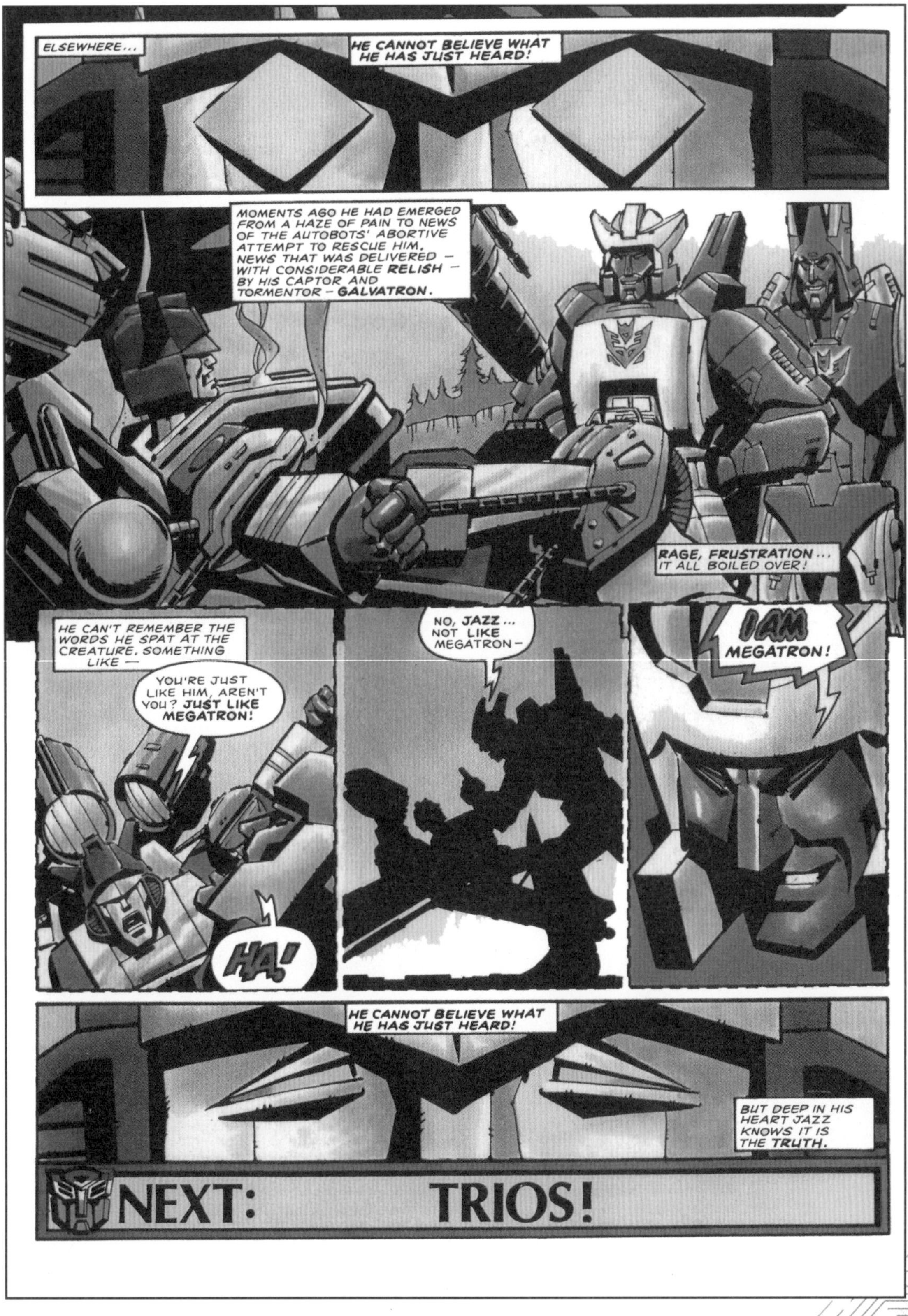
ELSEWHERE...
HE CANNOT BELIEVE WHAT HE HAS JUST HEARD!
MOMENTS AGO HE HAD EMERGED FROM A HAZE OF PAIN TO NEWS OF THE AUTOBOTS' ABORTIVE ATTEMPT TO RESCUE HIM. NEWS THAT WAS DELIVERED — WITH CONSIDERABLE RELISH — BY HIS CAPTOR AND TORMENTOR — GALVATRON.
RAGE, FRUSTRATION... IT ALL BOILED OVER!
HE CAN'T REMEMBER THE WORDS HE SPAT AT THE CREATURE. SOMETHING LIKE —
YOU'RE JUST LIKE HIM, AREN'T YOU? JUST LIKE MEGATRON!
HA!
NO, JAZZ... NOT LIKE MEGATRON —
I AM MEGATRON!
HE CANNOT BELIEVE WHAT HE HAS JUST HEARD!
BUT DEEP IN HIS HEART JAZZ KNOWS IT IS THE TRUTH.
NEXT: TRIOS!

As you'll have seen in our last few issues, the situation on Cyberton has reached crisis point for the remaining Autobots as they struggle to reclaim their homeworld from the conquering Decepticons. Okay, we know the situation now... and long-time readers will no doubt remember the state of play when Optimus Prime left Cyberton some four million years ago. But what happened in those intervening years? What brought the Autobots from a situation where they were holding their own against the Decepticons to their current position? Now it can be revealed, albeit somewhat briefly (four million years does not condense easily into one page!) as we take a look at the planet Cybertron – the middle years!

DOWNFALL!

With the disappearance of their leader and some of the most powerful Autobot warriors, the Autobot army fell into disarray. Though the *Council Of Autobot Elders* led by *High Councillor Traachon* – tried to bond their remaining soldiers together once more, it was the Decepticons (also bereft of their high command) who took the initiative. A young and ambitious War-Lord named *Trannis* seized control of the Decepticon army.

Sensing the Autobots' weakened state, Trannis systematically began to undo all the work Optimus Prime had done. City states that he had liberated fell in quick succession to a vicious and concerted campaign of terror, backed with brutal force. The Autobot army became scattered, with surviving units going underground to begin guerilla warfare. Despite his successes, Trannis reached the same deadlock experienced by his predecessor when he reached *Iacon*, the Autobots' capital city state. From the highly fortified city, the Autobots resisted all Trannis' attempts to capture Iacon. The deadlock remained for hundreds of thousands of years, until Trannis – now in almost total control of the rest of Cyberton – decided that Iacon simply wasn't worth capturing intact any more. That decided, he unleashed the full might of the Decepticon firepower against the city, almost levelling it in the process.

The Council of Autobot Elders met in emergency session and decided almost unanimously to surrender to the Decepticons rather than face utter annihilation. One council member, however, decided that he must fight on. Gathering a squad of over one hundred Autobots faithful to him, *Emirate Xaaron* fled Iacon through disused utility ducts. His fears concerning the Autobots'

surrender bore fruit when War-Lord Trannis marched triumphantly into the shattered shell of Iacon. His first act was to execute all members of the Council!

The Decepticons believed their victory to be total. Soon, Trannis reasoned, even the small pockets of resistance would be destroyed. Unknown to Trannis, over the next thousand or so years, Emirate Xaaron united all the scattered remnants of the Autobot army. They lay low, building in numbers and strength as Trannis grew progressively more complacent in his rule. Unknown to Xaaron, plans were afoot within the Decepticon high command to unseat Trannis, whom many Decepticons had felt had lost his killing edge. Xaaron therefore unwittingly aided the Decepticons when he sent his crack troop of commandos, *The Wreckers*, to assassinate Trannis. They succeeded, yet ultimately failed. With Trannis gone, the Decepticon, *Lord Straxus* arose to take his place. Straxus was merciless and relentless in his pursuit of the remaining Autobots and Xaaron's fragile position of power was shattered. Once more he and the Autobots had to flee into hiding.

The Autobot resistance continued to fight their guerila war over the following years, never relenting, never allowing the Decepticons a moment of peace. Now, the Autobot resistance is once more ready to strike back against the Decepticons in one mass concerted uprising. Will they succeed this time? Keep watching!

CYBERTRON: THE MIDDLE YEARS!

Originally printed in *Transformers UK* issue #83.

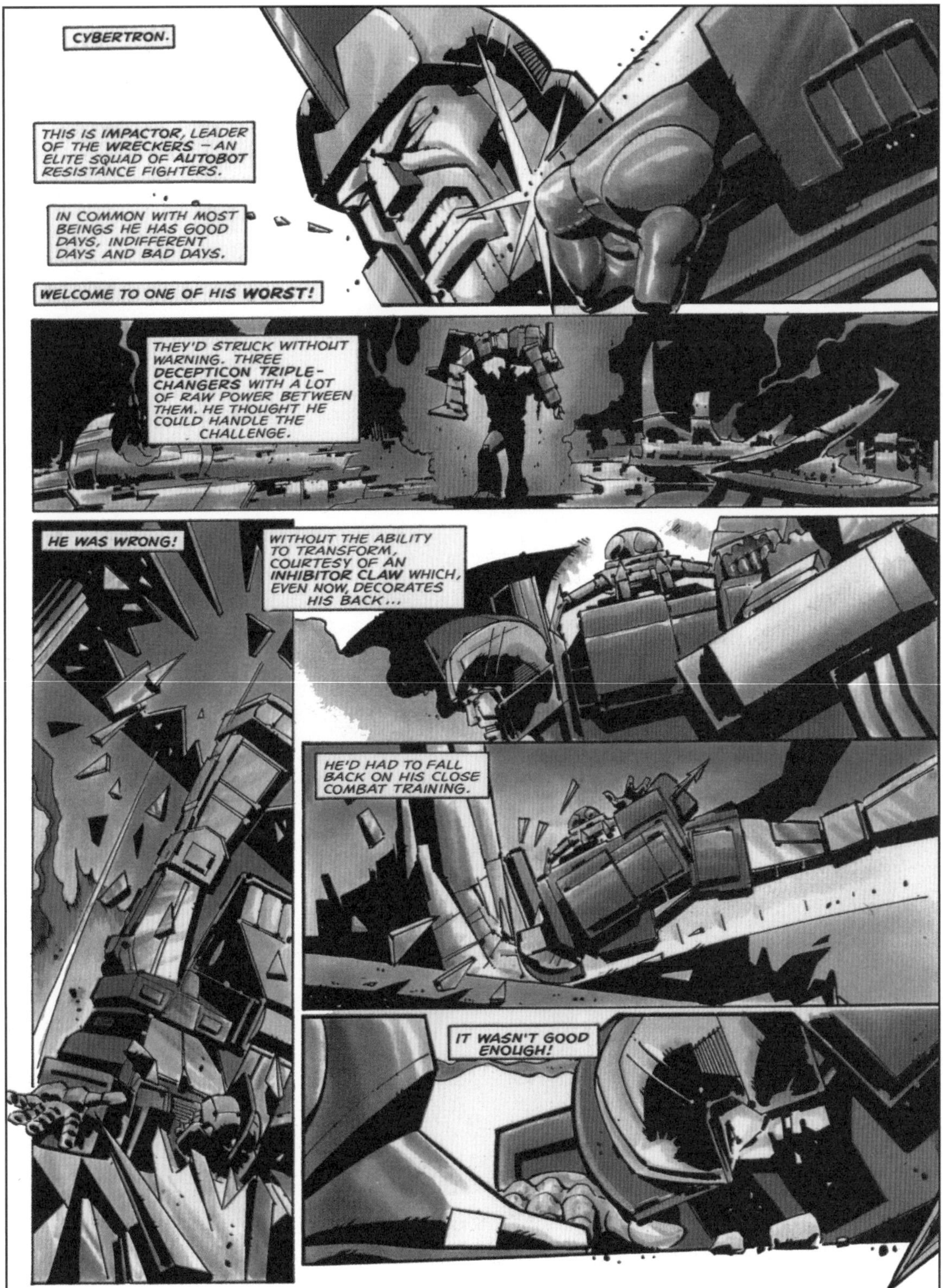

CYBERTRON.
THIS IS IMPACTOR, LEADER OF THE WRECKERS — AN ELITE SQUAD OF AUTOBOT RESISTANCE FIGHTERS.
IN COMMON WITH MOST BEINGS HE HAS GOOD DAYS, INDIFFERENT DAYS AND BAD DAYS.
WELCOME TO ONE OF HIS WORST!
THEY'D STRUCK WITHOUT WARNING. THREE DECEPTICON TRIPLE-CHANGERS WITH A LOT OF RAW POWER BETWEEN THEM. HE THOUGHT HE COULD HANDLE THE CHALLENGE.
HE WAS WRONG!
WITHOUT THE ABILITY TO TRANSFORM, COURTESY OF AN INHIBITOR CLAW WHICH, EVEN NOW, DECORATES HIS BACK...
HE'D HAD TO FALL BACK ON HIS CLOSE COMBAT TRAINING.
IT WASN'T GOOD ENOUGH!

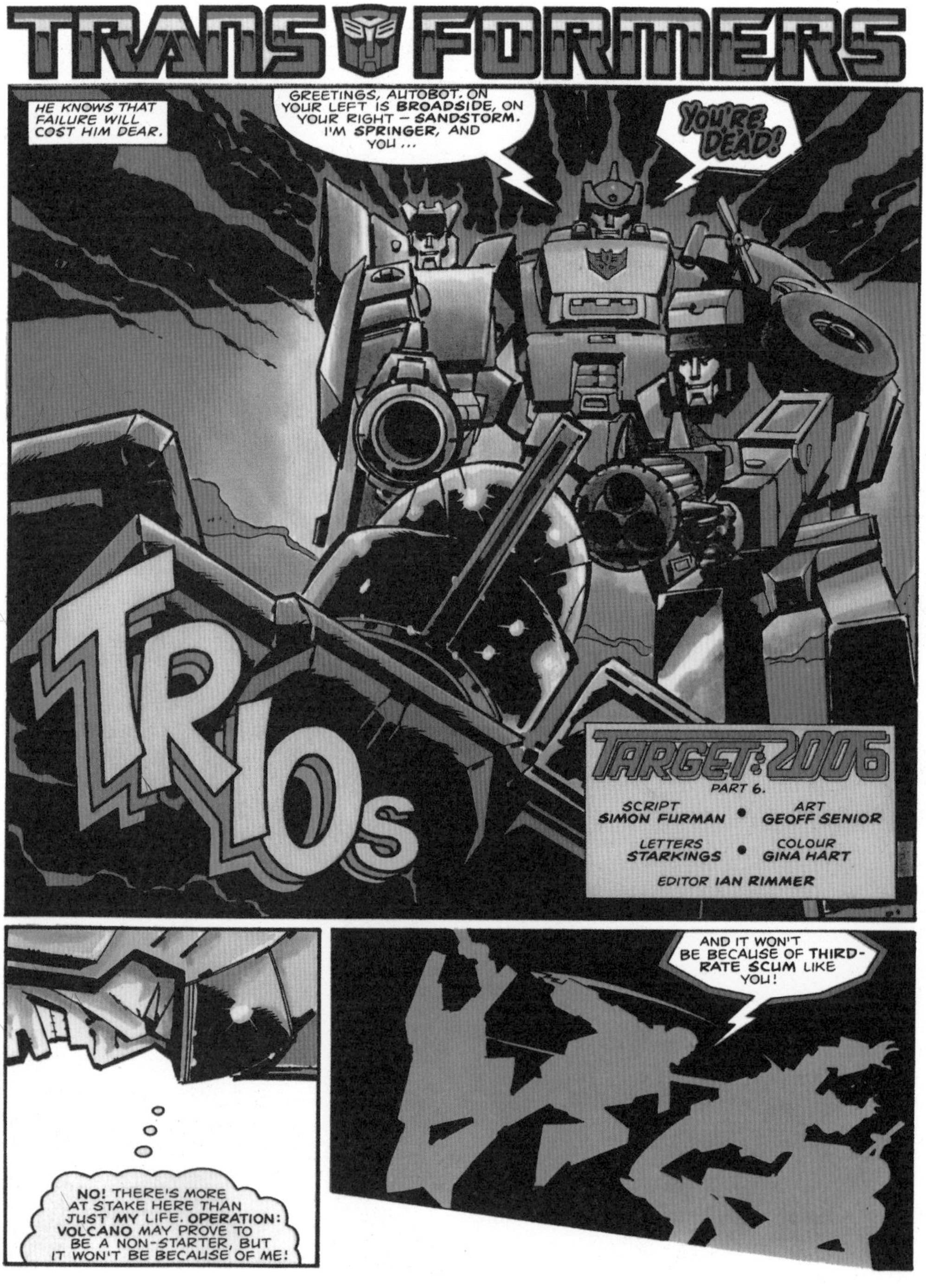
TRANSFORMERS
HE KNOWS THAT FAILURE WILL COST HIM DEAR.
GREETINGS, AUTOBOT. ON YOUR LEFT IS BROADSIDE, ON YOUR RIGHT – SANDSTORM. I'M SPRINGER, AND YOU ...
YOU'RE DEAD!
TRIOs
TARGET: 2006
PART 6.
SCRIPT SIMON FURMAN • ART GEOFF SENIOR
LETTERS STARKINGS • COLOUR GINA HART
EDITOR IAN RIMMER
NO! THERE'S MORE AT STAKE HERE THAN JUST MY LIFE. OPERATION: VOLCANO MAY PROVE TO BE A NON-STARTER, BUT IT WON'T BE BECAUSE OF ME!
AND IT WON'T BE BECAUSE OF THIRD-RATE SCUM LIKE YOU!

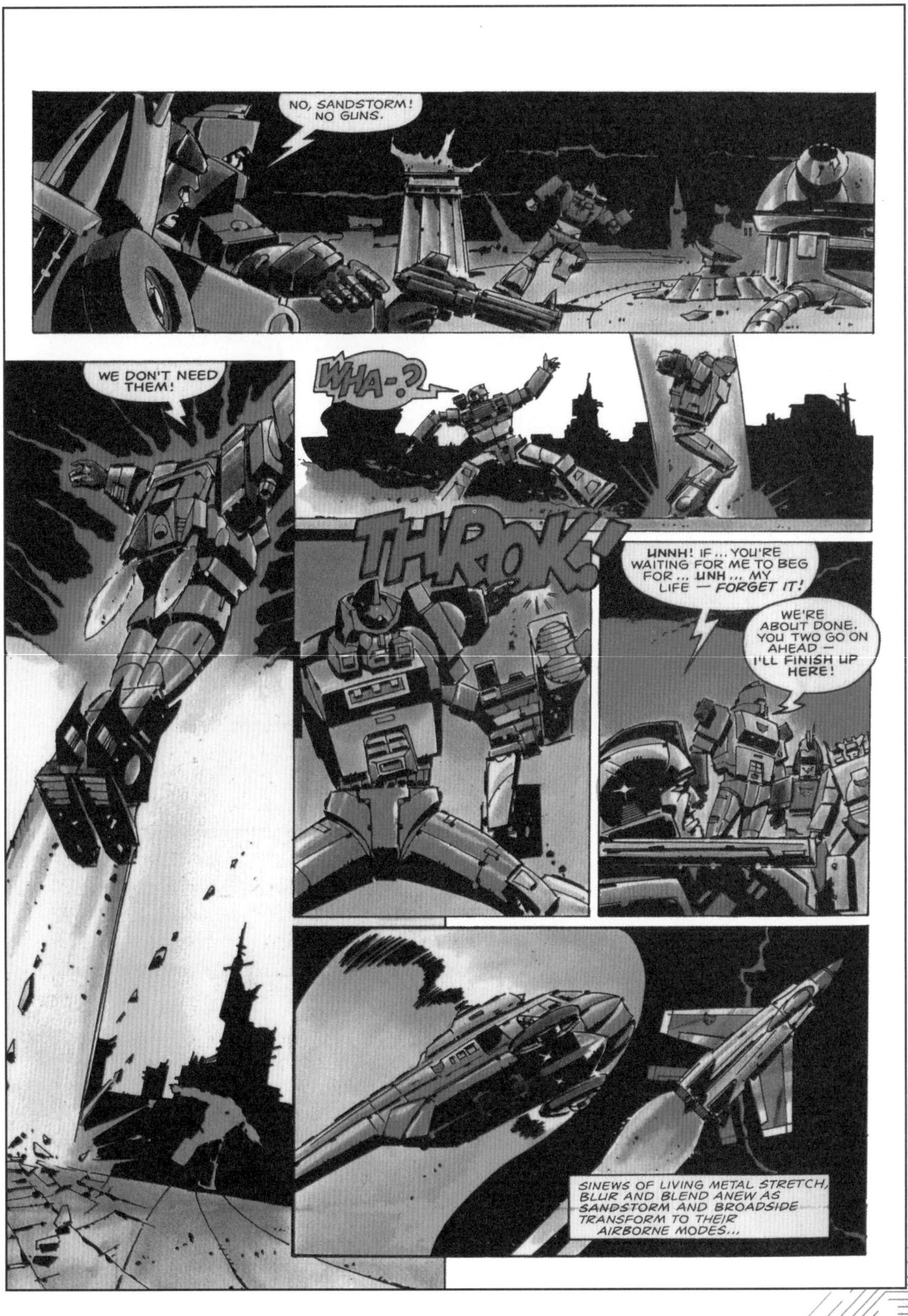
NO, SANDSTORM! NO GUNS.
WE DON'T NEED THEM!
WHA-?
THROK!
UNNH! IF... YOU'RE WAITING FOR ME TO BEG FOR... UNH... MY LIFE — FORGET IT!
WE'RE ABOUT DONE. YOU TWO GO ON AHEAD — I'LL FINISH UP HERE!
SINEWS OF LIVING METAL STRETCH, BLUR AND BLEND ANEW AS SANDSTORM AND BROADSIDE TRANSFORM TO THEIR AIRBORNE MODES...

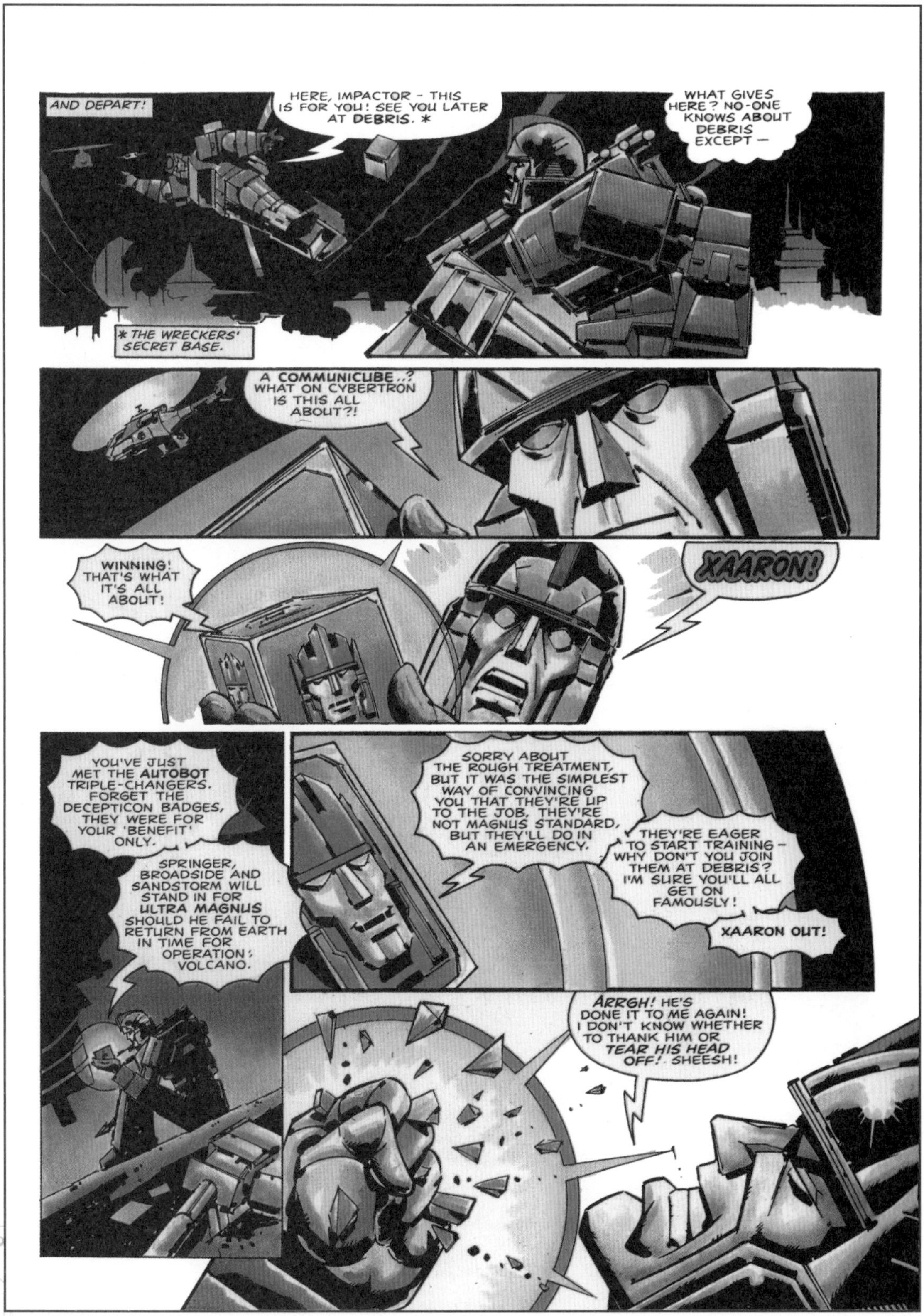
AND DEPART!
HERE, IMPACTOR - THIS IS FOR YOU! SEE YOU LATER AT DEBRIS. *
WHAT GIVES HERE? NO-ONE KNOWS ABOUT DEBRIS EXCEPT —
* THE WRECKERS' SECRET BASE.
A COMMUNICUBE..? WHAT ON CYBERTRON IS THIS ALL ABOUT?!
WINNING! THAT'S WHAT IT'S ALL ABOUT!
XAARON!
YOU'VE JUST MET THE AUTOBOT TRIPLE-CHANGERS. FORGET THE DECEPTICON BADGES, THEY WERE FOR YOUR 'BENEFIT' ONLY.
SPRINGER, BROADSIDE AND SANDSTORM WILL STAND IN FOR ULTRA MAGNUS SHOULD HE FAIL TO RETURN FROM EARTH IN TIME FOR OPERATION: VOLCANO.
SORRY ABOUT THE ROUGH TREATMENT, BUT IT WAS THE SIMPLEST WAY OF CONVINCING YOU THAT THEY'RE UP TO THE JOB. THEY'RE NOT MAGNUS STANDARD, BUT THEY'LL DO IN AN EMERGENCY.
THEY'RE EAGER TO START TRAINING - WHY DON'T YOU JOIN THEM AT DEBRIS? I'M SURE YOU'LL ALL GET ON FAMOUSLY!
XAARON OUT!
ARRGH! HE'S DONE IT TO ME AGAIN! I DON'T KNOW WHETHER TO THANK HIM OR TEAR HIS HEAD OFF! SHEESH!

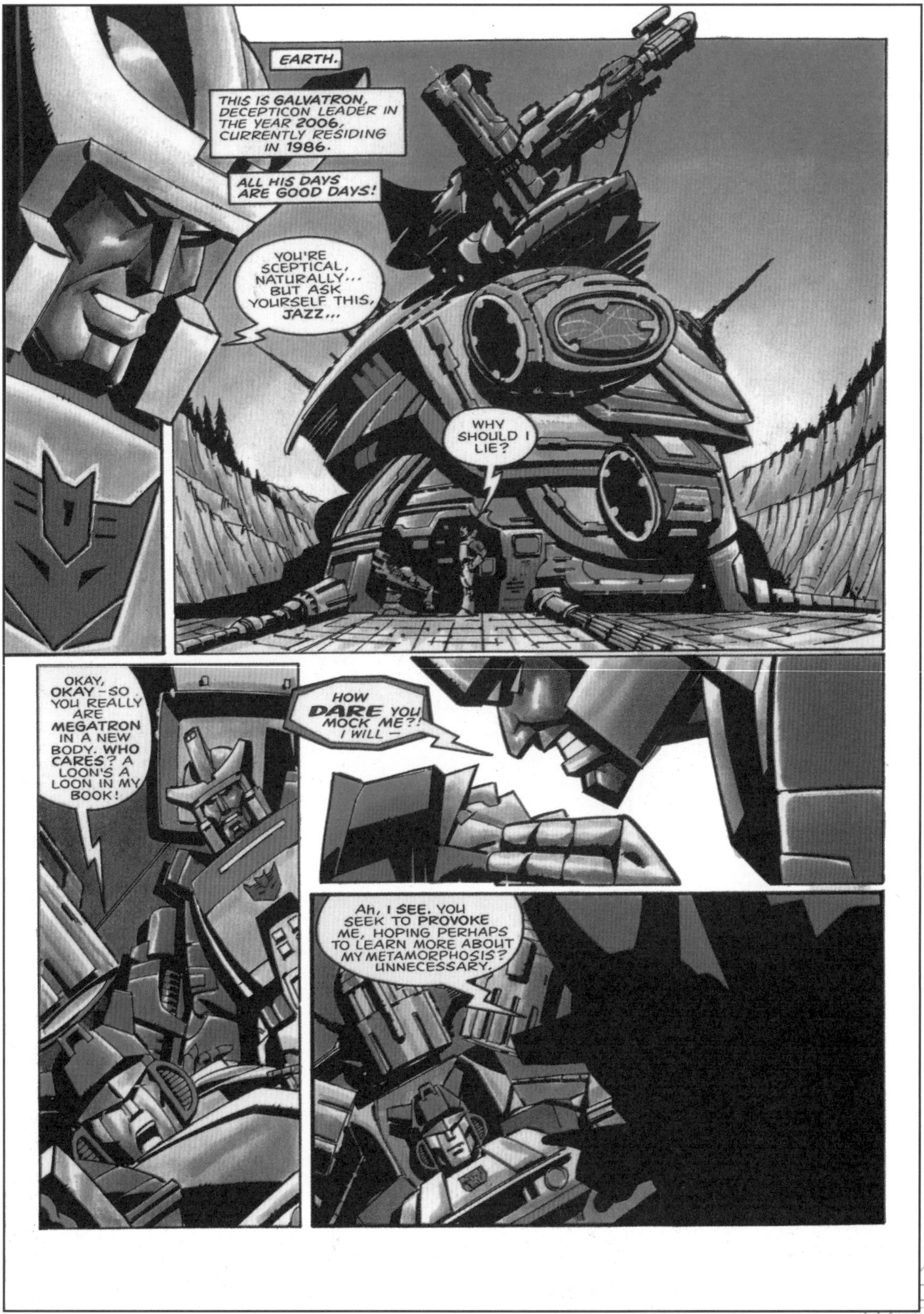

EARTH.
THIS IS GALVATRON, DECEPTICON LEADER IN THE YEAR 2006, CURRENTLY RESIDING IN 1986.
ALL HIS DAYS ARE GOOD DAYS!
YOU'RE SCEPTICAL, NATURALLY... BUT ASK YOURSELF THIS, JAZZ...
WHY SHOULD I LIE?
OKAY, OKAY -- SO YOU REALLY ARE MEGATRON IN A NEW BODY. WHO CARES? A LOON'S A LOON IN MY BOOK!
HOW DARE YOU MOCK ME?! I WILL --
Ah, I SEE. YOU SEEK TO PROVOKE ME, HOPING PERHAPS TO LEARN MORE ABOUT MY METAMORPHOSIS? UNNECESSARY.

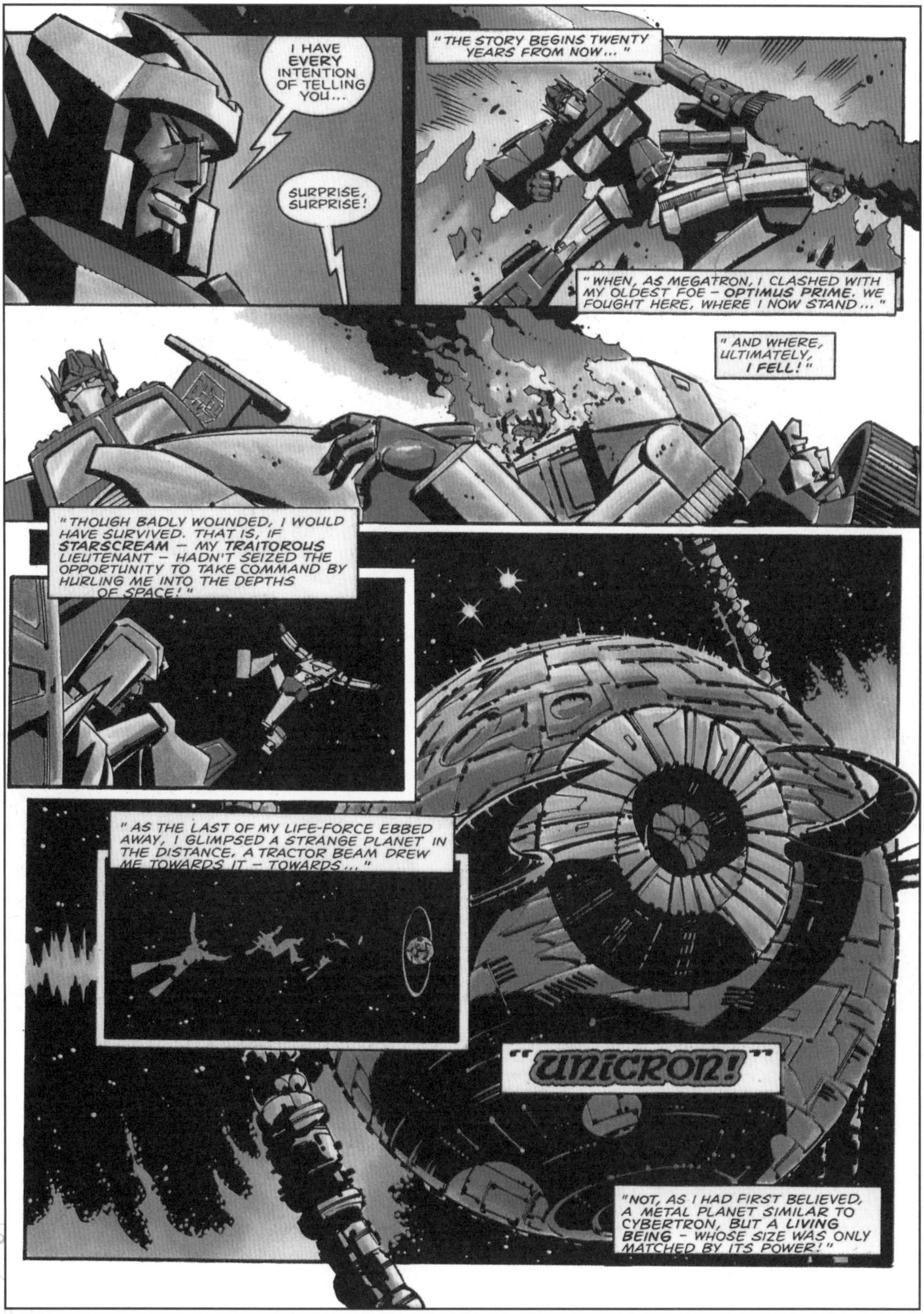
I HAVE EVERY INTENTION OF TELLING YOU...
SURPRISE, SURPRISE!
"THE STORY BEGINS TWENTY YEARS FROM NOW..."
"WHEN, AS MEGATRON, I CLASHED WITH MY OLDEST FOE – OPTIMUS PRIME. WE FOUGHT HERE, WHERE I NOW STAND..."
"AND WHERE, ULTIMATELY, I FELL!"
"THOUGH BADLY WOUNDED, I WOULD HAVE SURVIVED. THAT IS, IF STARSCREAM – MY TRAITOROUS LIEUTENANT – HADN'T SEIZED THE OPPORTUNITY TO TAKE COMMAND BY HURLING ME INTO THE DEPTHS OF SPACE!"
"AS THE LAST OF MY LIFE-FORCE EBBED AWAY, I GLIMPSED A STRANGE PLANET IN THE DISTANCE. A TRACTOR BEAM DREW ME TOWARDS IT – TOWARDS..."
"UNICRON!"
"NOT, AS I HAD FIRST BELIEVED, A METAL PLANET SIMILAR TO CYBERTRON, BUT A LIVING BEING – WHOSE SIZE WAS ONLY MATCHED BY ITS POWER!"

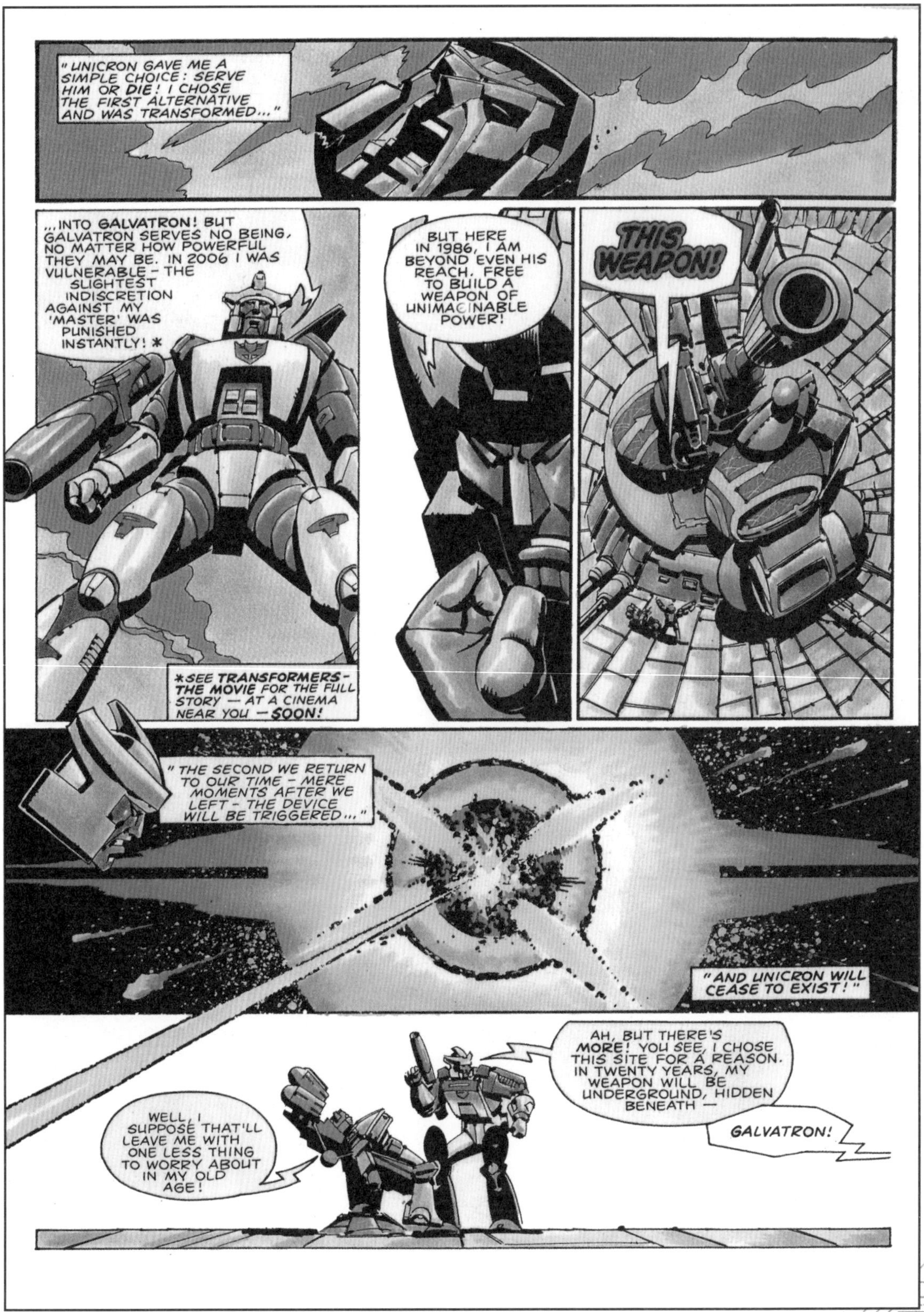
"UNICRON GAVE ME A SIMPLE CHOICE: SERVE HIM OR DIE! I CHOSE THE FIRST ALTERNATIVE AND WAS TRANSFORMED..."
...INTO GALVATRON! BUT GALVATRON SERVES NO BEING, NO MATTER HOW POWERFUL THEY MAY BE. IN 2006 I WAS VULNERABLE – THE SLIGHTEST INDISCRETION AGAINST MY 'MASTER' WAS PUNISHED INSTANTLY! *
*SEE TRANSFORMERS-THE MOVIE FOR THE FULL STORY — AT A CINEMA NEAR YOU —SOON!
BUT HERE IN 1986, I AM BEYOND EVEN HIS REACH. FREE TO BUILD A WEAPON OF UNIMAGINABLE POWER!
THIS WEAPON!
"THE SECOND WE RETURN TO OUR TIME - MERE MOMENTS AFTER WE LEFT - THE DEVICE WILL BE TRIGGERED..."
"AND UNICRON WILL CEASE TO EXIST!"
AH, BUT THERE'S MORE! YOU SEE, I CHOSE THIS SITE FOR A REASON. IN TWENTY YEARS, MY WEAPON WILL BE UNDERGROUND, HIDDEN BENEATH —
GALVATRON!
WELL, I SUPPOSE THAT'LL LEAVE ME WITH ONE LESS THING TO WORRY ABOUT IN MY OLD AGE!

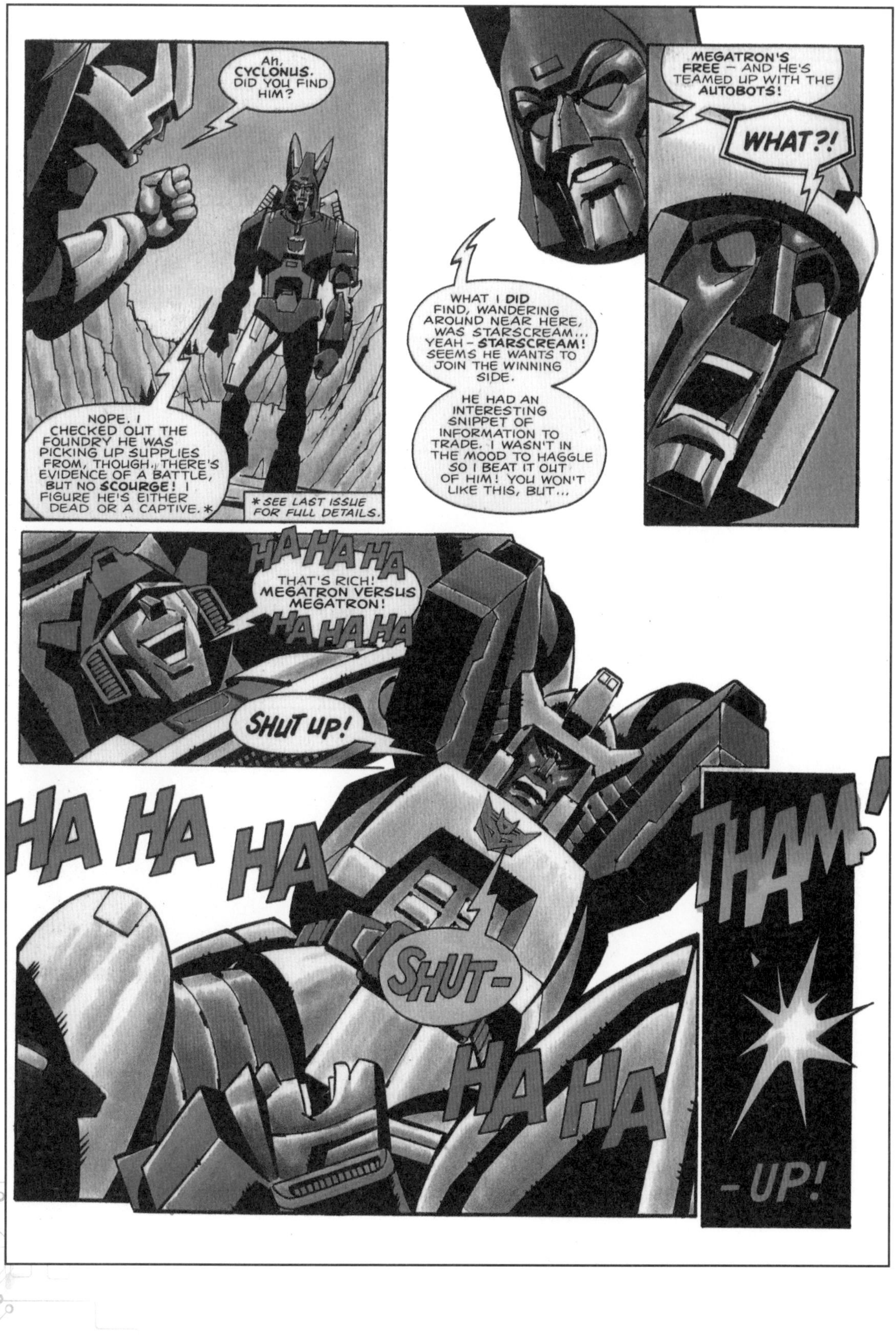

Ah, CYCLONUS. DID YOU FIND HIM?
NOPE. I CHECKED OUT THE FOUNDRY HE WAS PICKING UP SUPPLIES FROM, THOUGH. THERE'S EVIDENCE OF A BATTLE, BUT NO SCOURGE! I FIGURE HE'S EITHER DEAD OR A CAPTIVE.*
*SEE LAST ISSUE FOR FULL DETAILS.
WHAT I DID FIND, WANDERING AROUND NEAR HERE, WAS STARSCREAM... YEAH - STARSCREAM! SEEMS HE WANTS TO JOIN THE WINNING SIDE.
HE HAD AN INTERESTING SNIPPET OF INFORMATION TO TRADE. I WASN'T IN THE MOOD TO HAGGLE SO I BEAT IT OUT OF HIM! YOU WON'T LIKE THIS, BUT...
MEGATRON'S FREE — AND HE'S TEAMED UP WITH THE AUTOBOTS!
WHAT?!
HA HA HA HA
THAT'S RICH! MEGATRON VERSUS MEGATRON!
HA HA HA HA
SHUT UP!
HA HA HA HA
SHUT-
HA HA
THAM'
-UP!

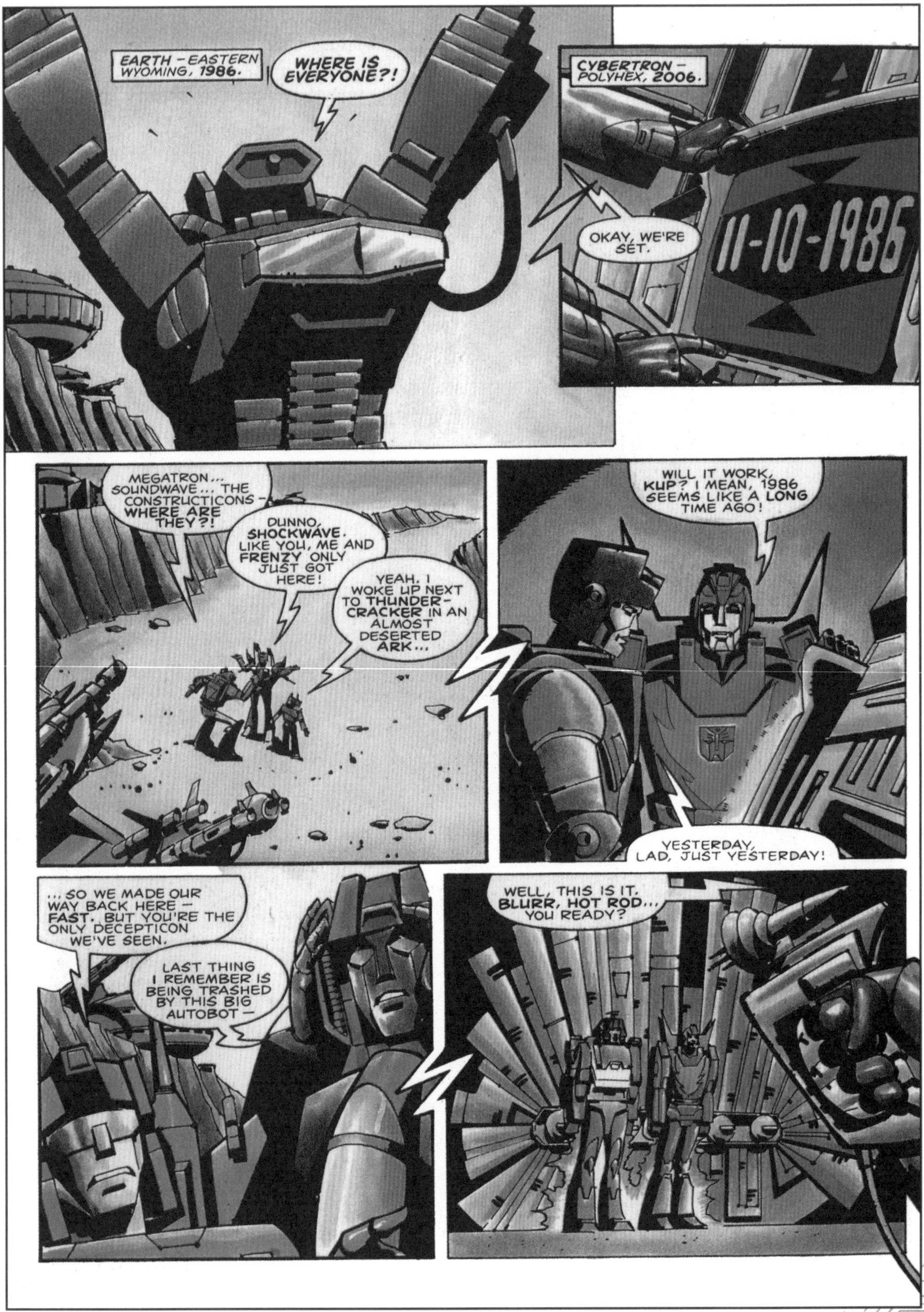
EARTH – EASTERN WYOMING, 1986.
WHERE IS EVERYONE?!
CYBERTRON – POLYHEX, 2006.
OKAY, WE'RE SET.
11-10-1986
MEGATRON... SOUNDWAVE... THE CONSTRUCTICONS – WHERE ARE THEY?!
DUNNO, SHOCKWAVE. LIKE YOU, ME AND FRENZY ONLY JUST GOT HERE!
YEAH. I WOKE UP NEXT TO THUNDER-CRACKER IN AN ALMOST DESERTED ARK...
WILL IT WORK, KUP? I MEAN, 1986 SEEMS LIKE A LONG TIME AGO!
YESTERDAY, LAD, JUST YESTERDAY!
...SO WE MADE OUR WAY BACK HERE – FAST. BUT YOU'RE THE ONLY DECEPTICON WE'VE SEEN.
LAST THING I REMEMBER IS BEING TRASHED BY THIS BIG AUTOBOT –
WELL, THIS IS IT. BLURR, HOT ROD... YOU READY?

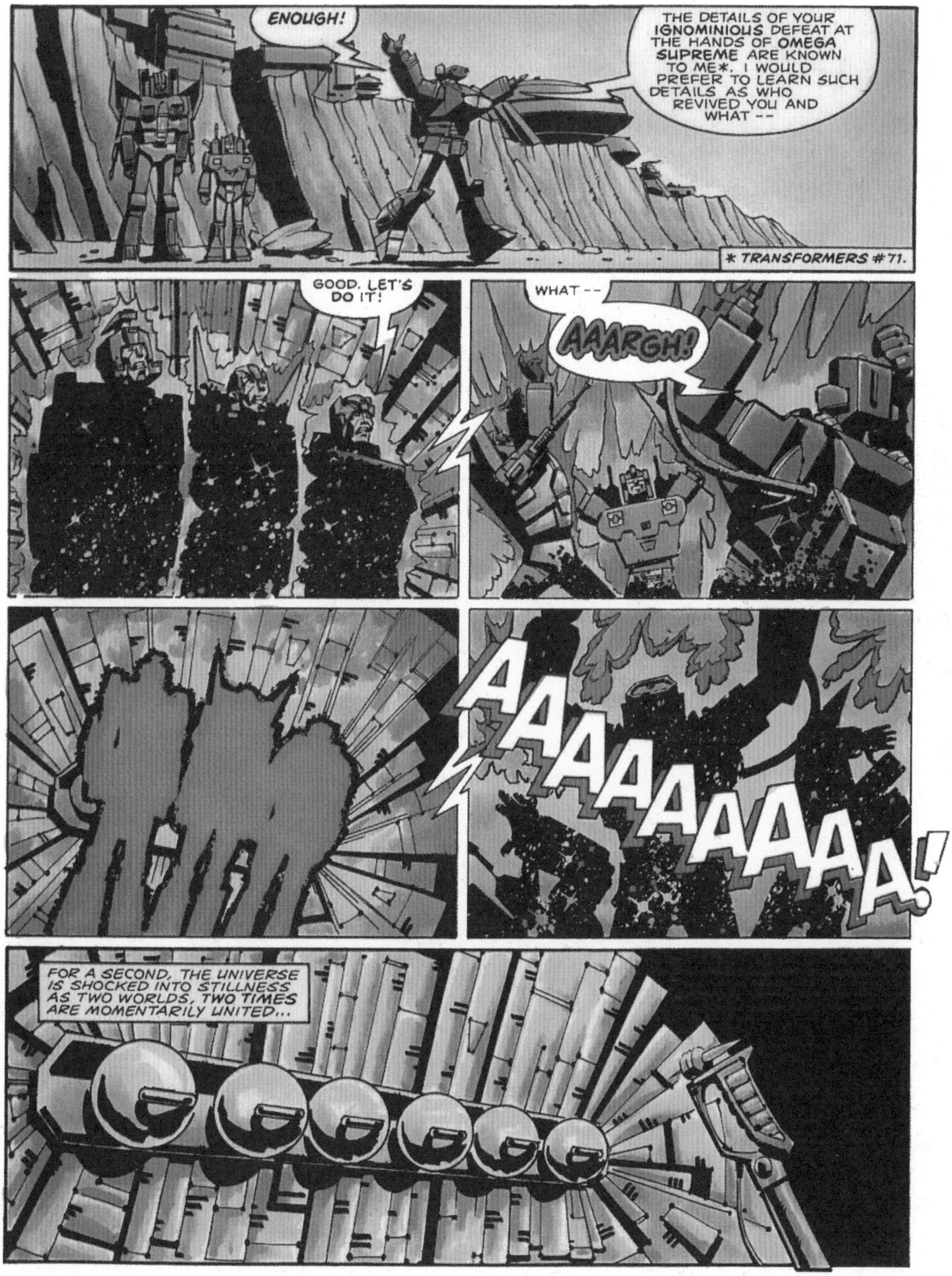

ENOUGH!
THE DETAILS OF YOUR IGNOMINIOUS DEFEAT AT THE HANDS OF OMEGA SUPREME ARE KNOWN TO ME*. I WOULD PREFER TO LEARN SUCH DETAILS AS WHO REVIVED YOU AND WHAT --
* TRANSFORMERS #71.
GOOD. LET'S DO IT!
WHAT --
AAARGH!
AAAAAAAAAA!
FOR A SECOND, THE UNIVERSE IS SHOCKED INTO STILLNESS AS TWO WORLDS, TWO TIMES ARE MOMENTARILY UNITED...

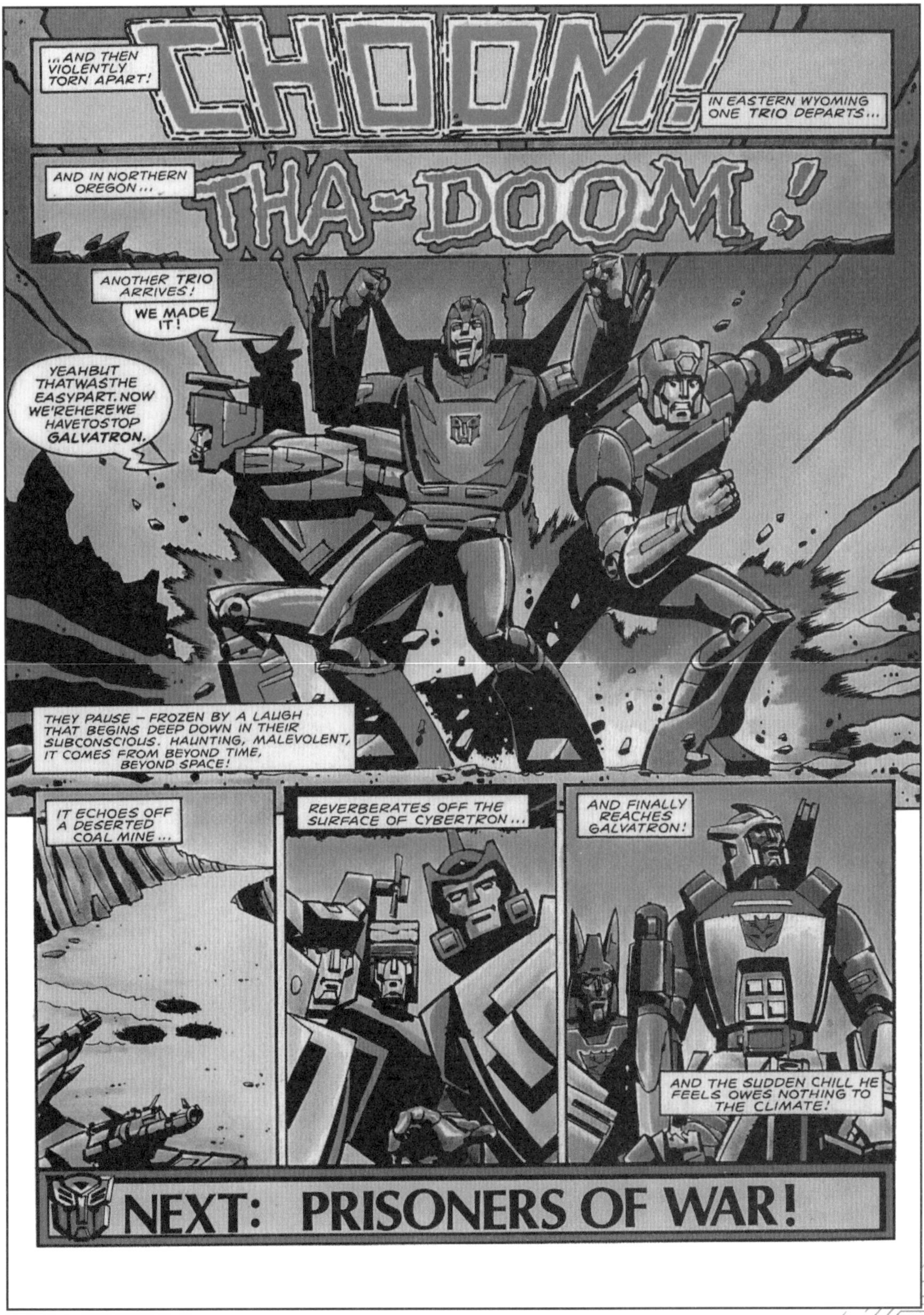
...AND THEN VIOLENTLY TORN APART!
CHOOM!
IN EASTERN WYOMING ONE TRIO DEPARTS...
AND IN NORTHERN OREGON...
THA-DOOM!
ANOTHER TRIO ARRIVES!
WE MADE IT!
YEAHBUT THATWASTHE EASYPART. NOW WE'REHEREWE HAVETOSTOP GALVATRON.
THEY PAUSE – FROZEN BY A LAUGH THAT BEGINS DEEP DOWN IN THEIR SUBCONSCIOUS. HAUNTING, MALEVOLENT, IT COMES FROM BEYOND TIME, BEYOND SPACE!
IT ECHOES OFF A DESERTED COAL MINE...
REVERBERATES OFF THE SURFACE OF CYBERTRON...
AND FINALLY REACHES GALVATRON!
AND THE SUDDEN CHILL HE FEELS OWES NOTHING TO THE CLIMATE!
NEXT: PRISONERS OF WAR!

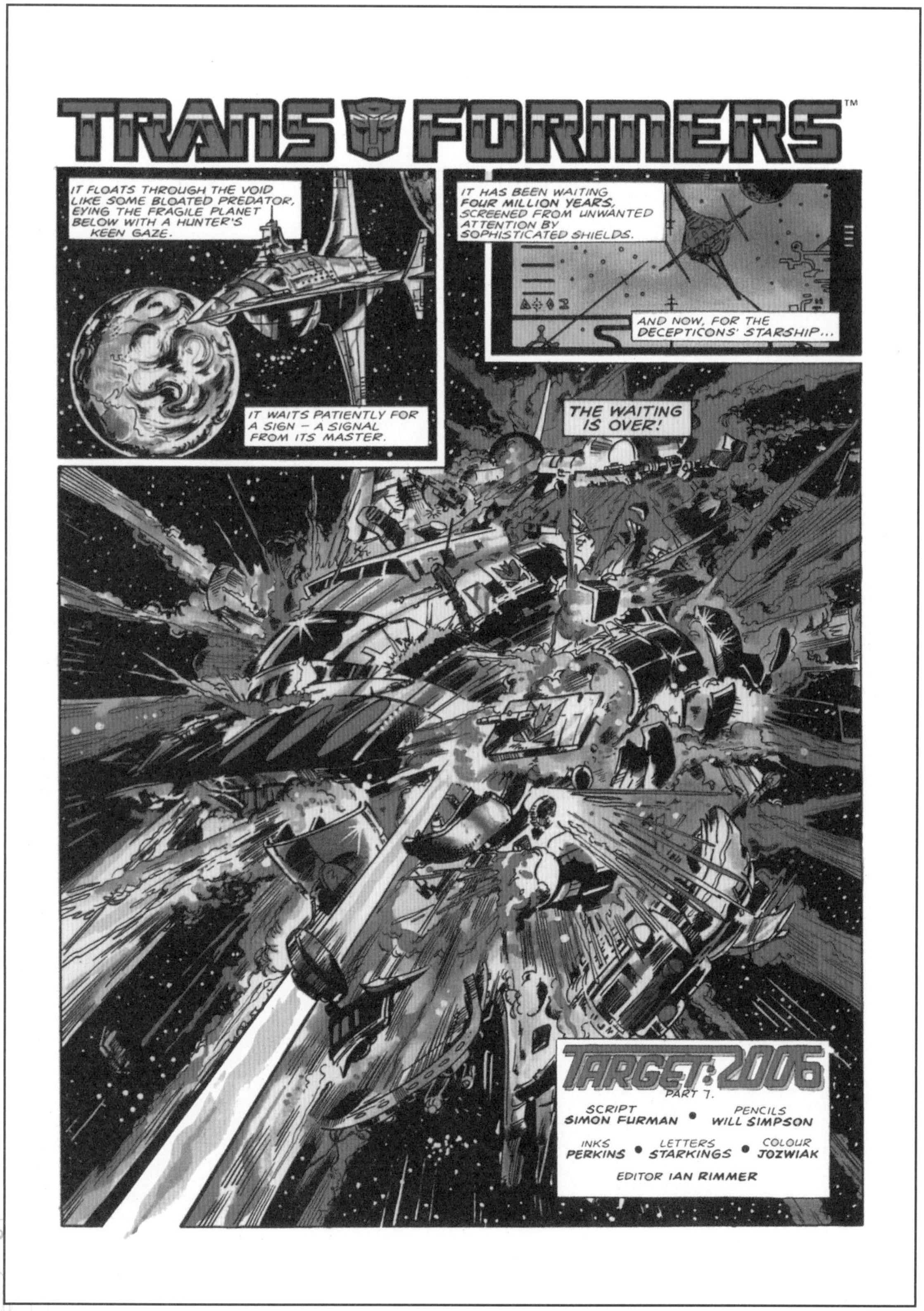
TRANSFORMERS™
IT FLOATS THROUGH THE VOID LIKE SOME BLOATED PREDATOR, EYING THE FRAGILE PLANET BELOW WITH A HUNTER'S KEEN GAZE.
IT WAITS PATIENTLY FOR A SIGN – A SIGNAL FROM ITS MASTER.
IT HAS BEEN WAITING FOUR MILLION YEARS, SCREENED FROM UNWANTED ATTENTION BY SOPHISTICATED SHIELDS.
AND NOW, FOR THE DECEPTICONS' STARSHIP...
THE WAITING IS OVER!
TARGET: 2006
PART 7.
SCRIPT SIMON FURMAN • PENCILS WILL SIMPSON
INKS PERKINS • LETTERS STARKINGS • COLOUR JOZWIAK
EDITOR IAN RIMMER

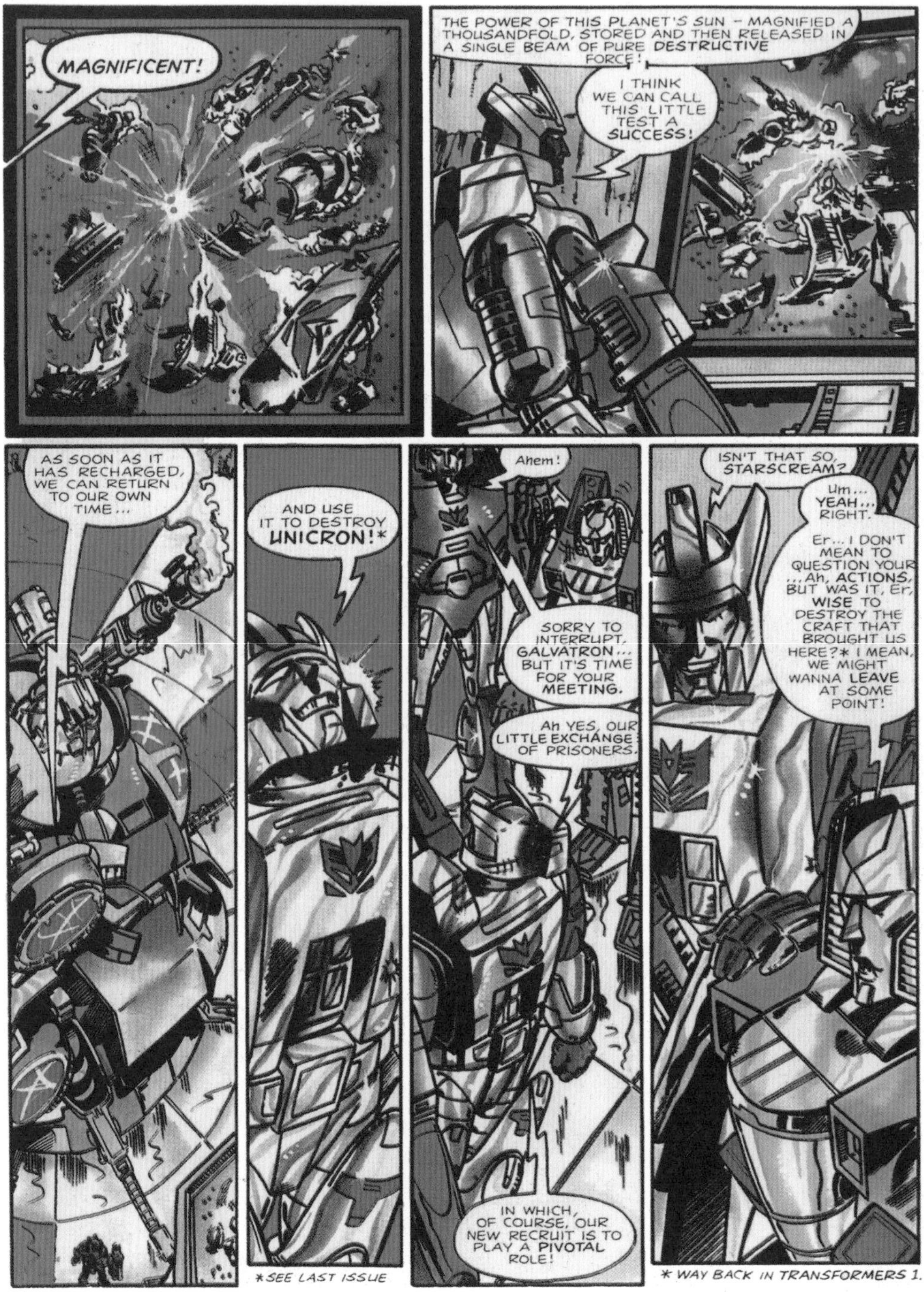
MAGNIFICENT!
THE POWER OF THIS PLANET'S SUN - MAGNIFIED A THOUSANDFOLD, STORED AND THEN RELEASED IN A SINGLE BEAM OF PURE DESTRUCTIVE FORCE!
I THINK WE CAN CALL THIS LITTLE TEST A SUCCESS!
AS SOON AS IT HAS RECHARGED, WE CAN RETURN TO OUR OWN TIME...
AND USE IT TO DESTROY UNICRON!*
*SEE LAST ISSUE
Ahem!
SORRY TO INTERRUPT, GALVATRON... BUT IT'S TIME FOR YOUR MEETING.
Ah YES, OUR LITTLE EXCHANGE OF PRISONERS.
IN WHICH, OF COURSE, OUR NEW RECRUIT IS TO PLAY A PIVOTAL ROLE!
ISN'T THAT SO, STARSCREAM?
Um... YEAH... RIGHT.
Er... I DON'T MEAN TO QUESTION YOUR ...Ah, ACTIONS, BUT WAS IT, Er, WISE TO DESTROY THE CRAFT THAT BROUGHT US HERE?* I MEAN, WE MIGHT WANNA LEAVE AT SOME POINT!
* WAY BACK IN TRANSFORMERS 1.

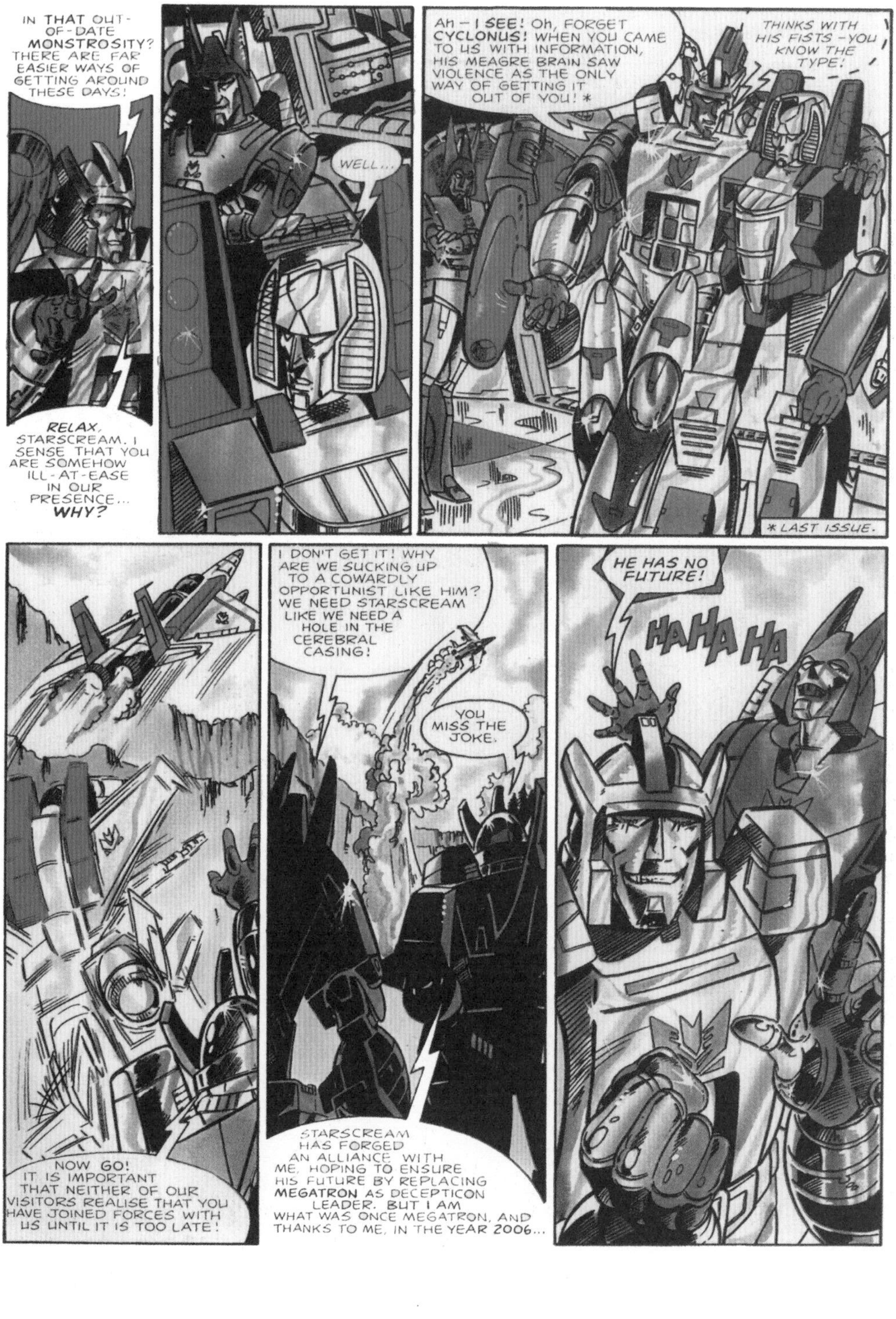

IN THAT OUT-OF-DATE MONSTROSITY? THERE ARE FAR EASIER WAYS OF GETTING AROUND THESE DAYS!
RELAX, STARSCREAM. I SENSE THAT YOU ARE SOMEHOW ILL-AT-EASE IN OUR PRESENCE... WHY?
WELL...
Ah – I SEE! Oh, FORGET CYCLONUS! WHEN YOU CAME TO US WITH INFORMATION, HIS MEAGRE BRAIN SAW VIOLENCE AS THE ONLY WAY OF GETTING IT OUT OF YOU! *
THINKS WITH HIS FISTS – YOU KNOW THE TYPE!
* LAST ISSUE.
NOW GO! IT IS IMPORTANT THAT NEITHER OF OUR VISITORS REALISE THAT YOU HAVE JOINED FORCES WITH US UNTIL IT IS TOO LATE!
I DON'T GET IT! WHY ARE WE SUCKING UP TO A COWARDLY OPPORTUNIST LIKE HIM? WE NEED STARSCREAM LIKE WE NEED A HOLE IN THE CEREBRAL CASING!
YOU MISS THE JOKE.
STARSCREAM HAS FORGED AN ALLIANCE WITH ME, HOPING TO ENSURE HIS FUTURE BY REPLACING MEGATRON AS DECEPTICON LEADER. BUT I AM WHAT WAS ONCE MEGATRON, AND THANKS TO ME, IN THE YEAR 2006...
HE HAS NO FUTURE!
HA HA HA HA

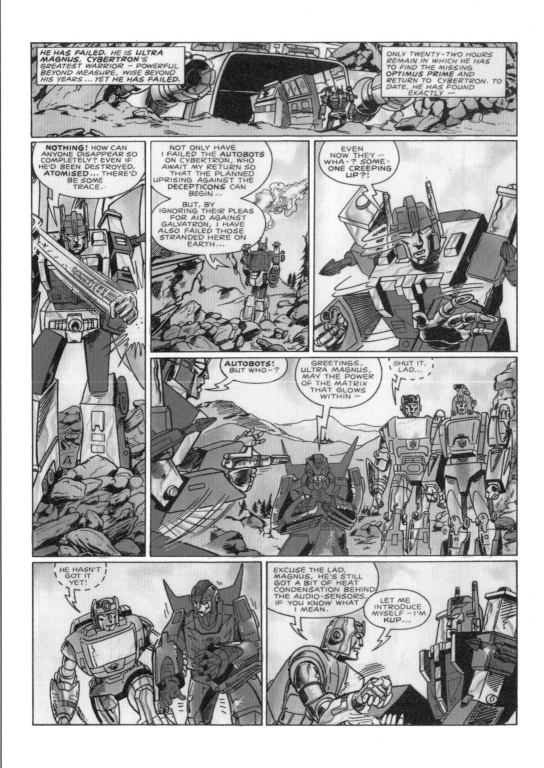

HE HAS FAILED. HE IS ULTRA MAGNUS, CYBERTRON'S GREATEST WARRIOR – POWERFUL BEYOND MEASURE, WISE BEYOND HIS YEARS ... YET HE HAS FAILED.

ONLY TWENTY-TWO HOURS REMAIN IN WHICH HE HAS TO FIND THE MISSING OPTIMUS PRIME AND RETURN TO CYBERTRON. TO DATE, HE HAS FOUND EXACTLY –

NOTHING! HOW CAN ANYONE DISAPPEAR SO COMPLETELY? EVEN IF HE'D BEEN DESTROYED, ATOMISED ... THERE'D BE SOME TRACE.'

NOT ONLY HAVE I FAILED THE AUTOBOTS ON CYBERTRON, WHO AWAIT MY RETURN SO THAT THE PLANNED UPRISING AGAINST THE DECEPTICONS CAN BEGIN ...

BUT, BY IGNORING THEIR PLEAS FOR AID AGAINST GALVATRON, I HAVE ALSO FAILED THOSE STRANDED HERE ON EARTH...

EVEN NOW THEY – WHA–? SOME– ONE CREEPING UP?!

AUTOBOTS! BUT WHO–?

GREETINGS, ULTRA MAGNUS, MAY THE POWER OF THE MATRIX THAT GLOWS WITHIN –

SHUT IT, LAD...

HE HASN'T GOT IT YET!

EXCUSE THE LAD, MAGNUS, HE'S STILL GOT A BIT OF HEAT CONDENSATION BEHIND THE AUDIO-SENSORS, IF YOU KNOW WHAT I MEAN.

LET ME INTRODUCE MYSELF – I'M KUP...

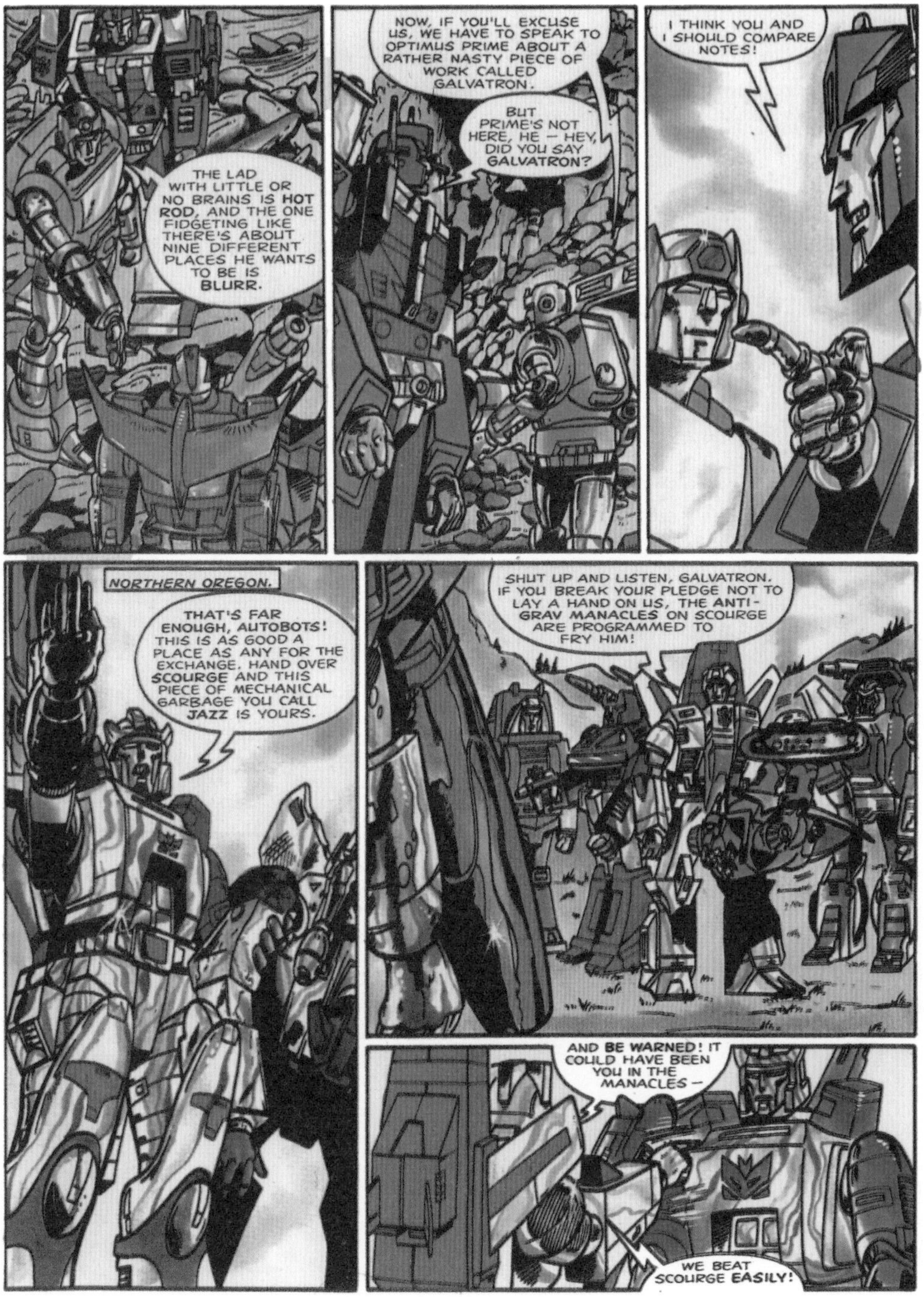
THE LAD WITH LITTLE OR NO BRAINS IS HOT ROD, AND THE ONE FIDGETING LIKE THERE'S ABOUT NINE DIFFERENT PLACES HE WANTS TO BE IS BLURR.
NOW, IF YOU'LL EXCUSE US, WE HAVE TO SPEAK TO OPTIMUS PRIME ABOUT A RATHER NASTY PIECE OF WORK CALLED GALVATRON.
BUT PRIME'S NOT HERE, HE — HEY, DID YOU SAY GALVATRON?
I THINK YOU AND I SHOULD COMPARE NOTES!
NORTHERN OREGON.
THAT'S FAR ENOUGH, AUTOBOTS! THIS IS AS GOOD A PLACE AS ANY FOR THE EXCHANGE. HAND OVER SCOURGE AND THIS PIECE OF MECHANICAL GARBAGE YOU CALL JAZZ IS YOURS.
SHUT UP AND LISTEN, GALVATRON. IF YOU BREAK YOUR PLEDGE NOT TO LAY A HAND ON US, THE ANTI-GRAV MANACLES ON SCOURGE ARE PROGRAMMED TO FRY HIM!
AND BE WARNED! IT COULD HAVE BEEN YOU IN THE MANACLES —
WE BEAT SCOURGE EASILY!

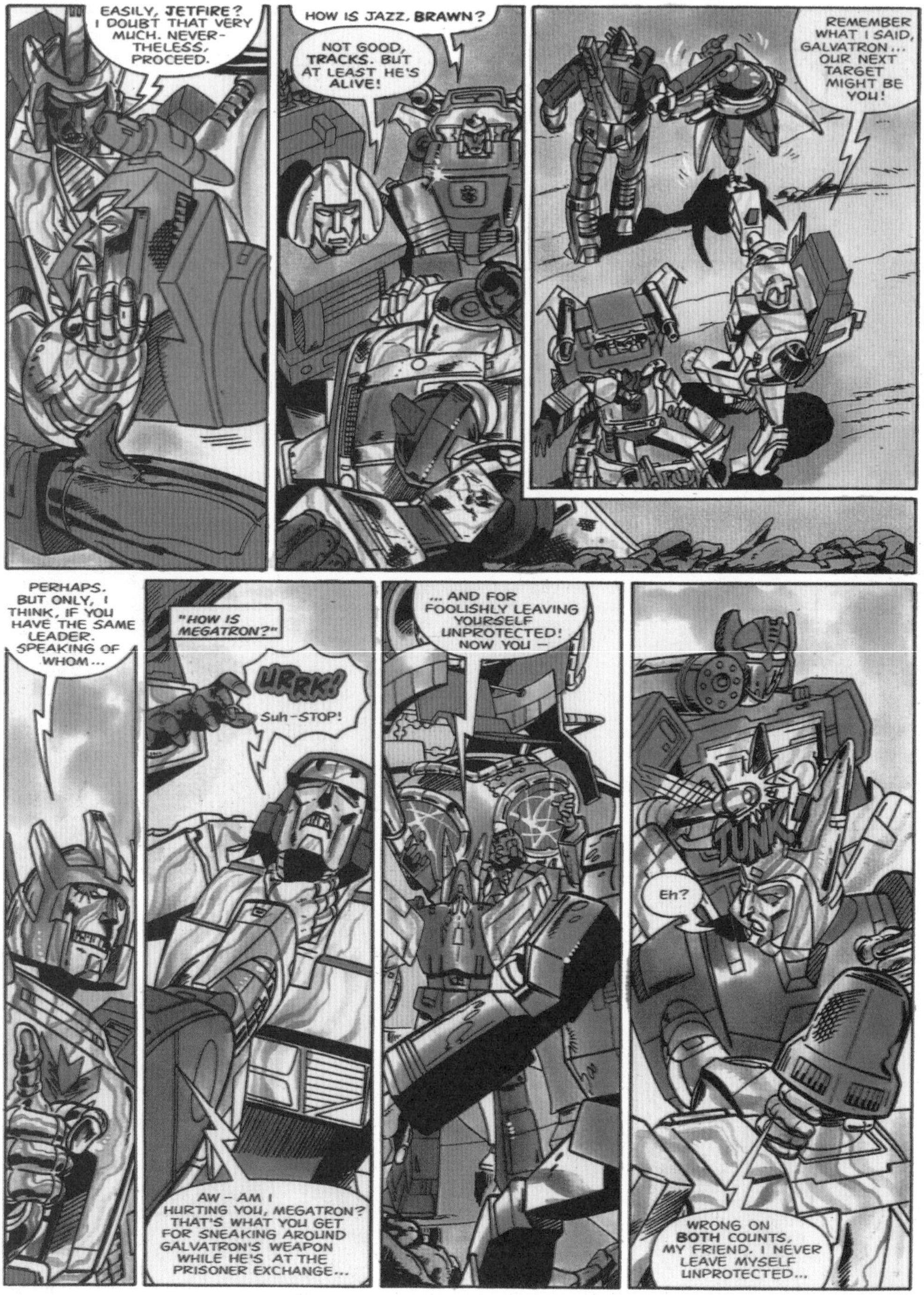
EASILY, JETFIRE? I DOUBT THAT VERY MUCH. NEVER-THELESS, PROCEED.
HOW IS JAZZ, BRAWN?
NOT GOOD, TRACKS. BUT AT LEAST HE'S ALIVE!
REMEMBER WHAT I SAID, GALVATRON... OUR NEXT TARGET MIGHT BE YOU!
PERHAPS. BUT ONLY, I THINK, IF YOU HAVE THE SAME LEADER. SPEAKING OF WHOM...
"HOW IS MEGATRON?"
URRK!
Suh-STOP!
AW - AM I HURTING YOU, MEGATRON? THAT'S WHAT YOU GET FOR SNEAKING AROUND GALVATRON'S WEAPON WHILE HE'S AT THE PRISONER EXCHANGE...
... AND FOR FOOLISHLY LEAVING YOURSELF UNPROTECTED! NOW YOU —
TUNK!
Eh?
WRONG ON BOTH COUNTS, MY FRIEND. I NEVER LEAVE MYSELF UNPROTECTED...

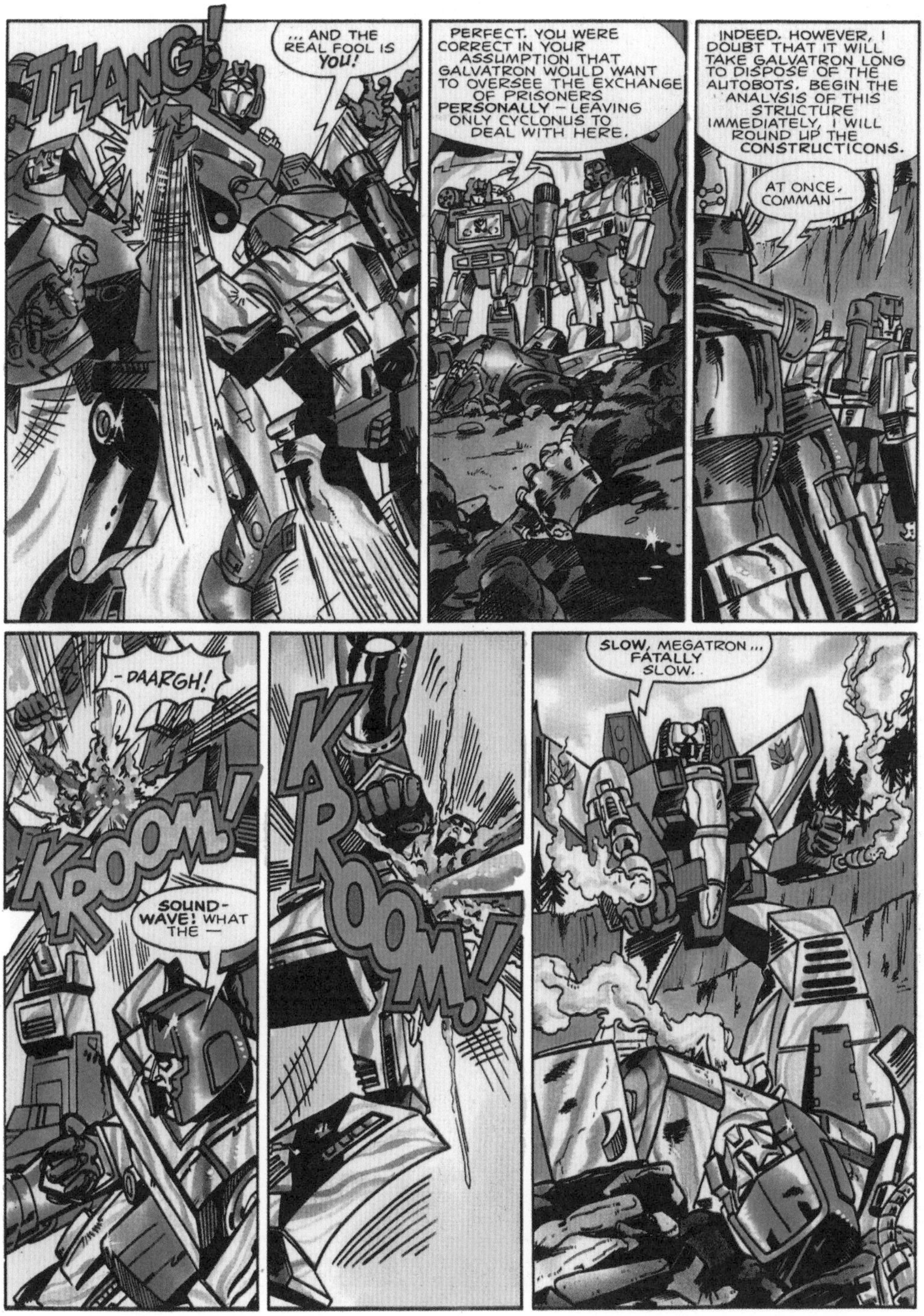
THANG!
... AND THE REAL FOOL IS YOU!
PERFECT. YOU WERE CORRECT IN YOUR ASSUMPTION THAT GALVATRON WOULD WANT TO OVERSEE THE EXCHANGE OF PRISONERS PERSONALLY — LEAVING ONLY CYCLONUS TO DEAL WITH HERE.
INDEED. HOWEVER, I DOUBT THAT IT WILL TAKE GALVATRON LONG TO DISPOSE OF THE AUTOBOTS. BEGIN THE ANALYSIS OF THIS STRUCTURE IMMEDIATELY, I WILL ROUND UP THE CONSTRUCTICONS.
AT ONCE, COMMAN —
-DAARGH!
KROOM!
SOUND-WAVE! WHAT THE —
KROOM!
SLOW, MEGATRON... FATALLY SLOW.

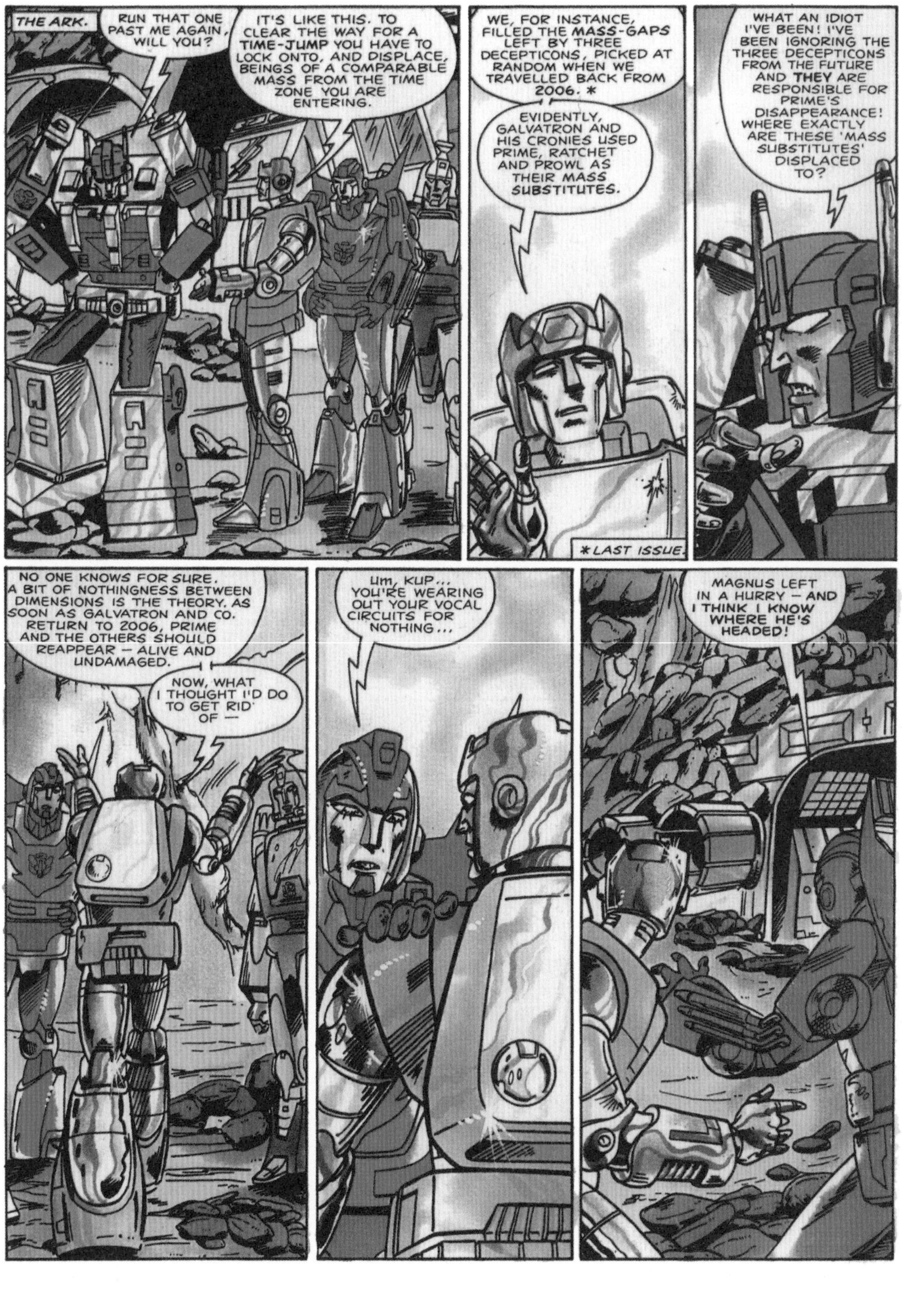
THE ARK.
RUN THAT ONE PAST ME AGAIN, WILL YOU?
IT'S LIKE THIS. TO CLEAR THE WAY FOR A TIME-JUMP YOU HAVE TO LOCK ONTO, AND DISPLACE, BEINGS OF A COMPARABLE MASS FROM THE TIME ZONE YOU ARE ENTERING.
WE, FOR INSTANCE, FILLED THE MASS-GAPS LEFT BY THREE DECEPTICONS, PICKED AT RANDOM WHEN WE TRAVELLED BACK FROM 2006. *
EVIDENTLY, GALVATRON AND HIS CRONIES USED PRIME, RATCHET AND PROWL AS THEIR MASS SUBSTITUTES.
*LAST ISSUE.
WHAT AN IDIOT I'VE BEEN! I'VE BEEN IGNORING THE THREE DECEPTICONS FROM THE FUTURE AND THEY ARE RESPONSIBLE FOR PRIME'S DISAPPEARANCE! WHERE EXACTLY ARE THESE 'MASS SUBSTITUTES' DISPLACED TO?
NO ONE KNOWS FOR SURE. A BIT OF NOTHINGNESS BETWEEN DIMENSIONS IS THE THEORY. AS SOON AS GALVATRON AND CO. RETURN TO 2006, PRIME AND THE OTHERS SHOULD REAPPEAR — ALIVE AND UNDAMAGED.
NOW, WHAT I THOUGHT I'D DO TO GET RID OF —
UM, KUP... YOU'RE WEARING OUT YOUR VOCAL CIRCUITS FOR NOTHING...
MAGNUS LEFT IN A HURRY — AND I THINK I KNOW WHERE HE'S HEADED!

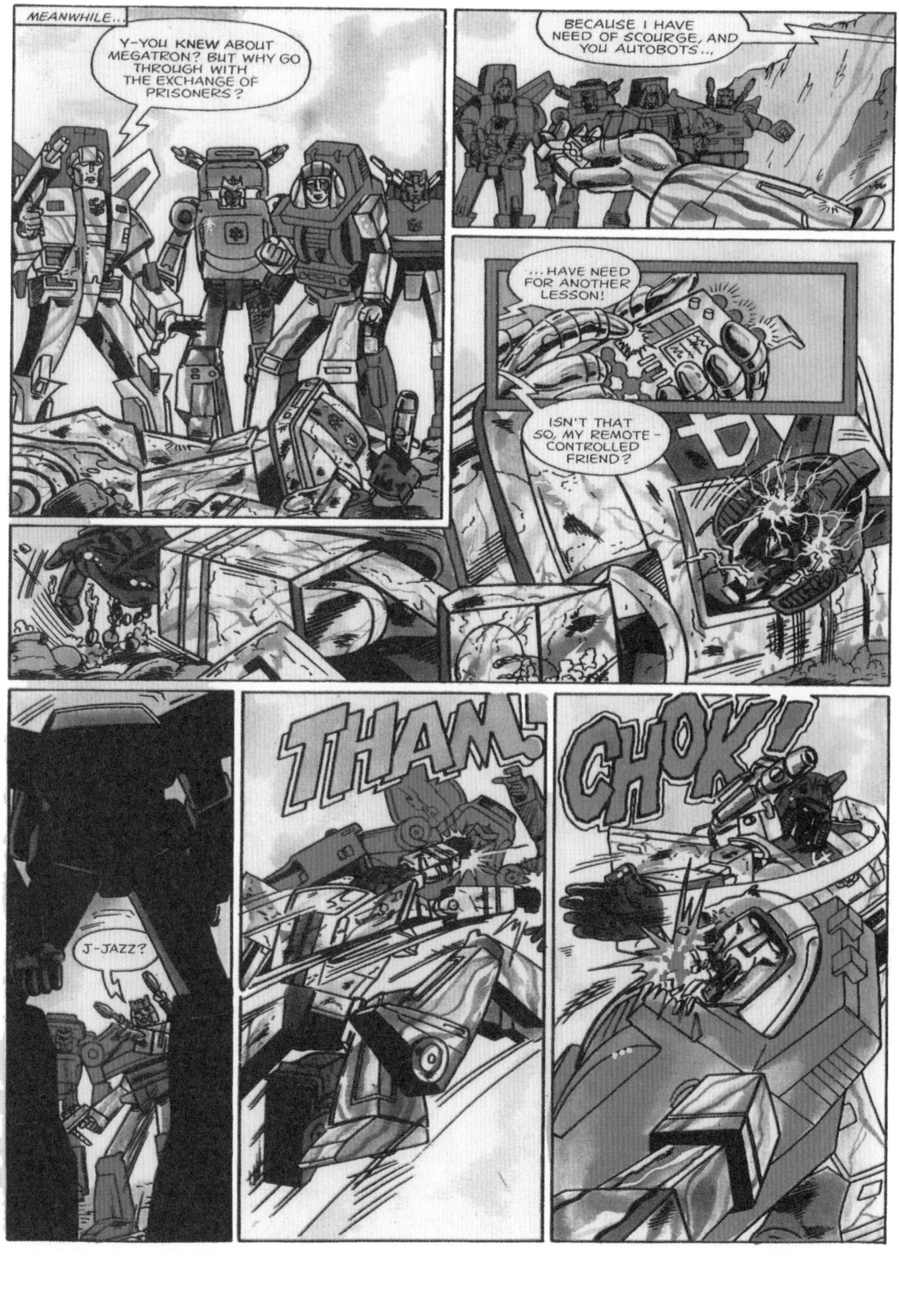
MEANWHILE...
Y-YOU KNEW ABOUT MEGATRON? BUT WHY GO THROUGH WITH THE EXCHANGE OF PRISONERS?
BECAUSE I HAVE NEED OF SCOURGE, AND YOU AUTOBOTS...
...HAVE NEED FOR ANOTHER LESSON!
ISN'T THAT SO, MY REMOTE-CONTROLLED FRIEND?
J-JAZZ?
THAM!
CHOK!

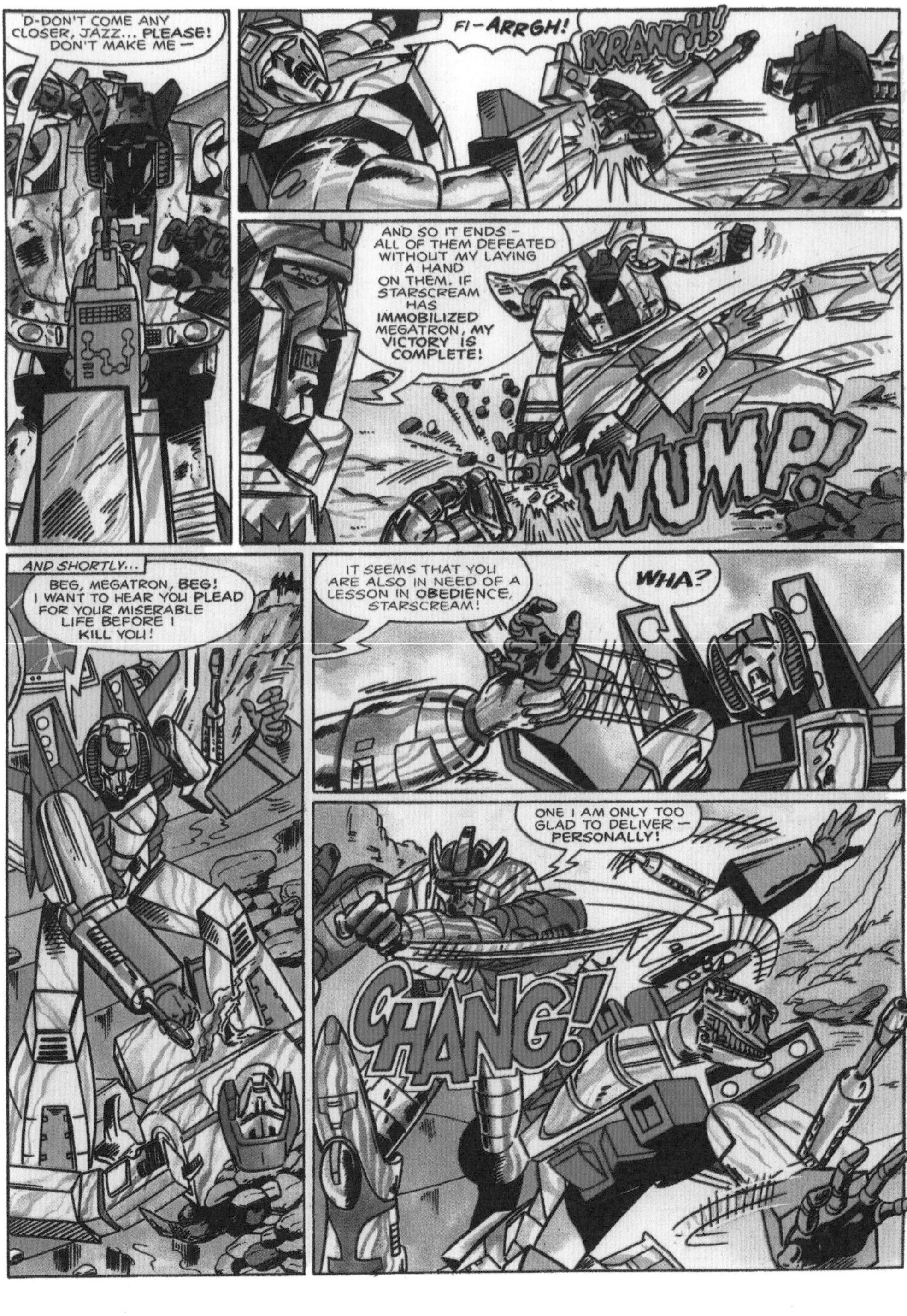

D-DON'T COME ANY CLOSER, JAZZ... PLEASE! DON'T MAKE ME —
FI-ARRGH!
KRANCH!!
AND SO IT ENDS — ALL OF THEM DEFEATED WITHOUT MY LAYING A HAND ON THEM. IF STARSCREAM HAS IMMOBILIZED MEGATRON, MY VICTORY IS COMPLETE!
WUMP!
AND SHORTLY...
BEG, MEGATRON, BEG! I WANT TO HEAR YOU PLEAD FOR YOUR MISERABLE LIFE BEFORE I KILL YOU!
IT SEEMS THAT YOU ARE ALSO IN NEED OF A LESSON IN OBEDIENCE, STARSCREAM!
WHA?
ONE I AM ONLY TOO GLAD TO DELIVER — PERSONALLY!
CHANG!

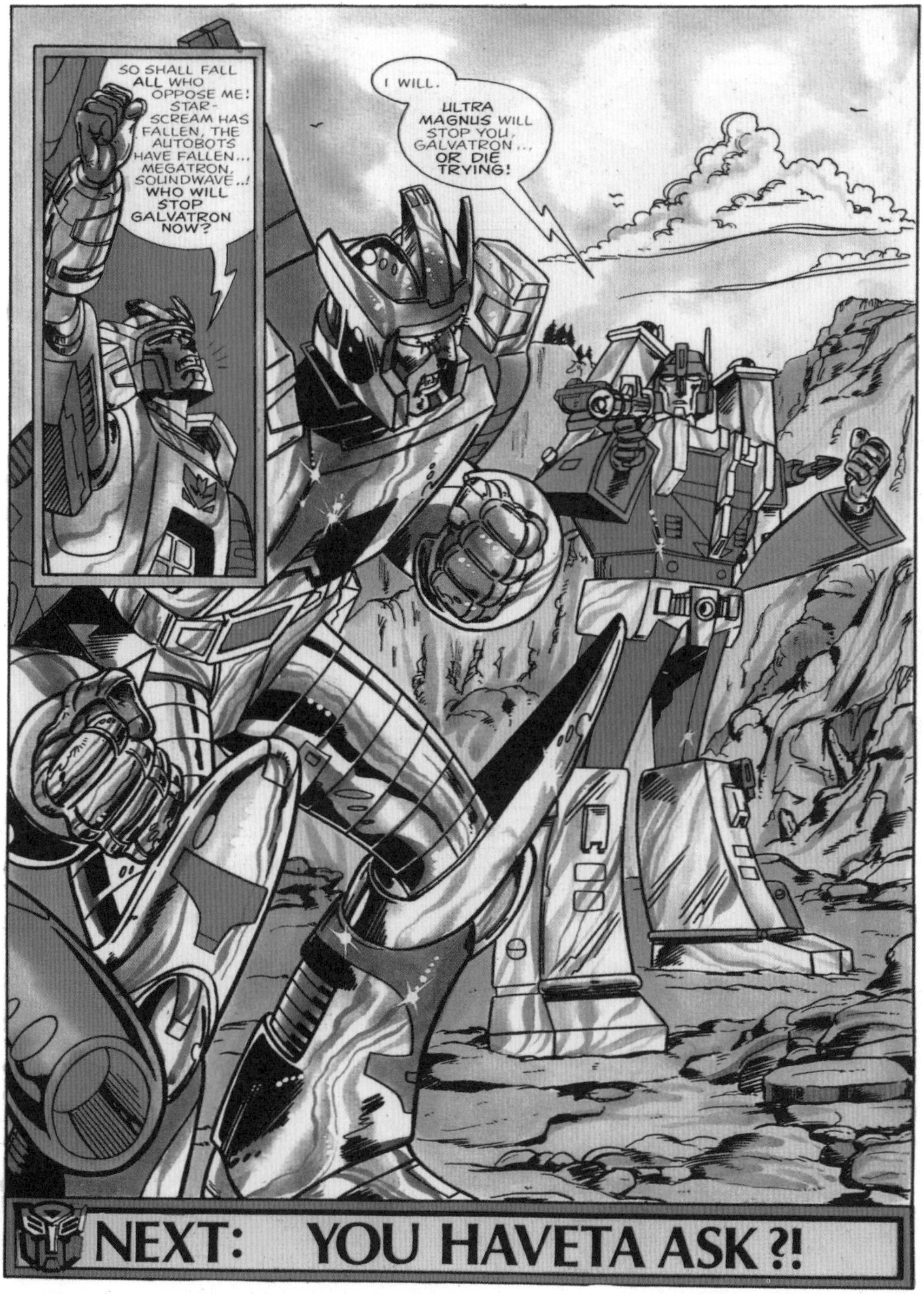
SO SHALL FALL ALL WHO OPPOSE ME! STAR-SCREAM HAS FALLEN, THE AUTOBOTS HAVE FALLEN... MEGATRON, SOUNDWAVE...! WHO WILL STOP GALVATRON NOW?
I WILL.
ULTRA MAGNUS WILL STOP YOU, GALVATRON... OR DIE TRYING!
NEXT: YOU HAVETA ASK ?!

GALVATRON.

HE CAME BACK FROM THE FUTURE TO 1986, AND BUILT A WEAPON OF TOMORROW. A WEAPON THAT WOULD ENSURE HIS RULE IN THE YEAR 2006.

MANY TRIED TO STOP HIM — BUT HIS HENCHMEN, **SCOURGE** AND **CYCLONUS**, THE OPPORTUNIST **STARSCREAM**, OR GALVATRON'S PUPPET, THE REMOTE-CONTROLLED AUTOBOT, **JAZZ** ...

...DEALT WITH ALL OPPOSITION ...

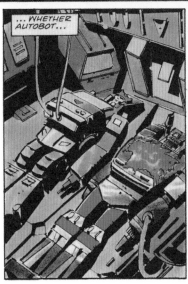

... WHETHER AUTOBOT...

...OR DECEPTICON.

NOW JUST ONE BEING STANDS BETWEEN GALVATRON AND TOTAL DOMINATION OF TWO PLANETS IN TWO ERAS ...

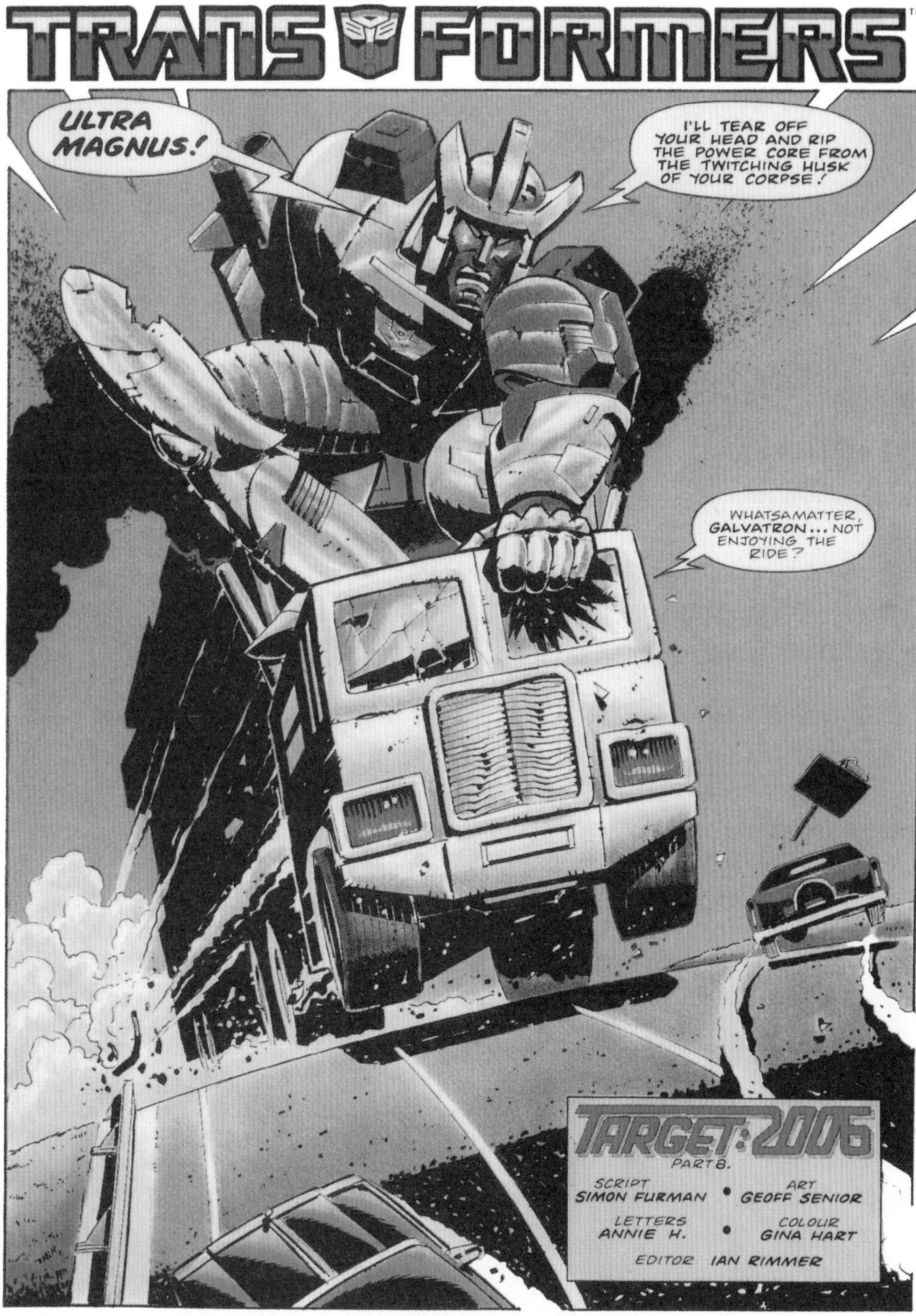
TRANSFORMERS™
ULTRA MAGNUS!
I'LL TEAR OFF YOUR HEAD AND RIP THE POWER CORE FROM THE TWITCHING HUSK OF YOUR CORPSE!
WHATSAMATTER, GALVATRON... NOT ENJOYING THE RIDE?
TARGET: 2006
PART 8.
SCRIPT SIMON FURMAN • ART GEOFF SENIOR
LETTERS ANNIE H. • COLOUR GINA HART
EDITOR IAN RIMMER

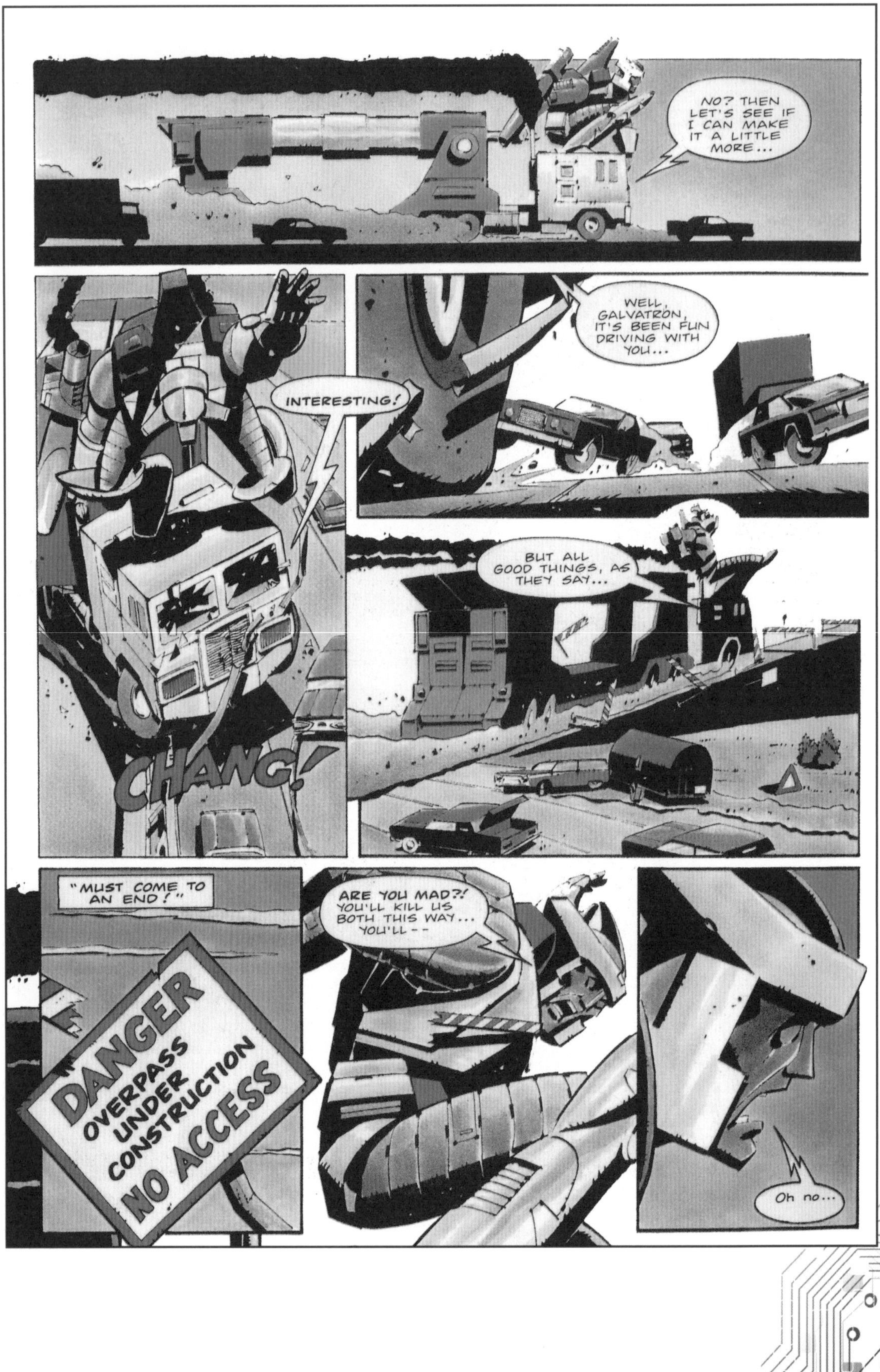
NO? THEN LET'S SEE IF I CAN MAKE IT A LITTLE MORE...
INTERESTING!
CHANG!
WELL, GALVATRON, IT'S BEEN FUN DRIVING WITH YOU...
BUT ALL GOOD THINGS, AS THEY SAY...
"MUST COME TO AN END!"
DANGER
OVERPASS UNDER CONSTRUCTION
NO ACCESS
ARE YOU MAD?! YOU'LL KILL US BOTH THIS WAY... YOU'LL--
Oh no...

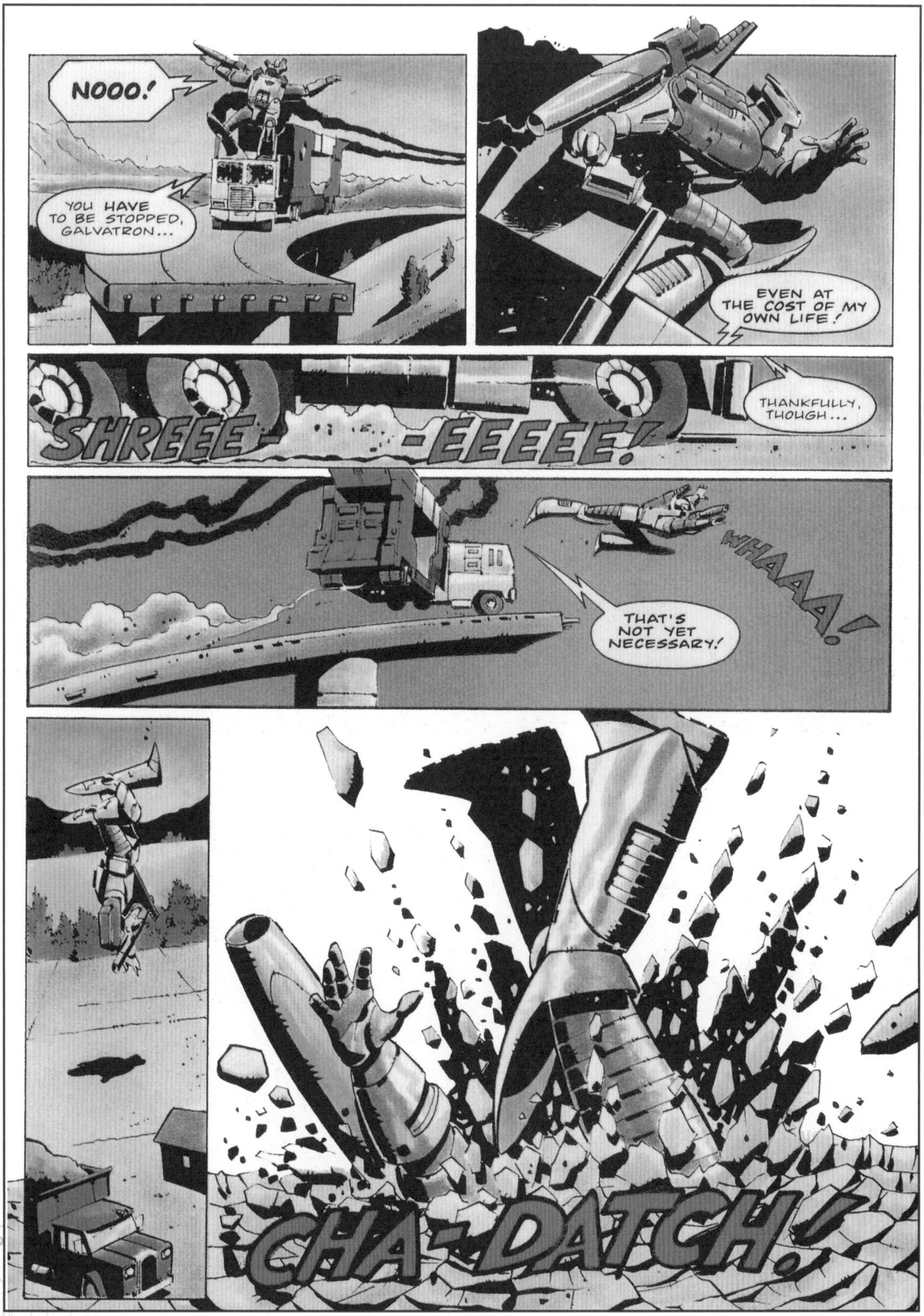
NOOO!
YOU HAVE TO BE STOPPED, GALVATRON...
EVEN AT THE COST OF MY OWN LIFE!
SHREEE- -EEEEEE!
THANKFULLY, THOUGH...
WHAAAA!
THAT'S NOT YET NECESSARY!
CHA-DATCH!

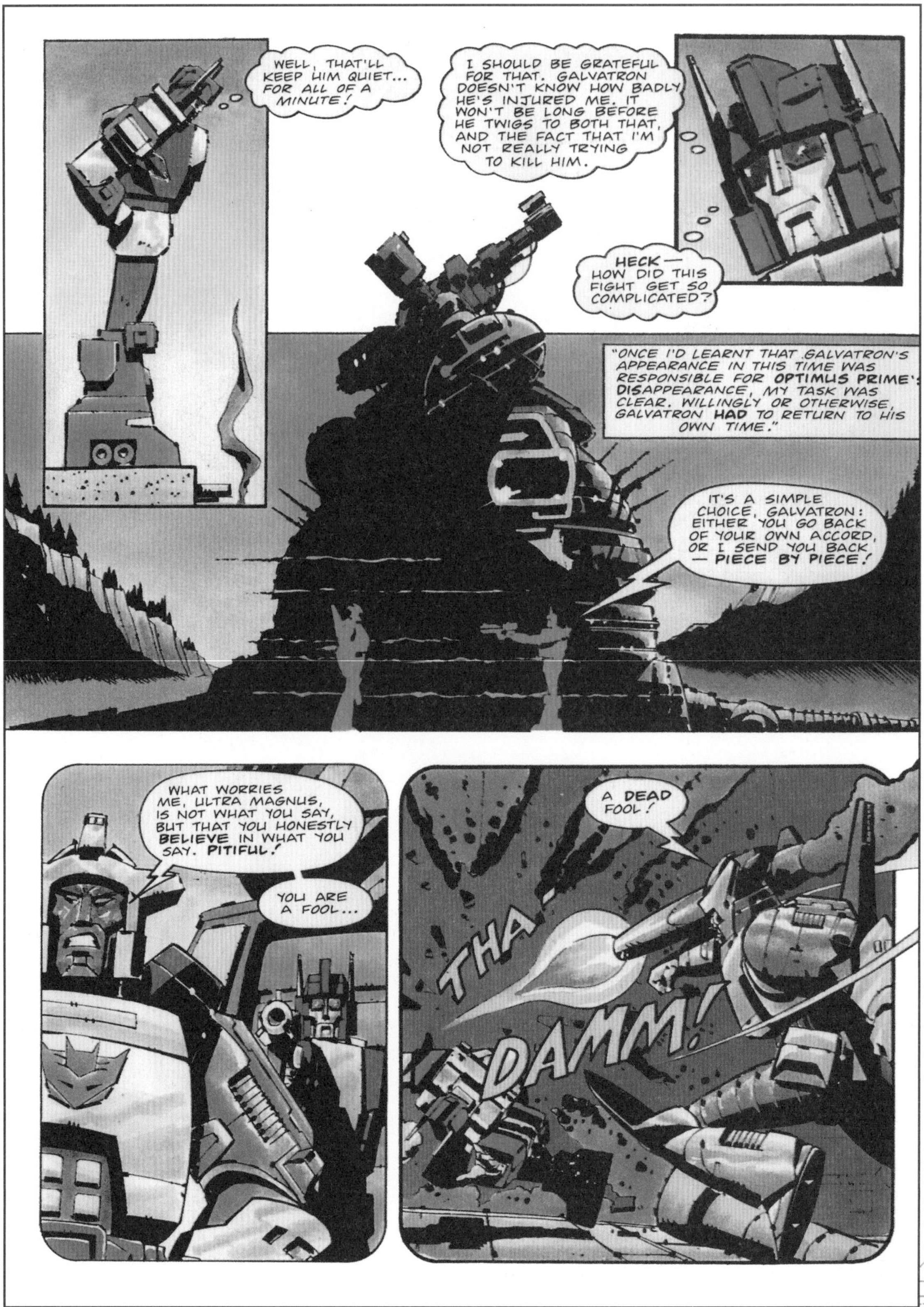

WELL, THAT'LL KEEP HIM QUIET... FOR ALL OF A MINUTE!
I SHOULD BE GRATEFUL FOR THAT. GALVATRON DOESN'T KNOW HOW BADLY HE'S INJURED ME. IT WON'T BE LONG BEFORE HE TWIGS TO BOTH THAT, AND THE FACT THAT I'M NOT REALLY TRYING TO KILL HIM.
HECK— HOW DID THIS FIGHT GET SO COMPLICATED?
"ONCE I'D LEARNT THAT GALVATRON'S APPEARANCE IN THIS TIME WAS RESPONSIBLE FOR OPTIMUS PRIME'S DISAPPEARANCE, MY TASK WAS CLEAR. WILLINGLY OR OTHERWISE, GALVATRON HAD TO RETURN TO HIS OWN TIME."
IT'S A SIMPLE CHOICE, GALVATRON: EITHER YOU GO BACK OF YOUR OWN ACCORD, OR I SEND YOU BACK — PIECE BY PIECE!
WHAT WORRIES ME, ULTRA MAGNUS, IS NOT WHAT YOU SAY, BUT THAT YOU HONESTLY BELIEVE IN WHAT YOU SAY. PITIFUL!
YOU ARE A FOOL...
A DEAD FOOL!
THA-DAMM!

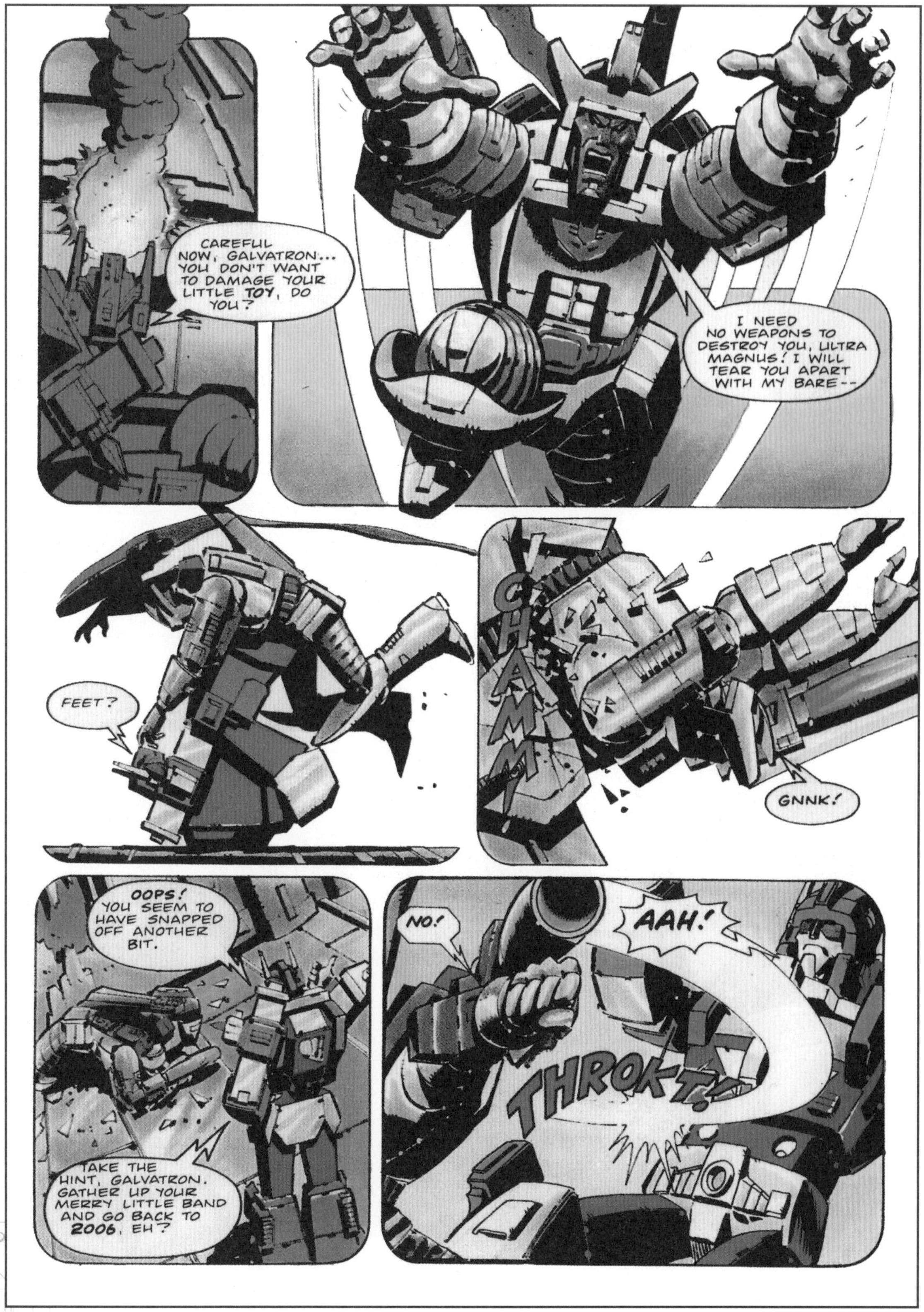
CAREFUL NOW, GALVATRON... YOU DON'T WANT TO DAMAGE YOUR LITTLE TOY, DO YOU?
I NEED NO WEAPONS TO DESTROY YOU, ULTRA MAGNUS! I WILL TEAR YOU APART WITH MY BARE--
FEET?
CHAMM
GNNK!
OOPS! YOU SEEM TO HAVE SNAPPED OFF ANOTHER BIT.
TAKE THE HINT, GALVATRON. GATHER UP YOUR MERRY LITTLE BAND AND GO BACK TO 2006, EH?
NO!
AAH!
THROKT!

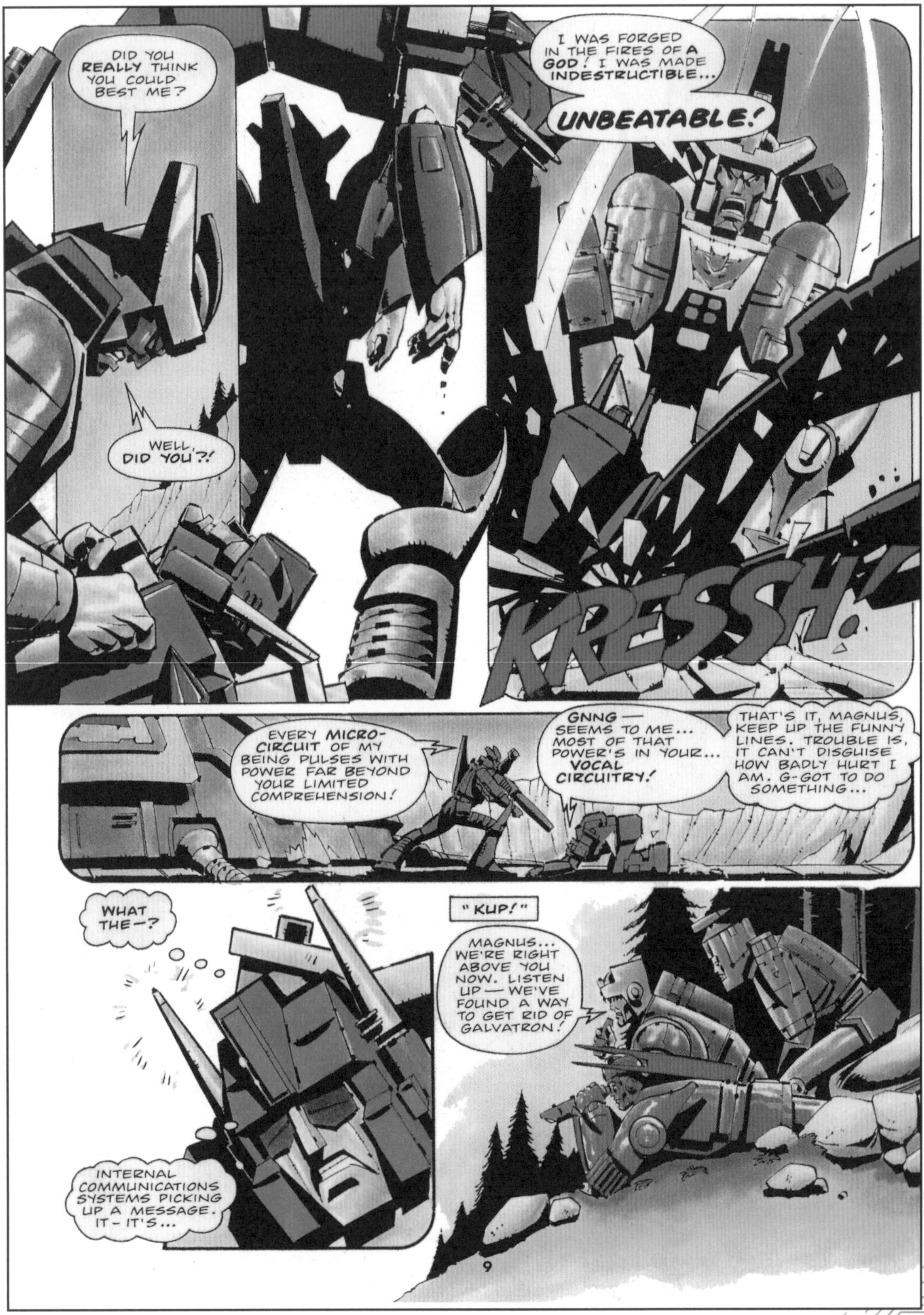
DID YOU REALLY THINK YOU COULD BEST ME?
WELL, DID YOU?!
I WAS FORGED IN THE FIRES OF A GOD! I WAS MADE INDESTRUCTIBLE...
UNBEATABLE!
KRESSH!
EVERY MICRO-CIRCUIT OF MY BEING PULSES WITH POWER FAR BEYOND YOUR LIMITED COMPREHENSION!
GNNG — SEEMS TO ME... MOST OF THAT POWER'S IN YOUR... VOCAL CIRCUITRY!
THAT'S IT, MAGNUS, KEEP UP THE FUNNY LINES. TROUBLE IS, IT CAN'T DISGUISE HOW BADLY HURT I AM. G-GOT TO DO SOMETHING...
WHAT THE—?
INTERNAL COMMUNICATIONS SYSTEMS PICKING UP A MESSAGE. IT - IT'S...
"KUP!"
MAGNUS... WE'RE RIGHT ABOVE YOU NOW. LISTEN UP — WE'VE FOUND A WAY TO GET RID OF GALVATRON!
9

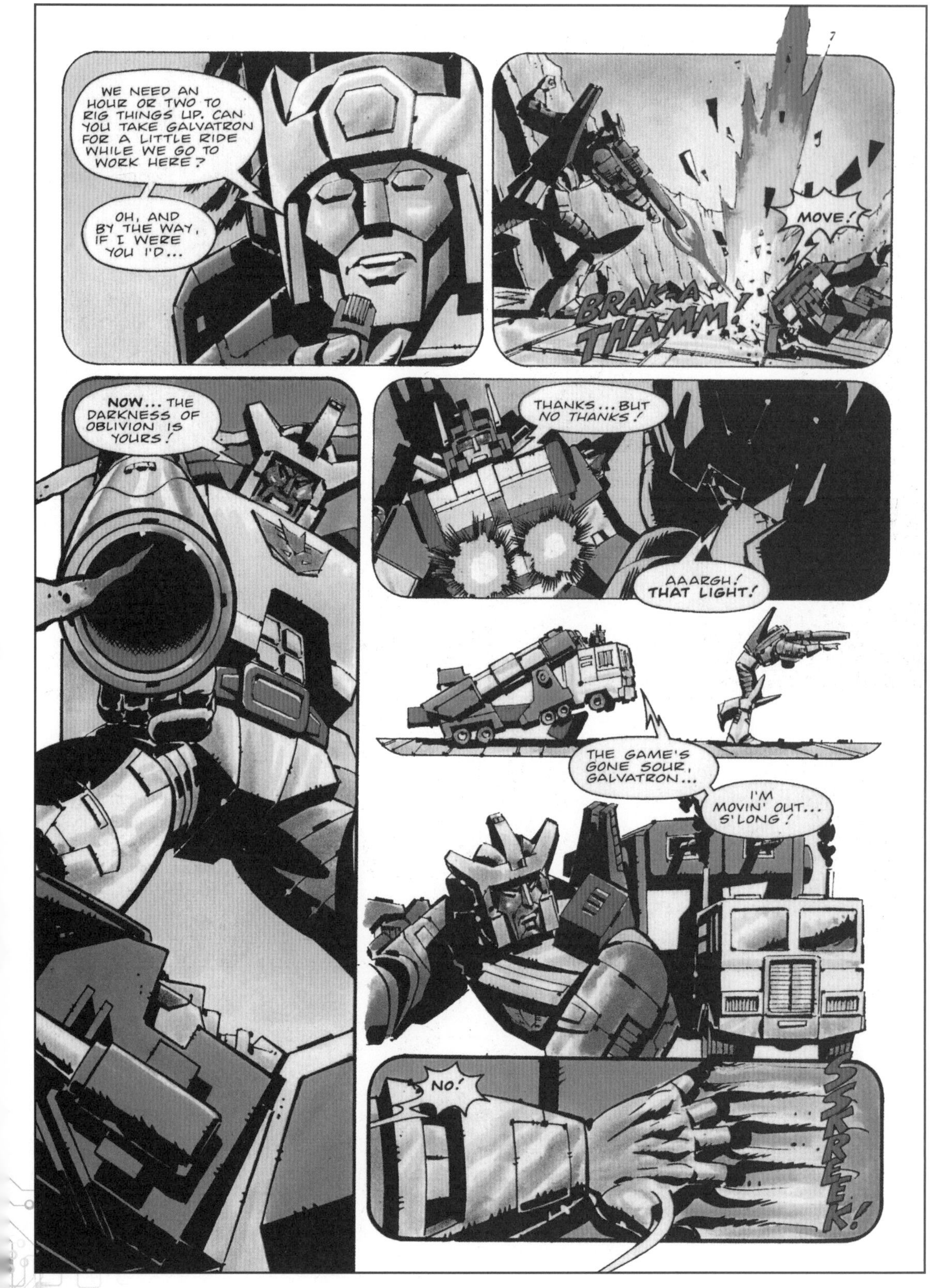
7
WE NEED AN HOUR OR TWO TO RIG THINGS UP. CAN YOU TAKE GALVATRON FOR A LITTLE RIDE WHILE WE GO TO WORK HERE?
OH, AND BY THE WAY, IF I WERE YOU I'D...
MOVE!
BRAK-A-! THAMM!
NOW... THE DARKNESS OF OBLIVION IS YOURS!
THANKS... BUT NO THANKS!
AAARGH! THAT LIGHT!
THE GAME'S GONE SOUR, GALVATRON...
I'M MOVIN' OUT... S'LONG!
NO!
SSKREEK!

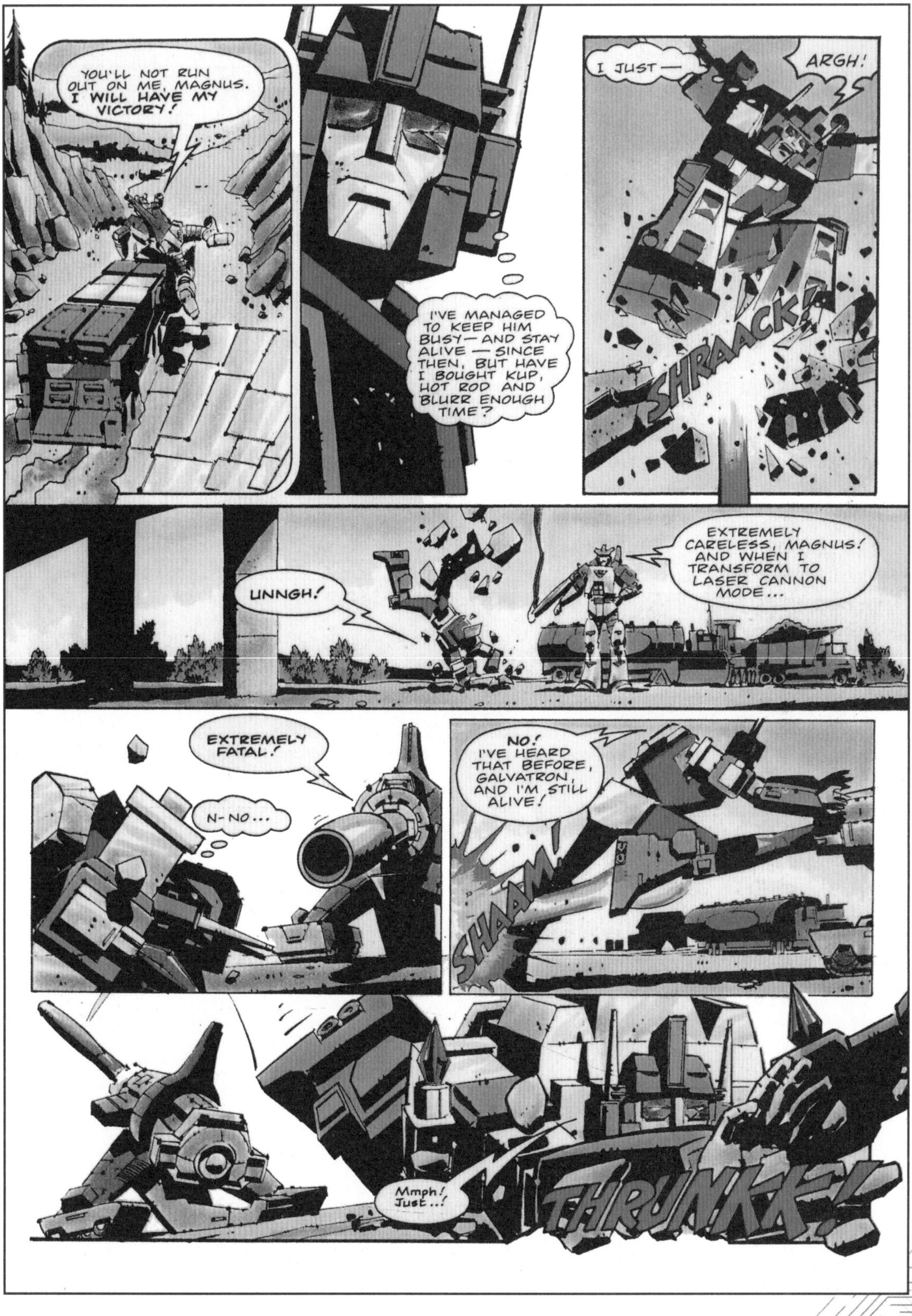
YOU'LL NOT RUN OUT ON ME, MAGNUS. I WILL HAVE MY VICTORY!
I'VE MANAGED TO KEEP HIM BUSY— AND STAY ALIVE — SINCE THEN, BUT HAVE I BOUGHT KUP, HOT ROD AND BLURR ENOUGH TIME?
I JUST—
ARGH!
SHRAACK!
UNNGH!
EXTREMELY CARELESS, MAGNUS! AND WHEN I TRANSFORM TO LASER CANNON MODE...
EXTREMELY FATAL!
N-NO...
NO! I'VE HEARD THAT BEFORE, GALVATRON, AND I'M STILL ALIVE!
SHAAM!
Mmph! Just...!
THRUNKK!

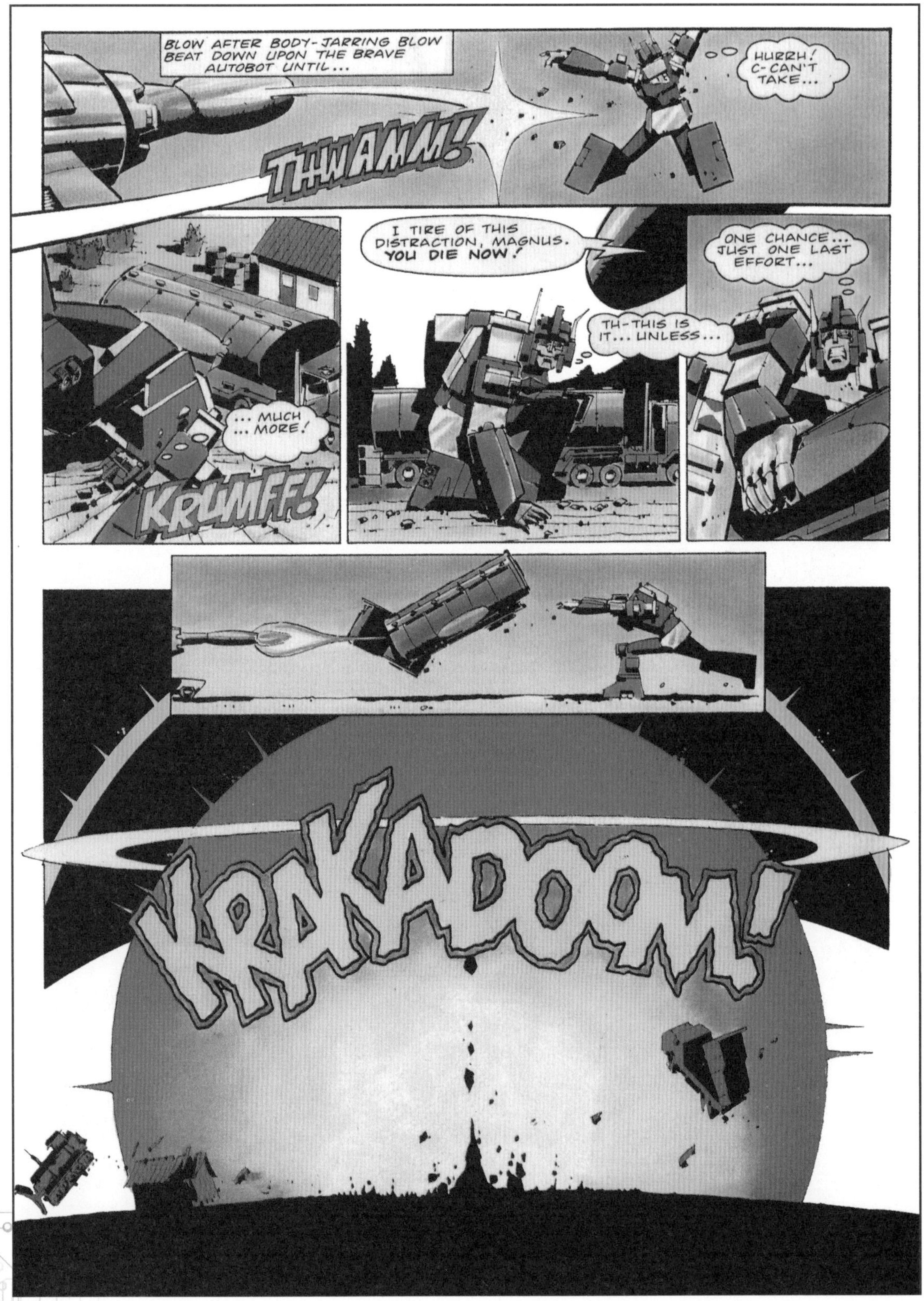
BLOW AFTER BODY-JARRING BLOW BEAT DOWN UPON THE BRAVE AUTOBOT UNTIL...
THWAMM!
HURRH! C-CAN'T TAKE...
...MUCH ...MORE!
KRUMFF!
I TIRE OF THIS DISTRACTION, MAGNUS. YOU DIE NOW!
TH-THIS IS IT... UNLESS...
ONE CHANCE... JUST ONE LAST EFFORT...
KRAKADOOM!

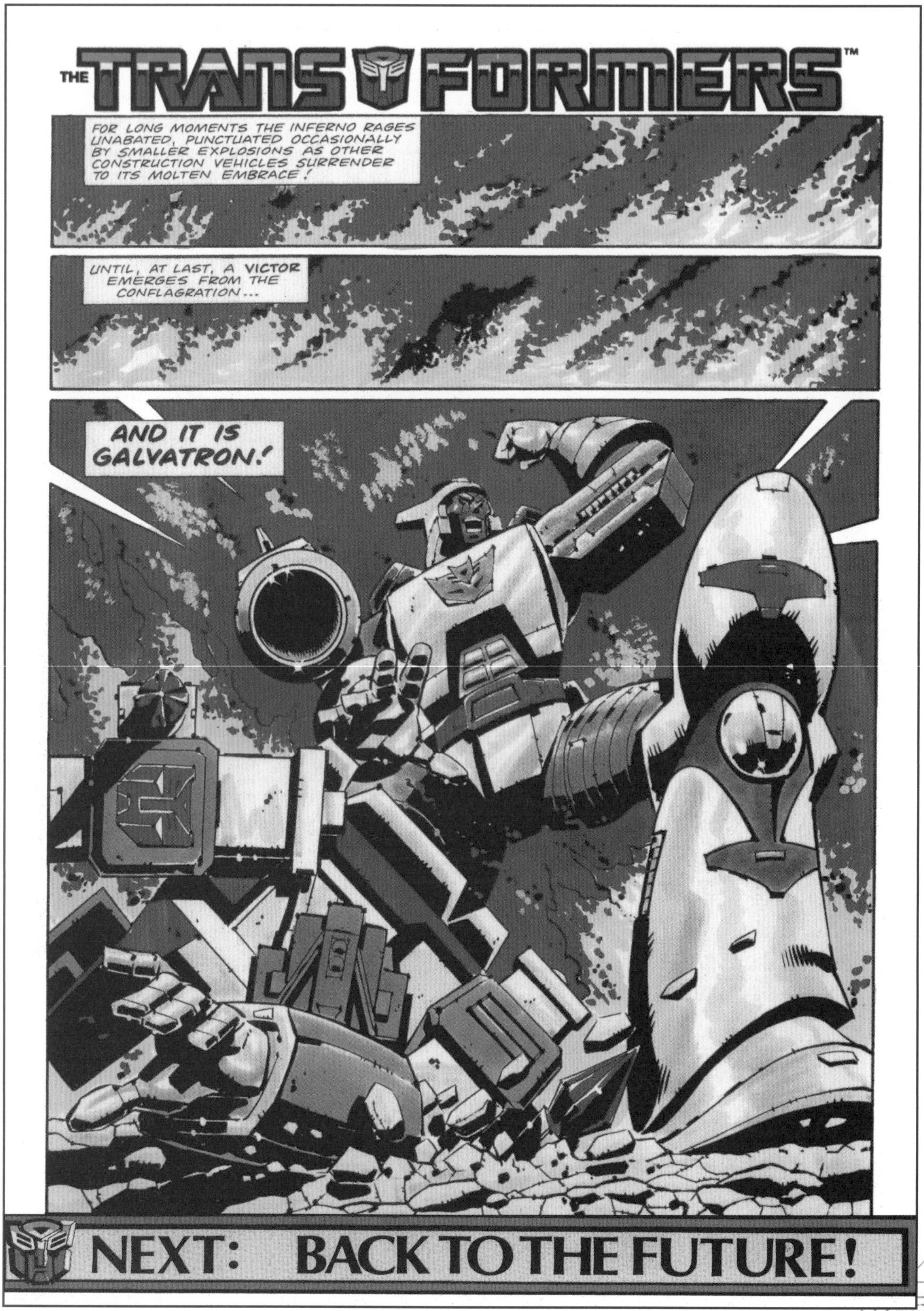
THE TRANSFORMERS
FOR LONG MOMENTS THE INFERNO RAGES UNABATED, PUNCTUATED OCCASIONALLY BY SMALLER EXPLOSIONS AS OTHER CONSTRUCTION VEHICLES SURRENDER TO ITS MOLTEN EMBRACE!
UNTIL, AT LAST, A VICTOR EMERGES FROM THE CONFLAGRATION...
AND IT IS GALVATRON!
NEXT: BACK TO THE FUTURE!

GALVATRON

INTRODUCING THE NEW LEADERS!

With our *Target:2006* story drawing to a close next issue, we felt it was high time we completed our little duo of New Leaders' profiles. Back in issue 81 we took an in-depth look at the Autobots' greatest warrior – Ultra Magnus. Now join us as the secrets of Galvatron are laid bare before your eyes and we take a little trip to the year 2006!

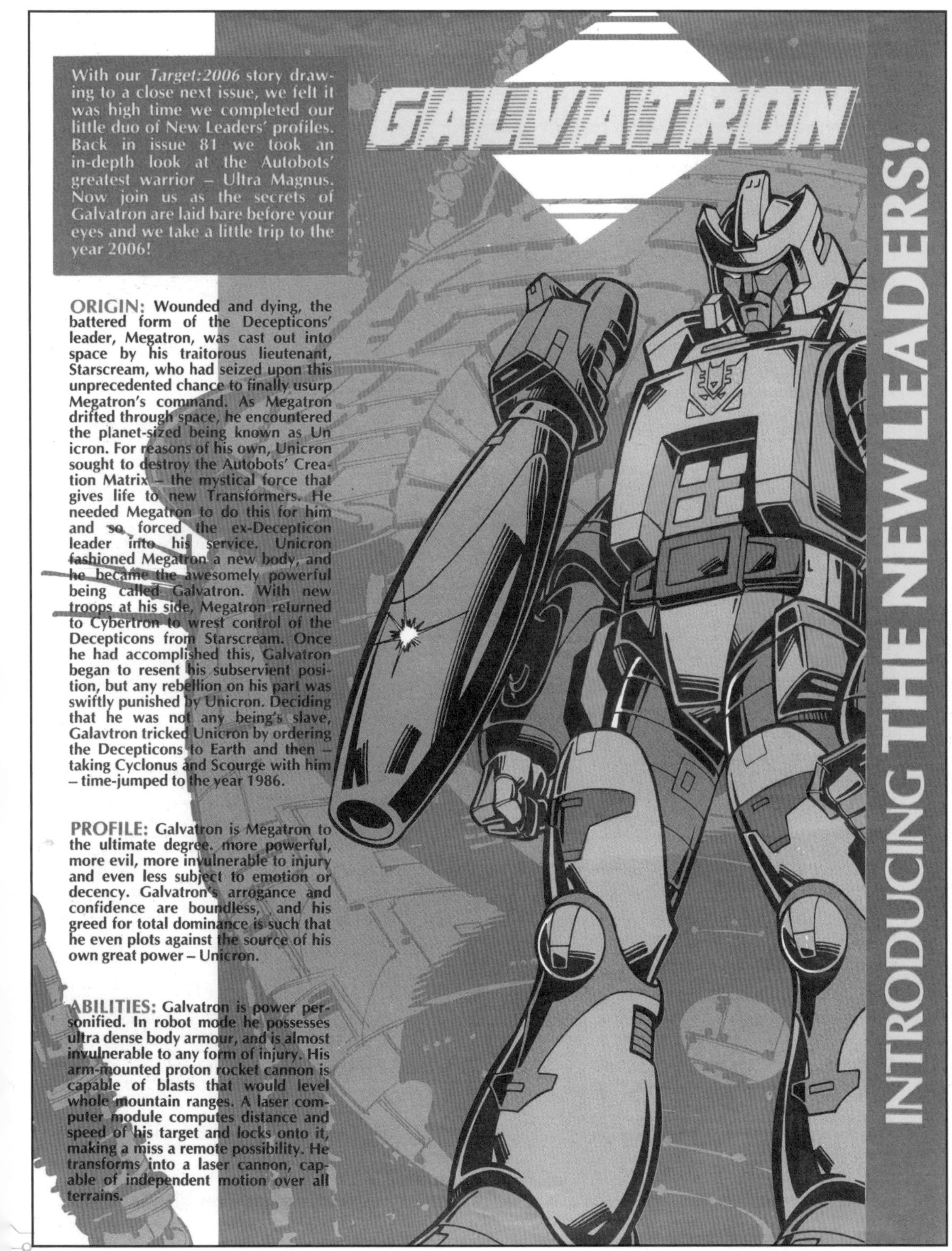

ORIGIN: Wounded and dying, the battered form of the Decepticons' leader, Megatron, was cast out into space by his traitorous lieutenant, Starscream, who had seized upon this unprecedented chance to finally usurp Megatron's command. As Megatron drifted through space, he encountered the planet-sized being known as Unicron. For reasons of his own, Unicron sought to destroy the Autobots' Creation Matrix – the mystical force that gives life to new Transformers. He needed Megatron to do this for him and so forced the ex-Decepticon leader into his service. Unicron fashioned Megatron a new body, and he became the awesomely powerful being called Galvatron. With new troops at his side, Megatron returned to Cybertron to wrest control of the Decepticons from Starscream. Once he had accomplished this, Galvatron began to resent his subservient position, but any rebellion on his part was swiftly punished by Unicron. Deciding that he was not any being's slave, Galavtron tricked Unicron by ordering the Decepticons to Earth and then – taking Cyclonus and Scourge with him – time-jumped to the year 1986.

PROFILE: Galvatron is Megatron to the ultimate degree. more powerful, more evil, more invulnerable to injury and even less subject to emotion or decency. Galvatron's arrogance and confidence are boundless, and his greed for total dominance is such that he even plots against the source of his own great power – Unicron.

ABILITIES: Galvatron is power personified. In robot mode he possesses ultra dense body armour, and is almost invulnerable to any form of injury. His arm-mounted proton rocket cannon is capable of blasts that would level whole mountain ranges. A laser computer module computes distance and speed of his target and locks onto it, making a miss a remote possibility. He transforms into a laser cannon, capable of independent motion over all terrains.

Originally printed in *Transformers UK* issue #87.

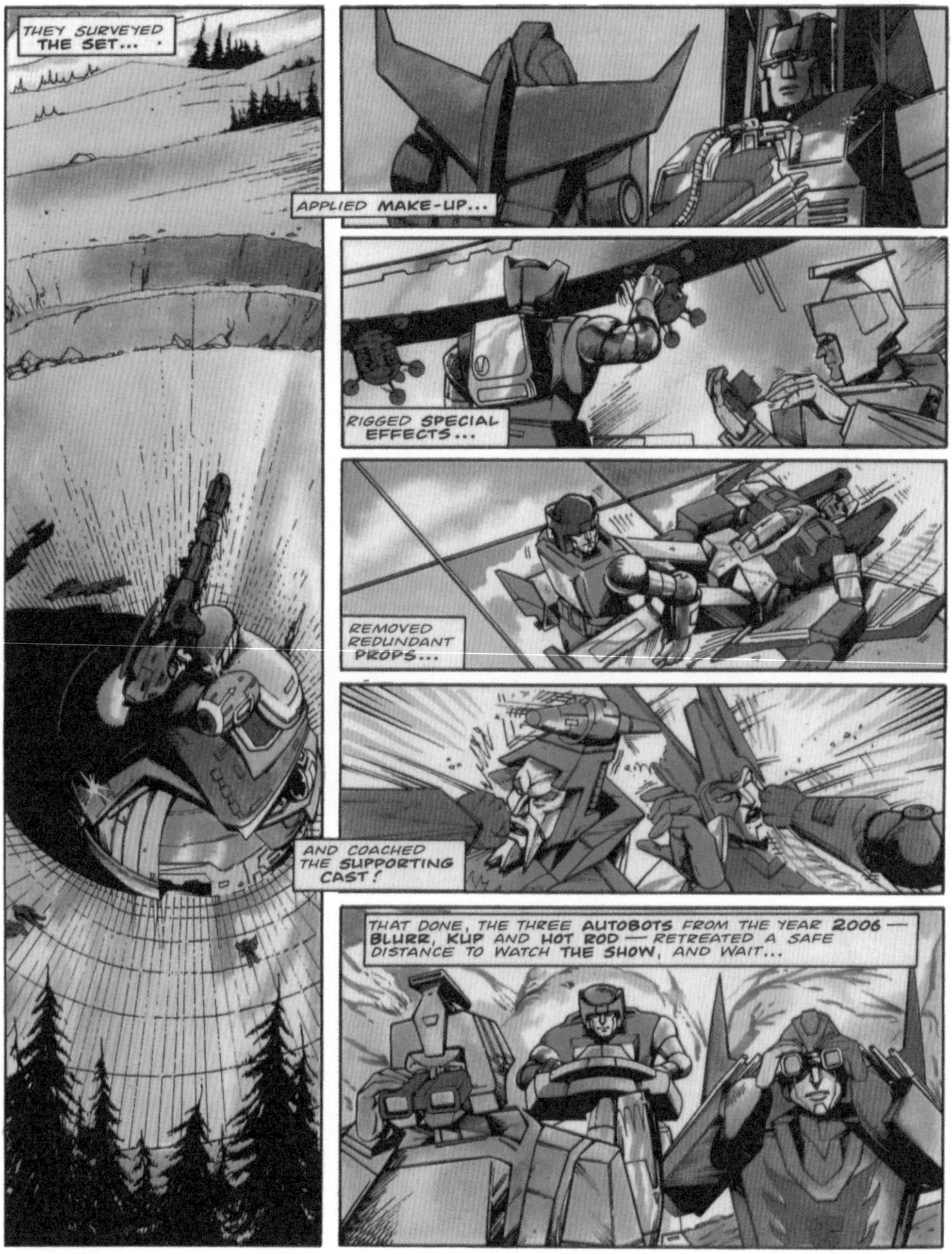
THEY SURVEYED THE SET...
APPLIED MAKE-UP...
RIGGED SPECIAL EFFECTS...
REMOVED REDUNDANT PROPS...
AND COACHED THE SUPPORTING CAST!
THAT DONE, THE THREE AUTOBOTS FROM THE YEAR 2006 — BLURR, KUP AND HOT ROD — RETREATED A SAFE DISTANCE TO WATCH THE SHOW, AND WAIT...

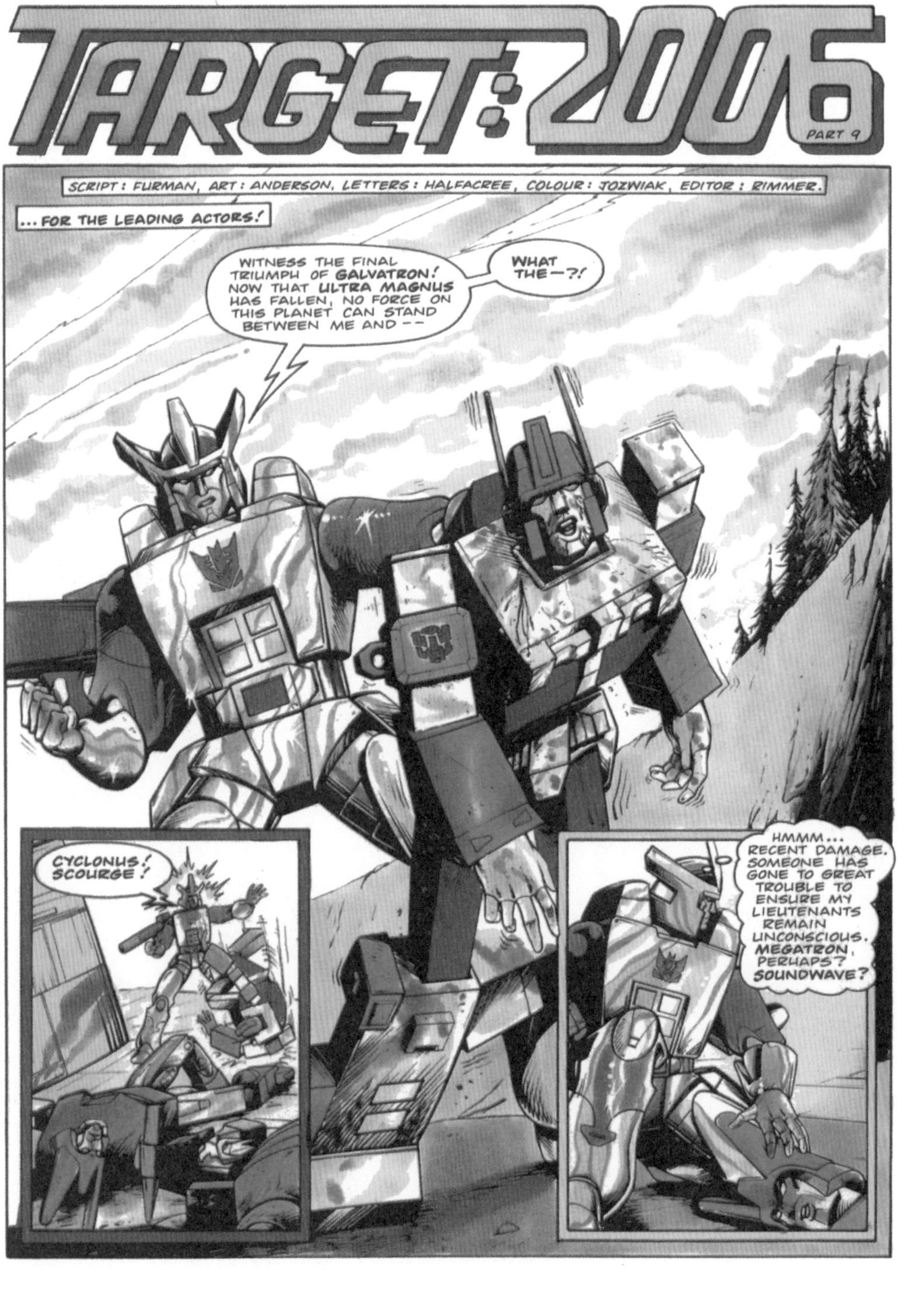
TARGET: 2006
PART 9
SCRIPT: FURMAN, ART: ANDERSON, LETTERS: HALFACREE, COLOUR: JOZWIAK, EDITOR: RIMMER.
...FOR THE LEADING ACTORS!
WITNESS THE FINAL TRIUMPH OF GALVATRON! NOW THAT ULTRA MAGNUS HAS FALLEN, NO FORCE ON THIS PLANET CAN STAND BETWEEN ME AND --
WHAT THE--?!
CYCLONUS! SCOURGE!
HMMM... RECENT DAMAGE. SOMEONE HAS GONE TO GREAT TROUBLE TO ENSURE MY LIEUTENANTS REMAIN UNCONSCIOUS. MEGATRON, PERHAPS? SOUNDWAVE?

NO. BOTH STILL LIE WHERE THEY FELL— ALIVE BUT DEFINITELY UNCONSCIOUS. THEN WHO—?

OF COURSE!

I SHOULD HAVE REALISED HE WAS NOT TO BE TRUSTED FOR EVEN THE FEW MOMENTS HE WAS OUT OF MY SIGHT!

DAMN YOU, STARSCREAM!

HIT IT!

OKAY, HE'S GOT THE RIGHT MESSAGE, I MEAN THE WRONG MESSAGE, I MEAN... AW HECK—

NO! WAIT!

MAGNUS HAS JUST PUT HIMSELF IN THE FIRING LINE!

UNGGH... H-HASN'T SEEN ME YET. HURT REAL BAD—ACK—IF I CAN JUST HOLD HIM FOR A WHILE... GIVE KUP AND THE OTHERS A CHANCE TO PUT WHAT-EVER THEIR PLAN IS INTO OPERATION!

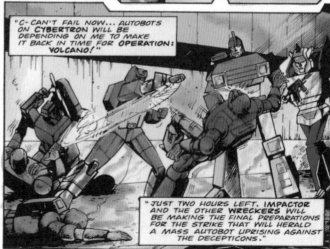

"C-CAN'T FAIL NOW... AUTOBOTS ON CYBERTRON WILL BE DEPENDING ON ME TO MAKE IT BACK IN TIME FOR OPERATION: VOLCANO!"

"JUST TWO HOURS LEFT. IMPACTOR AND THE OTHER WRECKERS WILL BE MAKING THE FINAL PREPARATIONS FOR THE STRIKE THAT WILL HERALD A MASS AUTOBOT UPRISING AGAINST THE DECEPTICONS."

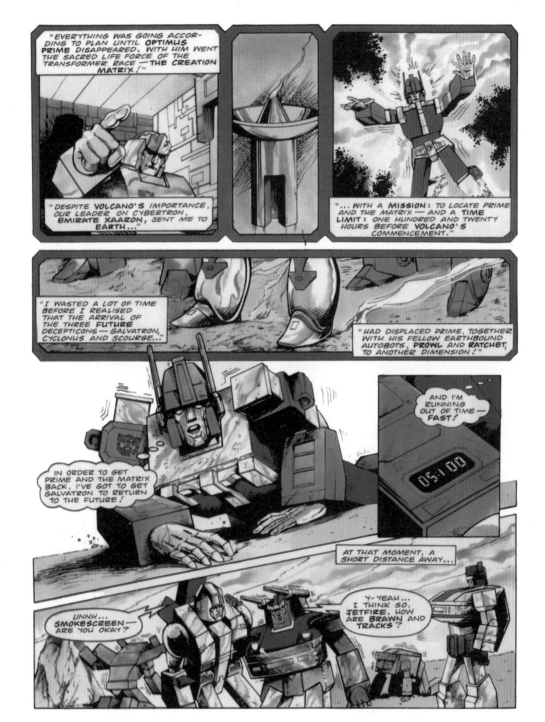

"EVERYTHING WAS GOING ACCORDING TO PLAN UNTIL OPTIMUS PRIME DISAPPEARED. WITH HIM WENT THE SACRED LIFE FORCE OF THE TRANSFORMER RACE — THE CREATION MATRIX!"

"DESPITE VOLCANO'S IMPORTANCE, OUR LEADER ON CYBERTRON, EMIRATE XAARON, SENT ME TO EARTH..."

"...WITH A MISSION: TO LOCATE PRIME AND THE MATRIX — AND A TIME LIMIT: ONE HUNDRED AND TWENTY HOURS BEFORE VOLCANO'S COMMENCEMENT."

"I WASTED A LOT OF TIME BEFORE I REALISED THAT THE ARRIVAL OF THE THREE FUTURE DECEPTICONS — GALVATRON, CYCLONUS AND SCOURGE..."

"HAD DISPLACED PRIME, TOGETHER WITH HIS FELLOW EARTHBOUND AUTOBOTS, PROWL AND RATCHET, TO ANOTHER DIMENSION!"

IN ORDER TO GET PRIME AND THE MATRIX BACK, I'VE GOT TO GET GALVATRON TO RETURN TO THE FUTURE!

AND I'M RUNNING OUT OF TIME — FAST!

05:10:00

AT THAT MOMENT, A SHORT DISTANCE AWAY...

UNNH... SMOKESCREEN— ARE YOU OKAY?

Y-YEAH... I THINK SO, JETFIRE. HOW ARE BRAWN AND TRACKS?

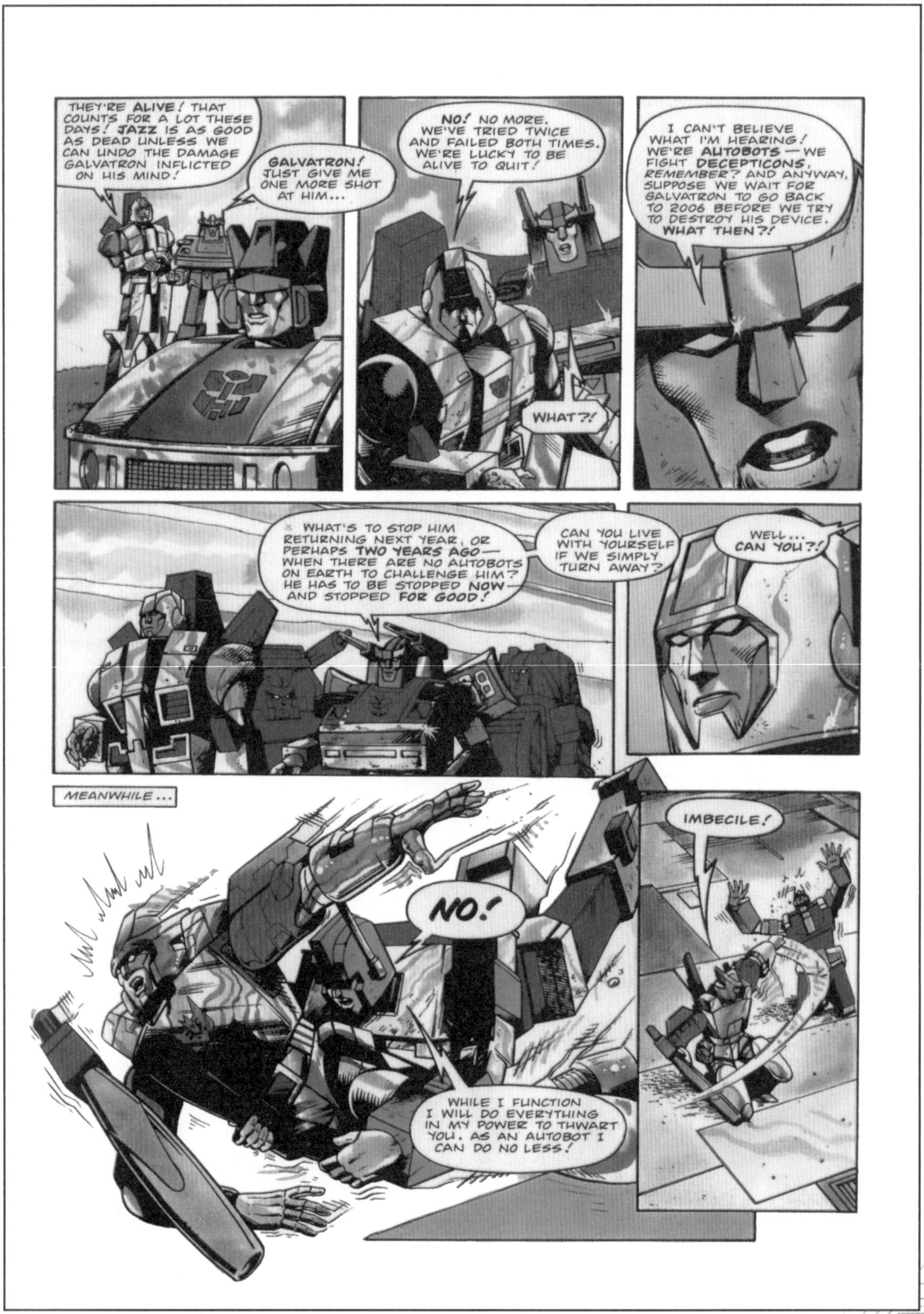
THEY'RE ALIVE! THAT COUNTS FOR A LOT THESE DAYS! JAZZ IS AS GOOD AS DEAD UNLESS WE CAN UNDO THE DAMAGE GALVATRON INFLICTED ON HIS MIND!
GALVATRON! JUST GIVE ME ONE MORE SHOT AT HIM...
NO! NO MORE. WE'VE TRIED TWICE AND FAILED BOTH TIMES. WE'RE LUCKY TO BE ALIVE TO QUIT!
WHAT?!
I CAN'T BELIEVE WHAT I'M HEARING! WE'RE AUTOBOTS — WE FIGHT DECEPTICONS, REMEMBER? AND ANYWAY, SUPPOSE WE WAIT FOR GALVATRON TO GO BACK TO 2006 BEFORE WE TRY TO DESTROY HIS DEVICE. WHAT THEN?!
WHAT'S TO STOP HIM RETURNING NEXT YEAR, OR PERHAPS TWO YEARS AGO— WHEN THERE ARE NO AUTOBOTS ON EARTH TO CHALLENGE HIM? HE HAS TO BE STOPPED NOW— AND STOPPED FOR GOOD!
CAN YOU LIVE WITH YOURSELF IF WE SIMPLY TURN AWAY?
WELL... CAN YOU?!
MEANWHILE...
NO!
WHILE I FUNCTION I WILL DO EVERYTHING IN MY POWER TO THWART YOU. AS AN AUTOBOT I CAN DO NO LESS!
IMBECILE!

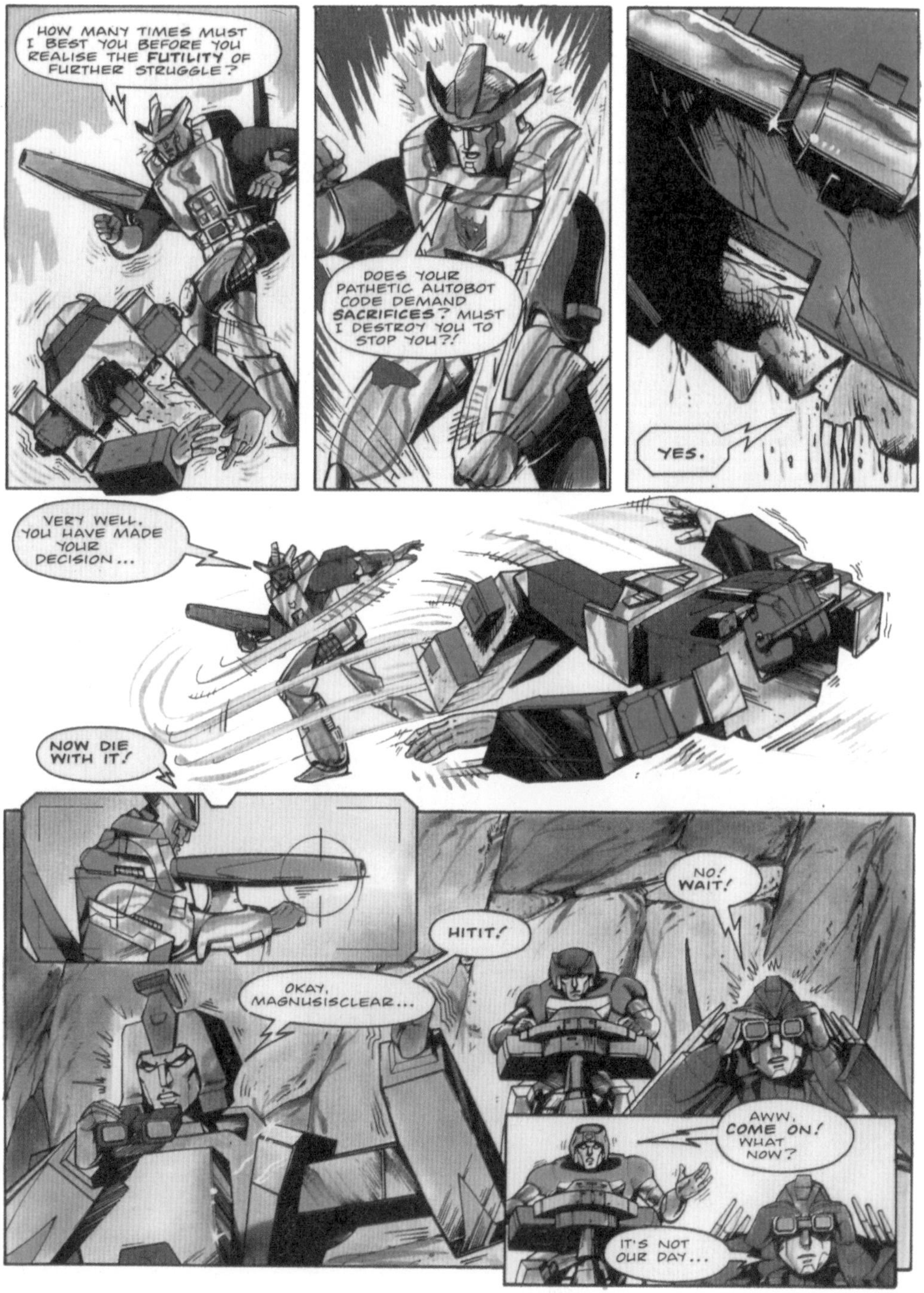
HOW MANY TIMES MUST I BEST YOU BEFORE YOU REALISE THE **FUTILITY** OF FURTHER STRUGGLE?
DOES YOUR PATHETIC AUTOBOT CODE DEMAND **SACRIFICES**? MUST I DESTROY YOU TO STOP YOU?!
YES.
VERY WELL. YOU HAVE MADE YOUR DECISION...
NOW DIE WITH IT!
NO! **WAIT!**
HITIT!
OKAY, MAGNUSISCLEAR...
AWW, **COME ON!** WHAT NOW?
IT'S NOT OUR DAY...

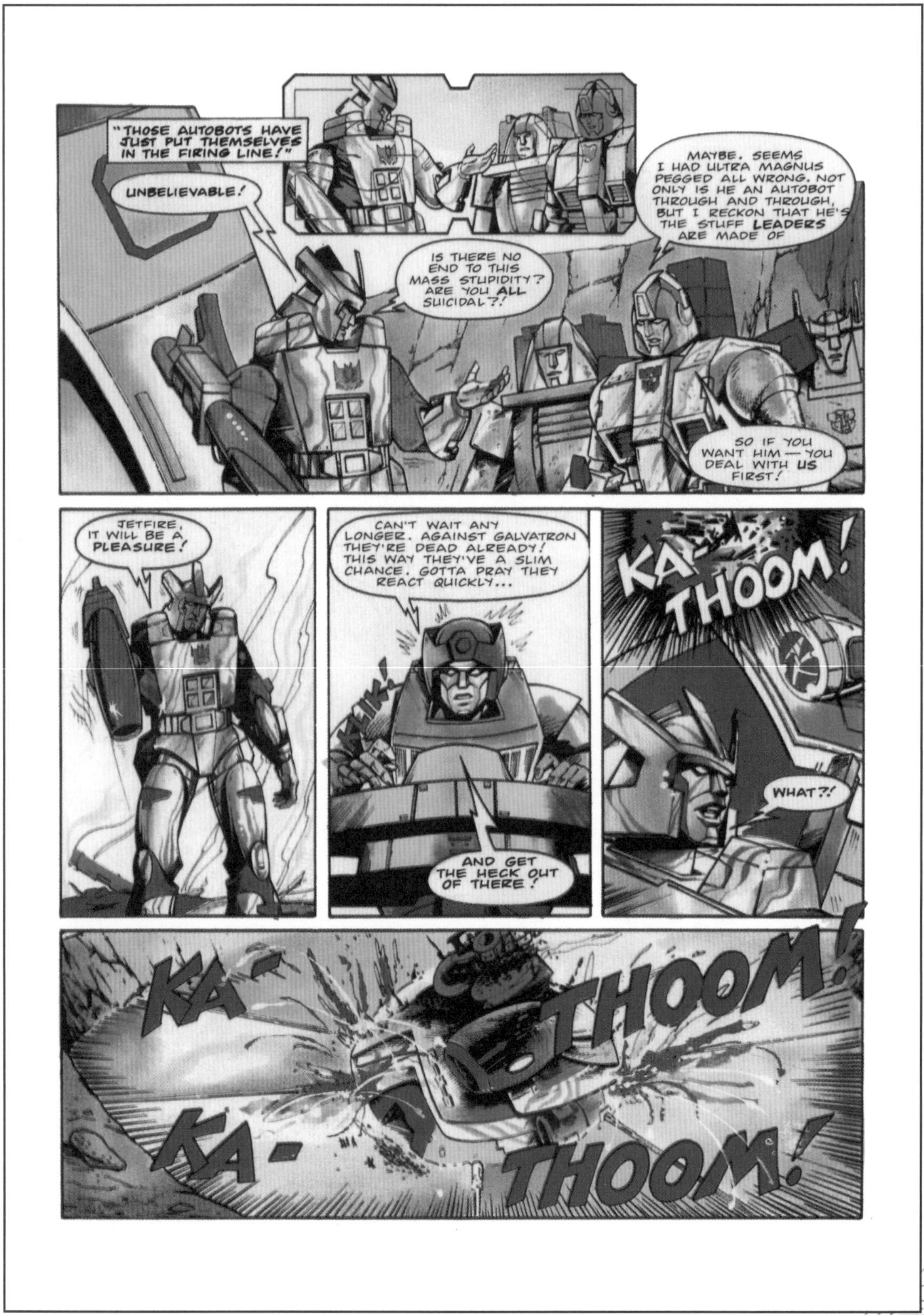
"THOSE AUTOBOTS HAVE JUST PUT THEMSELVES IN THE FIRING LINE!"
UNBELIEVABLE!
IS THERE NO END TO THIS MASS STUPIDITY? ARE YOU ALL SUICIDAL?!
MAYBE. SEEMS I HAD ULTRA MAGNUS PEGGED ALL WRONG. NOT ONLY IS HE AN AUTOBOT THROUGH AND THROUGH, BUT I RECKON THAT HE'S THE STUFF LEADERS ARE MADE OF
SO IF YOU WANT HIM — YOU DEAL WITH US FIRST!
JETFIRE, IT WILL BE A PLEASURE!
CAN'T WAIT ANY LONGER. AGAINST GALVATRON THEY'RE DEAD ALREADY! THIS WAY THEY'VE A SLIM CHANCE. GOTTA PRAY THEY REACT QUICKLY...
AND GET THE HECK OUT OF THERE!
KA-THOOM!
WHAT?!
KA-THOOM!
KA-THOOM!

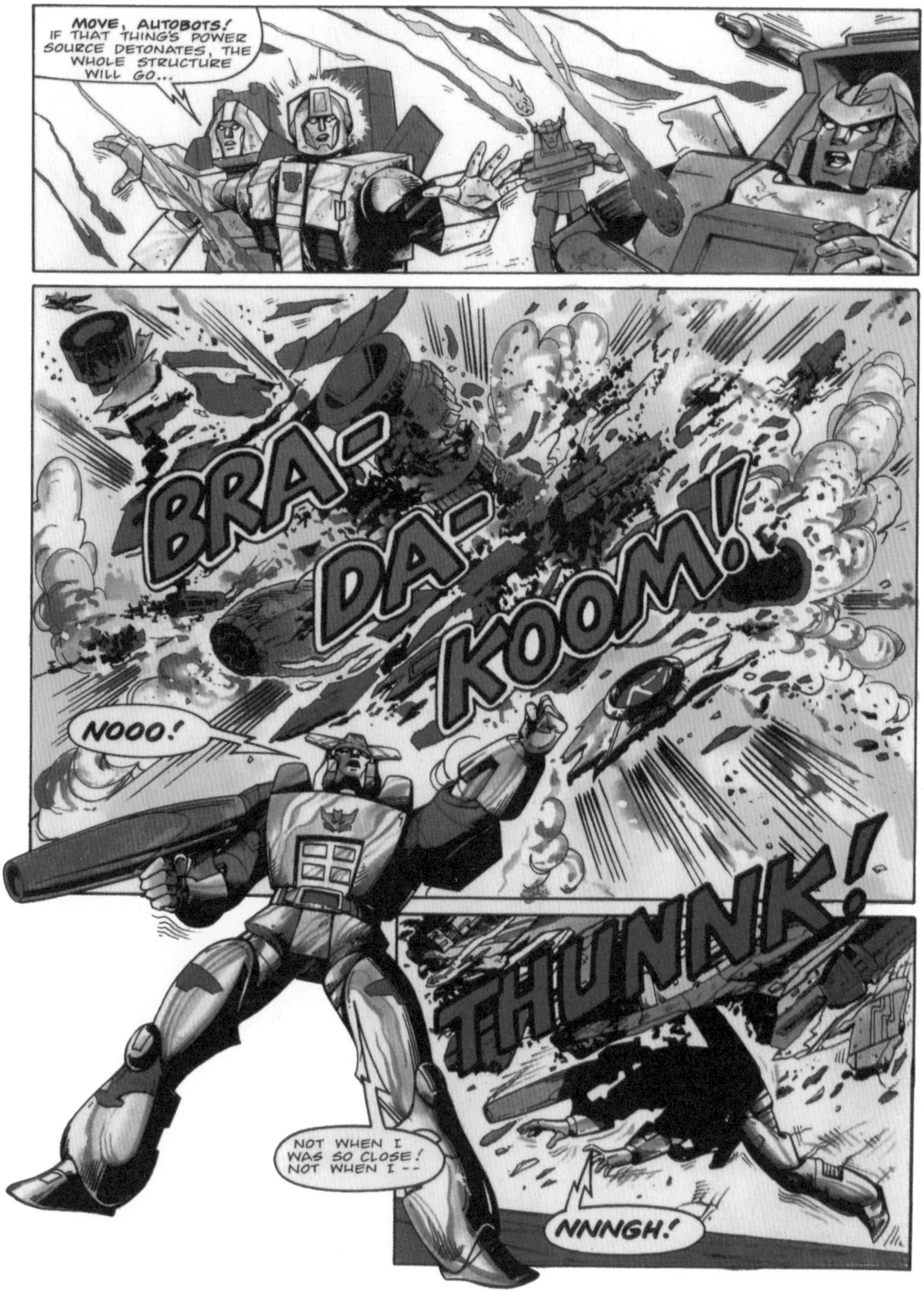

MOVE, AUTOBOTS! IF THAT THING'S POWER SOURCE DETONATES, THE WHOLE STRUCTURE WILL GO...
BRA-DA-KOOM!
NOOO!
THUNNK!
NOT WHEN I WAS SO CLOSE! NOT WHEN I --
NNNGH!

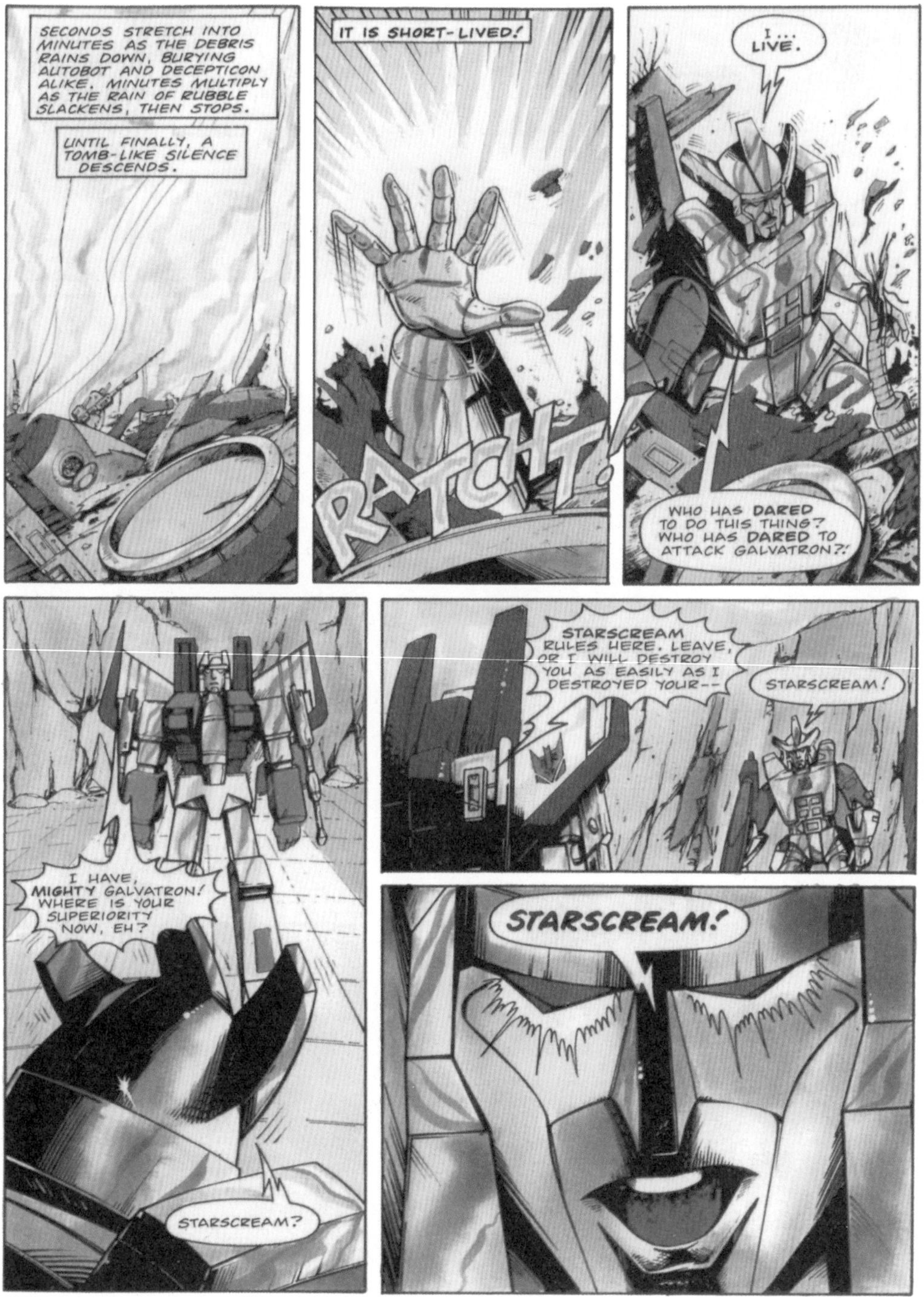
SECONDS STRETCH INTO MINUTES AS THE DEBRIS RAINS DOWN, BURYING AUTOBOT AND DECEPTICON ALIKE. MINUTES MULTIPLY AS THE RAIN OF RUBBLE SLACKENS, THEN STOPS.
UNTIL FINALLY, A TOMB-LIKE SILENCE DESCENDS.
IT IS SHORT-LIVED!
RATCHT!
I... LIVE.
WHO HAS DARED TO DO THIS THING? WHO HAS DARED TO ATTACK GALVATRON?!
I HAVE, MIGHTY GALVATRON! WHERE IS YOUR SUPERIORITY NOW, EH?
STARSCREAM?
STARSCREAM RULES HERE. LEAVE, OR I WILL DESTROY YOU AS EASILY AS I DESTROYED YOUR--
STARSCREAM!
STARSCREAM!

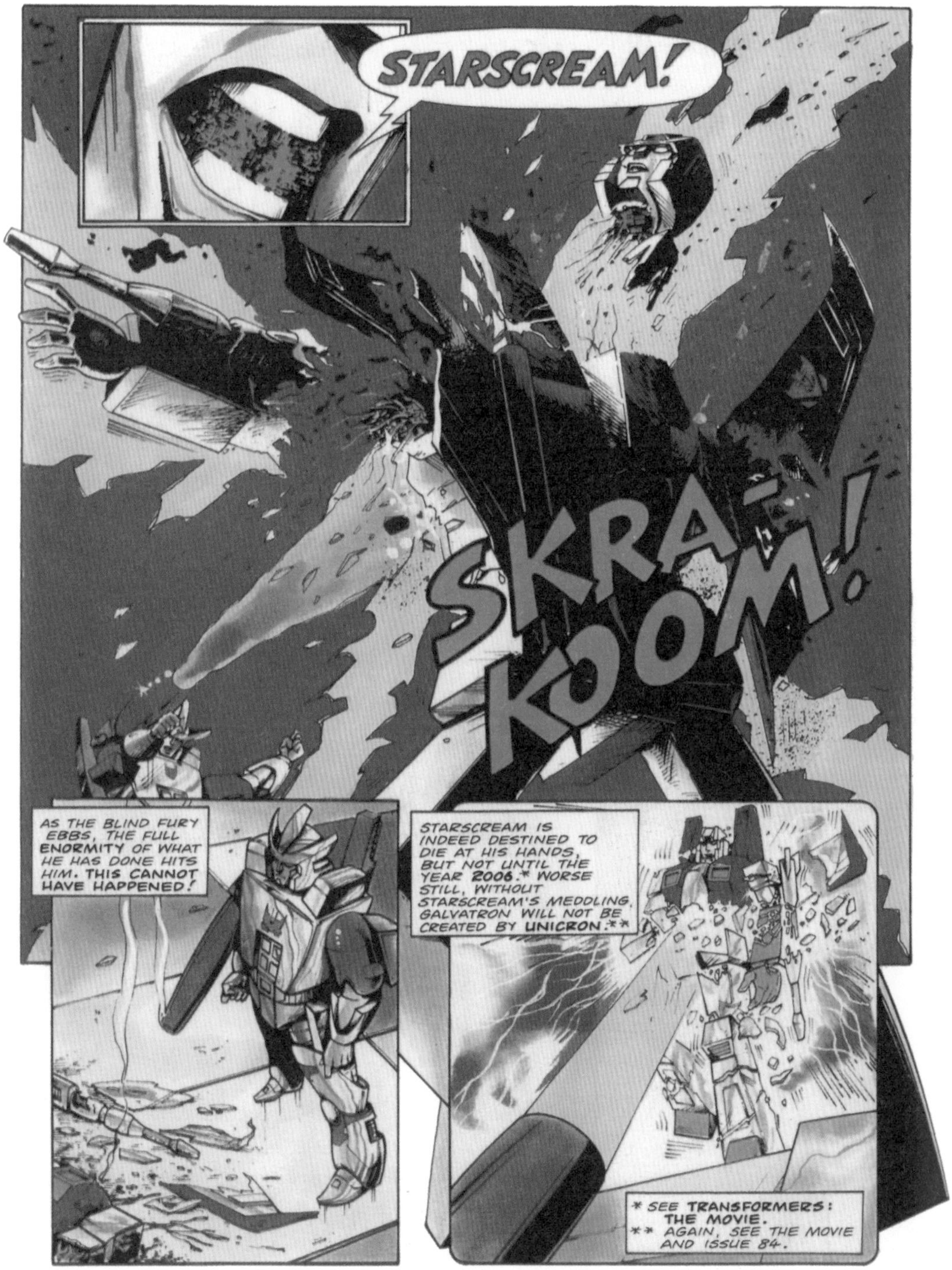

STARSCREAM!
SKRA-KOOM!
AS THE BLIND FURY EBBS, THE FULL ENORMITY OF WHAT HE HAS DONE HITS HIM. THIS CANNOT HAVE HAPPENED!
STARSCREAM IS INDEED DESTINED TO DIE AT HIS HANDS, BUT NOT UNTIL THE YEAR 2006.* WORSE STILL, WITHOUT STARSCREAM'S MEDDLING, GALVATRON WILL NOT BE CREATED BY UNICRON.**
* SEE TRANSFORMERS: THE MOVIE.
** AGAIN, SEE THE MOVIE AND ISSUE 84.

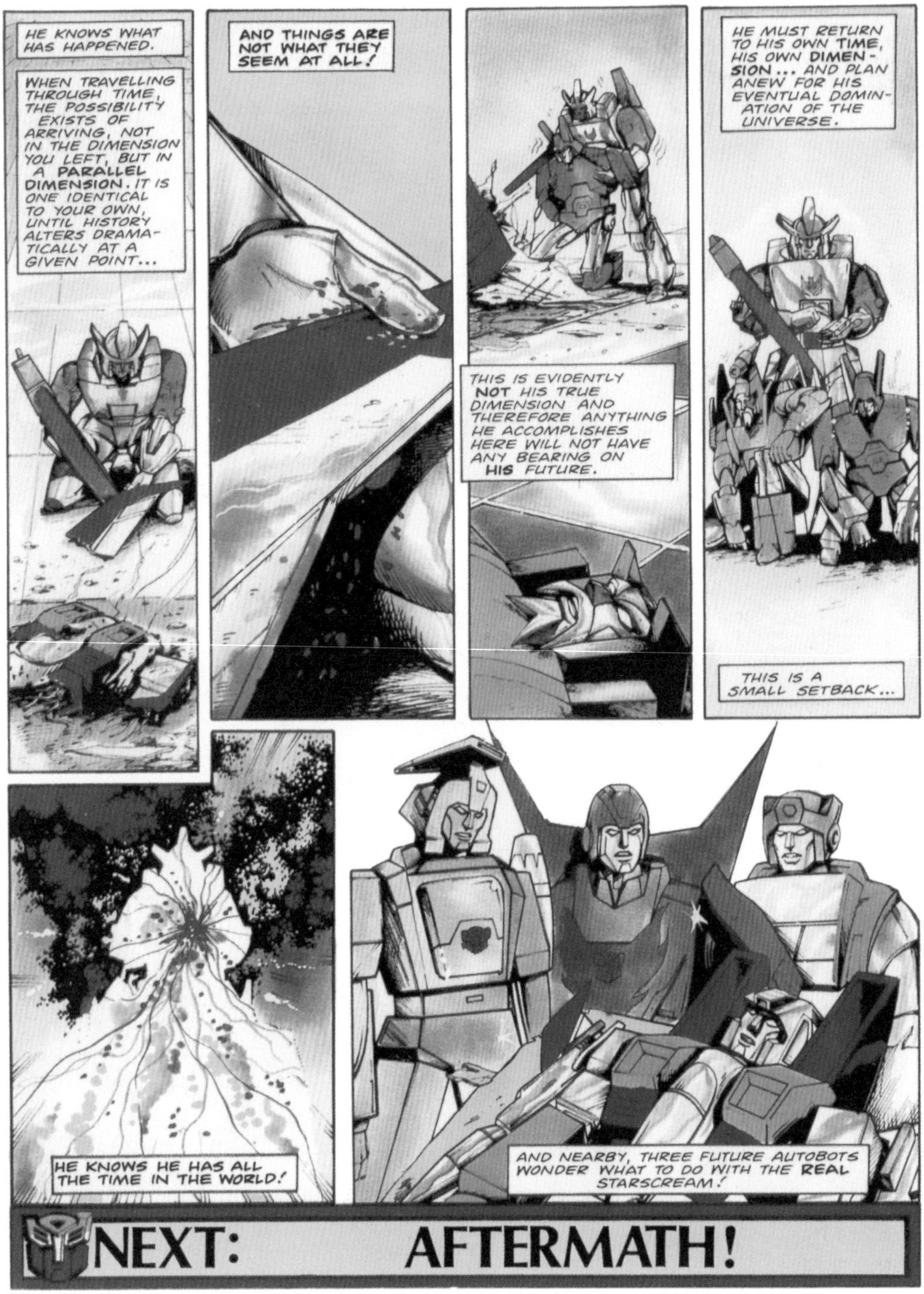

HE KNOWS WHAT HAS HAPPENED.
WHEN TRAVELLING THROUGH TIME, THE POSSIBILITY EXISTS OF ARRIVING, NOT IN THE DIMENSION YOU LEFT, BUT IN A PARALLEL DIMENSION. IT IS ONE IDENTICAL TO YOUR OWN, UNTIL HISTORY ALTERS DRAMATICALLY AT A GIVEN POINT...
AND THINGS ARE NOT WHAT THEY SEEM AT ALL!
THIS IS EVIDENTLY NOT HIS TRUE DIMENSION AND THEREFORE ANYTHING HE ACCOMPLISHES HERE WILL NOT HAVE ANY BEARING ON HIS FUTURE.
HE MUST RETURN TO HIS OWN TIME, HIS OWN DIMENSION... AND PLAN ANEW FOR HIS EVENTUAL DOMINATION OF THE UNIVERSE.
THIS IS A SMALL SETBACK...
HE KNOWS HE HAS ALL THE TIME IN THE WORLD!
AND NEARBY, THREE FUTURE AUTOBOTS WONDER WHAT TO DO WITH THE REAL STARSCREAM!
NEXT: AFTERMATH!

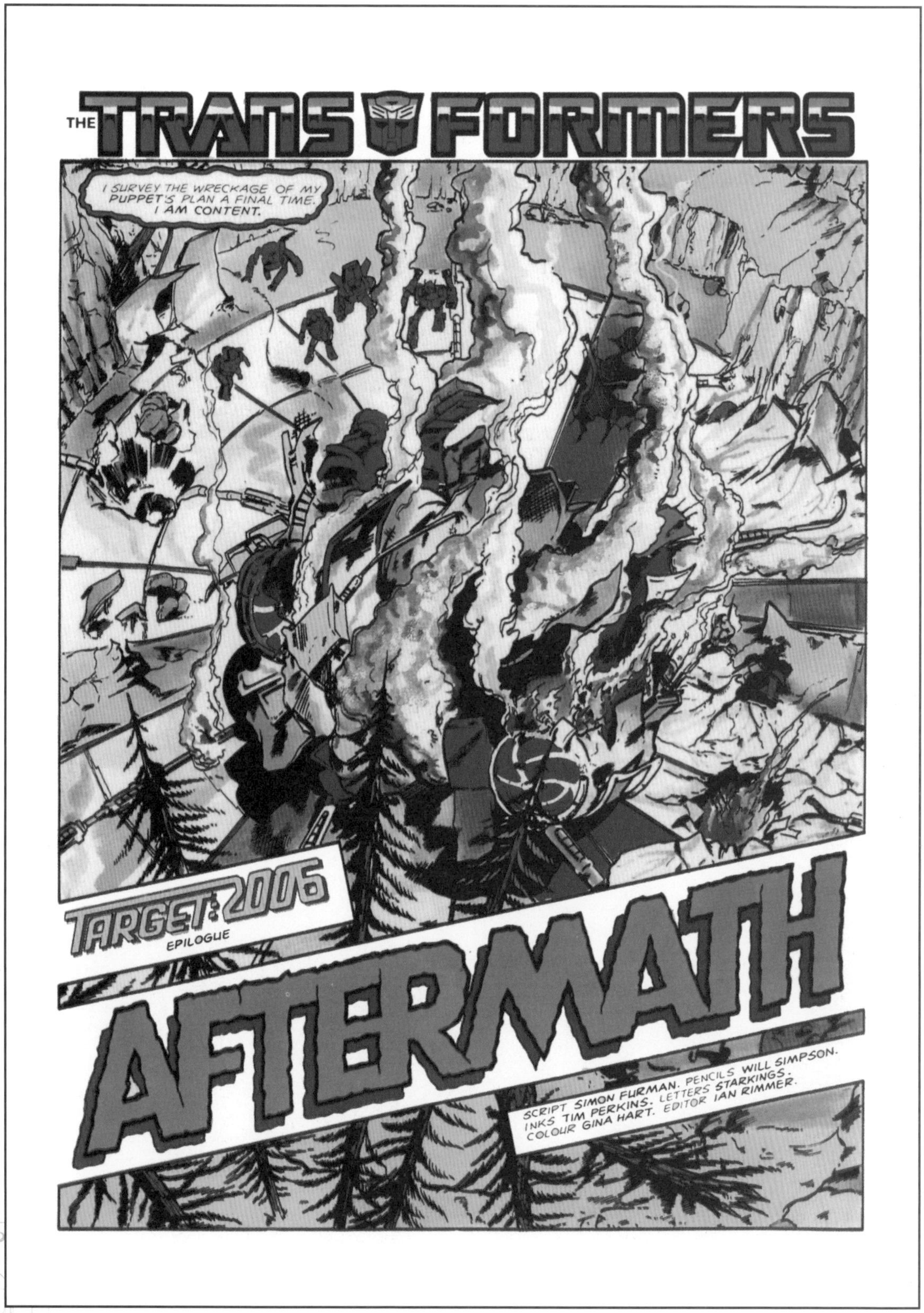
THE TRANSFORMERS
I SURVEY THE WRECKAGE OF MY PUPPET'S PLAN A FINAL TIME. I AM CONTENT.
TARGET: 2006
EPILOGUE
AFTERMATH
SCRIPT SIMON FURMAN. PENCILS WILL SIMPSON.
INKS TIM PERKINS. LETTERS STARKINGS.
COLOUR GINA HART. EDITOR IAN RIMMER.

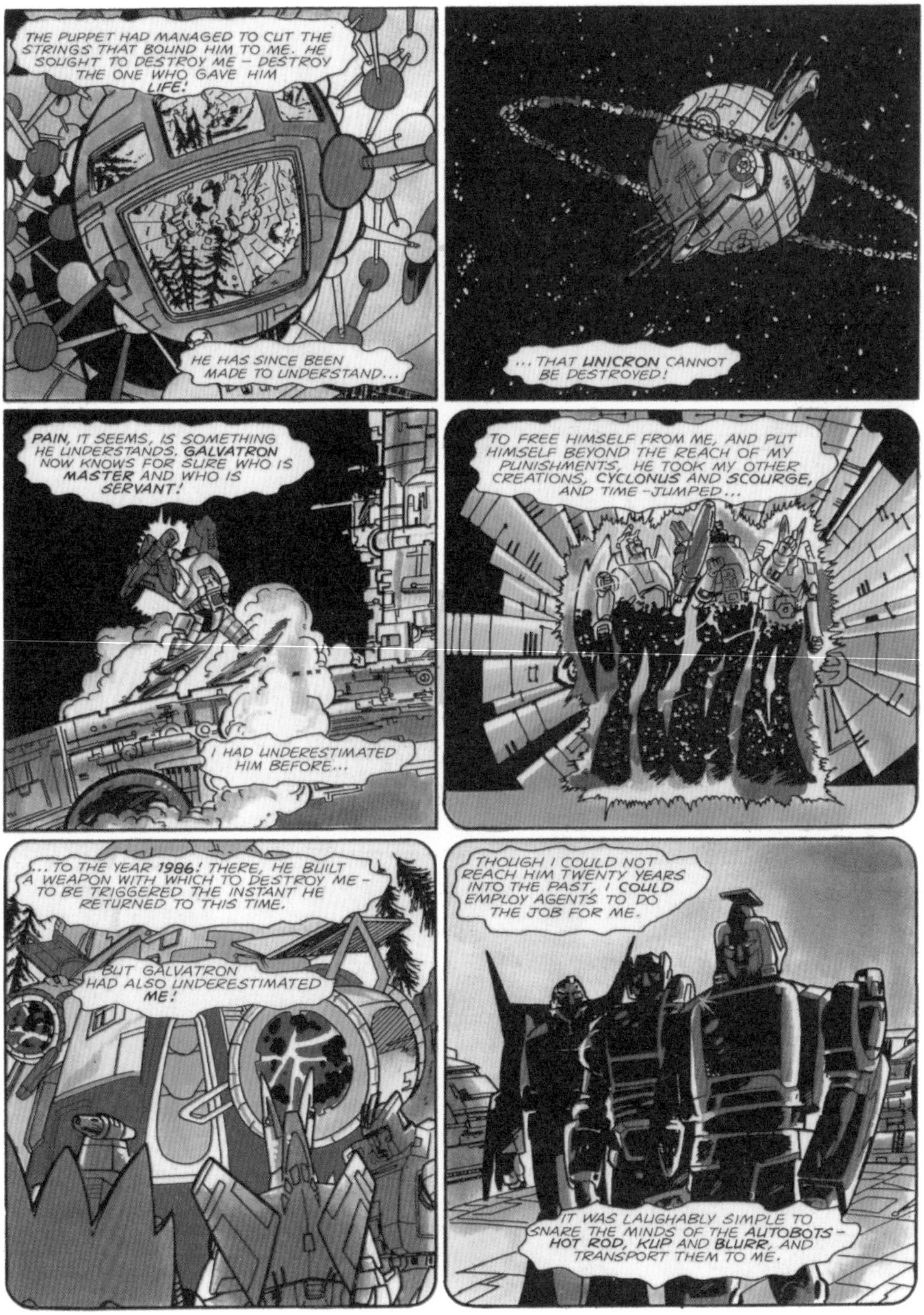
THE PUPPET HAD MANAGED TO CUT THE STRINGS THAT BOUND HIM TO ME. HE SOUGHT TO DESTROY ME – DESTROY THE ONE WHO GAVE HIM LIFE!
HE HAS SINCE BEEN MADE TO UNDERSTAND...
...THAT UNICRON CANNOT BE DESTROYED!
PAIN, IT SEEMS, IS SOMETHING HE UNDERSTANDS. GALVATRON NOW KNOWS FOR SURE WHO IS MASTER AND WHO IS SERVANT!
I HAD UNDERESTIMATED HIM BEFORE...
TO FREE HIMSELF FROM ME, AND PUT HIMSELF BEYOND THE REACH OF MY PUNISHMENTS, HE TOOK MY OTHER CREATIONS, CYCLONUS AND SCOURGE, AND TIME-JUMPED...
...TO THE YEAR 1986! THERE, HE BUILT A WEAPON WITH WHICH TO DESTROY ME – TO BE TRIGGERED THE INSTANT HE RETURNED TO THIS TIME.
BUT GALVATRON HAD ALSO UNDERESTIMATED ME!
THOUGH I COULD NOT REACH HIM TWENTY YEARS INTO THE PAST, I COULD EMPLOY AGENTS TO DO THE JOB FOR ME.
IT WAS LAUGHABLY SIMPLE TO SNARE THE MINDS OF THE AUTOBOTS – HOT ROD, KUP AND BLURR, AND TRANSPORT THEM TO ME.

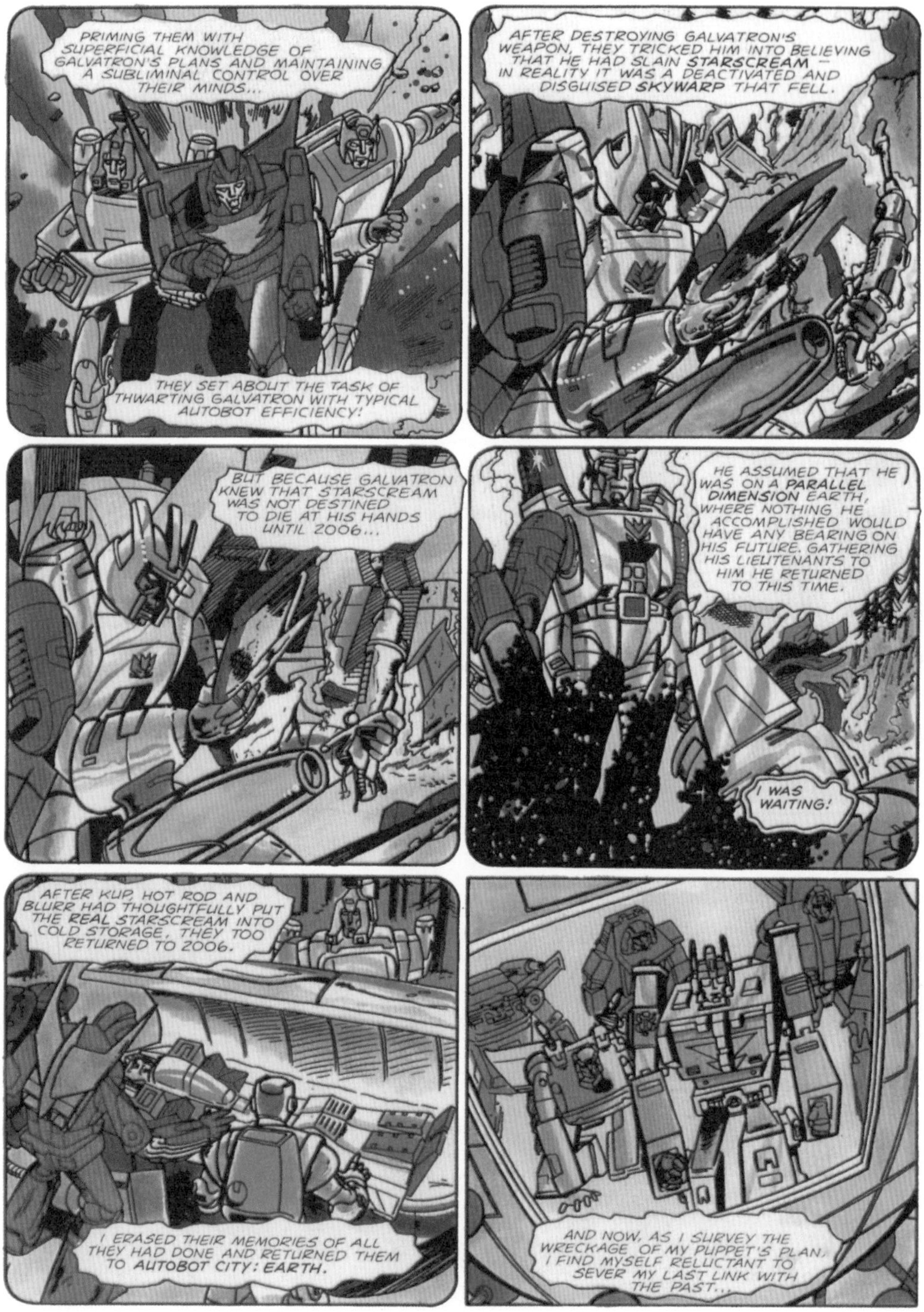
PRIMING THEM WITH SUPERFICIAL KNOWLEDGE OF GALVATRON'S PLANS AND MAINTAINING A SUBLIMINAL CONTROL OVER THEIR MINDS...
THEY SET ABOUT THE TASK OF THWARTING GALVATRON WITH TYPICAL AUTOBOT EFFICIENCY!
AFTER DESTROYING GALVATRON'S WEAPON, THEY TRICKED HIM INTO BELIEVING THAT HE HAD SLAIN STARSCREAM — IN REALITY IT WAS A DEACTIVATED AND DISGUISED SKYWARP THAT FELL.
BUT BECAUSE GALVATRON KNEW THAT STARSCREAM WAS NOT DESTINED TO DIE AT HIS HANDS UNTIL 2006...
HE ASSUMED THAT HE WAS ON A PARALLEL DIMENSION EARTH, WHERE NOTHING HE ACCOMPLISHED WOULD HAVE ANY BEARING ON HIS FUTURE. GATHERING HIS LIEUTENANTS TO HIM HE RETURNED TO THIS TIME.
I WAS WAITING!
AFTER KUP, HOT ROD AND BLURR HAD THOUGHTFULLY PUT THE REAL STARSCREAM INTO COLD STORAGE, THEY TOO RETURNED TO 2006.
I ERASED THEIR MEMORIES OF ALL THEY HAD DONE AND RETURNED THEM TO AUTOBOT CITY: EARTH.
AND NOW, AS I SURVEY THE WRECKAGE OF MY PUPPET'S PLAN, I FIND MYSELF RELUCTANT TO SEVER MY LAST LINK WITH THE PAST...

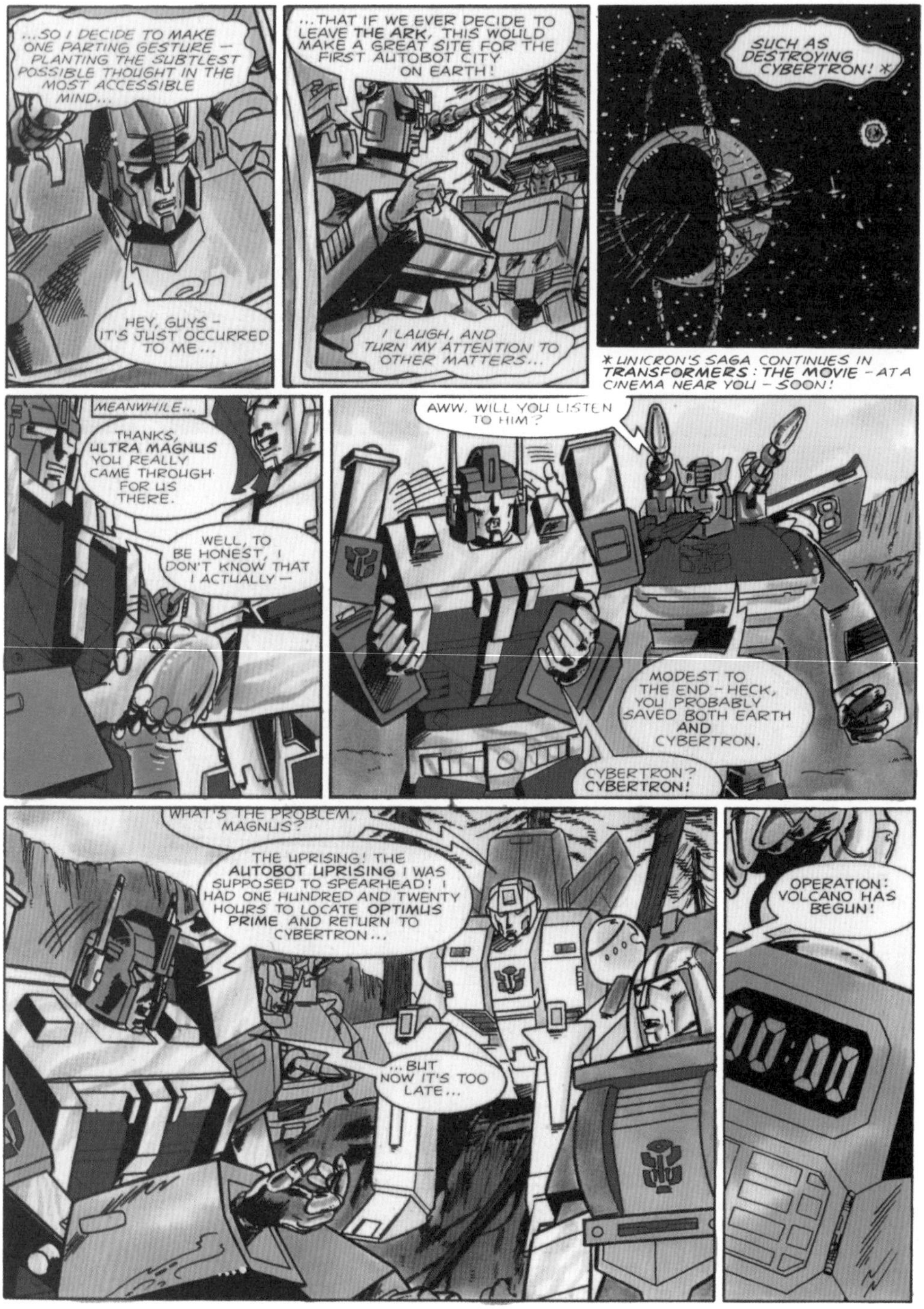
...SO I DECIDE TO MAKE ONE PARTING GESTURE — PLANTING THE SUBTLEST POSSIBLE THOUGHT IN THE MOST ACCESSIBLE MIND...
HEY, GUYS — IT'S JUST OCCURRED TO ME...
...THAT IF WE EVER DECIDE TO LEAVE THE ARK, THIS WOULD MAKE A GREAT SITE FOR THE FIRST AUTOBOT CITY ON EARTH!
I LAUGH, AND TURN MY ATTENTION TO OTHER MATTERS...
SUCH AS DESTROYING CYBERTRON! *
* UNICRON'S SAGA CONTINUES IN TRANSFORMERS: THE MOVIE - AT A CINEMA NEAR YOU - SOON!
MEANWHILE...
THANKS, ULTRA MAGNUS YOU REALLY CAME THROUGH FOR US THERE.
WELL, TO BE HONEST, I DON'T KNOW THAT I ACTUALLY —
AWW, WILL YOU LISTEN TO HIM?
MODEST TO THE END - HECK, YOU PROBABLY SAVED BOTH EARTH AND CYBERTRON.
CYBERTRON? CYBERTRON!
WHAT'S THE PROBLEM, MAGNUS?
THE UPRISING! THE AUTOBOT UPRISING I WAS SUPPOSED TO SPEARHEAD! I HAD ONE HUNDRED AND TWENTY HOURS TO LOCATE OPTIMUS PRIME AND RETURN TO CYBERTRON...
...BUT NOW IT'S TOO LATE...
OPERATION: VOLCANO HAS BEGUN!
00:00

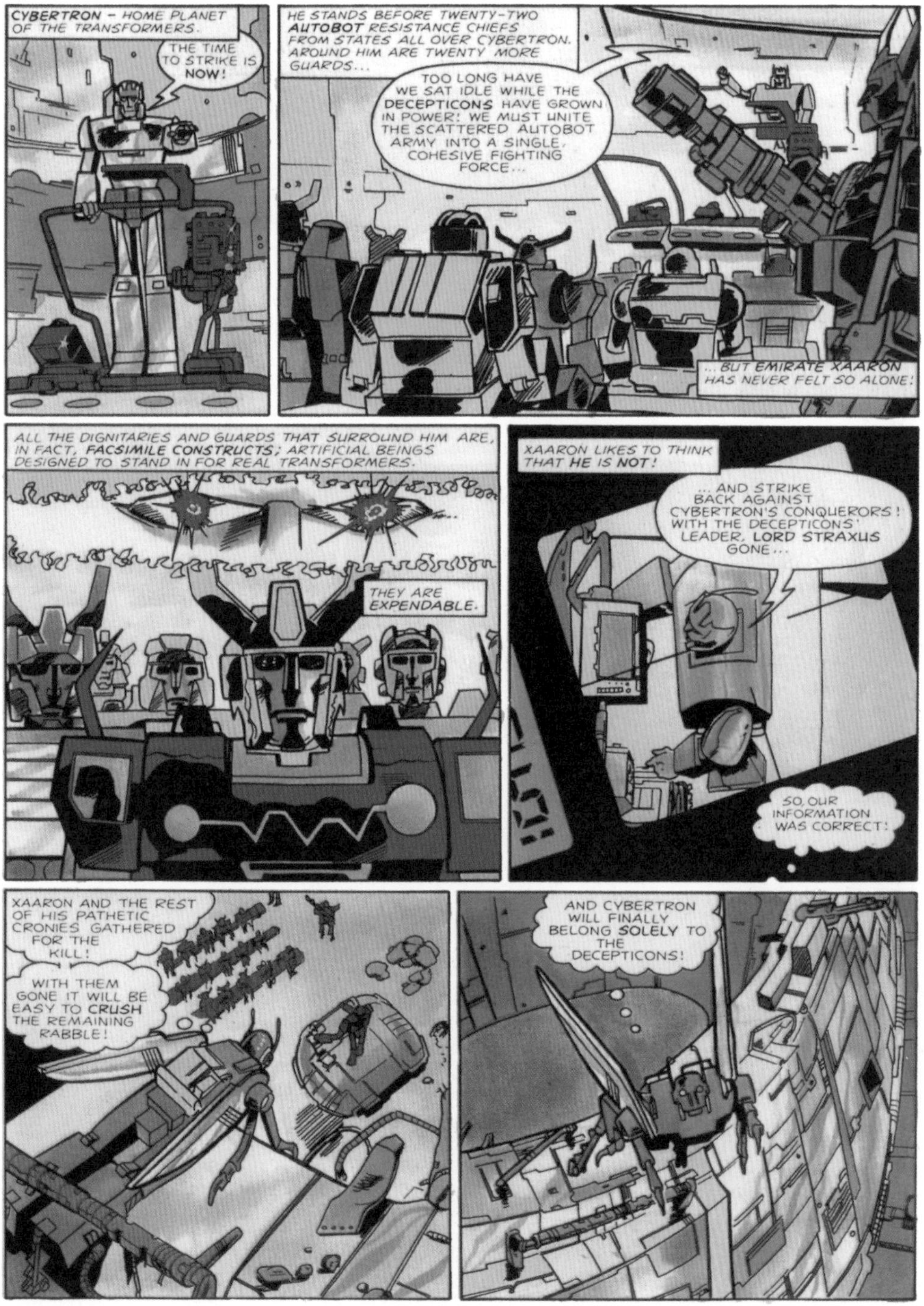
CYBERTRON – HOME PLANET OF THE TRANSFORMERS.
THE TIME TO STRIKE IS NOW!
HE STANDS BEFORE TWENTY-TWO AUTOBOT RESISTANCE CHIEFS FROM STATES ALL OVER CYBERTRON. AROUND HIM ARE TWENTY MORE GUARDS...
TOO LONG HAVE WE SAT IDLE WHILE THE DECEPTICONS HAVE GROWN IN POWER! WE MUST UNITE THE SCATTERED AUTOBOT ARMY INTO A SINGLE, COHESIVE FIGHTING FORCE...
...BUT EMIRATE XAARON HAS NEVER FELT SO ALONE!
ALL THE DIGNITARIES AND GUARDS THAT SURROUND HIM ARE, IN FACT, FACSIMILE CONSTRUCTS; ARTIFICIAL BEINGS DESIGNED TO STAND IN FOR REAL TRANSFORMERS.
THEY ARE EXPENDABLE.
XAARON LIKES TO THINK THAT HE IS NOT!
...AND STRIKE BACK AGAINST CYBERTRON'S CONQUERORS! WITH THE DECEPTICONS' LEADER, LORD STRAXUS GONE...
SO, OUR INFORMATION WAS CORRECT!
XAARON AND THE REST OF HIS PATHETIC CRONIES GATHERED FOR THE KILL!
WITH THEM GONE IT WILL BE EASY TO CRUSH THE REMAINING RABBLE!
AND CYBERTRON WILL FINALLY BELONG SOLELY TO THE DECEPTICONS!

BUT, WITHIN THE WALLS OF IACON'S IMPERIAL AMPHITHEATRE...

WELL?

IT'S WHAT WE'VE BEEN WAITING FOR, IMPACTOR. JUDGING BY THE SIZE OF OUR VISITOR, I'D SAY IT WAS ONE OF THE INSECTICONS.

IT DOESN'T MATTER WHICH — IF OUR LITTLE SET UP HAS SUCCEEDED, HE'LL BE BACK SHORTLY WITH THE OTHERS...

AND WE WRECKERS WILL BE WAITING FOR THEM!

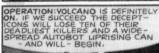

OPERATION:VOLCANO IS DEFINITELY ON. IF WE SUCCEED THE DECEPTICONS WILL LOSE TEN OF THEIR DEADLIEST KILLERS AND A WIDE-SPREAD AUTOBOT UPRISING CAN — AND WILL — BEGIN.

IF WE FAIL... WELL, I'M SURE I DON'T NEED TO TELL YOU WHAT THAT WOULD MEAN TO THE FUTURE OF THE AUTOBOTS HERE, ON CYBERTRON.

WHAT ABOUT ULTRA MAGNUS? DOESN'T HIS ABSENCE POINT TO THE FAILURE OF VOLCANO?

EVEN WITH SPRINGER, SANDSTORM AND BROADSIDE TO AUGMENT OUR STRENGTH WE'RE LIABLE TO BE OVERCOME BY SHEER WEIGHT OF NUMBERS!

WELL, ROADBUSTER... ALL I CAN SAY IS THAT IF ULTRA MAGNUS MEANS TO MAKE IT BACK FROM EARTH IN TIME TO AID US...

"HE'S CUTTING IT VERY FINE!"

EARTH — AND THE DECEPTICON, LASERBEAK, COMPLETES THE MOST DELICATE OF OPERATIONS.

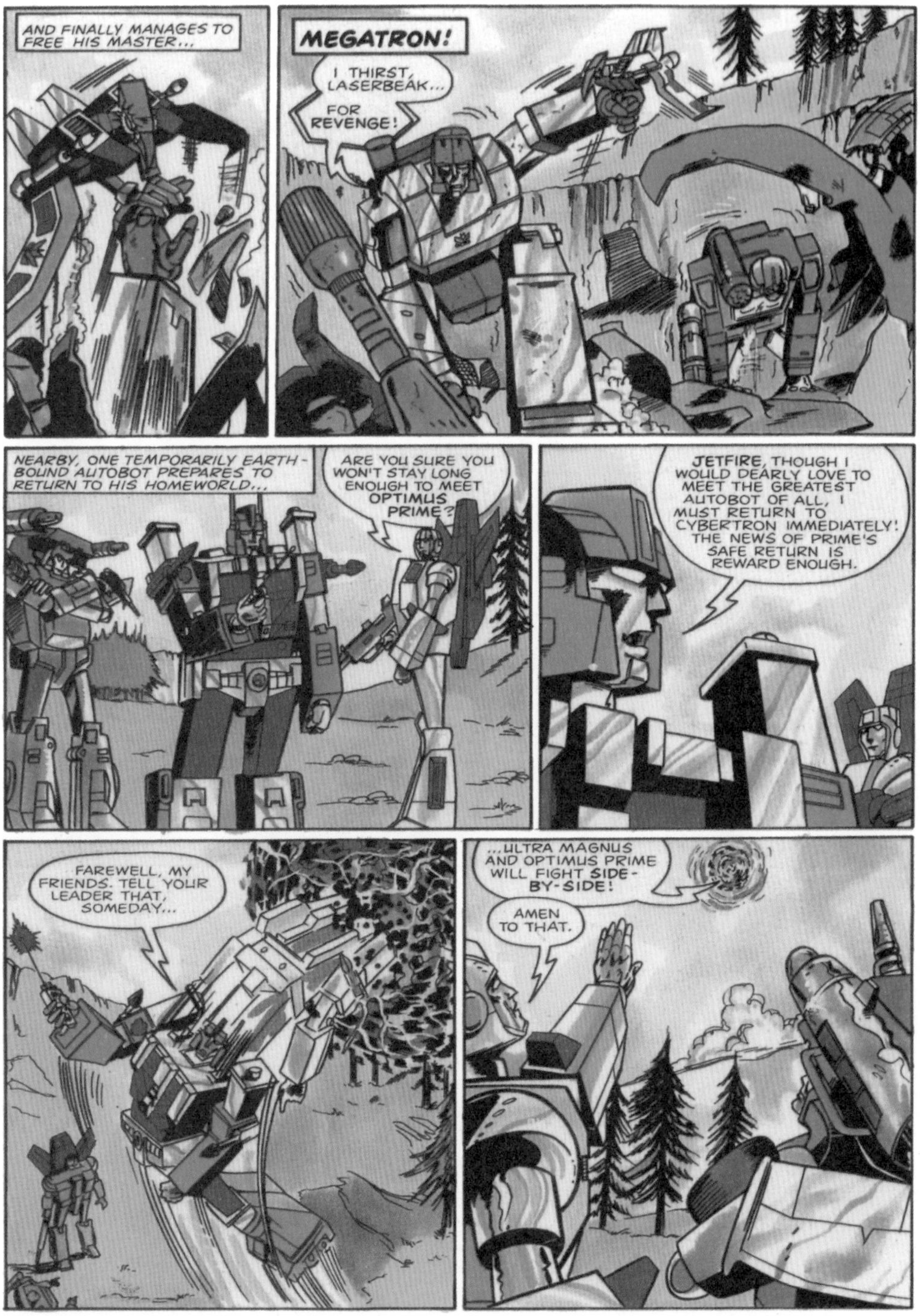
AND FINALLY MANAGES TO FREE HIS MASTER...
MEGATRON!
I THIRST, LASERBEAK...
FOR REVENGE!
NEARBY, ONE TEMPORARILY EARTH-BOUND AUTOBOT PREPARES TO RETURN TO HIS HOMEWORLD...
ARE YOU SURE YOU WON'T STAY LONG ENOUGH TO MEET OPTIMUS PRIME?
JETFIRE, THOUGH I WOULD DEARLY LOVE TO MEET THE GREATEST AUTOBOT OF ALL, I MUST RETURN TO CYBERTRON IMMEDIATELY! THE NEWS OF PRIME'S SAFE RETURN IS REWARD ENOUGH.
FAREWELL, MY FRIENDS. TELL YOUR LEADER THAT, SOMEDAY...
...ULTRA MAGNUS AND OPTIMUS PRIME WILL FIGHT SIDE-BY-SIDE!
AMEN TO THAT.

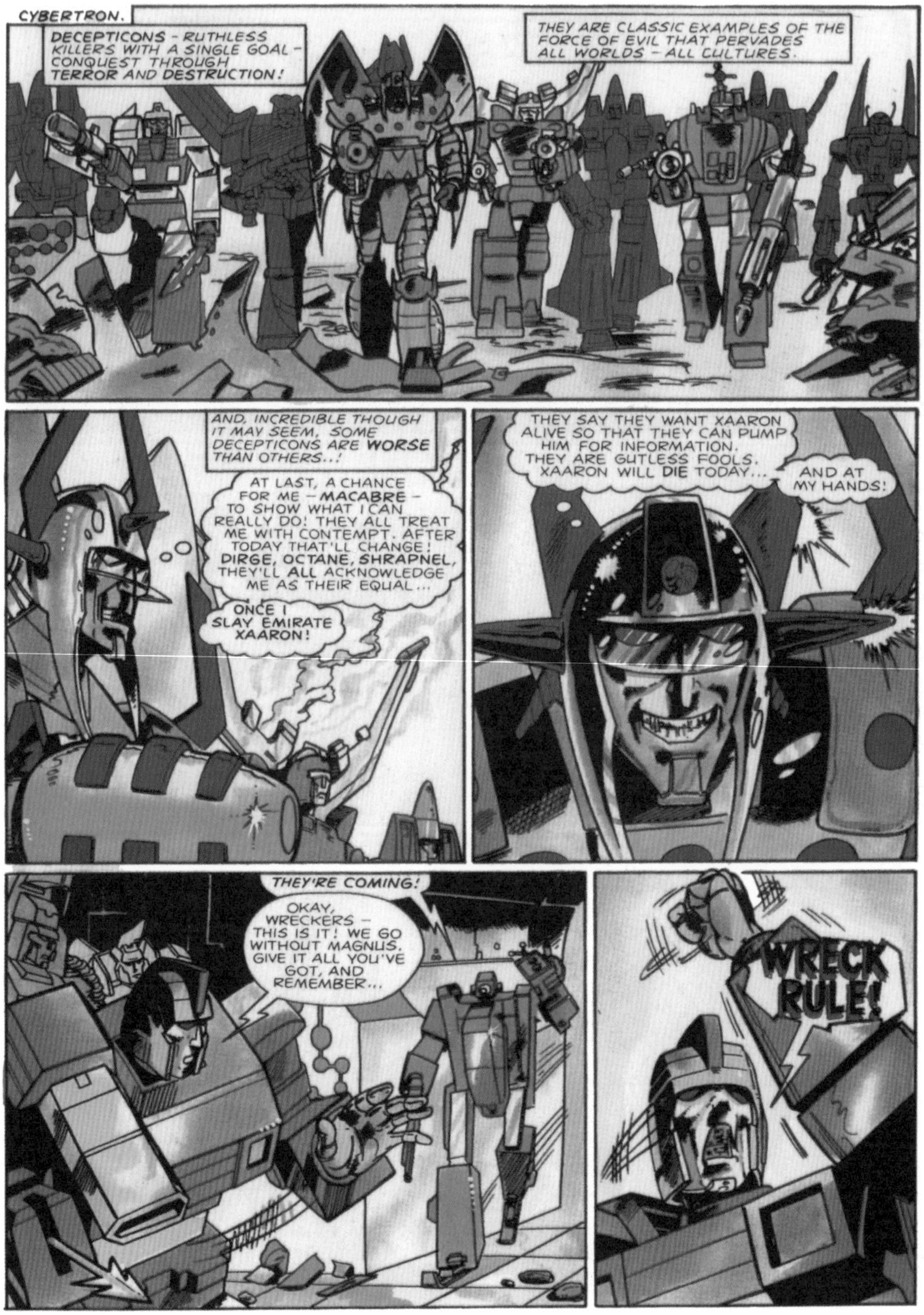
CYBERTRON.
DECEPTICONS - RUTHLESS KILLERS WITH A SINGLE GOAL - CONQUEST THROUGH TERROR AND DESTRUCTION!
THEY ARE CLASSIC EXAMPLES OF THE FORCE OF EVIL THAT PERVADES ALL WORLDS - ALL CULTURES.
AND, INCREDIBLE THOUGH IT MAY SEEM, SOME DECEPTICONS ARE WORSE THAN OTHERS...!
AT LAST, A CHANCE FOR ME - MACABRE - TO SHOW WHAT I CAN REALLY DO! THEY ALL TREAT ME WITH CONTEMPT. AFTER TODAY THAT'LL CHANGE! DIRGE, OCTANE, SHRAPNEL, THEY'LL ALL ACKNOWLEDGE ME AS THEIR EQUAL...
ONCE I SLAY EMIRATE XAARON!
THEY SAY THEY WANT XAARON ALIVE SO THAT THEY CAN PUMP HIM FOR INFORMATION. THEY ARE GUTLESS FOOLS. XAARON WILL DIE TODAY...
AND AT MY HANDS!
THEY'RE COMING!
OKAY, WRECKERS - THIS IS IT! WE GO WITHOUT MAGNUS. GIVE IT ALL YOU'VE GOT, AND REMEMBER...
WRECK AND RULE!

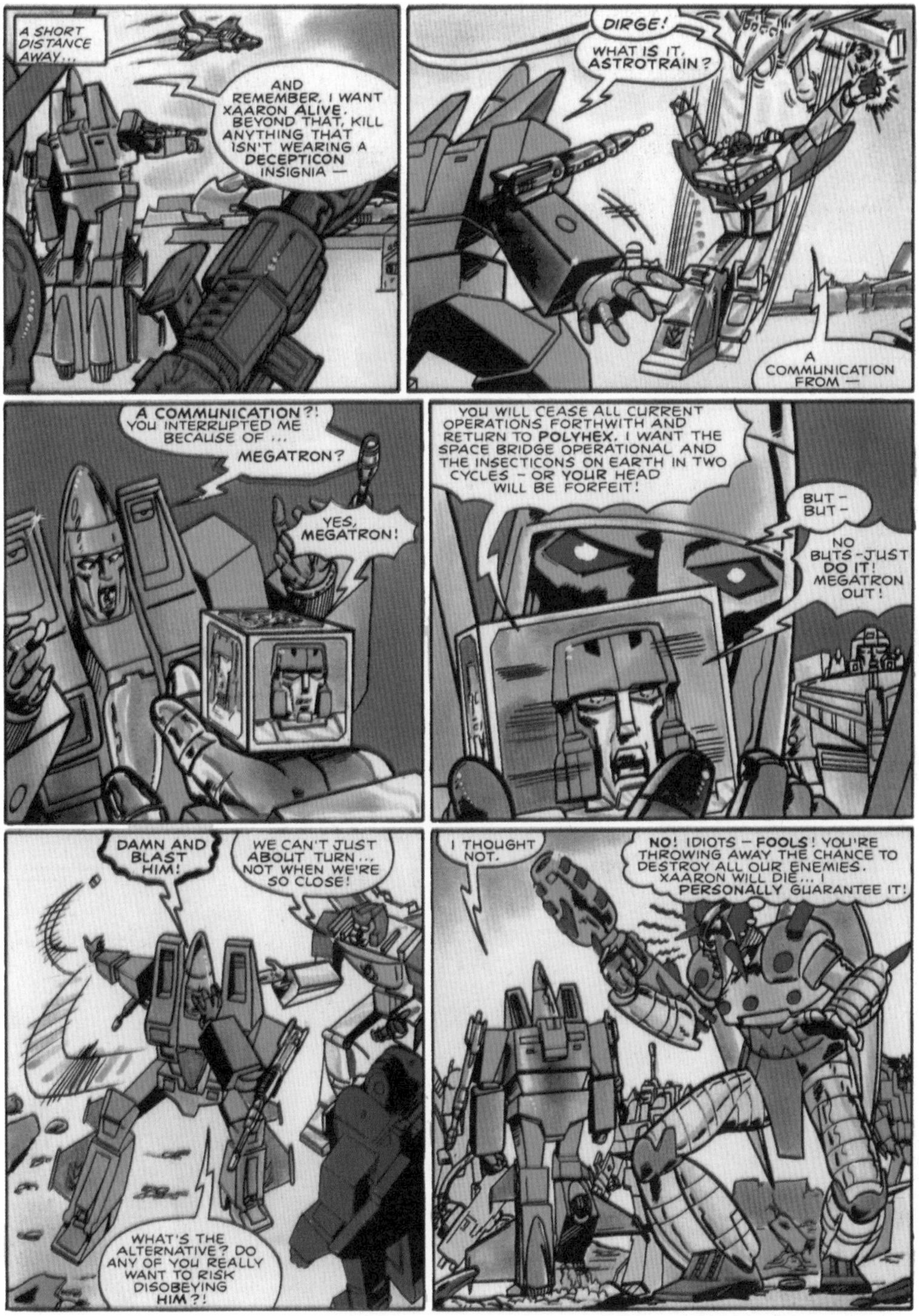

A SHORT DISTANCE AWAY...
AND REMEMBER, I WANT XAARON ALIVE. BEYOND THAT, KILL ANYTHING THAT ISN'T WEARING A DECEPTICON INSIGNIA —
DIRGE!
WHAT IS IT, ASTROTRAIN?
A COMMUNICATION FROM —
A COMMUNICATION?! YOU INTERRUPTED ME BECAUSE OF ... MEGATRON?
YES, MEGATRON!
YOU WILL CEASE ALL CURRENT OPERATIONS FORTHWITH AND RETURN TO POLYHEX. I WANT THE SPACE BRIDGE OPERATIONAL AND THE INSECTICONS ON EARTH IN TWO CYCLES - OR YOUR HEAD WILL BE FORFEIT!
BUT - BUT -
NO BUTS - JUST DO IT! MEGATRON OUT!
DAMN AND BLAST HIM!
WE CAN'T JUST ABOUT TURN... NOT WHEN WE'RE SO CLOSE!
WHAT'S THE ALTERNATIVE? DO ANY OF YOU REALLY WANT TO RISK DISOBEYING HIM?!
I THOUGHT NOT.
NO! IDIOTS — FOOLS! YOU'RE THROWING AWAY THE CHANCE TO DESTROY ALL OUR ENEMIES. XAARON WILL DIE... I PERSONALLY GUARANTEE IT!

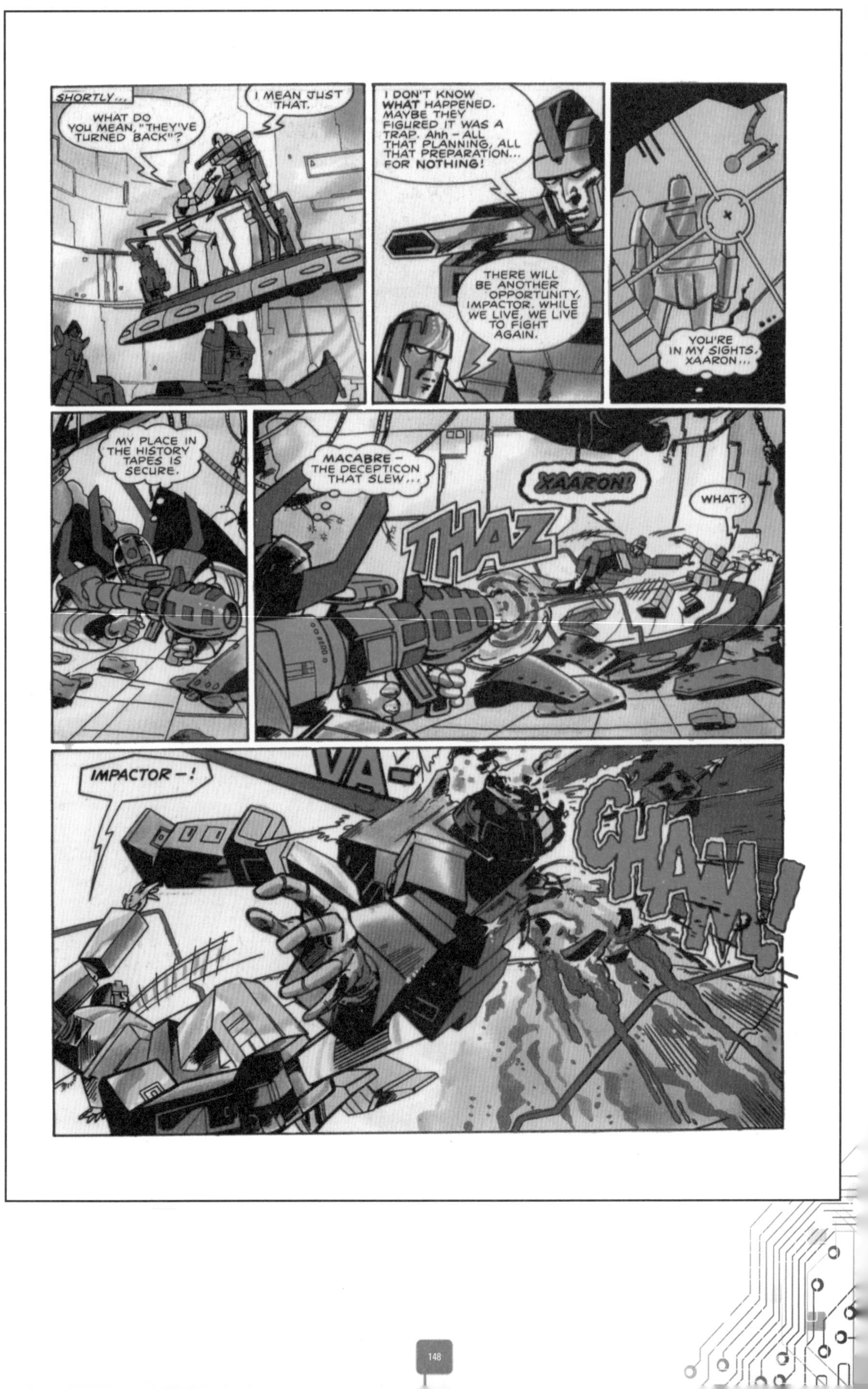

SHORTLY...
WHAT DO YOU MEAN, "THEY'VE TURNED BACK"?
I MEAN JUST THAT.
I DON'T KNOW WHAT HAPPENED. MAYBE THEY FIGURED IT WAS A TRAP. Ahh - ALL THAT PLANNING, ALL THAT PREPARATION... FOR NOTHING!
THERE WILL BE ANOTHER OPPORTUNITY, IMPACTOR. WHILE WE LIVE, WE LIVE TO FIGHT AGAIN.
YOU'RE IN MY SIGHTS, XAARON...
MY PLACE IN THE HISTORY TAPES IS SECURE.
MACABRE - THE DECEPTICON THAT SLEW...
XAARON!
WHAT?
THAZ
IMPACTOR -!
VA
CHAM!

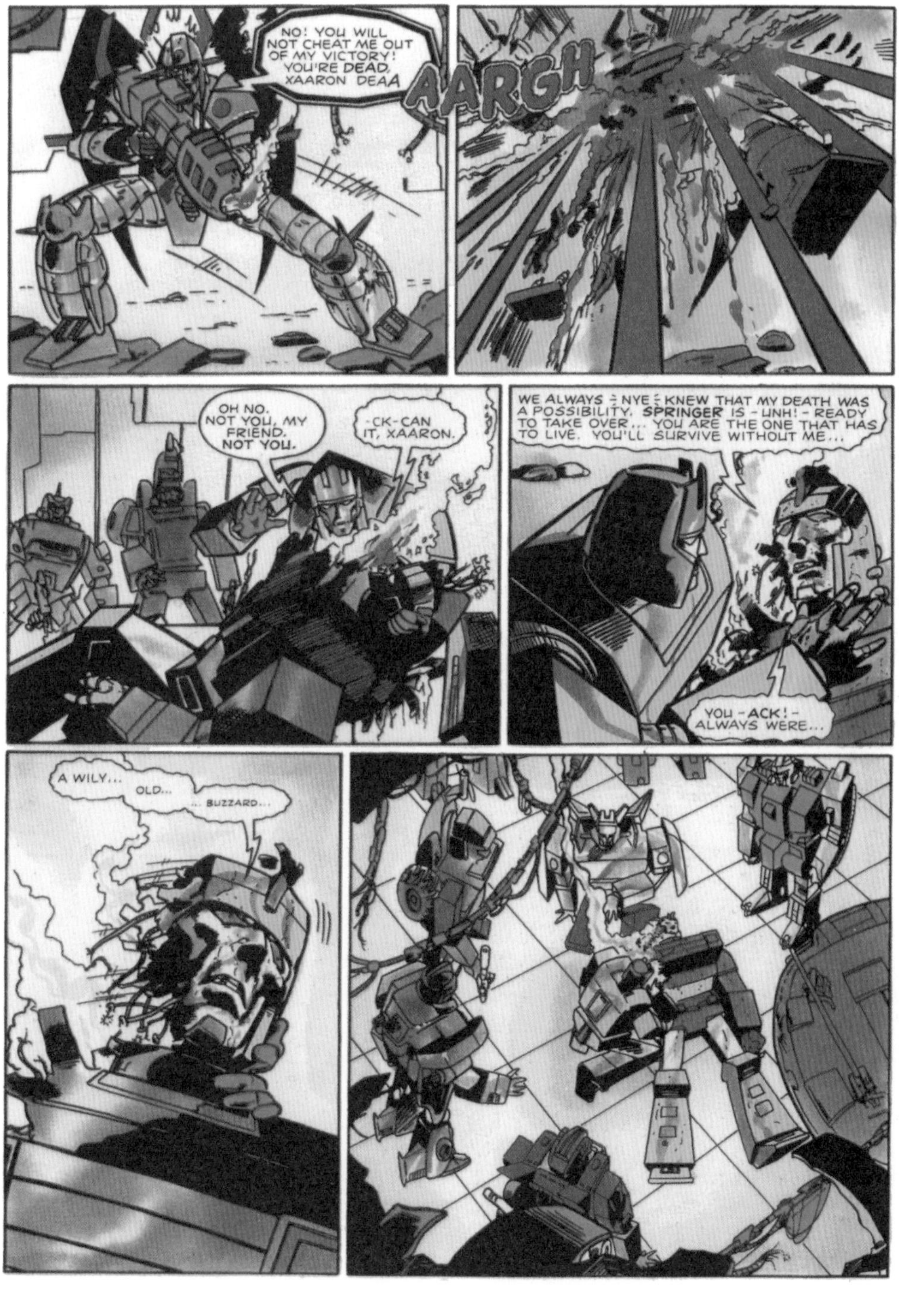
NO! YOU WILL NOT CHEAT ME OUT OF MY VICTORY! YOU'RE DEAD, XAARON DEAA
AARGH
OH NO. NOT YOU, MY FRIEND. NOT YOU.
-CK-CAN IT, XAARON.
WE ALWAYS -NYE- KNEW THAT MY DEATH WAS A POSSIBILITY. SPRINGER IS -UNH!- READY TO TAKE OVER... YOU ARE THE ONE THAT HAS TO LIVE. YOU'LL SURVIVE WITHOUT ME...
YOU -ACK!- ALWAYS WERE...
A WILY... OLD... ...BUZZARD...

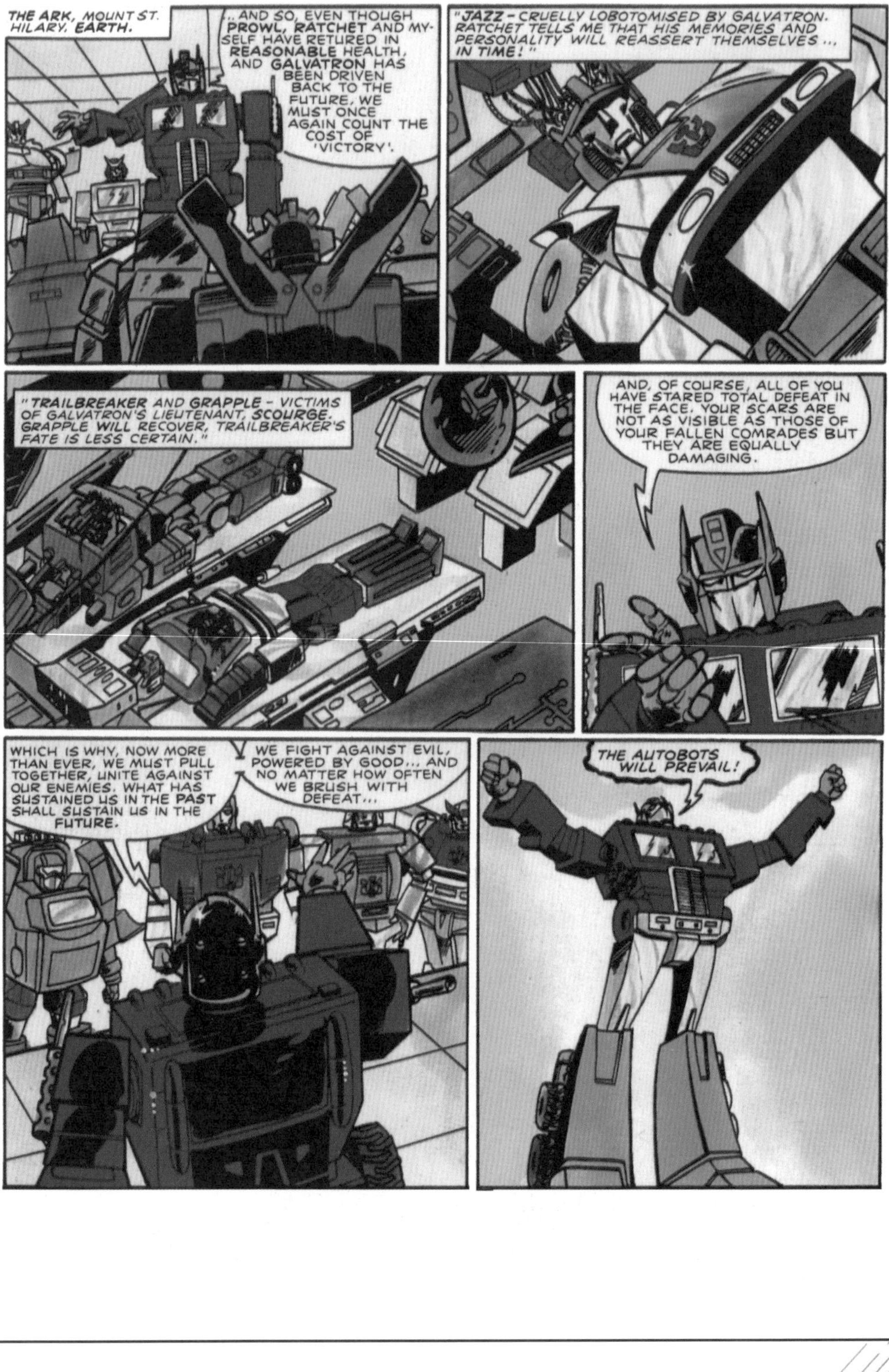
THE ARK, MOUNT ST. HILARY, EARTH.
... AND SO, EVEN THOUGH PROWL, RATCHET AND MYSELF HAVE RETURED IN REASONABLE HEALTH, AND GALVATRON HAS BEEN DRIVEN BACK TO THE FUTURE, WE MUST ONCE AGAIN COUNT THE COST OF 'VICTORY'.
"JAZZ - CRUELLY LOBOTOMISED BY GALVATRON. RATCHET TELLS ME THAT HIS MEMORIES AND PERSONALITY WILL REASSERT THEMSELVES ... IN TIME!"
"TRAILBREAKER AND GRAPPLE - VICTIMS OF GALVATRON'S LIEUTENANT, SCOURGE. GRAPPLE WILL RECOVER, TRAILBREAKER'S FATE IS LESS CERTAIN."
AND, OF COURSE, ALL OF YOU HAVE STARED TOTAL DEFEAT IN THE FACE. YOUR SCARS ARE NOT AS VISIBLE AS THOSE OF YOUR FALLEN COMRADES BUT THEY ARE EQUALLY DAMAGING.
WHICH IS WHY, NOW MORE THAN EVER, WE MUST PULL TOGETHER, UNITE AGAINST OUR ENEMIES. WHAT HAS SUSTAINED US IN THE PAST SHALL SUSTAIN US IN THE FUTURE.
WE FIGHT AGAINST EVIL, POWERED BY GOOD... AND NO MATTER HOW OFTEN WE BRUSH WITH DEFEAT...
THE AUTOBOTS WILL PREVAIL!

FILM 2006

With Grimlock

The movie event of the year opens this coming weekend (December 12th) at cinemas across the country. *Transformers: The Movie* is the biggest thing to happen to our warring mechanoids since the launch of this comic. It's ninety minutes of the very best in big screen animated action and adventure, featuring all the characters you've met in the comic and many more besides. But don't take our word for it! See what our resident letter answerer thought of the film as we present Grimlock's review of . . .

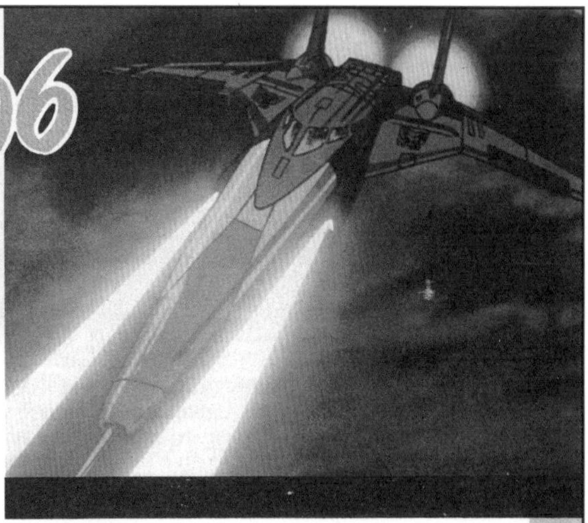

TRANSFORMERS: THE MOVIE!

Okay, kids – let's not mince words . . . this movie's utterly, utterly brilliant, so go and see it! I (not being someone who's easily impressed) was totally knocked for six by *Transformers: The Movie*. Why is it so good? Well, to find out, I suggest you not only study the great pics from the film I've printed here, but also read my step by step review. It's almost as good as the film itself!

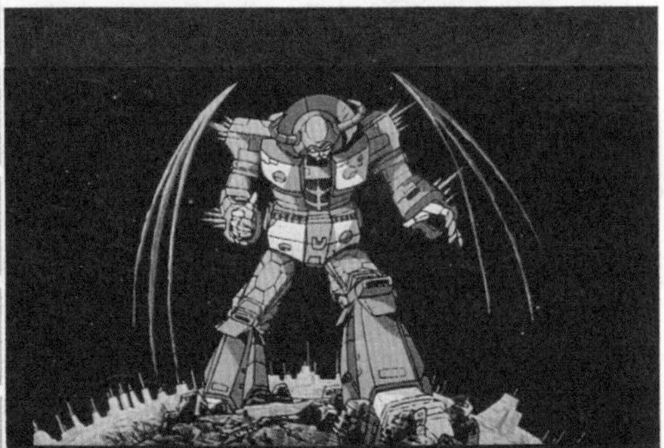

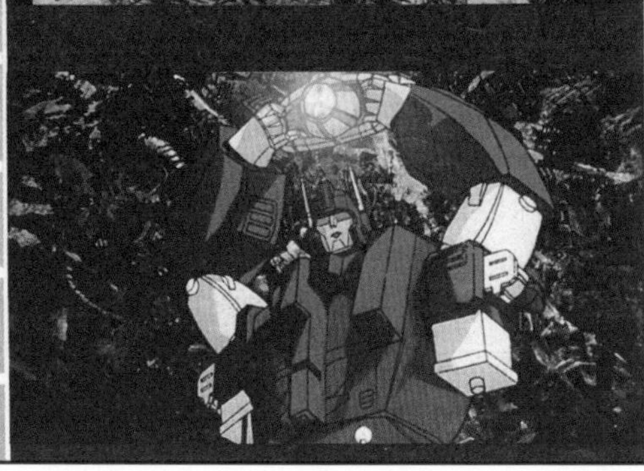

The Story: Set in the year 2006, the film reveals that those dirtwad Decepticons have been driven off Earth (probably by the Dinobots), but are still in control of Cybertron. Just as the Dinobots prepare to re-take Cybertron (from secret bases on Cybertron's moons), probably with minimal assistance from the Autobots, this giant planet-sized dirtwad called Unicron turns up and starts munching Cybertron's moons. Well, the Dinobots aren't about to stand for that, and – after successfully defending Autobot City: Earth from Megatron and the Decepticons – they turn their attentions to sorting out Unicron. The Autobots get in their way every now and then, and generally slow up the process of the Dinobots' battles. Oh yeah, along the way there's some pretty shocking developments for Optimus Prime and Megatron, the Creation matrix pops up everywhere, and there's lots and lots of terrific Transformers action! Basically though, the Dinobots are in it . . . so what more need be said?

Characters: You'll meet many of the new characters you saw during our Target: 2006 story – Galvatron, Ultra Magnus, Cyclonus, Scourge, Hot Rod, Kup, Blurr and Springer, to mention but a few – plus lots of others you haven't seen. For example, you can see Arcee (the first female Transformer), the new Decepticon cassette – Ratbat – and Blaster's cassettes – Ramhorn, Rewind, Eject and Steeljaw. There's plenty of your old favourites in there as well. Most importantly, of course, there's the Dinobots!

Animation: I found this quite breathtaking! (if I had breath to take, that is!) It flows with such speed and so smoothly, that you almost forget it is animation. The scale of some of the things you'll see is just beyond description! In the final analysis, however, the way they animate the Dinobots is what really makes it great!

Inaccuracies: After some of the goofs in the T.V. cartoon series, we were never gonna' get away with a totally flawless script. They still call Buster Spike, which is forgivable, BUT they also depict the Dinobots as slow-witted and semi-literate! It's just too much! I'm off to bust some heads over this!

To sum up, then, the thing – above all else – that makes this movie probably the greatest cinematic treat this century is, quite naturally, the Dinobots!*

*Editor's note: We would like to point out that the views expressed in this extremely unbiased review are not necessarily the views of the dumb stub – er, the editorial team.

16

Originally printed in *Transformers UK* issue #91.

Below:
Issue #90 (December 6th, 1986) • Cover by Herb Trimpe (re-use of *TFUS* #21, with new color by Robin Bouttell) • Reprints pages 12–22 of "Aerialbots Over America!" (*TFUS* issue #21) • Return of Circuit Breaker

Right:
Issue #91 (December 13th, 1986) • Cover by Phil Gascoine • Reprints pages 1–11 of "Heavy Traffic!" (*TFUS* issue #22) • The Stunticons are created • "Grim Grams" replaced by "Film 2006"

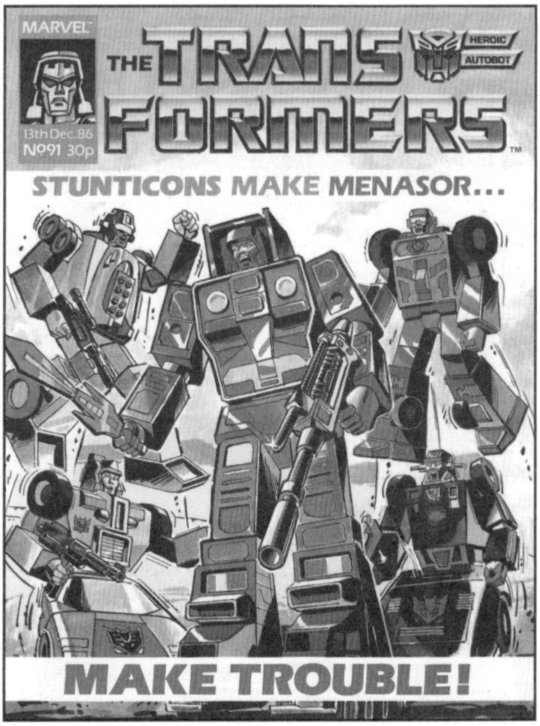
MARVEL
THE TRANSFORMERS
HEROIC AUTOBOT
13th Dec.86
No91 30p
STUNTICONS MAKE MENASOR...
MAKE TROUBLE!

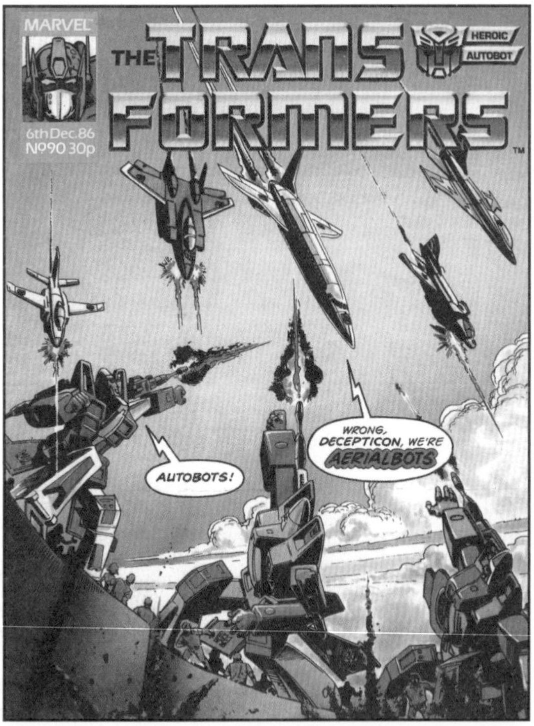
MARVEL
THE TRANSFORMERS
HEROIC AUTOBOT
6th Dec.86
No90 30p
AUTOBOTS!
WRONG, DECEPTICON, WE'RE AERIALBOTS

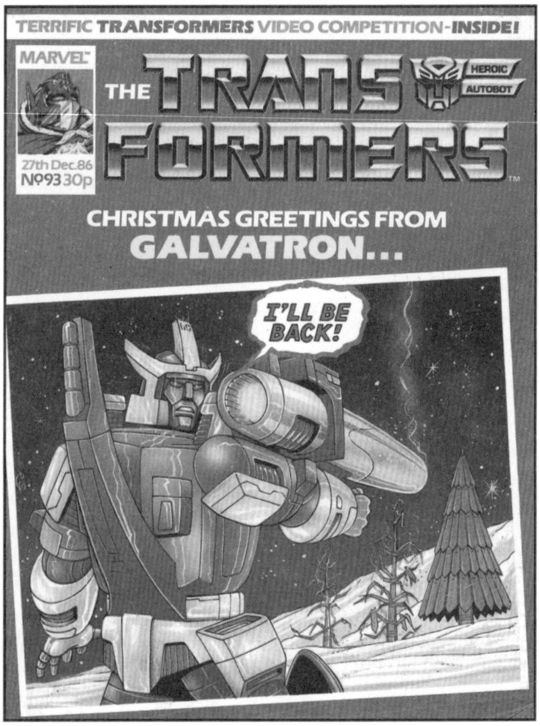
TERRIFIC TRANSFORMERS VIDEO COMPETITION-INSIDE!
MARVEL
THE TRANSFORMERS
HEROIC AUTOBOT
27th Dec.86
No93 30p
CHRISTMAS GREETINGS FROM GALVATRON...
I'LL BE BACK!

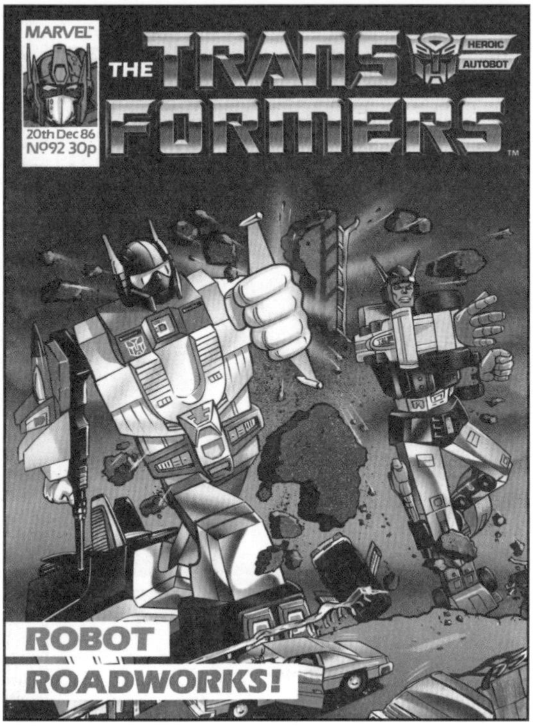
MARVEL
THE TRANSFORMERS
HEROIC AUTOBOT
20th Dec 86
No92 30p
ROBOT ROADWORKS!

Left:
Issue #92 (December 20th, 1986) • Cover by Lee Sullivan • Reprints pages 12–22 of "Heavy Traffic!" (*TFUS* issue #22) • The cover to *TFUS* #22, which featured a close-up of a barely-recognizable Menasor surrounded by a border full of superheroes (in celebration of Marvel's 25th anniversary) was the first not to be recycled for the UK comic.

Above:
Issue #93 (December 27th, 1986) • Cover by Robin Smith • "The Gift!" • "A to Z" features Beachcomber and Blades

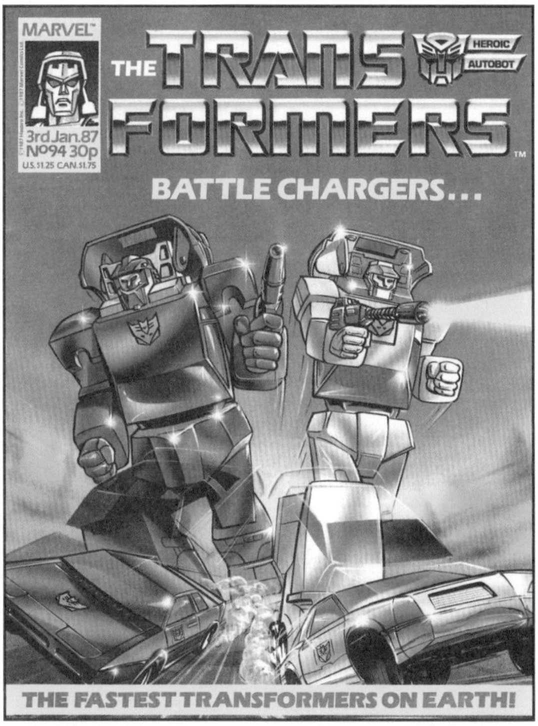
MARVEL
THE TRANSFORMERS
HEROIC AUTOBOT
3rd Jan.87
Nº94 30p
U.S.$1.25 CAN.$1.75
BATTLE CHARGERS...
THE FASTEST TRANSFORMERS ON EARTH!

Left:
Issue #94 (January 3rd, 1987) • Cover by Lee Sullivan • Reprints pages 1–11 of "Decepticon Graffiti!" (*TFUS* #23) • First appearance of Runabout and Runamuck

Below:
Issue #95 (January 10th, 1987) • Cover by Herb Trimpe (re-use of *TFUS* #23, with added speech balloons) • Reprints pages 12–22 of "Decepticon Graffiti!" (*TFUS* #23) • Last appearance of Donny Finkelberg/Robot Master

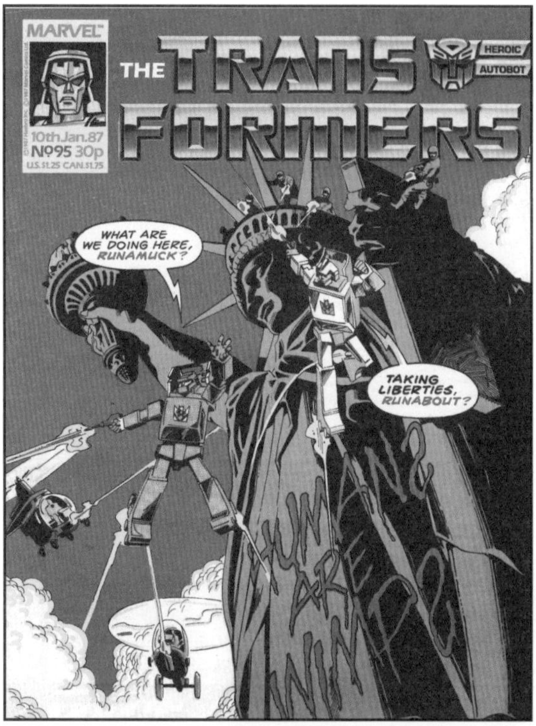
MARVEL
THE TRANSFORMERS
HEROIC AUTOBOT
10th Jan.87
Nº95 30p
U.S.$1.25 CAN.$1.75
WHAT ARE WE DOING HERE, RUNAMUCK?
TAKING LIBERTIES, RUNABOUT?

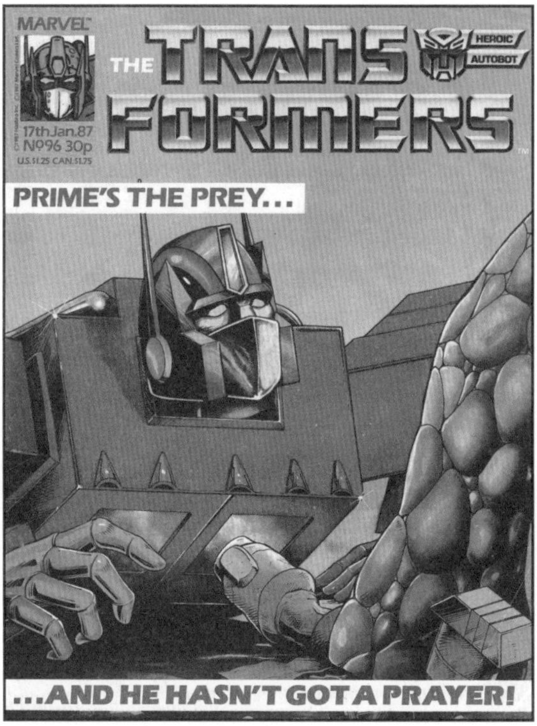
MARVEL
THE TRANSFORMERS
HEROIC AUTOBOT
17th Jan.87
Nº96 30p
U.S.$1.25 CAN.$1.75
PRIME'S THE PREY...
...AND HE HASN'T GOT A PRAYER!

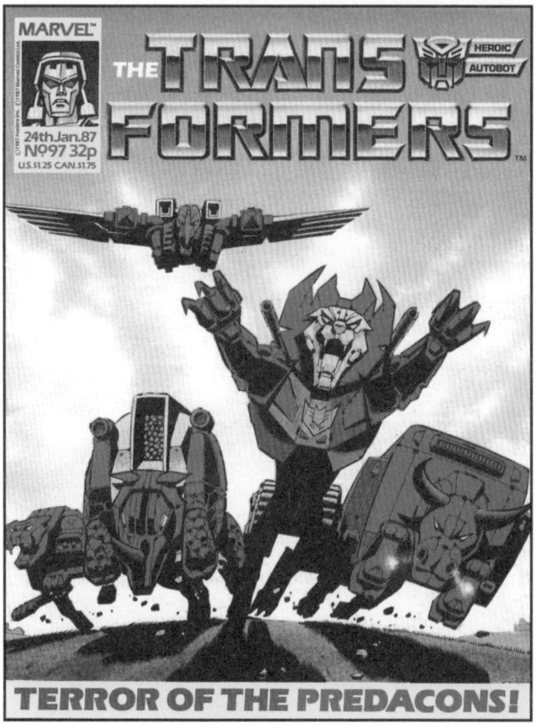
MARVEL
THE TRANSFORMERS
HEROIC AUTOBOT
24th Jan.87
Nº97 32p
U.S.$1.25 CAN.$1.75
TERROR OF THE PREDACONS!

Above:
Issue #96 (January 17th, 1987) • Cover by Jeff Anderson • "Prey!" Part 1 • First appearance of the Predacons • First issue to be distributed in the US

Right:
Issue #97 (January 24th, 1987) • Cover by Geoff Senior • "Prey!" Part 2 • First appearance of Predaking • Price increases to 32 pence

Below:
Issue #98 (January 31st, 1987) • Cover by Phil Gascoine • "…The Harder They Die!" • First appearance of Outback • Return of the Wreckers • Final "Spitfire and the Troubleshooters" back-up • Free gift: a Galvatron stick-on badge

Right:
Issue #99 (February 7th, 1987) • Cover by Lee Sullivan • "Under Fire!" • First appearance of Ratbat • Free gift: an Ultra Magnus stick-on badge • New "Action Force" (aka "G.I. JOE") back-up

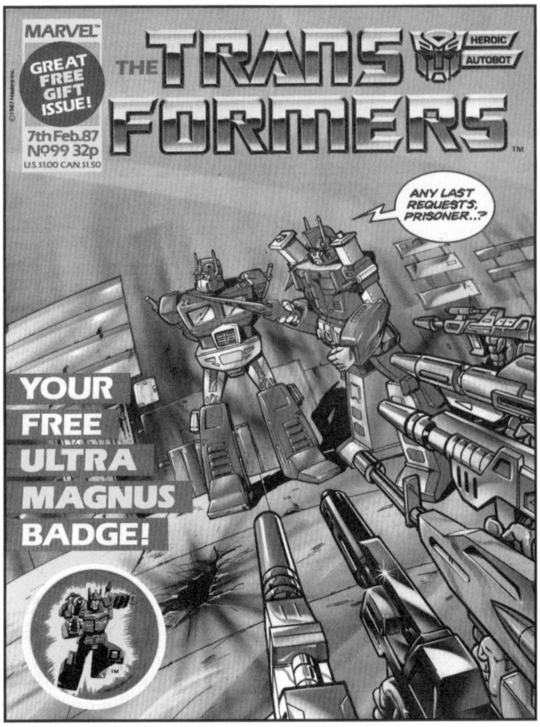
MARVEL
GREAT FREE GIFT ISSUE!
THE TRANSFORMERS
HEROIC AUTOBOT
7th Feb.87
Nº99 32p
U.S. $1.00 CAN. $1.50
ANY LAST REQUESTS, PRISONER..?
YOUR FREE ULTRA MAGNUS BADGE!

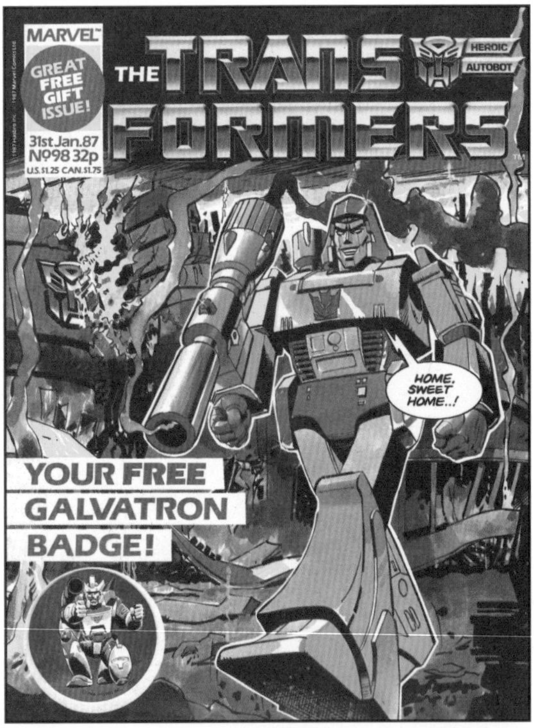
MARVEL
GREAT FREE GIFT ISSUE!
THE TRANSFORMERS
HEROIC AUTOBOT
31st Jan.87
Nº98 32p
U.S. $1.25 CAN. $1.75
HOME, SWEET HOME..!
YOUR FREE GALVATRON BADGE!

Below:
Issue #100 (February 14th, 1987) • Cover by Alan Davis • "Distant Thunder!" • Free gift: wrapround cover • 19-page lead strip • US price drops to $1.00 to match *TFUS*

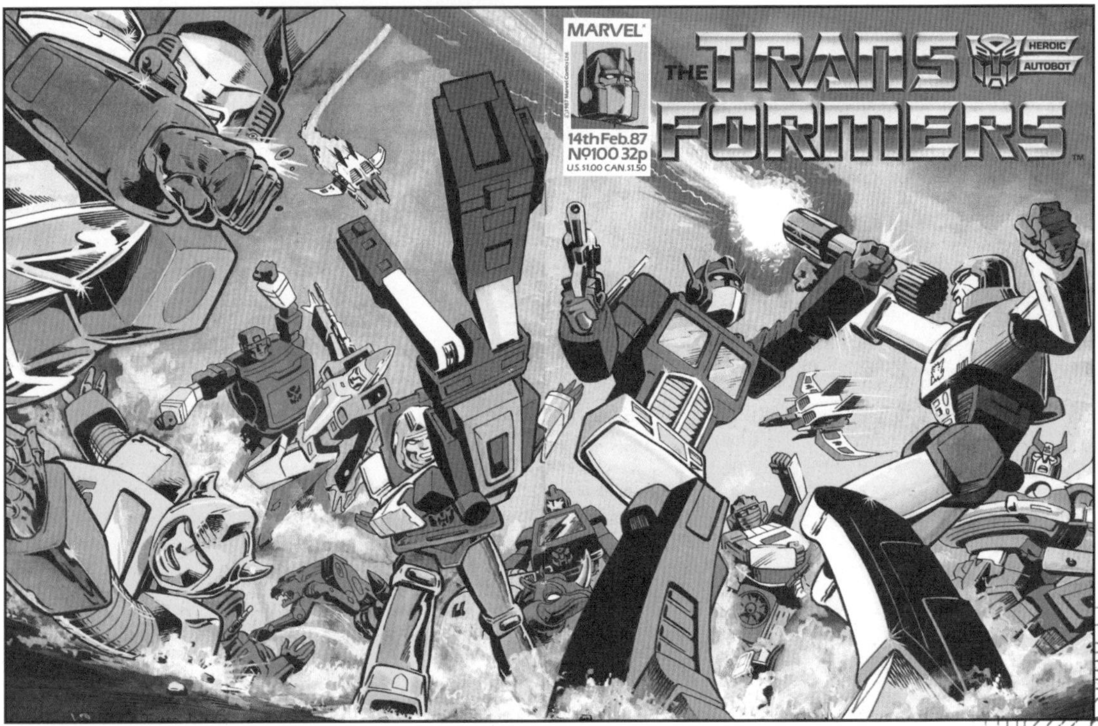
MARVEL
THE TRANSFORMERS
HEROIC AUTOBOT
14th Feb.87
Nº100 32p
U.S. $1.00 CAN. $1.50

All of the below were reprinted by Titan Books in 2004 (with a new cover by Lee Sullivan); and by IDW in 2009 as part of the "Best of UK" series (with new covers by Andrew Griffith)

PREY!

Originally printed in issues #96–97
Published January 17–24, 1987
Reprinted along with "...The Harder They Die!"
in *Collected Comics* #12 (June 1989), with a
new new cover by Andy Wildman

...THE HARDER THEY DIE!/ UNDER FIRE!

Originally printed in issues #98–99
Published January 31–February 7, 1987
"Under Fire!" reprinted with "Distant Thunder!"
in *Collected Comics* #13 (July 1989), re-using
the cover to issue #100

DISTANT THUNDER

Originally printed in issue #100
Published February 14, 1987

"It makes me shudder to think how close Galvatron came to **total victory**!"

From the opening pages of "Prey!", his first story since "Target: 2006," it's clear that Simon Furman is putting *TFUK*'s house in order: Optimus Prime watches footage of Scourge and of the arrival on Earth of Dirge, Thrust, and Ramjet, and moments later reflects on the havoc caused by Runabout and Runamuck—not to mention Galvatron. It makes for a scene heavy on flashbacks and thought balloons, but it serves to remind readers that *TFUK* was telling one big, interconnected story.

The two-part "Prey!" spearheaded the next batch of British material. Although broken up into two- and even one-part instalments, these nine issues read as a single epic story; and more than that, as a sequel of sorts to "Target: 2006."

"Yeah," confirms Furman. "I think we attacked them all as a block of story. By this point, after 'Target,' I wanted to tell a bigger story rather than lots of little stories. I think the only one that feels like its own story is the return of Galvatron ['Fallen Angel!']. But this whole set of stories was never going to be presented under one name; we approached this in the old style."

Thanks to the cast of characters, the locations, the team-ups, and the various confrontations, issues #96–104 (let's call it the "Prey" arc for ease of reference) read like *TFUK*'s Greatest Hits: as well as both Megatron and Optimus taking center stage for virtually the entire story

(something that in both UK and US stories happened less than one might have assumed) there was the return of the Wreckers, Lord Straxus, and the New Leaders; there was Magnus fighting alongside Optimus; and there was Galvatron versus the Dinobots… and all in the space of nine issues. One wonders whether Furman consciously decided to hold anything back for later.

"We never held back: we threw a ton of stuff into every story. But, that said, I think I was still setting stuff up—you can see with the Galvatron story we're seeding something else. Clearly we knew that Prime and Megatron were going out of the US story, so I'm pretty sure that's why we maneuvered Magnus to Earth and Galvatron back in time again; it was a case of, 'If we can't use Prime and Megatron again—if this is their swan song—then we'll put our guys back in the ring.' So even though we threw everything and the kitchen sink into this, there's a kind of planning ahead. At this point I knew our *next* story ['Wanted: Galvatron, Dead or Alive'] would see us going back to the future."

The apparent deaths of Optimus Prime and Megatron were only a few issues away (#106 and #108 respectively), and at this point there was no guarantee that either would return to the comics. In "Prey!", Optimus faces off against the Predacons before he and Megatron are swept across to Cybertron—a brief and bittersweet return home for the Autobot and Decepticon leaders.

"We wanted to go back to Cybertron," says Furman. "I'd always liked Bob [Budiansky]'s

THE TRANSFORMERS
IDW
ISSUE #1
$3.99
BEST OF UK
PREY

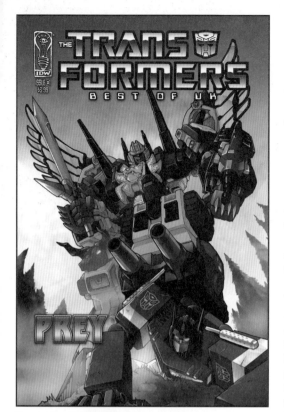

The cover to issue #1 of IDW's "Prey!" reprints.

MARVEL
TRANSFORMERS
SUMMER SPECIAL 75P
TM
HUNTER...
HUNTED!
COLLECTED COMICS 12

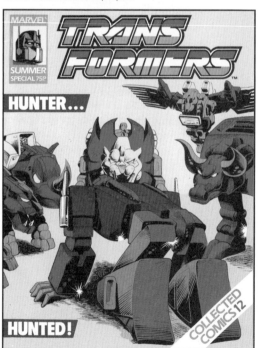

Collected Comics #12 was the last to feature an all-new cover.

'Return to Cybertron' story (reprinted in *TFUK* issues #66–69) and I'd enjoyed [the Cybertron scenes] in 'Target: 2006,' so I think it was just a no brainer to take Prime and Megatron back. They had to be removed from Earth anyway for the story to work in 'Prey!' so to take them back to Cybertron via a space bridge seemed like a logical step, as did tying them into Lord Straxus and the Wreckers and all of those other storylines we had simmering away on Cybertron—and in turn, the Cybertron stuff was all about getting Magnus to Earth."

The introduction of the Predacons in issue #96 is strange given that they were scheduled to make their "official" debut a few months later in the reprint of the *TFUS* story "Gone But Not Forgotten!" For the latter story to make sense, Furman had to invoke amnesia on Megatron's part. "Yes, we would have seen they were coming in issue #107," confirms Furman. "I'm sure we used them early because we thought 'if we're going to have Prime hunted, let's have him hunted by the Predacons.' They just fitted what we wanted for the story. And I also thought they were just really cool."

The first part of "Prey!" is surprisingly heavy on exposition, with dialog-driven scenes in the Ark and at the Decepticons' coal mine base, but then these first 11 pages have a lot of heave lifting to do in terms of setting up the hunt, the fake death of Optimus Prime, and the return to Cybertron of the two main characters. It's all worth it, of course, and the last panel—a floored and weaponless Prime surrounded by the Predacons and a grinning Megatron—is a great cliffhanger. Almost as a counterbalance, part two of the story is virtually wall-to-wall action; and it ends on an even better cliffhanger, with the discovery of Prime's dismembered corpse.

What must readers have thought when, a week later, they rejoined the story to find Optimus Prime, alive and well, strolling through the burnt-out streets of Cybertron, rescuing Mini-Autobots and accidentally impaling generic Decepticons?

"...The Harder They Die!" features some of Geoff Senior's most impressive artwork. Whether it's Megatron pulling the handgun from his waist compartment, or Prime's face as he stands over the ruins of Iacon, or the Death's Head-esque Guardian droid, there are many panels to cherish.

The reintroduction of Straxus, meanwhile, is evidence that Furman is happy to resurrect characters, particularly villains, if he thinks it will give long-time readers a buzz. It's almost as if he's raking through the embers of old US stories, rescuing the good stuff, and bolstering his UK cast.

Issue #100's extra-long "Distant Thunder!" uses Prime's nursing of the injured Outback as a framing device for a long flashback that finally

THE GIFT

Originally printed in issue #93
Published December 27, 1986
Reprinted in *Collected Comics* #11
(November 1988)

James Hill wrote his last *Transformers* story shortly after "The Return of the Transformers" for the 1986/7 *Annual*; both tales featured Jetfire, the first Autobot to have been created on Earth (albeit as a Decepticon, originally). A self-contained festive story in the tradition of "Christmas Breaker!" a year earlier, it is notable for being the last British strip to feature Buster Witwicky; indeed, with its references to older stories such as "DIS-Integrated Circuits!" (from issues #33–34) and "Brainstorm!" (#37–38), the strip has a decidedly old-school feel—and is all the better for it. Continuity-conscious Hill has certainly done his homework: within these 11 pages are references to G. B. Blackrock, Robot Master, the Primal Program, and the Celestial Spires.

"The Gift" was artist Martin Griffiths' try-out script for Marvel UK. Although he didn't work on any other interior strips, he went on to provide the covers to issues #103 and #143. Also making his one and only appearance in *TFUK* was letterer Robin Riggs.

As if the story wasn't distinct enough already, "The Gift" marks the arrival of Steve White, whose sharp, bold colors would become a visual hallmark over the next 100+ issues.

Finally, issue #93 is also notable for having a cover that has no connection to the story inside (apart from the metallic Christmas tree); only six weeks after his departure in "Target: 2006," *TFUK* was teasing/reassuring readers that Galvatron would return–as indeed he would in issue #101.

reveals what happened to the Autobots and Decepticons who were displaced by time-travelers in "Target: 2006." The story of the peaceful Cloran and Zenag's violent invaders was foreshadowed in part 1 of "Prey!", when Shockwave (tantalisingly) says, "I have seen a side of Optimus Prime you could never dream of. When we fought in that murky little dimension I came to understand why we have never convincingly beaten him."

Furman admits that he didn't have "Distant Thunder!" in mind when he wrote "Target: 2006": "Whether there was a letter from a reader or whether in our own mind we thought we'd never explained where [Prime and Co.] had been, it just felt like it was a story that needed telling."

Whilst in no way disappointing, "Distant Thunder!" makes for a strange 100th issue story. It's true that in Prime, Shockwave, Ratchet, and Prowl some big name characters are put under the spotlight (and it is fitting, when considering the dozens of new Autobots and Decepticons that had been introduced since the early days of the comic, that issue #100 focused on Transformers who had been around since the very beginning), but readers may have been expecting the all-out Autobot/Decepticon battle promised by Alan Davis' waparound cover.

"It is a strange choice for a hundredth story," Furman concedes, "and looking back knowing what I know now I wonder whether I'd do something different and relegate 'Distant Thunder' to an 11-pager. It's offbeat, yeah. It's an oddity amongst the stories before and after.

"It's also one of the few examples I can pinpoint of my just mercilessly ripping something off. The conclusion when Prime turns his back on the ape creature and denies his existence is lifted completely from the end of *A Nightmare of Elm Street*. Completely. The heroine turns her back on Freddy Krueger, says 'I don't believe in you, you can't harm me,' and he slashes at her with his claws and they pass right through her."

What "Distant Thunder" does well—and this does feel appropriate, given that it's the hundredth issue—is convey Prime's wisdom and compassion. By his actions in the past and his words in the present, we are reminded what makes Optimus so special. The fact that he would be dead in six issues' time gave subsequent readings of the story an added poignancy.

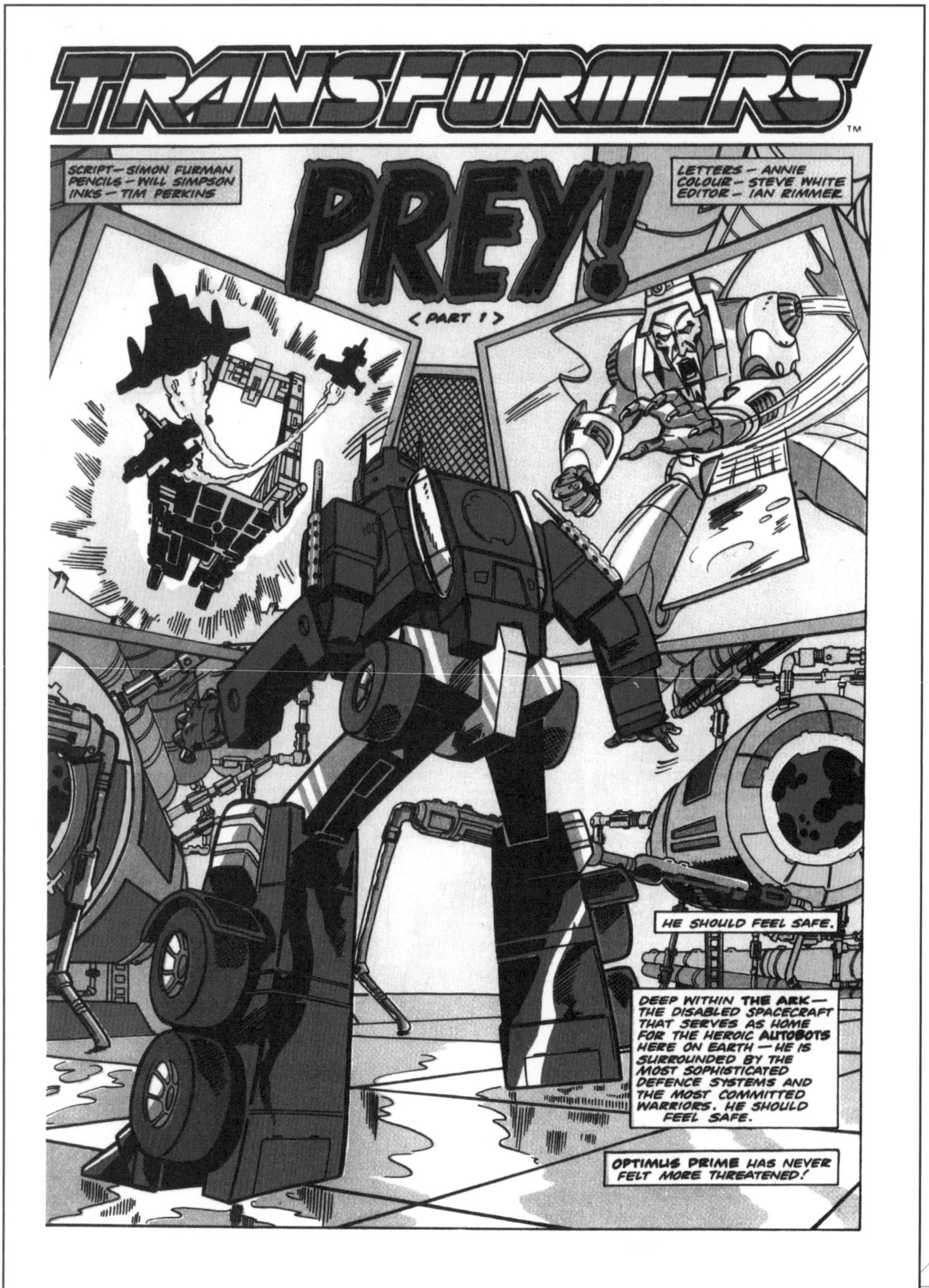
TRANSFORMERS
TM
SCRIPT—SIMON FURMAN
PENCILS—WILL SIMPSON
INKS—TIM PERKINS
PREY!
< PART 1 >
LETTERS—ANNIE
COLOUR—STEVE WHITE
EDITOR—IAN RIMMER
HE SHOULD FEEL SAFE.
DEEP WITHIN THE ARK—THE DISABLED SPACECRAFT THAT SERVES AS HOME FOR THE HEROIC AUTOBOTS HERE ON EARTH—HE IS SURROUNDED BY THE MOST SOPHISTICATED DEFENCE SYSTEMS AND THE MOST COMMITTED WARRIORS. HE SHOULD FEEL SAFE.
OPTIMUS PRIME HAS NEVER FELT MORE THREATENED!

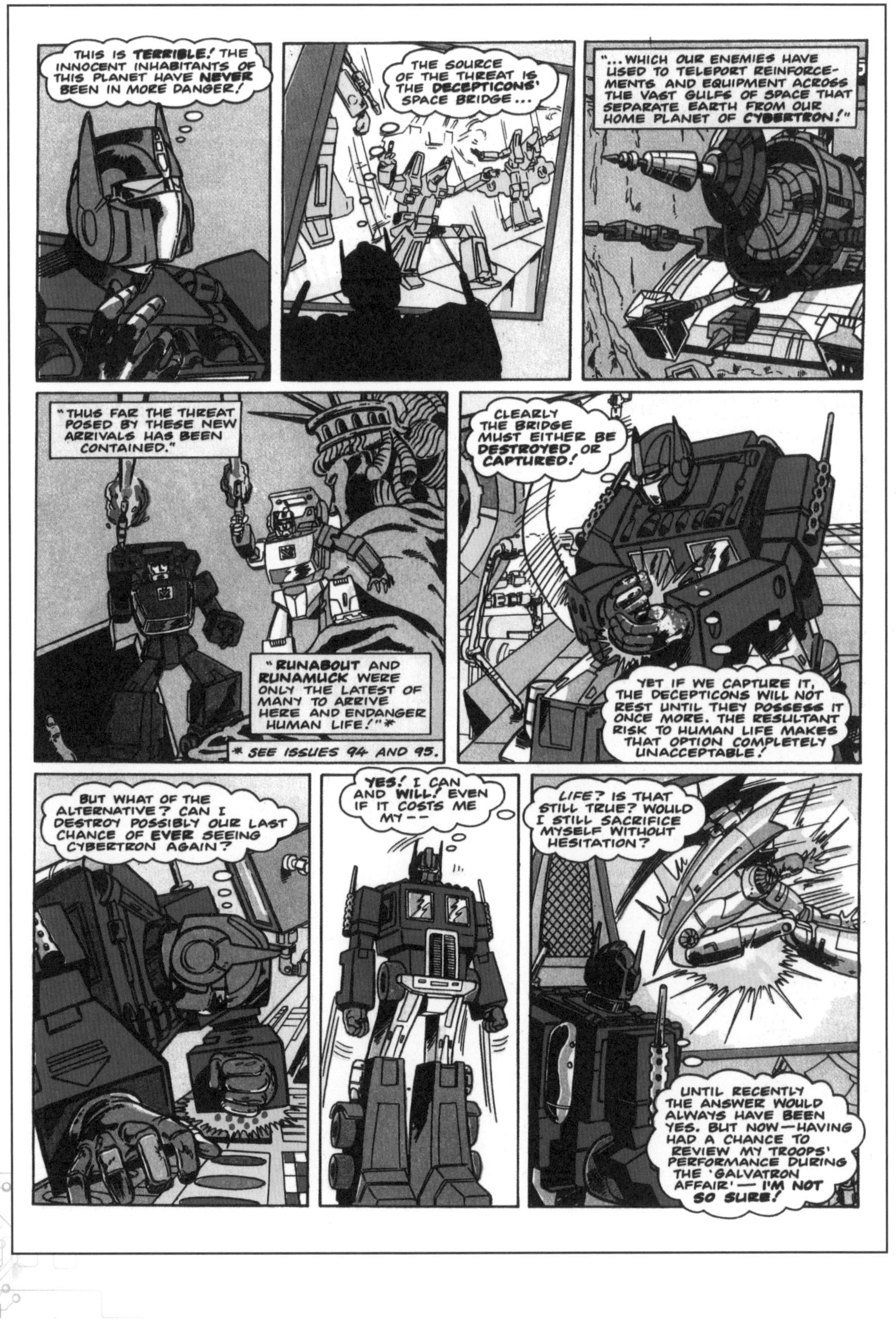

THIS IS TERRIBLE! THE INNOCENT INHABITANTS OF THIS PLANET HAVE NEVER BEEN IN MORE DANGER!
THE SOURCE OF THE THREAT IS THE DECEPTICONS' SPACE BRIDGE...
"...WHICH OUR ENEMIES HAVE USED TO TELEPORT REINFORCEMENTS AND EQUIPMENT ACROSS THE VAST GULFS OF SPACE THAT SEPARATE EARTH FROM OUR HOME PLANET OF CYBERTRON!"
"THUS FAR THE THREAT POSED BY THESE NEW ARRIVALS HAS BEEN CONTAINED."
"RUNABOUT AND RUNAMUCK WERE ONLY THE LATEST OF MANY TO ARRIVE HERE AND ENDANGER HUMAN LIFE!"*
* SEE ISSUES 94 AND 95.
CLEARLY THE BRIDGE MUST EITHER BE DESTROYED OR CAPTURED!
YET IF WE CAPTURE IT, THE DECEPTICONS WILL NOT REST UNTIL THEY POSSESS IT ONCE MORE. THE RESULTANT RISK TO HUMAN LIFE MAKES THAT OPTION COMPLETELY UNACCEPTABLE!
BUT WHAT OF THE ALTERNATIVE? CAN I DESTROY POSSIBLY OUR LAST CHANCE OF EVER SEEING CYBERTRON AGAIN?
YES! I CAN AND WILL! EVEN IF IT COSTS ME MY--
LIFE? IS THAT STILL TRUE? WOULD I STILL SACRIFICE MYSELF WITHOUT HESITATION?
UNTIL RECENTLY THE ANSWER WOULD ALWAYS HAVE BEEN YES. BUT NOW—HAVING HAD A CHANCE TO REVIEW MY TROOPS' PERFORMANCE DURING THE 'GALVATRON AFFAIR'— I'M NOT SO SURE!

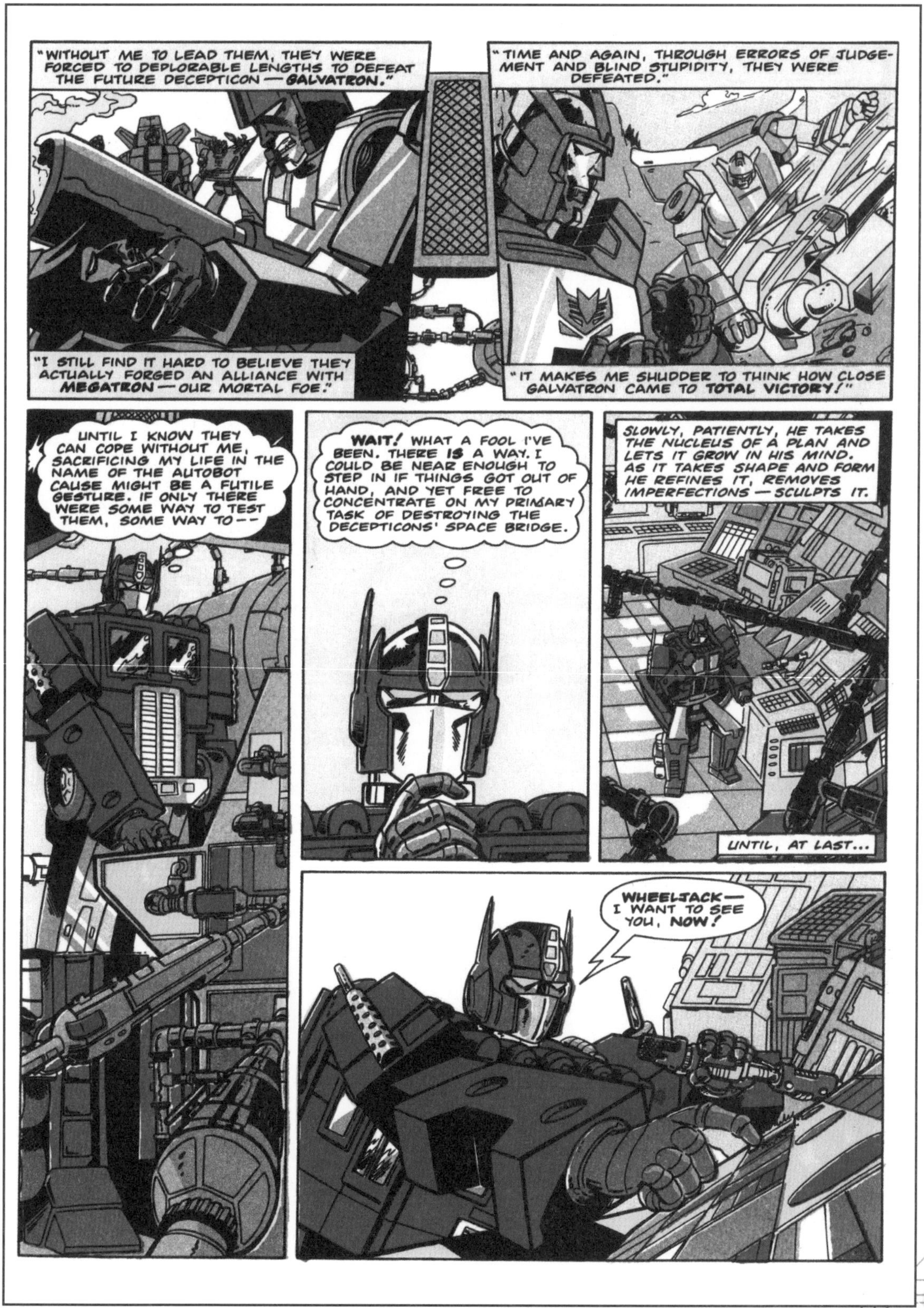
"WITHOUT ME TO LEAD THEM, THEY WERE FORCED TO DEPLORABLE LENGTHS TO DEFEAT THE FUTURE DECEPTICON — GALVATRON."
"I STILL FIND IT HARD TO BELIEVE THEY ACTUALLY FORGED AN ALLIANCE WITH MEGATRON — OUR MORTAL FOE."
"TIME AND AGAIN, THROUGH ERRORS OF JUDGEMENT AND BLIND STUPIDITY, THEY WERE DEFEATED."
"IT MAKES ME SHUDDER TO THINK HOW CLOSE GALVATRON CAME TO TOTAL VICTORY!"
UNTIL I KNOW THEY CAN COPE WITHOUT ME, SACRIFICING MY LIFE IN THE NAME OF THE AUTOBOT CAUSE MIGHT BE A FUTILE GESTURE. IF ONLY THERE WERE SOME WAY TO TEST THEM, SOME WAY TO--
WAIT! WHAT A FOOL I'VE BEEN. THERE IS A WAY. I COULD BE NEAR ENOUGH TO STEP IN IF THINGS GOT OUT OF HAND, AND YET FREE TO CONCENTRATE ON MY PRIMARY TASK OF DESTROYING THE DECEPTICONS' SPACE BRIDGE.
SLOWLY, PATIENTLY, HE TAKES THE NUCLEUS OF A PLAN AND LETS IT GROW IN HIS MIND. AS IT TAKES SHAPE AND FORM HE REFINES IT, REMOVES IMPERFECTIONS — SCULPTS IT.
UNTIL, AT LAST...
WHEELJACK — I WANT TO SEE YOU, NOW!

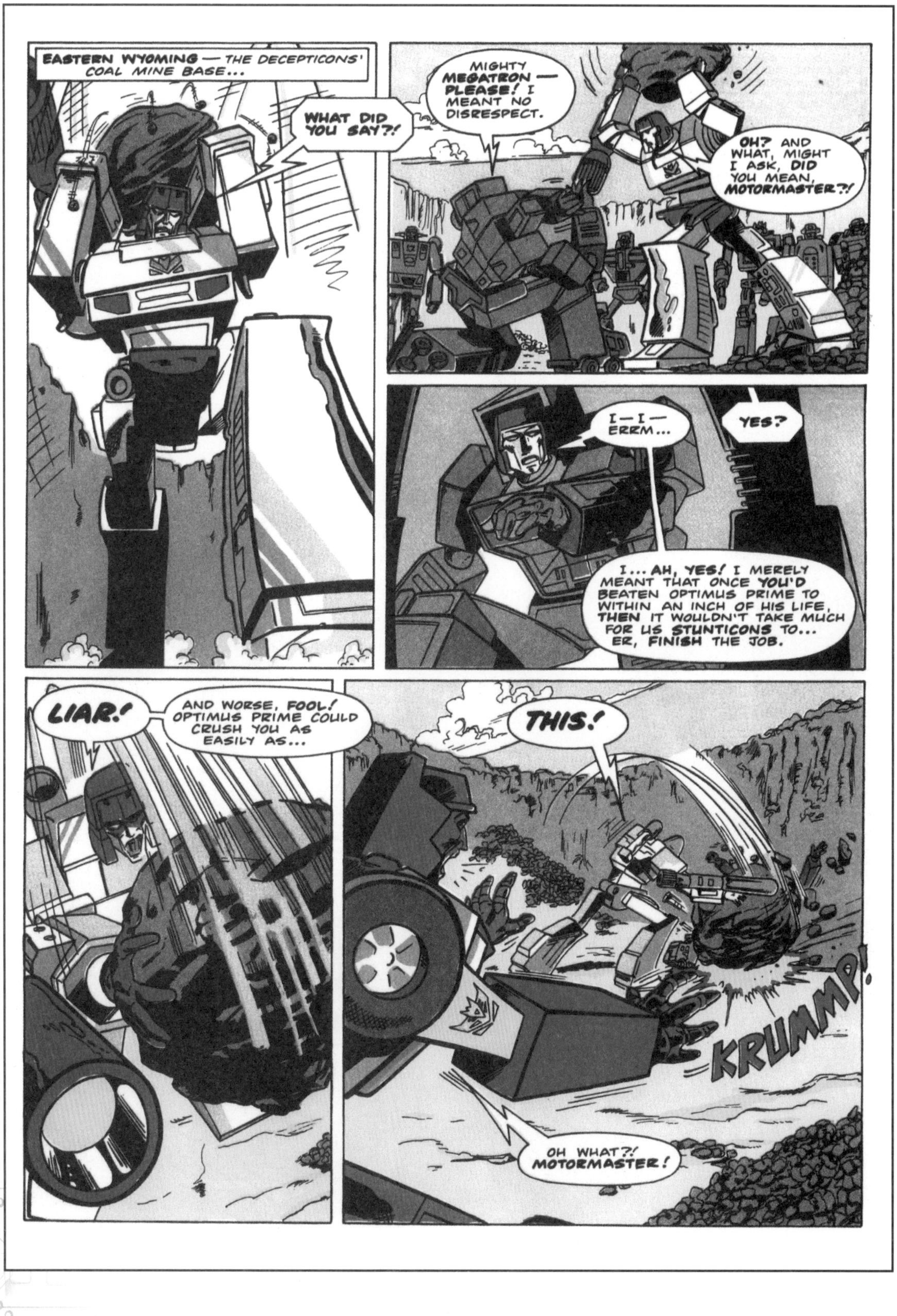

EASTERN WYOMING — THE DECEPTICONS' COAL MINE BASE...
WHAT DID YOU SAY?!
MIGHTY MEGATRON — PLEASE! I MEANT NO DISRESPECT.
OH? AND WHAT, MIGHT I ASK, DID YOU MEAN, MOTORMASTER?!
I—I— ERRM...
YES?
I... AH, YES! I MERELY MEANT THAT ONCE YOU'D BEATEN OPTIMUS PRIME TO WITHIN AN INCH OF HIS LIFE, THEN IT WOULDN'T TAKE MUCH FOR US STUNTICONS TO... ER, FINISH THE JOB.
LIAR!
AND WORSE, FOOL! OPTIMUS PRIME COULD CRUSH YOU AS EASILY AS...
THIS!
KRUMMP!
OH WHAT?! MOTORMASTER!

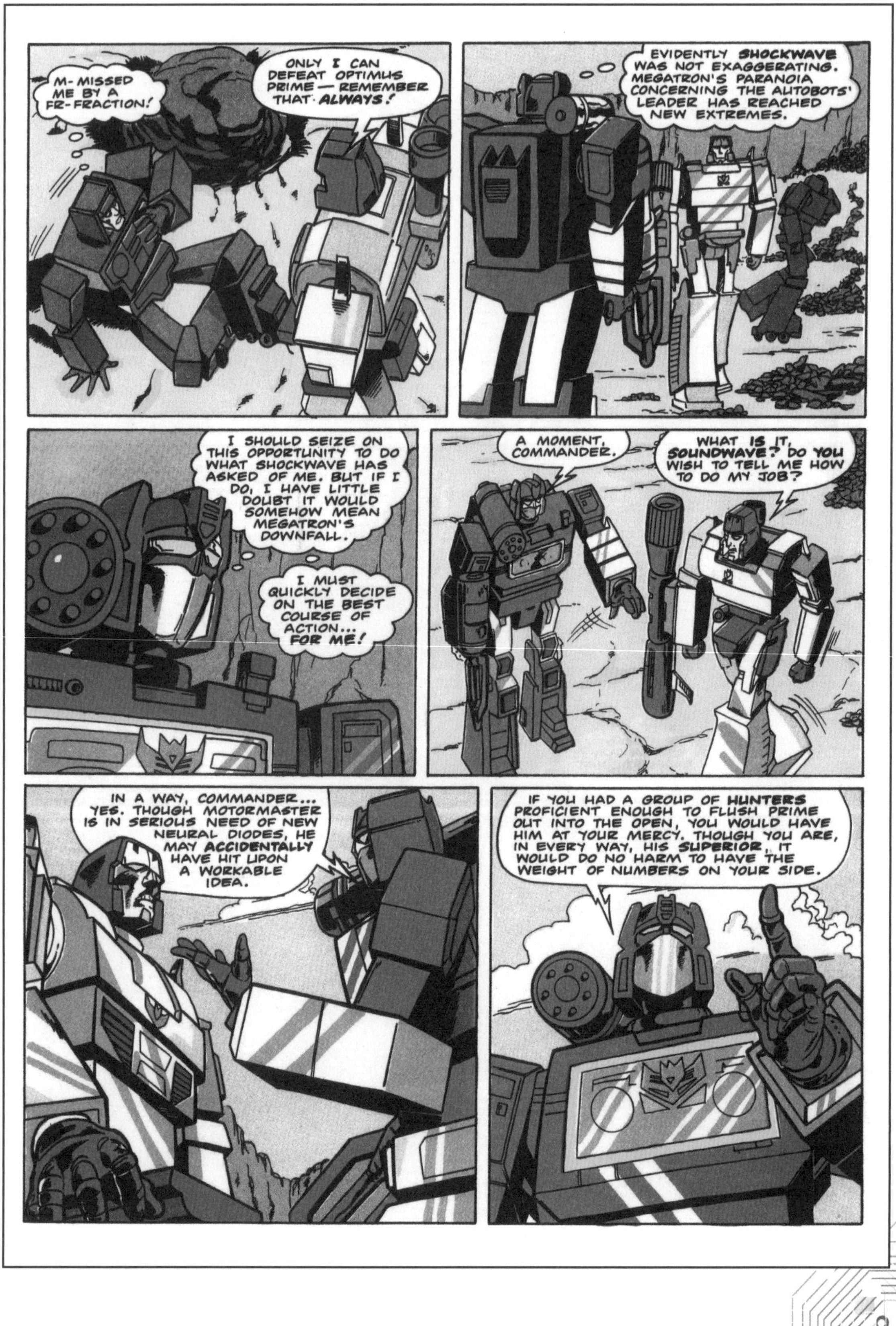

M-MISSED ME BY A FR-FRACTION!
ONLY I CAN DEFEAT OPTIMUS PRIME — REMEMBER THAT · ALWAYS!
EVIDENTLY SHOCKWAVE WAS NOT EXAGGERATING. MEGATRON'S PARANOIA CONCERNING THE AUTOBOTS' LEADER HAS REACHED NEW EXTREMES.
I SHOULD SEIZE ON THIS OPPORTUNITY TO DO WHAT SHOCKWAVE HAS ASKED OF ME. BUT IF I DO, I HAVE LITTLE DOUBT IT WOULD SOMEHOW MEAN MEGATRON'S DOWNFALL.
I MUST QUICKLY DECIDE ON THE BEST COURSE OF ACTION... FOR ME!
A MOMENT, COMMANDER.
WHAT IS IT, SOUNDWAVE? DO YOU WISH TO TELL ME HOW TO DO MY JOB?
IN A WAY, COMMANDER... YES. THOUGH MOTORMASTER IS IN SERIOUS NEED OF NEW NEURAL DIODES, HE MAY ACCIDENTALLY HAVE HIT UPON A WORKABLE IDEA.
IF YOU HAD A GROUP OF HUNTERS PROFICIENT ENOUGH TO FLUSH PRIME OUT INTO THE OPEN, YOU WOULD HAVE HIM AT YOUR MERCY. THOUGH YOU ARE, IN EVERY WAY, HIS SUPERIOR, IT WOULD DO NO HARM TO HAVE THE WEIGHT OF NUMBERS ON YOUR SIDE.

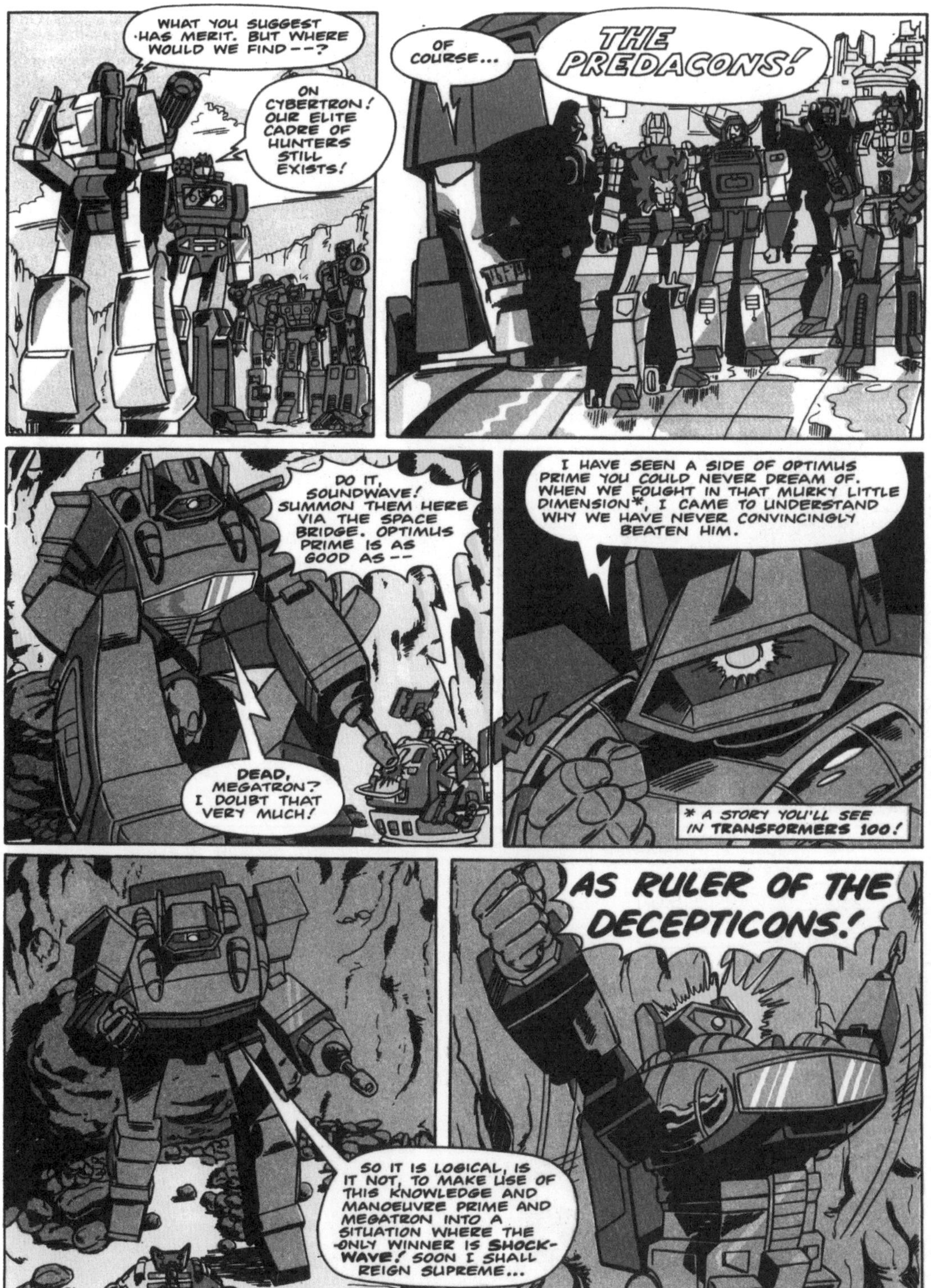
WHAT YOU SUGGEST HAS MERIT. BUT WHERE WOULD WE FIND --?
ON CYBERTRON! OUR ELITE CADRE OF HUNTERS STILL EXISTS!
OF COURSE...
THE PREDACONS!
DO IT, SOUNDWAVE! SUMMON THEM HERE VIA THE SPACE BRIDGE. OPTIMUS PRIME IS AS GOOD AS --
DEAD, MEGATRON? I DOUBT THAT VERY MUCH!
I HAVE SEEN A SIDE OF OPTIMUS PRIME YOU COULD NEVER DREAM OF. WHEN WE FOUGHT IN THAT MURKY LITTLE DIMENSION*, I CAME TO UNDERSTAND WHY WE HAVE NEVER CONVINCINGLY BEATEN HIM.
* A STORY YOU'LL SEE IN TRANSFORMERS 100!
SO IT IS LOGICAL, IS IT NOT, TO MAKE USE OF THIS KNOWLEDGE AND MANOEUVRE PRIME AND MEGATRON INTO A SITUATION WHERE THE ONLY WINNER IS SHOCKWAVE! SOON I SHALL REIGN SUPREME...
AS RULER OF THE DECEPTICONS!

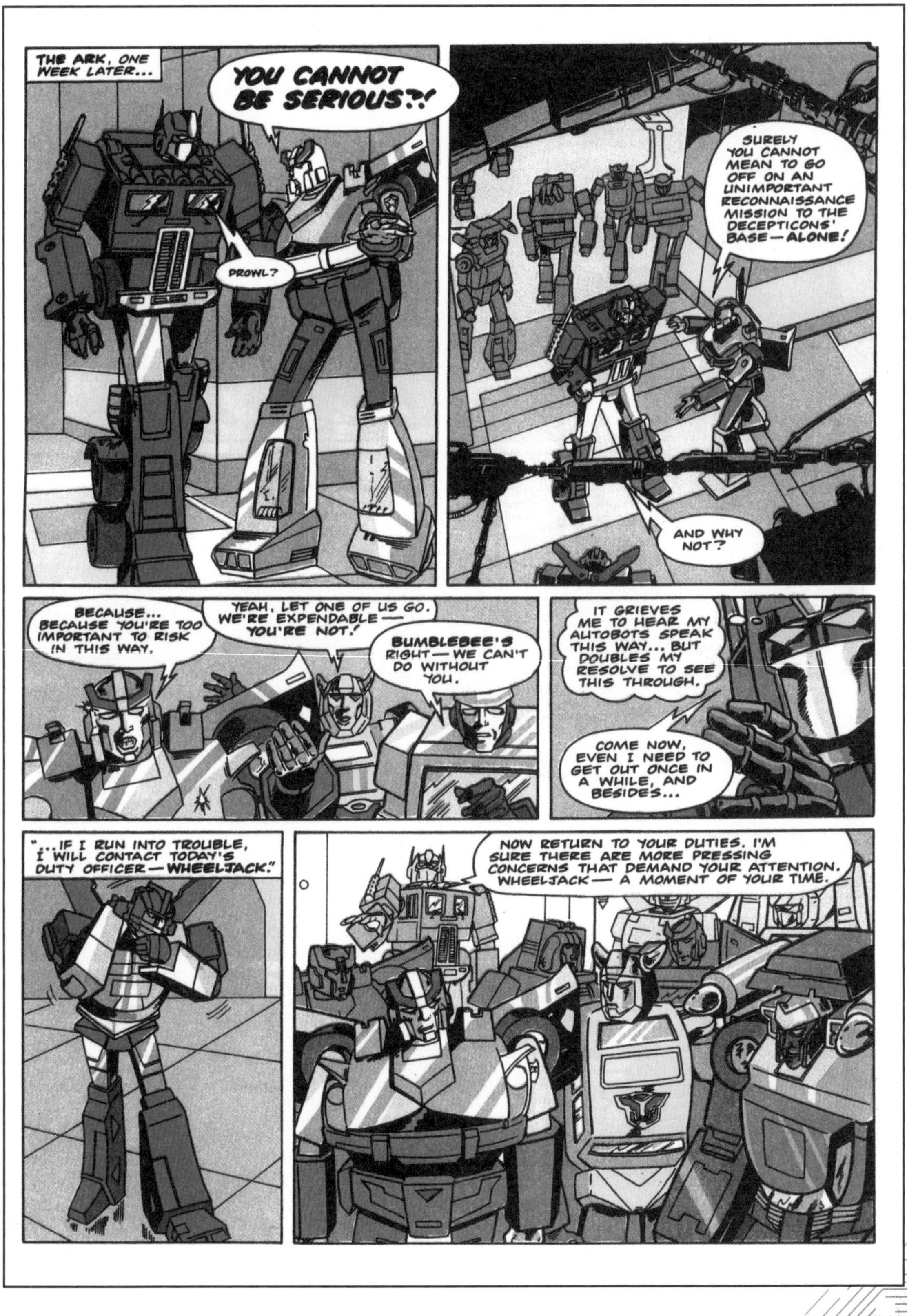

THE ARK, ONE WEEK LATER...
YOU CANNOT BE SERIOUS?!
PROWL?
SURELY YOU CANNOT MEAN TO GO OFF ON AN UNIMPORTANT RECONNAISSANCE MISSION TO THE DECEPTICONS' BASE—ALONE!
AND WHY NOT?
BECAUSE... BECAUSE YOU'RE TOO IMPORTANT TO RISK IN THIS WAY.
YEAH, LET ONE OF US GO. WE'RE EXPENDABLE— YOU'RE NOT!
BUMBLEBEE'S RIGHT—WE CAN'T DO WITHOUT YOU.
IT GRIEVES ME TO HEAR MY AUTOBOTS SPEAK THIS WAY... BUT DOUBLES MY RESOLVE TO SEE THIS THROUGH.
COME NOW, EVEN I NEED TO GET OUT ONCE IN A WHILE, AND BESIDES...
"...IF I RUN INTO TROUBLE, I WILL CONTACT TODAY'S DUTY OFFICER—WHEELJACK."
NOW RETURN TO YOUR DUTIES. I'M SURE THERE ARE MORE PRESSING CONCERNS THAT DEMAND YOUR ATTENTION. WHEELJACK— A MOMENT OF YOUR TIME.

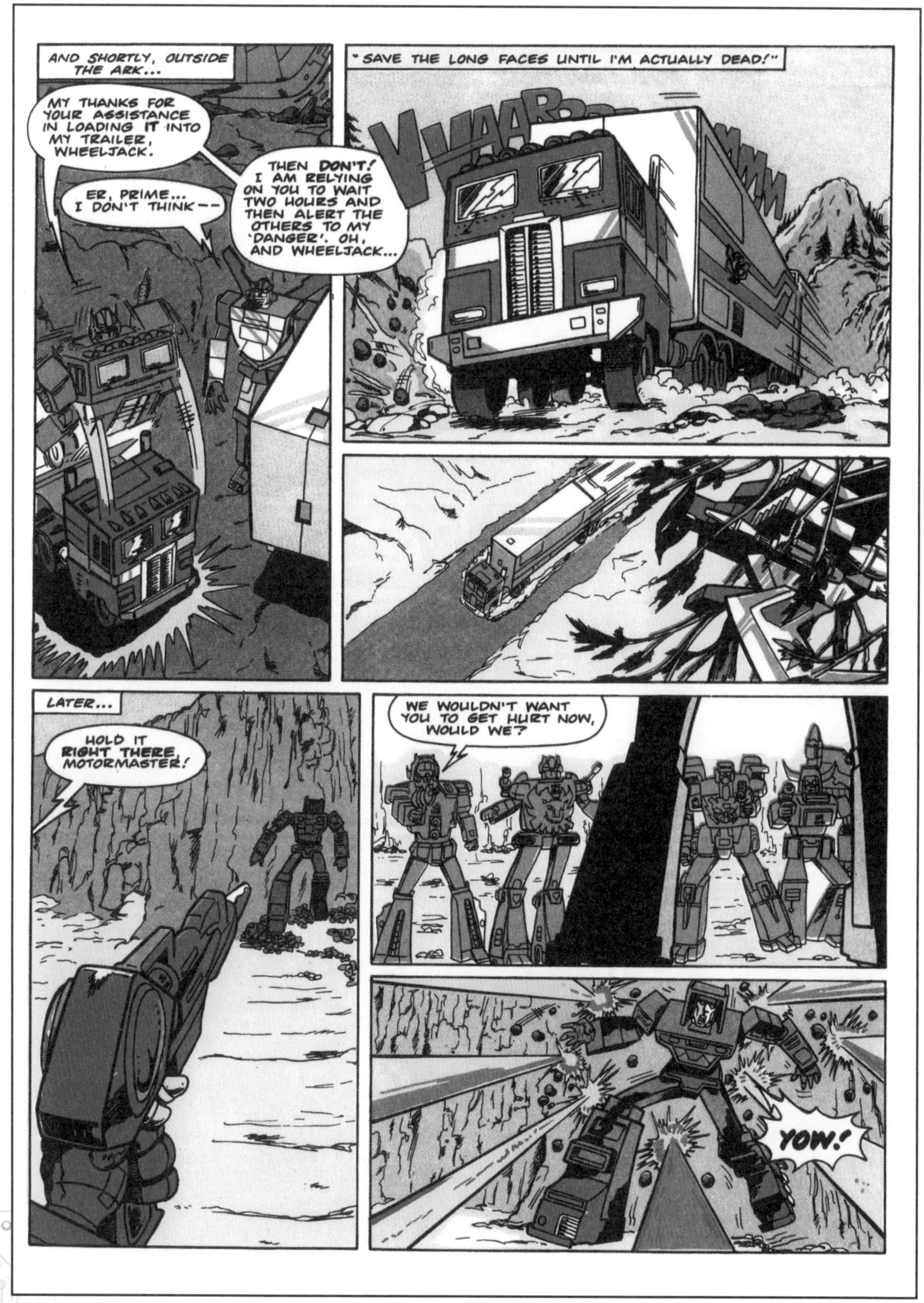

AND SHORTLY, OUTSIDE THE ARK...
MY THANKS FOR YOUR ASSISTANCE IN LOADING IT INTO MY TRAILER, WHEELJACK.
ER, PRIME... I DON'T THINK--
THEN DON'T! I AM RELYING ON YOU TO WAIT TWO HOURS AND THEN ALERT THE OTHERS TO MY 'DANGER'. OH, AND WHEELJACK...
"SAVE THE LONG FACES UNTIL I'M ACTUALLY DEAD!"
LATER...
HOLD IT RIGHT THERE, MOTORMASTER!
WE WOULDN'T WANT YOU TO GET HURT NOW, WOULD WE?
YOW!

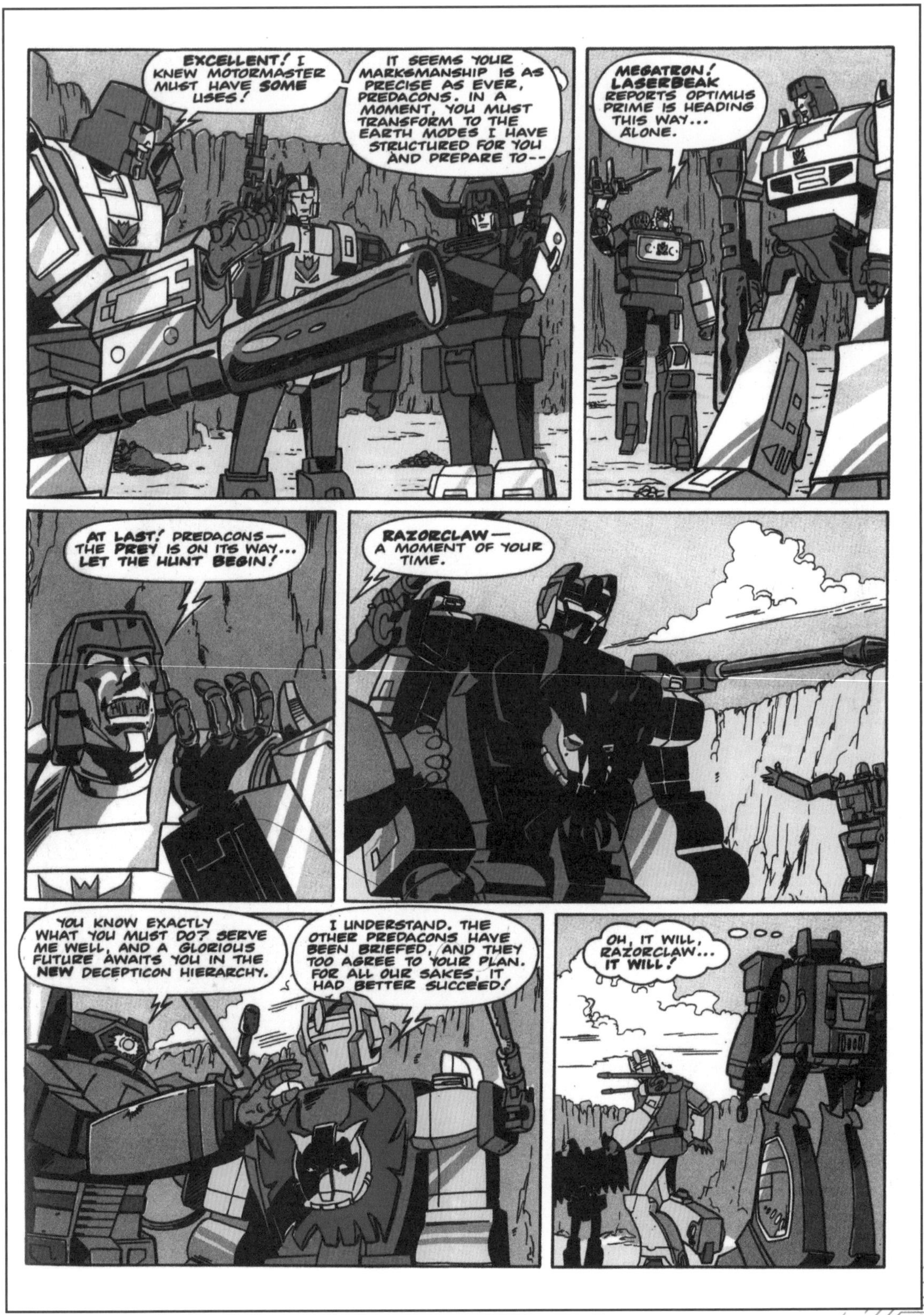
EXCELLENT! I KNEW MOTORMASTER MUST HAVE SOME USES!
IT SEEMS YOUR MARKSMANSHIP IS AS PRECISE AS EVER, PREDACONS. IN A MOMENT, YOU MUST TRANSFORM TO THE EARTH MODES I HAVE STRUCTURED FOR YOU AND PREPARE TO--
MEGATRON! LASERBEAK REPORTS OPTIMUS PRIME IS HEADING THIS WAY... ALONE.
AT LAST! PREDACONS— THE PREY IS ON ITS WAY... LET THE HUNT BEGIN!
RAZORCLAW— A MOMENT OF YOUR TIME.
YOU KNOW EXACTLY WHAT YOU MUST DO? SERVE ME WELL, AND A GLORIOUS FUTURE AWAITS YOU IN THE NEW DECEPTICON HIERARCHY.
I UNDERSTAND. THE OTHER PREDACONS HAVE BEEN BRIEFED, AND THEY TOO AGREE TO YOUR PLAN. FOR ALL OUR SAKES, IT HAD BETTER SUCCEED!
OH, IT WILL, RAZORCLAW... IT WILL!

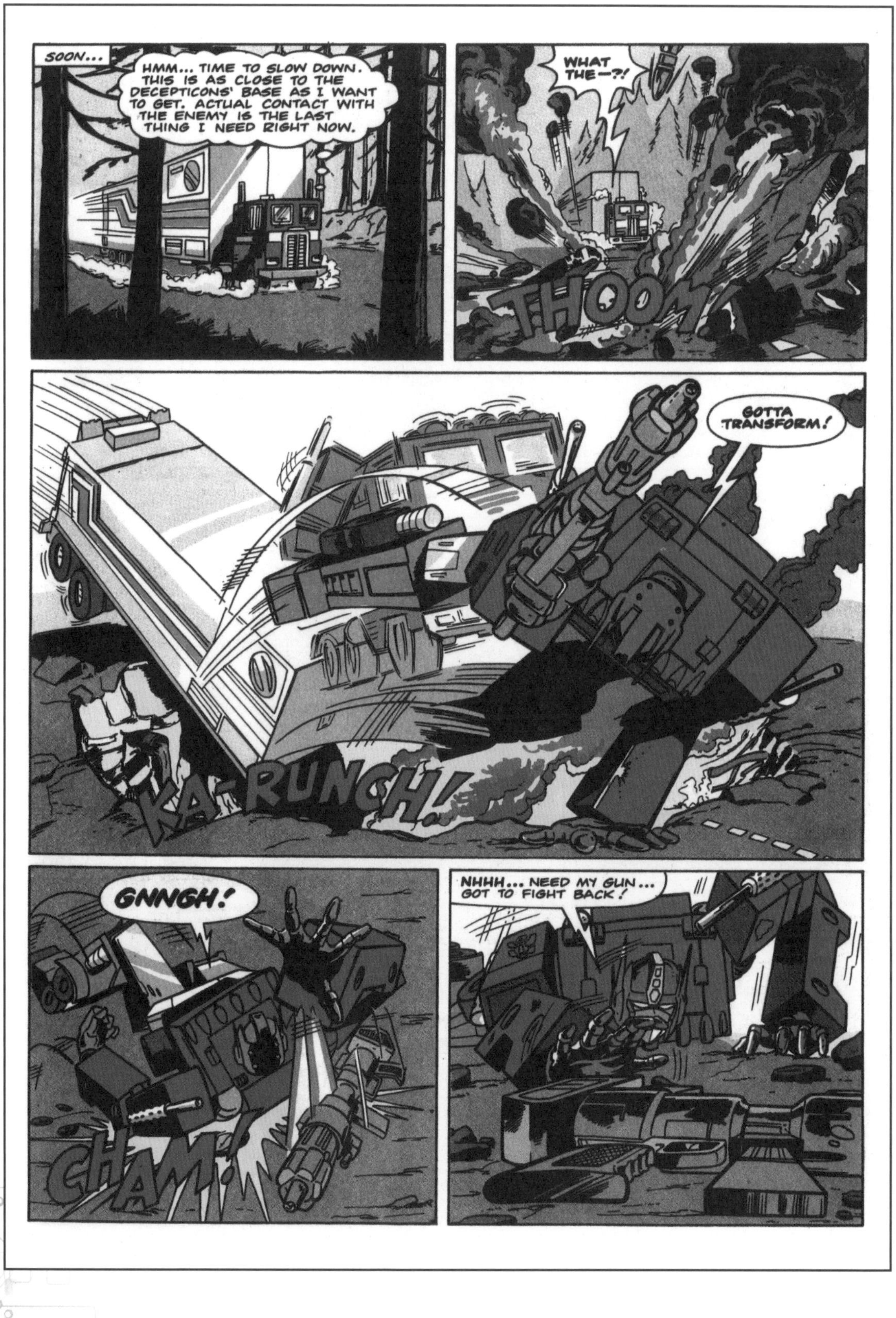
SOON...
HMM... TIME TO SLOW DOWN. THIS IS AS CLOSE TO THE DECEPTICONS' BASE AS I WANT TO GET. ACTUAL CONTACT WITH THE ENEMY IS THE LAST THING I NEED RIGHT NOW.
WHAT THE—?!
THOOM
GOTTA TRANSFORM!
KA-RUNCH!
GNNGH!
CHAM
NHHH... NEED MY GUN... GOT TO FIGHT BACK!

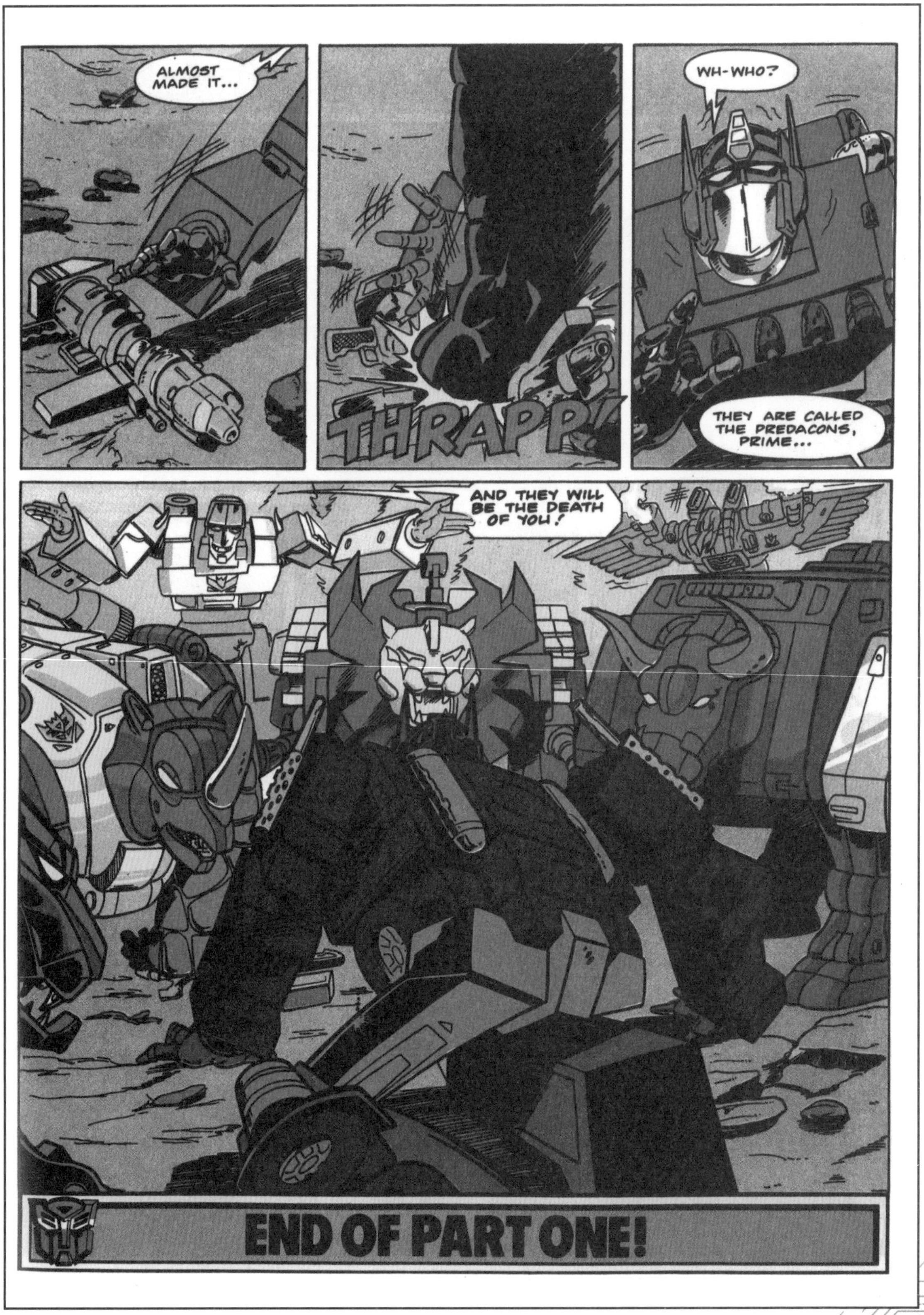
ALMOST MADE IT...
THRAPP!
WH-WHO?
THEY ARE CALLED THE PREDACONS, PRIME...
AND THEY WILL BE THE DEATH OF YOU!
END OF PART ONE!

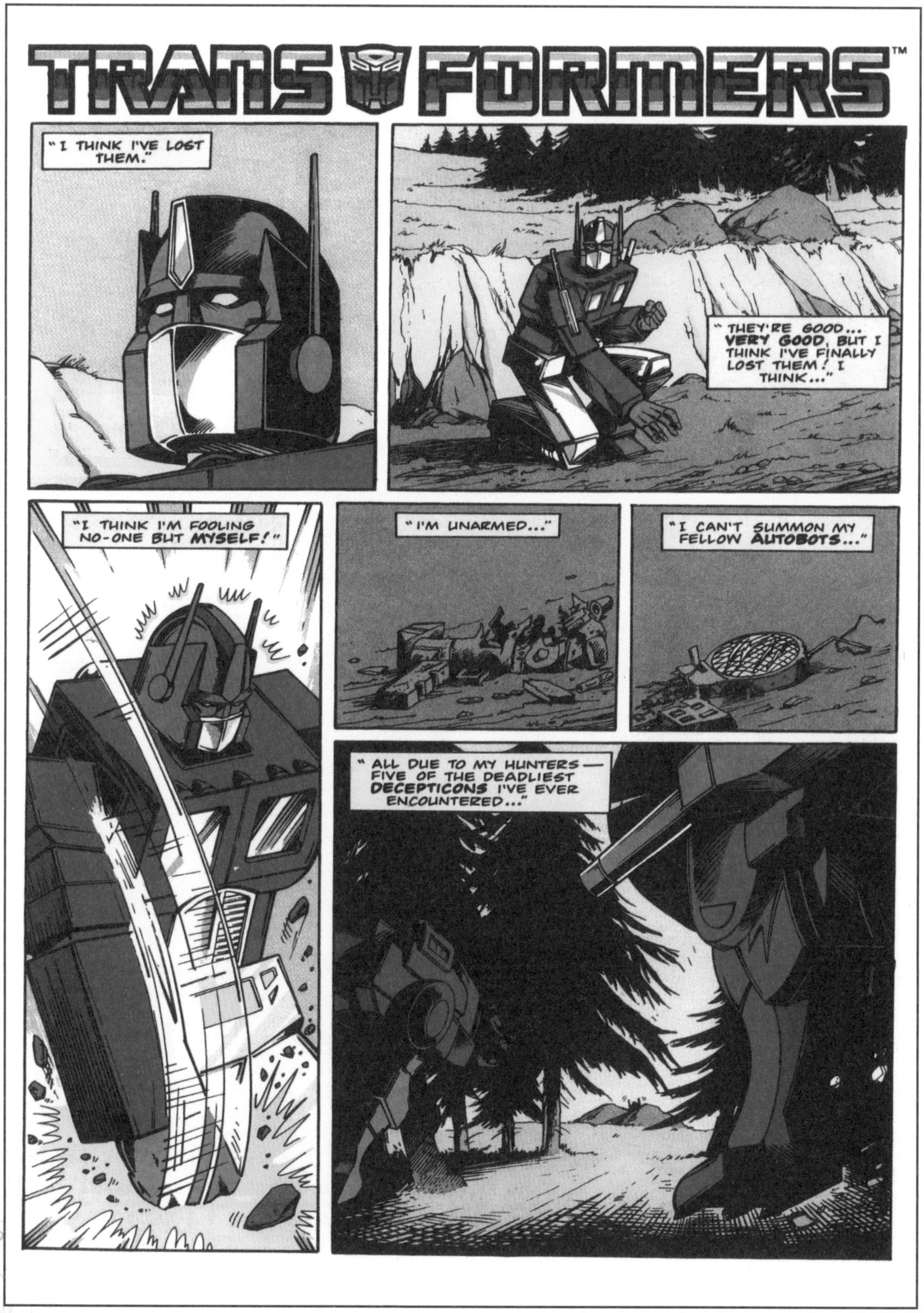
TRANSFORMERS™
"I THINK I'VE LOST THEM."
"THEY'RE GOOD... VERY GOOD, BUT I THINK I'VE FINALLY LOST THEM! I THINK..."
"I THINK I'M FOOLING NO-ONE BUT MYSELF!"
"I'M UNARMED..."
"I CAN'T SUMMON MY FELLOW AUTOBOTS..."
"ALL DUE TO MY HUNTERS— FIVE OF THE DEADLIEST DECEPTICONS I'VE EVER ENCOUNTERED..."

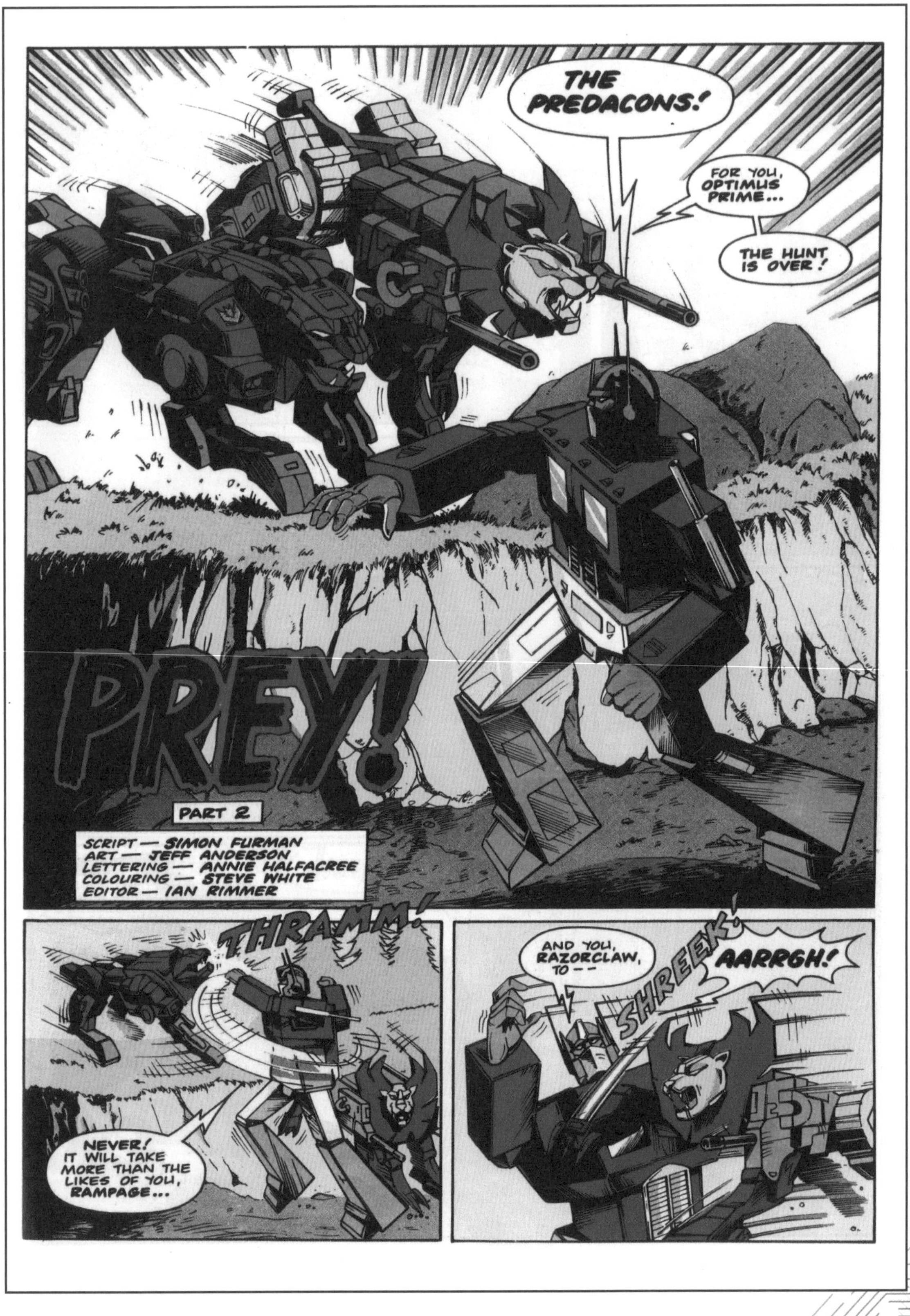
THE PREDACONS!
FOR YOU, OPTIMUS PRIME...
THE HUNT IS OVER!
PREY!
PART 2
SCRIPT — SIMON FURMAN
ART — JEFF ANDERSON
LETTERING — ANNIE HALFACREE
COLOURING — STEVE WHITE
EDITOR — IAN RIMMER
THRAMM!
NEVER! IT WILL TAKE MORE THAN THE LIKES OF YOU, RAMPAGE...
AND YOU, RAZORCLAW, TO --
SHREEK!
AARRGH!

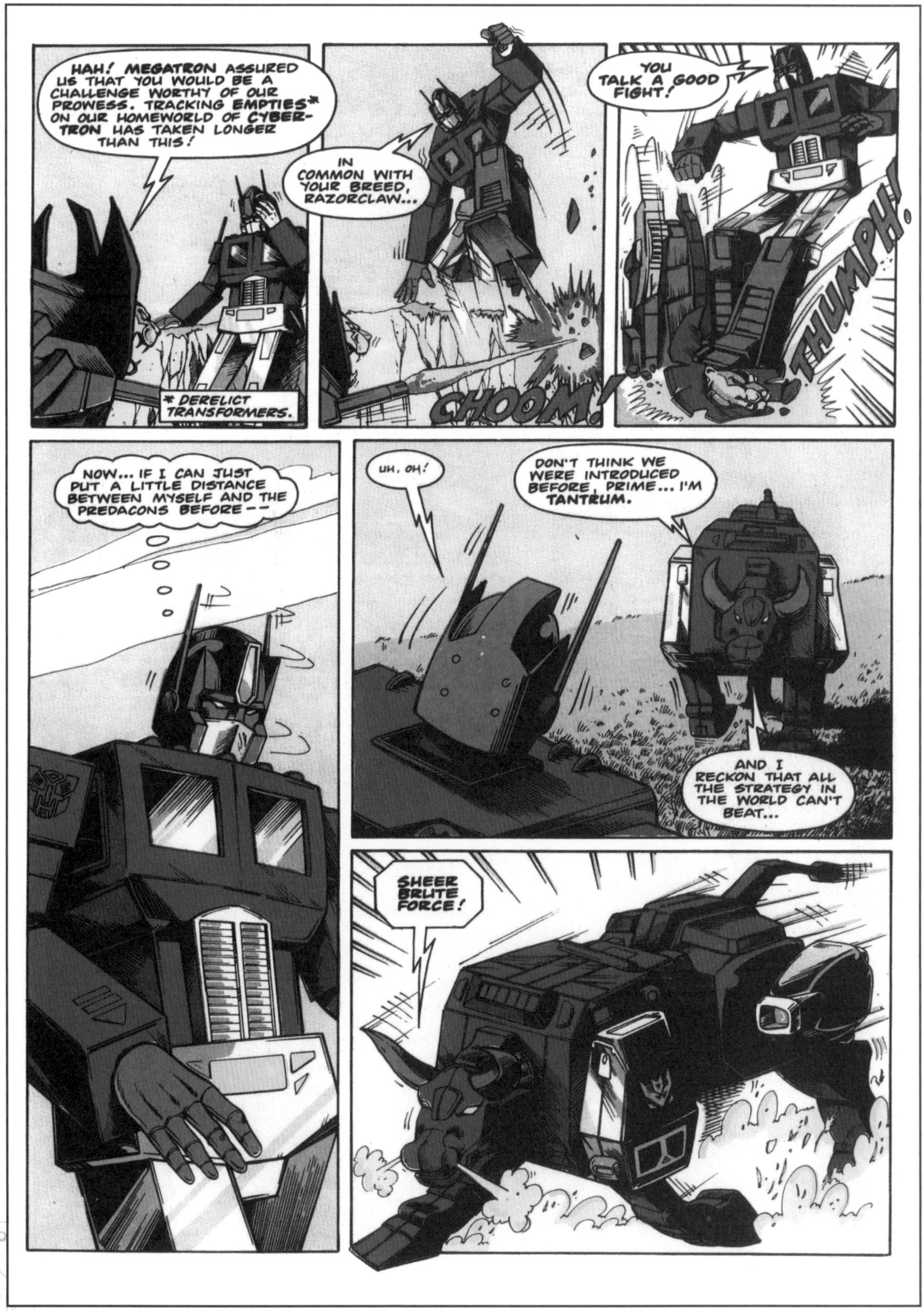

HAH! MEGATRON ASSURED US THAT YOU WOULD BE A CHALLENGE WORTHY OF OUR PROWESS. TRACKING EMPTIES* ON OUR HOMEWORLD OF CYBERTRON HAS TAKEN LONGER THAN THIS!
*DERELICT TRANSFORMERS.
IN COMMON WITH YOUR BREED, RAZORCLAW...
CHOOM!
YOU TALK A GOOD FIGHT!
THUMPH!
NOW... IF I CAN JUST PUT A LITTLE DISTANCE BETWEEN MYSELF AND THE PREDACONS BEFORE--
UH, OH!
DON'T THINK WE WERE INTRODUCED BEFORE, PRIME... I'M TANTRUM.
AND I RECKON THAT ALL THE STRATEGY IN THE WORLD CAN'T BEAT...
SHEER BRUTE FORCE!

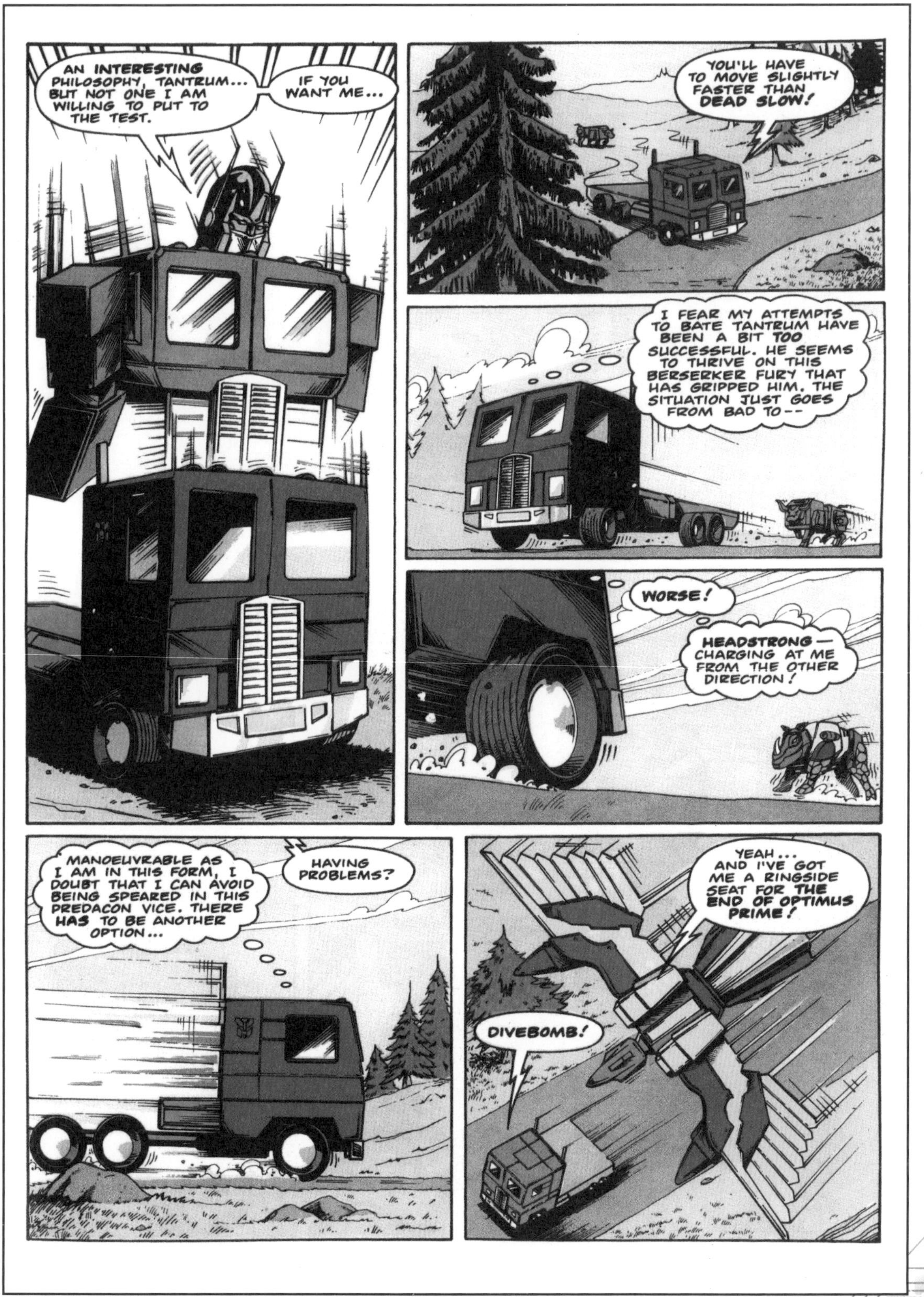
AN INTERESTING PHILOSOPHY, TANTRUM... BUT NOT ONE I AM WILLING TO PUT TO THE TEST.
IF YOU WANT ME...
YOU'LL HAVE TO MOVE SLIGHTLY FASTER THAN DEAD SLOW!
I FEAR MY ATTEMPTS TO BATE TANTRUM HAVE BEEN A BIT TOO SUCCESSFUL. HE SEEMS TO THRIVE ON THIS BERSERKER FURY THAT HAS GRIPPED HIM. THE SITUATION JUST GOES FROM BAD TO--
WORSE!
HEADSTRONG— CHARGING AT ME FROM THE OTHER DIRECTION!
MANOEUVRABLE AS I AM IN THIS FORM, I DOUBT THAT I CAN AVOID BEING SPEARED IN THIS PREDACON VICE. THERE HAS TO BE ANOTHER OPTION...
HAVING PROBLEMS?
YEAH... AND I'VE GOT ME A RINGSIDE SEAT FOR THE END OF OPTIMUS PRIME!
DIVEBOMB!

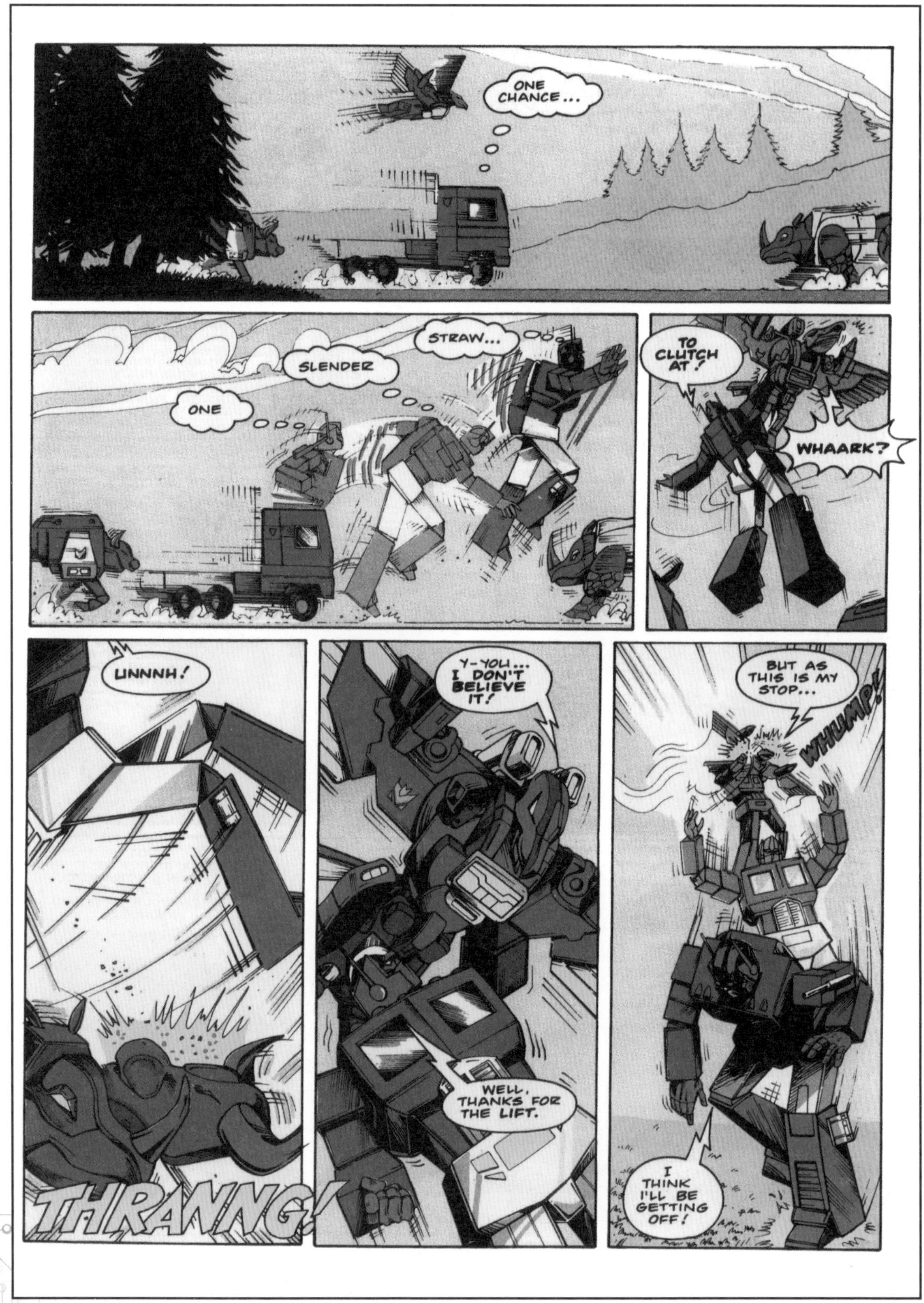
ONE CHANCE...
ONE
SLENDER
STRAW...
TO CLUTCH AT!
WHAARK?
UNNNH!
THRANNG!
Y-YOU... I DON'T BELIEVE IT!
WELL, THANKS FOR THE LIFT.
BUT AS THIS IS MY STOP...
WHUMP!
I THINK I'LL BE GETTING OFF!

I SUSPECT I HAVE STRETCHED THE GRACE OF WHATEVER GUARDIAN SPIRIT WATCHES OVER ME TO THE LIMIT AND WAY, WAY BEYOND! I'VE MANAGED TO DELAY THE PREDACONS... NOW ALL I HAVE TO DO IS *STOP* THEM.

THE IRONY INHERENT IN THIS SITUATION DOES NOT ESCAPE ME!

MY PLAN WAS TO CREATE THE *ILLUSION* OF MY DEATH, BUT THESE EVENTS MAY WELL END WITH THE *REAL THING!*

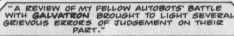

"A REVIEW OF MY FELLOW AUTOBOTS' BATTLE WITH **GALVATRON** BROUGHT TO LIGHT SEVERAL GRIEVOUS ERRORS OF JUDGEMENT ON THEIR PART."

"NOT LEAST OF WHICH WAS SIDING WITH THE DECEPTICONS' LEADER—MEGATRON!"

"I DECIDED THAT THE AUTOBOTS WOULD HAVE TO LEARN TO FUNCTION WITHOUT ME. WITH THE ASSISTANCE OF MY CHIEF ENGINEER, **WHEEL-JACK**, I SET ABOUT PREPARING A NECESSARY DECEPTION."

"BUT BEFORE I COULD FULLY PUT MY PLAN INTO ACTION, I FOUND MYSELF UNDER ATTACK FROM MEGATRON, BACKED UP BY THE PREDACONS."

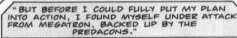

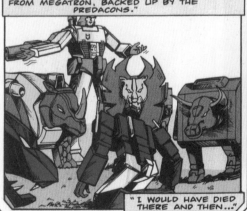

"I WOULD HAVE DIED THERE AND THEN..."

"...HAD NOT MEGATRON WISHED TO SEE ME SQUIRM ONE FINAL TIME. RELYING ON THE PREDACONS' REPUTATION AS TRACKERS..."

"I WAS GIVEN TEN MINUTES START BEFORE **THE HUNT** BEGAN!"

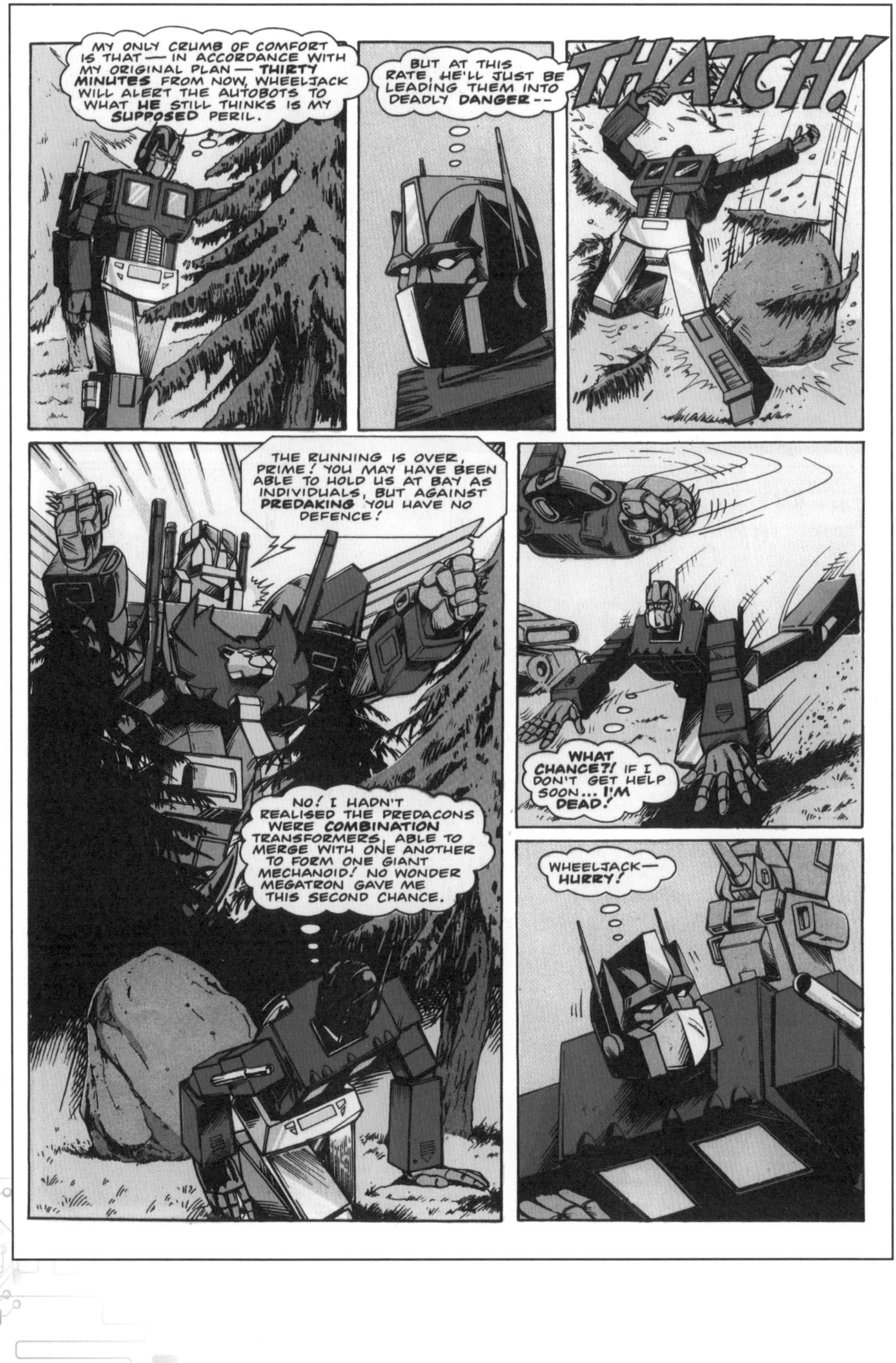

MY ONLY CRUMB OF COMFORT IS THAT — IN ACCORDANCE WITH MY ORIGINAL PLAN — THIRTY MINUTES FROM NOW, WHEELJACK WILL ALERT THE AUTOBOTS TO WHAT HE STILL THINKS IS MY SUPPOSED PERIL.
BUT AT THIS RATE, HE'LL JUST BE LEADING THEM INTO DEADLY DANGER--
THATCH!
THE RUNNING IS OVER, PRIME! YOU MAY HAVE BEEN ABLE TO HOLD US AT BAY AS INDIVIDUALS, BUT AGAINST PREDAKING YOU HAVE NO DEFENCE!
NO! I HADN'T REALISED THE PREDACONS WERE COMBINATION TRANSFORMERS, ABLE TO MERGE WITH ONE ANOTHER TO FORM ONE GIANT MECHANOID! NO WONDER MEGATRON GAVE ME THIS SECOND CHANCE.
WHAT CHANCE?! IF I DON'T GET HELP SOON... I'M DEAD!
WHEELJACK— HURRY!

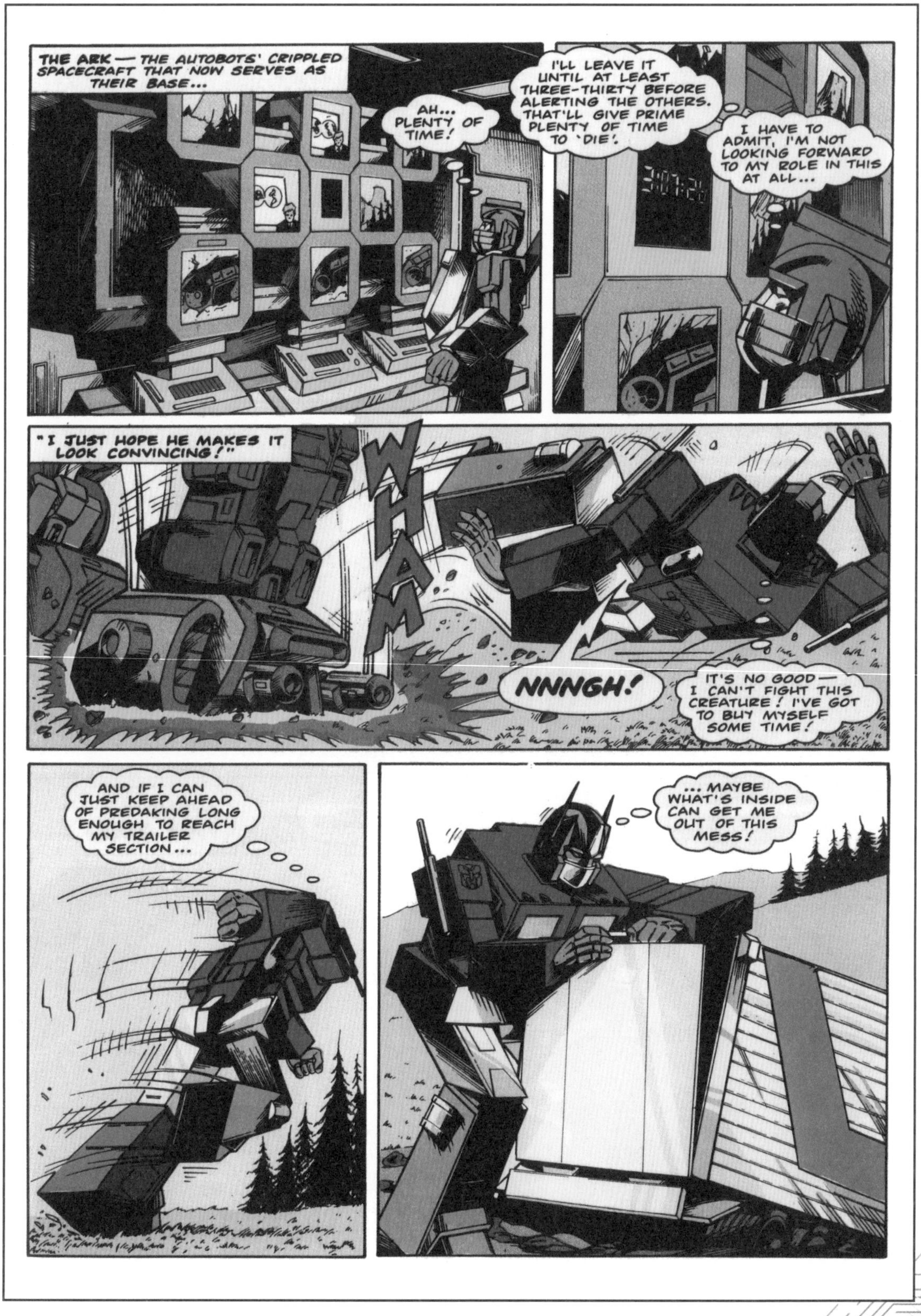

THE ARK — THE AUTOBOTS' CRIPPLED SPACECRAFT THAT NOW SERVES AS THEIR BASE...
AH... PLENTY OF TIME!
I'LL LEAVE IT UNTIL AT LEAST THREE-THIRTY BEFORE ALERTING THE OTHERS. THAT'LL GIVE PRIME PLENTY OF TIME TO 'DIE'.
I HAVE TO ADMIT, I'M NOT LOOKING FORWARD TO MY ROLE IN THIS AT ALL...
"I JUST HOPE HE MAKES IT LOOK CONVINCING!"
WHAM
NNNGH!
IT'S NO GOOD — I CAN'T FIGHT THIS CREATURE! I'VE GOT TO BUY MYSELF SOME TIME!
AND IF I CAN JUST KEEP AHEAD OF PREDAKING LONG ENOUGH TO REACH MY TRAILER SECTION...
...MAYBE WHAT'S INSIDE CAN GET ME OUT OF THIS MESS!

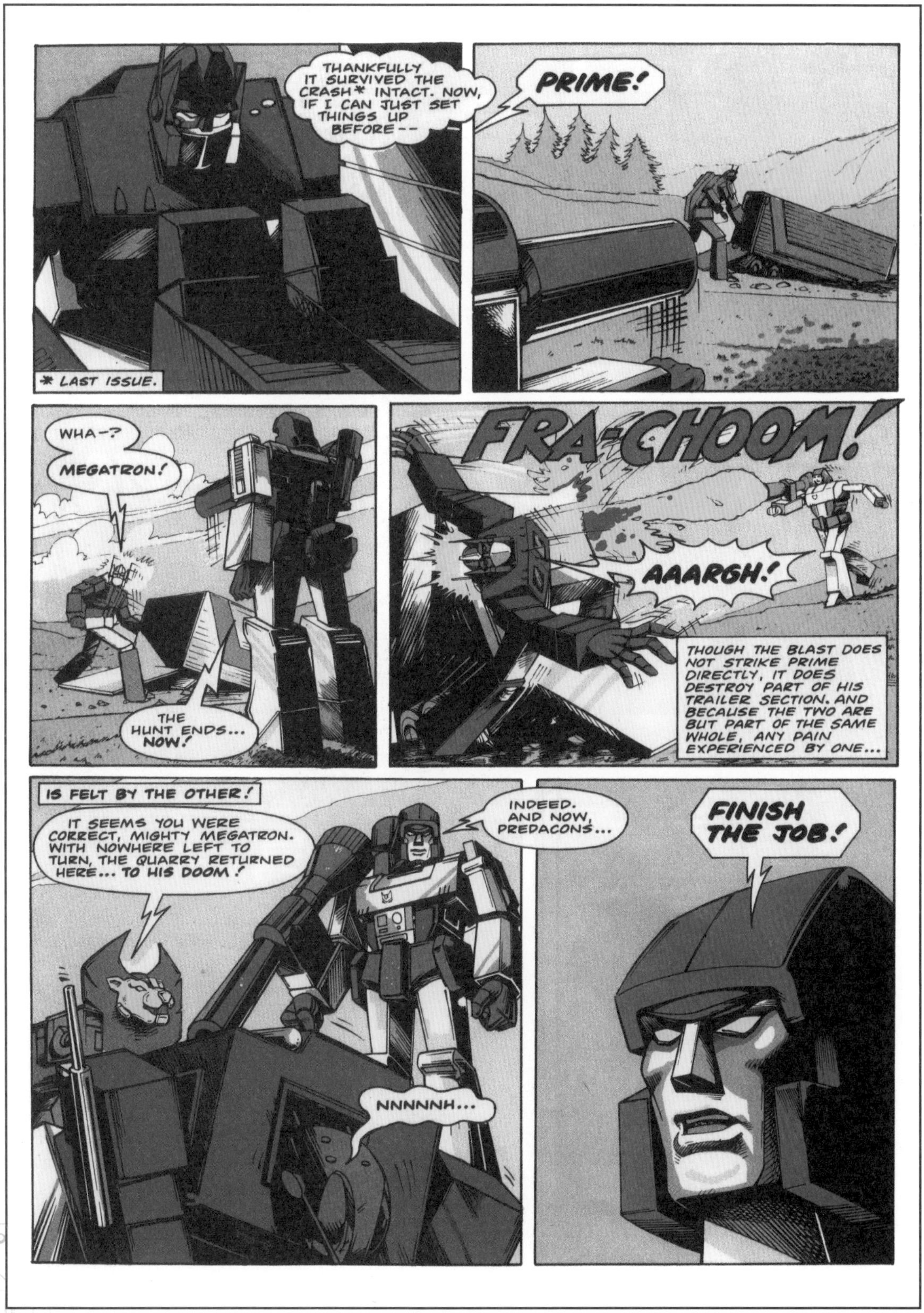

THANKFULLY IT SURVIVED THE CRASH* INTACT. NOW, IF I CAN JUST SET THINGS UP BEFORE--
* LAST ISSUE.
PRIME!
WHA-?
MEGATRON!
THE HUNT ENDS... NOW!
FRA-CHOOM!
AAARGH!
THOUGH THE BLAST DOES NOT STRIKE PRIME DIRECTLY, IT DOES DESTROY PART OF HIS TRAILER SECTION. AND BECAUSE THE TWO ARE BUT PART OF THE SAME WHOLE, ANY PAIN EXPERIENCED BY ONE...
IS FELT BY THE OTHER!
IT SEEMS YOU WERE CORRECT, MIGHTY MEGATRON. WITH NOWHERE LEFT TO TURN, THE QUARRY RETURNED HERE... TO HIS DOOM!
INDEED. AND NOW, PREDACONS...
NNNNNH...
FINISH THE JOB!

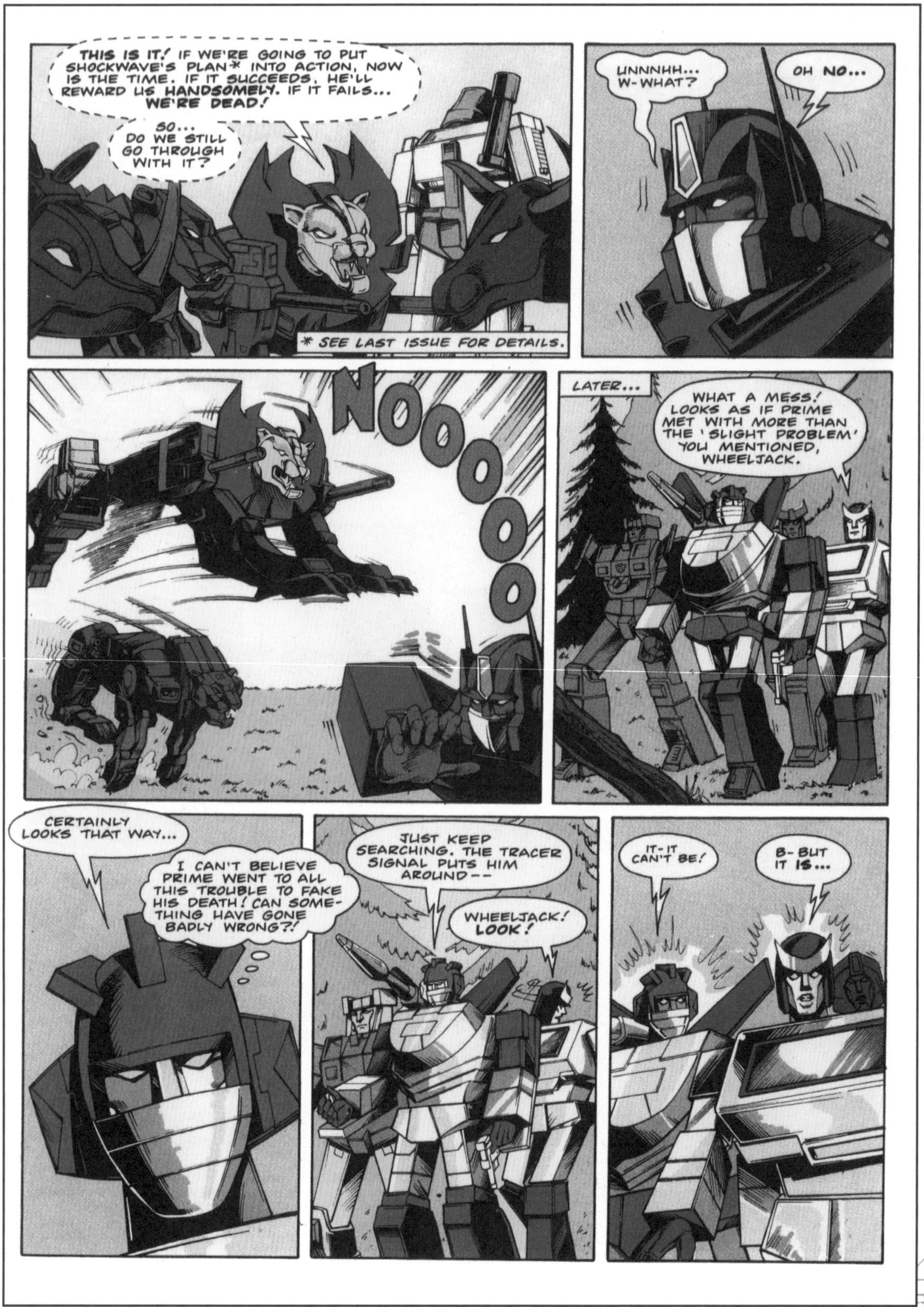
THIS IS IT! IF WE'RE GOING TO PUT SHOCKWAVE'S PLAN* INTO ACTION, NOW IS THE TIME. IF IT SUCCEEDS, HE'LL REWARD US HANDSOMELY. IF IT FAILS... WE'RE DEAD!
SO... DO WE STILL GO THROUGH WITH IT?
* SEE LAST ISSUE FOR DETAILS.
UNNNHH... W-WHAT?
OH NO...
NOOOOOO
LATER...
WHAT A MESS! LOOKS AS IF PRIME MET WITH MORE THAN THE 'SLIGHT PROBLEM' YOU MENTIONED, WHEELJACK.
CERTAINLY LOOKS THAT WAY...
I CAN'T BELIEVE PRIME WENT TO ALL THIS TROUBLE TO FAKE HIS DEATH! CAN SOMETHING HAVE GONE BADLY WRONG?!
JUST KEEP SEARCHING. THE TRACER SIGNAL PUTS HIM AROUND--
WHEELJACK! LOOK!
IT-IT CAN'T BE!
B-BUT IT IS...

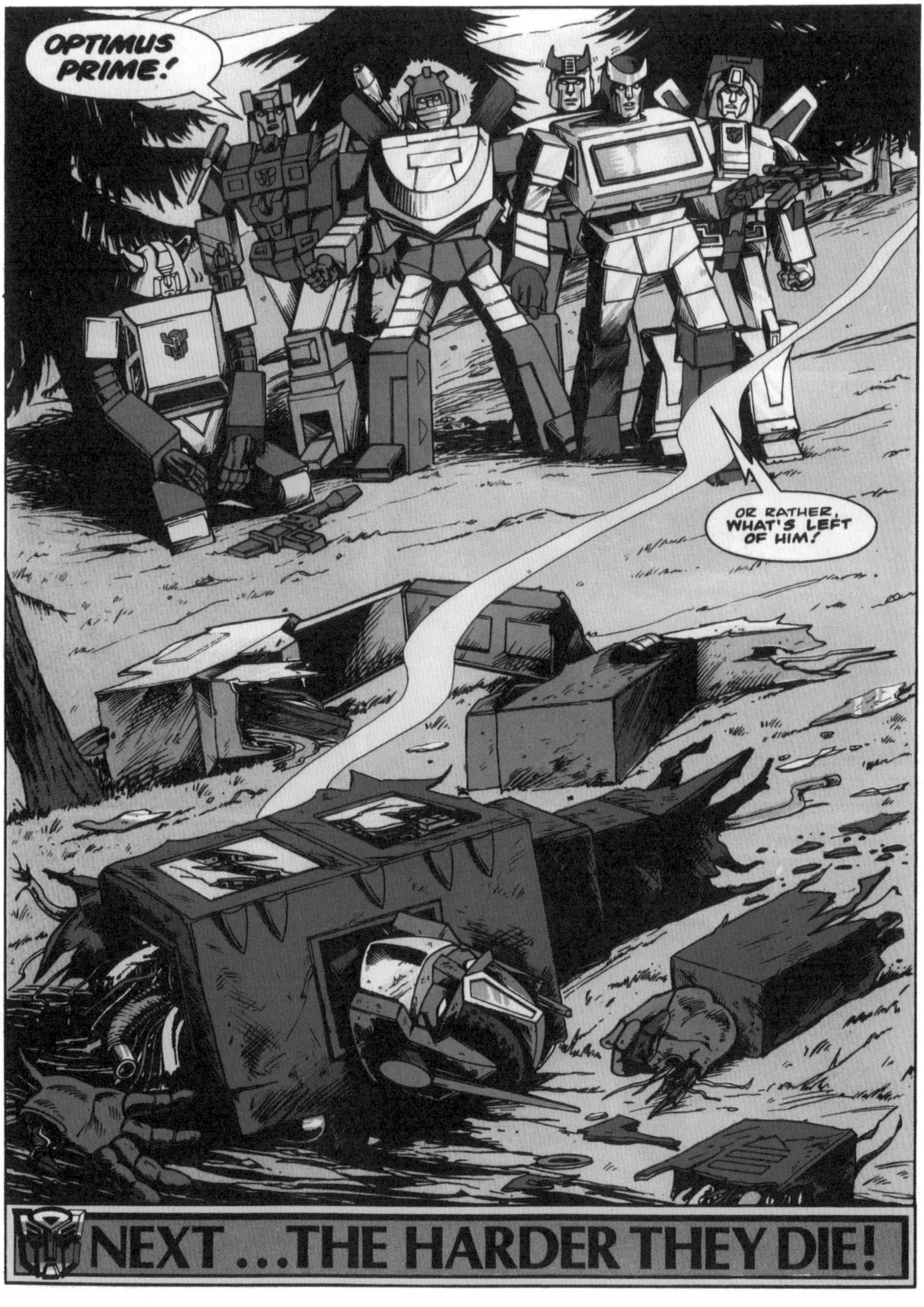
OPTIMUS PRIME!
OR RATHER, WHAT'S LEFT OF HIM!
NEXT ...THE HARDER THEY DIE!

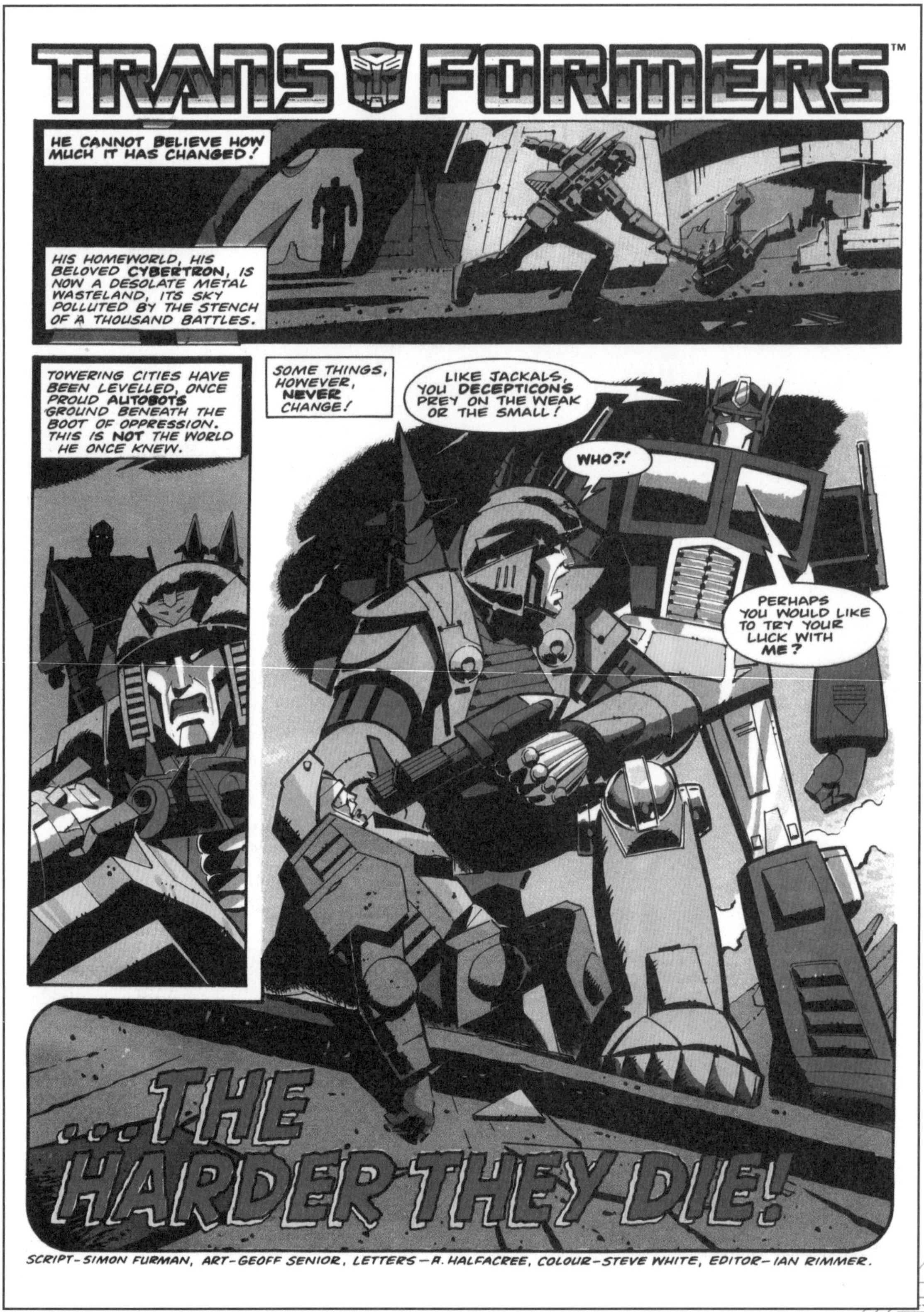
TRANSFORMERS™
HE CANNOT BELIEVE HOW MUCH IT HAS CHANGED!
HIS HOMEWORLD, HIS BELOVED CYBERTRON, IS NOW A DESOLATE METAL WASTELAND, ITS SKY POLLUTED BY THE STENCH OF A THOUSAND BATTLES.
TOWERING CITIES HAVE BEEN LEVELLED, ONCE PROUD AUTOBOTS GROUND BENEATH THE BOOT OF OPPRESSION. THIS IS NOT THE WORLD HE ONCE KNEW.
SOME THINGS, HOWEVER, NEVER CHANGE!
LIKE JACKALS, YOU DECEPTICONS PREY ON THE WEAK OR THE SMALL!
WHO?!
PERHAPS YOU WOULD LIKE TO TRY YOUR LUCK WITH ME?
...THE HARDER THEY DIE!
SCRIPT-SIMON FURMAN, ART-GEOFF SENIOR, LETTERS-R. HALFACREE, COLOUR-STEVE WHITE, EDITOR-IAN RIMMER.

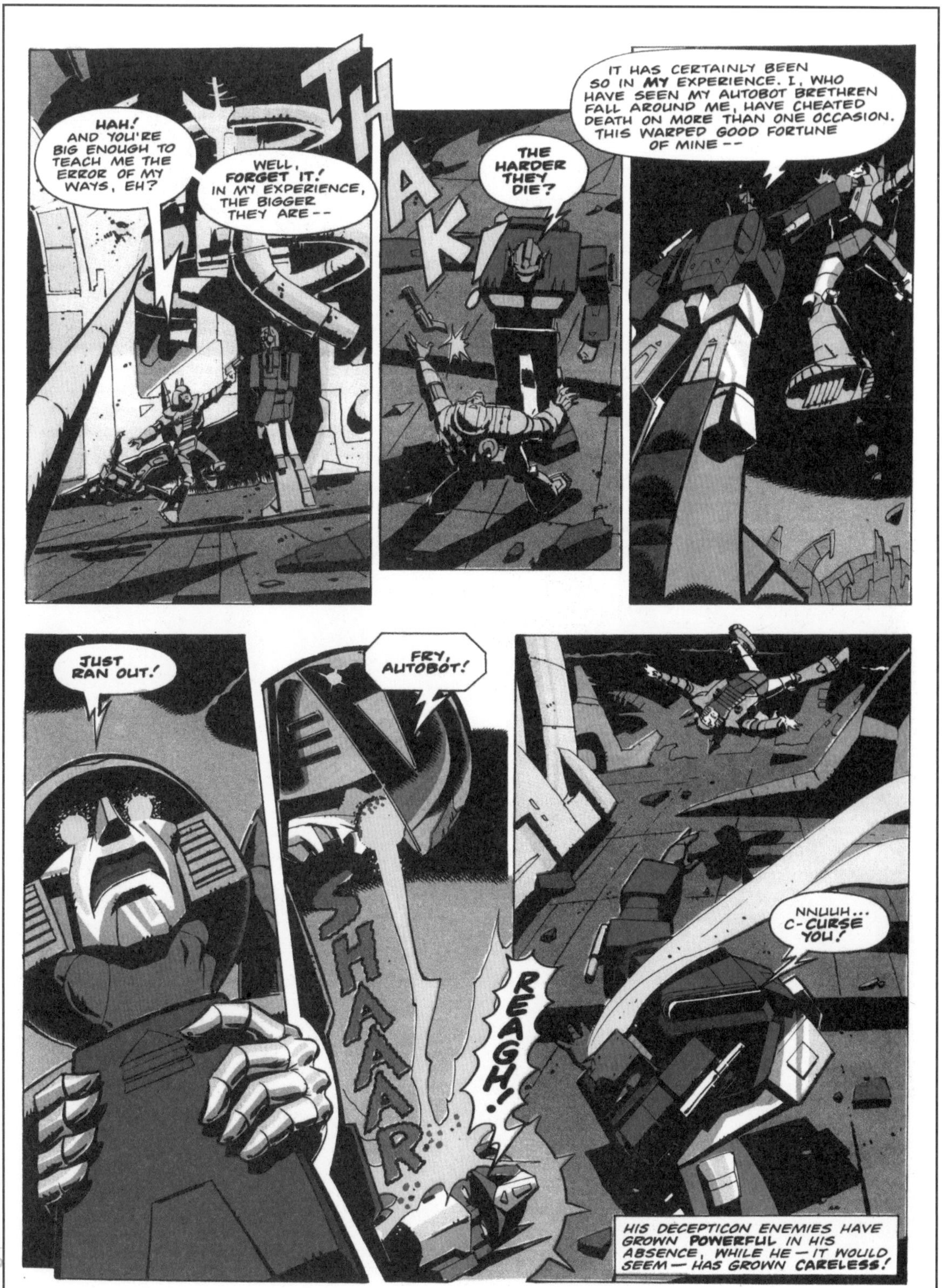
HAH! AND YOU'RE BIG ENOUGH TO TEACH ME THE ERROR OF MY WAYS, EH?
WELL, FORGET IT! IN MY EXPERIENCE, THE BIGGER THEY ARE--
THAK!
THE HARDER THEY DIE?
IT HAS CERTAINLY BEEN SO IN MY EXPERIENCE. I, WHO HAVE SEEN MY AUTOBOT BRETHREN FALL AROUND ME, HAVE CHEATED DEATH ON MORE THAN ONE OCCASION. THIS WARPED GOOD FORTUNE OF MINE--
JUST RAN OUT!
FRY, AUTOBOT!
SHAAAR
REAGH!
NNUUH... C-CURSE YOU!
HIS DECEPTICON ENEMIES HAVE GROWN POWERFUL IN HIS ABSENCE, WHILE HE — IT WOULD SEEM — HAS GROWN CARELESS!

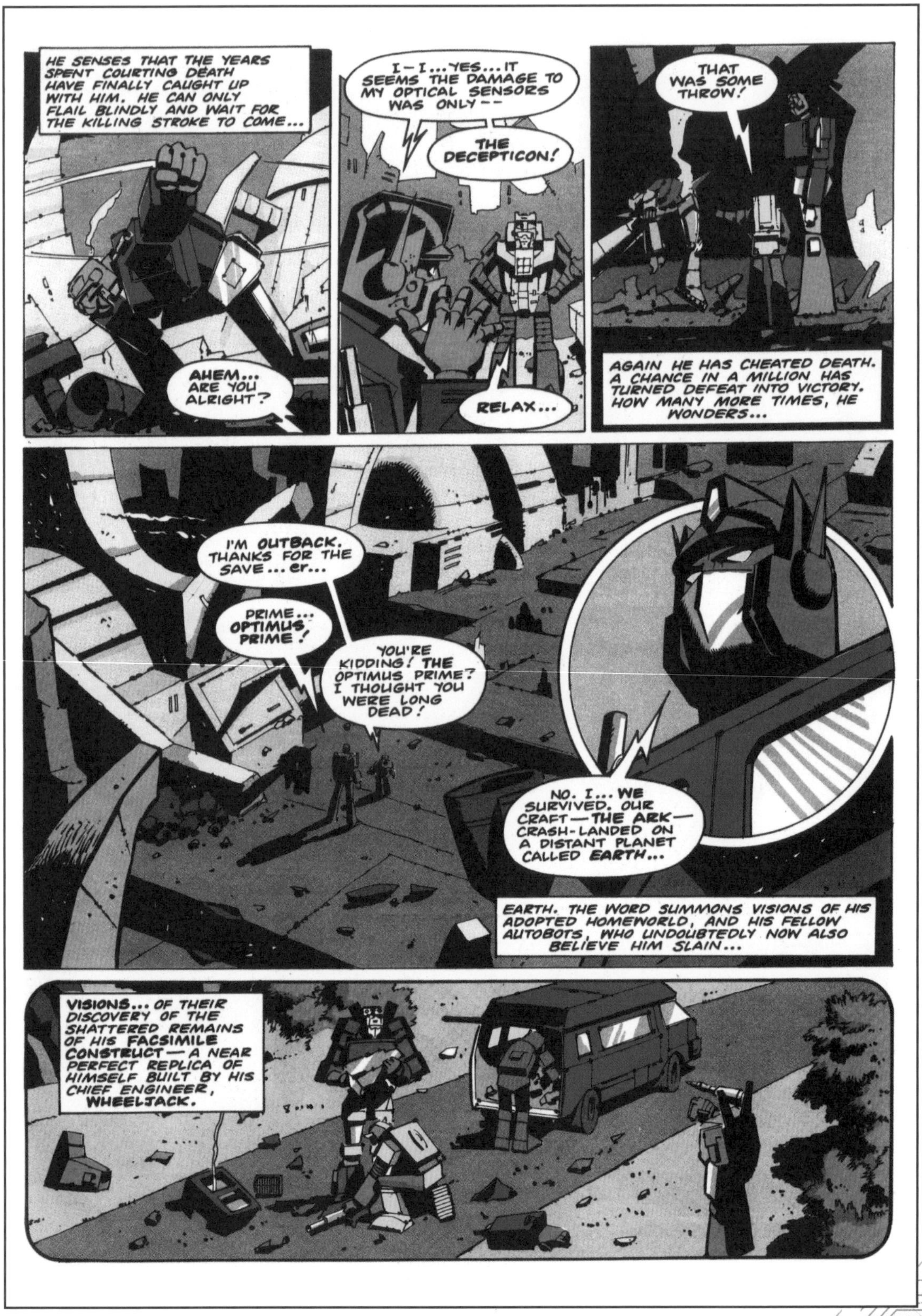
HE SENSES THAT THE YEARS SPENT COURTING DEATH HAVE FINALLY CAUGHT UP WITH HIM. HE CAN ONLY FLAIL BLINDLY AND WAIT FOR THE KILLING STROKE TO COME...
AHEM... ARE YOU ALRIGHT?
I-I... YES... IT SEEMS THE DAMAGE TO MY OPTICAL SENSORS WAS ONLY--
THE DECEPTICON!
RELAX...
THAT WAS SOME THROW!
AGAIN HE HAS CHEATED DEATH. A CHANCE IN A MILLION HAS TURNED DEFEAT INTO VICTORY. HOW MANY MORE TIMES, HE WONDERS...
I'M OUTBACK. THANKS FOR THE SAVE... er...
PRIME... OPTIMUS PRIME!
YOU'RE KIDDING! THE OPTIMUS PRIME? I THOUGHT YOU WERE LONG DEAD!
NO. I... WE SURVIVED. OUR CRAFT—THE ARK—CRASH-LANDED ON A DISTANT PLANET CALLED EARTH...
EARTH. THE WORD SUMMONS VISIONS OF HIS ADOPTED HOMEWORLD, AND HIS FELLOW AUTOBOTS, WHO UNDOUBTEDLY NOW ALSO BELIEVE HIM SLAIN...
VISIONS... OF THEIR DISCOVERY OF THE SHATTERED REMAINS OF HIS FACSIMILE CONSTRUCT—A NEAR PERFECT REPLICA OF HIMSELF BUILT BY HIS CHIEF ENGINEER, WHEELJACK.

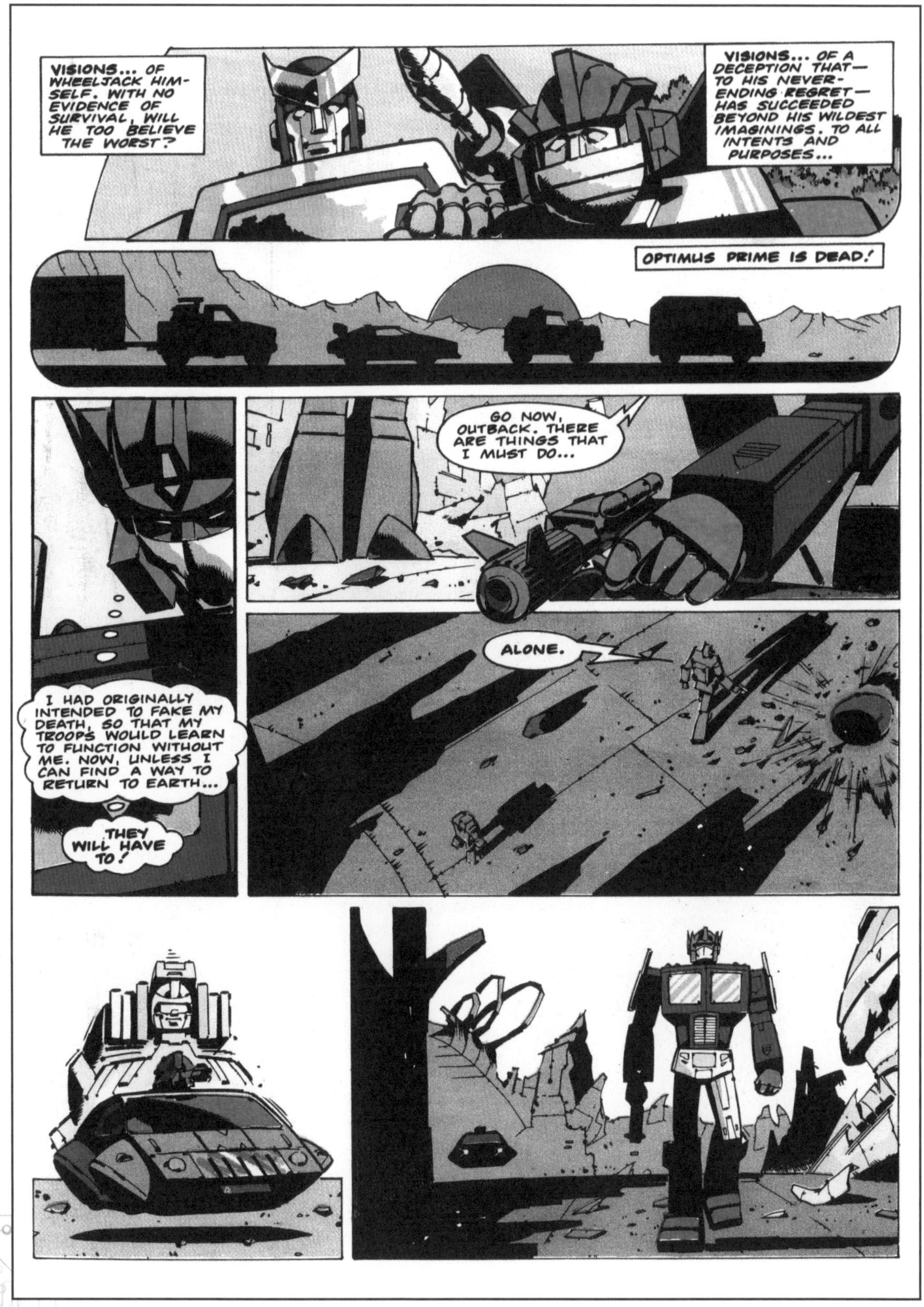
VISIONS... OF WHEELJACK HIMSELF. WITH NO EVIDENCE OF SURVIVAL, WILL HE TOO BELIEVE THE WORST?
VISIONS... OF A DECEPTION THAT— TO HIS NEVER-ENDING REGRET— HAS SUCCEEDED BEYOND HIS WILDEST IMAGININGS. TO ALL INTENTS AND PURPOSES...
OPTIMUS PRIME IS DEAD!
GO NOW, OUTBACK. THERE ARE THINGS THAT I MUST DO...
ALONE.
I HAD ORIGINALLY INTENDED TO FAKE MY DEATH, SO THAT MY TROOPS WOULD LEARN TO FUNCTION WITHOUT ME. NOW, UNLESS I CAN FIND A WAY TO RETURN TO EARTH...
THEY WILL HAVE TO!

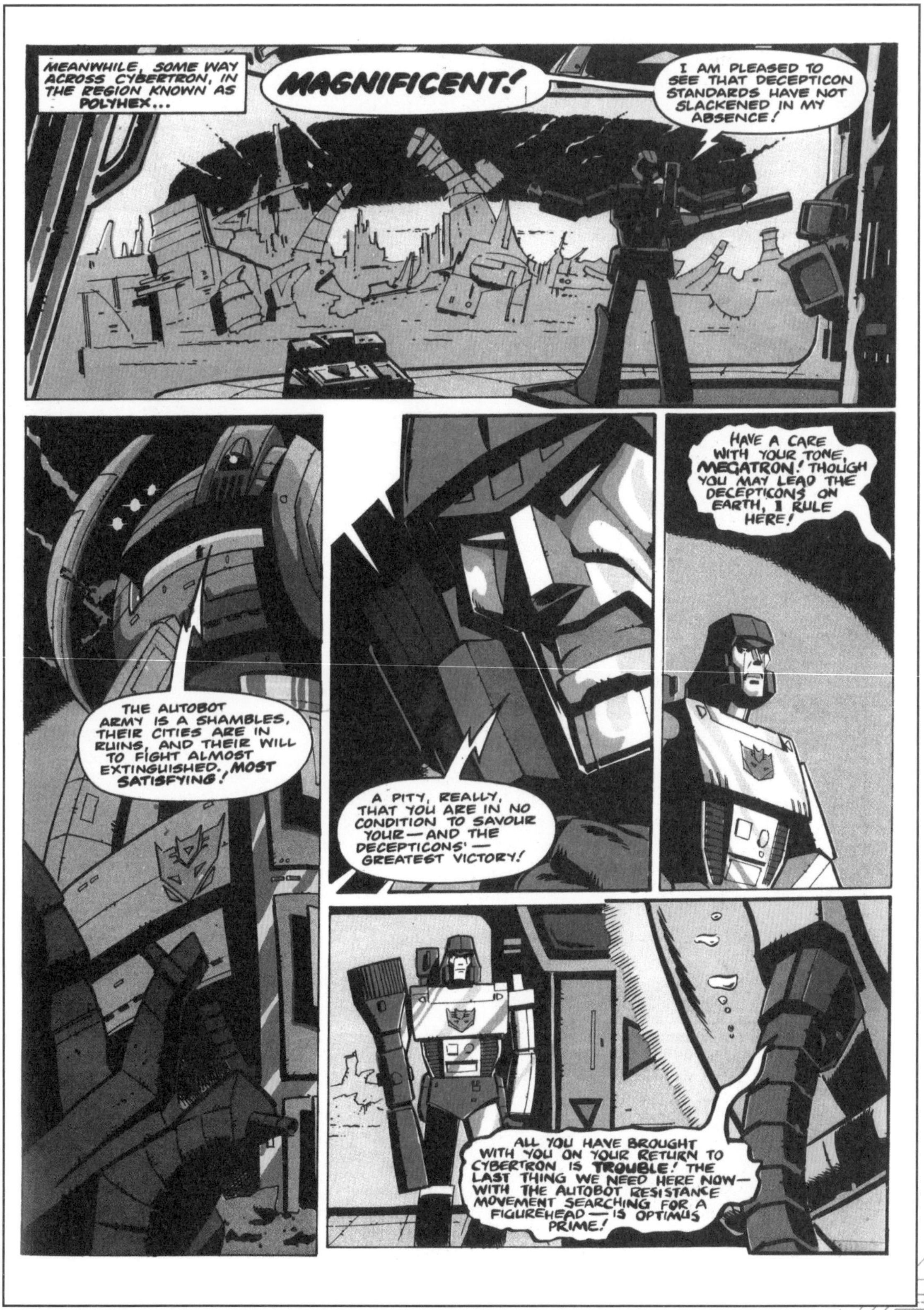
MEANWHILE, SOME WAY ACROSS CYBERTRON, IN THE REGION KNOWN AS POLYHEX...
MAGNIFICENT!
I AM PLEASED TO SEE THAT DECEPTICON STANDARDS HAVE NOT SLACKENED IN MY ABSENCE!
THE AUTOBOT ARMY IS A SHAMBLES, THEIR CITIES ARE IN RUINS, AND THEIR WILL TO FIGHT ALMOST EXTINGUISHED. MOST SATISFYING!
A PITY, REALLY, THAT YOU ARE IN NO CONDITION TO SAVOUR YOUR—AND THE DECEPTICONS'—GREATEST VICTORY!
HAVE A CARE WITH YOUR TONE, MEGATRON! THOUGH YOU MAY LEAD THE DECEPTICONS ON EARTH, I RULE HERE!
ALL YOU HAVE BROUGHT WITH YOU ON YOUR RETURN TO CYBERTRON IS TROUBLE! THE LAST THING WE NEED HERE NOW—WITH THE AUTOBOT RESISTANCE MOVEMENT SEARCHING FOR A FIGUREHEAD—IS OPTIMUS PRIME!

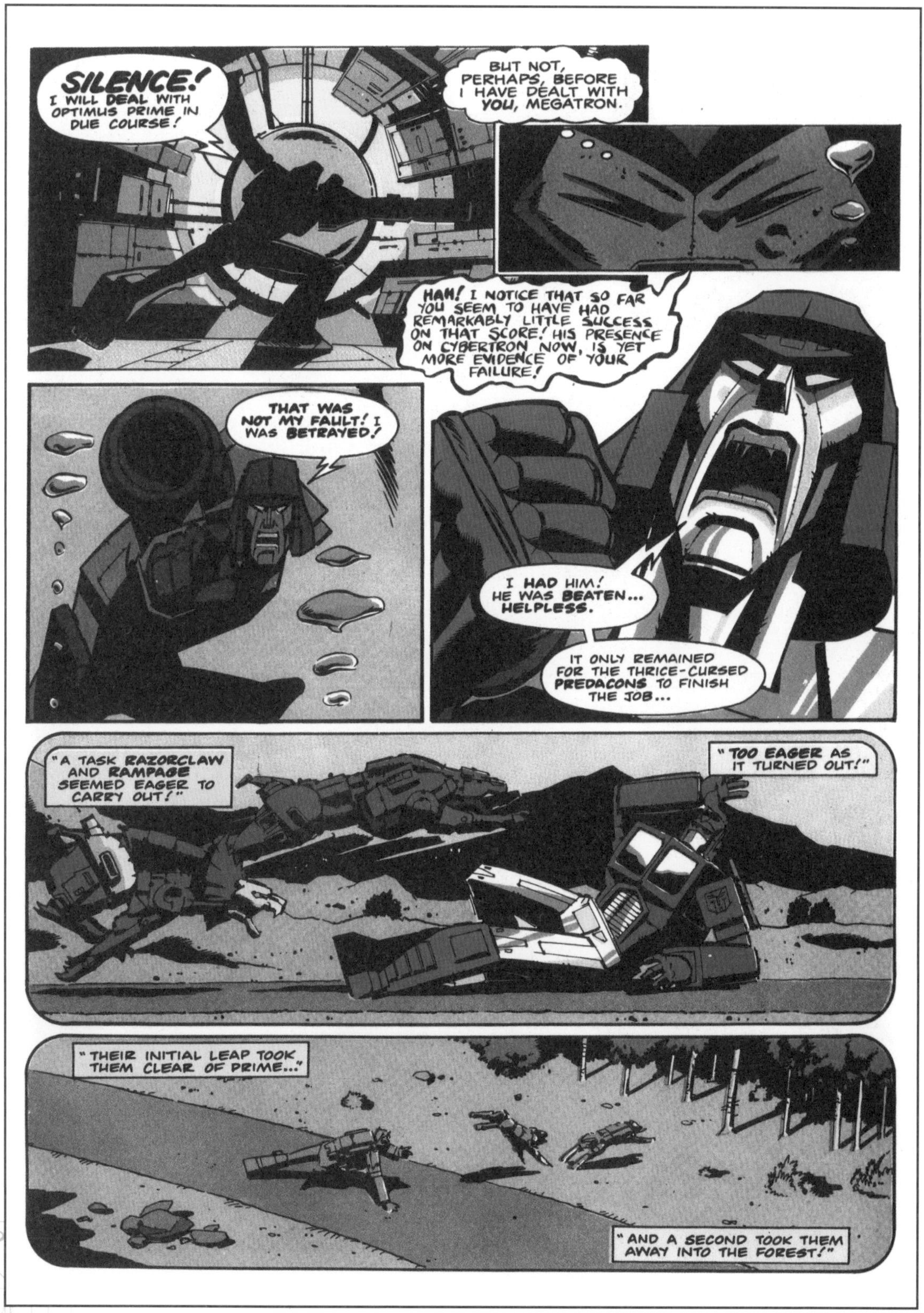
SILENCE! I WILL DEAL WITH OPTIMUS PRIME IN DUE COURSE!
BUT NOT, PERHAPS, BEFORE I HAVE DEALT WITH YOU, MEGATRON.
HAH! I NOTICE THAT SO FAR YOU SEEM TO HAVE HAD REMARKABLY LITTLE SUCCESS ON THAT SCORE! HIS PRESENCE ON CYBERTRON NOW, IS YET MORE EVIDENCE OF YOUR FAILURE!
THAT WAS NOT MY FAULT! I WAS BETRAYED!
I HAD HIM! HE WAS BEATEN... HELPLESS.
IT ONLY REMAINED FOR THE THRICE-CURSED PREDACONS TO FINISH THE JOB...
"A TASK RAZORCLAW AND RAMPAGE SEEMED EAGER TO CARRY OUT!"
"TOO EAGER AS IT TURNED OUT!"
"THEIR INITIAL LEAP TOOK THEM CLEAR OF PRIME..."
"AND A SECOND TOOK THEM AWAY INTO THE FOREST!"

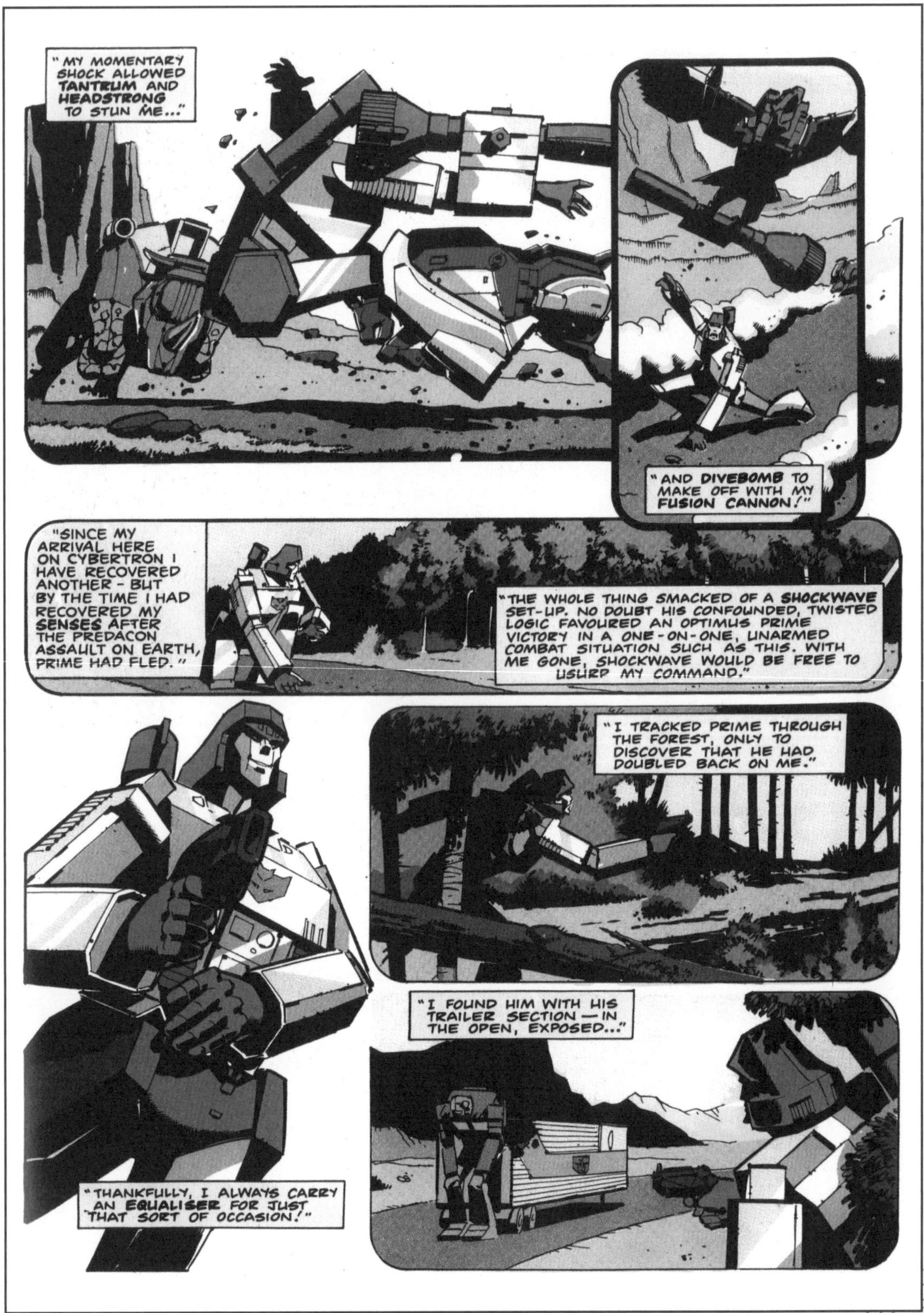
"MY MOMENTARY SHOCK ALLOWED TANTRUM AND HEADSTRONG TO STUN ME..."
"AND DIVEBOMB TO MAKE OFF WITH MY FUSION CANNON!"
"SINCE MY ARRIVAL HERE ON CYBERTRON I HAVE RECOVERED ANOTHER - BUT BY THE TIME I HAD RECOVERED MY SENSES AFTER THE PREDACON ASSAULT ON EARTH, PRIME HAD FLED."
"THE WHOLE THING SMACKED OF A SHOCKWAVE SET-UP. NO DOUBT HIS CONFOUNDED, TWISTED LOGIC FAVOURED AN OPTIMUS PRIME VICTORY IN A ONE-ON-ONE, UNARMED COMBAT SITUATION SUCH AS THIS. WITH ME GONE, SHOCKWAVE WOULD BE FREE TO USURP MY COMMAND."
"I TRACKED PRIME THROUGH THE FOREST, ONLY TO DISCOVER THAT HE HAD DOUBLED BACK ON ME."
"THANKFULLY, I ALWAYS CARRY AN EQUALISER FOR JUST THAT SORT OF OCCASION!"
"I FOUND HIM WITH HIS TRAILER SECTION — IN THE OPEN, EXPOSED..."

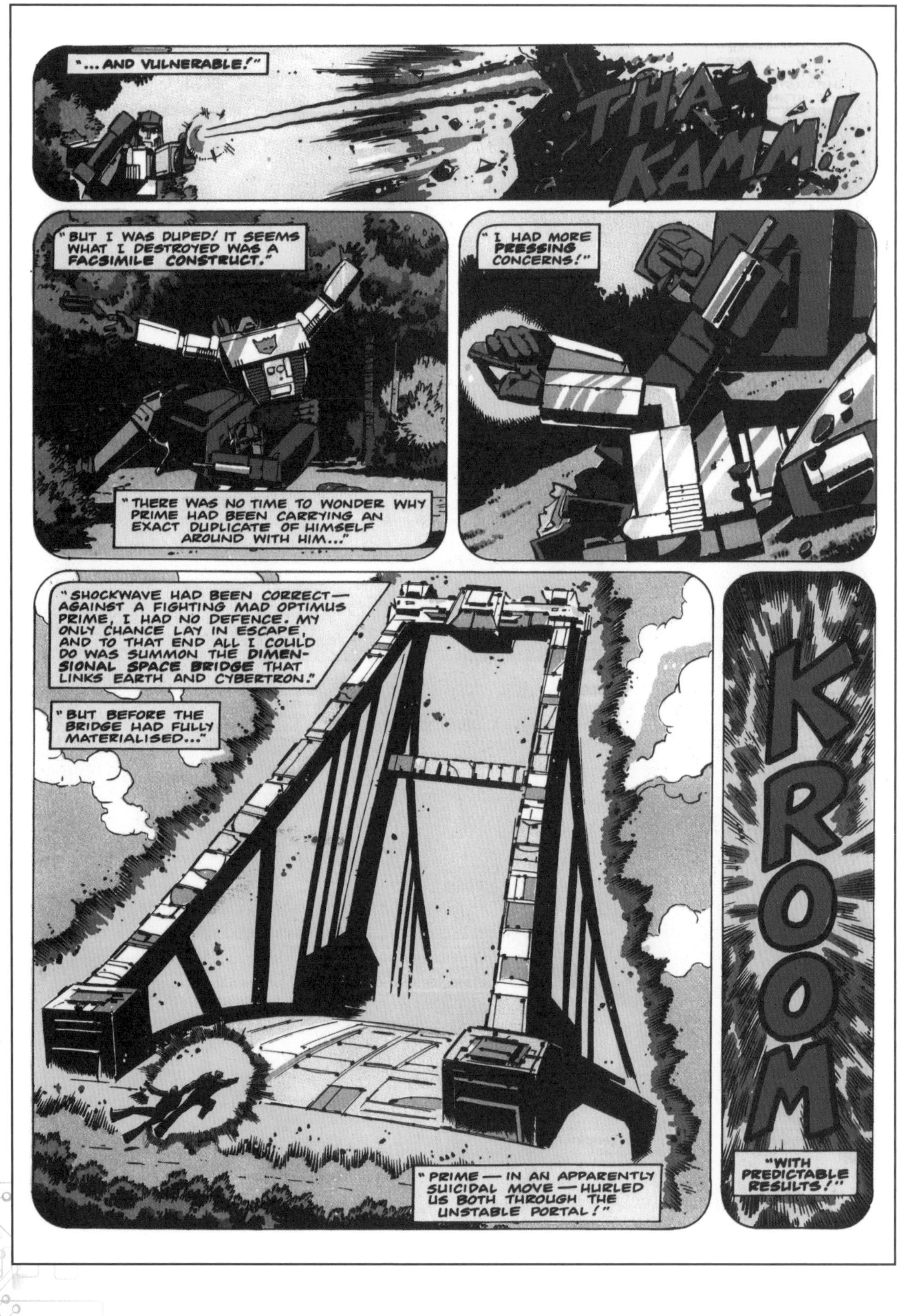
"...AND VULNERABLE!"
THA-KAMM!
"BUT I WAS DUPED! IT SEEMS WHAT I DESTROYED WAS A FACSIMILE CONSTRUCT."
"THERE WAS NO TIME TO WONDER WHY PRIME HAD BEEN CARRYING AN EXACT DUPLICATE OF HIMSELF AROUND WITH HIM..."
"I HAD MORE PRESSING CONCERNS!"
"SHOCKWAVE HAD BEEN CORRECT— AGAINST A FIGHTING MAD OPTIMUS PRIME, I HAD NO DEFENCE. MY ONLY CHANCE LAY IN ESCAPE, AND TO THAT END ALL I COULD DO WAS SUMMON THE DIMENSIONAL SPACE BRIDGE THAT LINKS EARTH AND CYBERTRON."
"BUT BEFORE THE BRIDGE HAD FULLY MATERIALISED..."
"PRIME — IN AN APPARENTLY SUICIDAL MOVE — HURLED US BOTH THROUGH THE UNSTABLE PORTAL!"
KROOM
"WITH PREDICTABLE RESULTS!"

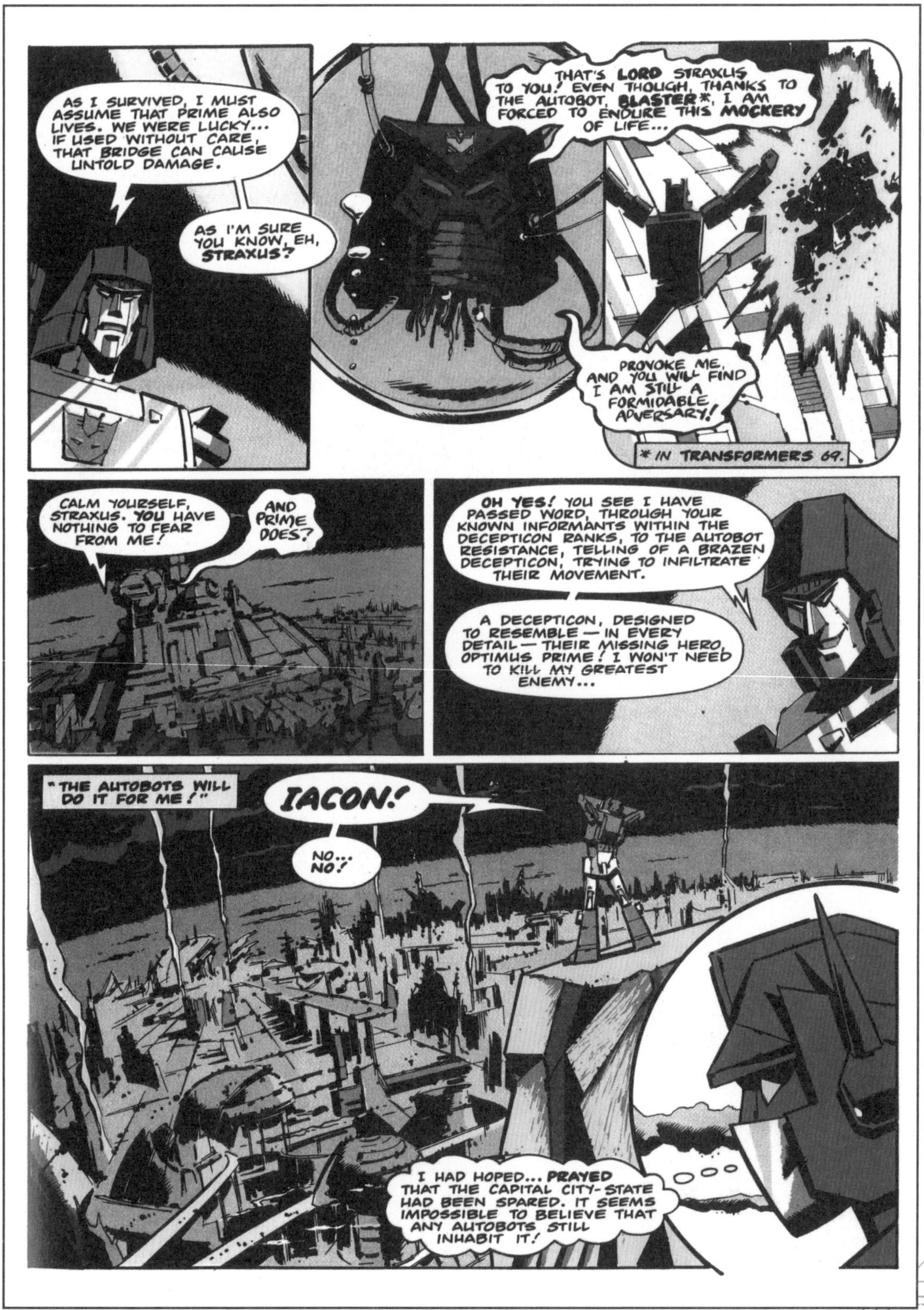

AS I SURVIVED, I MUST ASSUME THAT PRIME ALSO LIVES. WE WERE LUCKY... IF USED WITHOUT CARE, THAT BRIDGE CAN CAUSE UNTOLD DAMAGE.
AS I'M SURE YOU KNOW, EH, STRAXUS?
THAT'S LORD STRAXUS TO YOU! EVEN THOUGH, THANKS TO THE AUTOBOT, BLASTER*, I AM FORCED TO ENDURE THIS MOCKERY OF LIFE...
PROVOKE ME, AND YOU WILL FIND I AM STILL A FORMIDABLE ADVERSARY!
* IN TRANSFORMERS 69.
CALM YOURSELF, STRAXUS. YOU HAVE NOTHING TO FEAR FROM ME!
AND PRIME DOES?
OH YES! YOU SEE I HAVE PASSED WORD, THROUGH YOUR KNOWN INFORMANTS WITHIN THE DECEPTICON RANKS, TO THE AUTOBOT RESISTANCE, TELLING OF A BRAZEN DECEPTICON, TRYING TO INFILTRATE THEIR MOVEMENT.
A DECEPTICON, DESIGNED TO RESEMBLE — IN EVERY DETAIL — THEIR MISSING HERO, OPTIMUS PRIME! I WON'T NEED TO KILL MY GREATEST ENEMY...
"THE AUTOBOTS WILL DO IT FOR ME!"
IACON!
NO... NO!
I HAD HOPED... PRAYED THAT THE CAPITAL CITY-STATE HAD BEEN SPARED. IT SEEMS IMPOSSIBLE TO BELIEVE THAT ANY AUTOBOTS STILL INHABIT IT!

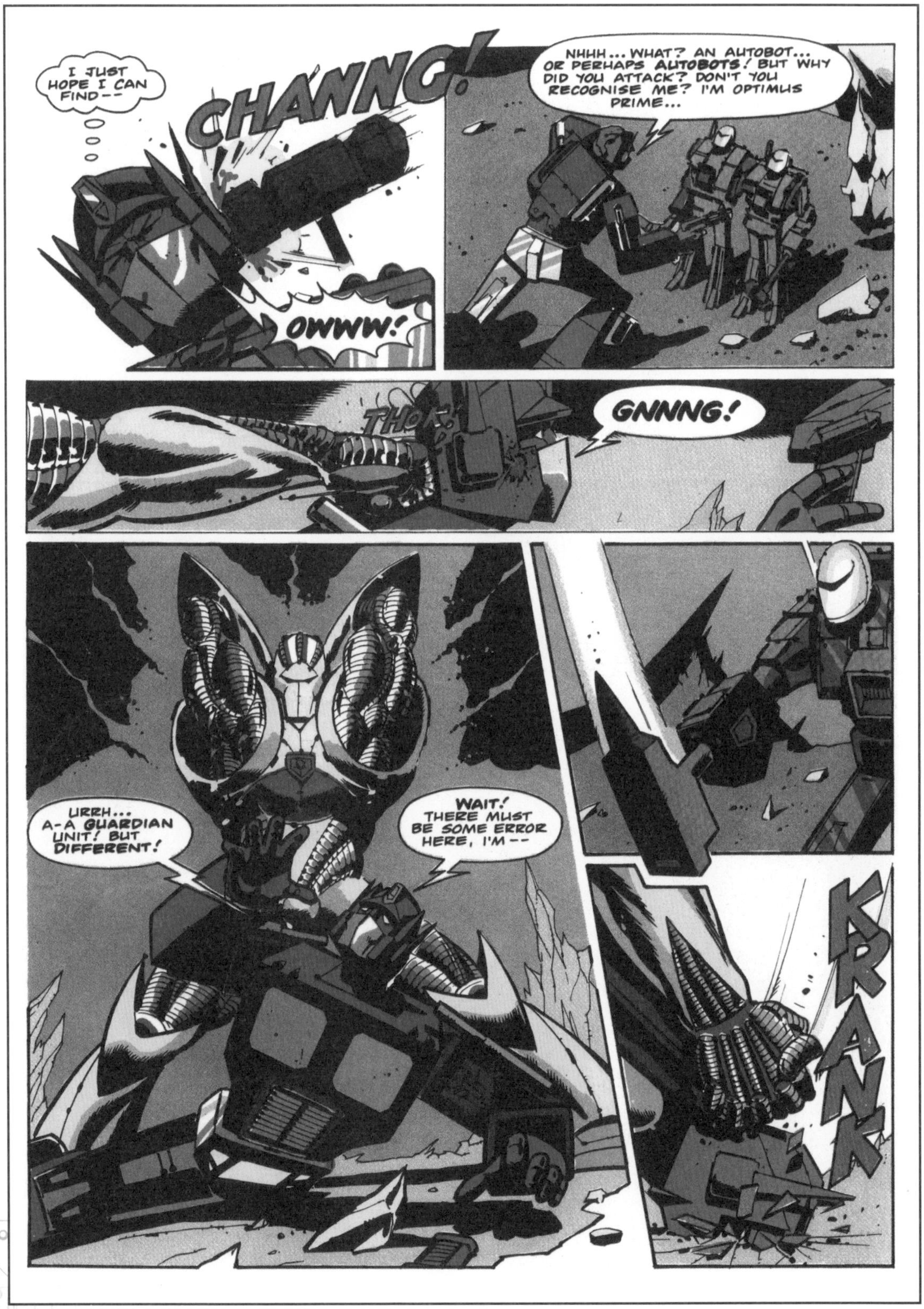

I JUST HOPE I CAN FIND--
CHANNG!
OWWW!
NHHH... WHAT? AN AUTOBOT... OR PERHAPS AUTOBOTS! BUT WHY DID YOU ATTACK? DON'T YOU RECOGNISE ME? I'M OPTIMUS PRIME...
GNNNG!
URRH... A-A GUARDIAN UNIT! BUT DIFFERENT!
WAIT! THERE MUST BE SOME ERROR HERE, I'M --
KRANK

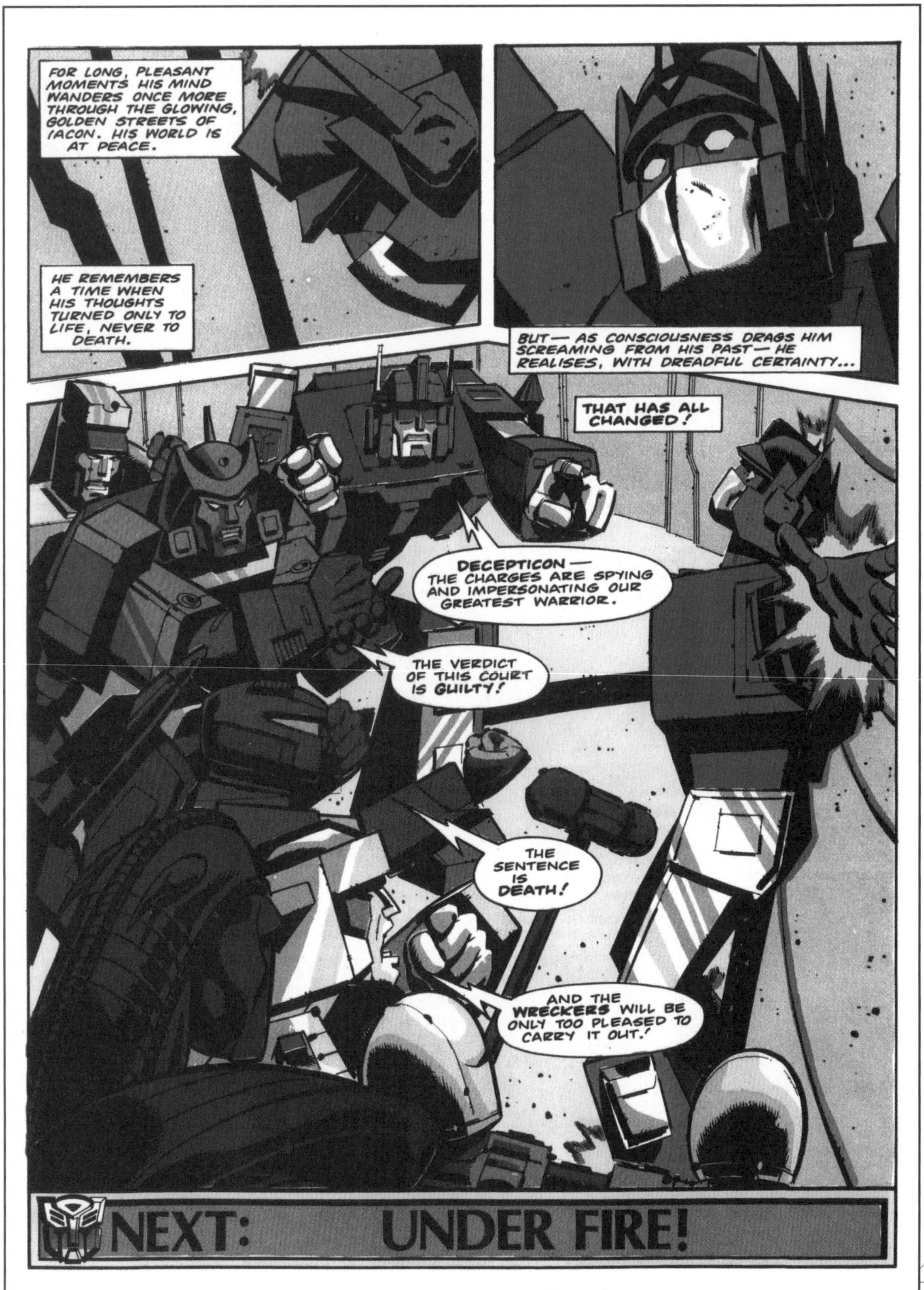
FOR LONG, PLEASANT MOMENTS HIS MIND WANDERS ONCE MORE THROUGH THE GLOWING, GOLDEN STREETS OF IACON. HIS WORLD IS AT PEACE.
HE REMEMBERS A TIME WHEN HIS THOUGHTS TURNED ONLY TO LIFE, NEVER TO DEATH.
BUT— AS CONSCIOUSNESS DRAGS HIM SCREAMING FROM HIS PAST— HE REALISES, WITH DREADFUL CERTAINTY...
THAT HAS ALL CHANGED!
DECEPTICON— THE CHARGES ARE SPYING AND IMPERSONATING OUR GREATEST WARRIOR.
THE VERDICT OF THIS COURT IS GUILTY!
THE SENTENCE IS DEATH!
AND THE WRECKERS WILL BE ONLY TOO PLEASED TO CARRY IT OUT!
NEXT: UNDER FIRE!

TRANSFORMERS™

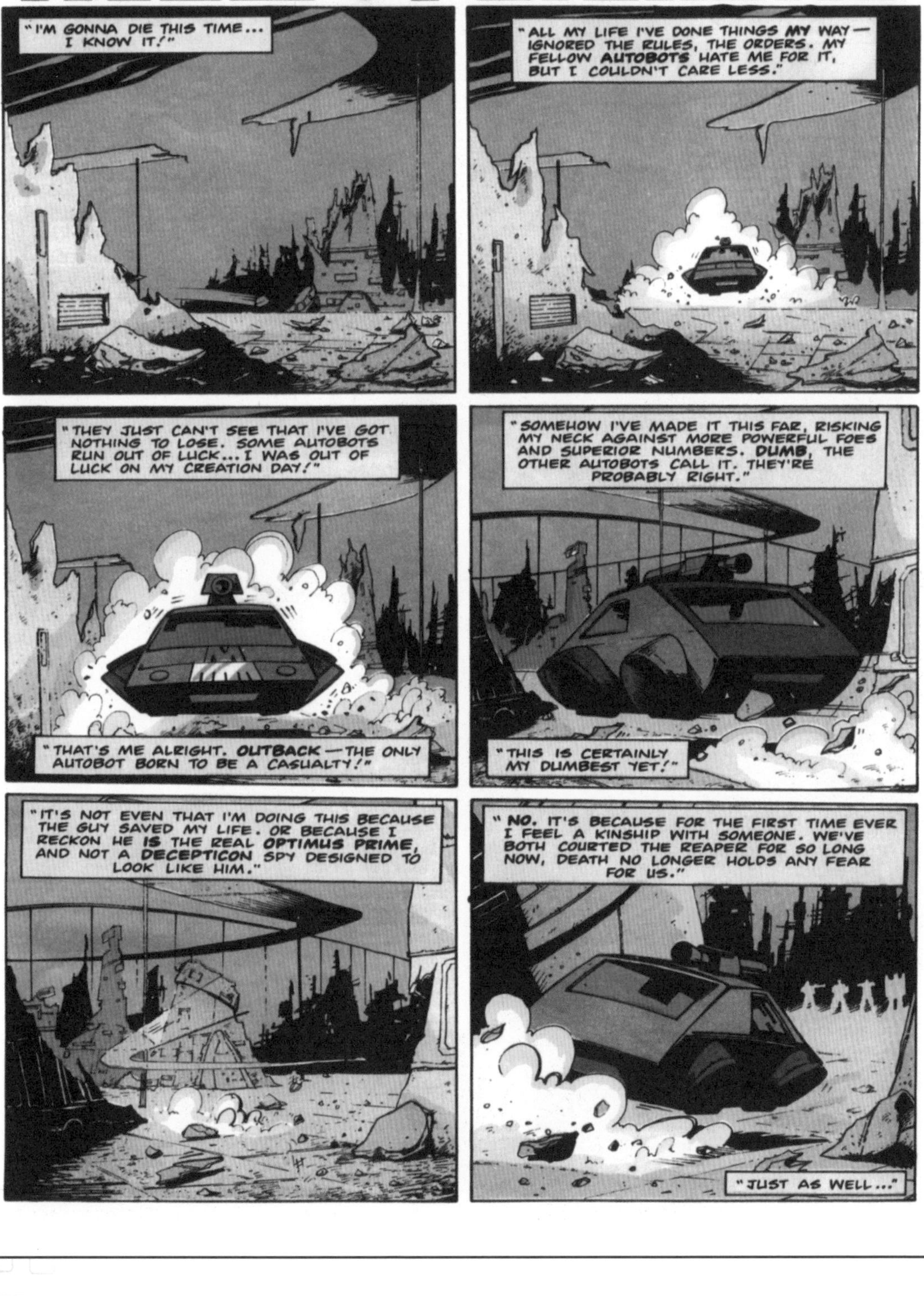
"I'M GONNA DIE THIS TIME... I KNOW IT!"
"ALL MY LIFE I'VE DONE THINGS MY WAY— IGNORED THE RULES, THE ORDERS. MY FELLOW AUTOBOTS HATE ME FOR IT, BUT I COULDN'T CARE LESS."
"THEY JUST CAN'T SEE THAT I'VE GOT NOTHING TO LOSE. SOME AUTOBOTS RUN OUT OF LUCK... I WAS OUT OF LUCK ON MY CREATION DAY!"
"THAT'S ME ALRIGHT. OUTBACK—THE ONLY AUTOBOT BORN TO BE A CASUALTY!"
"SOMEHOW I'VE MADE IT THIS FAR, RISKING MY NECK AGAINST MORE POWERFUL FOES AND SUPERIOR NUMBERS. DUMB, THE OTHER AUTOBOTS CALL IT. THEY'RE PROBABLY RIGHT."
"THIS IS CERTAINLY MY DUMBEST YET!"
"IT'S NOT EVEN THAT I'M DOING THIS BECAUSE THE GUY SAVED MY LIFE. OR BECAUSE I RECKON HE IS THE REAL OPTIMUS PRIME, AND NOT A DECEPTICON SPY DESIGNED TO LOOK LIKE HIM."
"NO. IT'S BECAUSE FOR THE FIRST TIME EVER I FEEL A KINSHIP WITH SOMEONE. WE'VE BOTH COURTED THE REAPER FOR SO LONG NOW, DEATH NO LONGER HOLDS ANY FEAR FOR US."
"JUST AS WELL..."

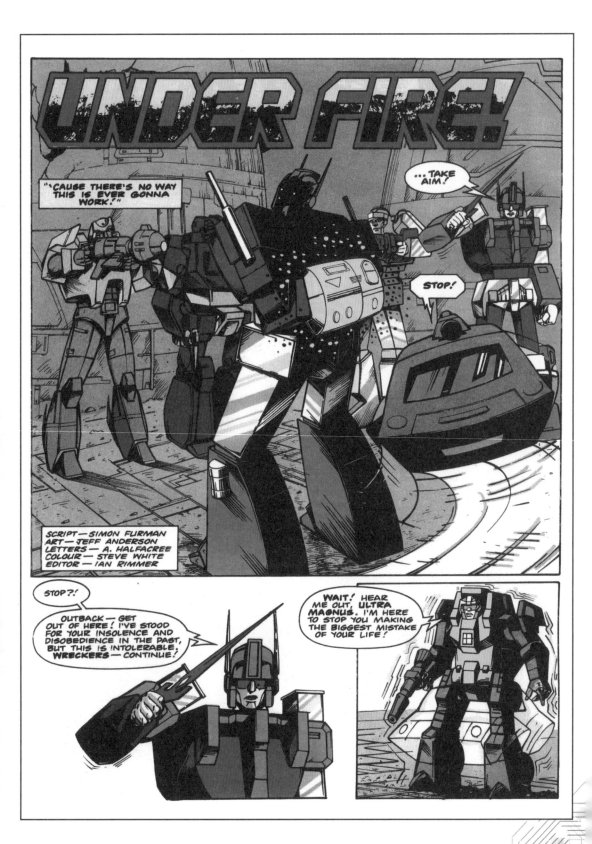

UNDER FIRE!

"'CAUSE THERE'S NO WAY THIS IS EVER GONNA WORK.'"

...TAKE AIM!

STOP!

SCRIPT — SIMON FURMAN
ART — JEFF ANDERSON
LETTERS — A. HALFACREE
COLOUR — STEVE WHITE
EDITOR — IAN RIMMER

STOP?!

OUTBACK — GET OUT OF HERE! I'VE STOOD FOR YOUR INSOLENCE AND DISOBEDIENCE IN THE PAST, BUT THIS IS INTOLERABLE! WRECKERS — CONTINUE!

WAIT! HEAR ME OUT, ULTRA MAGNUS. I'M HERE TO STOP YOU MAKING THE BIGGEST MISTAKE OF YOUR LIFE!

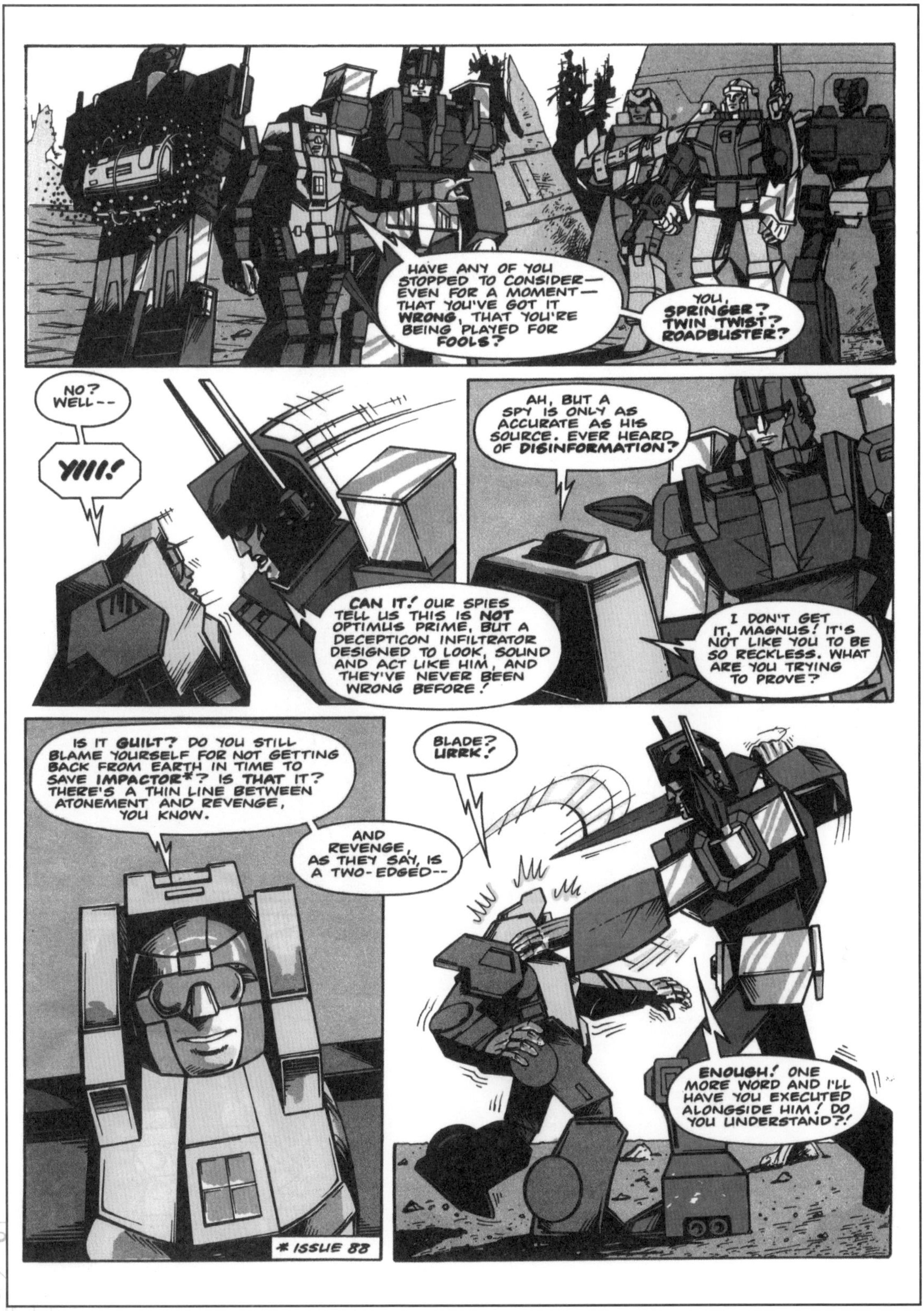
HAVE ANY OF YOU STOPPED TO CONSIDER— EVEN FOR A MOMENT— THAT YOU'VE GOT IT WRONG, THAT YOU'RE BEING PLAYED FOR FOOLS?
YOU, SPRINGER? TWIN TWIST? ROADBUSTER?
NO? WELL--
YIII!
CAN IT! OUR SPIES TELL US THIS IS NOT OPTIMUS PRIME, BUT A DECEPTICON INFILTRATOR DESIGNED TO LOOK, SOUND AND ACT LIKE HIM, AND THEY'VE NEVER BEEN WRONG BEFORE!
AH, BUT A SPY IS ONLY AS ACCURATE AS HIS SOURCE. EVER HEARD OF DISINFORMATION?
I DON'T GET IT, MAGNUS! IT'S NOT LIKE YOU TO BE SO RECKLESS. WHAT ARE YOU TRYING TO PROVE?
IS IT GUILT? DO YOU STILL BLAME YOURSELF FOR NOT GETTING BACK FROM EARTH IN TIME TO SAVE IMPACTOR*? IS THAT IT? THERE'S A THIN LINE BETWEEN ATONEMENT AND REVENGE, YOU KNOW.
AND REVENGE, AS THEY SAY, IS A TWO-EDGED--
* ISSUE 88
BLADE? URRK!
ENOUGH! ONE MORE WORD AND I'LL HAVE YOU EXECUTED ALONGSIDE HIM! DO YOU UNDERSTAND?!

WHOA, THERE! I GET THE MESSAGE. JUST THOUGHT YOU'D LIKE TO HEAR MY OPINION, THAT'S ALL.

WELL, SORRY, PAL. I TRIED. LOOKS AS THOUGH YOU'LL HAVE TO TAKE...

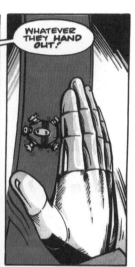

WHATEVER THEY HAND OUT!

WHA—?

THE ENERGY RESTRAINTS— THEY'RE GONE. I CAN...

MOVE!

FWOOOOSH!

LOOK OUT!

UNNH...GAS PARTICLE BOMB... GHAAAK!

C-CAN'T SEE...

BROOMF!

HYACK!

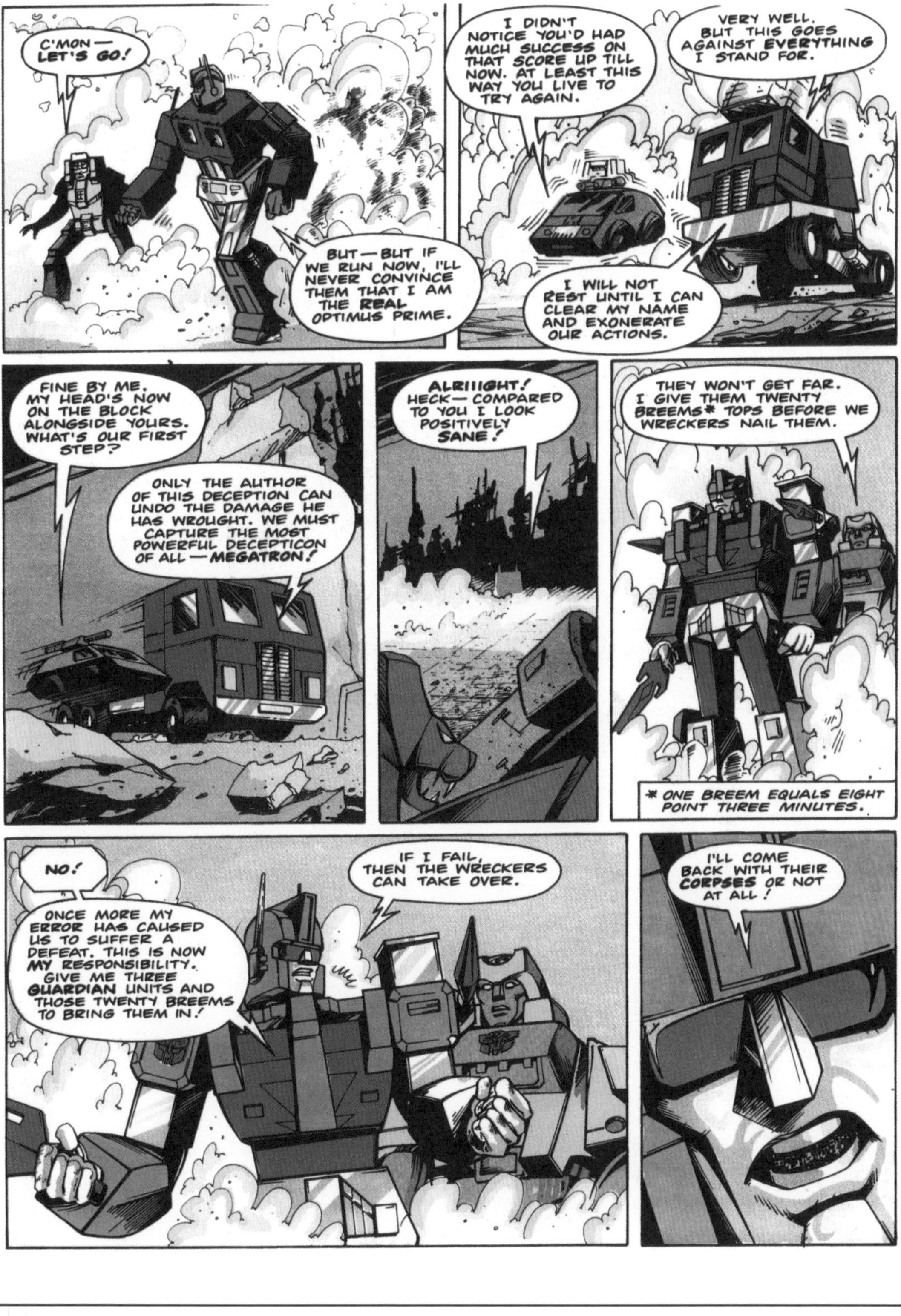

C'MON— LET'S GO!
BUT—BUT IF WE RUN NOW, I'LL NEVER CONVINCE THEM THAT I AM THE REAL OPTIMUS PRIME.
I DIDN'T NOTICE YOU'D HAD MUCH SUCCESS ON THAT SCORE UP TILL NOW. AT LEAST THIS WAY YOU LIVE TO TRY AGAIN.
VERY WELL. BUT THIS GOES AGAINST EVERYTHING I STAND FOR.
I WILL NOT REST UNTIL I CAN CLEAR MY NAME AND EXONERATE OUR ACTIONS.
FINE BY ME. MY HEAD'S NOW ON THE BLOCK ALONGSIDE YOURS. WHAT'S OUR FIRST STEP?
ONLY THE AUTHOR OF THIS DECEPTION CAN UNDO THE DAMAGE HE HAS WROUGHT. WE MUST CAPTURE THE MOST POWERFUL DECEPTICON OF ALL—MEGATRON!
ALRIIIGHT! HECK—COMPARED TO YOU I LOOK POSITIVELY SANE!
THEY WON'T GET FAR. I GIVE THEM TWENTY BREEMS* TOPS BEFORE WE WRECKERS NAIL THEM.
* ONE BREEM EQUALS EIGHT POINT THREE MINUTES.
NO!
ONCE MORE MY ERROR HAS CAUSED US TO SUFFER A DEFEAT. THIS IS NOW MY RESPONSIBILITY. GIVE ME THREE GUARDIAN UNITS AND THOSE TWENTY BREEMS TO BRING THEM IN!
IF I FAIL, THEN THE WRECKERS CAN TAKE OVER.
I'LL COME BACK WITH THEIR CORPSES OR NOT AT ALL!

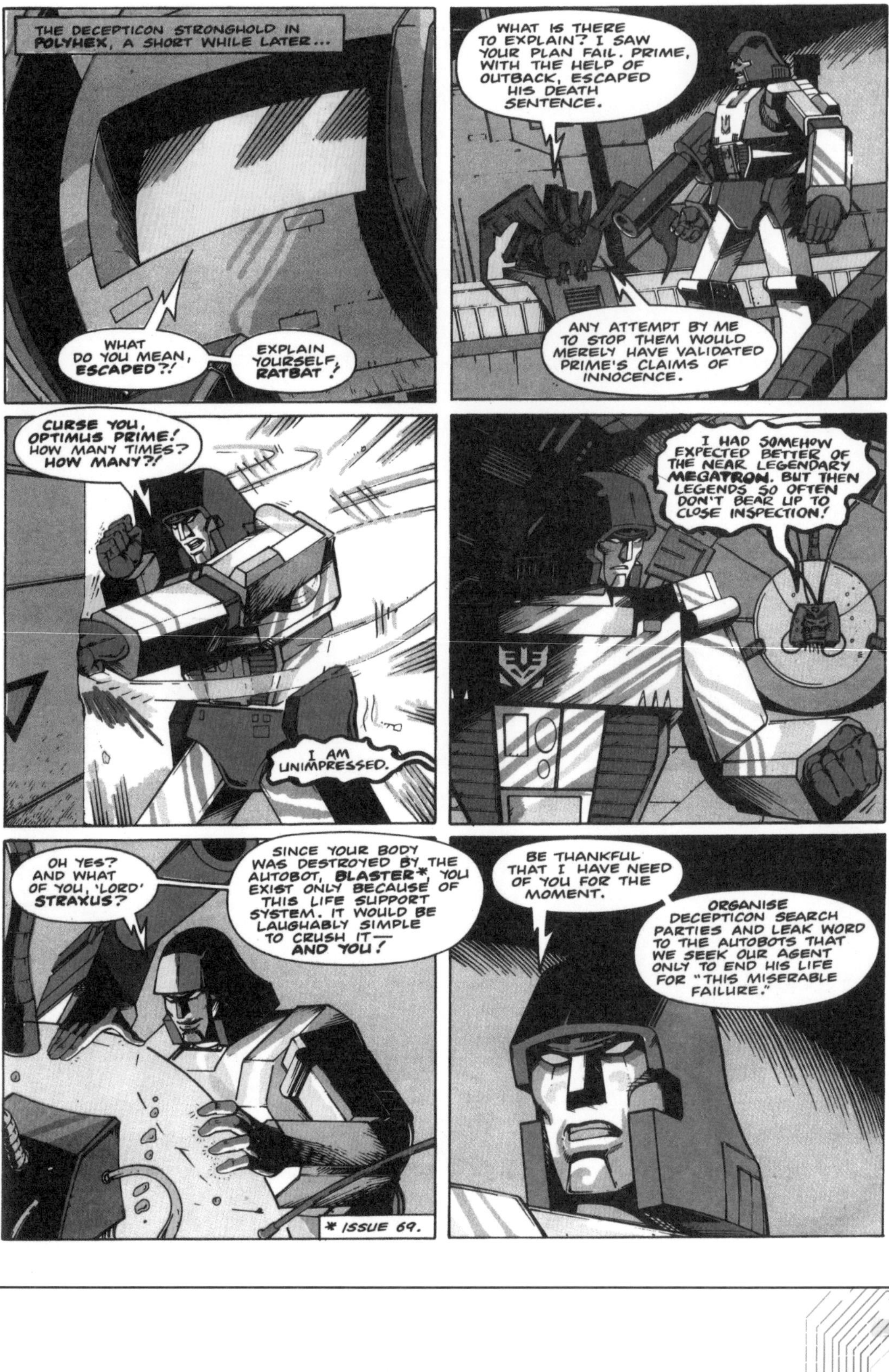

THE DECEPTICON STRONGHOLD IN POLYHEX, A SHORT WHILE LATER...
WHAT DO YOU MEAN, ESCAPED?!
EXPLAIN YOURSELF, RATBAT!
WHAT IS THERE TO EXPLAIN? I SAW YOUR PLAN FAIL. PRIME, WITH THE HELP OF OUTBACK, ESCAPED HIS DEATH SENTENCE.
ANY ATTEMPT BY ME TO STOP THEM WOULD MERELY HAVE VALIDATED PRIME'S CLAIMS OF INNOCENCE.
CURSE YOU, OPTIMUS PRIME! HOW MANY TIMES? HOW MANY?!
I AM UNIMPRESSED.
I HAD SOMEHOW EXPECTED BETTER OF THE NEAR LEGENDARY MEGATRON. BUT THEN LEGENDS SO OFTEN DON'T BEAR UP TO CLOSE INSPECTION!
OH YES? AND WHAT OF YOU, 'LORD' STRAXUS?
SINCE YOUR BODY WAS DESTROYED BY THE AUTOBOT, BLASTER*, YOU EXIST ONLY BECAUSE OF THIS LIFE SUPPORT SYSTEM. IT WOULD BE LAUGHABLY SIMPLE TO CRUSH IT— AND YOU!
* ISSUE 69.
BE THANKFUL THAT I HAVE NEED OF YOU FOR THE MOMENT.
ORGANISE DECEPTICON SEARCH PARTIES AND LEAK WORD TO THE AUTOBOTS THAT WE SEEK OUR AGENT ONLY TO END HIS LIFE FOR "THIS MISERABLE FAILURE."

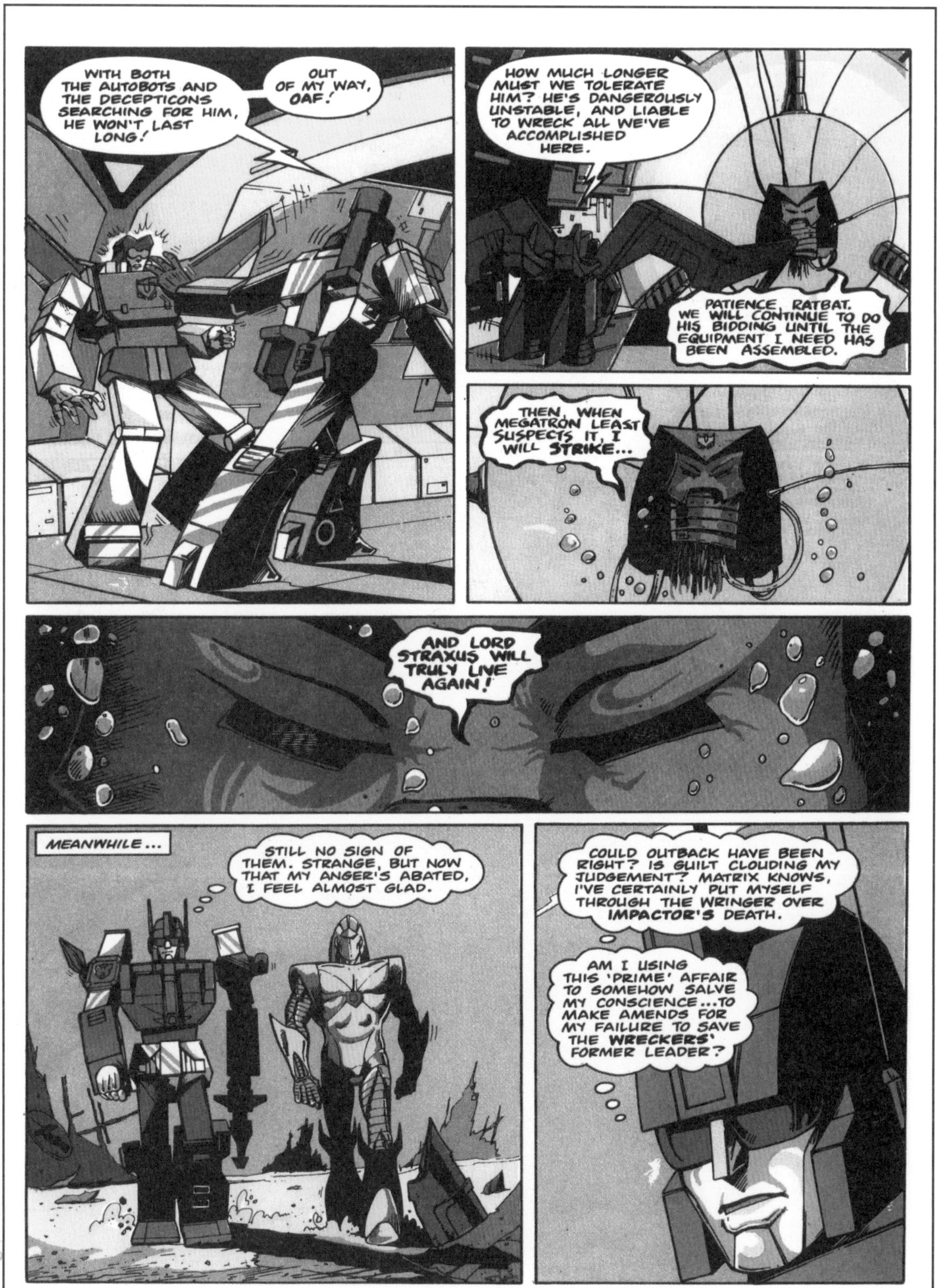
WITH BOTH THE AUTOBOTS AND THE DECEPTICONS SEARCHING FOR HIM, HE WON'T LAST LONG!
OUT OF MY WAY, OAF!
HOW MUCH LONGER MUST WE TOLERATE HIM? HE'S DANGEROUSLY UNSTABLE, AND LIABLE TO WRECK ALL WE'VE ACCOMPLISHED HERE.
PATIENCE RATBAT. WE WILL CONTINUE TO DO HIS BIDDING UNTIL THE EQUIPMENT I NEED HAS BEEN ASSEMBLED.
THEN, WHEN MEGATRON LEAST SUSPECTS IT, I WILL STRIKE...
AND LORD STRAXUS WILL TRULY LIVE AGAIN!
MEANWHILE...
STILL NO SIGN OF THEM. STRANGE, BUT NOW THAT MY ANGER'S ABATED, I FEEL ALMOST GLAD.
COULD OUTBACK HAVE BEEN RIGHT? IS GUILT CLOUDING MY JUDGEMENT? MATRIX KNOWS, I'VE CERTAINLY PUT MYSELF THROUGH THE WRINGER OVER IMPACTOR'S DEATH.
AM I USING THIS 'PRIME' AFFAIR TO SOMEHOW SALVE MY CONSCIENCE...TO MAKE AMENDS FOR MY FAILURE TO SAVE THE WRECKERS' FORMER LEADER?

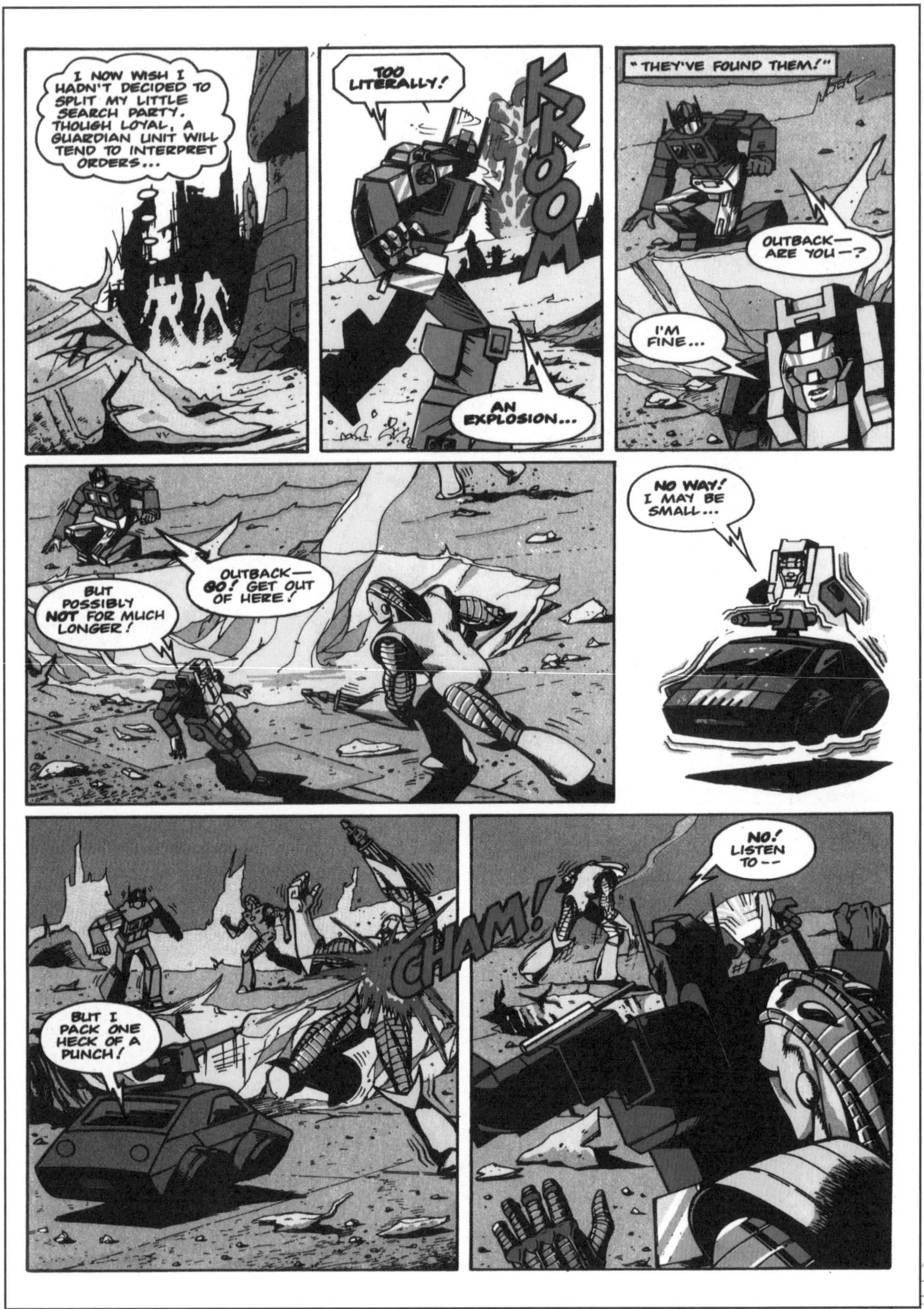
I NOW WISH I HADN'T DECIDED TO SPLIT MY LITTLE SEARCH PARTY. THOUGH LOYAL, A GUARDIAN UNIT WILL TEND TO INTERPRET ORDERS...
TOO LITERALLY!
KROOOM
AN EXPLOSION...
"THEY'VE FOUND THEM!"
OUTBACK— ARE YOU—?
I'M FINE...
OUTBACK— GO! GET OUT OF HERE!
BUT POSSIBLY NOT FOR MUCH LONGER!
NO WAY! I MAY BE SMALL...
BUT I PACK ONE HECK OF A PUNCH!
CHAM!
NO! LISTEN TO --

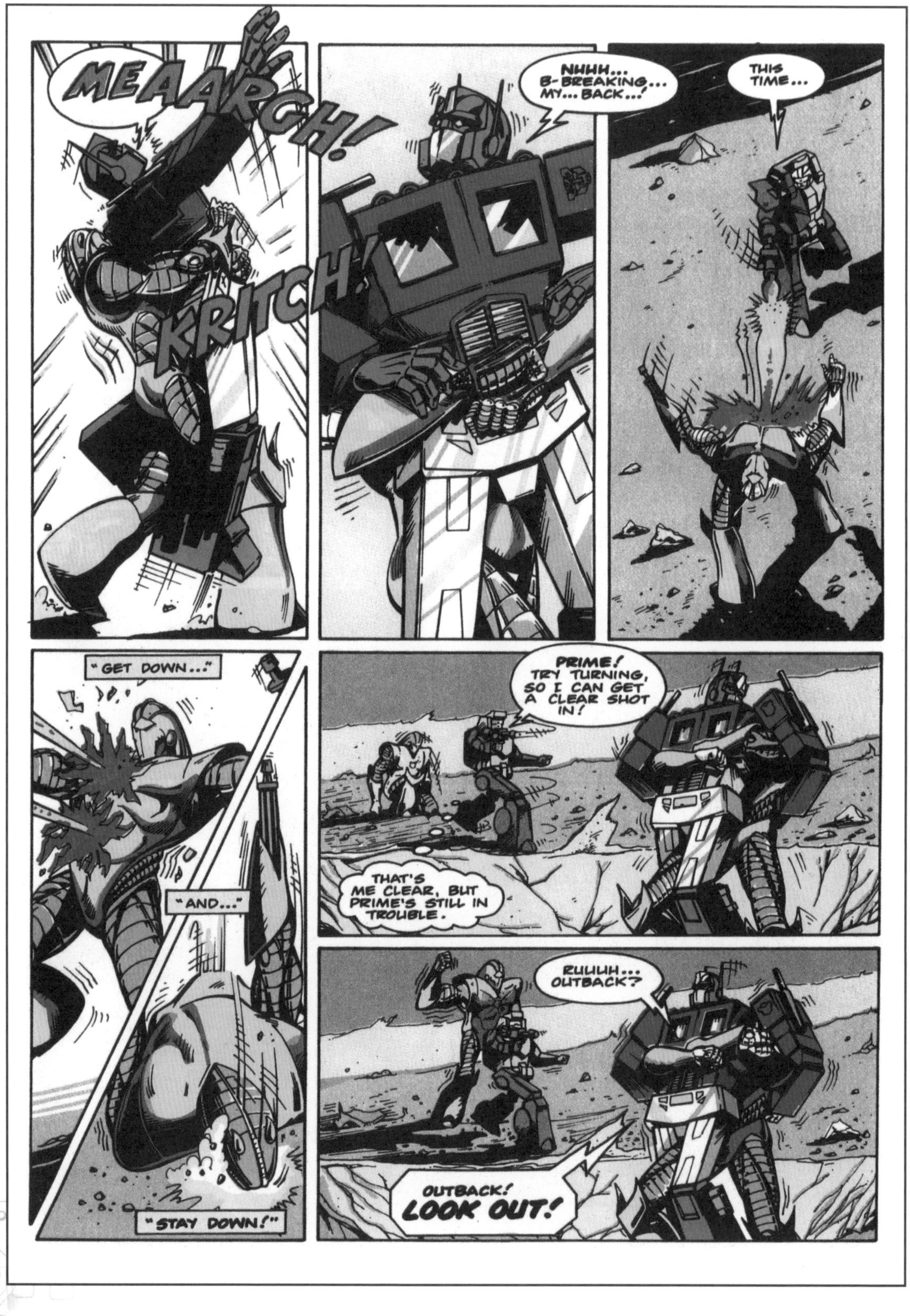
MEAARGH!
KRITCH!
NHHH... B-BREAKING... MY... BACK...!
THIS TIME...
"GET DOWN..."
"AND..."
"STAY DOWN!"
PRIME! TRY TURNING, SO I CAN GET A CLEAR SHOT IN!
THAT'S ME CLEAR, BUT PRIME'S STILL IN TROUBLE.
RUUUH... OUTBACK?
OUTBACK! LOOK OUT!

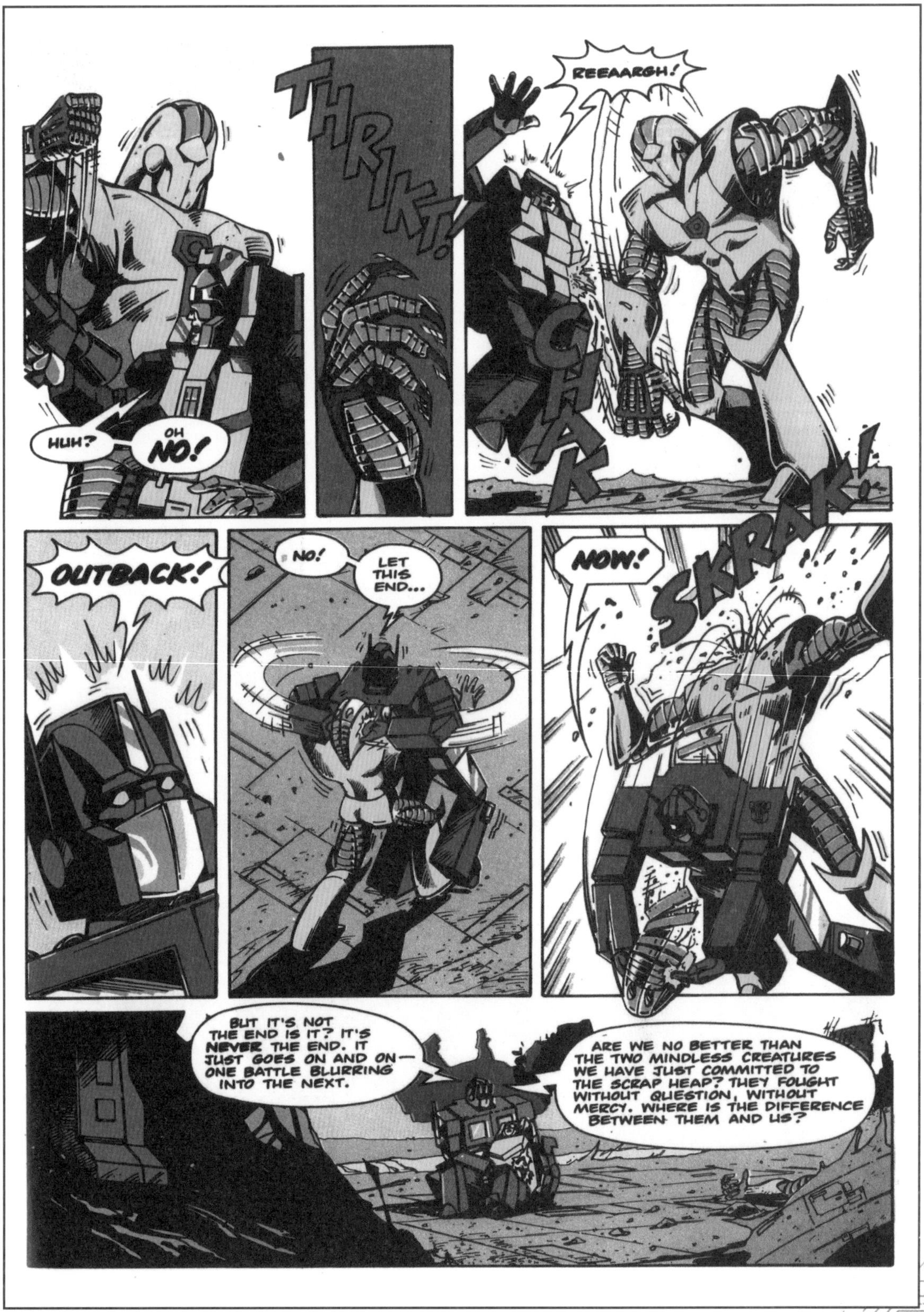
HUH?
OH NO!
THRIKT!
REEAARGH!
CHAK
SKRAK!
OUTBACK!
NO!
LET THIS END...
NOW!
BUT IT'S NOT THE END IS IT? IT'S NEVER THE END. IT JUST GOES ON AND ON— ONE BATTLE BLURRING INTO THE NEXT.
ARE WE NO BETTER THAN THE TWO MINDLESS CREATURES WE HAVE JUST COMMITTED TO THE SCRAP HEAP? THEY FOUGHT WITHOUT QUESTION, WITHOUT MERCY. WHERE IS THE DIFFERENCE BETWEEN THEM AND US?

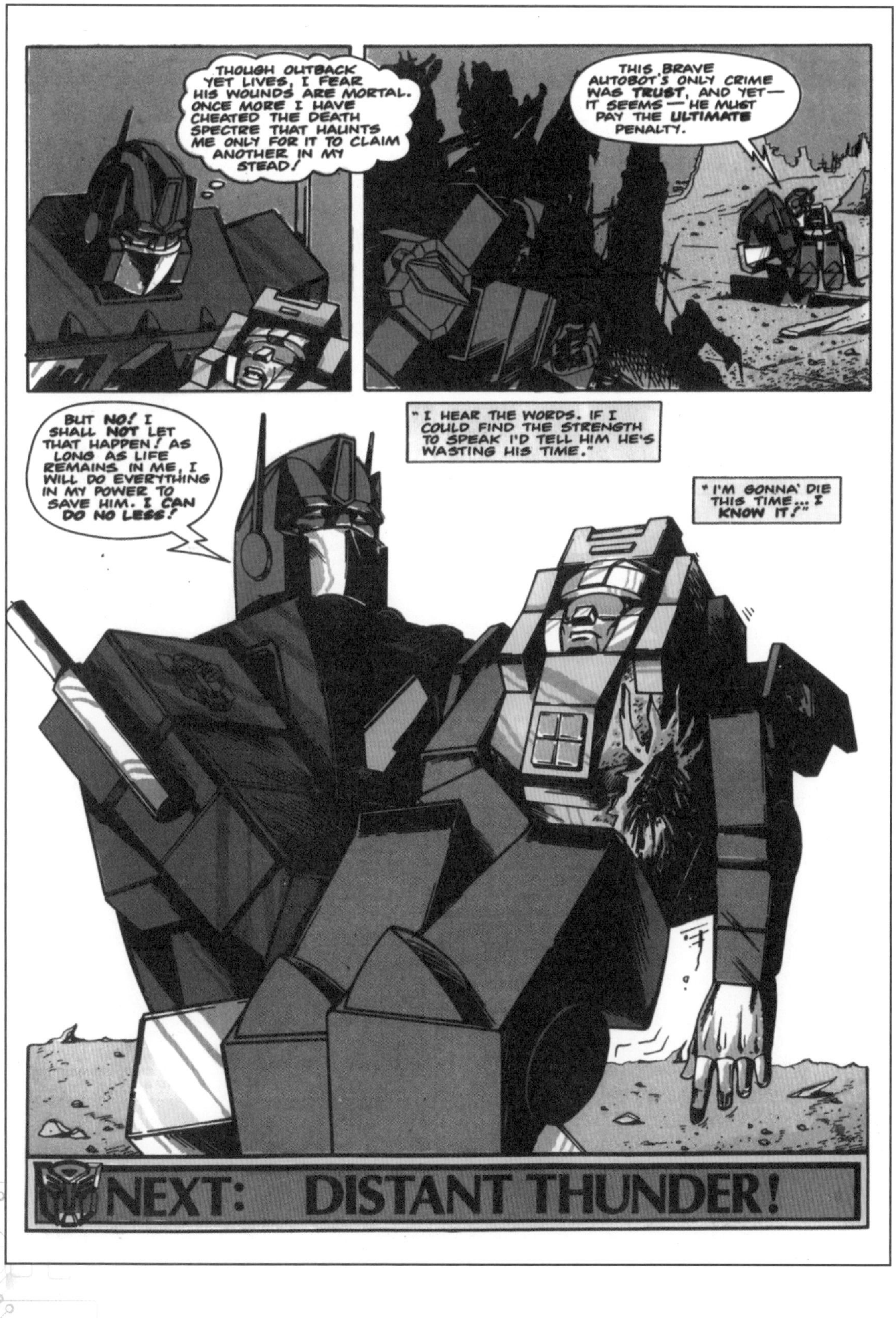
THOUGH OUTBACK YET LIVES, I FEAR HIS WOUNDS ARE MORTAL. ONCE MORE I HAVE CHEATED THE DEATH SPECTRE THAT HAUNTS ME ONLY FOR IT TO CLAIM ANOTHER IN MY STEAD!
THIS BRAVE AUTOBOT'S ONLY CRIME WAS TRUST, AND YET— IT SEEMS—HE MUST PAY THE ULTIMATE PENALTY.
BUT NO! I SHALL NOT LET THAT HAPPEN! AS LONG AS LIFE REMAINS IN ME, I WILL DO EVERYTHING IN MY POWER TO SAVE HIM. I CAN DO NO LESS!
"I HEAR THE WORDS. IF I COULD FIND THE STRENGTH TO SPEAK I'D TELL HIM HE'S WASTING HIS TIME."
"I'M GONNA' DIE THIS TIME... I KNOW IT!"
NEXT: DISTANT THUNDER!

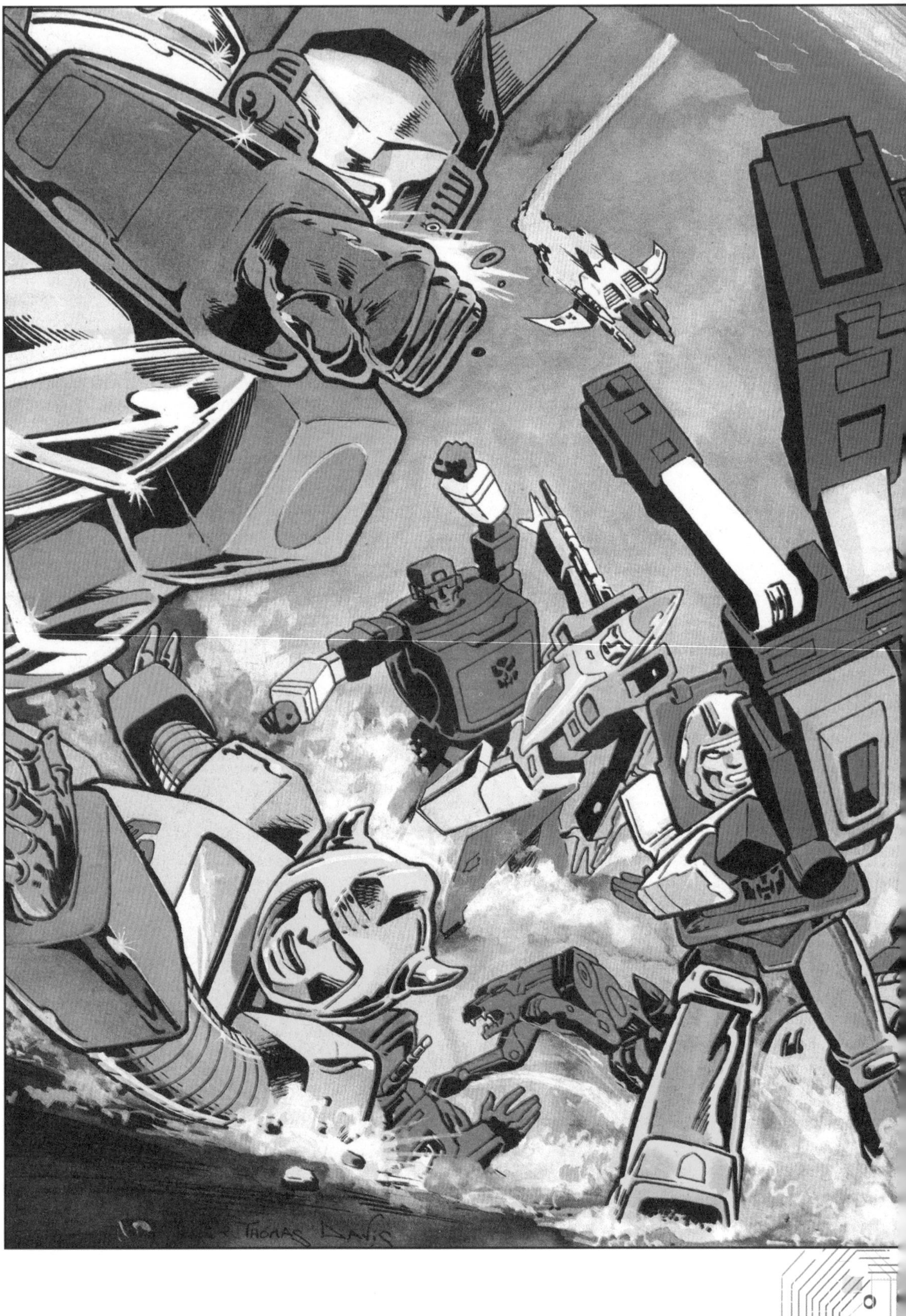

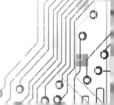

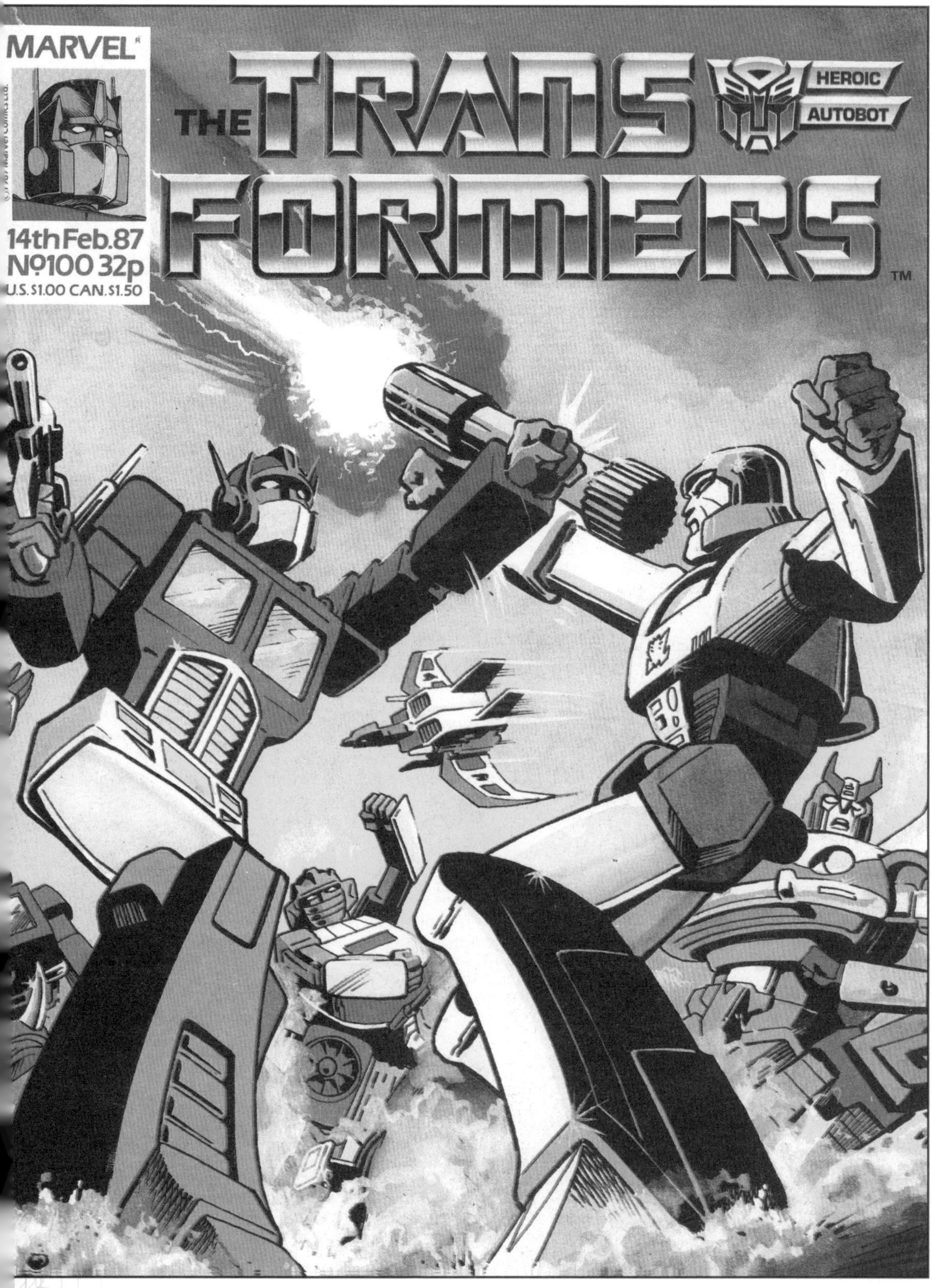

MARVEL
THE TRANSFORMERS
HEROIC AUTOBOT
14th Feb.87
No.100 32p
U.S.$1.00 CAN.$1.50
TM

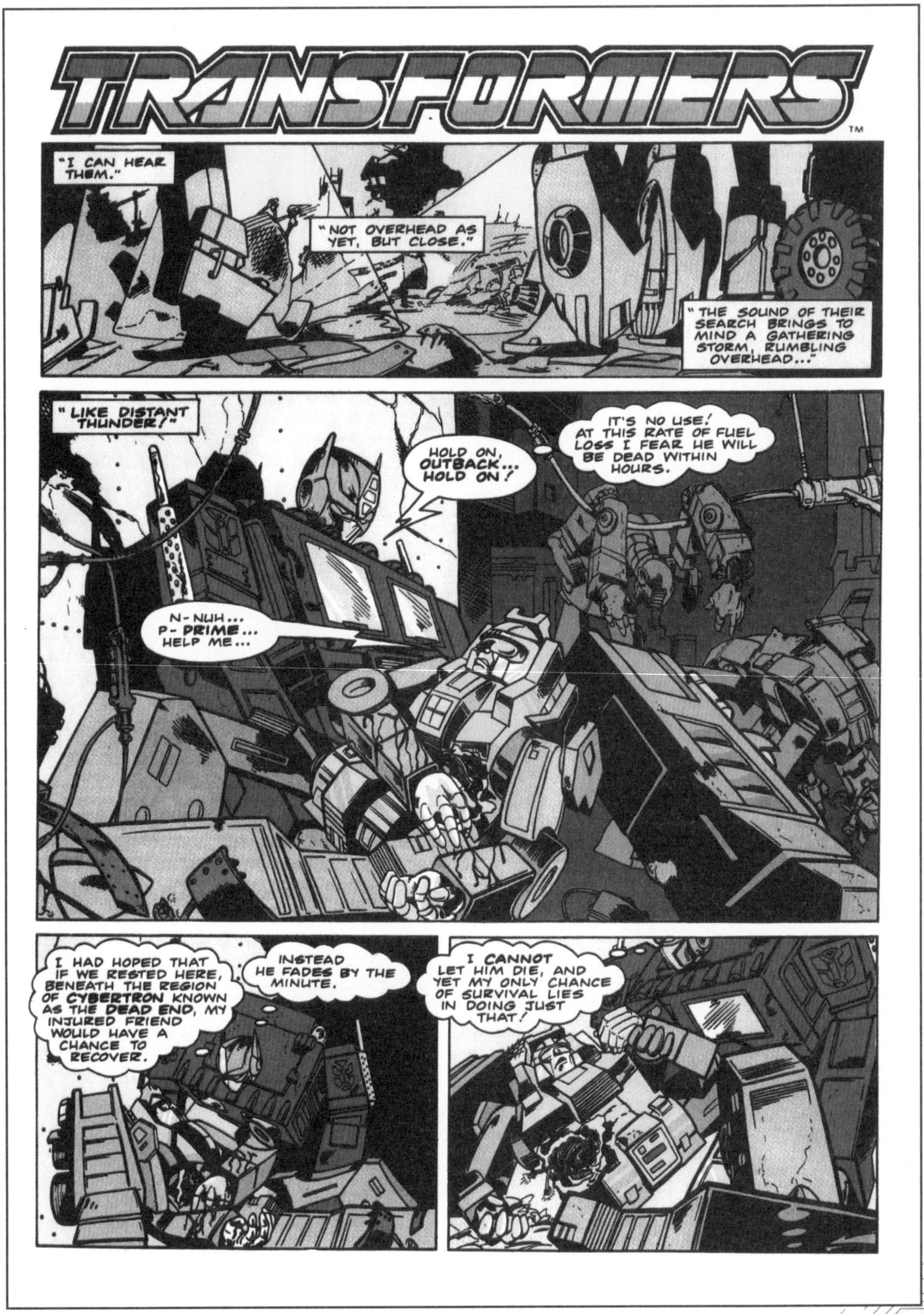
TRANSFORMERS
TM
"I CAN HEAR THEM."
"NOT OVERHEAD AS YET, BUT CLOSE."
"THE SOUND OF THEIR SEARCH BRINGS TO MIND A GATHERING STORM, RUMBLING OVERHEAD..."
"LIKE DISTANT THUNDER!"
HOLD ON, OUTBACK... HOLD ON!
IT'S NO USE! AT THIS RATE OF FUEL LOSS I FEAR HE WILL BE DEAD WITHIN HOURS.
N-NUH... P-PRIME... HELP ME...
I HAD HOPED THAT IF WE RESTED HERE, BENEATH THE REGION OF CYBERTRON KNOWN AS THE DEAD END, MY INJURED FRIEND WOULD HAVE A CHANCE TO RECOVER.
INSTEAD HE FADES BY THE MINUTE.
I CANNOT LET HIM DIE, AND YET MY ONLY CHANCE OF SURVIVAL LIES IN DOING JUST THAT!

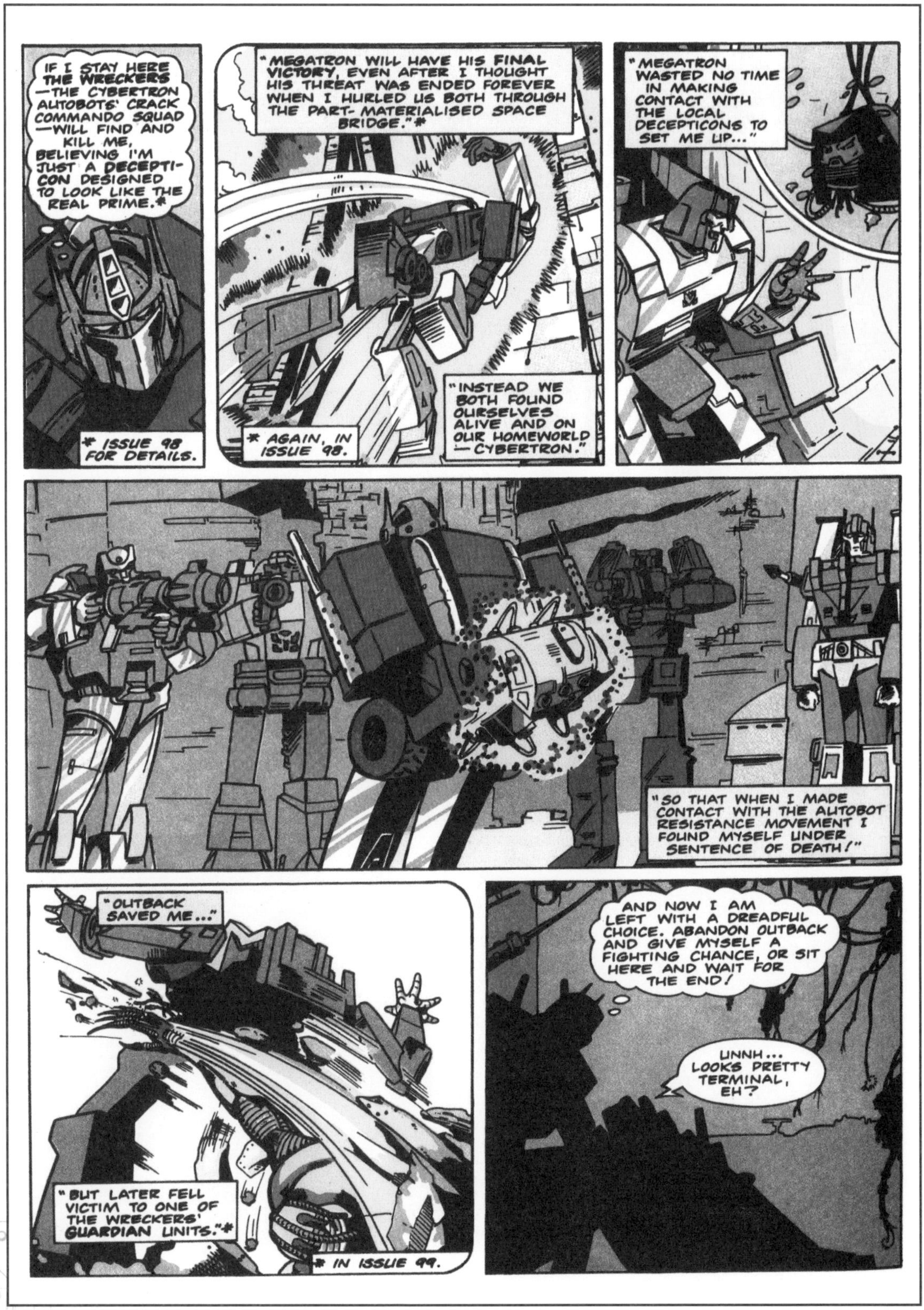
IF I STAY HERE THE WRECKERS —THE CYBERTRON AUTOBOTS' CRACK COMMANDO SQUAD —WILL FIND AND KILL ME, BELIEVING I'M JUST A DECEPTICON DESIGNED TO LOOK LIKE THE REAL PRIME.*
* ISSUE 98 FOR DETAILS.
"MEGATRON WILL HAVE HIS FINAL VICTORY, EVEN AFTER I THOUGHT HIS THREAT WAS ENDED FOREVER WHEN I HURLED US BOTH THROUGH THE PART-MATERIALISED SPACE BRIDGE."*
* AGAIN, IN ISSUE 98.
"INSTEAD WE BOTH FOUND OURSELVES ALIVE AND ON OUR HOMEWORLD —CYBERTRON."
"MEGATRON WASTED NO TIME IN MAKING CONTACT WITH THE LOCAL DECEPTICONS TO SET ME UP..."
"SO THAT WHEN I MADE CONTACT WITH THE AUTOBOT RESISTANCE MOVEMENT I FOUND MYSELF UNDER SENTENCE OF DEATH!"
"OUTBACK SAVED ME..."
"BUT LATER FELL VICTIM TO ONE OF THE WRECKERS' GUARDIAN UNITS."*
* IN ISSUE 99.
AND NOW I AM LEFT WITH A DREADFUL CHOICE. ABANDON OUTBACK AND GIVE MYSELF A FIGHTING CHANCE, OR SIT HERE AND WAIT FOR THE END!
UNNH... LOOKS PRETTY TERMINAL, EH?

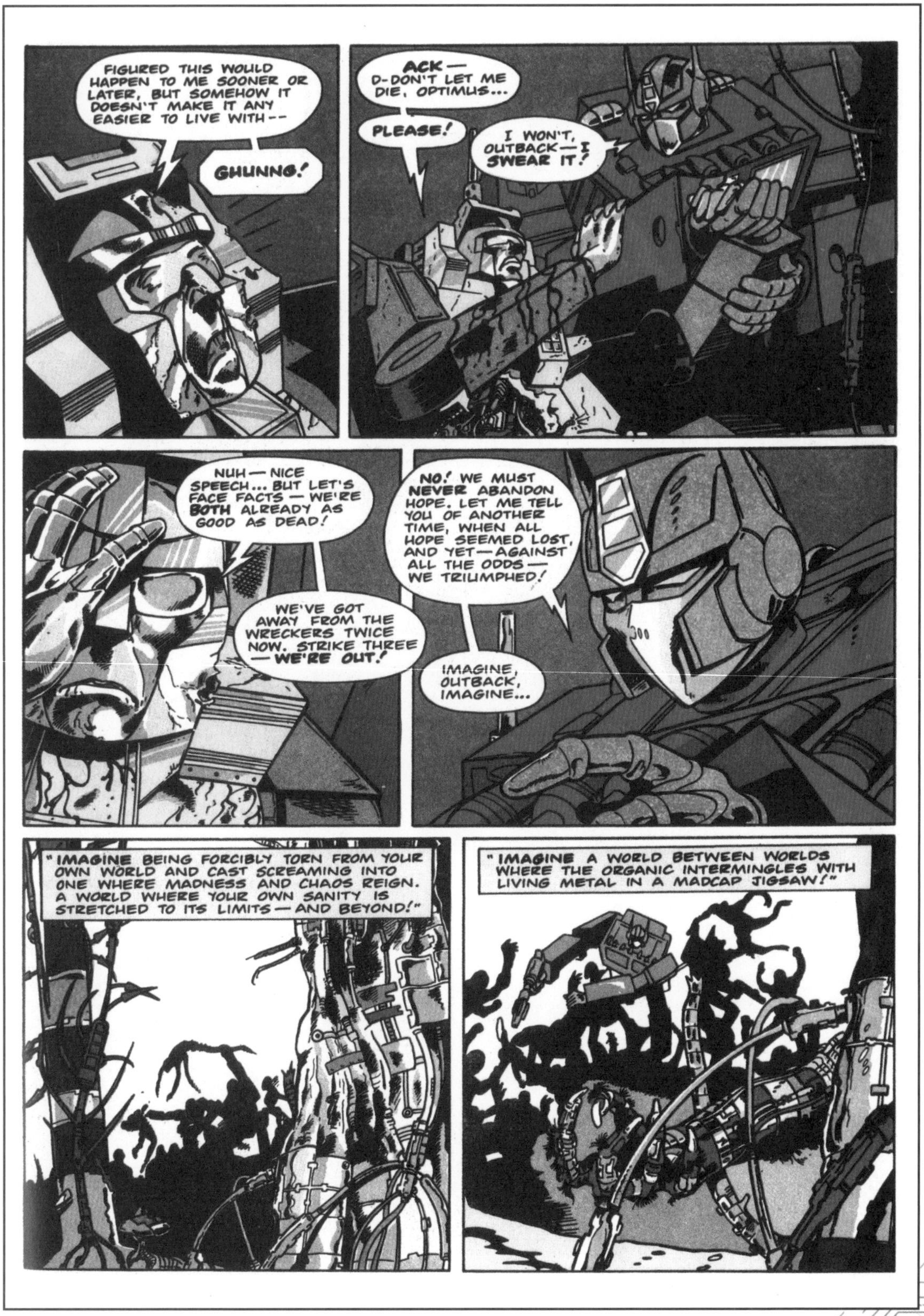

FIGURED THIS WOULD HAPPEN TO ME SOONER OR LATER, BUT SOMEHOW IT DOESN'T MAKE IT ANY EASIER TO LIVE WITH--
GHUNNG!
ACK— D-DON'T LET ME DIE, OPTIMUS...
PLEASE!
I WON'T, OUTBACK—I SWEAR IT!
NUH—NICE SPEECH... BUT LET'S FACE FACTS—WE'RE BOTH ALREADY AS GOOD AS DEAD!
WE'VE GOT AWAY FROM THE WRECKERS TWICE NOW. STRIKE THREE —WE'RE OUT!
NO! WE MUST NEVER ABANDON HOPE. LET ME TELL YOU OF ANOTHER TIME, WHEN ALL HOPE SEEMED LOST, AND YET—AGAINST ALL THE ODDS—WE TRIUMPHED!
IMAGINE, OUTBACK, IMAGINE...
"IMAGINE BEING FORCIBLY TORN FROM YOUR OWN WORLD AND CAST SCREAMING INTO ONE WHERE MADNESS AND CHAOS REIGN. A WORLD WHERE YOUR OWN SANITY IS STRETCHED TO ITS LIMITS—AND BEYOND!"
"IMAGINE A WORLD BETWEEN WORLDS WHERE THE ORGANIC INTERMINGLES WITH LIVING METAL IN A MADCAP JIGSAW!"

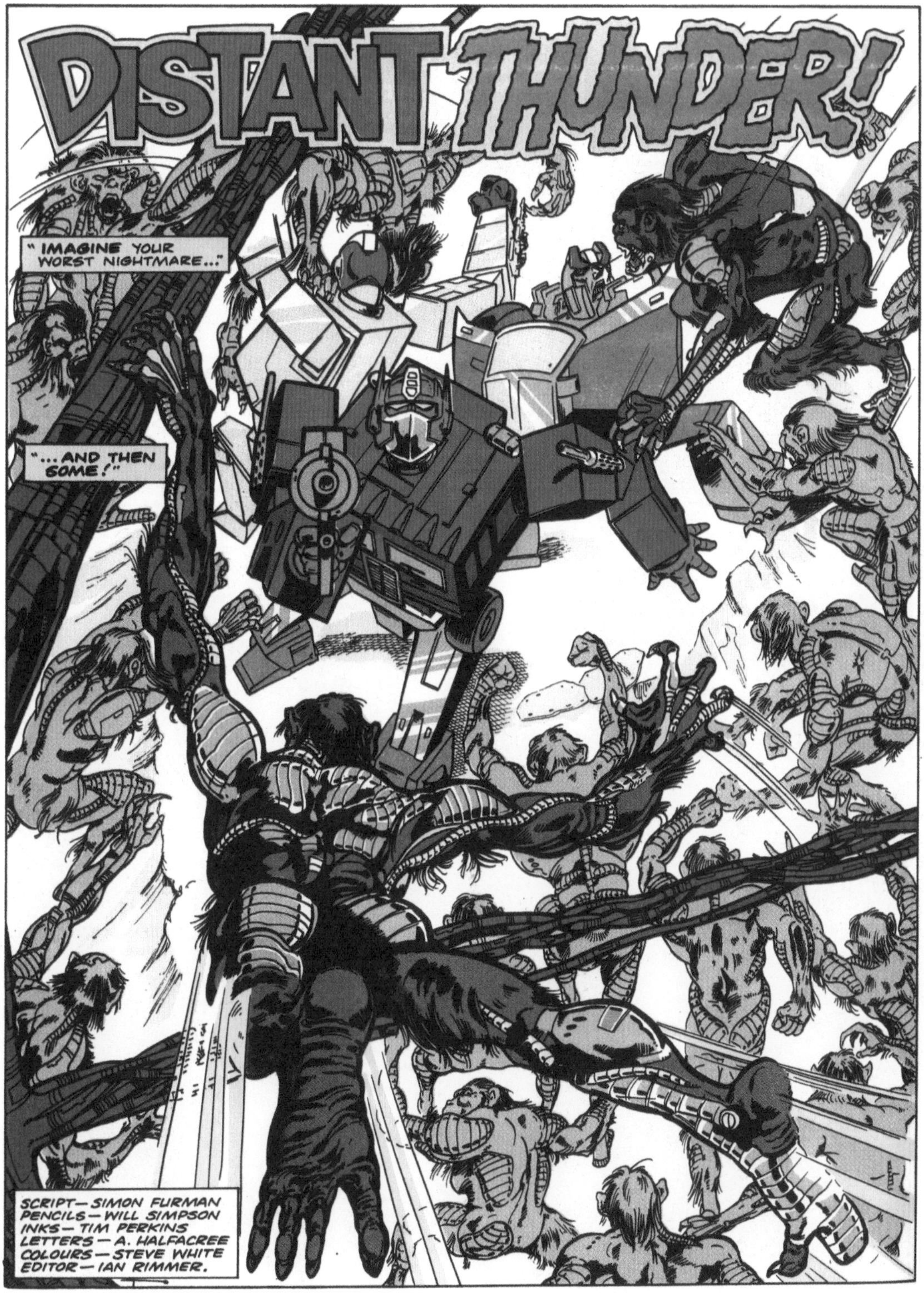
DISTANT THUNDER!
"IMAGINE YOUR WORST NIGHTMARE..."
"...AND THEN SOME!"
SCRIPT—SIMON FURMAN
PENCILS—WILL SIMPSON
INKS—TIM PERKINS
LETTERS—A. HALFACREE
COLOURS—STEVE WHITE
EDITOR—IAN RIMMER.

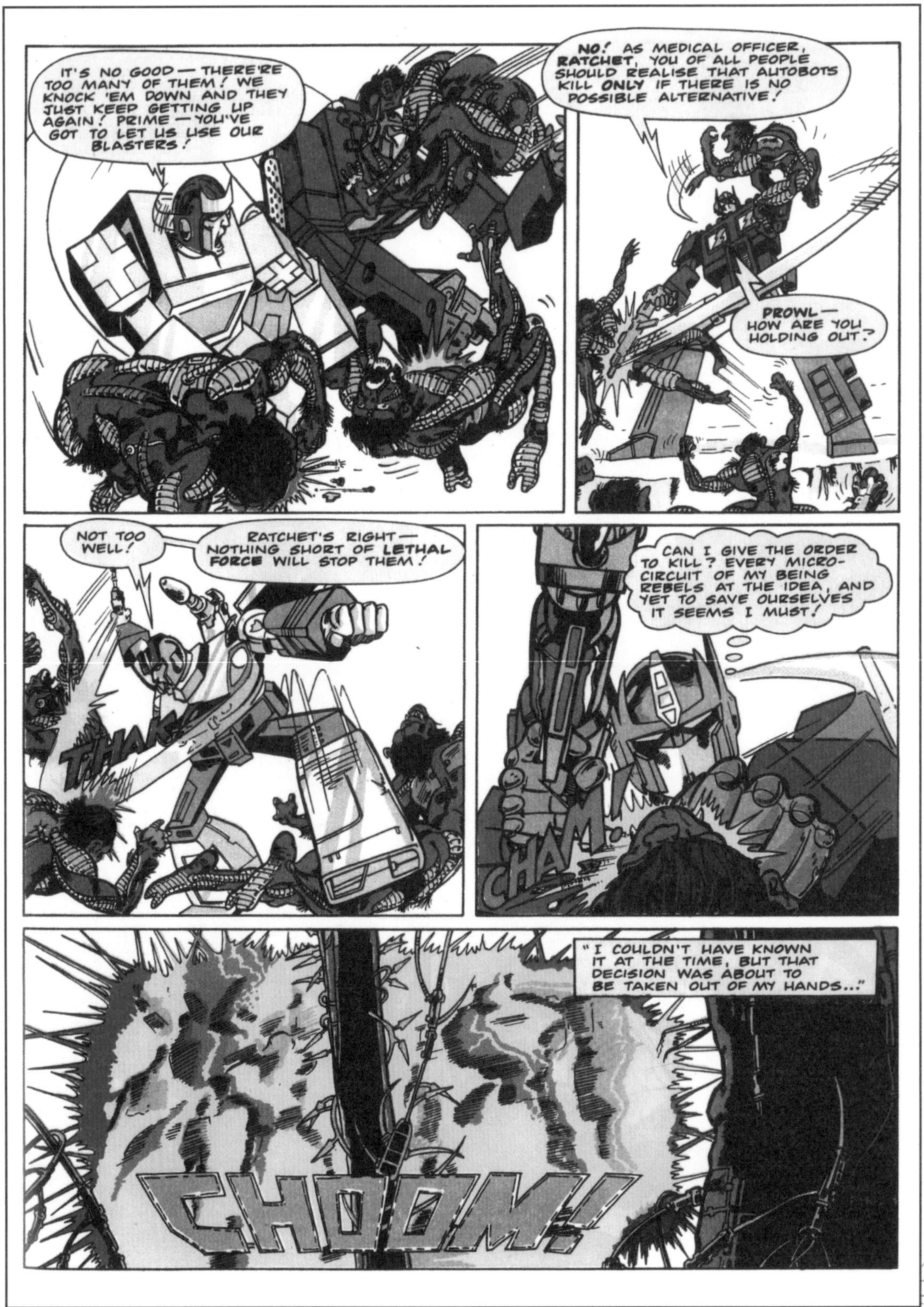
IT'S NO GOOD — THERE'RE TOO MANY OF THEM! WE KNOCK 'EM DOWN AND THEY JUST KEEP GETTING UP AGAIN! PRIME — YOU'VE GOT TO LET US USE OUR BLASTERS!
NO! AS MEDICAL OFFICER, RATCHET, YOU OF ALL PEOPLE SHOULD REALISE THAT AUTOBOTS KILL ONLY IF THERE IS NO POSSIBLE ALTERNATIVE!
PROWL — HOW ARE YOU HOLDING OUT?
NOT TOO WELL!
RATCHET'S RIGHT — NOTHING SHORT OF LETHAL FORCE WILL STOP THEM!
THAK
CAN I GIVE THE ORDER TO KILL? EVERY MICRO-CIRCUIT OF MY BEING REBELS AT THE IDEA, AND YET TO SAVE OURSELVES IT SEEMS I MUST!
CHAM
"I COULDN'T HAVE KNOWN IT AT THE TIME, BUT THAT DECISION WAS ABOUT TO BE TAKEN OUT OF MY HANDS..."
CHOOM!

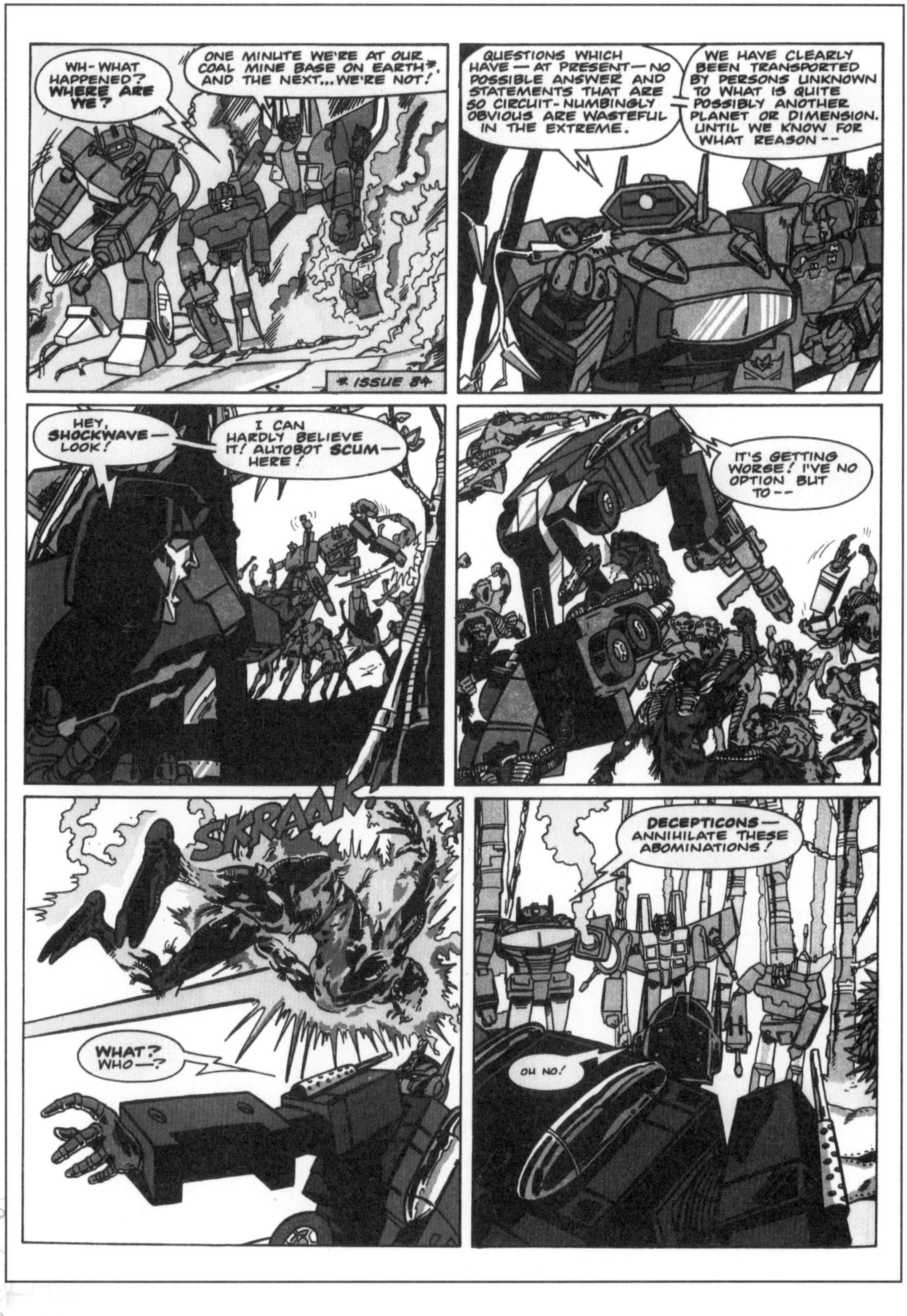
WH-WHAT HAPPENED? WHERE ARE WE?
ONE MINUTE WE'RE AT OUR COAL MINE BASE ON EARTH*, AND THE NEXT... WE'RE NOT!
* ISSUE 84
QUESTIONS WHICH HAVE — AT PRESENT — NO POSSIBLE ANSWER AND STATEMENTS THAT ARE SO CIRCUIT-NUMBINGLY OBVIOUS ARE WASTEFUL IN THE EXTREME.
WE HAVE CLEARLY BEEN TRANSPORTED BY PERSONS UNKNOWN TO WHAT IS QUITE POSSIBLY ANOTHER PLANET OR DIMENSION. UNTIL WE KNOW FOR WHAT REASON --
HEY, SHOCKWAVE — LOOK!
I CAN HARDLY BELIEVE IT! AUTOBOT SCUM — HERE!
IT'S GETTING WORSE! I'VE NO OPTION BUT TO --
SKRAAK!
WHAT? WHO —?
DECEPTICONS — ANNIHILATE THESE ABOMINATIONS!
OH NO!

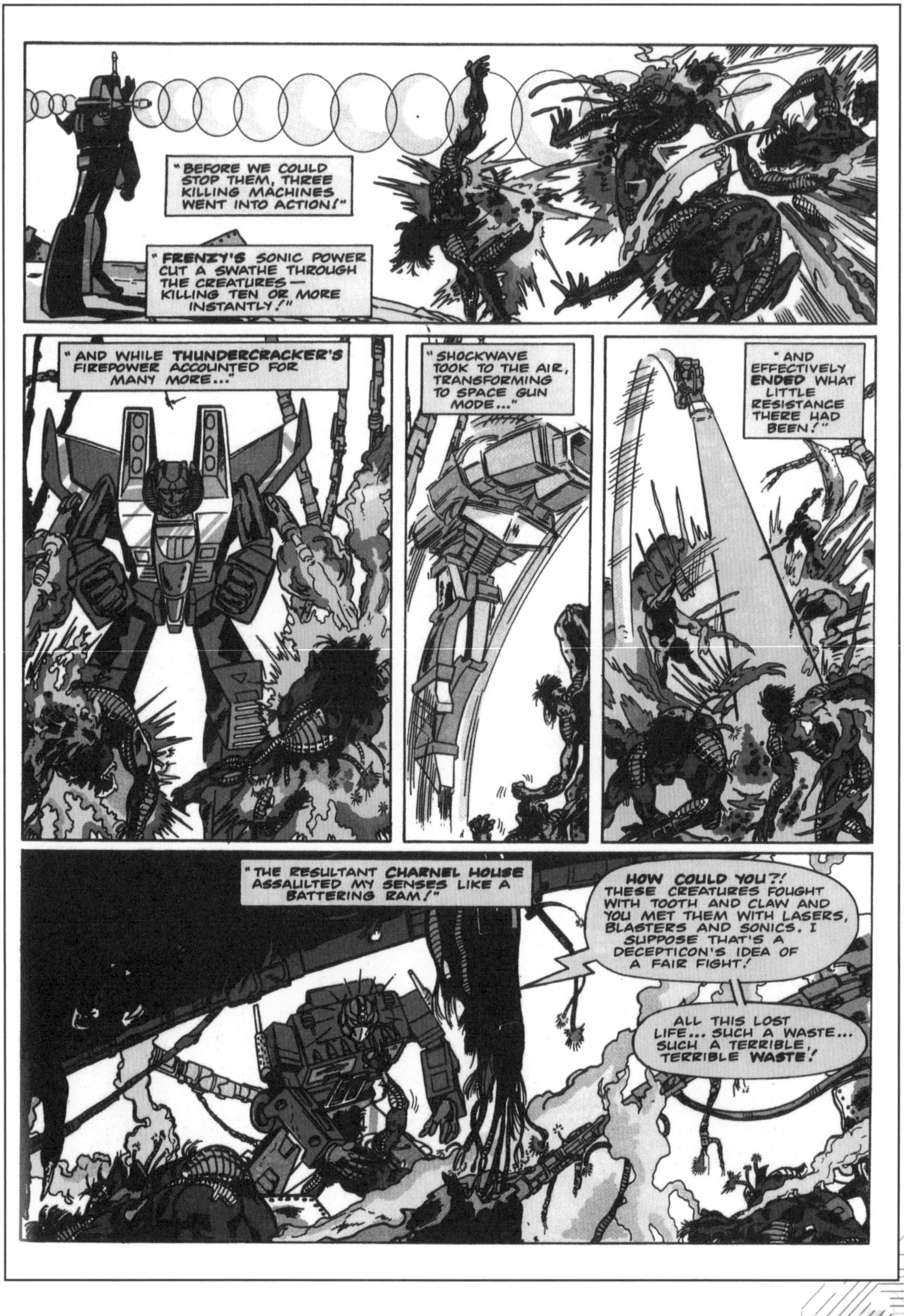
"BEFORE WE COULD STOP THEM, THREE KILLING MACHINES WENT INTO ACTION!"
"FRENZY'S SONIC POWER CUT A SWATHE THROUGH THE CREATURES— KILLING TEN OR MORE INSTANTLY!"
"AND WHILE THUNDERCRACKER'S FIREPOWER ACCOUNTED FOR MANY MORE..."
"SHOCKWAVE TOOK TO THE AIR, TRANSFORMING TO SPACE GUN MODE..."
"AND EFFECTIVELY ENDED WHAT LITTLE RESISTANCE THERE HAD BEEN!"
"THE RESULTANT CHARNEL HOUSE ASSAULTED MY SENSES LIKE A BATTERING RAM!"
HOW COULD YOU?! THESE CREATURES FOUGHT WITH TOOTH AND CLAW AND YOU MET THEM WITH LASERS, BLASTERS AND SONICS. I SUPPOSE THAT'S A DECEPTICON'S IDEA OF A FAIR FIGHT!
ALL THIS LOST LIFE... SUCH A WASTE... SUCH A TERRIBLE, TERRIBLE WASTE!

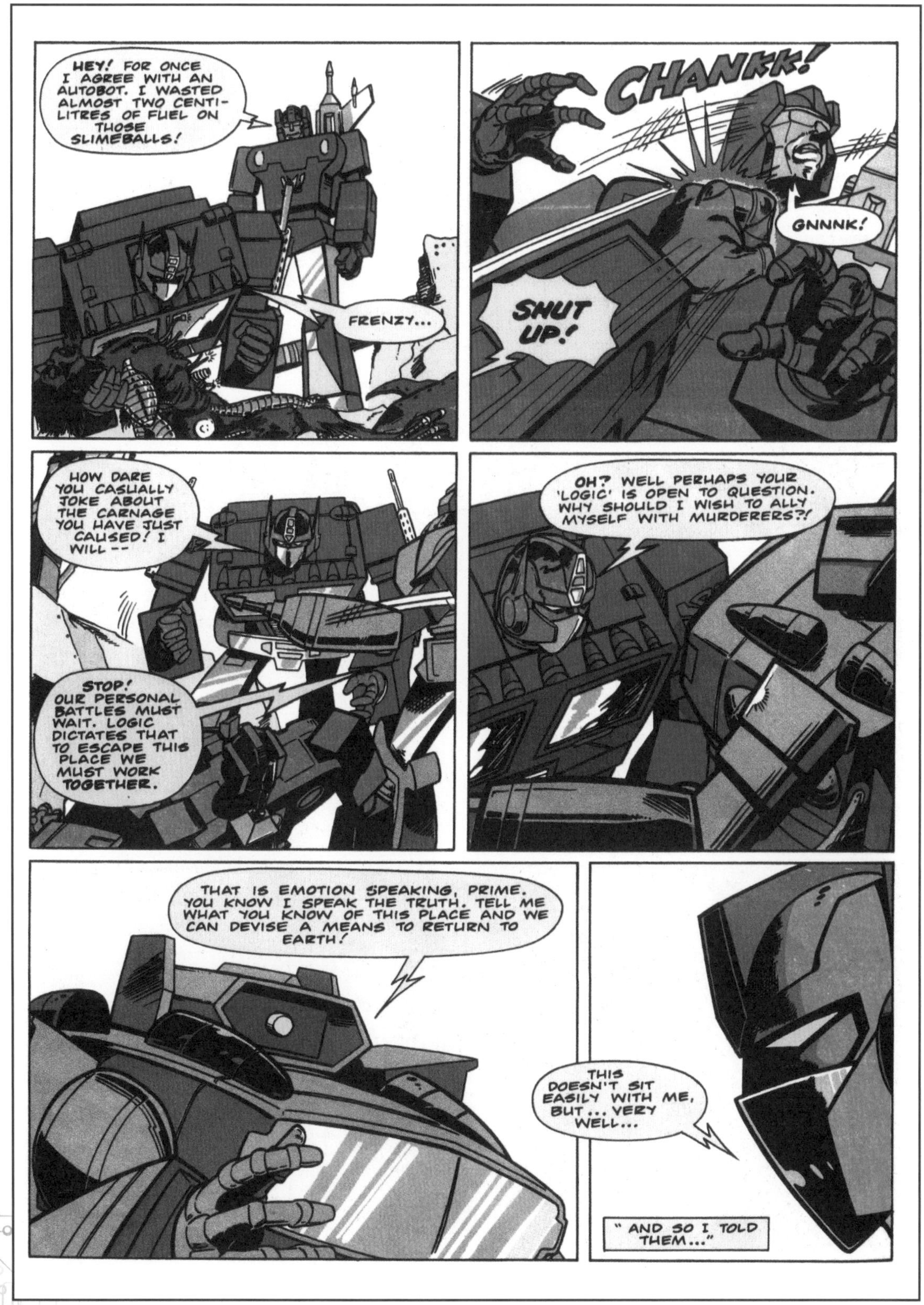
HEY! FOR ONCE I AGREE WITH AN AUTOBOT. I WASTED ALMOST TWO CENTILITRES OF FUEL ON THOSE SLIMEBALLS!
FRENZY...
CHANKK!
GNNNK!
SHUT UP!
HOW DARE YOU CASUALLY JOKE ABOUT THE CARNAGE YOU HAVE JUST CAUSED! I WILL --
STOP! OUR PERSONAL BATTLES MUST WAIT. LOGIC DICTATES THAT TO ESCAPE THIS PLACE WE MUST WORK TOGETHER.
OH? WELL PERHAPS YOUR 'LOGIC' IS OPEN TO QUESTION. WHY SHOULD I WISH TO ALLY MYSELF WITH MURDERERS?!
THAT IS EMOTION SPEAKING, PRIME. YOU KNOW I SPEAK THE TRUTH. TELL ME WHAT YOU KNOW OF THIS PLACE AND WE CAN DEVISE A MEANS TO RETURN TO EARTH!
THIS DOESN'T SIT EASILY WITH ME, BUT... VERY WELL...
"AND SO I TOLD THEM..."

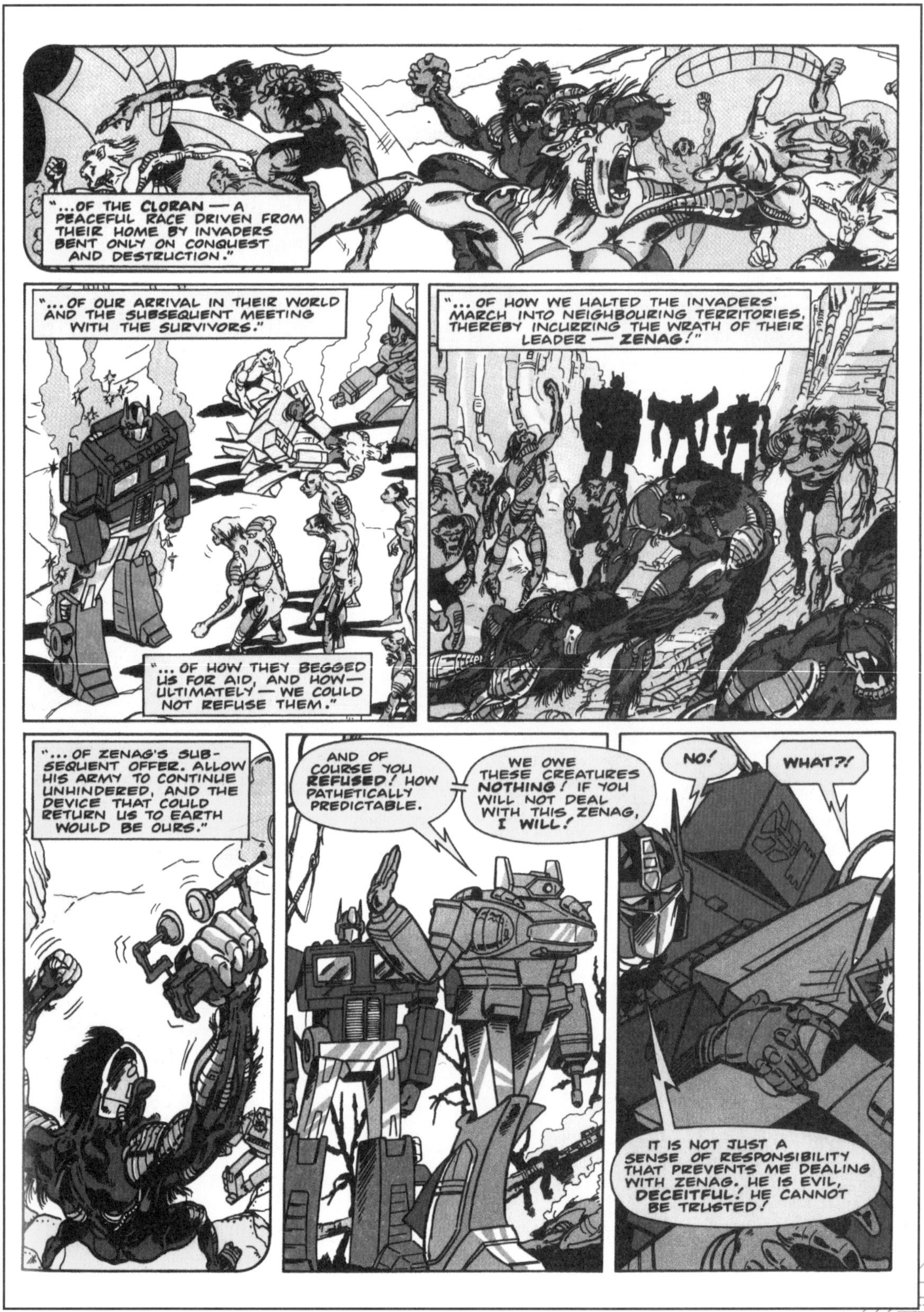
"...OF THE CLORAN — A PEACEFUL RACE DRIVEN FROM THEIR HOME BY INVADERS BENT ONLY ON CONQUEST AND DESTRUCTION."
"...OF OUR ARRIVAL IN THEIR WORLD AND THE SUBSEQUENT MEETING WITH THE SURVIVORS."
"...OF HOW THEY BEGGED US FOR AID, AND HOW— ULTIMATELY— WE COULD NOT REFUSE THEM."
"...OF HOW WE HALTED THE INVADERS' MARCH INTO NEIGHBOURING TERRITORIES, THEREBY INCURRING THE WRATH OF THEIR LEADER — ZENAG!"
"...OF ZENAG'S SUBSEQUENT OFFER. ALLOW HIS ARMY TO CONTINUE UNHINDERED, AND THE DEVICE THAT COULD RETURN US TO EARTH WOULD BE OURS."
AND OF COURSE YOU REFUSED! HOW PATHETICALLY PREDICTABLE.
WE OWE THESE CREATURES NOTHING! IF YOU WILL NOT DEAL WITH THIS ZENAG, I WILL!
NO!
WHAT?!
IT IS NOT JUST A SENSE OF RESPONSIBILITY THAT PREVENTS ME DEALING WITH ZENAG. HE IS EVIL, DECEITFUL! HE CANNOT BE TRUSTED!

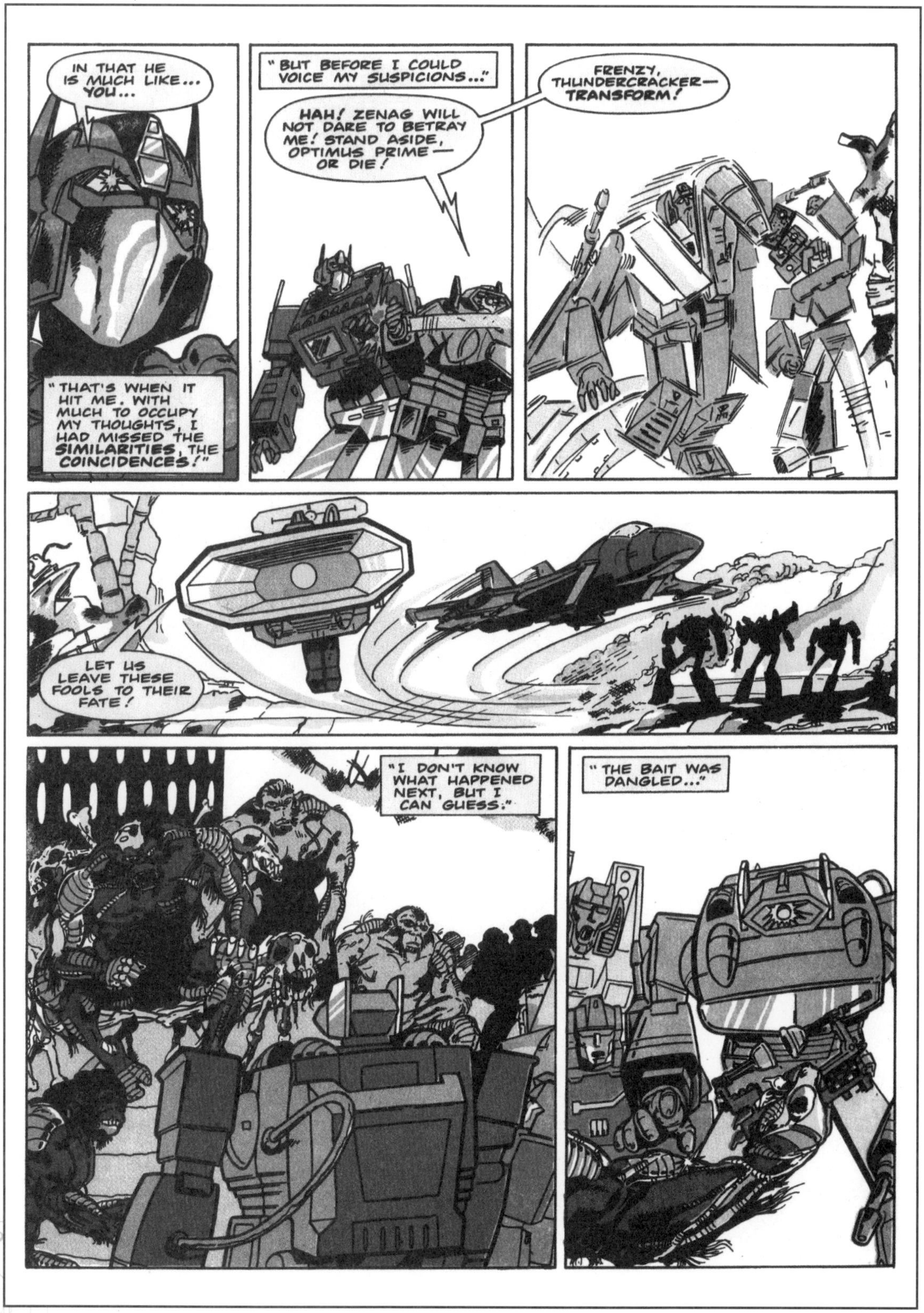
IN THAT HE IS MUCH LIKE... YOU...
"THAT'S WHEN IT HIT ME. WITH MUCH TO OCCUPY MY THOUGHTS, I HAD MISSED THE SIMILARITIES, THE COINCIDENCES!"
"BUT BEFORE I COULD VOICE MY SUSPICIONS..."
HAH! ZENAG WILL NOT DARE TO BETRAY ME! STAND ASIDE, OPTIMUS PRIME — OR DIE!
FRENZY, THUNDERCRACKER — TRANSFORM!
LET US LEAVE THESE FOOLS TO THEIR FATE!
"I DON'T KNOW WHAT HAPPENED NEXT, BUT I CAN GUESS:"
"THE BAIT WAS DANGLED..."

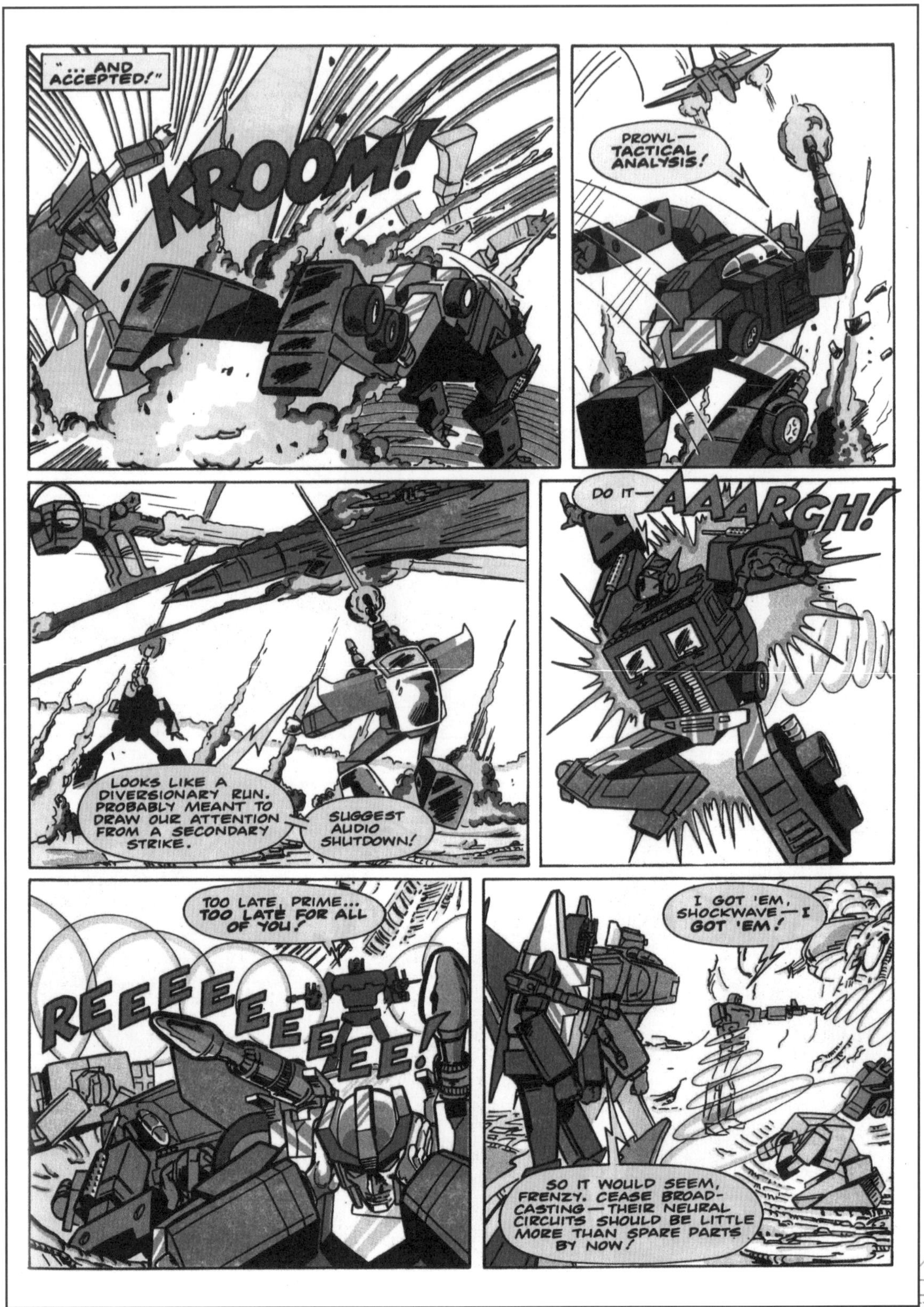
"... AND ACCEPTED!"
KROOM!
PROWL— TACTICAL ANALYSIS!
LOOKS LIKE A DIVERSIONARY RUN, PROBABLY MEANT TO DRAW OUR ATTENTION FROM A SECONDARY STRIKE.
SUGGEST AUDIO SHUTDOWN!
DO IT—
AAARCH!
TOO LATE, PRIME... TOO LATE FOR ALL OF YOU!
REEEEEEEEEEE!
I GOT 'EM, SHOCKWAVE— I GOT 'EM!
SO IT WOULD SEEM, FRENZY. CEASE BROAD-CASTING—THEIR NEURAL CIRCUITS SHOULD BE LITTLE MORE THAN SPARE PARTS BY NOW!

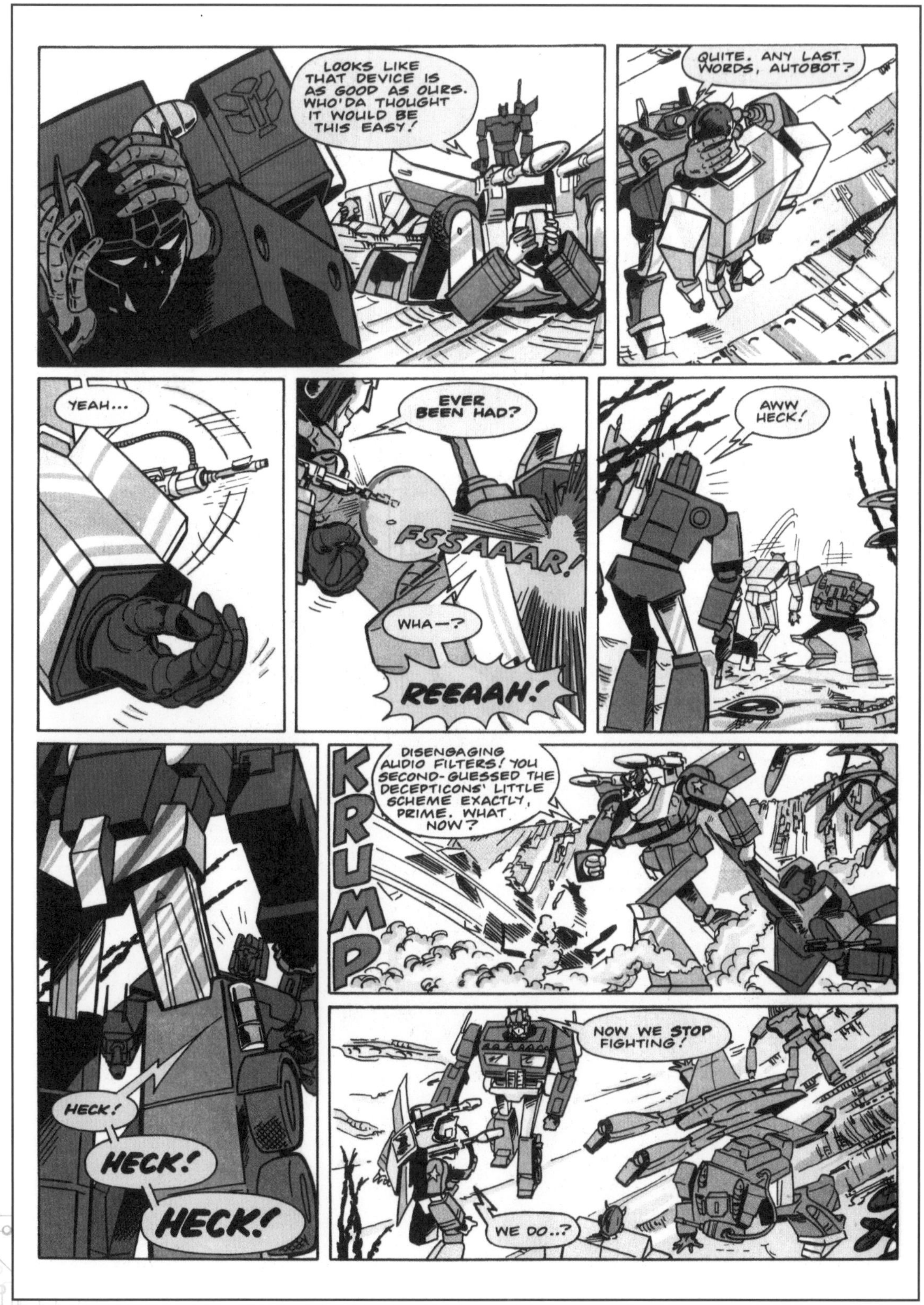

LOOKS LIKE THAT DEVICE IS AS GOOD AS OURS. WHO'DA THOUGHT IT WOULD BE THIS EASY!
QUITE. ANY LAST WORDS, AUTOBOT?
YEAH...
EVER BEEN HAD?
FSSAAAAR!
WHA--?
REEAAH!
AWW HECK!
HECK!
HECK!
HECK!
KRUMP
DISENGAGING AUDIO FILTERS! YOU SECOND-GUESSED THE DECEPTICONS' LITTLE SCHEME EXACTLY, PRIME. WHAT NOW?
NOW WE STOP FIGHTING!
WE DO..?

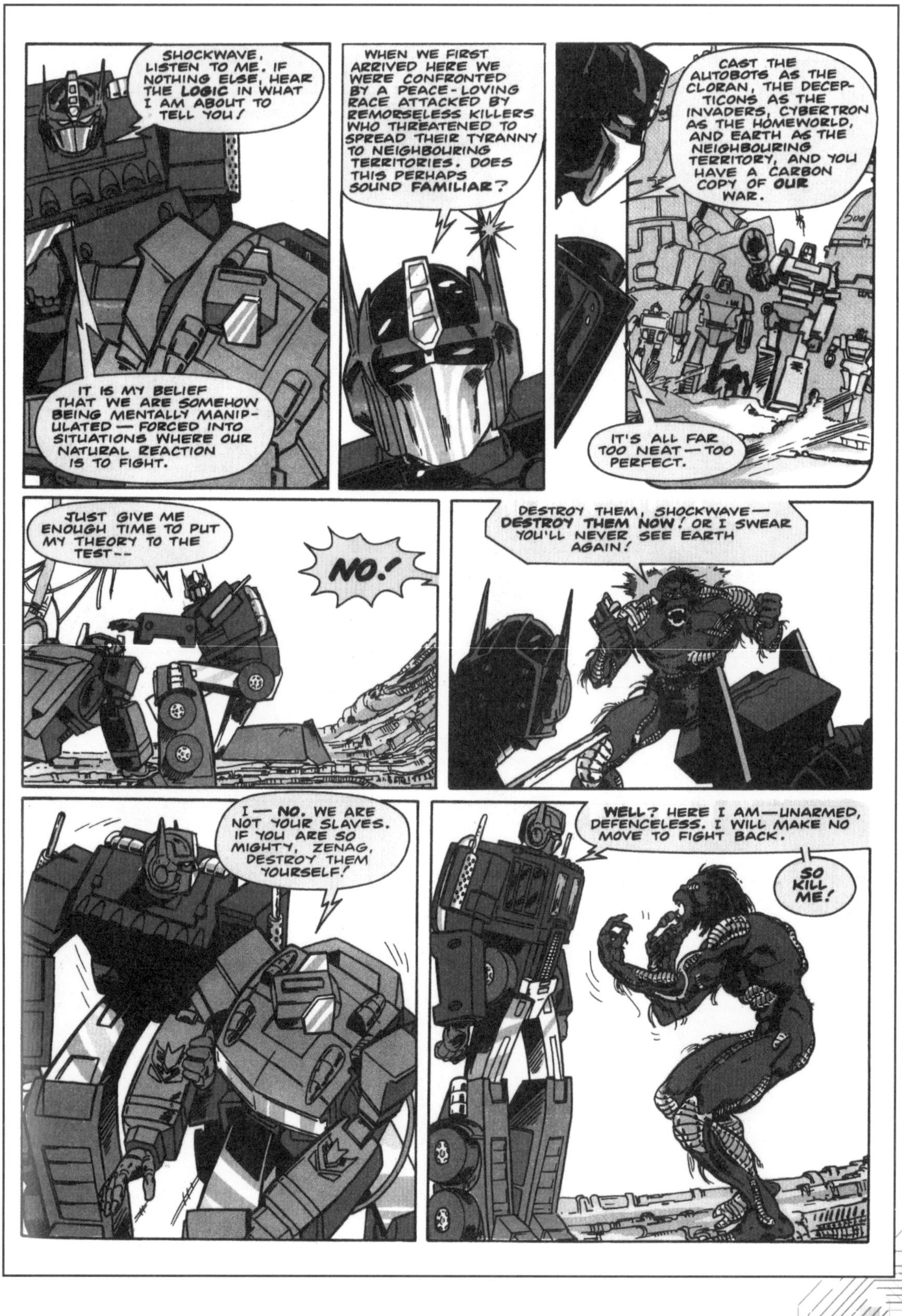
SHOCKWAVE, LISTEN TO ME. IF NOTHING ELSE, HEAR THE LOGIC IN WHAT I AM ABOUT TO TELL YOU!
IT IS MY BELIEF THAT WE ARE SOMEHOW BEING MENTALLY MANIP-ULATED — FORCED INTO SITUATIONS WHERE OUR NATURAL REACTION IS TO FIGHT.
WHEN WE FIRST ARRIVED HERE WE WERE CONFRONTED BY A PEACE-LOVING RACE ATTACKED BY REMORSELESS KILLERS WHO THREATENED TO SPREAD THEIR TYRANNY TO NEIGHBOURING TERRITORIES. DOES THIS PERHAPS SOUND FAMILIAR?
CAST THE AUTOBOTS AS THE CLORAN, THE DECEP-TICONS AS THE INVADERS, CYBERTRON AS THE HOMEWORLD, AND EARTH AS THE NEIGHBOURING TERRITORY, AND YOU HAVE A CARBON COPY OF OUR WAR.
IT'S ALL FAR TOO NEAT — TOO PERFECT.
JUST GIVE ME ENOUGH TIME TO PUT MY THEORY TO THE TEST--
NO!
DESTROY THEM, SHOCKWAVE — DESTROY THEM NOW! OR I SWEAR YOU'LL NEVER SEE EARTH AGAIN!
I — NO. WE ARE NOT YOUR SLAVES. IF YOU ARE SO MIGHTY, ZENAG, DESTROY THEM YOURSELF!
WELL? HERE I AM — UNARMED, DEFENCELESS. I WILL MAKE NO MOVE TO FIGHT BACK.
SO KILL ME!

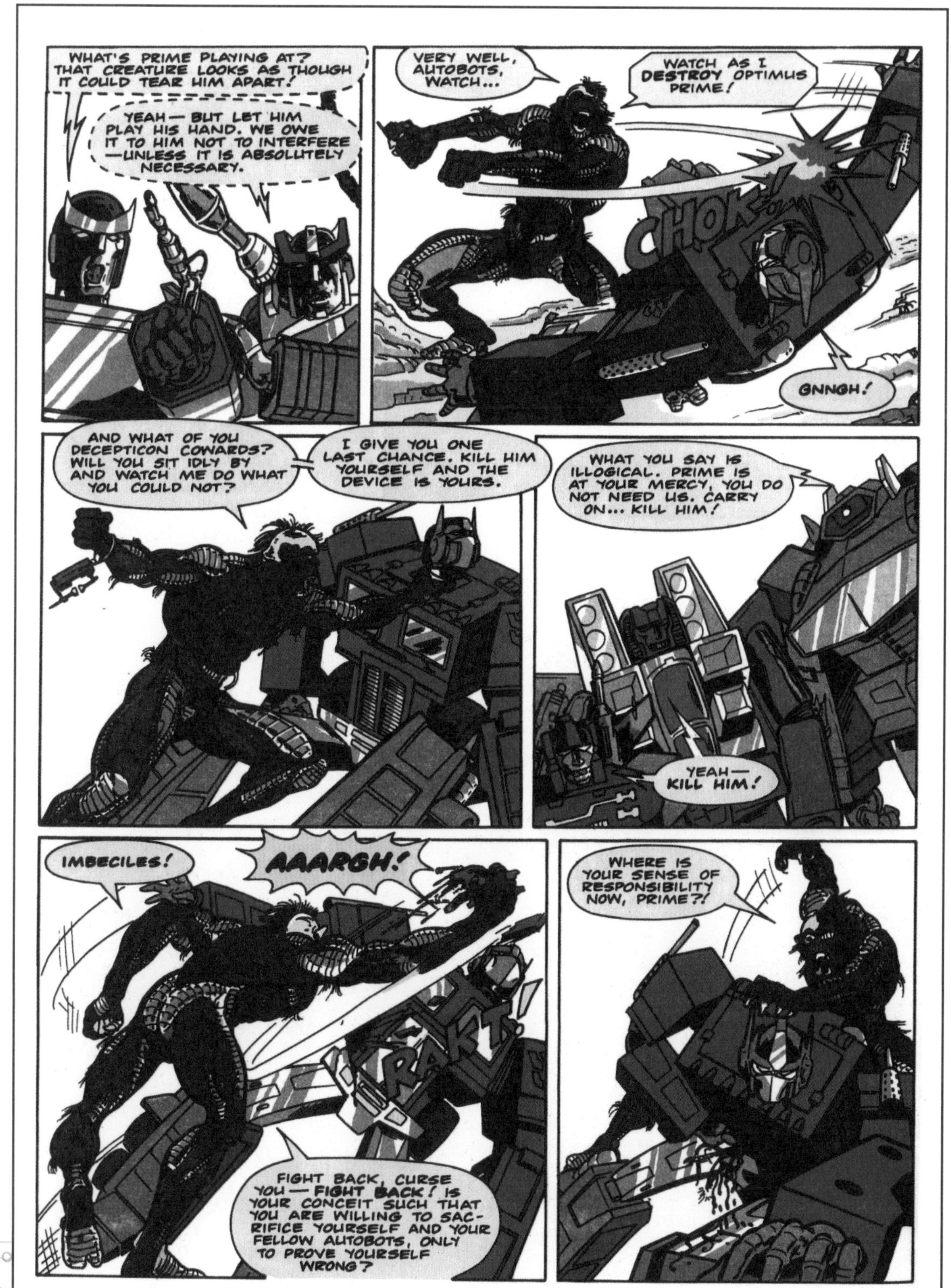

WHAT'S PRIME PLAYING AT? THAT CREATURE LOOKS AS THOUGH IT COULD TEAR HIM APART!
YEAH — BUT LET HIM PLAY HIS HAND. WE OWE IT TO HIM NOT TO INTERFERE — UNLESS IT IS ABSOLUTELY NECESSARY.
VERY WELL, AUTOBOTS, WATCH...
WATCH AS I DESTROY OPTIMUS PRIME!
CHOK!
GNNGH!
AND WHAT OF YOU DECEPTICON COWARDS? WILL YOU SIT IDLY BY AND WATCH ME DO WHAT YOU COULD NOT?
I GIVE YOU ONE LAST CHANCE. KILL HIM YOURSELF AND THE DEVICE IS YOURS.
WHAT YOU SAY IS ILLOGICAL. PRIME IS AT YOUR MERCY, YOU DO NOT NEED US. CARRY ON... KILL HIM!
YEAH — KILL HIM!
IMBECILES!
AAARGH!
RAKT!
FIGHT BACK, CURSE YOU — FIGHT BACK! IS YOUR CONCEIT SUCH THAT YOU ARE WILLING TO SACRIFICE YOURSELF AND YOUR FELLOW AUTOBOTS, ONLY TO PROVE YOURSELF WRONG?
WHERE IS YOUR SENSE OF RESPONSIBILITY NOW, PRIME?!

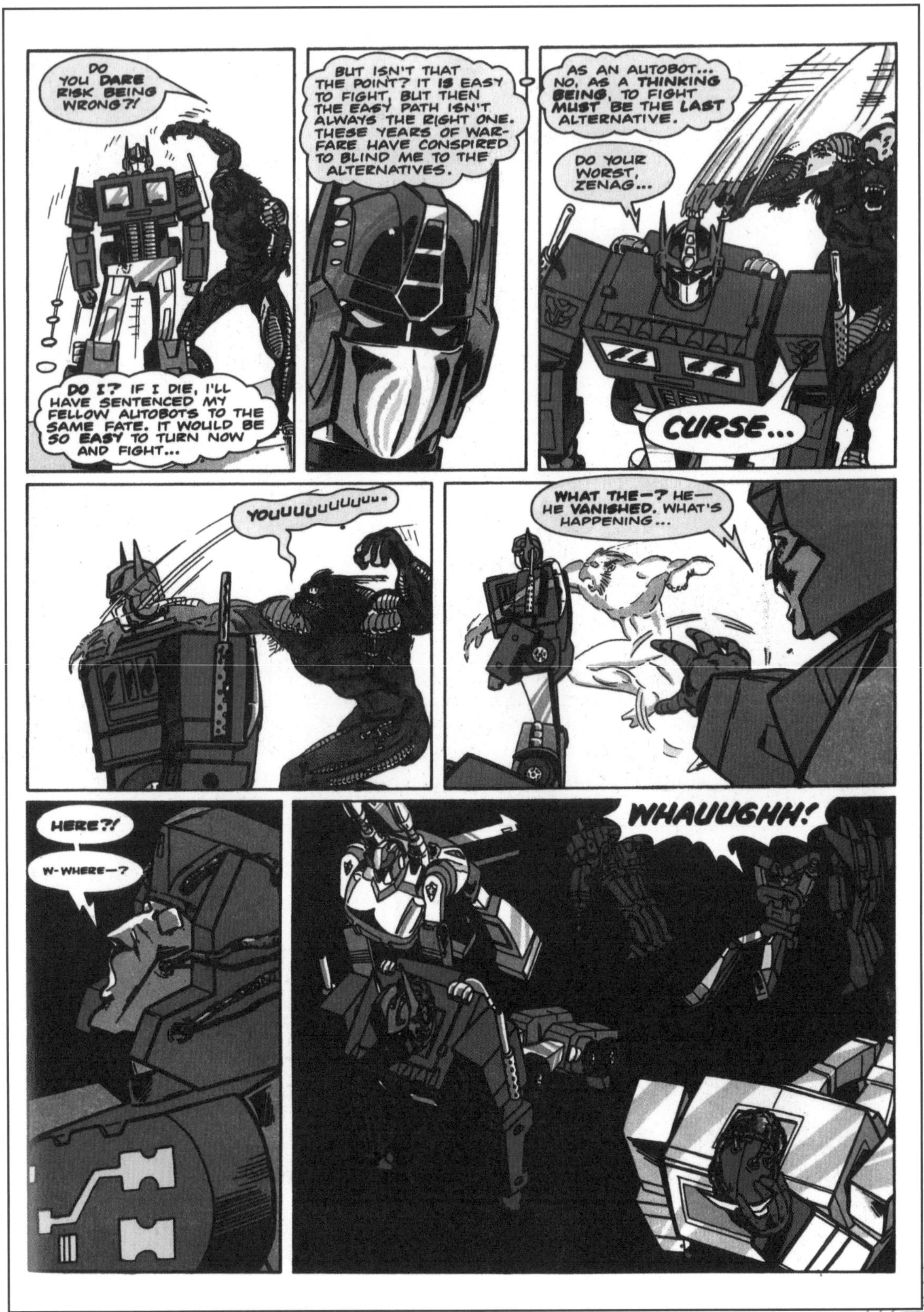
DO YOU DARE RISK BEING WRONG?!
DO I? IF I DIE, I'LL HAVE SENTENCED MY FELLOW AUTOBOTS TO THE SAME FATE. IT WOULD BE SO EASY TO TURN NOW AND FIGHT...
BUT ISN'T THAT THE POINT? IT IS EASY TO FIGHT, BUT THEN THE EASY PATH ISN'T ALWAYS THE RIGHT ONE. THESE YEARS OF WARFARE HAVE CONSPIRED TO BLIND ME TO THE ALTERNATIVES.
AS AN AUTOBOT... NO, AS A THINKING BEING, TO FIGHT MUST BE THE LAST ALTERNATIVE.
DO YOUR WORST, ZENAG...
CURSE...
YOUUUUUUUUU..
WHAT THE--? HE-- HE VANISHED. WHAT'S HAPPENING...
HERE?!
W-WHERE--?
WHAUUGHH!

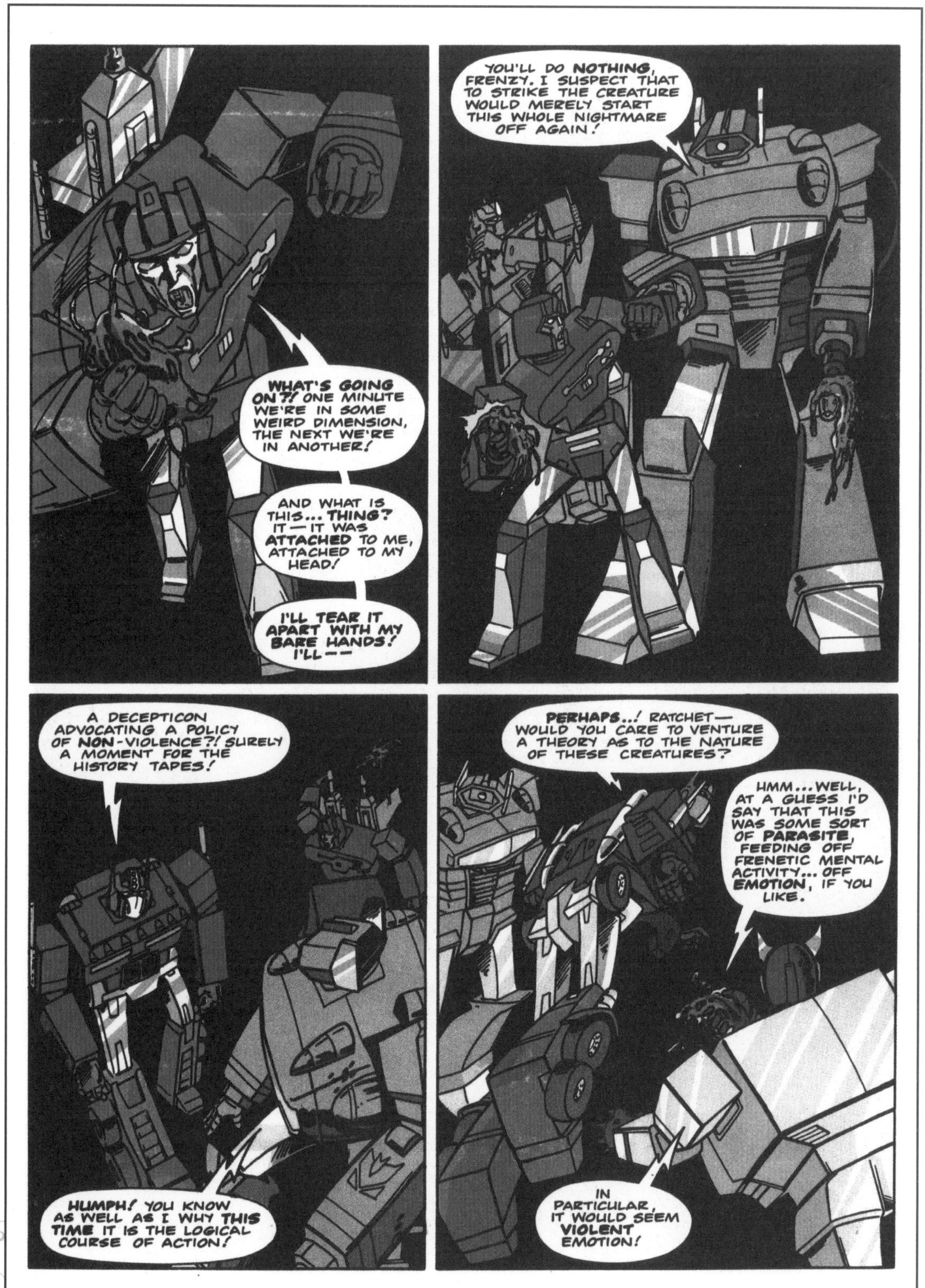
WHAT'S GOING ON?! ONE MINUTE WE'RE IN SOME WEIRD DIMENSION, THE NEXT WE'RE IN ANOTHER!
AND WHAT IS THIS... THING? IT—IT WAS ATTACHED TO ME, ATTACHED TO MY HEAD!
I'LL TEAR IT APART WITH MY BARE HANDS! I'LL--
YOU'LL DO NOTHING, FRENZY. I SUSPECT THAT TO STRIKE THE CREATURE WOULD MERELY START THIS WHOLE NIGHTMARE OFF AGAIN!
A DECEPTICON ADVOCATING A POLICY OF NON-VIOLENCE?! SURELY A MOMENT FOR THE HISTORY TAPES!
HUMPH! YOU KNOW AS WELL AS I WHY THIS TIME IT IS THE LOGICAL COURSE OF ACTION!
PERHAPS...! RATCHET— WOULD YOU CARE TO VENTURE A THEORY AS TO THE NATURE OF THESE CREATURES?
HMM... WELL, AT A GUESS I'D SAY THAT THIS WAS SOME SORT OF PARASITE, FEEDING OFF FRENETIC MENTAL ACTIVITY... OFF EMOTION, IF YOU LIKE.
IN PARTICULAR, IT WOULD SEEM VIOLENT EMOTION!

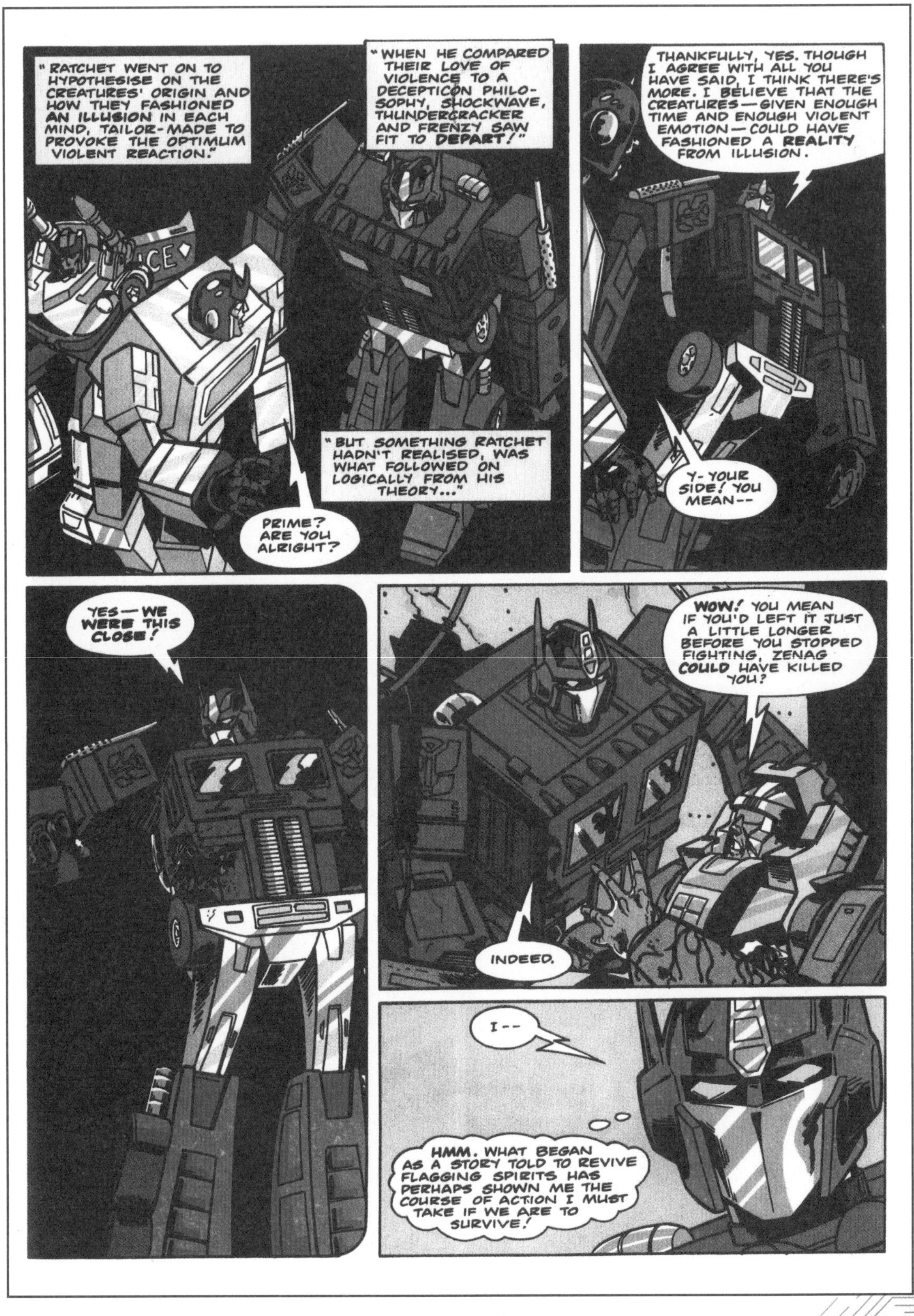
"RATCHET WENT ON TO HYPOTHESISE ON THE CREATURES' ORIGIN AND HOW THEY FASHIONED AN ILLUSION IN EACH MIND, TAILOR-MADE TO PROVOKE THE OPTIMUM VIOLENT REACTION."
"WHEN HE COMPARED THEIR LOVE OF VIOLENCE TO A DECEPTICON PHILOSOPHY, SHOCKWAVE, THUNDERCRACKER AND FRENZY SAW FIT TO DEPART!"
"BUT SOMETHING RATCHET HADN'T REALISED, WAS WHAT FOLLOWED ON LOGICALLY FROM HIS THEORY..."
PRIME? ARE YOU ALRIGHT?
THANKFULLY, YES. THOUGH I AGREE WITH ALL YOU HAVE SAID, I THINK THERE'S MORE. I BELIEVE THAT THE CREATURES—GIVEN ENOUGH TIME AND ENOUGH VIOLENT EMOTION—COULD HAVE FASHIONED A REALITY FROM ILLUSION.
Y-YOUR SIDE! YOU MEAN--
YES—WE WERE THIS CLOSE!
WOW! YOU MEAN IF YOU'D LEFT IT JUST A LITTLE LONGER BEFORE YOU STOPPED FIGHTING, ZENAG COULD HAVE KILLED YOU?
INDEED.
I--
HMM. WHAT BEGAN AS A STORY TOLD TO REVIVE FLAGGING SPIRITS HAS PERHAPS SHOWN ME THE COURSE OF ACTION I MUST TAKE IF WE ARE TO SURVIVE!

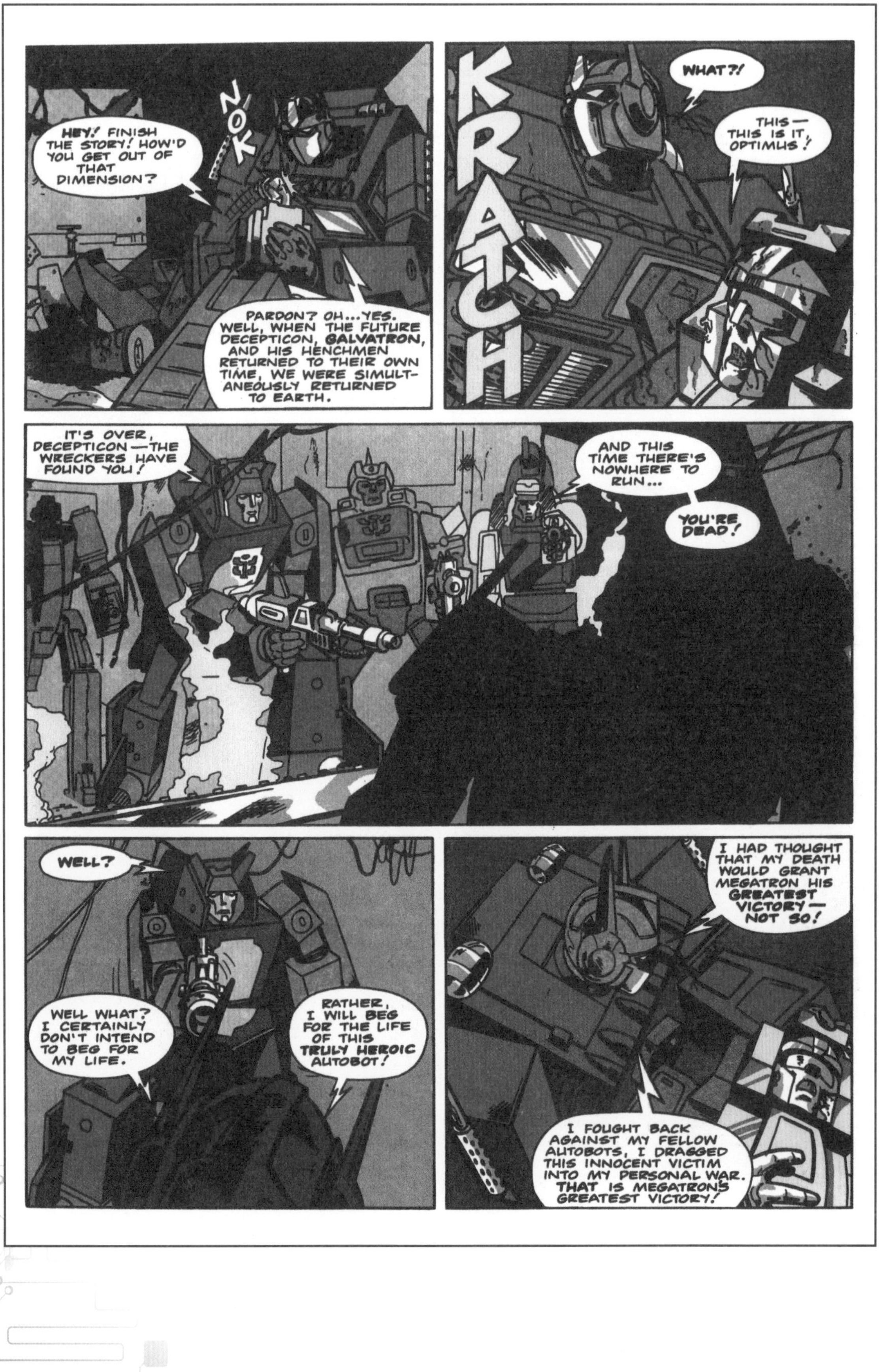
NOK
HEY! FINISH THE STORY! HOW'D YOU GET OUT OF THAT DIMENSION?
PARDON? OH... YES. WELL, WHEN THE FUTURE DECEPTICON, GALVATRON, AND HIS HENCHMEN RETURNED TO THEIR OWN TIME, WE WERE SIMULT-ANEOUSLY RETURNED TO EARTH.
KRATCH
WHAT?!
THIS— THIS IS IT, OPTIMUS!
IT'S OVER, DECEPTICON—THE WRECKERS HAVE FOUND YOU!
AND THIS TIME THERE'S NOWHERE TO RUN...
YOU'RE DEAD!
WELL?
WELL WHAT? I CERTAINLY DON'T INTEND TO BEG FOR MY LIFE.
RATHER, I WILL BEG FOR THE LIFE OF THIS TRULY HEROIC AUTOBOT!
I HAD THOUGHT THAT MY DEATH WOULD GRANT MEGATRON HIS GREATEST VICTORY—NOT SO!
I FOUGHT BACK AGAINST MY FELLOW AUTOBOTS, I DRAGGED THIS INNOCENT VICTIM INTO MY PERSONAL WAR. THAT IS MEGATRON'S GREATEST VICTORY!

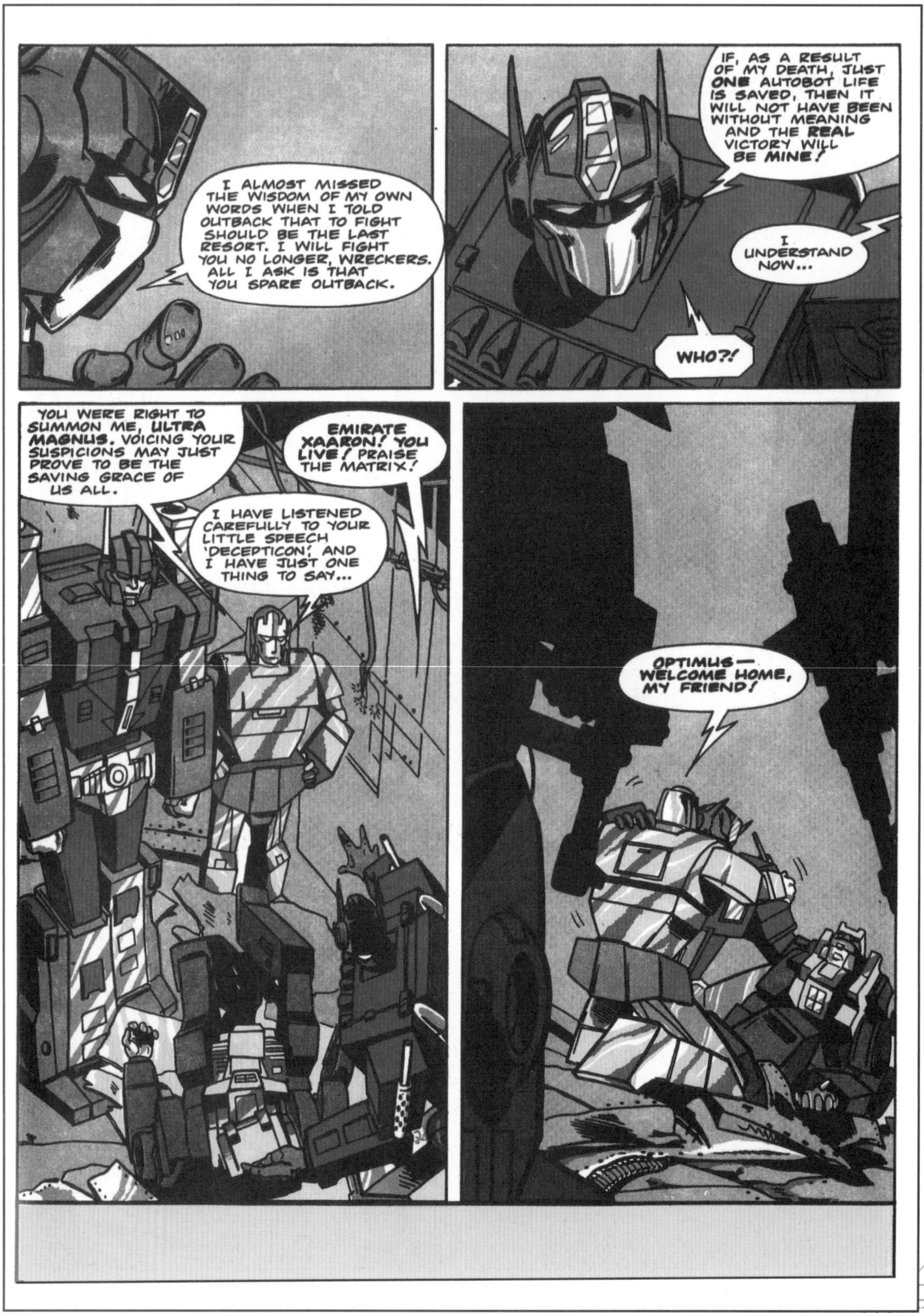
I ALMOST MISSED THE WISDOM OF MY OWN WORDS WHEN I TOLD OUTBACK THAT TO FIGHT SHOULD BE THE LAST RESORT. I WILL FIGHT YOU NO LONGER, WRECKERS. ALL I ASK IS THAT YOU SPARE OUTBACK.
IF, AS A RESULT OF MY DEATH, JUST ONE AUTOBOT LIFE IS SAVED, THEN IT WILL NOT HAVE BEEN WITHOUT MEANING AND THE REAL VICTORY WILL BE MINE!
I UNDERSTAND NOW...
WHO?!
YOU WERE RIGHT TO SUMMON ME, ULTRA MAGNUS. VOICING YOUR SUSPICIONS MAY JUST PROVE TO BE THE SAVING GRACE OF US ALL.
EMIRATE XAARON! YOU LIVE! PRAISE THE MATRIX!
I HAVE LISTENED CAREFULLY TO YOUR LITTLE SPEECH 'DECEPTICON', AND I HAVE JUST ONE THING TO SAY...
OPTIMUS— WELCOME HOME, MY FRIEND!

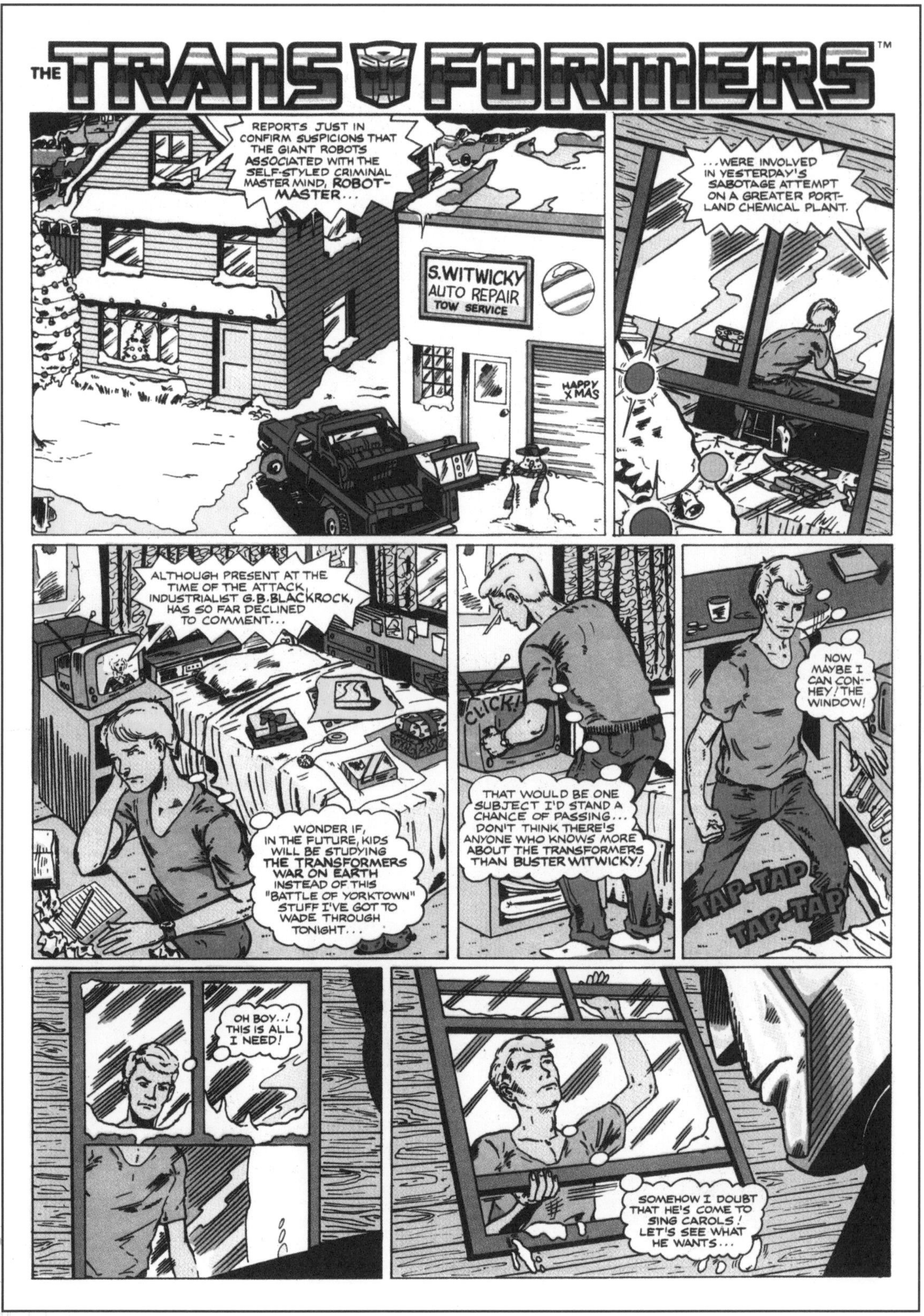
THE TRANSFORMERS ™
REPORTS JUST IN CONFIRM SUSPICIONS THAT THE GIANT ROBOTS ASSOCIATED WITH THE SELF-STYLED CRIMINAL MASTER MIND, ROBOT-MASTER...
S. WITWICKY AUTO REPAIR TOW SERVICE
HAPPY X MAS
...WERE INVOLVED IN YESTERDAY'S SABOTAGE ATTEMPT ON A GREATER PORTLAND CHEMICAL PLANT.
ALTHOUGH PRESENT AT THE TIME OF THE ATTACK, INDUSTRIALIST G.B. BLACKROCK, HAS SO FAR DECLINED TO COMMENT...
WONDER IF, IN THE FUTURE, KIDS WILL BE STUDYING THE TRANSFORMERS WAR ON EARTH INSTEAD OF THIS "BATTLE OF YORKTOWN" STUFF I'VE GOT TO WADE THROUGH TONIGHT...
CLICK!
THAT WOULD BE ONE SUBJECT I'D STAND A CHANCE OF PASSING... DON'T THINK THERE'S ANYONE WHO KNOWS MORE ABOUT THE TRANSFORMERS THAN BUSTER WITWICKY!
NOW MAYBE I CAN CON-- HEY! THE WINDOW!
TAP-TAP
TAP-TAP
OH BOY..! THIS IS ALL I NEED!
SOMEHOW I DOUBT THAT HE'S COME TO SING CAROLS! LET'S SEE WHAT HE WANTS...

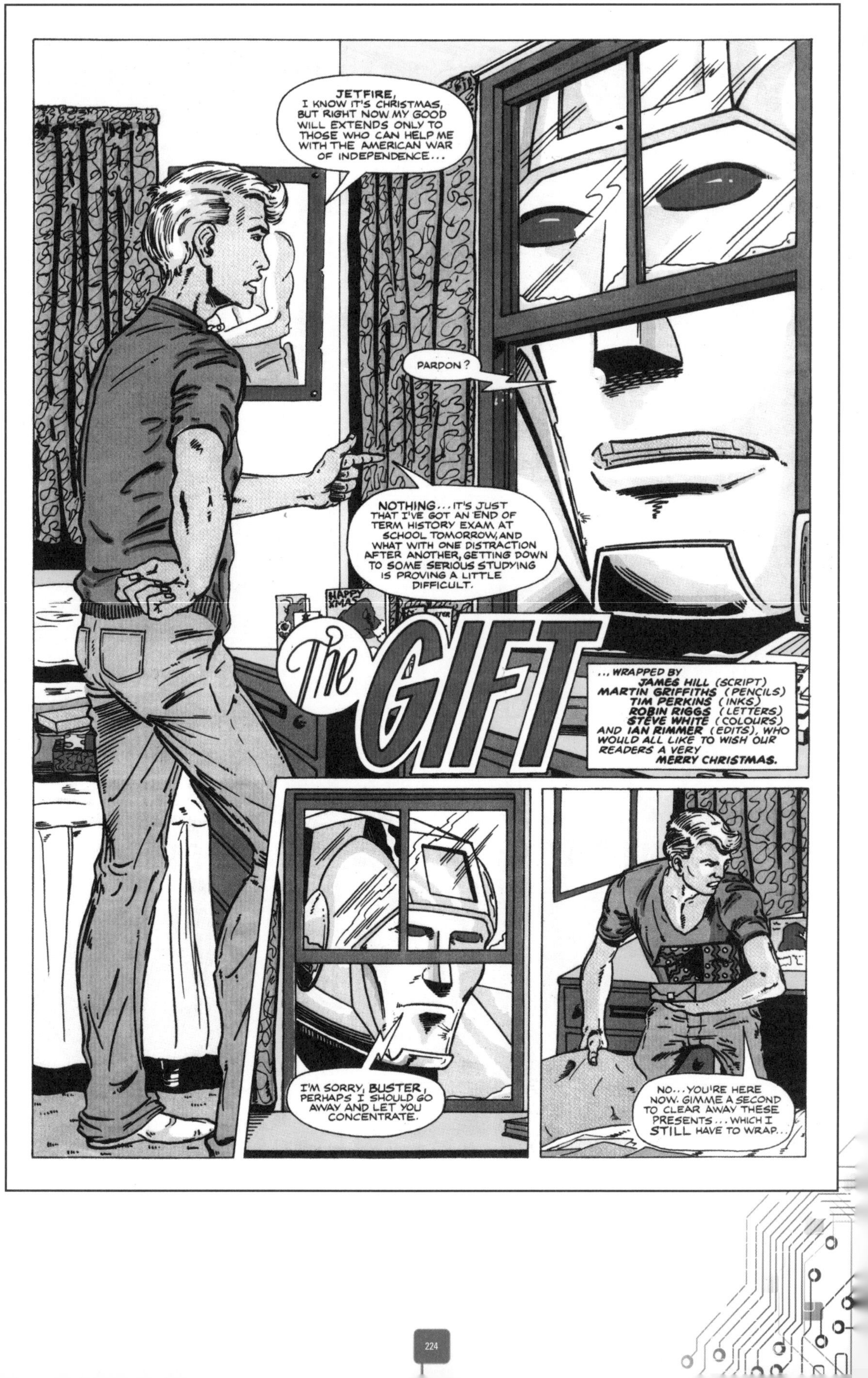
JETFIRE, I KNOW IT'S CHRISTMAS, BUT RIGHT NOW MY GOOD WILL EXTENDS ONLY TO THOSE WHO CAN HELP ME WITH THE AMERICAN WAR OF INDEPENDENCE...
PARDON?
NOTHING... IT'S JUST THAT I'VE GOT AN END OF TERM HISTORY EXAM AT SCHOOL TOMORROW, AND WHAT WITH ONE DISTRACTION AFTER ANOTHER, GETTING DOWN TO SOME SERIOUS STUDYING IS PROVING A LITTLE DIFFICULT.
HAPPY XMAS
The GIFT
...WRAPPED BY JAMES HILL (SCRIPT) MARTIN GRIFFITHS (PENCILS) TIM PERKINS (INKS) ROBIN RIGGS (LETTERS) STEVE WHITE (COLOURS) AND IAN RIMMER (EDITS), WHO WOULD ALL LIKE TO WISH OUR READERS A VERY MERRY CHRISTMAS.
I'M SORRY, BUSTER, PERHAPS I SHOULD GO AWAY AND LET YOU CONCENTRATE.
NO... YOU'RE HERE NOW. GIMME A SECOND TO CLEAR AWAY THESE PRESENTS... WHICH I STILL HAVE TO WRAP...

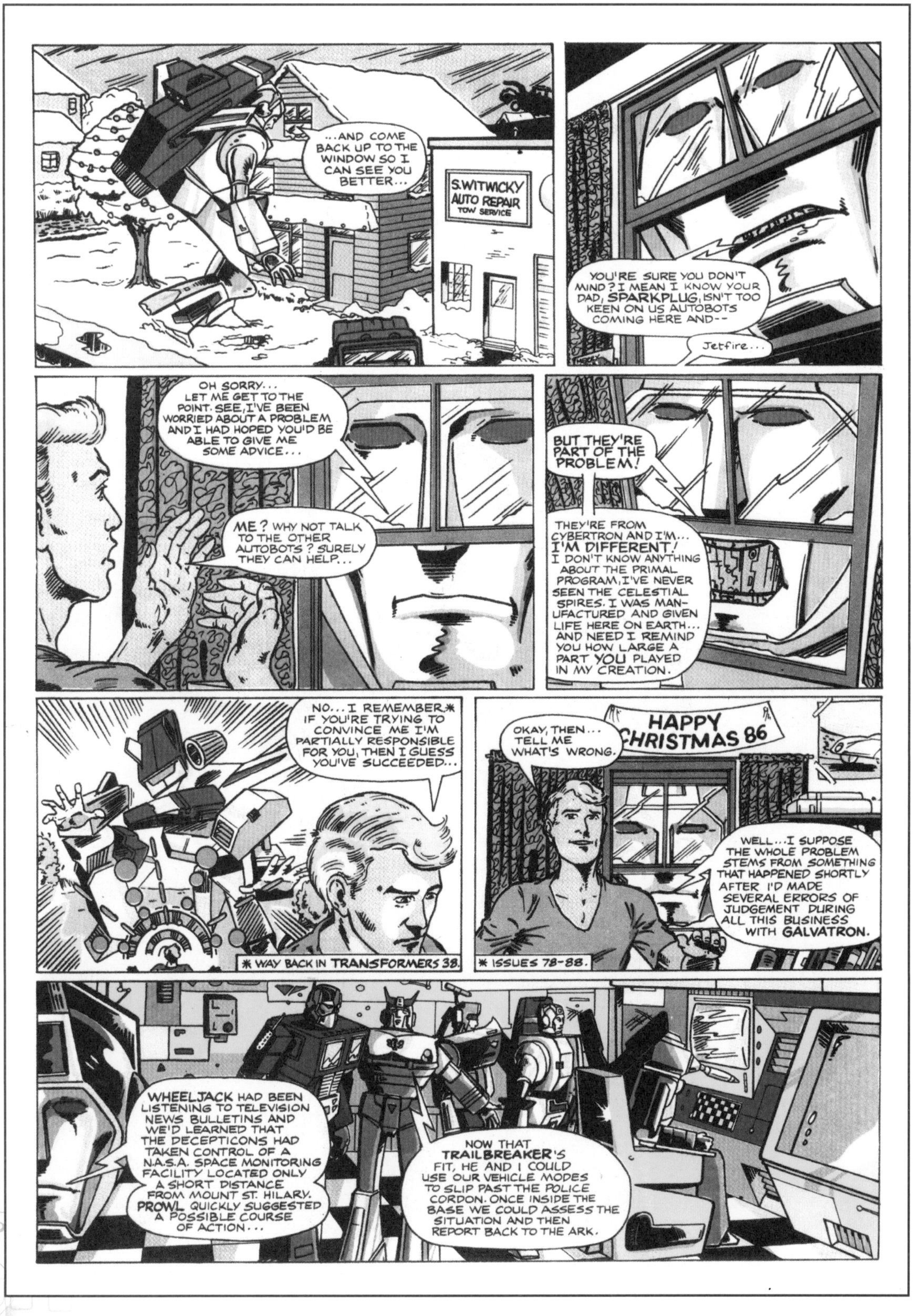
...AND COME BACK UP TO THE WINDOW SO I CAN SEE YOU BETTER...
S. WITWICKY AUTO REPAIR TOW SERVICE
YOU'RE SURE YOU DON'T MIND? I MEAN I KNOW YOUR DAD, SPARKPLUG, ISN'T TOO KEEN ON US AUTOBOTS COMING HERE AND--
Jetfire...
OH SORRY... LET ME GET TO THE POINT. SEE, I'VE BEEN WORRIED ABOUT A PROBLEM AND I HAD HOPED YOU'D BE ABLE TO GIVE ME SOME ADVICE...
ME? WHY NOT TALK TO THE OTHER AUTOBOTS? SURELY THEY CAN HELP...
BUT THEY'RE PART OF THE PROBLEM!
THEY'RE FROM CYBERTRON AND I'M... I'M DIFFERENT! I DON'T KNOW ANYTHING ABOUT THE PRIMAL PROGRAM, I'VE NEVER SEEN THE CELESTIAL SPIRES. I WAS MAN-UFACTURED AND GIVEN LIFE HERE ON EARTH... AND NEED I REMIND YOU HOW LARGE A PART YOU PLAYED IN MY CREATION.
NO... I REMEMBER.* IF YOU'RE TRYING TO CONVINCE ME I'M PARTIALLY RESPONSIBLE FOR YOU, THEN I GUESS YOU'VE SUCCEEDED...
* WAY BACK IN TRANSFORMERS 38.
HAPPY CHRISTMAS 86
OKAY, THEN... TELL ME WHAT'S WRONG.
WELL... I SUPPOSE THE WHOLE PROBLEM STEMS FROM SOMETHING THAT HAPPENED SHORTLY AFTER I'D MADE SEVERAL ERRORS OF JUDGEMENT DURING ALL THIS BUSINESS WITH GALVATRON.
* ISSUES 78-88.
WHEELJACK HAD BEEN LISTENING TO TELEVISION NEWS BULLETINS AND WE'D LEARNED THAT THE DECEPTICONS HAD TAKEN CONTROL OF A N.A.S.A. SPACE MONITORING FACILITY LOCATED ONLY A SHORT DISTANCE FROM MOUNT ST. HILARY. PROWL QUICKLY SUGGESTED A POSSIBLE COURSE OF ACTION...
NOW THAT TRAILBREAKER'S FIT, HE AND I COULD USE OUR VEHICLE MODES TO SLIP PAST THE POLICE CORDON. ONCE INSIDE THE BASE WE COULD ASSESS THE SITUATION AND THEN REPORT BACK TO THE ARK.

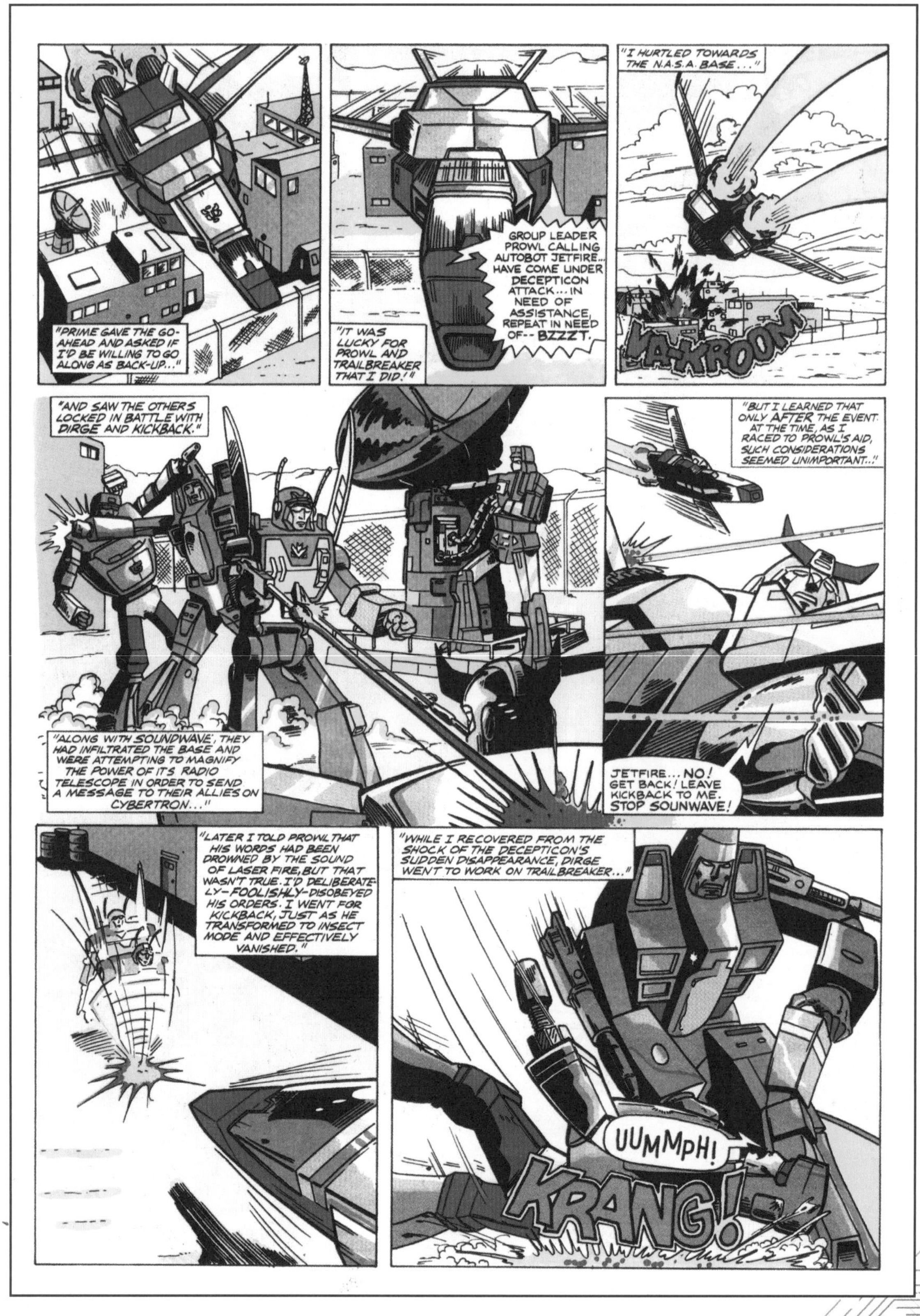
"PRIME GAVE THE GO-AHEAD AND ASKED IF I'D BE WILLING TO GO ALONG AS BACK-UP..."
"IT WAS LUCKY FOR PROWL AND TRAILBREAKER THAT I DID!"
GROUP LEADER PROWL CALLING AUTOBOT JETFIRE... HAVE COME UNDER DECEPTICON ATTACK... IN NEED OF ASSISTANCE, REPEAT IN NEED OF-- BZZZT.
"I HURTLED TOWARDS THE N.A.S.A. BASE..."
VA-KROOM
"AND SAW THE OTHERS LOCKED IN BATTLE WITH DIRGE AND KICKBACK."
"ALONG WITH SOUNDWAVE, THEY HAD INFILTRATED THE BASE AND WERE ATTEMPTING TO MAGNIFY THE POWER OF IT'S RADIO TELESCOPE IN ORDER TO SEND A MESSAGE TO THEIR ALLIES ON CYBERTRON..."
"BUT I LEARNED THAT ONLY AFTER THE EVENT. AT THE TIME, AS I RACED TO PROWL'S AID, SUCH CONSIDERATIONS SEEMED UNIMPORTANT..."
JETFIRE... NO! GET BACK! LEAVE KICKBACK TO ME. STOP SOUNWAVE!
"LATER I TOLD PROWL THAT HIS WORDS HAD BEEN DROWNED BY THE SOUND OF LASER FIRE, BUT THAT WASN'T TRUE. I'D DELIBERATE-LY--FOOLISHLY--DISOBEYED HIS ORDERS. I WENT FOR KICKBACK, JUST AS HE TRANSFORMED TO INSECT MODE AND EFFECTIVELY VANISHED."
"WHILE I RECOVERED FROM THE SHOCK OF THE DECEPTICON'S SUDDEN DISAPPEARANCE, DIRGE WENT TO WORK ON TRAILBREAKER..."
UUMMPH!
KRANG!

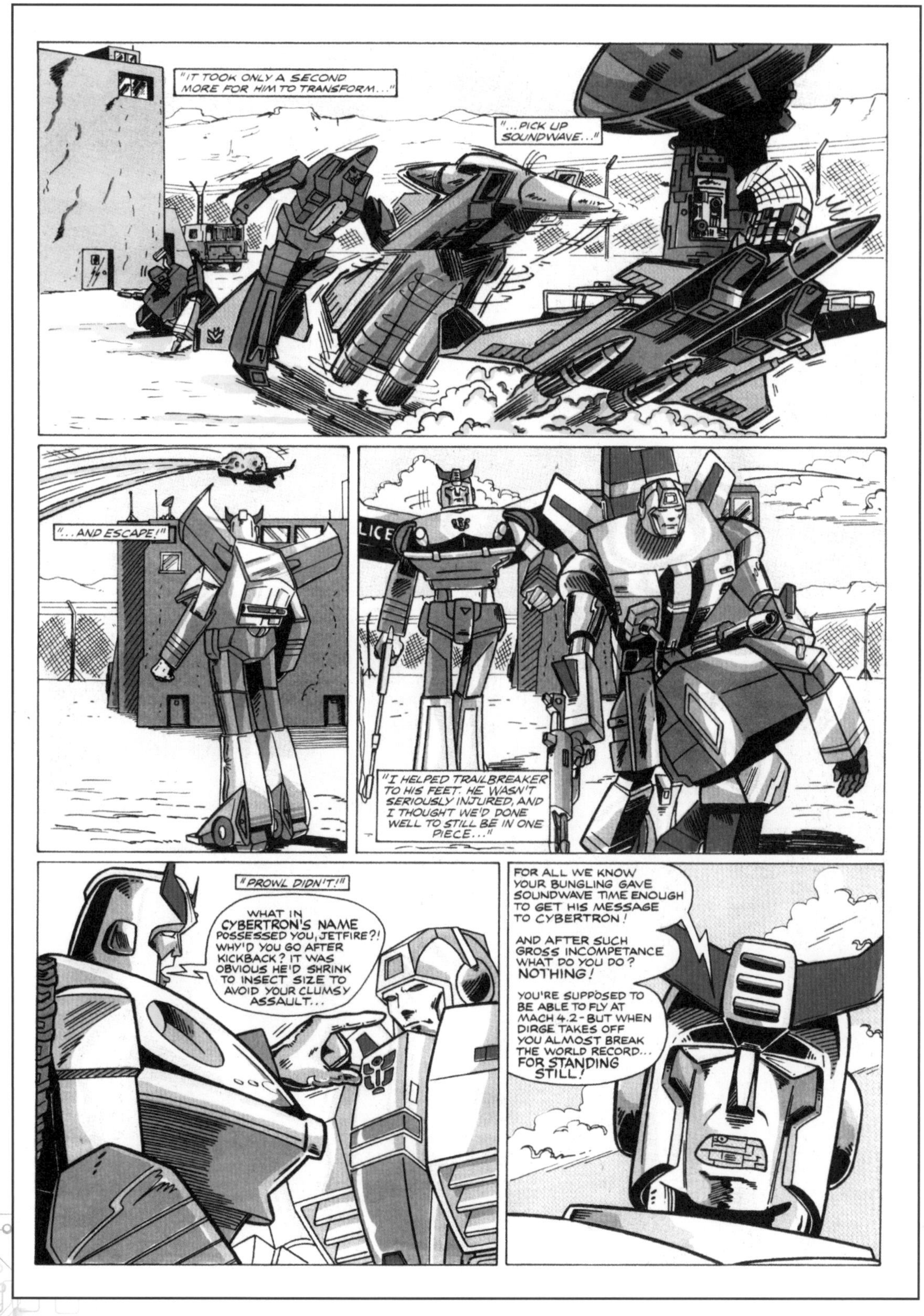
"IT TOOK ONLY A SECOND MORE FOR HIM TO TRANSFORM..."
"...PICK UP SOUNDWAVE..."
"...AND ESCAPE!"
"I HELPED TRAILBREAKER TO HIS FEET. HE WASN'T SERIOUSLY INJURED, AND I THOUGHT WE'D DONE WELL TO STILL BE IN ONE PIECE..."
"PROWL DIDN'T!"
WHAT IN CYBERTRON'S NAME POSSESSED YOU, JETFIRE?! WHY'D YOU GO AFTER KICKBACK? IT WAS OBVIOUS HE'D SHRINK TO INSECT SIZE TO AVOID YOUR CLUMSY ASSAULT...
FOR ALL WE KNOW YOUR BUNGLING GAVE SOUNDWAVE TIME ENOUGH TO GET HIS MESSAGE TO CYBERTRON!
AND AFTER SUCH GROSS INCOMPETANCE WHAT DO YOU DO? NOTHING!
YOU'RE SUPPOSED TO BE ABLE TO FLY AT MACH 4.2 - BUT WHEN DIRGE TAKES OFF YOU ALMOST BREAK THE WORLD RECORD... FOR STANDING STILL!

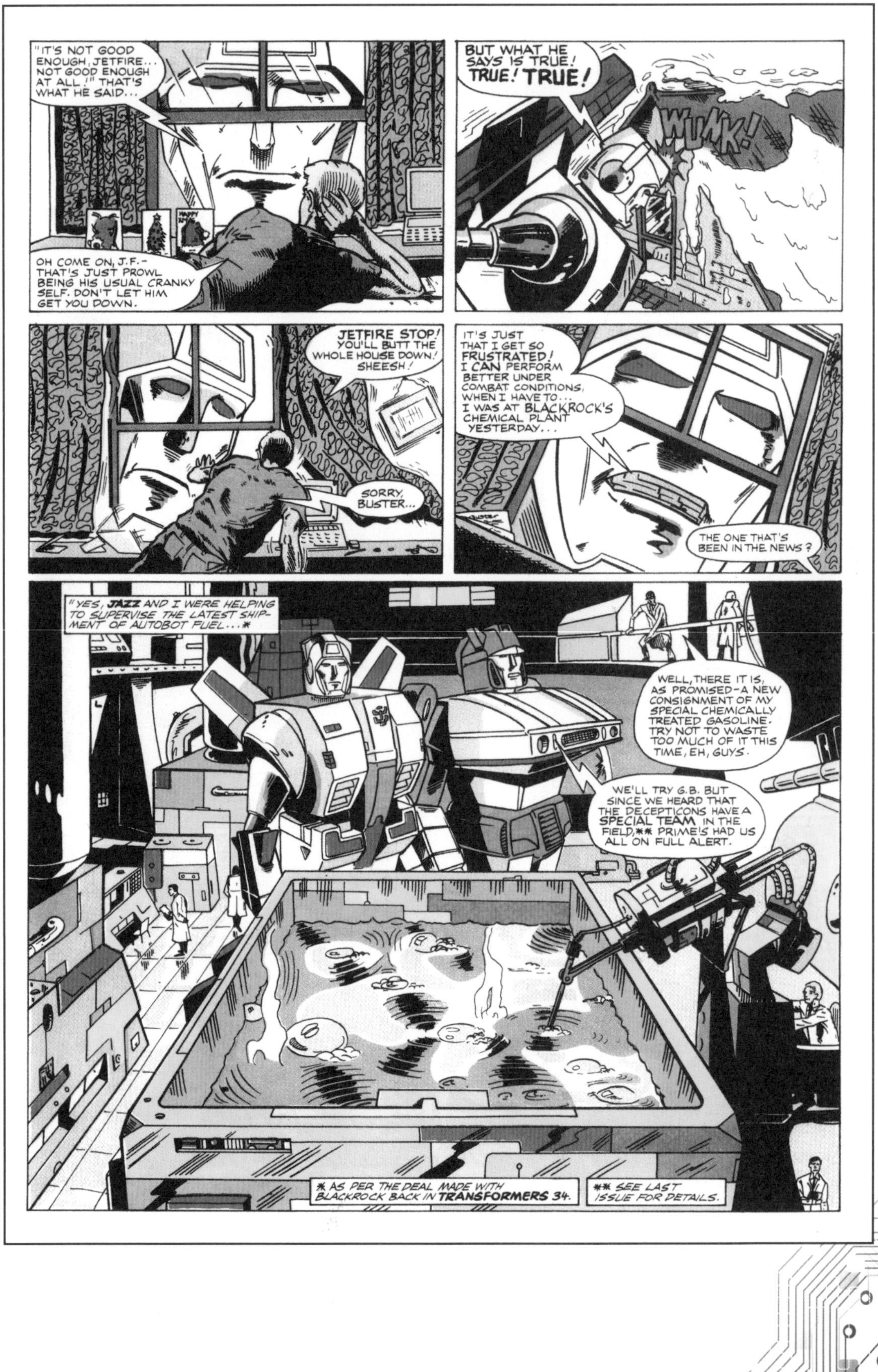

"IT'S NOT GOOD ENOUGH, JETFIRE... NOT GOOD ENOUGH AT ALL!" THAT'S WHAT HE SAID...
OH COME ON, J.F.- THAT'S JUST PROWL BEING HIS USUAL CRANKY SELF. DON'T LET HIM GET YOU DOWN.
BUT WHAT HE SAYS IS TRUE! TRUE! TRUE!
WUNK!
JETFIRE STOP! YOU'LL BUTT THE WHOLE HOUSE DOWN! SHEESH!
SORRY, BUSTER...
IT'S JUST THAT I GET SO FRUSTRATED! I CAN PERFORM BETTER UNDER COMBAT CONDITIONS, WHEN I HAVE TO... I WAS AT BLACKROCK'S CHEMICAL PLANT YESTERDAY...
THE ONE THAT'S BEEN IN THE NEWS?
"YES, JAZZ AND I WERE HELPING TO SUPERVISE THE LATEST SHIPMENT OF AUTOBOT FUEL...*
WELL, THERE IT IS, AS PROMISED-A NEW CONSIGNMENT OF MY SPECIAL CHEMICALLY TREATED GASOLINE. TRY NOT TO WASTE TOO MUCH OF IT THIS TIME, EH, GUYS.
WE'LL TRY G.B. BUT SINCE WE HEARD THAT THE DECEPTICONS HAVE A SPECIAL TEAM IN THE FIELD,** PRIME'S HAD US ALL ON FULL ALERT.
* AS PER THE DEAL MADE WITH BLACKROCK BACK IN TRANSFORMERS 34.
** SEE LAST ISSUE FOR DETAILS.

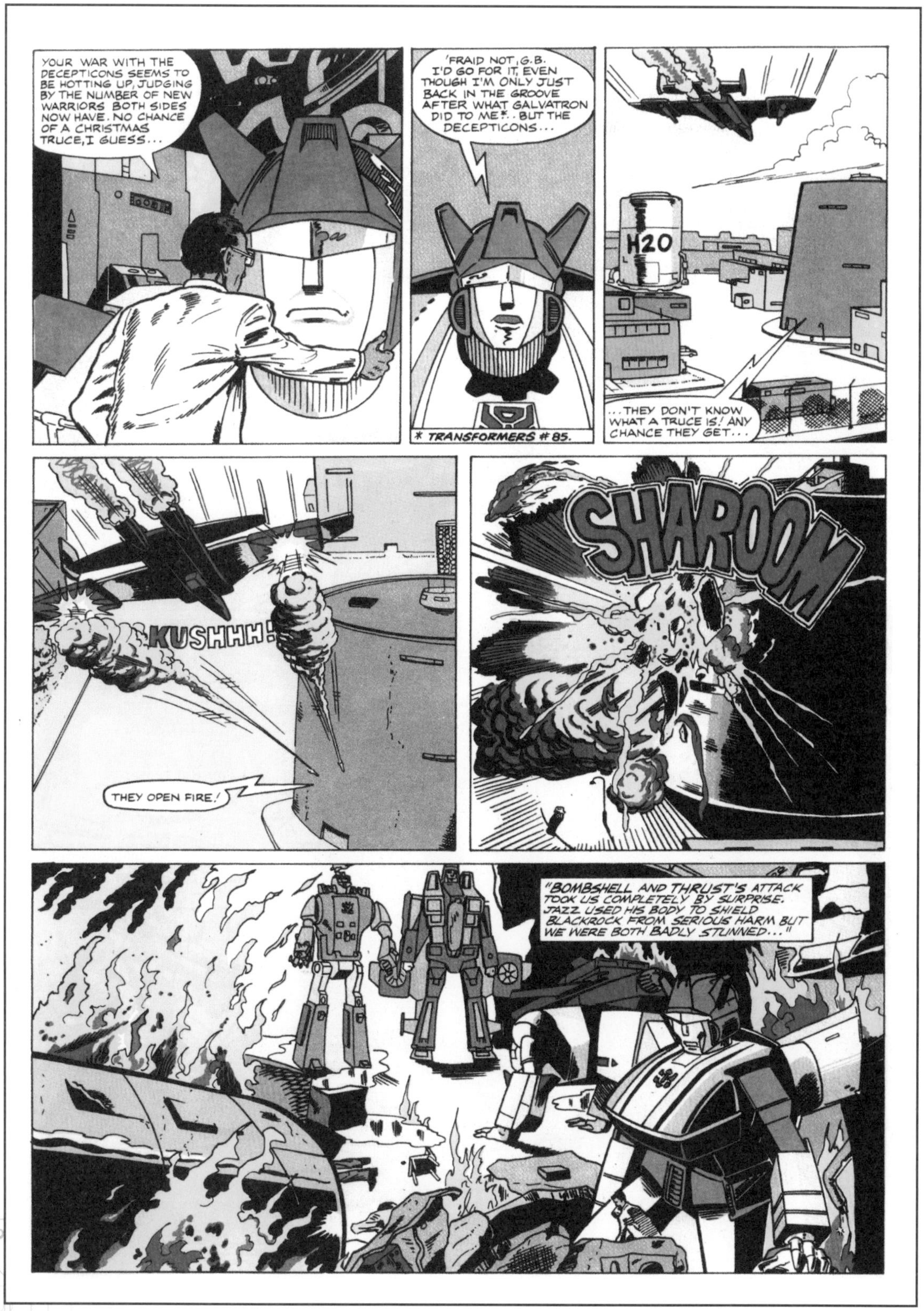
YOUR WAR WITH THE DECEPTICONS SEEMS TO BE HOTTING UP, JUDGING BY THE NUMBER OF NEW WARRIORS BOTH SIDES NOW HAVE. NO CHANCE OF A CHRISTMAS TRUCE, I GUESS...
'FRAID NOT, G.B. I'D GO FOR IT, EVEN THOUGH I'M ONLY JUST BACK IN THE GROOVE AFTER WHAT GALVATRON DID TO ME*.. BUT THE DECEPTICONS...
* TRANSFORMERS # 85.
H2O
...THEY DON'T KNOW WHAT A TRUCE IS! ANY CHANCE THEY GET...
KUSHHH!
THEY OPEN FIRE!
SHAROOM
"BOMBSHELL AND THRUST'S ATTACK TOOK US COMPLETELY BY SURPRISE. JAZZ USED HIS BODY TO SHIELD BLACKROCK FROM SERIOUS HARM BUT WE WERE BOTH BADLY STUNNED..."

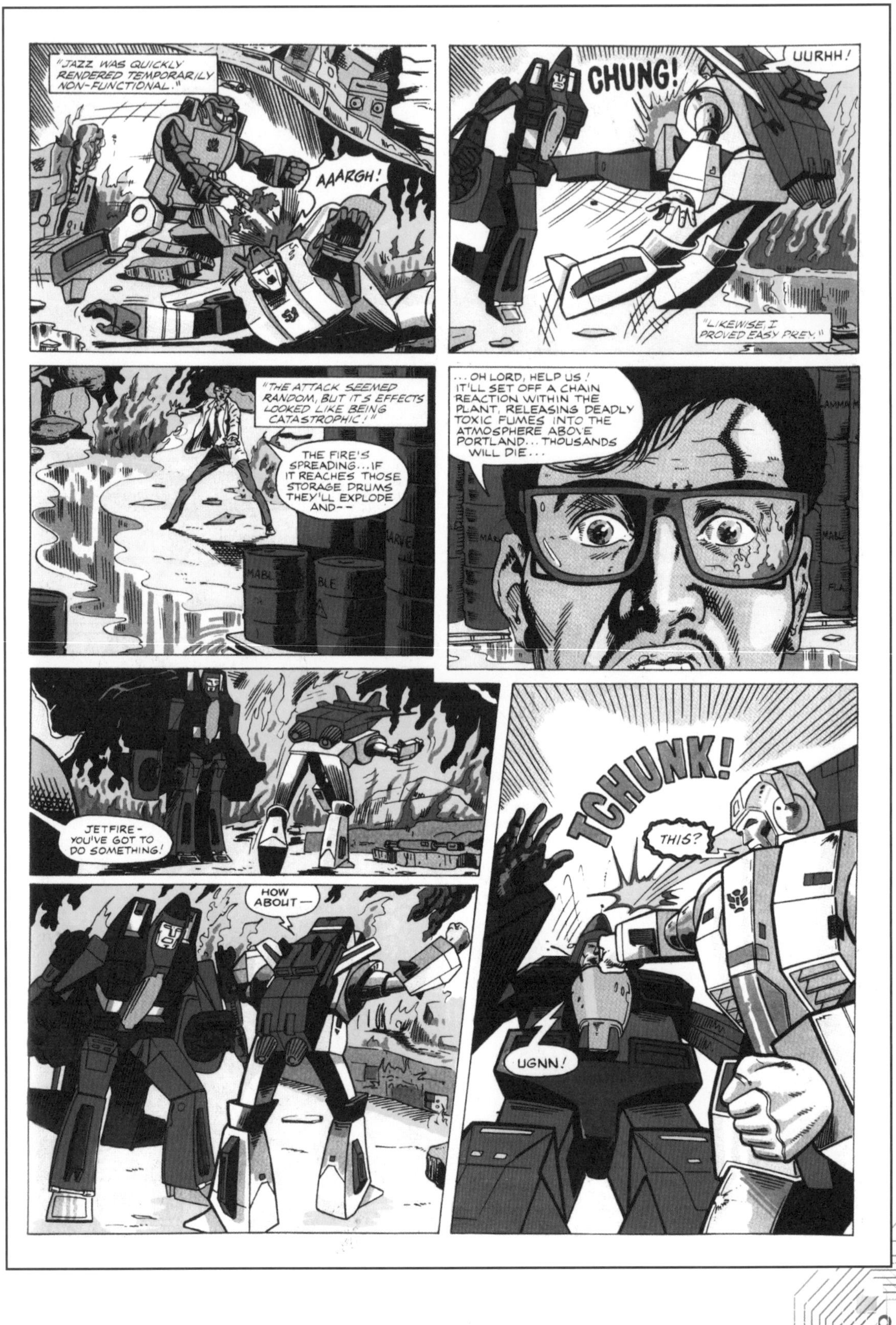

"JAZZ WAS QUICKLY RENDERED TEMPORARILY NON-FUNCTIONAL."
AAARGH!
CHUNG!
UURHH!
"LIKEWISE, I PROVED EASY PREY."
"THE ATTACK SEEMED RANDOM, BUT IT'S EFFECTS LOOKED LIKE BEING CATASTROPHIC!"
THE FIRE'S SPREADING... IF IT REACHES THOSE STORAGE DRUMS THEY'LL EXPLODE AND--
...OH LORD, HELP US! IT'LL SET OFF A CHAIN REACTION WITHIN THE PLANT, RELEASING DEADLY TOXIC FUMES INTO THE ATMOSPHERE ABOVE PORTLAND... THOUSANDS WILL DIE...
JETFIRE-YOU'VE GOT TO DO SOMETHING!
HOW ABOUT—
TCHUNK!
THIS?
UGNN!

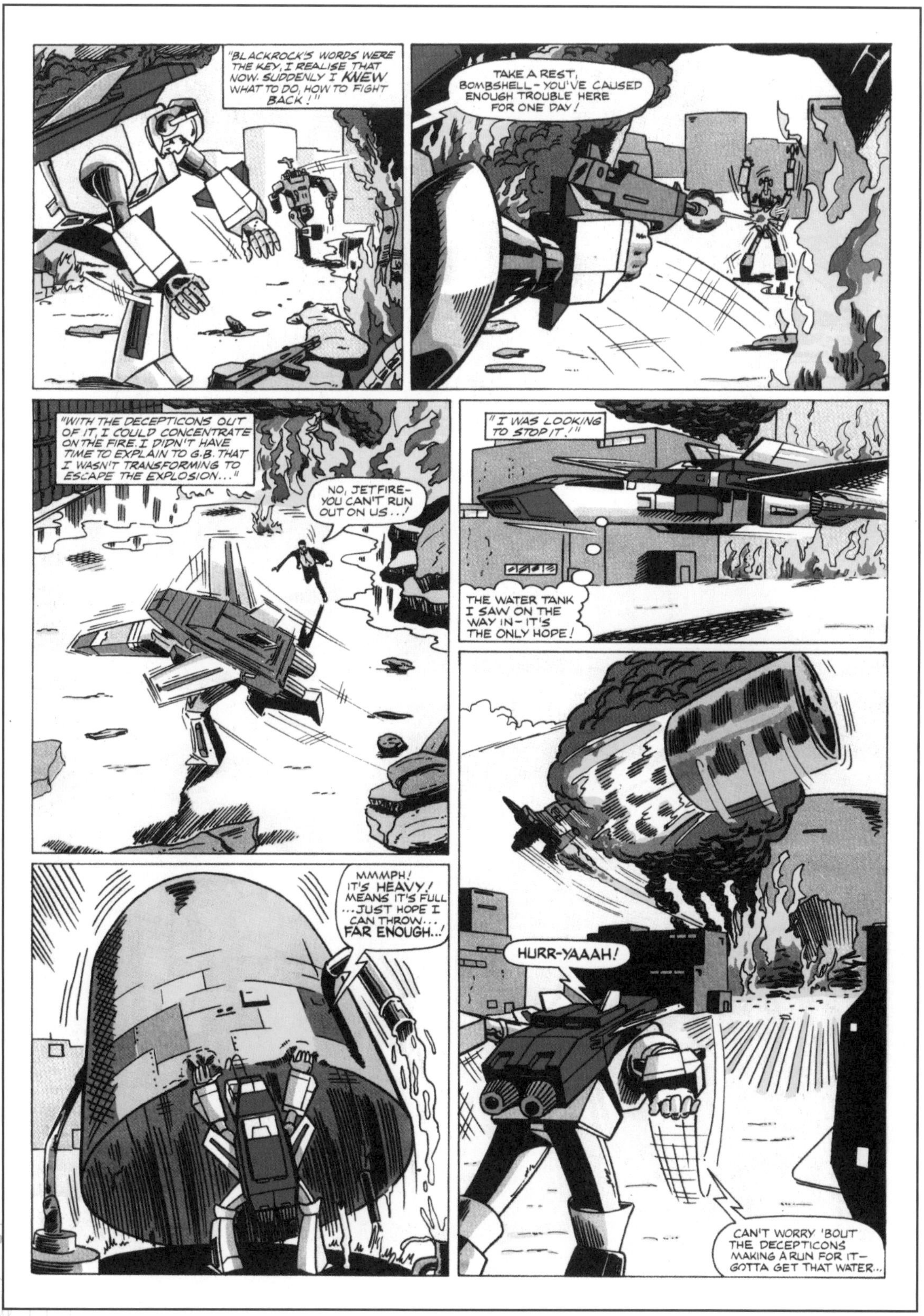

"BLACKROCK'S WORDS WERE THE KEY, I REALISE THAT NOW. SUDDENLY I KNEW WHAT TO DO, HOW TO FIGHT BACK!"
TAKE A REST, BOMBSHELL - YOU'VE CAUSED ENOUGH TROUBLE HERE FOR ONE DAY!
"WITH THE DECEPTICONS OUT OF IT, I COULD CONCENTRATE ON THE FIRE. I DIDN'T HAVE TIME TO EXPLAIN TO G.B. THAT I WASN'T TRANSFORMING TO ESCAPE THE EXPLOSION..."
NO, JETFIRE- YOU CAN'T RUN OUT ON US...!
"I WAS LOOKING TO STOP IT!"
THE WATER TANK I SAW ON THE WAY IN - IT'S THE ONLY HOPE!
MMMPH! IT'S HEAVY! MEANS IT'S FULL ...JUST HOPE I CAN THROW... FAR ENOUGH...!
HURR-YAAAH!
CAN'T WORRY 'BOUT THE DECEPTICONS MAKING A RUN FOR IT- GOTTA GET THAT WATER...

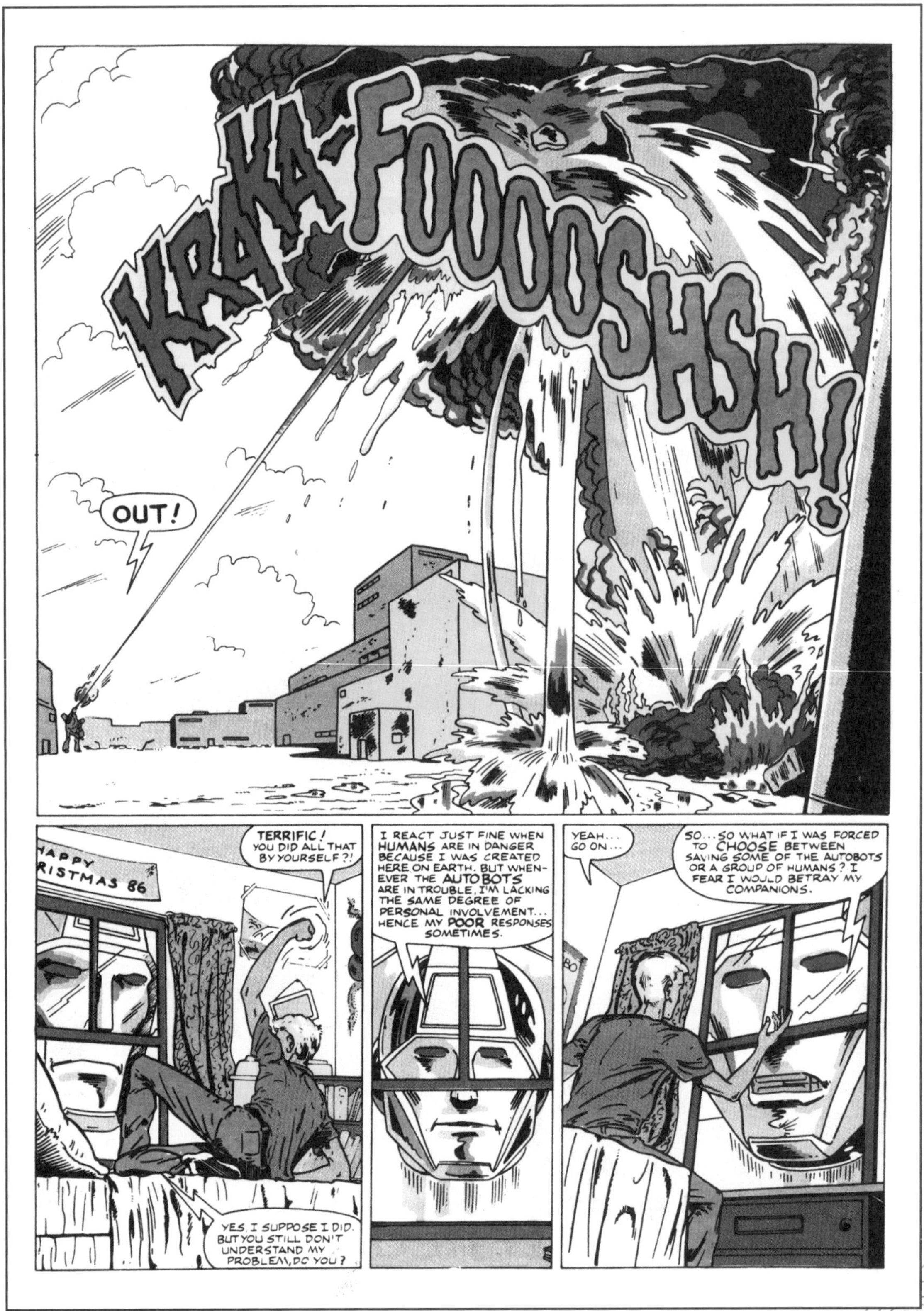
KRAKA-FOOOOSHSH!
OUT!
HAPPY
RISTMAS 86
TERRIFIC! YOU DID ALL THAT BY YOURSELF?!
YES. I SUPPOSE I DID. BUT YOU STILL DON'T UNDERSTAND MY PROBLEM, DO YOU?
I REACT JUST FINE WHEN HUMANS ARE IN DANGER BECAUSE I WAS CREATED HERE ON EARTH. BUT WHENEVER THE AUTOBOTS ARE IN TROUBLE, I'M LACKING THE SAME DEGREE OF PERSONAL INVOLVEMENT... HENCE MY POOR RESPONSES SOMETIMES.
YEAH... GO ON...
SO... SO WHAT IF I WAS FORCED TO CHOOSE BETWEEN SAVING SOME OF THE AUTOBOTS OR A GROUP OF HUMANS? I FEAR I WOULD BETRAY MY COMPANIONS.

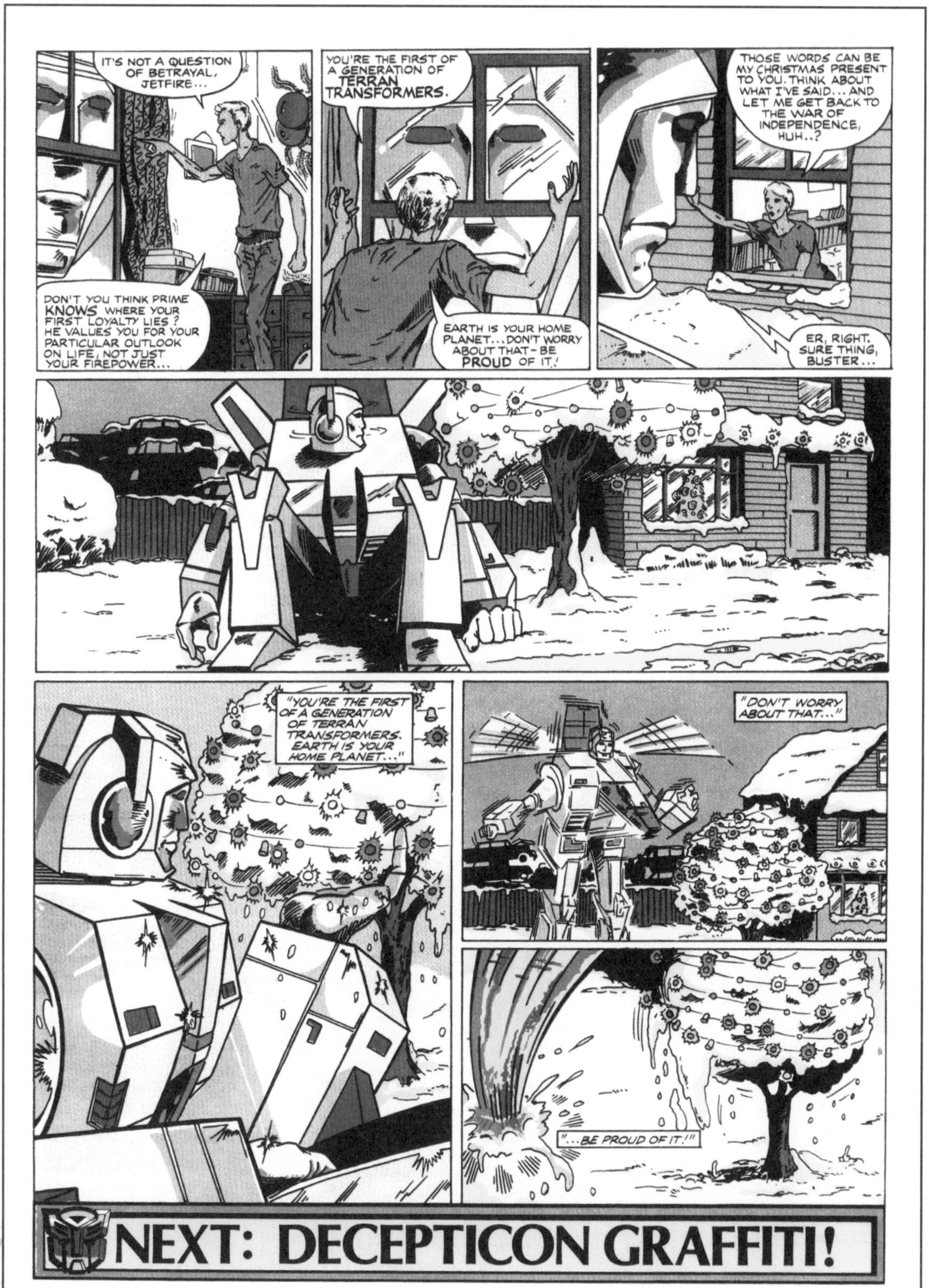
IT'S NOT A QUESTION OF BETRAYAL, JETFIRE...
DON'T YOU THINK PRIME KNOWS WHERE YOUR FIRST LOYALTY LIES? HE VALUES YOU FOR YOUR PARTICULAR OUTLOOK ON LIFE, NOT JUST YOUR FIREPOWER...
YOU'RE THE FIRST OF A GENERATION OF TERRAN TRANSFORMERS.
EARTH IS YOUR HOME PLANET... DON'T WORRY ABOUT THAT- BE PROUD OF IT.!
THOSE WORDS CAN BE MY CHRISTMAS PRESENT TO YOU. THINK ABOUT WHAT I'VE SAID... AND LET ME GET BACK TO THE WAR OF INDEPENDENCE, HUH..?
ER, RIGHT. SURE THING, BUSTER...
"YOU'RE THE FIRST OF A GENERATION OF TERRAN TRANSFORMERS. EARTH IS YOUR HOME PLANET..."
"DON'T WORRY ABOUT THAT..."
"...BE PROUD OF IT!"
NEXT: DECEPTICON GRAFFITI!

Below:
Issue #101 (February 21st, 1987) • Cover by Lee Sullivan • "Fallen Angel!" Part 1 • "A to Z" features Blaster and Blast-Off • Skids is sent to Limbo • Galvatron returns

Right:
Issue #102 (February 28th, 1987) • Cover by Geoff Senior • "Fallen Angel!" Part 2 • "Action Force" back-up ends

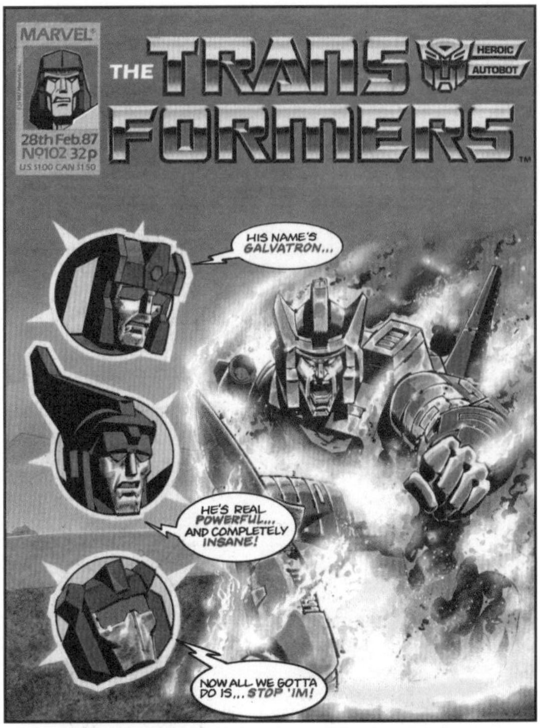
MARVEL
THE TRANSFORMERS
HEROIC AUTOBOT
28th Feb.87
Nº102 32p
HIS NAME'S GALVATRON...
HE'S REAL POWERFUL... AND COMPLETELY INSANE!
NOW ALL WE GOTTA DO IS... STOP 'IM!

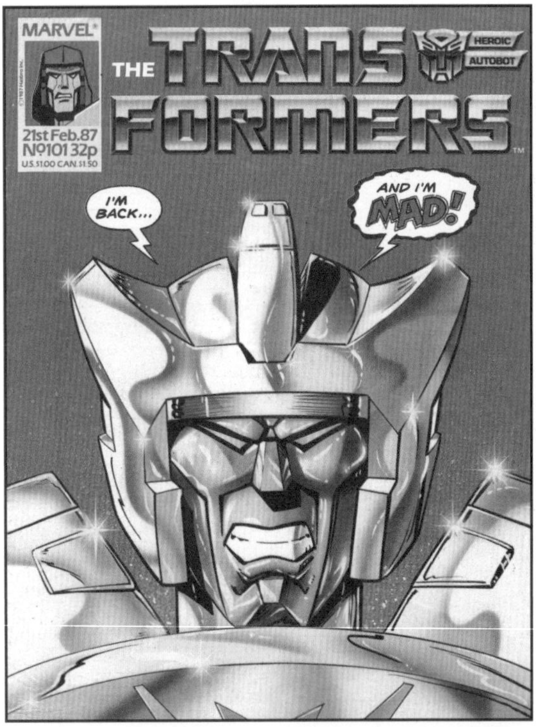
MARVEL
THE TRANSFORMERS
HEROIC AUTOBOT
21st Feb.87
Nº101 32p
I'M BACK...
AND I'M MAD!

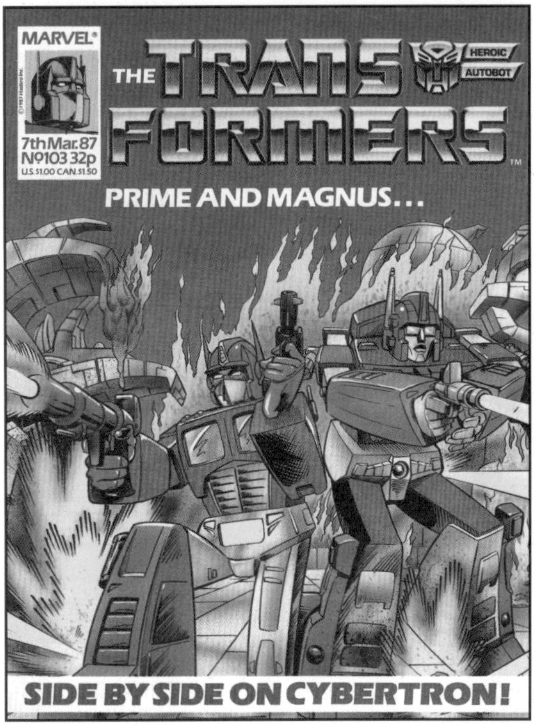
MARVEL
THE TRANSFORMERS
HEROIC AUTOBOT
7th Mar.87
Nº103 32p
PRIME AND MAGNUS...
SIDE BY SIDE ON CYBERTRON!

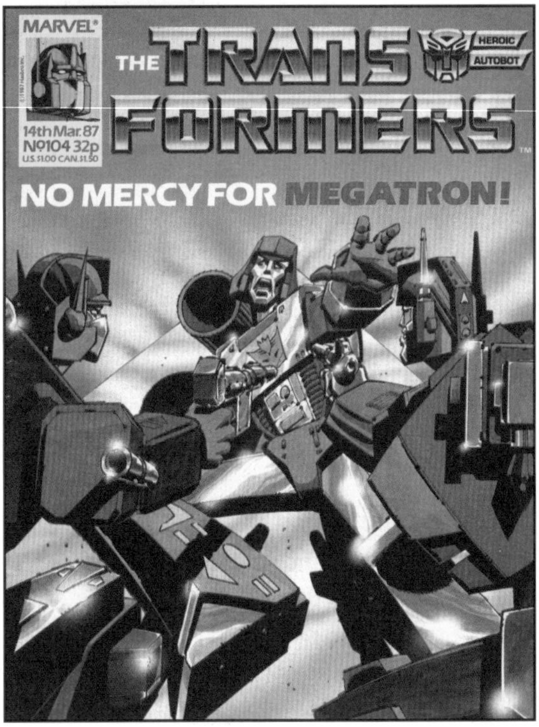
MARVEL
THE TRANSFORMERS
HEROIC AUTOBOT
14th Mar.87
Nº104 32p
NO MERCY FOR MEGATRON!

Left:
Issue #103 (March 7th, 1987) • Cover by Martin Griffiths and Robin Bouttell • "Resurrection!" Part 1 • Megatron and Straxus mind-swap • First appearance of Tailgate • "Inhumanoids" back-up begins

Above:
Issue #104 (March 14th, 1987) • Cover by Geoff Senior • "Resurrection!" Part 2

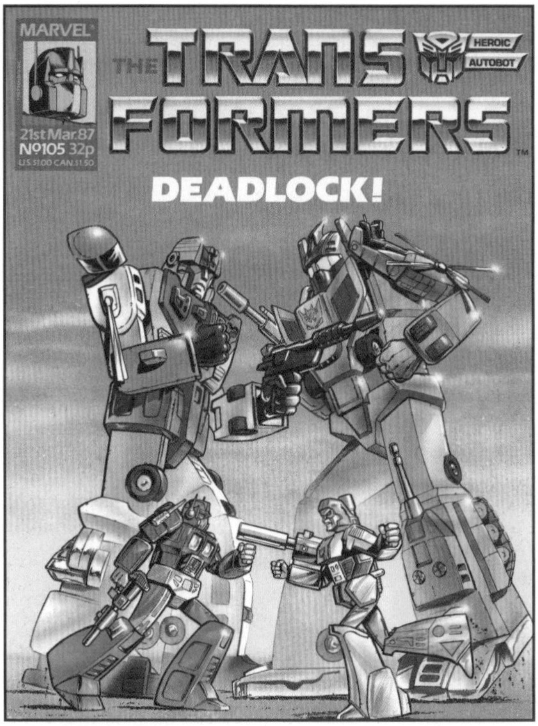
MARVEL
THE TRANSFORMERS
HEROIC AUTOBOT
21st Mar. 87
Nº105 32p
U.S.$1.00 CAN.$1.50
DEADLOCK!

Left:
Issue #105 (March 21st, 1987) • Cover by Lee Sullivan • Reprints pages 1–11 of "Afterdeath!" (*TFUS* #24) • First "real life" appearance of the Protectobots and Combaticons, and Ethan Zachary

Below:
Issue #106 (March 28th, 1986) • Cover by Herb Trimpe (re-use of *TFUS* #24, recolored by Robin Bouttell) • Reprints pages 12–22 of "Afterdeath!" (*TFUS* #24) • Death of Optimus Prime

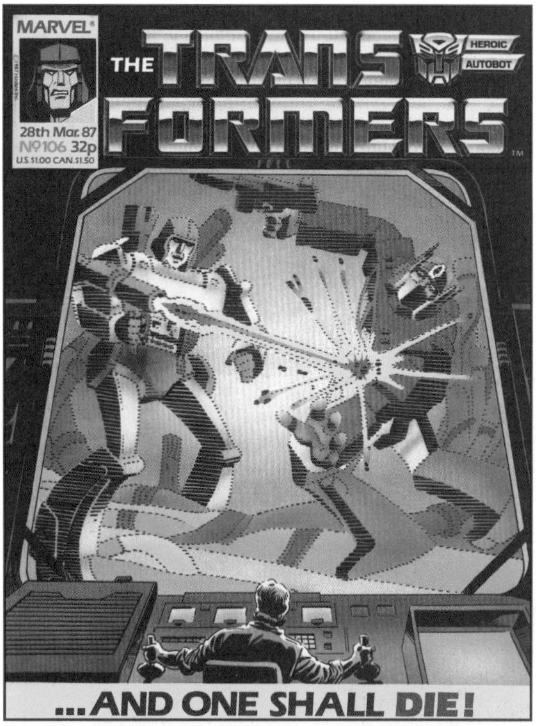
MARVEL
THE TRANSFORMERS
HEROIC AUTOBOT
28th Mar. 87
Nº106 32p
U.S.$1.00 CAN.$1.50
...AND ONE SHALL DIE!

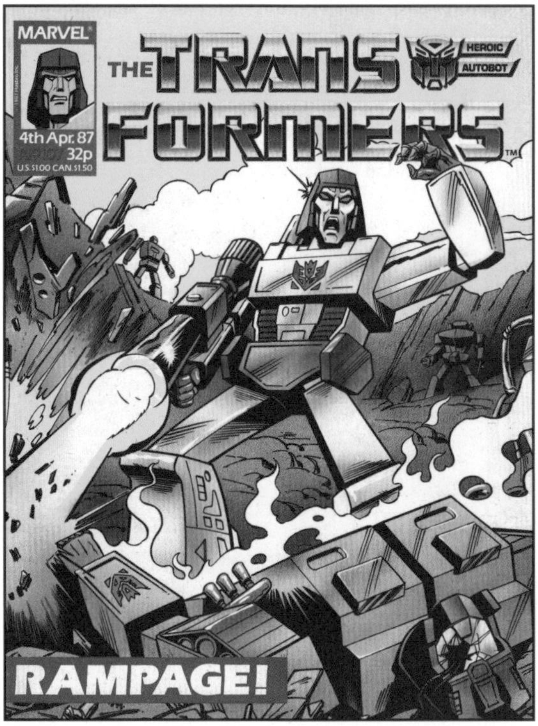
MARVEL
THE TRANSFORMERS
HEROIC AUTOBOT
4th Apr. 87
32p
U.S.$1.00 CAN.$1.50
RAMPAGE!

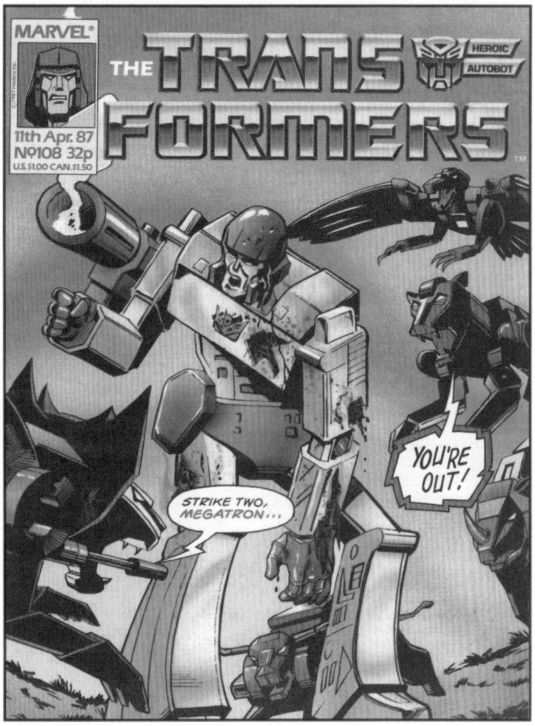
MARVEL
THE TRANSFORMERS
HEROIC AUTOBOT
11th Apr. 87
Nº108 32p
U.S.$1.00 CAN.$1.50
YOU'RE OUT!
STRIKE TWO, MEGATRON...

Above:
Issue #107 (April 4th, 1987) • Cover by David Hine • Reprints pages 1–11 of "Gone But Not Forgotten!" (*TFUS* #25) • Edited out of the US reprint was reference to the hydrothermocline—a tie-in to the *G.I. JOE/Transformers* crossover that, at the time, was not going to be reprinted in the UK

Right:
Issue #108 (April 11th, 1987) • Cover by Herb Trimpe (re-use of *TFUS* #24, recolored by Robin Bouttell) • Reprints pages 12–22 of "Gone But Not Forgotten!" (*TFUS* #25) • "Death" of Megatron • Dialog edited to account for the prior appearance of the Predacons in "Prey!" • "A to Z" features Blitzwing and Bluestreak

Below:
Issue #109 (April 18th, 1987) • Cover by Herb Trimpe • Reprints pages 1–11 of "Funeral for a Friend!" (*TFUS* #26) • Skids is removed from a crowd shot on Page 2: in UK continuity he's still in Limbo • First appearance of The Mechanic

Right:
Issue #110 (April 25th, 1987) • Cover by Jeff Anderson • Reprints pages 12–22 of "Funeral for a Friend!" (*TFUS* #26)

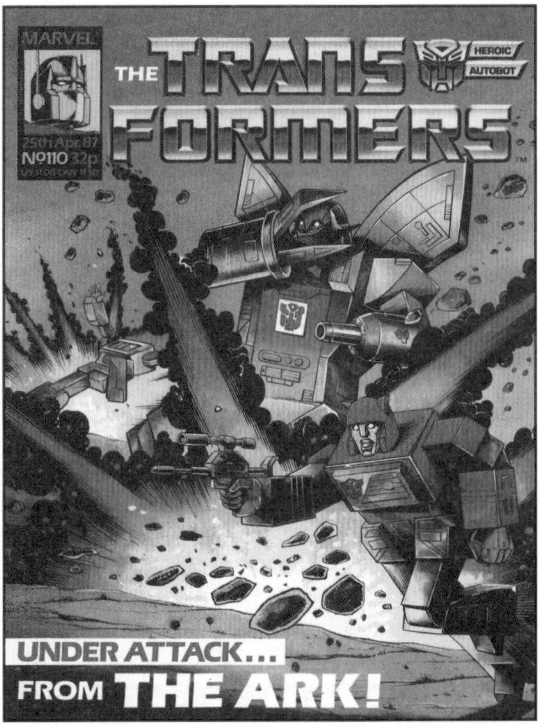
MARVEL
THE TRANSFORMERS
HEROIC AUTOBOT
25th Apr. 87
No110 32p
UNDER ATTACK...
FROM THE ARK!

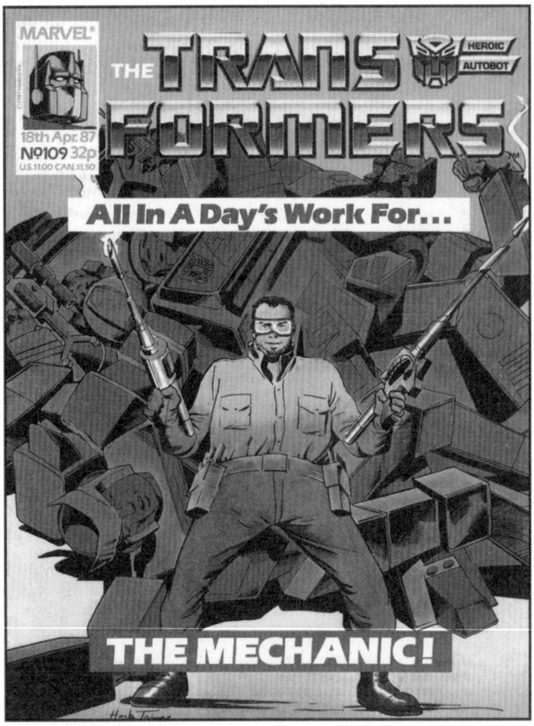
MARVEL
THE TRANSFORMERS
HEROIC AUTOBOT
18th Apr. 87
No109 32p
U.S.$1.00 CAN.$1.50
All In A Day's Work For...
THE MECHANIC!

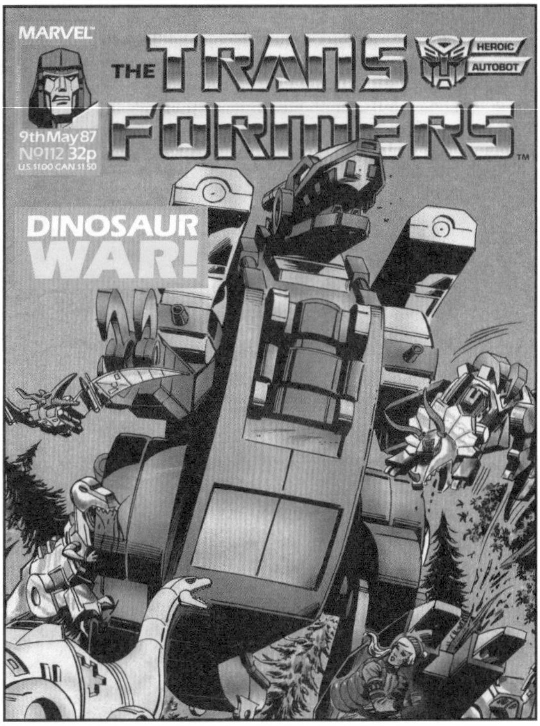
MARVEL
THE TRANSFORMERS
HEROIC AUTOBOT
9th May 87
No112 32p
U.S.$1.00 CAN.$1.50
DINOSAUR WAR!

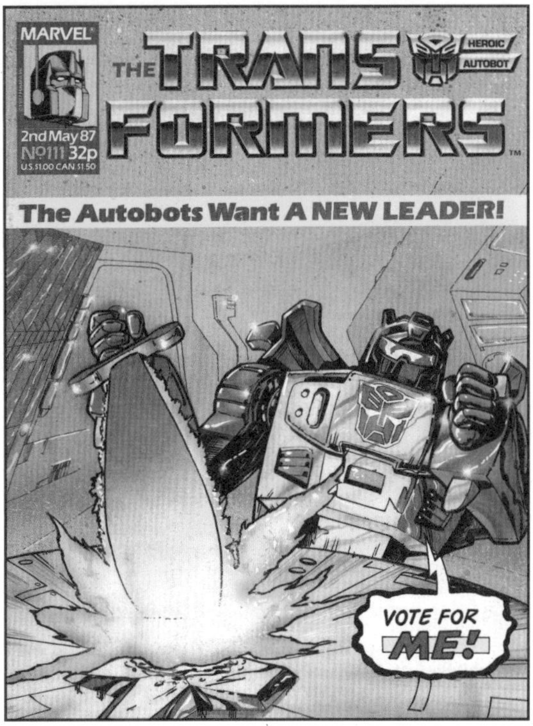
MARVEL
THE TRANSFORMERS
HEROIC AUTOBOT
2nd May 87
No111 32p
U.S.$1.00 CAN.$1.50
The Autobots Want A NEW LEADER!
VOTE FOR ME!

Left:
Issue #111 (May 2nd, 1987) • Cover by Lee Sullivan • Reprints pages 1–11 of "King of the Hill!" (*TFUS* #27) • First appearance of Trypticon

Above:
Issue #112 (May 9th, 1987) • Cover by Herb Trimpe (re-use of *TFUS* #27 recolored by Tim Perkins) • Reprints pages 12–22 of "King of the Hill!" (*TFUS* #27) • Grimlock made Autobot leader • First appearance of Wipe-Out

FALLEN ANGEL

Originally printed in issues #101–102
Published February 21–28, 1987
Reprinted in the 1990 *Transformers Annual* and in the
2003 Titan Books trade paperback *Fallen Angel*

RESURRECTION

Originally printed in issues #103–104
Published March 7–14, 1987
Reprinted in issues #229–232 (July/August 1989)
and in IDW's "Best of UK: Prey" (2009)

"Die, Rodimus Prime—**DIE!**"

The return of Galvatron in "Fallen Angel" seems perfectly timed: the centenary issue is out of the way, and we're charging into the next 100 issues with the reappearance of a character who was already a readers' favorite. It's as if *TFUK* is saying, "Yeah, the first hundred issues were good, but wait until you see what we've got lined up now!"

Galvatron's return coincides with that of the Dinobots, who had last been seen in issue #77. Furman had deliberately excluded Grimlock and Co. from "Target: 2006" for fear that they would be overexposed, but he couldn't keep away from his favorite characters for long. And the fact that the Dinobots had walked out on the Autobots allowed Furman to engineer a short, brutal Dinobot/Galvatron confrontation rather than tell another 10-part tale. In other words, it felt as if the official sequel to "Target: 2006" was still to come.

Furman had long had it in mind that the Dinobots would fight Galvatron: "I just thought that if we were going to bring back Galvatron and not have him fight Optimus Prime or Ultra Magnus, then Grimlock was next in the pecking order—and I wanted to get the Dinobots back into the storyline anyway."

"Fallen Angel" is the first in a long line of post-*Movie* stories that would end with issue #254's "White Fire," over a hundred and fifty issues later. We're treated to the first in-comic glimpse of Rodimus Prime and robot-mode Unicron, but

the Galvatron who crash-lands on the Earth of 1987 is not the Galvatron we remember… "We didn't want him to be the same character after the Movie," explains Furman when asked what happened to the cool, calm, almost detached Galvatron of "Target: 2006." "At the end of the Movie he's beaten and hurled into space, and we wanted there to be some kind of repercussions of that. So in 'Fallen Angel' we say he's had a rough ride back… he crash lands and he attacks the Dinobots without even thinking who they are."

Also, following his defeat at the hands of Rodimus Prime at the end of the Movie, Galvatron was no longer unbeatable. "His invulnerability is dented in the Movie," agrees Furman. "And then after that he jumps back [to 1987] and gets the sonic attack [courtesy of Blaster], and he's basically got some kind of mental problem after that. It all goes downhill from there."

Geoff Senior's artwork in Part 1 is astonishing—it's obvious that Galvatron has already become one of his favorite characters to draw. And although his panel composition is more restrained than in "Target: 2006," his trademark heavy inking is, if anything, more pronounced. Jeff Anderson, meanwhile, puts in some of his best work in Part 2, with his portrayal of Galvatron succumbing to Blaster's sonic attack being a highlight.

In amongst Galvatron and the Dinobots and Shockwave's Decepticons we have a third

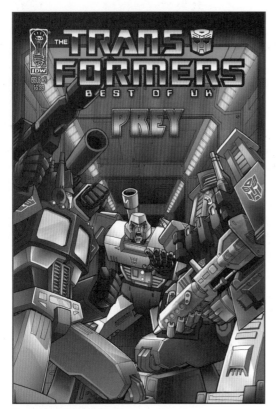

THE
TRANSFORMERS
BEST OF UK
PREY
IDW
The cover to issue #4 of IDW's "Prey!" reprints.

surprising return: Professor Morris and his robot surrogate, Centurion. Morris is apparently killed in Part 1 but reappears in Part 2 as a voice inside Swoop's head. His reappearance sets up the dilemma at the center of the story: should Swoop surrender control of his body to Morris so they can both get revenge on Galvatron? Although an apparently sentient Centurion is rebuilt in issue #125, we never hear from Morris again—something that Furman regrets.

"We never properly finished the Morris story and that's a real disappointment to me— you know, is he still shut in that room? I'd intended to continue that particular story but it just never happened."

The two-part "Resurrection!" (issues #103–104) completes the story arc begun in issue #96 and sends Optimus Prime and Megatron back to Earth with Magnus in tow. But before that point, the Megatron/Straxus power play reaches a violent and surreal climax, as the Polyhexian tyrant attempts to take over the Decepticon leader's body.

Straxus' protracted take-over bid is one of the most memorable Transformers sequences ever, thanks both to Furman's decision to stretch the pain and confusion across three intense pages, and to artist Will Simpson's frankly startling visuals. The image of Megatron's elongated mouth and the devilish glee with which he crushes Straxus' head are enough to give readers nightmares.

The Straxus/Megatron dynamic would resurface in "Salvage" (issues #160–161) and "Two Megatrons" (issues #243–244), the latter tale used to bridge a colossal gulf in US/UK continuity. "I don't think we realized how their relationship was going to play out at this stage," admits Furman, who considers the introduction of Straxus into the UK continuity as a "bolt-on that worked… it gave us an out later on when we had to explain why there were two Megatrons running about."

"Resurrection!" ends with Prime and Magnus breaking into Polyhex and confronting a disoriented Megatron. Long-time readers would have recognized Megatron's anti-matter powers from "Raiders of the Last Ark!", printed way back in issues #18–21. "I've never understood why it was never used more," says Furman. "It was a really cool ability!"

The final issue of the "Prey" arc has to do so much—get Prime, Megatron, and Magnus to Earth; address the question of whether Straxus succeded in taking over Megatron; put the Predacons back on Cybertron and pre-emptively explain why Megatron wouldn't recognize them in a few issues' time—that the big set pieces have to be scaled back. In an instalment double the size, the wonderfully dramatic moment when the space bridge materializes inside the Decepticons' base would have commanded a splash page or two.

Furman, of course, manages to weave all the story threads together neatly, and by the end of issue #104 has achieved what he set out to do: give Megatron and Optimus a fast-paced, high-stakes, planet-hopping *TFUK* send off.

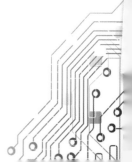

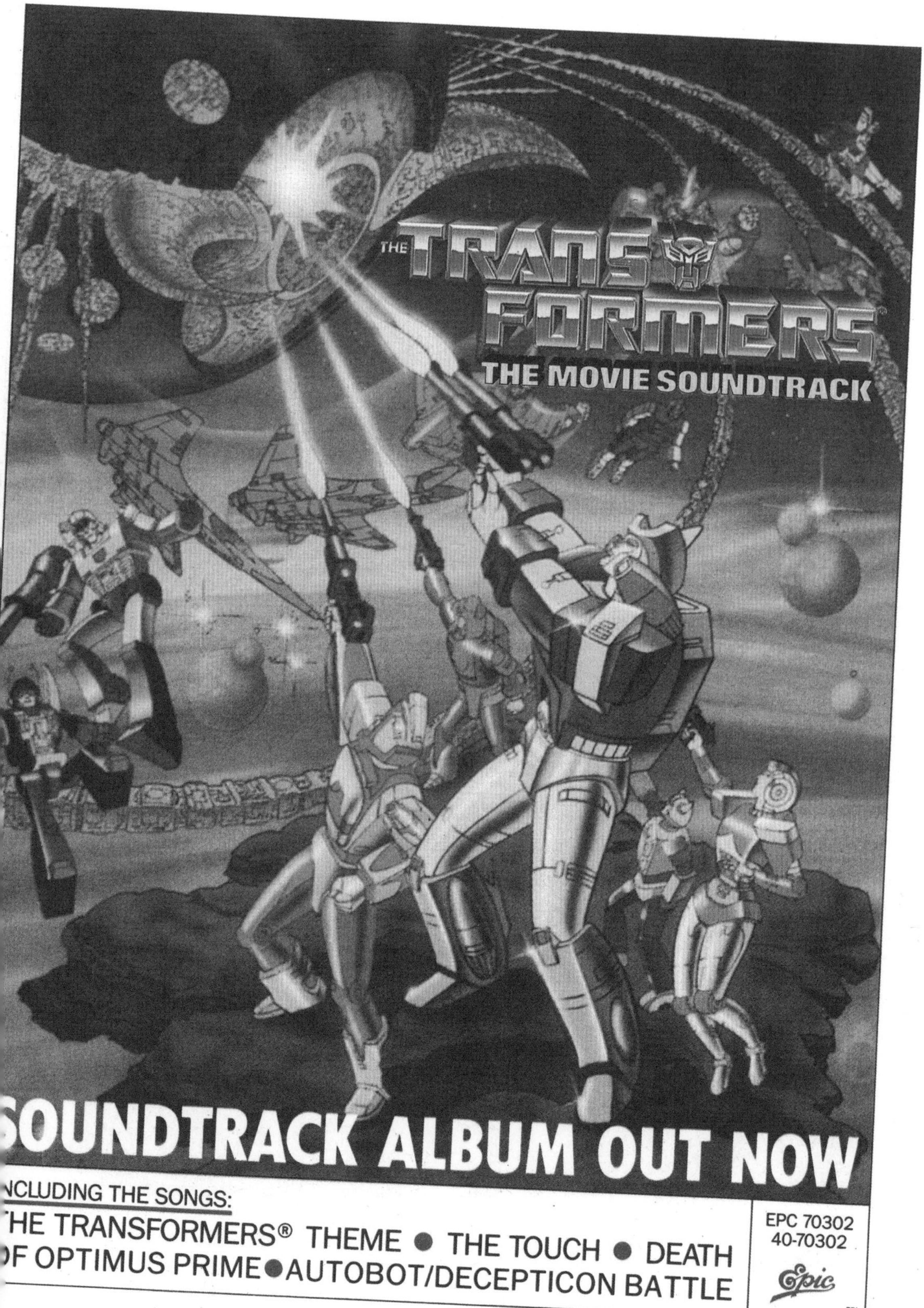
THE TRANSFORMERS
THE MOVIE SOUNDTRACK
SOUNDTRACK ALBUM OUT NOW
NCLUDING THE SONGS:
HE TRANSFORMERS® THEME ● THE TOUCH ● DEATH
F OPTIMUS PRIME ● AUTOBOT/DECEPTICON BATTLE
EPC 70302
40-70302
Epic
DPA

Transformers The Movie soundtrack ad.

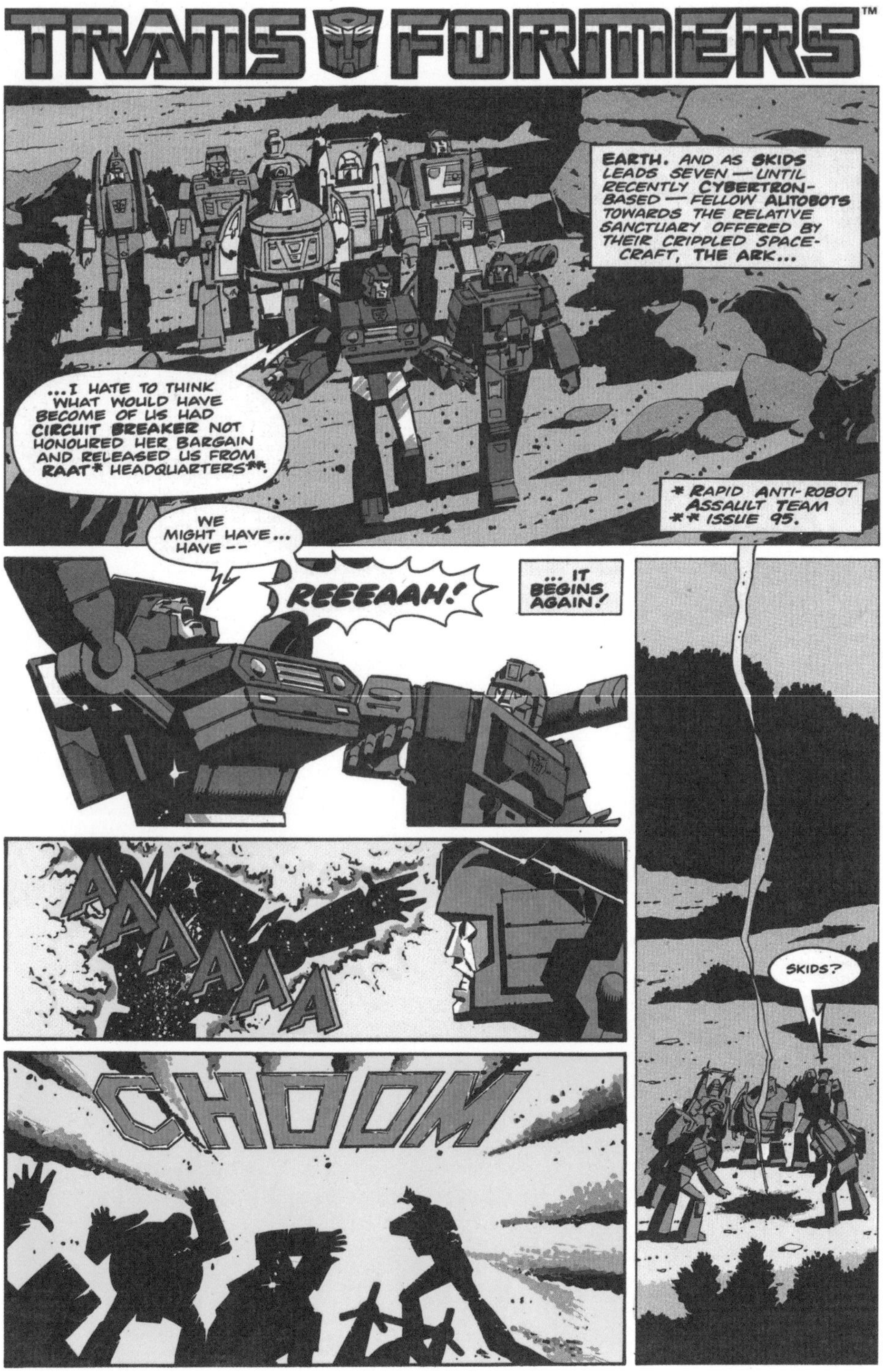
TRANSFORMERS™
EARTH. AND AS SKIDS LEADS SEVEN — UNTIL RECENTLY CYBERTRON-BASED — FELLOW AUTOBOTS TOWARDS THE RELATIVE SANCTUARY OFFERED BY THEIR CRIPPLED SPACE-CRAFT, THE ARK...
...I HATE TO THINK WHAT WOULD HAVE BECOME OF US HAD CIRCUIT BREAKER NOT HONOURED HER BARGAIN AND RELEASED US FROM RAAT* HEADQUARTERS**.
* RAPID ANTI-ROBOT ASSAULT TEAM
** ISSUE 95.
WE MIGHT HAVE... HAVE --
REEEAAAH!
... IT BEGINS AGAIN!
AAAAAAA
CHOOM
SKIDS?

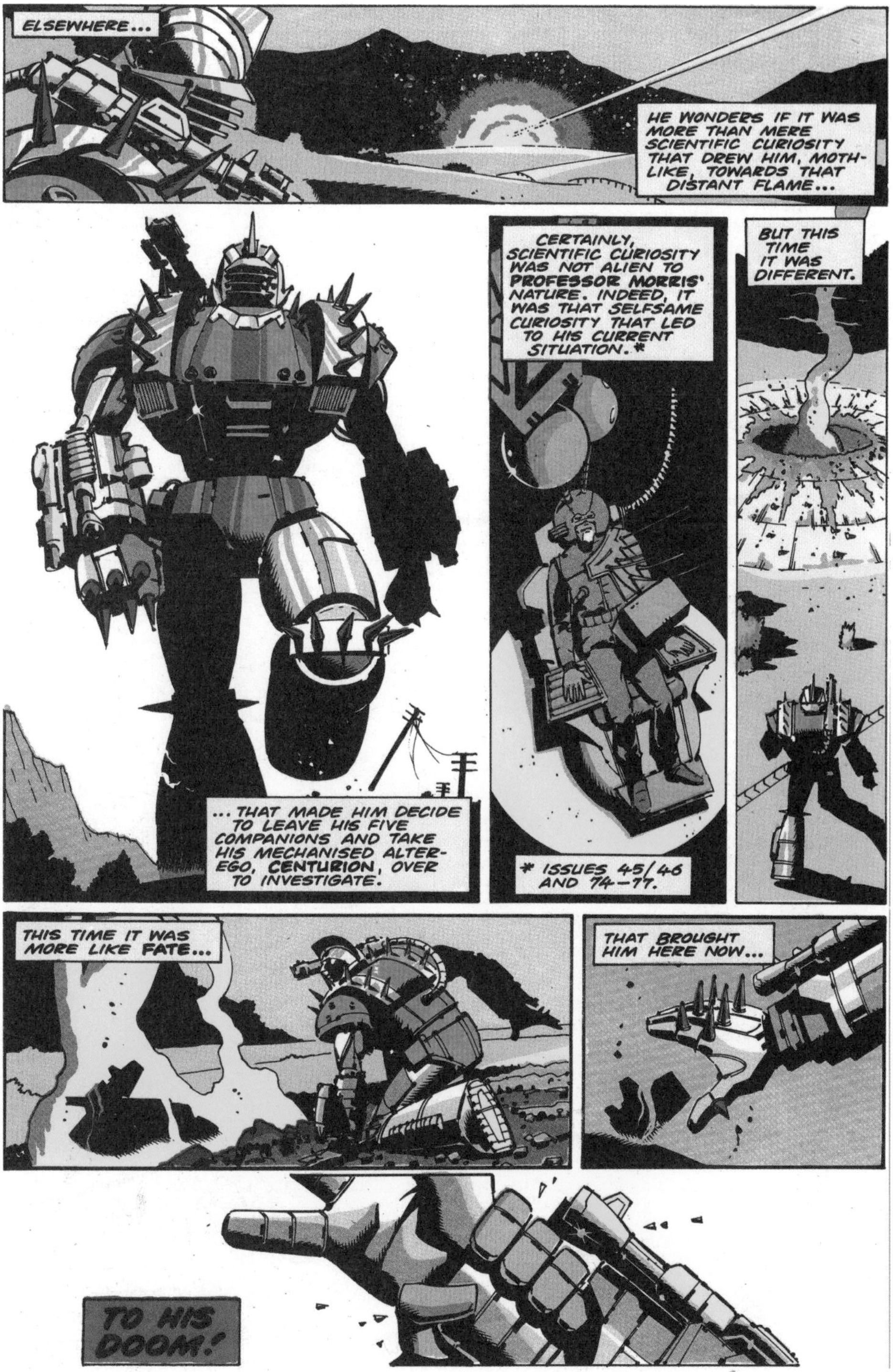
ELSEWHERE...
HE WONDERS IF IT WAS MORE THAN MERE SCIENTIFIC CURIOSITY THAT DREW HIM, MOTH-LIKE, TOWARDS THAT DISTANT FLAME...
...THAT MADE HIM DECIDE TO LEAVE HIS FIVE COMPANIONS AND TAKE HIS MECHANISED ALTER-EGO, CENTURION, OVER TO INVESTIGATE.
CERTAINLY, SCIENTIFIC CURIOSITY WAS NOT ALIEN TO PROFESSOR MORRIS' NATURE. INDEED, IT WAS THAT SELFSAME CURIOSITY THAT LED TO HIS CURRENT SITUATION.*
* ISSUES 45/46 AND 74-77.
BUT THIS TIME IT WAS DIFFERENT.
THIS TIME IT WAS MORE LIKE FATE...
THAT BROUGHT HIM HERE NOW...
TO HIS DOOM!

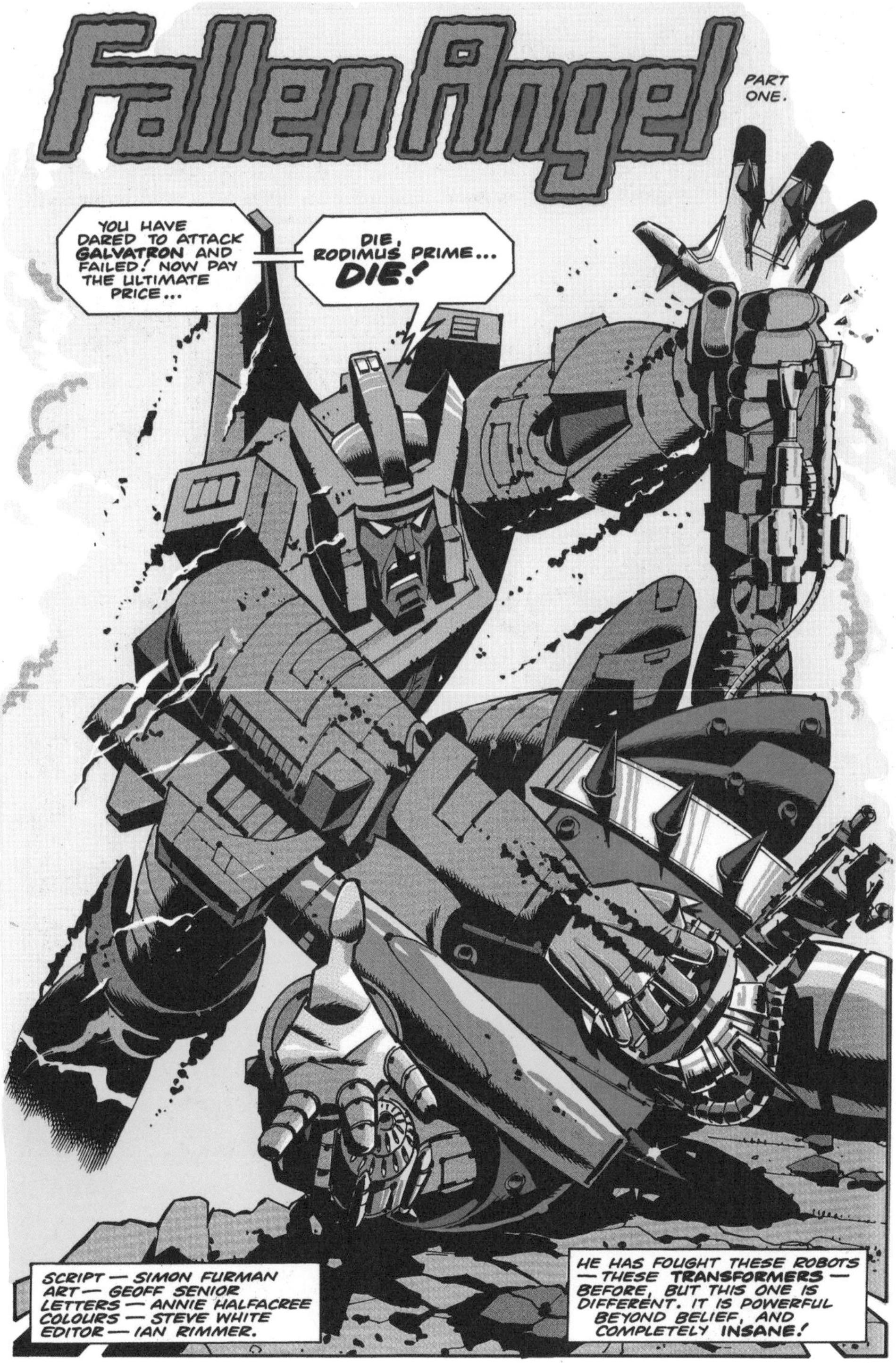
Fallen Angel
PART ONE.
YOU HAVE DARED TO ATTACK GALVATRON AND FAILED! NOW PAY THE ULTIMATE PRICE...
DIE, RODIMUS PRIME... DIE!
SCRIPT — SIMON FURMAN
ART — GEOFF SENIOR
LETTERS — ANNIE HALFACREE
COLOURS — STEVE WHITE
EDITOR — IAN RIMMER.
HE HAS FOUGHT THESE ROBOTS — THESE TRANSFORMERS — BEFORE, BUT THIS ONE IS DIFFERENT. IT IS POWERFUL BEYOND BELIEF, AND COMPLETELY INSANE!

8

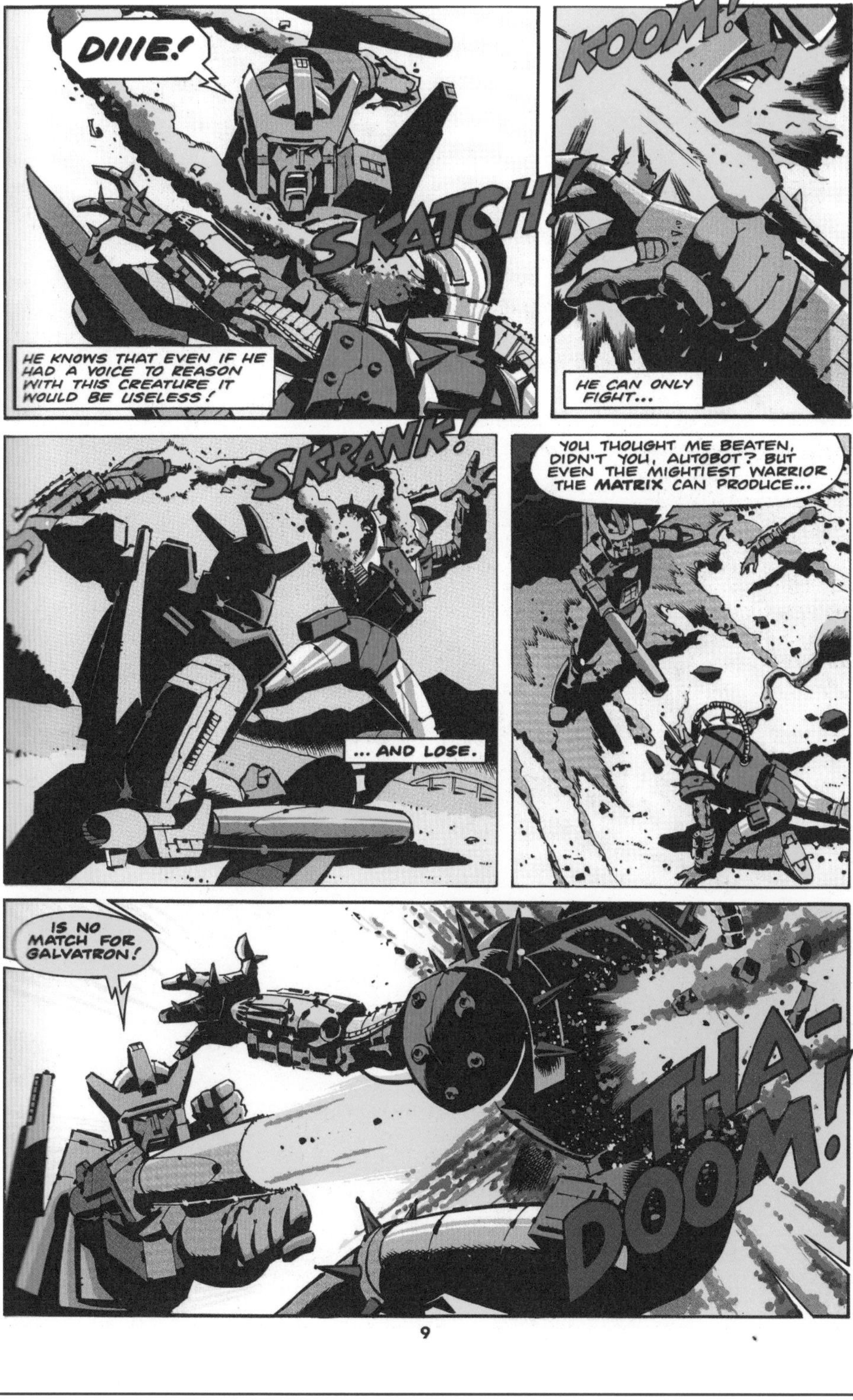
DIIIE!
SKATCH!
HE KNOWS THAT EVEN IF HE HAD A VOICE TO REASON WITH THIS CREATURE IT WOULD BE USELESS!
KOOM!
HE CAN ONLY FIGHT...
SKRANK!
... AND LOSE.
YOU THOUGHT ME BEATEN, DIDN'T YOU, AUTOBOT? BUT EVEN THE MIGHTIEST WARRIOR THE MATRIX CAN PRODUCE...
IS NO MATCH FOR GALVATRON!
THA-DOOM!

9

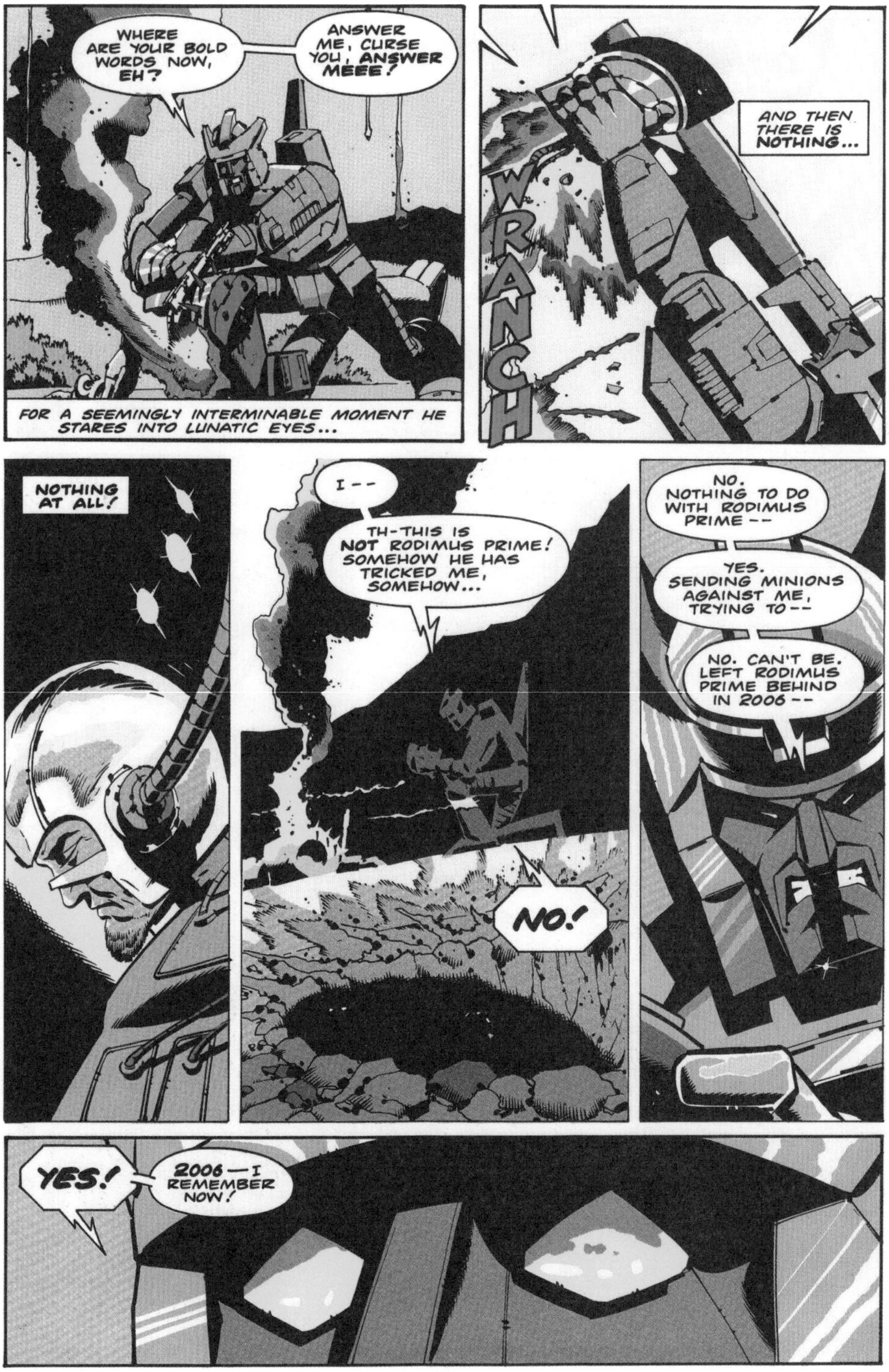
WHERE ARE YOUR BOLD WORDS NOW, EH?
ANSWER ME, CURSE YOU, ANSWER MEEE!
FOR A SEEMINGLY INTERMINABLE MOMENT HE STARES INTO LUNATIC EYES...
AND THEN THERE IS NOTHING...
WRANCH
NOTHING AT ALL!
I --
TH-THIS IS NOT RODIMUS PRIME! SOMEHOW HE HAS TRICKED ME, SOMEHOW...
NO!
NO. NOTHING TO DO WITH RODIMUS PRIME --
YES. SENDING MINIONS AGAINST ME, TRYING TO --
NO. CAN'T BE. LEFT RODIMUS PRIME BEHIND IN 2006 --
YES!
2006 — I REMEMBER NOW!

10

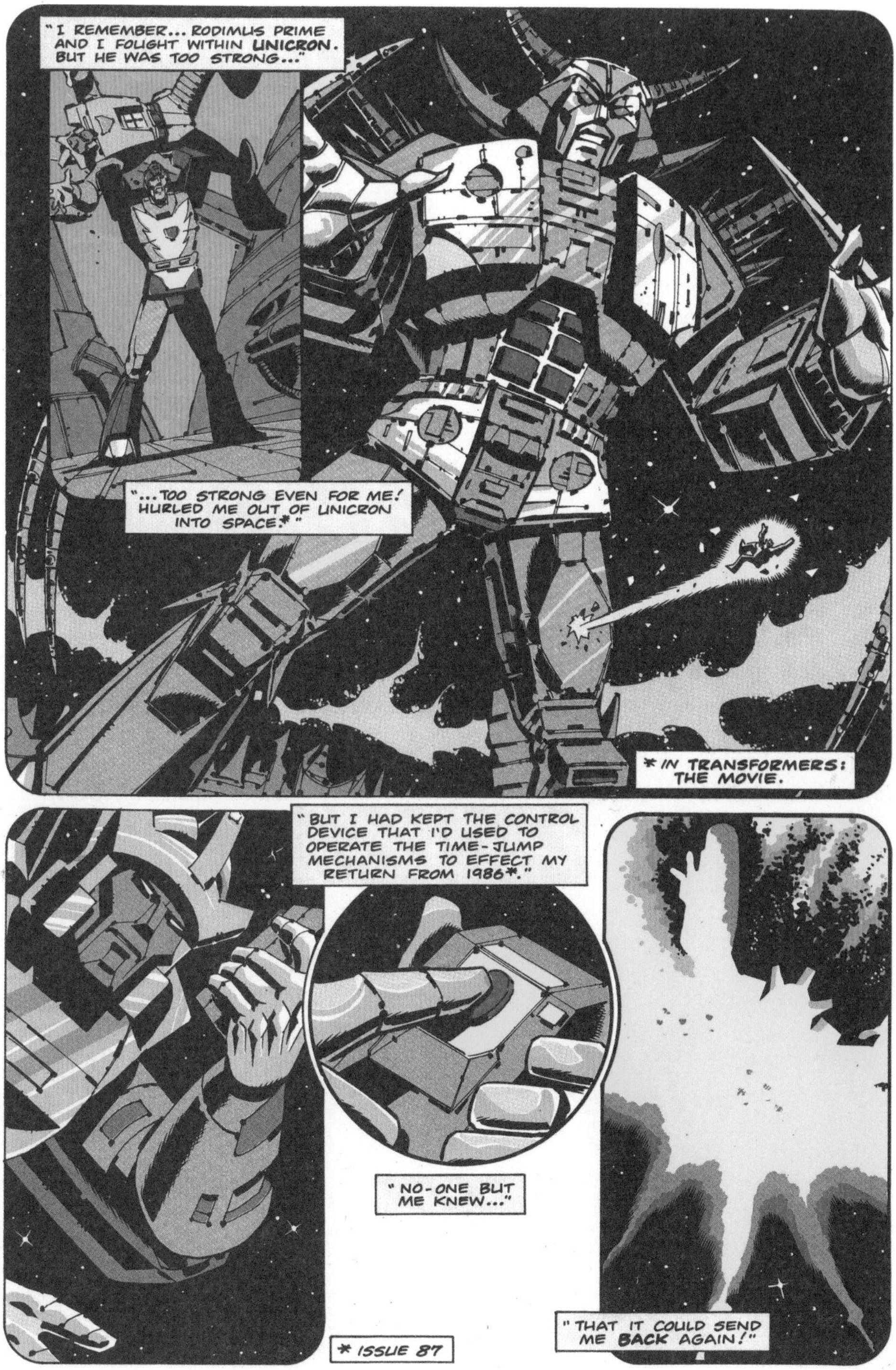
"I REMEMBER... RODIMUS PRIME AND I FOUGHT WITHIN UNICRON. BUT HE WAS TOO STRONG..."
"...TOO STRONG EVEN FOR ME! HURLED ME OUT OF UNICRON INTO SPACE*."
* IN TRANSFORMERS: THE MOVIE.
"BUT I HAD KEPT THE CONTROL DEVICE THAT I'D USED TO OPERATE THE TIME-JUMP MECHANISMS TO EFFECT MY RETURN FROM 1986*."
"NO-ONE BUT ME KNEW..."
* ISSUE 87
"THAT IT COULD SEND ME BACK AGAIN!"

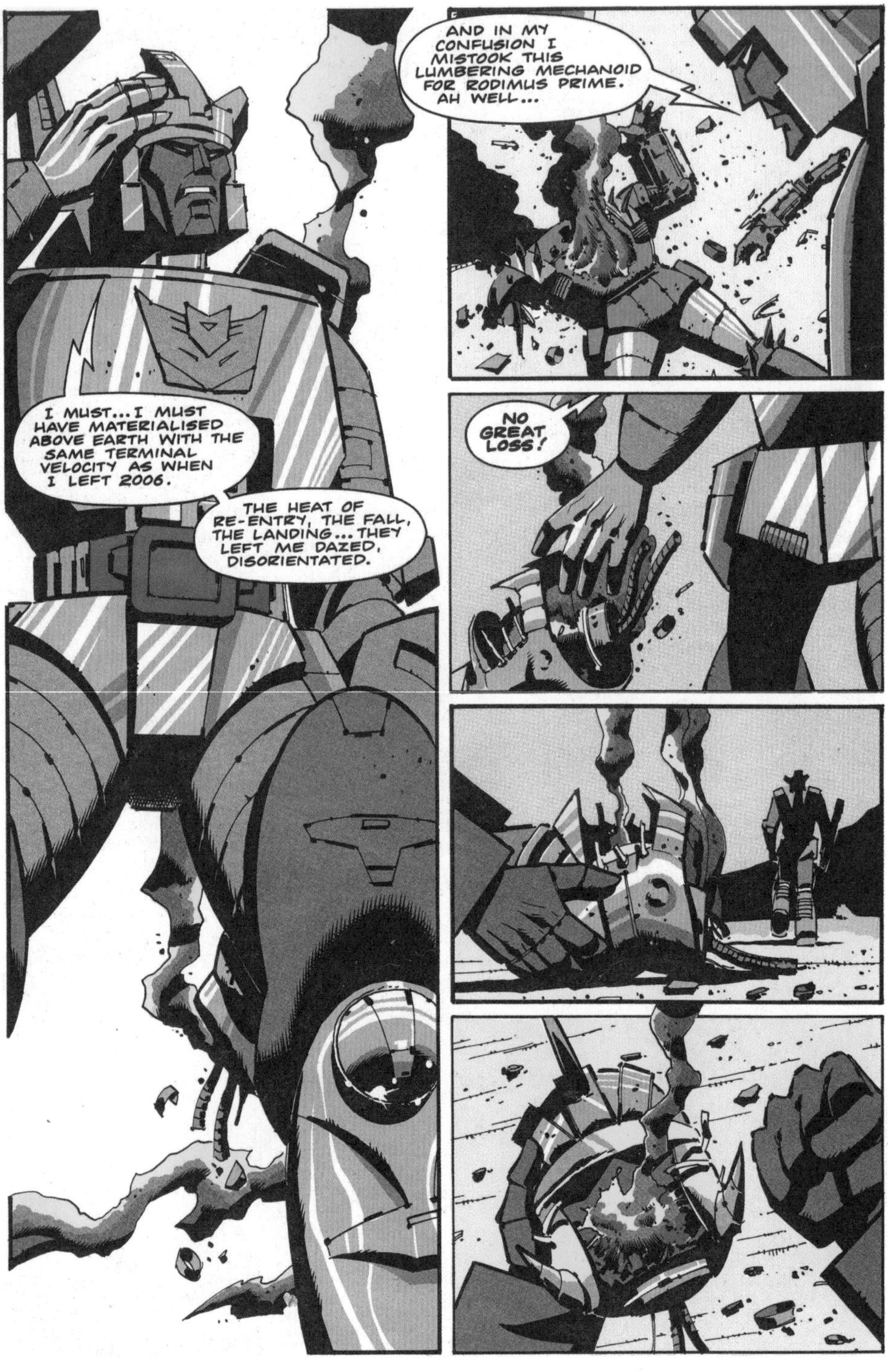
I MUST... I MUST HAVE MATERIALISED ABOVE EARTH WITH THE SAME TERMINAL VELOCITY AS WHEN I LEFT 2006.
THE HEAT OF RE-ENTRY, THE FALL, THE LANDING... THEY LEFT ME DAZED, DISORIENTATED.
AND IN MY CONFUSION I MISTOOK THIS LUMBERING MECHANOID FOR RODIMUS PRIME. AH WELL...
NO GREAT LOSS!

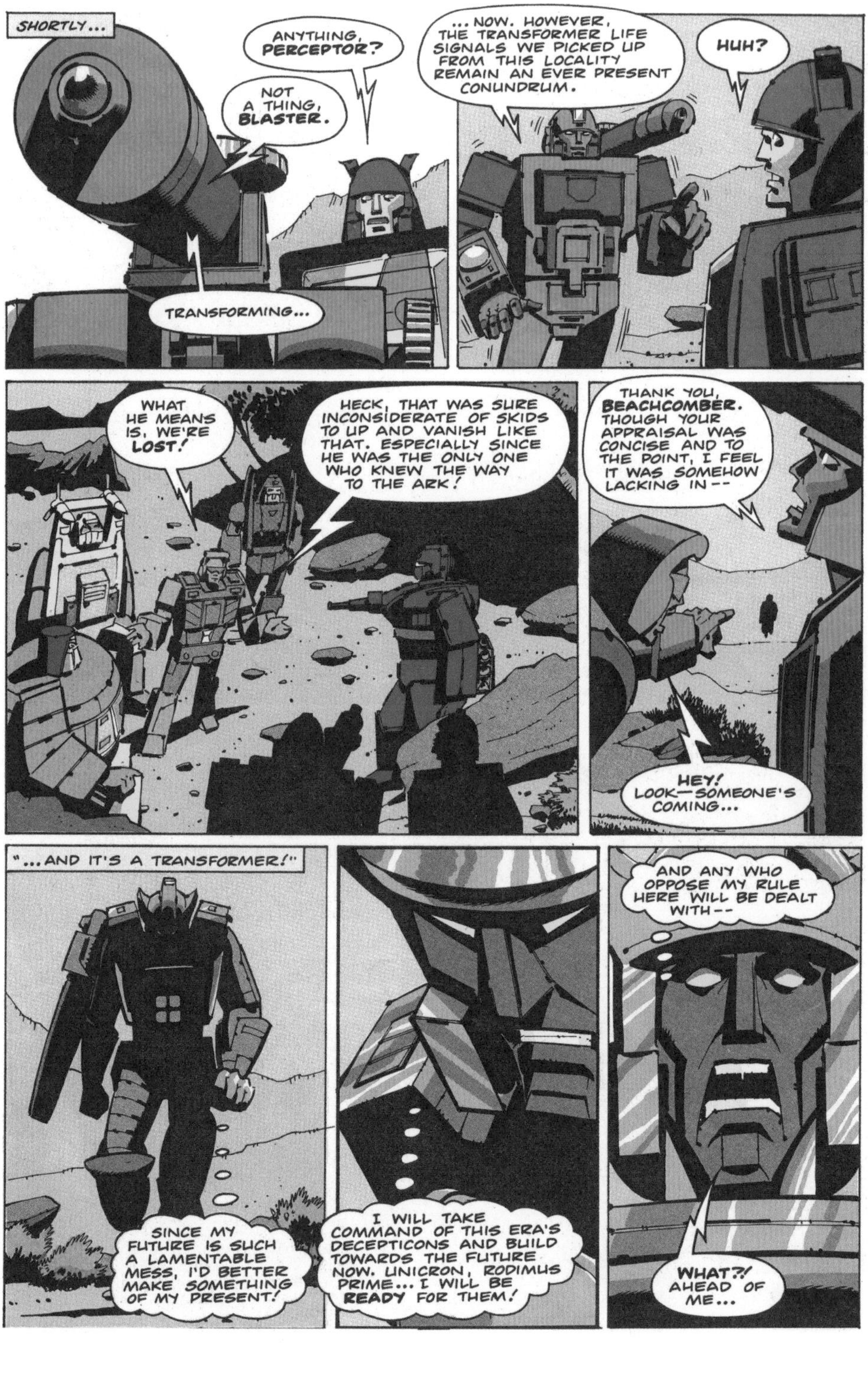
SHORTLY...
ANYTHING, PERCEPTOR?
NOT A THING, BLASTER.
TRANSFORMING...
...NOW. HOWEVER, THE TRANSFORMER LIFE SIGNALS WE PICKED UP FROM THIS LOCALITY REMAIN AN EVER PRESENT CONUNDRUM.
HUH?
WHAT HE MEANS IS, WE'RE LOST!
HECK, THAT WAS SURE INCONSIDERATE OF SKIDS TO UP AND VANISH LIKE THAT. ESPECIALLY SINCE HE WAS THE ONLY ONE WHO KNEW THE WAY TO THE ARK!
THANK YOU, BEACHCOMBER. THOUGH YOUR APPRAISAL WAS CONCISE AND TO THE POINT, I FEEL IT WAS SOMEHOW LACKING IN--
HEY! LOOK—SOMEONE'S COMING...
"...AND IT'S A TRANSFORMER!"
SINCE MY FUTURE IS SUCH A LAMENTABLE MESS, I'D BETTER MAKE SOMETHING OF MY PRESENT!
I WILL TAKE COMMAND OF THIS ERA'S DECEPTICONS AND BUILD TOWARDS THE FUTURE NOW. UNICRON, RODIMUS PRIME... I WILL BE READY FOR THEM!
AND ANY WHO OPPOSE MY RULE HERE WILL BE DEALT WITH--
WHAT?! AHEAD OF ME...

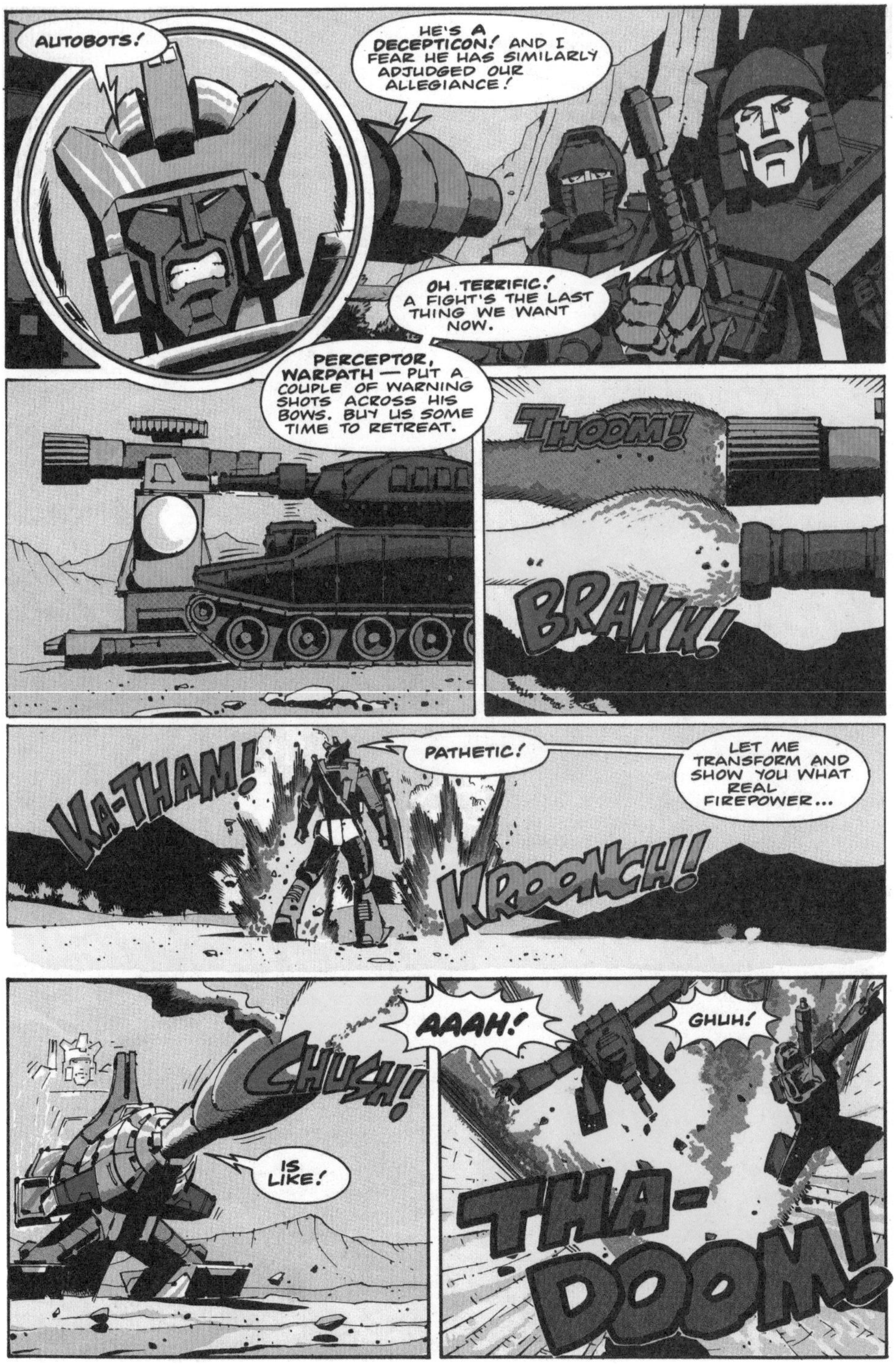
AUTOBOTS!
HE'S A DECEPTICON! AND I FEAR HE HAS SIMILARLY ADJUDGED OUR ALLEGIANCE!
OH TERRIFIC! A FIGHT'S THE LAST THING WE WANT NOW.
PERCEPTOR, WARPATH — PUT A COUPLE OF WARNING SHOTS ACROSS HIS BOWS. BUY US SOME TIME TO RETREAT.
THOOM!
BRAKK!
KA-THAM!
PATHETIC!
LET ME TRANSFORM AND SHOW YOU WHAT REAL FIREPOWER...
KROONCH!
CHUSH!
IS LIKE!
AAAH!
GHUH!
THA-DOOM!

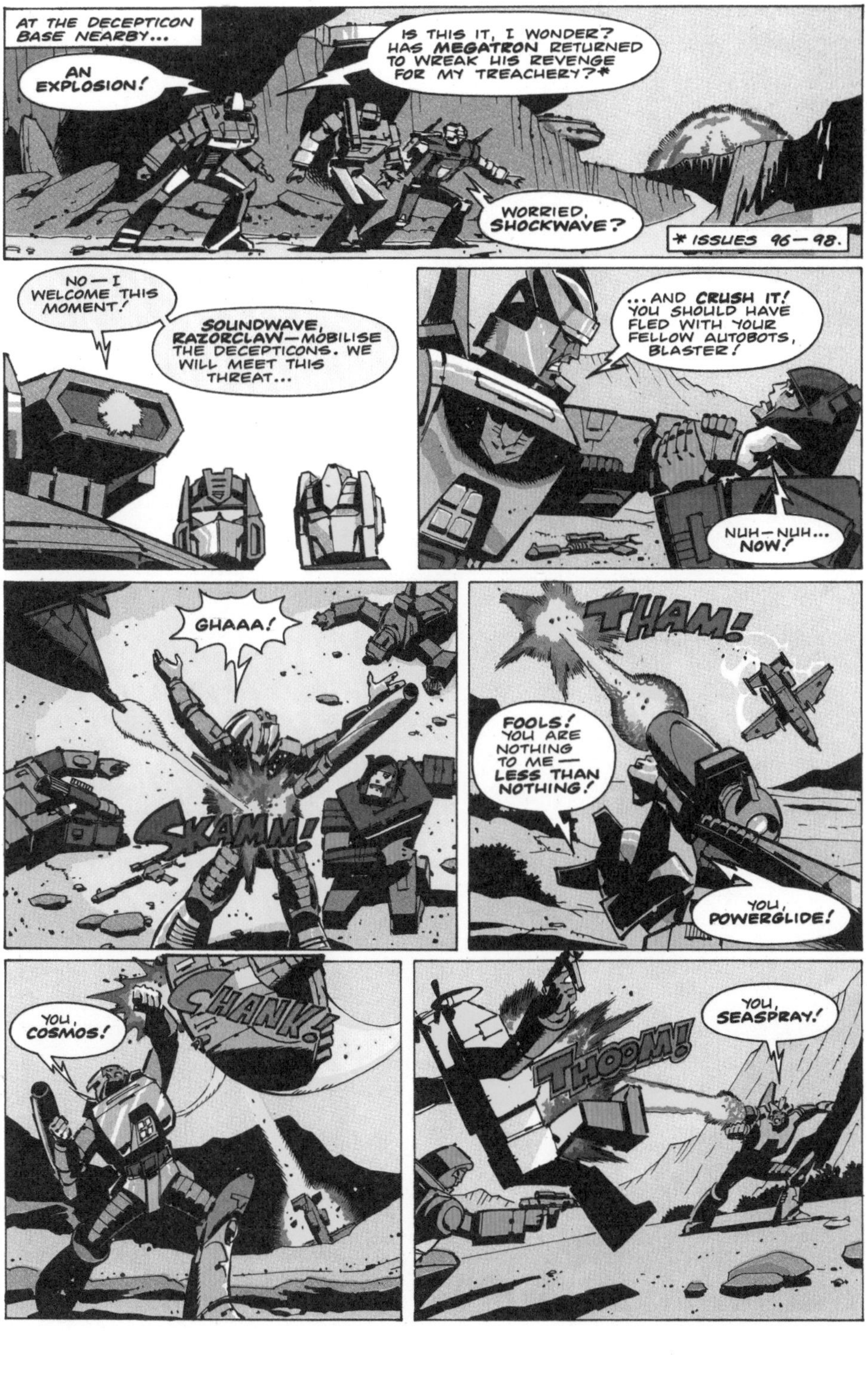
AT THE DECEPTICON BASE NEARBY...
AN EXPLOSION!
IS THIS IT, I WONDER? HAS MEGATRON RETURNED TO WREAK HIS REVENGE FOR MY TREACHERY?*
WORRIED, SHOCKWAVE?
* ISSUES 96—98.
NO—I WELCOME THIS MOMENT!
SOUNDWAVE, RAZORCLAW—MOBILISE THE DECEPTICONS. WE WILL MEET THIS THREAT...
...AND CRUSH IT! YOU SHOULD HAVE FLED WITH YOUR FELLOW AUTOBOTS, BLASTER!
NUH—NUH... NOW!
GHAAA!
SKAMM!
THAM!
FOOLS! YOU ARE NOTHING TO ME—LESS THAN NOTHING!
YOU, POWERGLIDE!
YOU, COSMOS!
CHANK!
THOOM!
YOU, SEASPRAY!

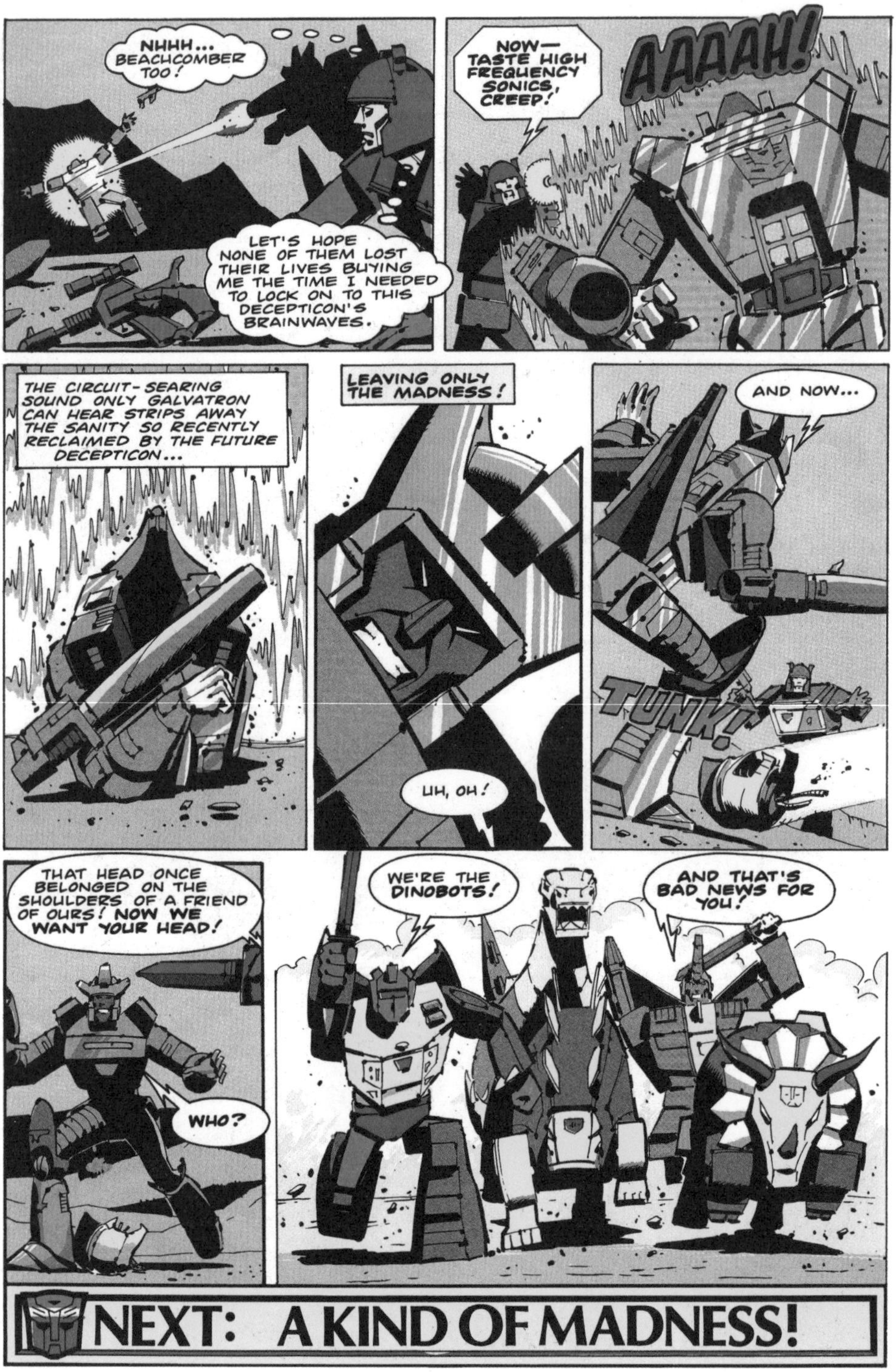
NHHH... BEACHCOMBER TOO!
LET'S HOPE NONE OF THEM LOST THEIR LIVES BUYING ME THE TIME I NEEDED TO LOCK ON TO THIS DECEPTICON'S BRAINWAVES.
NOW— TASTE HIGH FREQUENCY SONICS, CREEP!
AAAAH!
THE CIRCUIT-SEARING SOUND ONLY GALVATRON CAN HEAR STRIPS AWAY THE SANITY SO RECENTLY RECLAIMED BY THE FUTURE DECEPTICON...
LEAVING ONLY THE MADNESS!
UH, OH!
AND NOW...
TUNK!
THAT HEAD ONCE BELONGED ON THE SHOULDERS OF A FRIEND OF OURS! NOW WE WANT YOUR HEAD!
WHO?
WE'RE THE DINOBOTS!
AND THAT'S BAD NEWS FOR YOU!
NEXT: A KIND OF MADNESS!

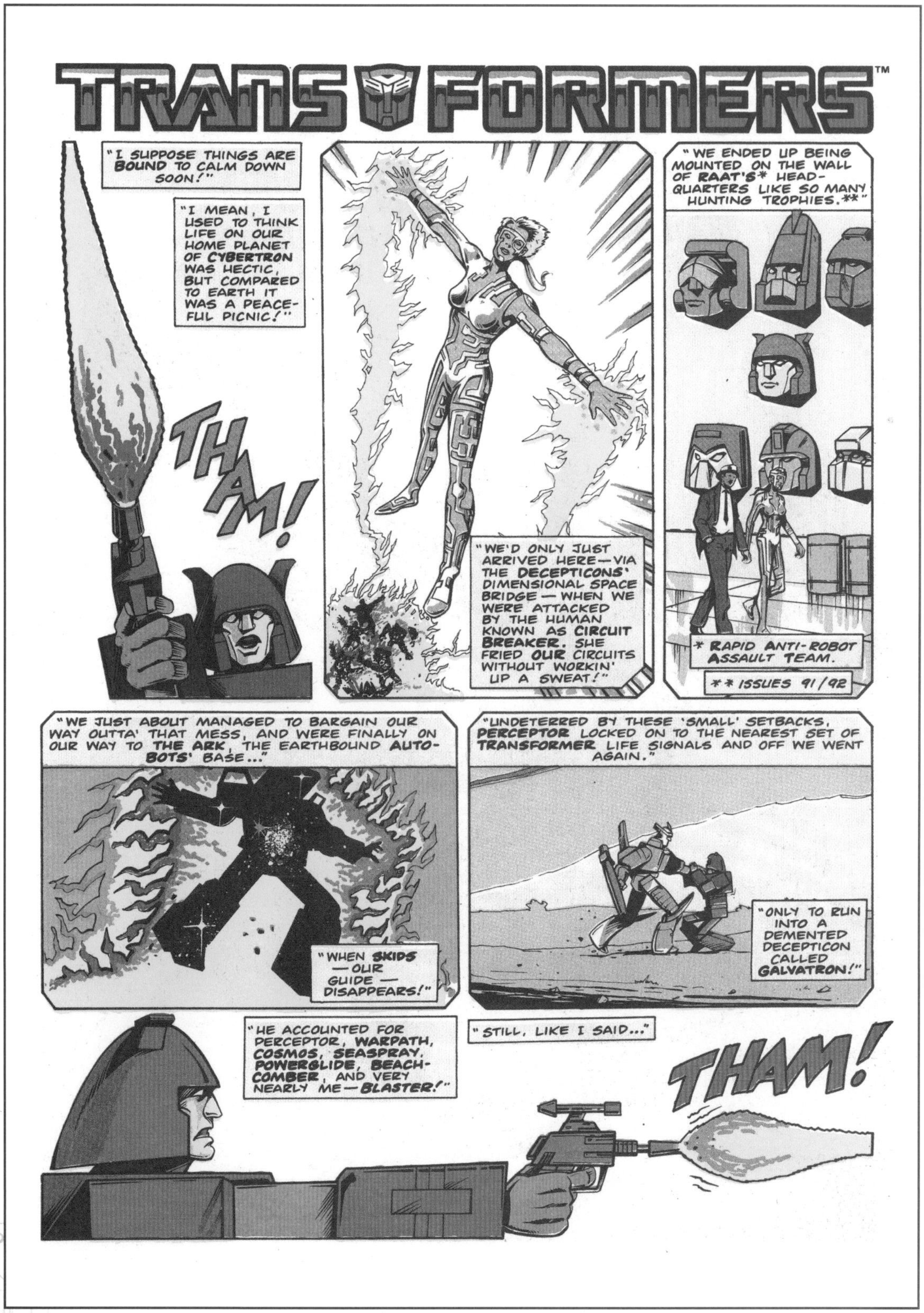
TRANSFORMERS™
"I SUPPOSE THINGS ARE BOUND TO CALM DOWN SOON!"
"I MEAN, I USED TO THINK LIFE ON OUR HOME PLANET OF CYBERTRON WAS HECTIC, BUT COMPARED TO EARTH IT WAS A PEACEFUL PICNIC!"
THAM!
"WE'D ONLY JUST ARRIVED HERE—VIA THE DECEPTICONS' DIMENSIONAL SPACE BRIDGE—WHEN WE WERE ATTACKED BY THE HUMAN KNOWN AS CIRCUIT BREAKER. SHE FRIED OUR CIRCUITS WITHOUT WORKIN' UP A SWEAT!"
"WE ENDED UP BEING MOUNTED ON THE WALL OF RAAT'S* HEAD-QUARTERS LIKE SO MANY HUNTING TROPHIES.**"
* RAPID ANTI-ROBOT ASSAULT TEAM.
** ISSUES 91/92
"WE JUST ABOUT MANAGED TO BARGAIN OUR WAY OUTTA' THAT MESS, AND WERE FINALLY ON OUR WAY TO THE ARK, THE EARTHBOUND AUTOBOTS' BASE..."
"WHEN SKIDS—OUR GUIDE—DISAPPEARS!"
"UNDETERRED BY THESE 'SMALL' SETBACKS, PERCEPTOR LOCKED ON TO THE NEAREST SET OF TRANSFORMER LIFE SIGNALS AND OFF WE WENT AGAIN."
"ONLY TO RUN INTO A DEMENTED DECEPTICON CALLED GALVATRON!"
"HE ACCOUNTED FOR PERCEPTOR, WARPATH, COSMOS, SEASPRAY, POWERGLIDE, BEACHCOMBER, AND VERY NEARLY ME—BLASTER!"
"STILL, LIKE I SAID..."
THAM!

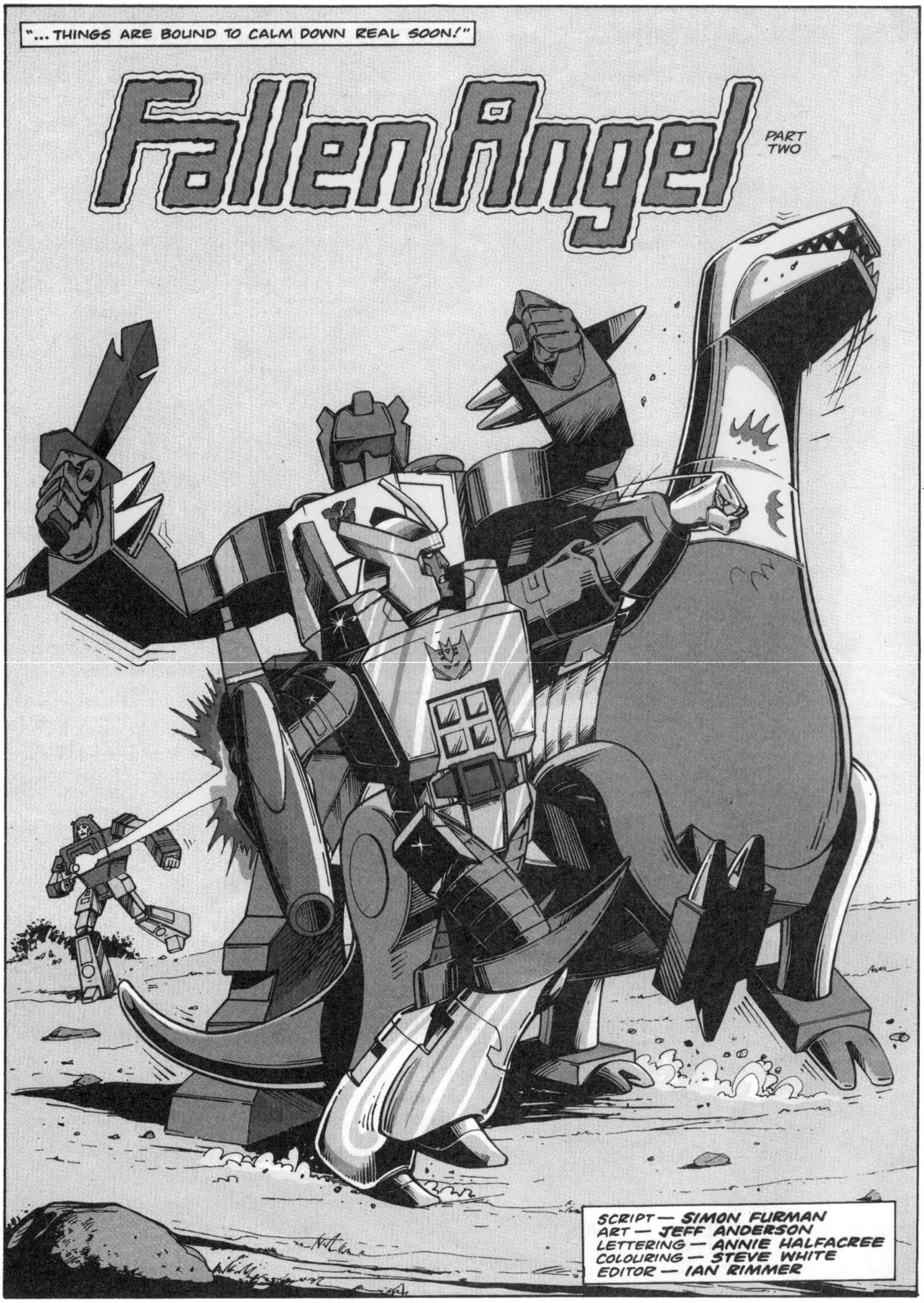
"... THINGS ARE BOUND TO CALM DOWN REAL SOON!"
Fallen Angel
PART TWO
SCRIPT — SIMON FURMAN
ART — JEFF ANDERSON
LETTERING — ANNIE HALFACREE
COLOURING — STEVE WHITE
EDITOR — IAN RIMMER

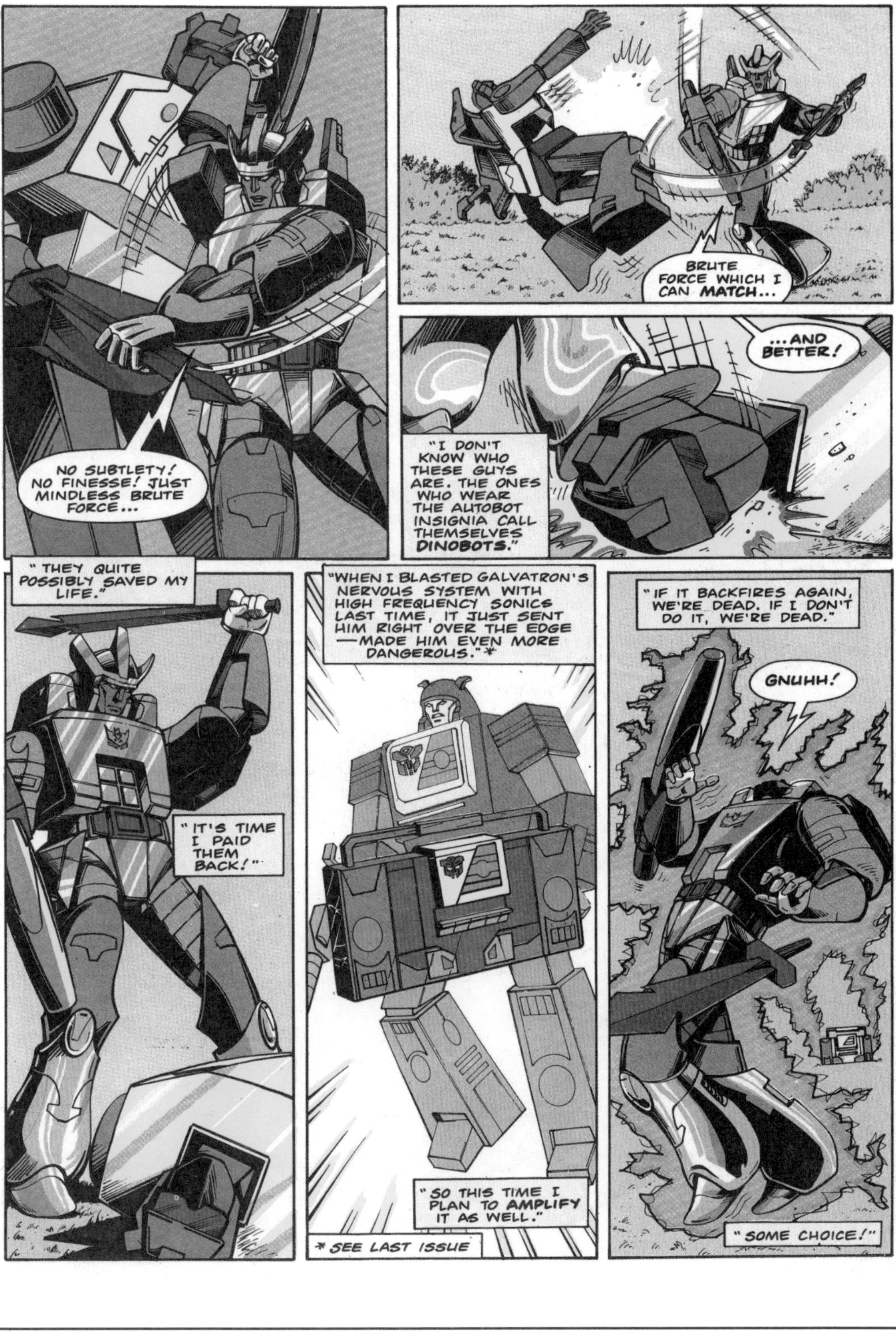
NO SUBTLETY! NO FINESSE! JUST MINDLESS BRUTE FORCE...
BRUTE FORCE WHICH I CAN MATCH...
...AND BETTER!
"I DON'T KNOW WHO THESE GUYS ARE. THE ONES WHO WEAR THE AUTOBOT INSIGNIA CALL THEMSELVES DINOBOTS."
"THEY QUITE POSSIBLY SAVED MY LIFE."
"IT'S TIME I PAID THEM BACK!"
"WHEN I BLASTED GALVATRON'S NERVOUS SYSTEM WITH HIGH FREQUENCY SONICS LAST TIME, IT JUST SENT HIM RIGHT OVER THE EDGE —MADE HIM EVEN MORE DANGEROUS."*
"SO THIS TIME I PLAN TO AMPLIFY IT AS WELL."
*SEE LAST ISSUE
"IF IT BACKFIRES AGAIN, WE'RE DEAD. IF I DON'T DO IT, WE'RE DEAD."
GNUHH!
"SOME CHOICE!"

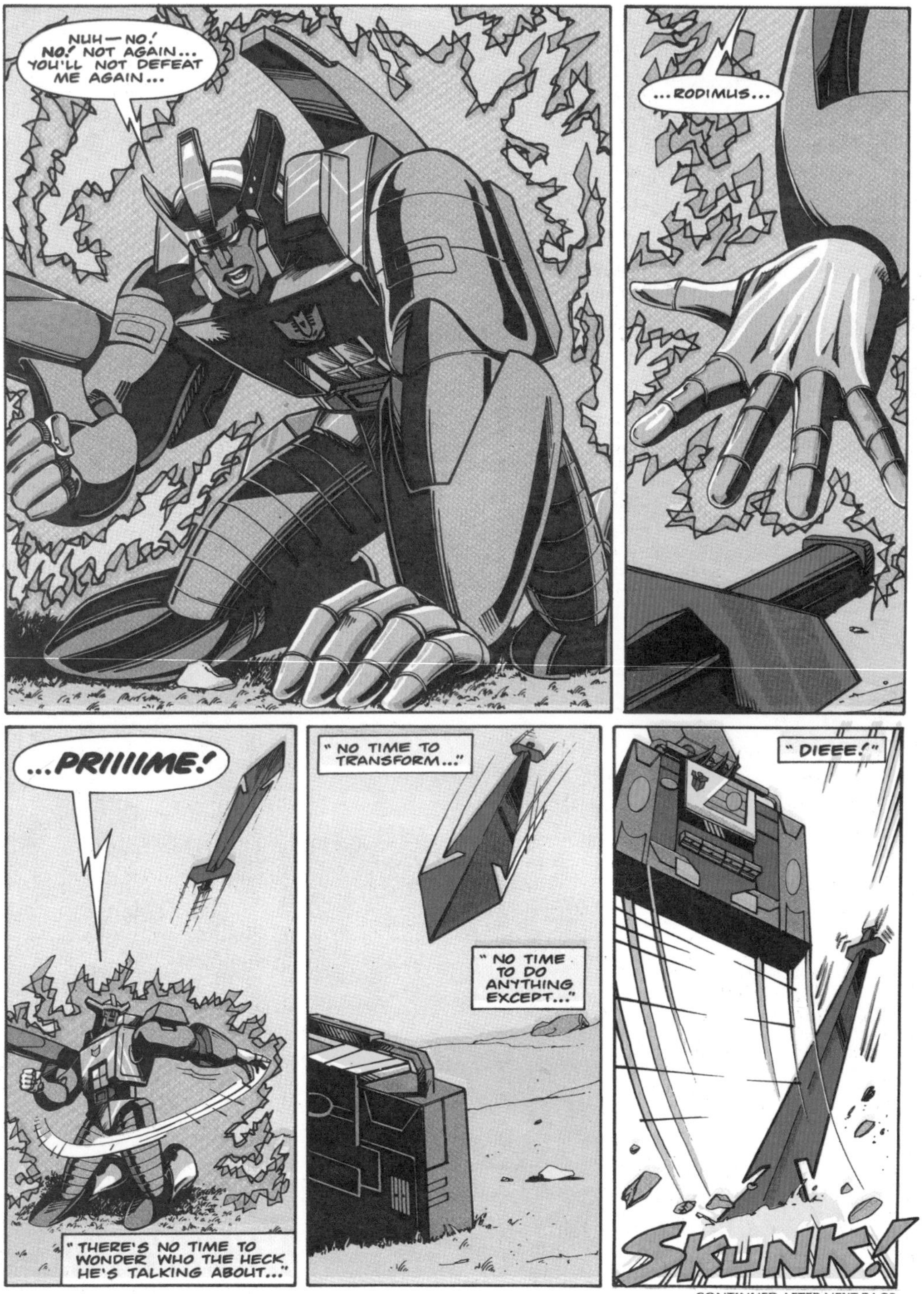
NUH—NO! NO! NOT AGAIN... YOU'LL NOT DEFEAT ME AGAIN...
...RODIMUS...
...PRIIIIME!
"THERE'S NO TIME TO WONDER WHO THE HECK HE'S TALKING ABOUT..."
"NO TIME TO TRANSFORM..."
"NO TIME TO DO ANYTHING EXCEPT..."
"DIEEE!"
SKUNK!

CONTINUED AFTER NEXT PAGE

PHEW! THANKS FOR THE SAVE!
GUESS I MADE A REAL MESS OF THAT, DIDN'T I... ER...
THE NAME'S SWOOP. AND NO, YOU DIDN'T MAKE A MESS OF ANYTHING...
"YOUR DIVERSION HAS GIVEN US DINOBOTS THE TIME WE NEED..."
"FOR SNARL TO GET IN POSITION..."
"AND OUR LEADER, GRIMLOCK, TO MAKE THE FIRST ATTACK!"
CHANG!
"NOW SLUDGE FOLLOWS IT UP..."
"AND SLAG MAKES IT REAL HOT FOR THAT GUY!"
"SO—WHAT DO YOU RECKON TO THE DINOBOTS IN ACTION, EH?"
INCREDIBLE!
I CAME HERE EXPECTING TO CONFRONT MEGATRON, AND I FIND THIS!

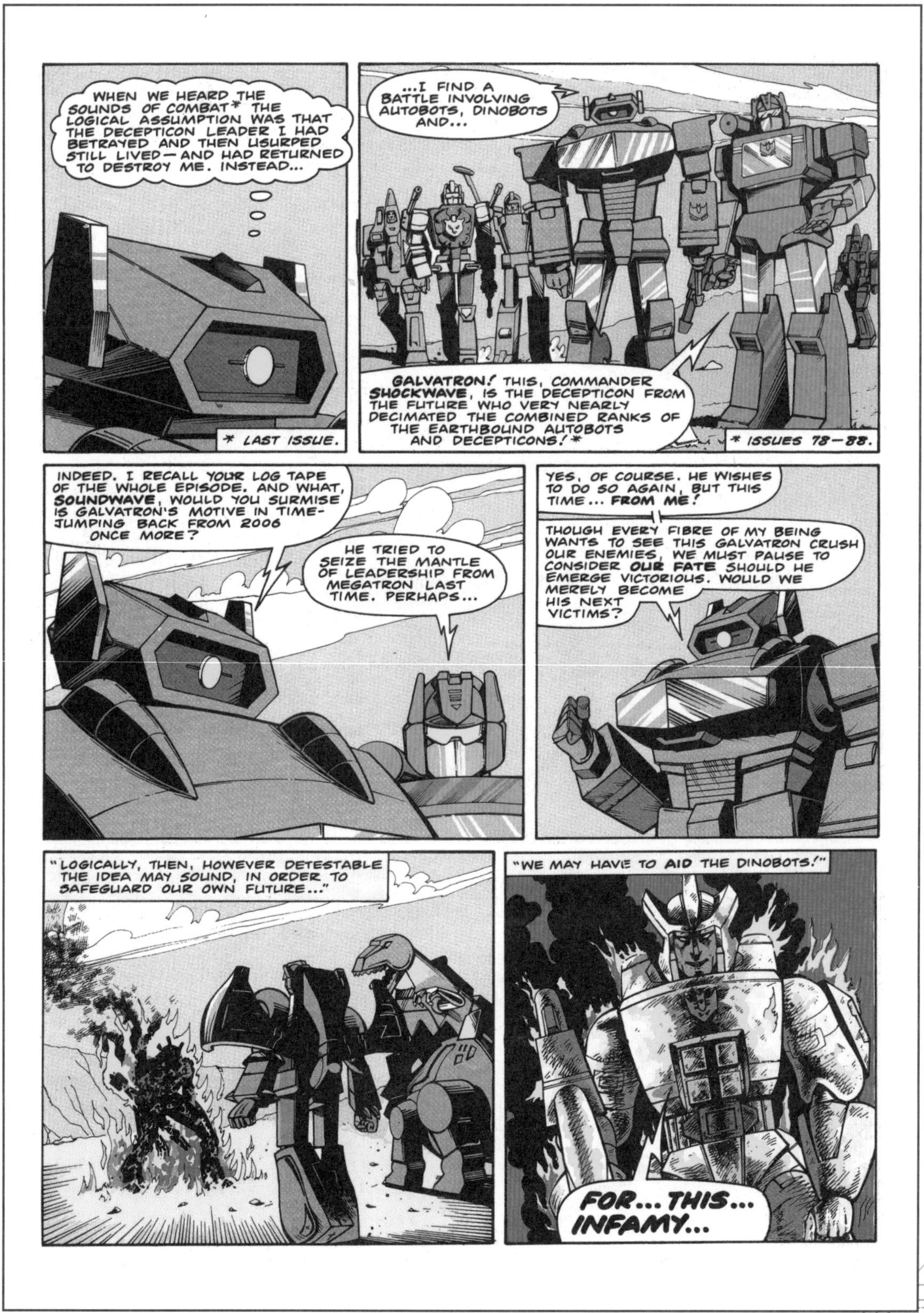
WHEN WE HEARD THE SOUNDS OF COMBAT* THE LOGICAL ASSUMPTION WAS THAT THE DECEPTICON LEADER I HAD BETRAYED AND THEN USURPED STILL LIVED— AND HAD RETURNED TO DESTROY ME. INSTEAD...
* LAST ISSUE.
...I FIND A BATTLE INVOLVING AUTOBOTS, DINOBOTS AND...
GALVATRON! THIS, COMMANDER SHOCKWAVE, IS THE DECEPTICON FROM THE FUTURE WHO VERY NEARLY DECIMATED THE COMBINED RANKS OF THE EARTHBOUND AUTOBOTS AND DECEPTICONS! *
* ISSUES 78—88.
INDEED. I RECALL YOUR LOG TAPE OF THE WHOLE EPISODE. AND WHAT, SOUNDWAVE, WOULD YOU SURMISE IS GALVATRON'S MOTIVE IN TIME-JUMPING BACK FROM 2006 ONCE MORE?
HE TRIED TO SEIZE THE MANTLE OF LEADERSHIP FROM MEGATRON LAST TIME. PERHAPS...
YES, OF COURSE. HE WISHES TO DO SO AGAIN, BUT THIS TIME... FROM ME!
THOUGH EVERY FIBRE OF MY BEING WANTS TO SEE THIS GALVATRON CRUSH OUR ENEMIES, WE MUST PAUSE TO CONSIDER OUR FATE SHOULD HE EMERGE VICTORIOUS. WOULD WE MERELY BECOME HIS NEXT VICTIMS?
"LOGICALLY, THEN, HOWEVER DETESTABLE THE IDEA MAY SOUND, IN ORDER TO SAFEGUARD OUR OWN FUTURE..."
"WE MAY HAVE TO AID THE DINOBOTS!"
FOR... THIS... INFAMY...

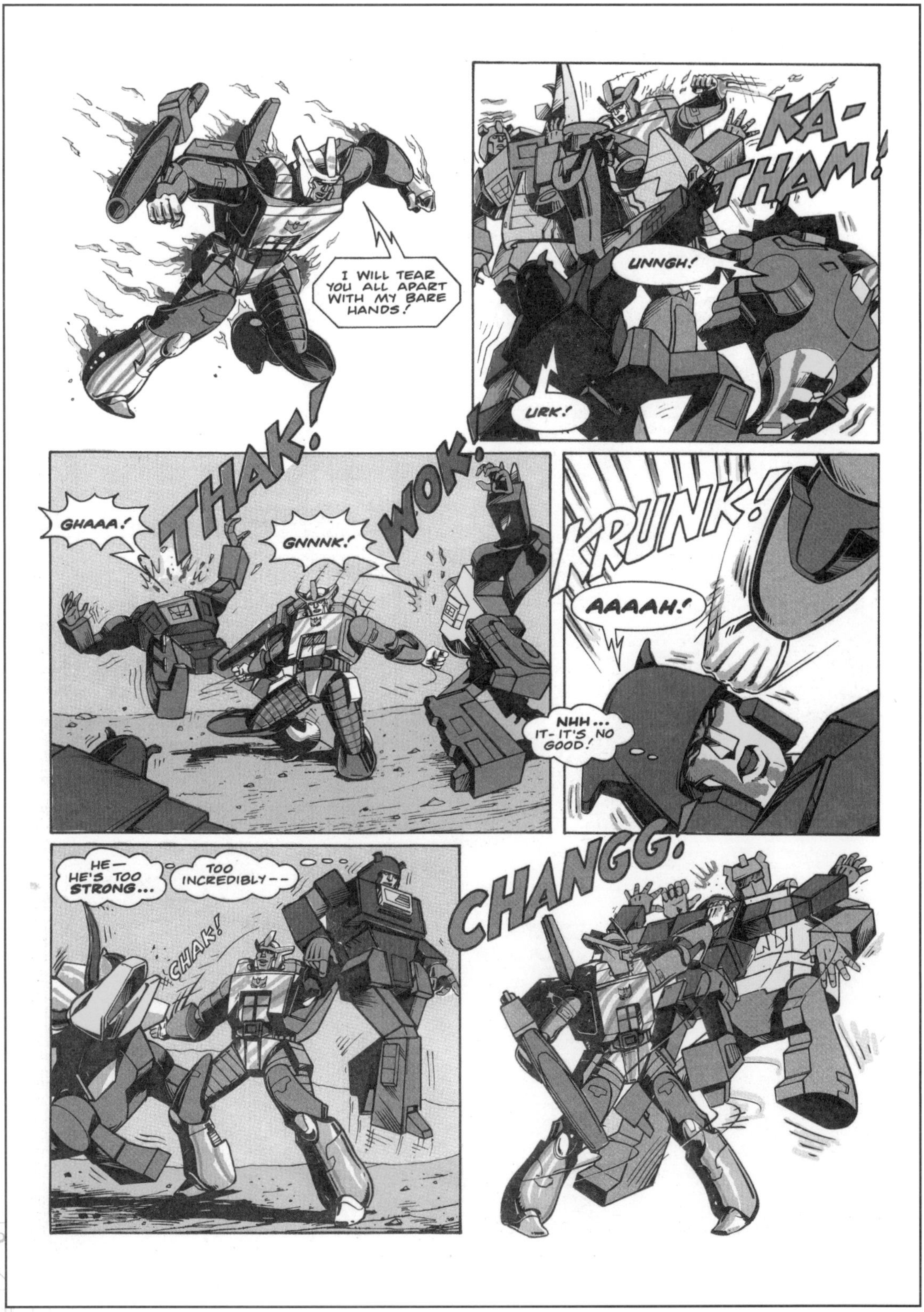
I WILL TEAR YOU ALL APART WITH MY BARE HANDS!
KA-THAM!
UNNGH!
URK!
THAK!
WOK!
GHAAA!
GNNNK!
KRUNK!
AAAAH!
NHH... IT- IT'S NO GOOD!
HE— HE'S TOO STRONG...
TOO INCREDIBLY--
CHAK!
CHANGG!

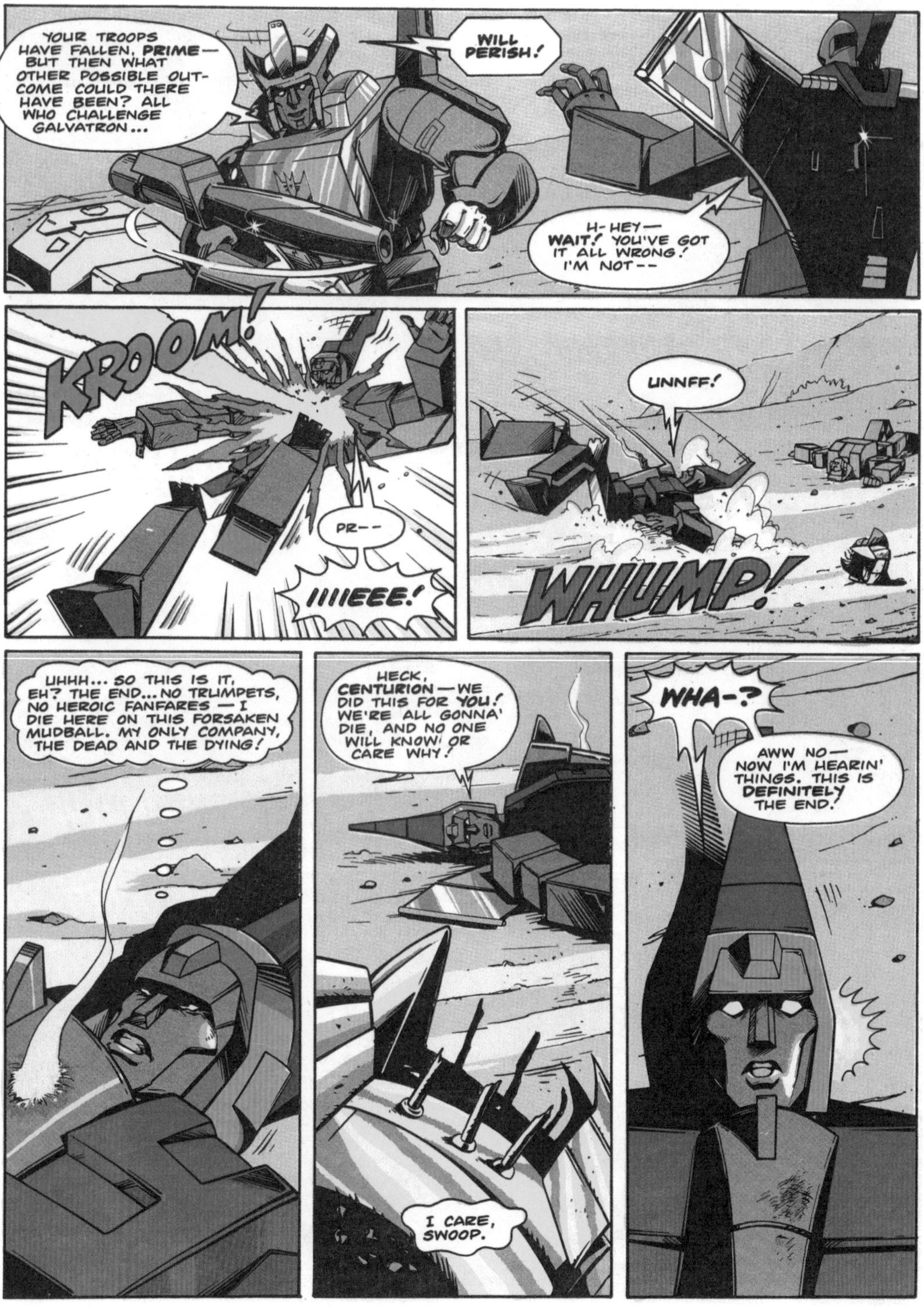
YOUR TROOPS HAVE FALLEN, PRIME— BUT THEN WHAT OTHER POSSIBLE OUT-COME COULD THERE HAVE BEEN? ALL WHO CHALLENGE GALVATRON...
WILL PERISH!
H-HEY— WAIT! YOU'VE GOT IT ALL WRONG! I'M NOT--
KROOM!
PR--
IIIIEEE!
UNNFF!
WHUMP!
UHHH... SO THIS IS IT, EH? THE END... NO TRUMPETS, NO HEROIC FANFARES — I DIE HERE ON THIS FORSAKEN MUDBALL. MY ONLY COMPANY, THE DEAD AND THE DYING!
HECK, CENTURION—WE DID THIS FOR YOU! WE'RE ALL GONNA' DIE, AND NO ONE WILL KNOW OR CARE WHY!
I CARE, SWOOP.
WHA-?
AWW NO— NOW I'M HEARIN' THINGS. THIS IS DEFINITELY THE END.

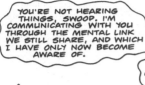

YOU'RE NOT HEARING THINGS, SWOOP. I'M COMMUNICATING WITH YOU THROUGH THE MENTAL LINK WE STILL SHARE, AND WHICH I HAVE ONLY NOW BECOME AWARE OF.

YOU SEE, SWOOP, I AM CENTURION, BUT I AM ALSO...

PROFESSOR MORRIS— THE MAN WHO ONCE POSSESSED YOUR BODY AND TURNED YOU AGAINST YOUR FELLOW AUTOBOTS*.

UNTIL NOW I HAD FELT IT PRUDENT TO KEEP THIS FACT FROM YOU!

* ISSUES 45/46

BUT THANKS TO THE DECEPTICON YOU CALL GALVATRON, CENTURION IS LITTLE MORE THAN SCRAP METAL.* AND I WANT REVENGE!

* LAST ISSUE.

YOU'RE WOUNDED, CONCUSSED AND IN SHOCK. YOU CAN'T FIGHT BACK— I CAN!

LET ME TAKE OVER— POSSESS YOUR BODY ONCE MORE. TOGETHER WE CAN DEFEAT THIS MONSTER!

N-NO... I CAN'T! NOT AFTER LAST TIME! I CAN'T ALLOW YOU IN MY HEAD AGAIN — I JUST CAN'T!

NO? WELL THEN, JUST LIE THERE AND ADMIT DEFEAT...

LIE THERE AND WATCH YOUR FELLOW DINOBOTS FALL!

LIE THERE AND REMEMBER THAT I OFFERED YOU A CHANCE!

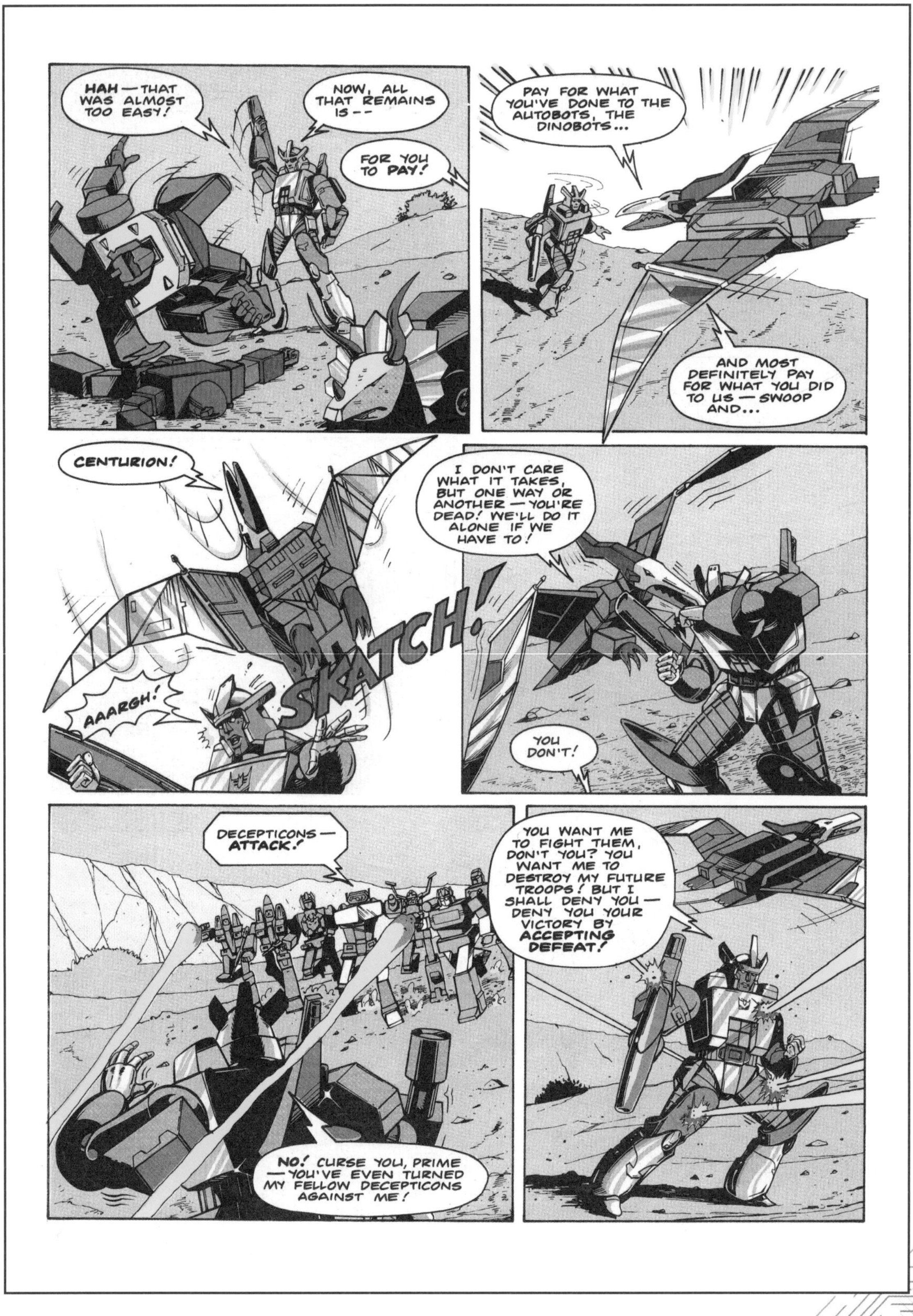
HAH — THAT WAS ALMOST TOO EASY!
NOW, ALL THAT REMAINS IS --
FOR YOU TO PAY!
PAY FOR WHAT YOU'VE DONE TO THE AUTOBOTS, THE DINOBOTS...
AND MOST DEFINITELY PAY FOR WHAT YOU DID TO US — SWOOP AND...
CENTURION!
SKATCH!
AAARGH!
I DON'T CARE WHAT IT TAKES, BUT ONE WAY OR ANOTHER — YOU'RE DEAD! WE'LL DO IT ALONE IF WE HAVE TO!
YOU DON'T!
DECEPTICONS — ATTACK!
NO! CURSE YOU, PRIME — YOU'VE EVEN TURNED MY FELLOW DECEPTICONS AGAINST ME!
YOU WANT ME TO FIGHT THEM, DON'T YOU? YOU WANT ME TO DESTROY MY FUTURE TROOPS! BUT I SHALL DENY YOU — DENY YOU YOUR VICTORY BY ACCEPTING DEFEAT!

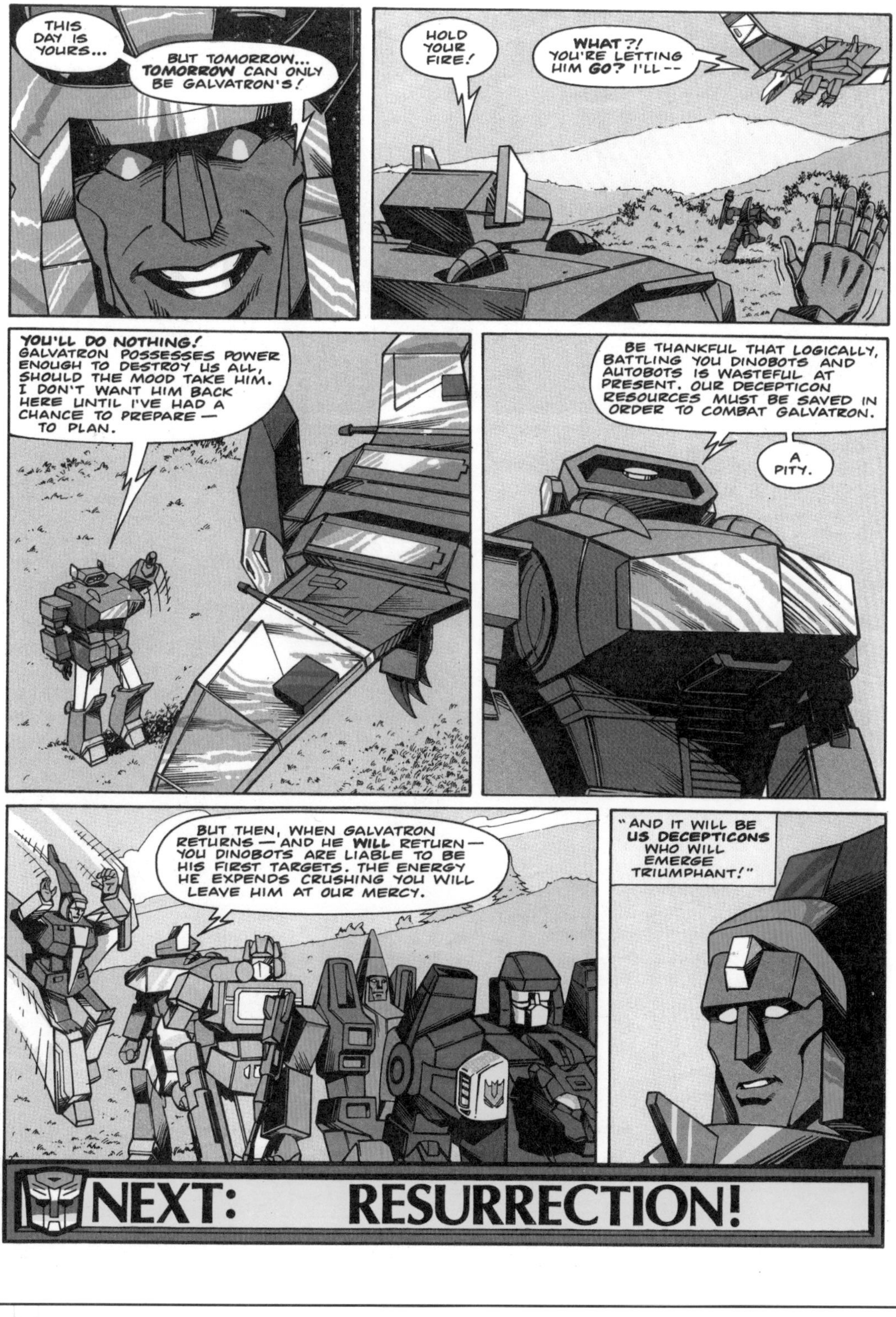
THIS DAY IS YOURS...
BUT TOMORROW... TOMORROW CAN ONLY BE GALVATRON'S!
HOLD YOUR FIRE!
WHAT?! YOU'RE LETTING HIM GO? I'LL --
YOU'LL DO NOTHING! GALVATRON POSSESSES POWER ENOUGH TO DESTROY US ALL, SHOULD THE MOOD TAKE HIM. I DON'T WANT HIM BACK HERE UNTIL I'VE HAD A CHANCE TO PREPARE — TO PLAN.
BE THANKFUL THAT LOGICALLY, BATTLING YOU DINOBOTS AND AUTOBOTS IS WASTEFUL AT PRESENT. OUR DECEPTICON RESOURCES MUST BE SAVED IN ORDER TO COMBAT GALVATRON.
A PITY.
BUT THEN, WHEN GALVATRON RETURNS — AND HE WILL RETURN — YOU DINOBOTS ARE LIABLE TO BE HIS FIRST TARGETS. THE ENERGY HE EXPENDS CRUSHING YOU WILL LEAVE HIM AT OUR MERCY.
"AND IT WILL BE US DECEPTICONS WHO WILL EMERGE TRIUMPHANT!"
NEXT: RESURRECTION!

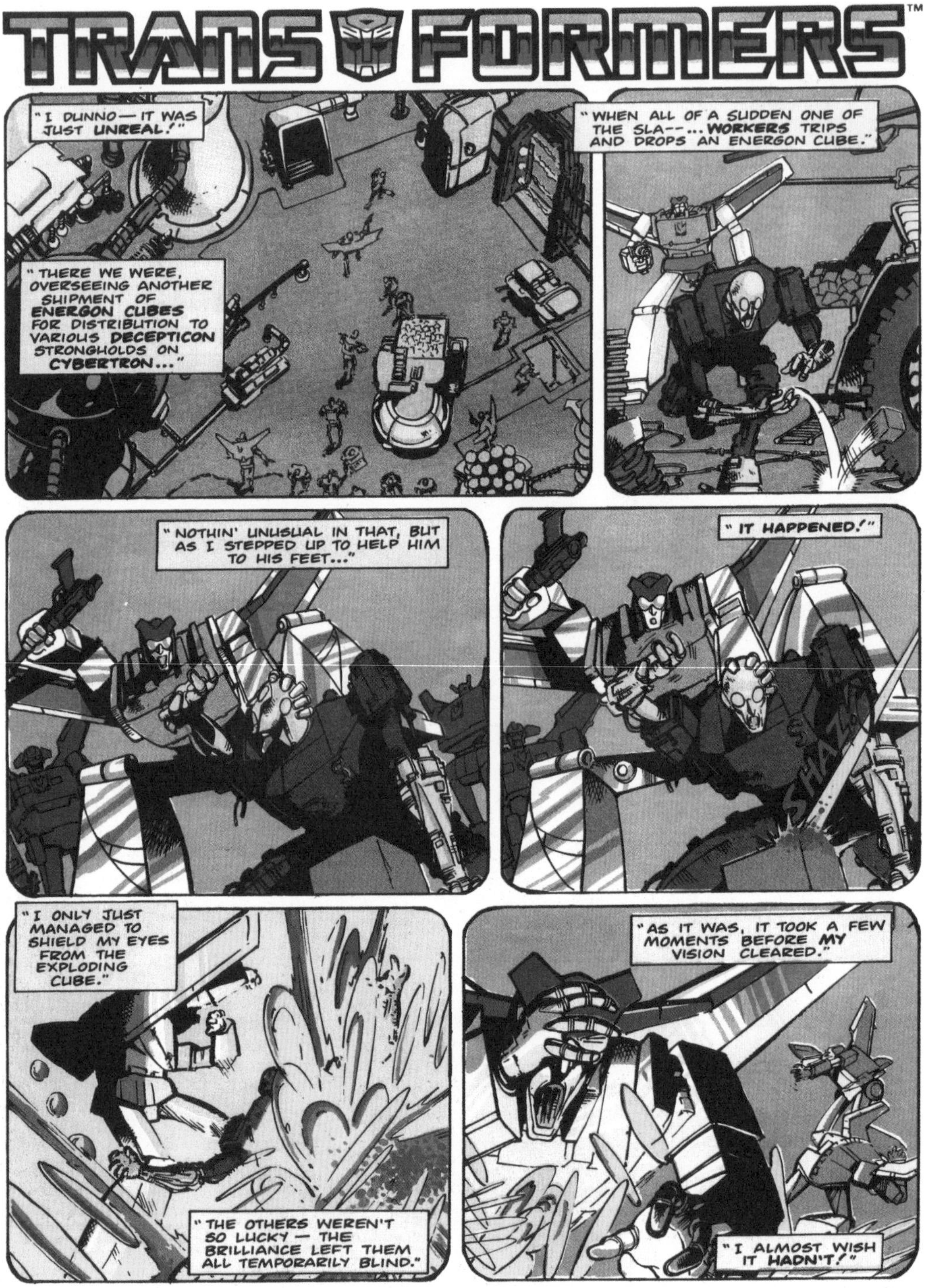
"I DUNNO— IT WAS JUST UNREAL!"
"THERE WE WERE, OVERSEEING ANOTHER SHIPMENT OF ENERGON CUBES FOR DISTRIBUTION TO VARIOUS DECEPTICON STRONGHOLDS ON CYBERTRON..."
"WHEN ALL OF A SUDDEN ONE OF THE SLA--...WORKERS TRIPS AND DROPS AN ENERGON CUBE."
"NOTHIN' UNUSUAL IN THAT, BUT AS I STEPPED UP TO HELP HIM TO HIS FEET..."
"IT HAPPENED!"
SHAZ
"I ONLY JUST MANAGED TO SHIELD MY EYES FROM THE EXPLODING CUBE."
"THE OTHERS WEREN'T SO LUCKY — THE BRILLIANCE LEFT THEM ALL TEMPORARILY BLIND."
"AS IT WAS, IT TOOK A FEW MOMENTS BEFORE MY VISION CLEARED."
"I ALMOST WISH IT HADN'T!"

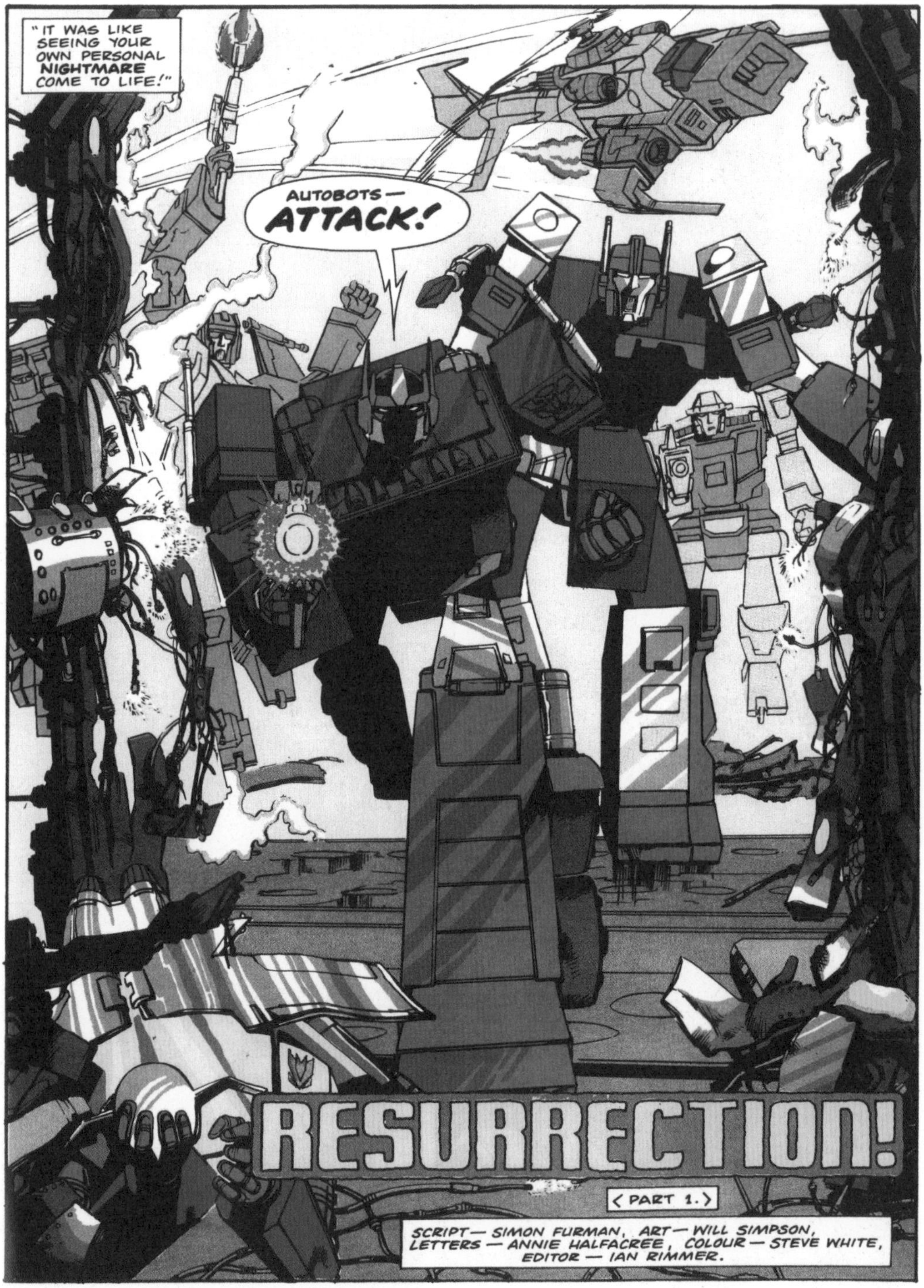
"IT WAS LIKE SEEING YOUR OWN PERSONAL NIGHTMARE COME TO LIFE!"
AUTOBOTS— ATTACK!
RESURRECTION!
< PART 1. >
SCRIPT— SIMON FURMAN, ART— WILL SIMPSON, LETTERS — ANNIE HALFACREE, COLOUR — STEVE WHITE, EDITOR — IAN RIMMER.

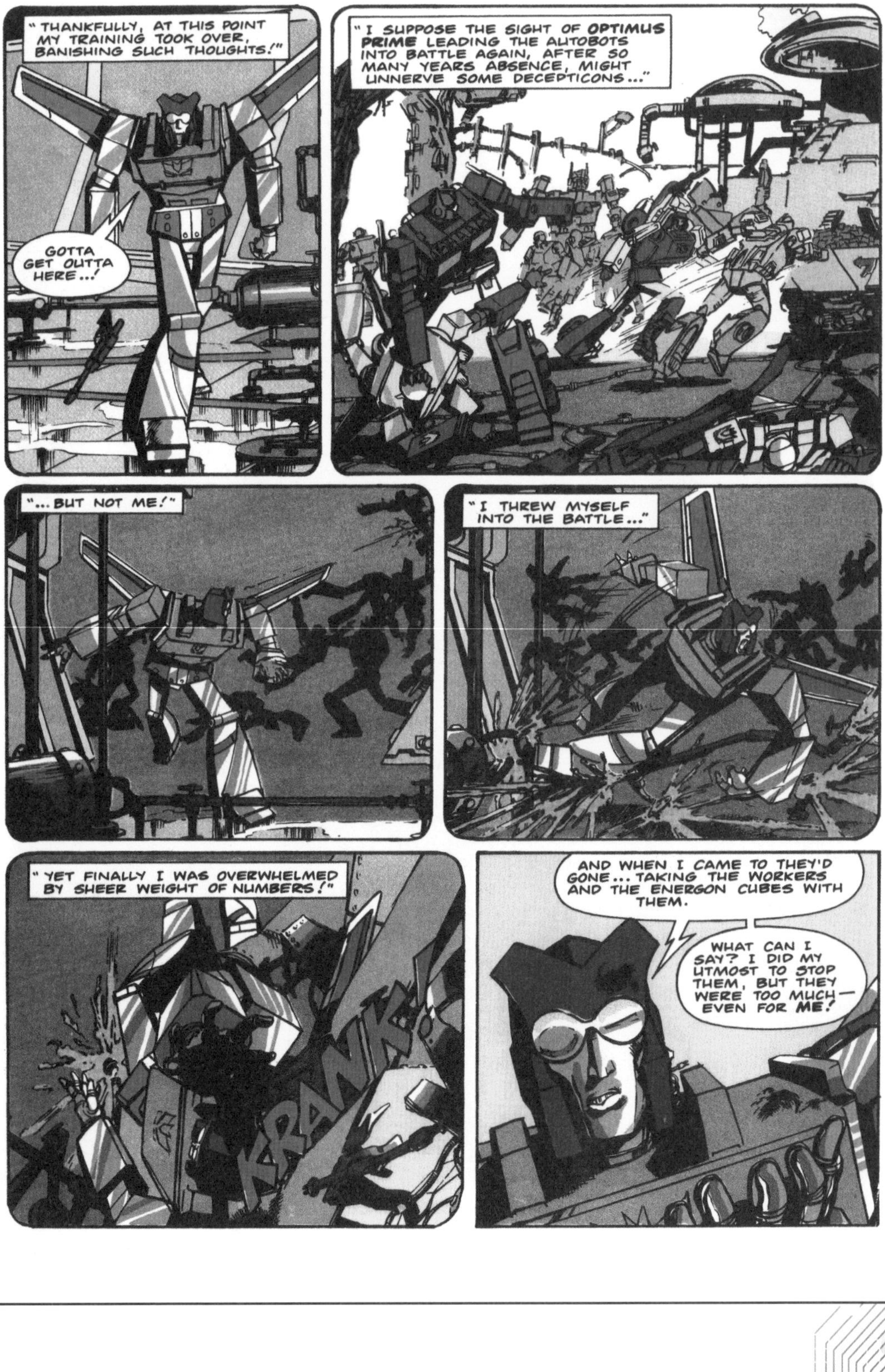
"THANKFULLY, AT THIS POINT MY TRAINING TOOK OVER, BANISHING SUCH THOUGHTS!"
GOTTA GET OUTTA HERE...!
"I SUPPOSE THE SIGHT OF OPTIMUS PRIME LEADING THE AUTOBOTS INTO BATTLE AGAIN, AFTER SO MANY YEARS ABSENCE, MIGHT UNNERVE SOME DECEPTICONS..."
"...BUT NOT ME!"
"I THREW MYSELF INTO THE BATTLE..."
"YET FINALLY I WAS OVERWHELMED BY SHEER WEIGHT OF NUMBERS!"
KRANK!
AND WHEN I CAME TO THEY'D GONE... TAKING THE WORKERS AND THE ENERGON CUBES WITH THEM.
WHAT CAN I SAY? I DID MY UTMOST TO STOP THEM, BUT THEY WERE TOO MUCH— EVEN FOR ME!

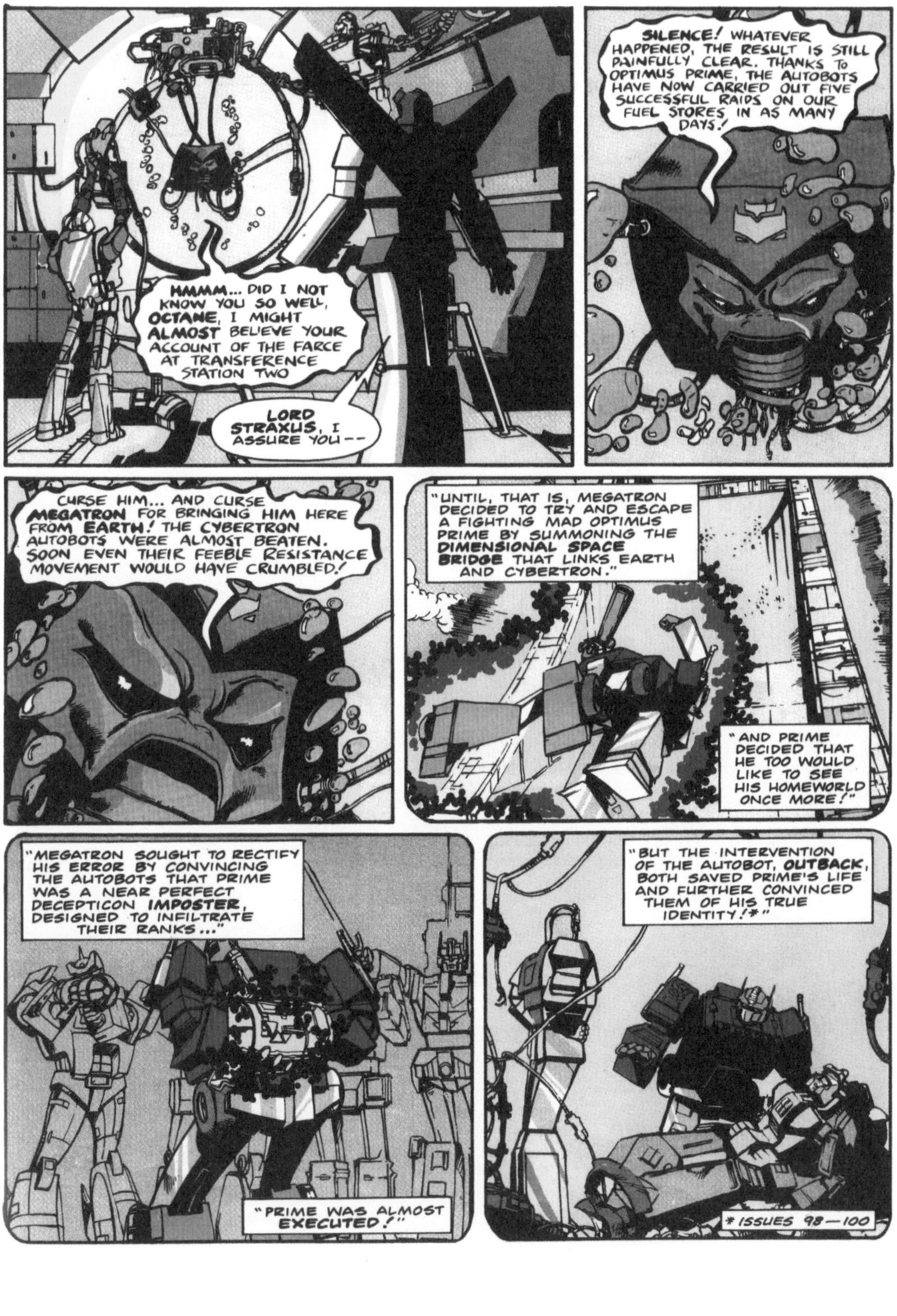
HMMM... DID I NOT KNOW YOU SO WELL, OCTANE, I MIGHT ALMOST BELIEVE YOUR ACCOUNT OF THE FARCE AT TRANSFERENCE STATION TWO
LORD STRAXUS, I ASSURE YOU--
SILENCE! WHATEVER HAPPENED, THE RESULT IS STILL PAINFULLY CLEAR. THANKS TO OPTIMUS PRIME, THE AUTOBOTS HAVE NOW CARRIED OUT FIVE SUCCESSFUL RAIDS ON OUR FUEL STORES IN AS MANY DAYS!
CURSE HIM... AND CURSE MEGATRON FOR BRINGING HIM HERE FROM EARTH! THE CYBERTRON AUTOBOTS WERE ALMOST BEATEN. SOON EVEN THEIR FEEBLE RESISTANCE MOVEMENT WOULD HAVE CRUMBLED!
"UNTIL, THAT IS, MEGATRON DECIDED TO TRY AND ESCAPE A FIGHTING MAD OPTIMUS PRIME BY SUMMONING THE DIMENSIONAL SPACE BRIDGE THAT LINKS EARTH AND CYBERTRON."
"AND PRIME DECIDED THAT HE TOO WOULD LIKE TO SEE HIS HOMEWORLD ONCE MORE!"
"MEGATRON SOUGHT TO RECTIFY HIS ERROR BY CONVINCING THE AUTOBOTS THAT PRIME WAS A NEAR PERFECT DECEPTICON IMPOSTER, DESIGNED TO INFILTRATE THEIR RANKS..."
"PRIME WAS ALMOST EXECUTED!"
"BUT THE INTERVENTION OF THE AUTOBOT, OUTBACK, BOTH SAVED PRIME'S LIFE AND FURTHER CONVINCED THEM OF HIS TRUE IDENTITY!*"
*ISSUES 98—100

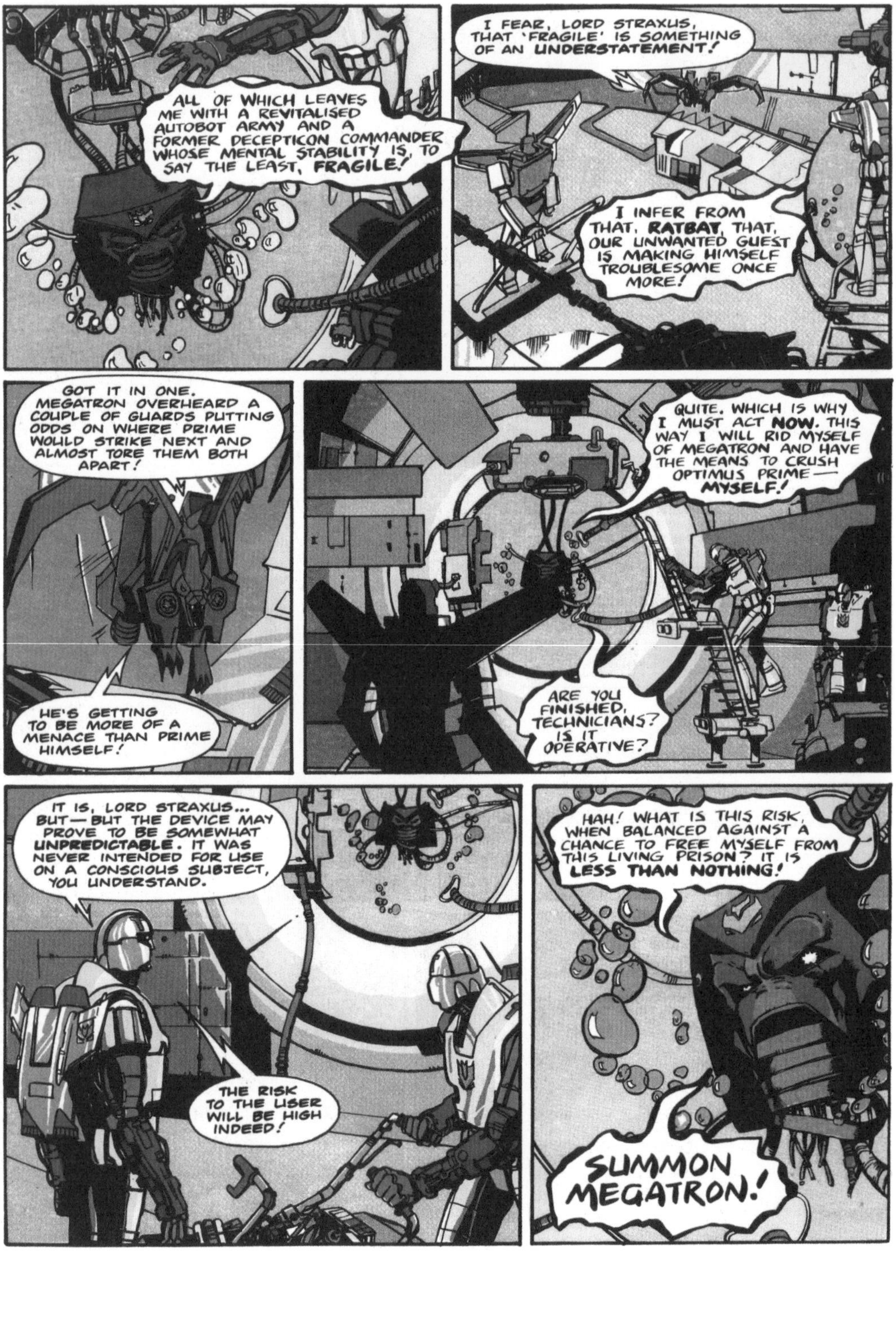
ALL OF WHICH LEAVES ME WITH A REVITALISED AUTOBOT ARMY AND A FORMER DECEPTICON COMMANDER WHOSE MENTAL STABILITY IS, TO SAY THE LEAST, FRAGILE!
I FEAR, LORD STRAXUS, THAT 'FRAGILE' IS SOMETHING OF AN UNDERSTATEMENT!
I INFER FROM THAT, RATBAT, THAT, OUR UNWANTED GUEST IS MAKING HIMSELF TROUBLESOME ONCE MORE!
GOT IT IN ONE. MEGATRON OVERHEARD A COUPLE OF GUARDS PUTTING ODDS ON WHERE PRIME WOULD STRIKE NEXT AND ALMOST TORE THEM BOTH APART!
HE'S GETTING TO BE MORE OF A MENACE THAN PRIME HIMSELF!
QUITE. WHICH IS WHY I MUST ACT NOW. THIS WAY I WILL RID MYSELF OF MEGATRON AND HAVE THE MEANS TO CRUSH OPTIMUS PRIME— MYSELF!
ARE YOU FINISHED, TECHNICIANS? IS IT OPERATIVE?
IT IS, LORD STRAXUS... BUT—BUT THE DEVICE MAY PROVE TO BE SOMEWHAT UNPREDICTABLE. IT WAS NEVER INTENDED FOR USE ON A CONSCIOUS SUBJECT, YOU UNDERSTAND.
THE RISK TO THE USER WILL BE HIGH INDEED!
HAH! WHAT IS THIS RISK, WHEN BALANCED AGAINST A CHANCE TO FREE MYSELF FROM THIS LIVING PRISON? IT IS LESS THAN NOTHING!
SUMMON MEGATRON!

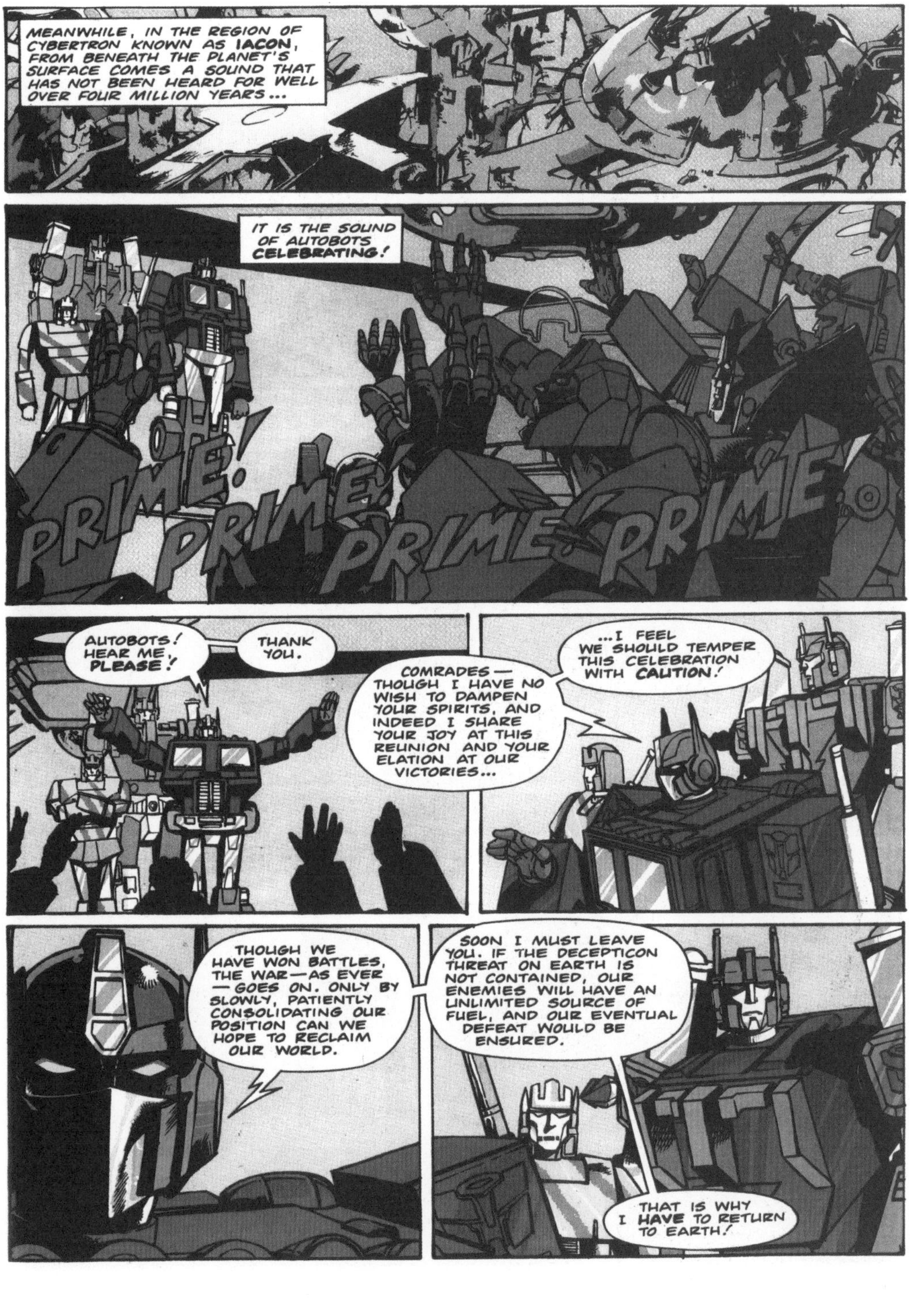
MEANWHILE, IN THE REGION OF CYBERTRON KNOWN AS IACON, FROM BENEATH THE PLANET'S SURFACE COMES A SOUND THAT HAS NOT BEEN HEARD FOR WELL OVER FOUR MILLION YEARS...
IT IS THE SOUND OF AUTOBOTS CELEBRATING!
PRIME! PRIME! PRIME! PRIME
AUTOBOTS! HEAR ME, PLEASE!
THANK YOU.
COMRADES— THOUGH I HAVE NO WISH TO DAMPEN YOUR SPIRITS, AND INDEED I SHARE YOUR JOY AT THIS REUNION AND YOUR ELATION AT OUR VICTORIES...
...I FEEL WE SHOULD TEMPER THIS CELEBRATION WITH CAUTION!
THOUGH WE HAVE WON BATTLES, THE WAR—AS EVER —GOES ON. ONLY BY SLOWLY, PATIENTLY CONSOLIDATING OUR POSITION CAN WE HOPE TO RECLAIM OUR WORLD.
SOON I MUST LEAVE YOU. IF THE DECEPTICON THREAT ON EARTH IS NOT CONTAINED, OUR ENEMIES WILL HAVE AN UNLIMITED SOURCE OF FUEL, AND OUR EVENTUAL DEFEAT WOULD BE ENSURED.
THAT IS WHY I HAVE TO RETURN TO EARTH!

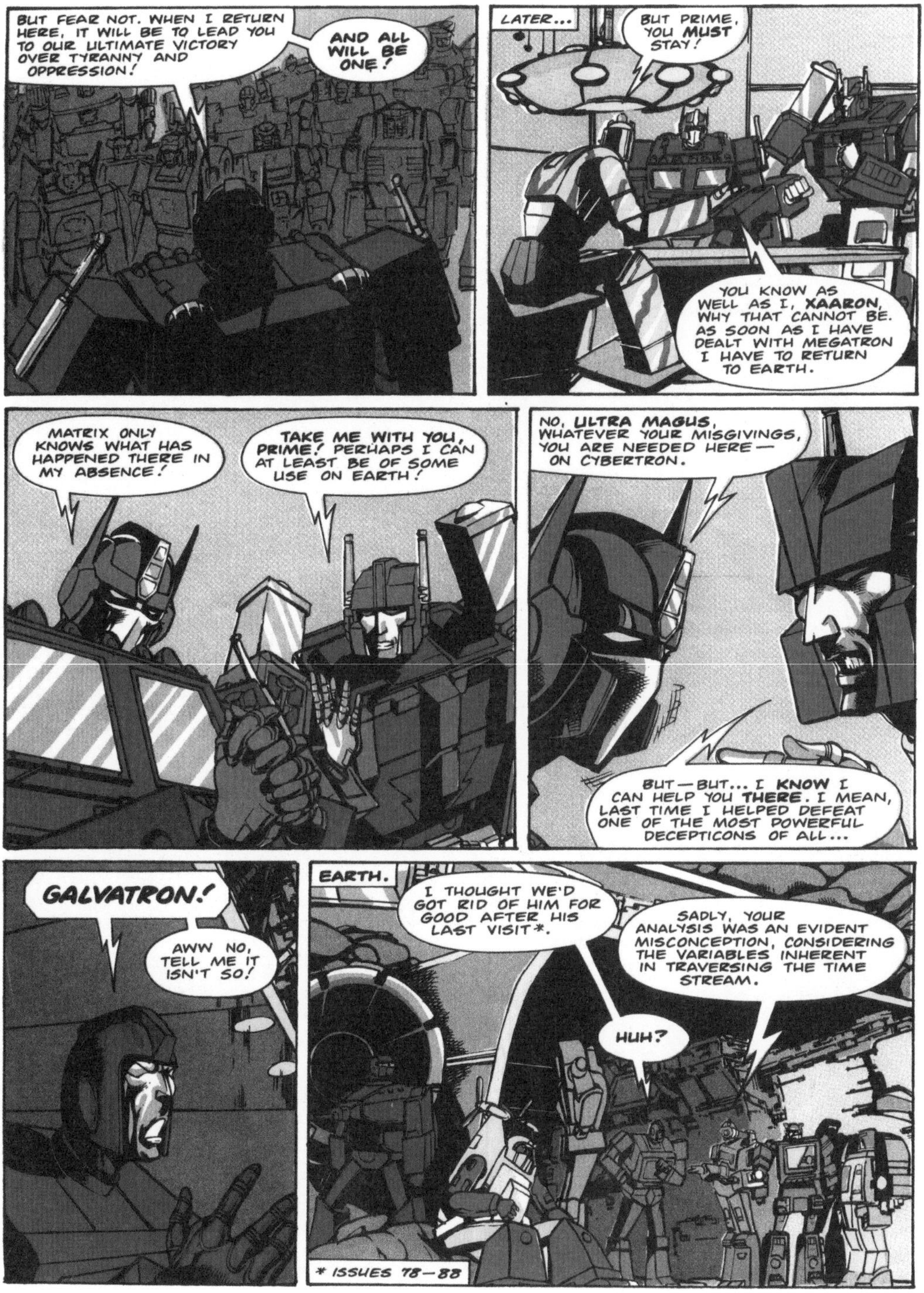
BUT FEAR NOT. WHEN I RETURN HERE, IT WILL BE TO LEAD YOU TO OUR ULTIMATE VICTORY OVER TYRANNY AND OPPRESSION!
AND ALL WILL BE ONE!
LATER...
BUT PRIME, YOU MUST STAY!
YOU KNOW AS WELL AS I, XAARON, WHY THAT CANNOT BE. AS SOON AS I HAVE DEALT WITH MEGATRON I HAVE TO RETURN TO EARTH.
MATRIX ONLY KNOWS WHAT HAS HAPPENED THERE IN MY ABSENCE!
TAKE ME WITH YOU, PRIME! PERHAPS I CAN AT LEAST BE OF SOME USE ON EARTH!
NO, ULTRA MAGUS, WHATEVER YOUR MISGIVINGS, YOU ARE NEEDED HERE — ON CYBERTRON.
BUT — BUT... I KNOW I CAN HELP YOU THERE. I MEAN, LAST TIME I HELPED DEFEAT ONE OF THE MOST POWERFUL DECEPTICONS OF ALL...
GALVATRON!
AWW NO, TELL ME IT ISN'T SO!
EARTH.
I THOUGHT WE'D GOT RID OF HIM FOR GOOD AFTER HIS LAST VISIT*.
SADLY, YOUR ANALYSIS WAS AN EVIDENT MISCONCEPTION, CONSIDERING THE VARIABLES INHERENT IN TRAVERSING THE TIME STREAM.
HUH?
* ISSUES 78—88

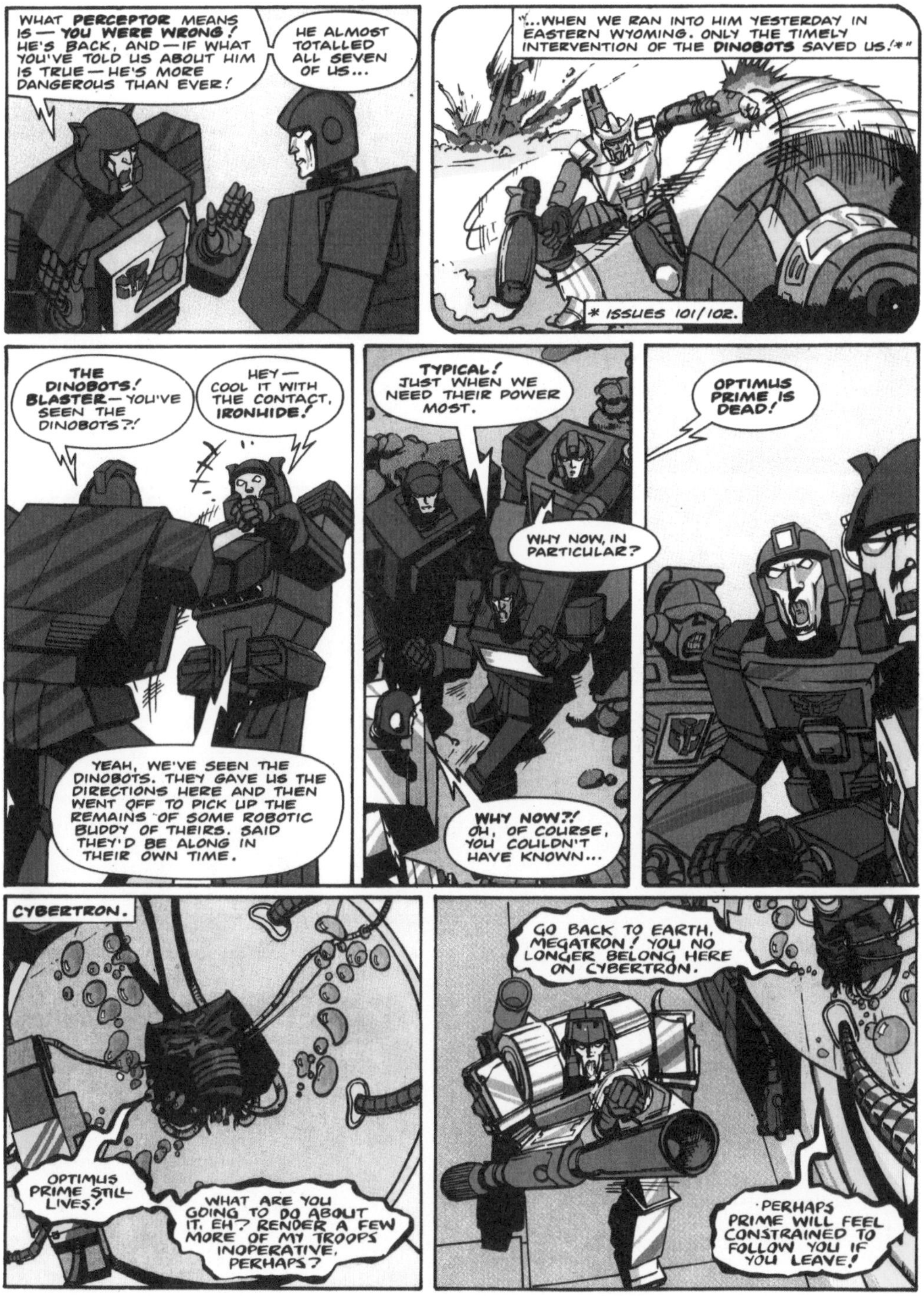

WHAT PERCEPTOR MEANS IS — YOU WERE WRONG! HE'S BACK, AND — IF WHAT YOU'VE TOLD US ABOUT HIM IS TRUE — HE'S MORE DANGEROUS THAN EVER!
HE ALMOST TOTALLED ALL SEVEN OF US...
"...WHEN WE RAN INTO HIM YESTERDAY IN EASTERN WYOMING. ONLY THE TIMELY INTERVENTION OF THE DINOBOTS SAVED US!*"
* ISSUES 101/102.
THE DINOBOTS! BLASTER — YOU'VE SEEN THE DINOBOTS?!
HEY — COOL IT WITH THE CONTACT, IRONHIDE!
YEAH, WE'VE SEEN THE DINOBOTS. THEY GAVE US THE DIRECTIONS HERE AND THEN WENT OFF TO PICK UP THE REMAINS OF SOME ROBOTIC BUDDY OF THEIRS. SAID THEY'D BE ALONG IN THEIR OWN TIME.
TYPICAL! JUST WHEN WE NEED THEIR POWER MOST.
WHY NOW, IN PARTICULAR?
WHY NOW?! OH, OF COURSE, YOU COULDN'T HAVE KNOWN...
OPTIMUS PRIME IS DEAD!
CYBERTRON.
OPTIMUS PRIME STILL LIVES!
WHAT ARE YOU GOING TO DO ABOUT IT, EH? RENDER A FEW MORE OF MY TROOPS INOPERATIVE, PERHAPS?
GO BACK TO EARTH, MEGATRON! YOU NO LONGER BELONG HERE ON CYBERTRON.
PERHAPS PRIME WILL FEEL CONSTRAINED TO FOLLOW YOU IF YOU LEAVE!

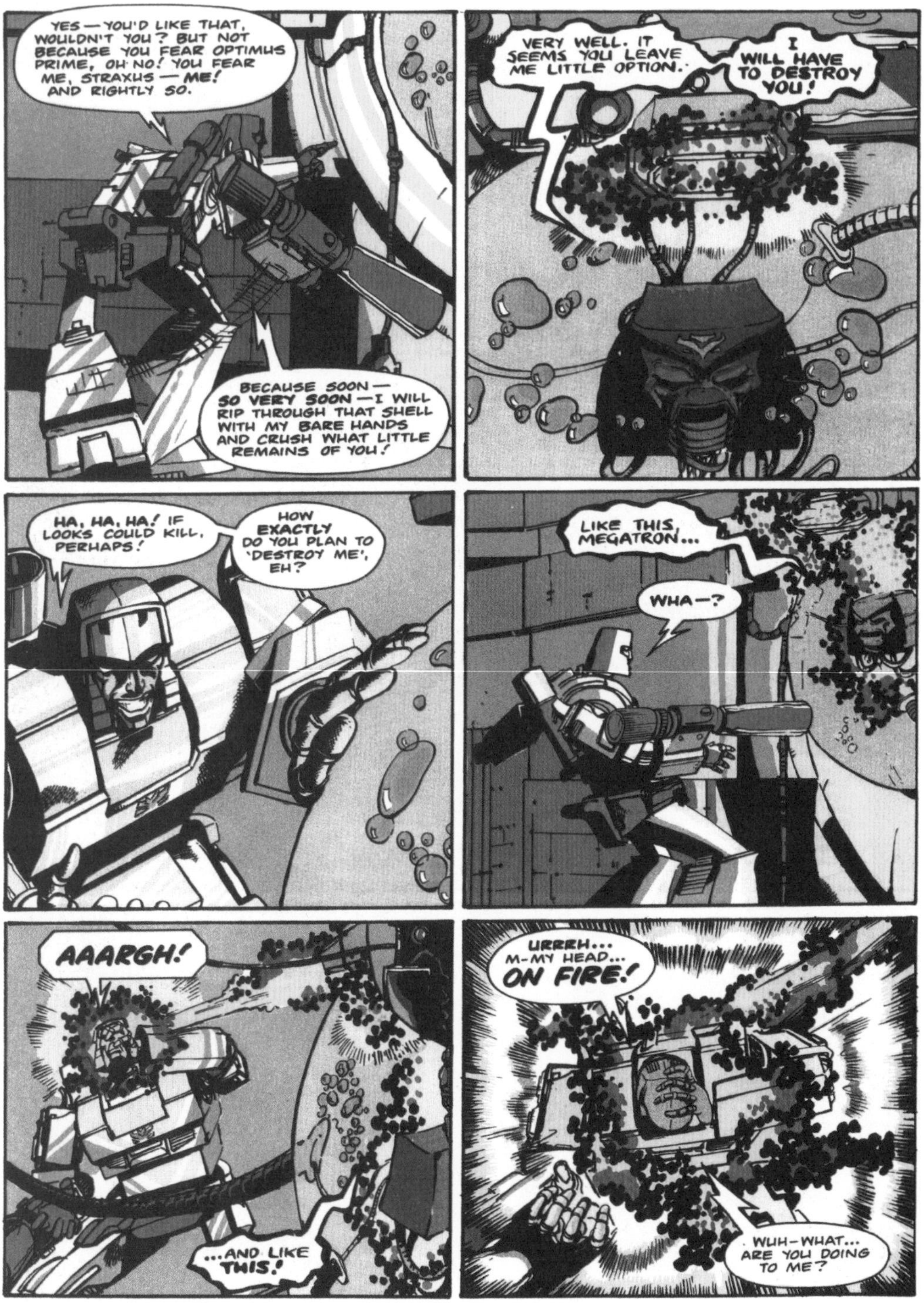

YES — YOU'D LIKE THAT, WOULDN'T YOU? BUT NOT BECAUSE YOU FEAR OPTIMUS PRIME, OH NO! YOU FEAR ME, STRAXUS — ME! AND RIGHTLY SO.
BECAUSE SOON — SO VERY SOON — I WILL RIP THROUGH THAT SHELL WITH MY BARE HANDS AND CRUSH WHAT LITTLE REMAINS OF YOU!
VERY WELL. IT SEEMS YOU LEAVE ME LITTLE OPTION.
I WILL HAVE TO DESTROY YOU!
HA, HA, HA! IF LOOKS COULD KILL, PERHAPS!
HOW EXACTLY DO YOU PLAN TO 'DESTROY ME', EH?
LIKE THIS, MEGATRON...
WHA—?
AAARGH!
...AND LIKE THIS!
URRRH... M-MY HEAD... ON FIRE!
WUH-WHAT... ARE YOU DOING TO ME?

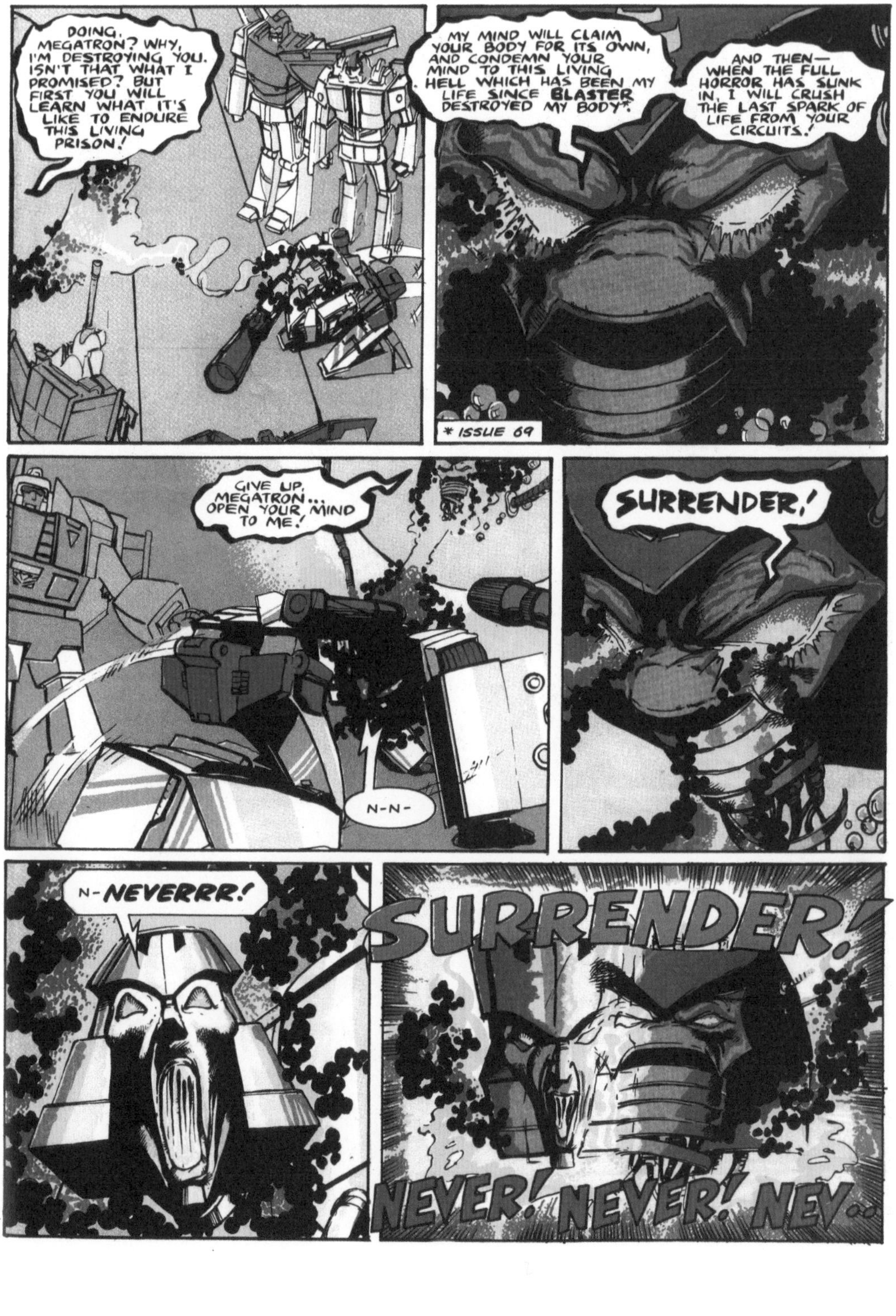
DOING, MEGATRON? WHY, I'M DESTROYING YOU. ISN'T THAT WHAT I PROMISED? BUT FIRST YOU WILL LEARN WHAT IT'S LIKE TO ENDURE THIS LIVING PRISON!
MY MIND WILL CLAIM YOUR BODY FOR ITS OWN, AND CONDEMN YOUR MIND TO THIS LIVING HELL WHICH HAS BEEN MY LIFE SINCE BLASTER DESTROYED MY BODY*.
AND THEN— WHEN THE FULL HORROR HAS SUNK IN, I WILL CRUSH THE LAST SPARK OF LIFE FROM YOUR CIRCUITS!
* ISSUE 69
GIVE UP, MEGATRON... OPEN YOUR MIND TO ME!
N-N-
SURRENDER!
N-NEVERRR!
SURRENDER!
NEVER! NEVER! NEV...

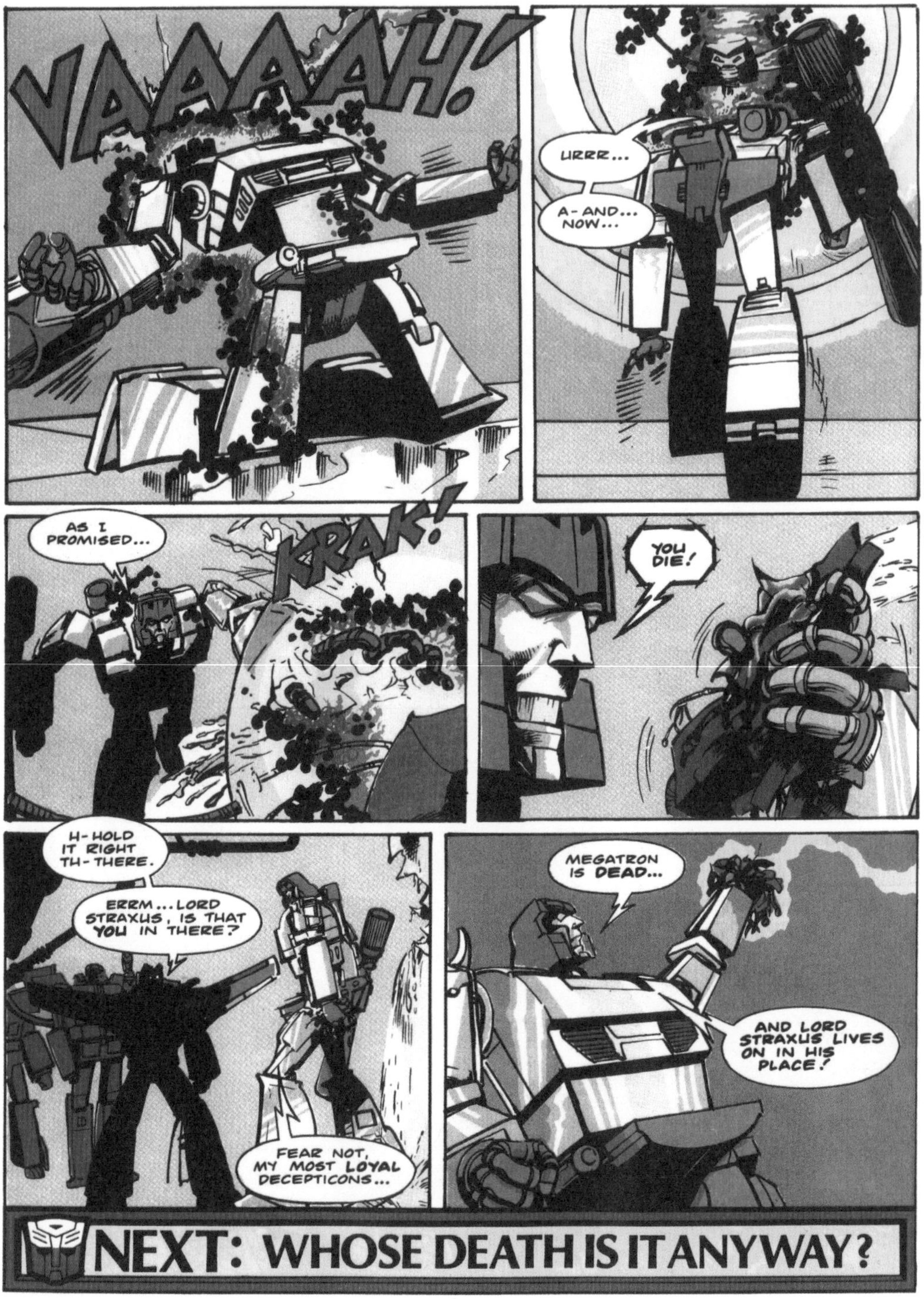
VAAAAH!
URRR...
A-AND... NOW...
AS I PROMISED...
KRAK!
YOU DIE!
H-HOLD IT RIGHT TH-THERE.
ERRM...LORD STRAXUS, IS THAT YOU IN THERE?
FEAR NOT, MY MOST LOYAL DECEPTICONS...
MEGATRON IS DEAD...
AND LORD STRAXUS LIVES ON IN HIS PLACE!
NEXT: WHOSE DEATH IS IT ANYWAY?

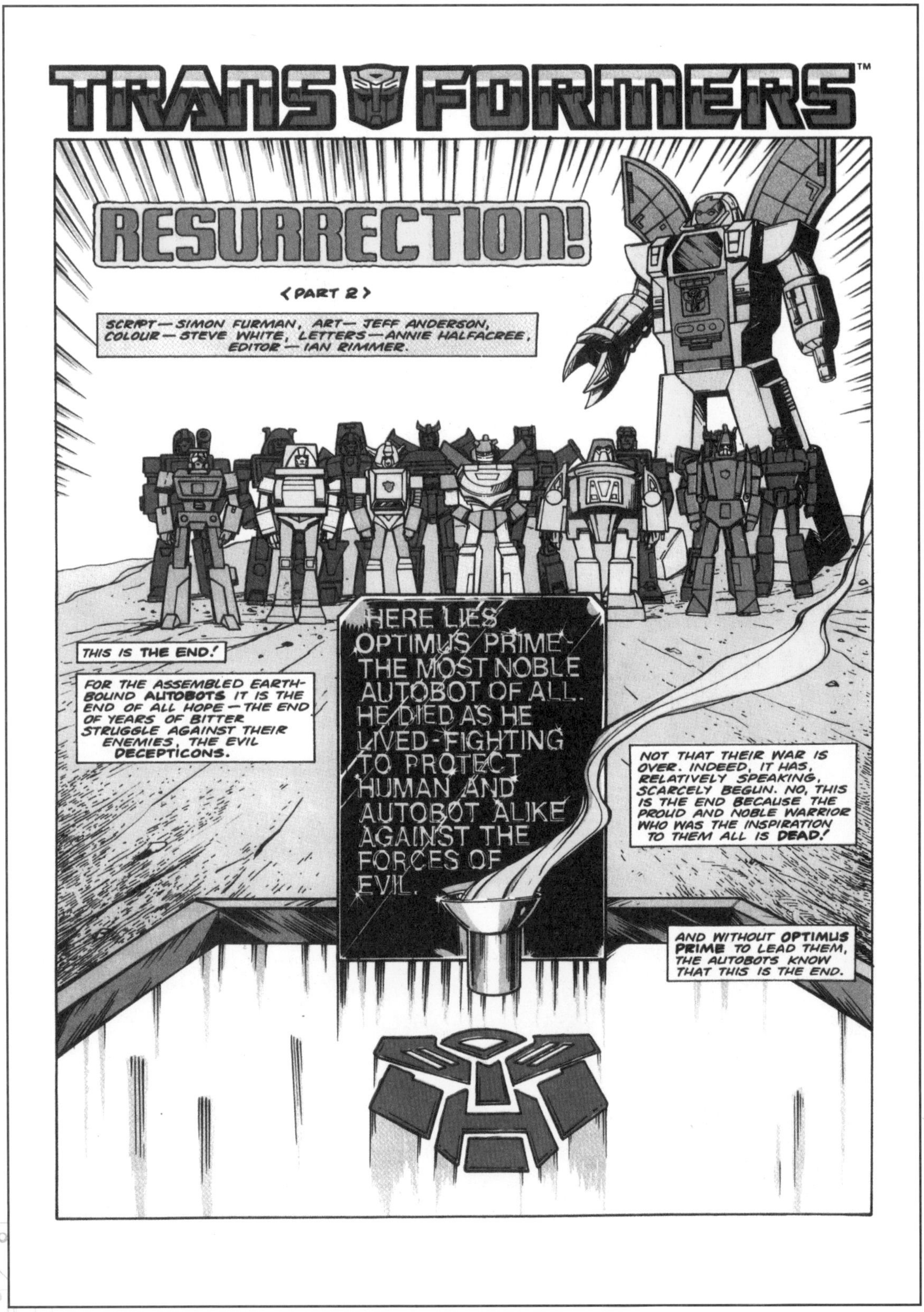
TRANSFORMERS™
RESURRECTION!
‹PART 2›
SCRIPT—SIMON FURMAN, ART—JEFF ANDERSON, COLOUR—STEVE WHITE, LETTERS—ANNIE HALFACREE, EDITOR—IAN RIMMER.
THIS IS THE END!
FOR THE ASSEMBLED EARTH-BOUND AUTOBOTS IT IS THE END OF ALL HOPE—THE END OF YEARS OF BITTER STRUGGLE AGAINST THEIR ENEMIES, THE EVIL DECEPTICONS.
HERE LIES OPTIMUS PRIME - THE MOST NOBLE AUTOBOT OF ALL. HE DIED AS HE LIVED - FIGHTING TO PROTECT HUMAN AND AUTOBOT ALIKE AGAINST THE FORCES OF EVIL.
NOT THAT THEIR WAR IS OVER. INDEED, IT HAS, RELATIVELY SPEAKING, SCARCELY BEGUN. NO, THIS IS THE END BECAUSE THE PROUD AND NOBLE WARRIOR WHO WAS THE INSPIRATION TO THEM ALL IS DEAD!
AND WITHOUT OPTIMUS PRIME TO LEAD THEM, THE AUTOBOTS KNOW THAT THIS IS THE END.

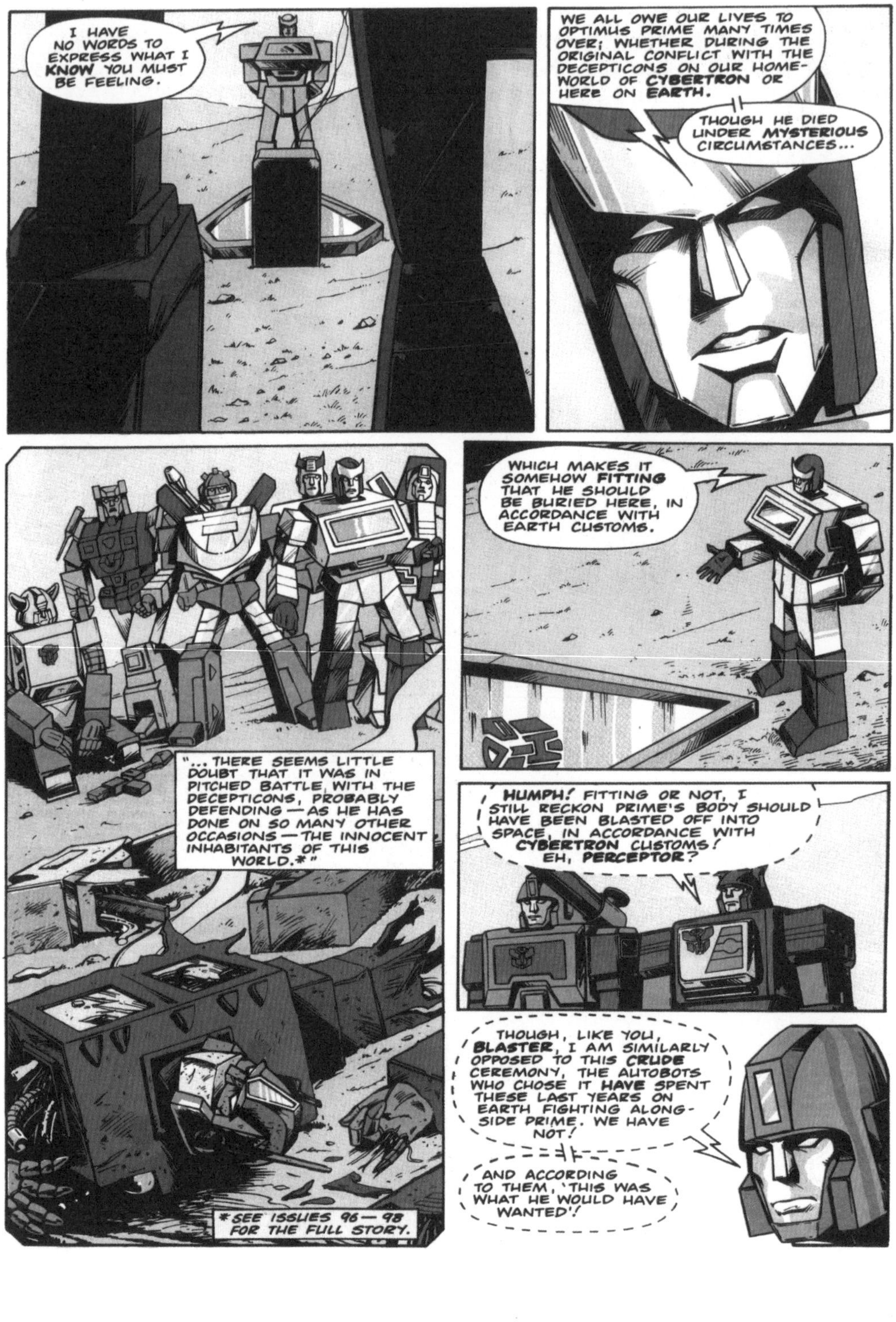

I HAVE NO WORDS TO EXPRESS WHAT I KNOW YOU MUST BE FEELING.
WE ALL OWE OUR LIVES TO OPTIMUS PRIME MANY TIMES OVER; WHETHER DURING THE ORIGINAL CONFLICT WITH THE DECEPTICONS ON OUR HOME-WORLD OF CYBERTRON OR HERE ON EARTH.
THOUGH HE DIED UNDER MYSTERIOUS CIRCUMSTANCES...
"...THERE SEEMS LITTLE DOUBT THAT IT WAS IN PITCHED BATTLE WITH THE DECEPTICONS, PROBABLY DEFENDING—AS HE HAS DONE ON SO MANY OTHER OCCASIONS—THE INNOCENT INHABITANTS OF THIS WORLD.*"
*SEE ISSUES 96—98 FOR THE FULL STORY.
WHICH MAKES IT SOMEHOW FITTING THAT HE SHOULD BE BURIED HERE, IN ACCORDANCE WITH EARTH CUSTOMS.
HUMPH! FITTING OR NOT, I STILL RECKON PRIME'S BODY SHOULD HAVE BEEN BLASTED OFF INTO SPACE, IN ACCORDANCE WITH CYBERTRON CUSTOMS! EH, PERCEPTOR?
THOUGH, LIKE YOU, BLASTER, I AM SIMILARLY OPPOSED TO THIS CRUDE CEREMONY, THE AUTOBOTS WHO CHOSE IT HAVE SPENT THESE LAST YEARS ON EARTH FIGHTING ALONG-SIDE PRIME. WE HAVE NOT!
AND ACCORDING TO THEM, 'THIS WAS WHAT HE WOULD HAVE WANTED'!

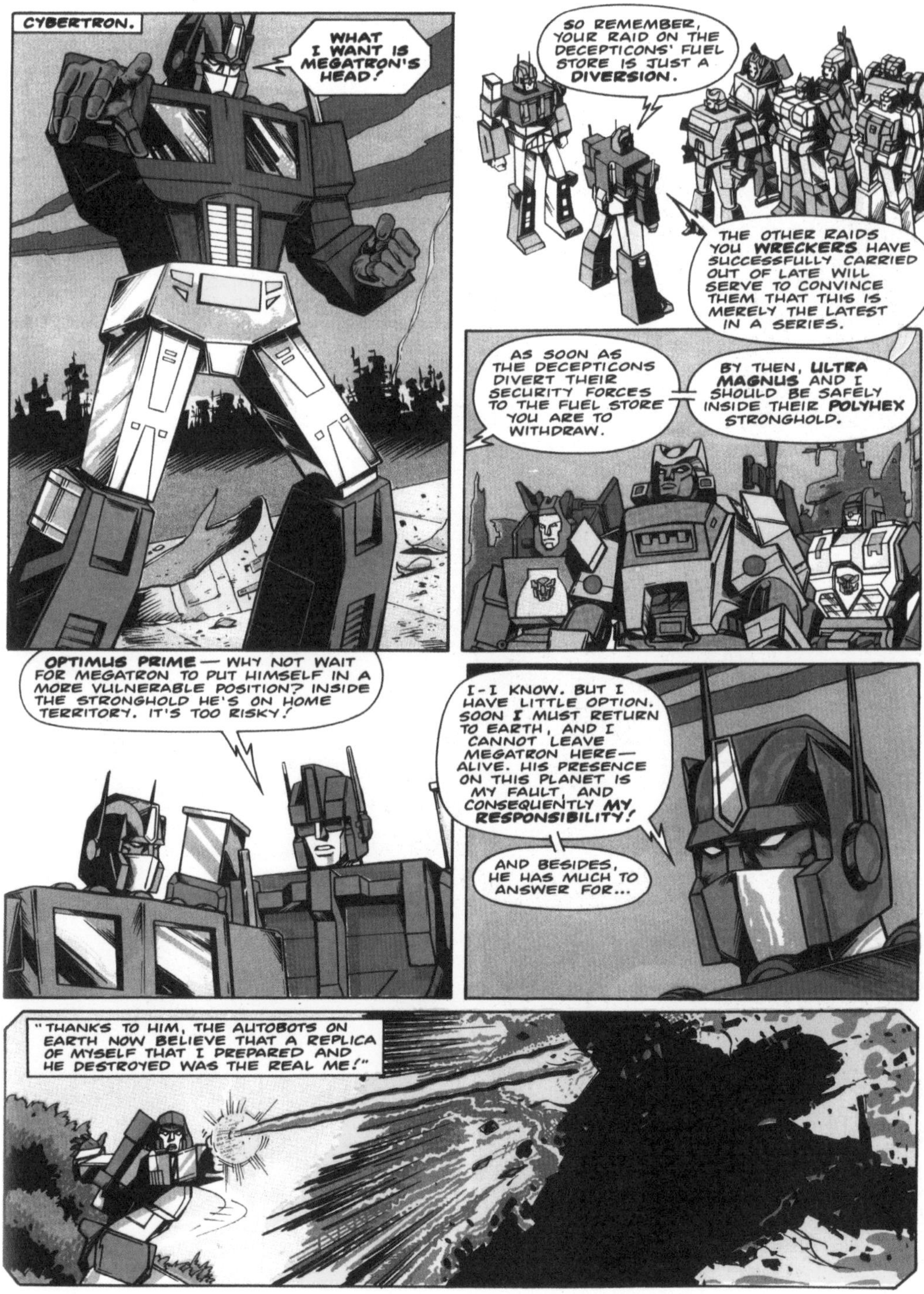
CYBERTRON.
WHAT I WANT IS MEGATRON'S HEAD!
SO REMEMBER, YOUR RAID ON THE DECEPTICONS' FUEL STORE IS JUST A DIVERSION.
THE OTHER RAIDS YOU WRECKERS HAVE SUCCESSFULLY CARRIED OUT OF LATE WILL SERVE TO CONVINCE THEM THAT THIS IS MERELY THE LATEST IN A SERIES.
AS SOON AS THE DECEPTICONS DIVERT THEIR SECURITY FORCES TO THE FUEL STORE YOU ARE TO WITHDRAW.
BY THEN, ULTRA MAGNUS AND I SHOULD BE SAFELY INSIDE THEIR POLYHEX STRONGHOLD.
OPTIMUS PRIME— WHY NOT WAIT FOR MEGATRON TO PUT HIMSELF IN A MORE VULNERABLE POSITION? INSIDE THE STRONGHOLD HE'S ON HOME TERRITORY. IT'S TOO RISKY!
I-I KNOW. BUT I HAVE LITTLE OPTION. SOON I MUST RETURN TO EARTH, AND I CANNOT LEAVE MEGATRON HERE— ALIVE. HIS PRESENCE ON THIS PLANET IS MY FAULT, AND CONSEQUENTLY MY RESPONSIBILITY!
AND BESIDES, HE HAS MUCH TO ANSWER FOR...
"THANKS TO HIM, THE AUTOBOTS ON EARTH NOW BELIEVE THAT A REPLICA OF MYSELF THAT I PREPARED AND HE DESTROYED WAS THE REAL ME!"

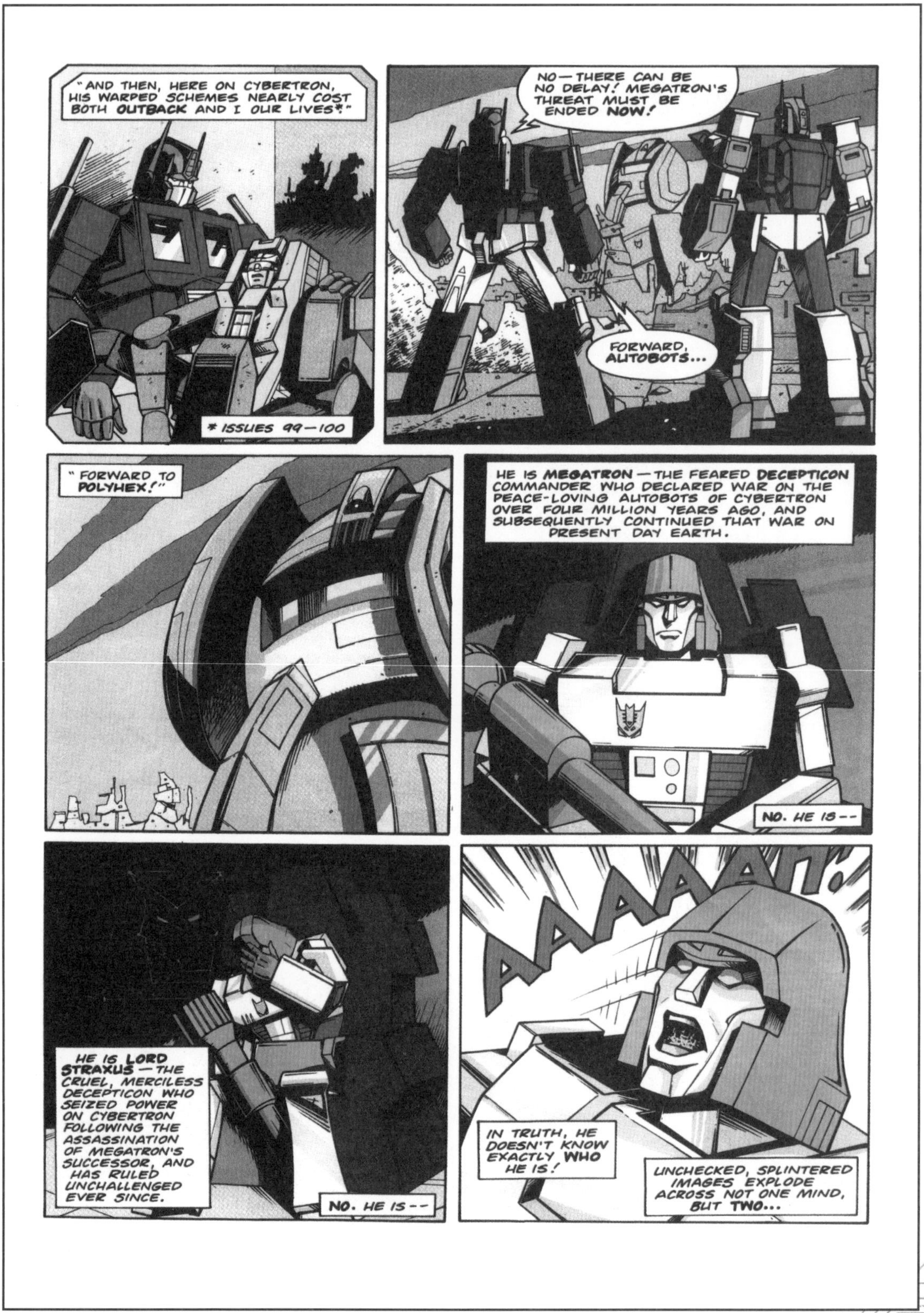
"AND THEN, HERE ON CYBERTRON, HIS WARPED SCHEMES NEARLY COST BOTH OUTBACK AND I OUR LIVES*."
* ISSUES 99—100
NO—THERE CAN BE NO DELAY! MEGATRON'S THREAT MUST BE ENDED NOW!
FORWARD, AUTOBOTS...
"FORWARD TO POLYHEX!"
HE IS MEGATRON—THE FEARED DECEPTICON COMMANDER WHO DECLARED WAR ON THE PEACE-LOVING AUTOBOTS OF CYBERTRON OVER FOUR MILLION YEARS AGO, AND SUBSEQUENTLY CONTINUED THAT WAR ON PRESENT DAY EARTH.
NO. HE IS--
HE IS LORD STRAXUS—THE CRUEL, MERCILESS DECEPTICON WHO SEIZED POWER ON CYBERTRON FOLLOWING THE ASSASSINATION OF MEGATRON'S SUCCESSOR, AND HAS RULED UNCHALLENGED EVER SINCE.
NO. HE IS--
AAAAAAH!
IN TRUTH, HE DOESN'T KNOW EXACTLY WHO HE IS!
UNCHECKED, SPLINTERED IMAGES EXPLODE ACROSS NOT ONE MIND, BUT TWO...

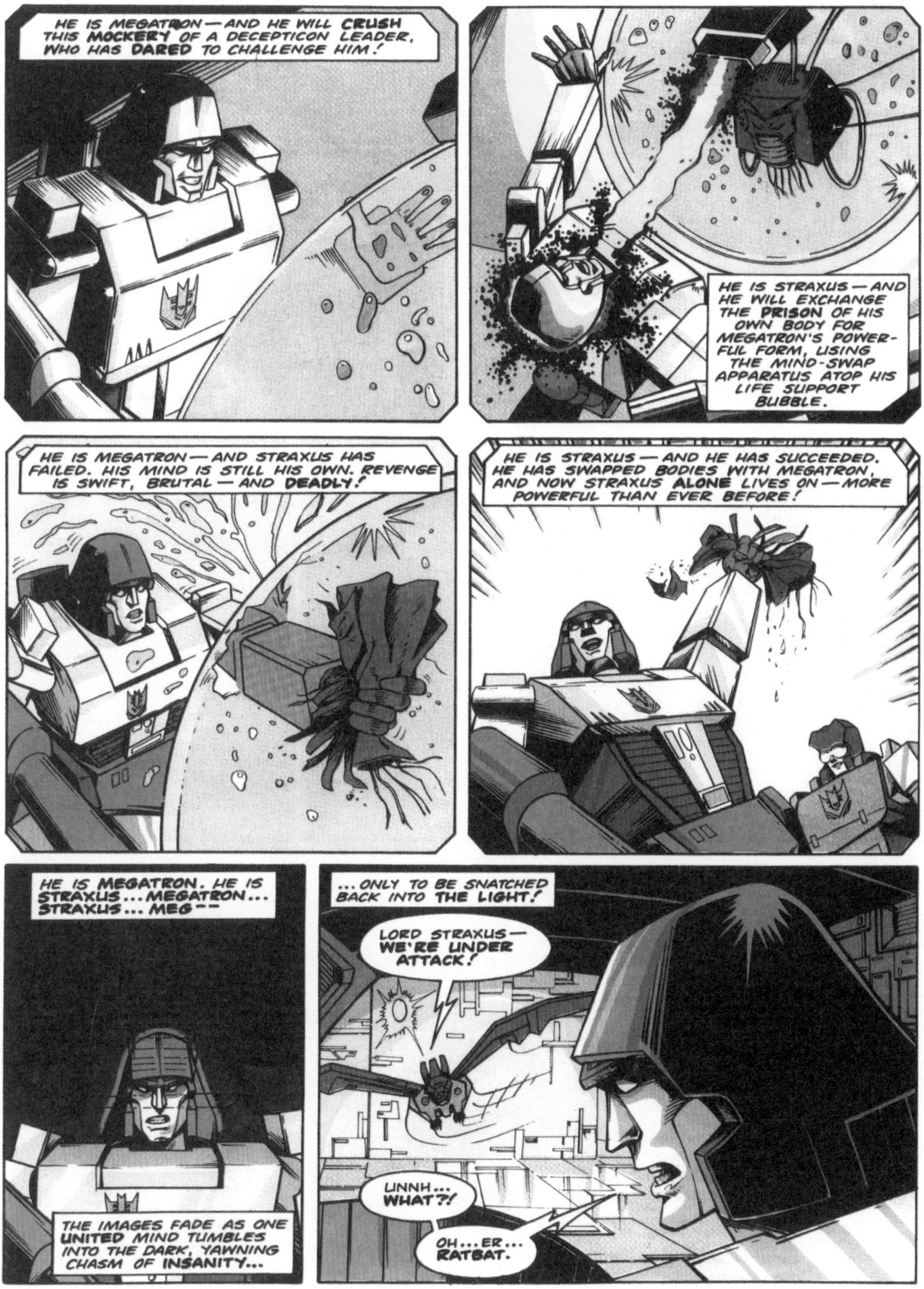
HE IS MEGATRON — AND HE WILL CRUSH THIS MOCKERY OF A DECEPTICON LEADER, WHO HAS DARED TO CHALLENGE HIM!
HE IS STRAXUS — AND HE WILL EXCHANGE THE PRISON OF HIS OWN BODY FOR MEGATRON'S POWERFUL FORM, USING THE MIND-SWAP APPARATUS ATOP HIS LIFE SUPPORT BUBBLE.
HE IS MEGATRON — AND STRAXUS HAS FAILED. HIS MIND IS STILL HIS OWN. REVENGE IS SWIFT, BRUTAL — AND DEADLY!
HE IS STRAXUS — AND HE HAS SUCCEEDED. HE HAS SWAPPED BODIES WITH MEGATRON, AND NOW STRAXUS ALONE LIVES ON — MORE POWERFUL THAN EVER BEFORE!
HE IS MEGATRON. HE IS STRAXUS... MEGATRON... STRAXUS... MEG--
THE IMAGES FADE AS ONE UNITED MIND TUMBLES INTO THE DARK, YAWNING CHASM OF INSANITY...
...ONLY TO BE SNATCHED BACK INTO THE LIGHT!
LORD STRAXUS — WE'RE UNDER ATTACK!
UNNH... WHAT?!
OH... ER... RATBAT.

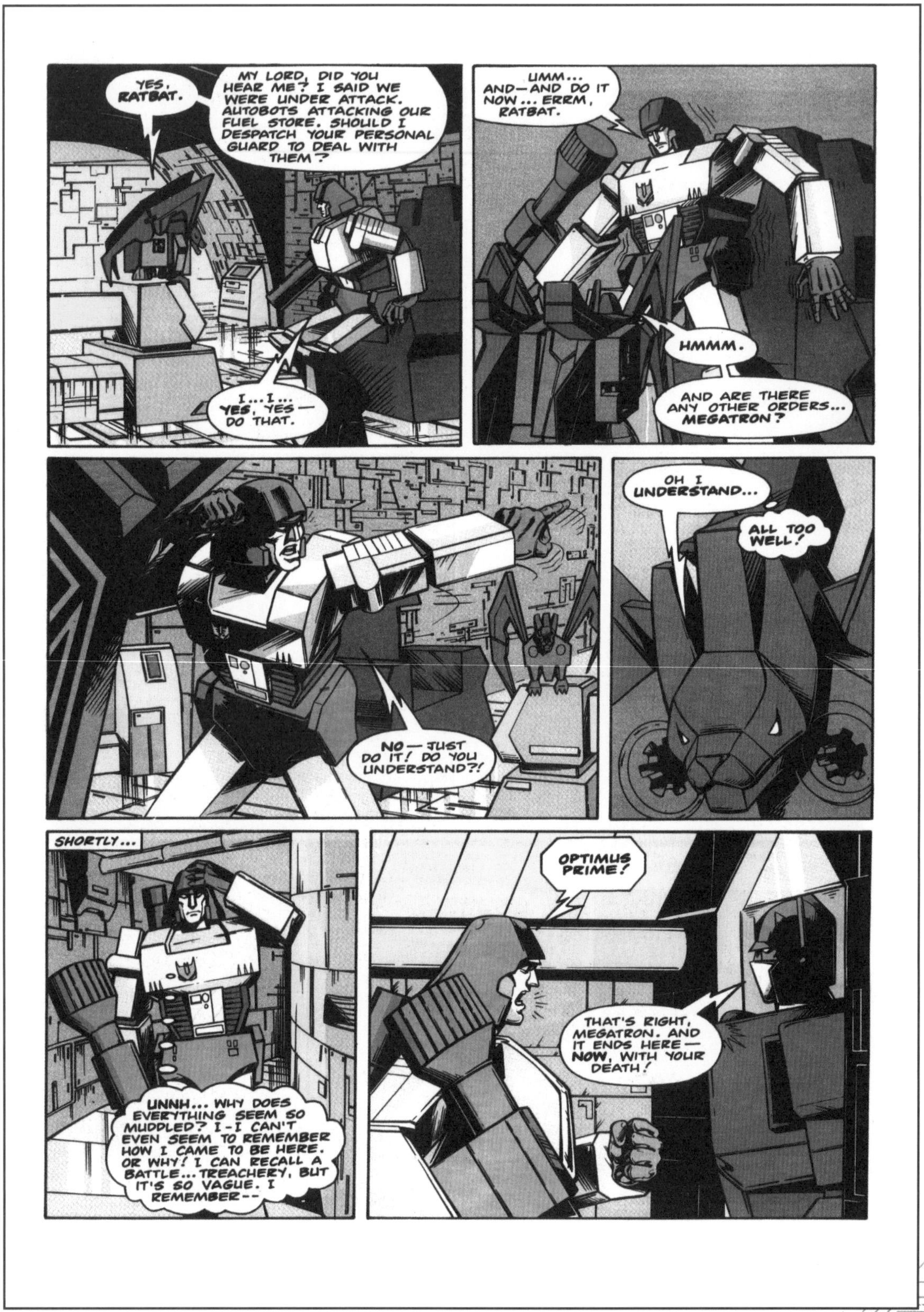
YES, RATBAT.
MY LORD, DID YOU HEAR ME? I SAID WE WERE UNDER ATTACK. AUTOBOTS ATTACKING OUR FUEL STORE. SHOULD I DESPATCH YOUR PERSONAL GUARD TO DEAL WITH THEM?
I... I... YES, YES— DO THAT.
UMM... AND—AND DO IT NOW... ERRM, RATBAT.
HMMM.
AND ARE THERE ANY OTHER ORDERS... MEGATRON?
NO— JUST DO IT! DO YOU UNDERSTAND?!
OH I UNDERSTAND...
ALL TOO WELL!
SHORTLY...
UNNH... WHY DOES EVERYTHING SEEM SO MUDDLED? I-I CAN'T EVEN SEEM TO REMEMBER HOW I CAME TO BE HERE. OR WHY! I CAN RECALL A BATTLE... TREACHERY, BUT IT'S SO VAGUE. I REMEMBER--
OPTIMUS PRIME!
THAT'S RIGHT, MEGATRON. AND IT ENDS HERE— NOW, WITH YOUR DEATH!

HOW TRUE, BUT IT IS YOU WHO WILL FALL, OPTIMUS PRIME!

SOMEHOW, DECEPTICON...

THAM!

I DON'T THINK SO!

GHAAA!

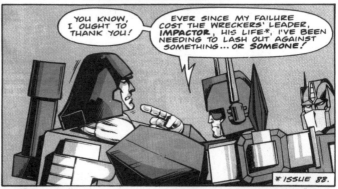

YOU KNOW, I OUGHT TO THANK YOU!

EVER SINCE MY FAILURE COST THE WRECKERS' LEADER, IMPACTOR*, HIS LIFE*, I'VE BEEN NEEDING TO LASH OUT AGAINST SOMETHING...OR SOMEONE!

* ISSUE 88.

KRANK!

THE DESIRE TO RIGHT MY 'WRONG' WAS CAUSING ME TO MAKE GRIEVOUS ERRORS OF JUDGEMENT — ONE OF WHICH ALMOST RESULTED IN PRIME'S EXECUTION!*

* ISSUE 99.

BUT NOW — THANKS TO YOU, AND TO PRIME FOR LETTING ME HAVE FIRST CRACK AT YOU — I CAN GET IT ALL OUT OF MY SYSTEM...

AND DO TWO WORLDS A SERVICE...

BY DESTROYING MEGATRON!

CHANG!

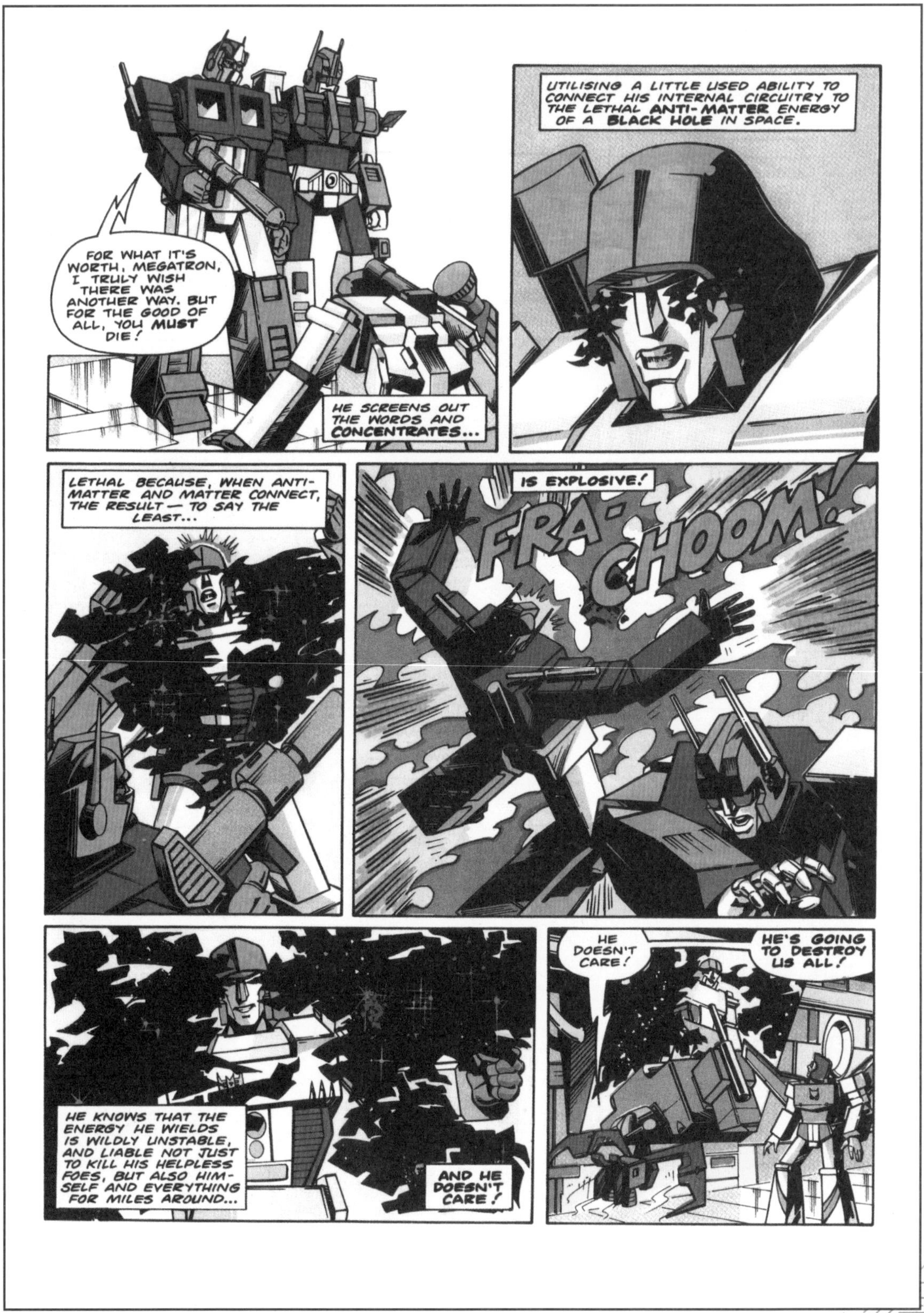

FOR WHAT IT'S WORTH, MEGATRON, I TRULY WISH THERE WAS ANOTHER WAY. BUT FOR THE GOOD OF ALL, YOU MUST DIE!
HE SCREENS OUT THE WORDS AND CONCENTRATES...
UTILISING A LITTLE USED ABILITY TO CONNECT HIS INTERNAL CIRCUITRY TO THE LETHAL ANTI-MATTER ENERGY OF A BLACK HOLE IN SPACE.
LETHAL BECAUSE, WHEN ANTI-MATTER AND MATTER CONNECT, THE RESULT — TO SAY THE LEAST...
IS EXPLOSIVE!
FRA-CHOOM!
HE KNOWS THAT THE ENERGY HE WIELDS IS WILDLY UNSTABLE, AND LIABLE NOT JUST TO KILL HIS HELPLESS FOES, BUT ALSO HIMSELF AND EVERYTHING FOR MILES AROUND...
AND HE DOESN'T CARE!
HE DOESN'T CARE!
HE'S GOING TO DESTROY US ALL!

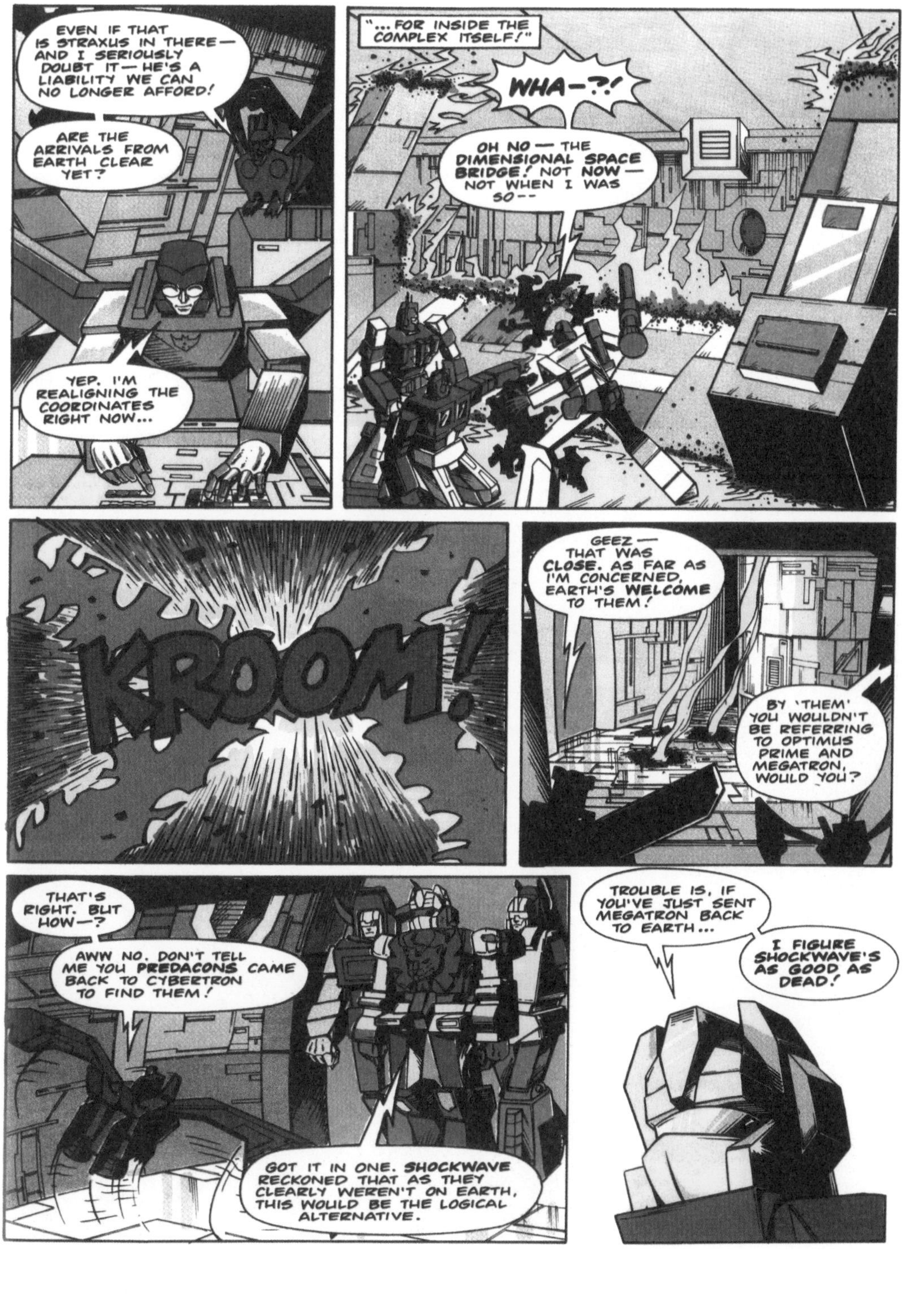
EVEN IF THAT IS STRAXUS IN THERE— AND I SERIOUSLY DOUBT IT—HE'S A LIABILITY WE CAN NO LONGER AFFORD!
ARE THE ARRIVALS FROM EARTH CLEAR YET?
YEP. I'M REALIGNING THE COORDINATES RIGHT NOW...
"...FOR INSIDE THE COMPLEX ITSELF!"
WHA-?!
OH NO—THE DIMENSIONAL SPACE BRIDGE! NOT NOW—NOT WHEN I WAS SO--
KROOM!
GEEZ—THAT WAS CLOSE. AS FAR AS I'M CONCERNED, EARTH'S WELCOME TO THEM!
BY 'THEM' YOU WOULDN'T BE REFERRING TO OPTIMUS PRIME AND MEGATRON, WOULD YOU?
THAT'S RIGHT. BUT HOW—?
AWW NO. DON'T TELL ME YOU PREDACONS CAME BACK TO CYBERTRON TO FIND THEM!
GOT IT IN ONE. SHOCKWAVE RECKONED THAT AS THEY CLEARLY WEREN'T ON EARTH, THIS WOULD BE THE LOGICAL ALTERNATIVE.
TROUBLE IS, IF YOU'VE JUST SENT MEGATRON BACK TO EARTH...
I FIGURE SHOCKWAVE'S AS GOOD AS DEAD!

EARTH — THE DECEPTICONS' COAL MINE BASE.

TH- THERE WAS THIS BLINDING FLASH... AND THEN... WELL, HE WAS JUST *THERE.* HE --

SILENCE, FRENZY!

GREETINGS, MEGATRON. I KNOW I CAN EXPECT NO MERCY FOR...FOR--

FOR *WHAT?!* FOR ACCOMPLISHING NEXT TO NOTHING IN MY ABSENCE? IT SEEMS I CANNOT ENTRUST EVEN THE SIMPLEST TASK TO YOU, *SHOCKWAVE?*

RETURN TO YOUR DUTIES, I WILL DEAL WITH THE AUTOBOTS — *MY WAY!*

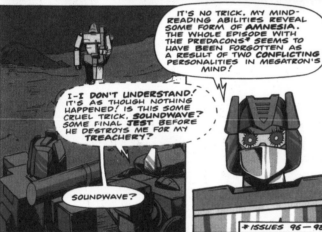

IT'S NO TRICK. MY MIND-READING ABILITIES REVEAL SOME FORM OF AMNESIA. THE WHOLE EPISODE WITH THE PREDACONS* SEEMS TO HAVE BEEN FORGOTTEN AS A RESULT OF TWO *CONFLICTING* PERSONALITIES IN MEGATRON'S MIND!

I-I DON'T UNDERSTAND! IT'S AS THOUGH NOTHING HAPPENED! IS THIS SOME CRUEL TRICK, SOUNDWAVE? SOME FINAL *JEST* BEFORE HE DESTROYS ME FOR MY TREACHERY?

SOUNDWAVE?

ISSUES 96 — 98

EXCELLENT! IT WAS FORTUITOUS INDEED THAT I SENT THE PREDACONS BACK TO CYBERTRON. IT SEEMS I AM BACK TO SQUARE ONE WITH MEGATRON...

UNTIL NEXT TIME!

ELSEWHERE...

I-I STILL CAN'T BELIEVE IT. HE'S REALLY GONE! I DUNNO, WITHOUT OPTIMUS PRIME THE FUTURE LOOKS...

BRIGHT?!

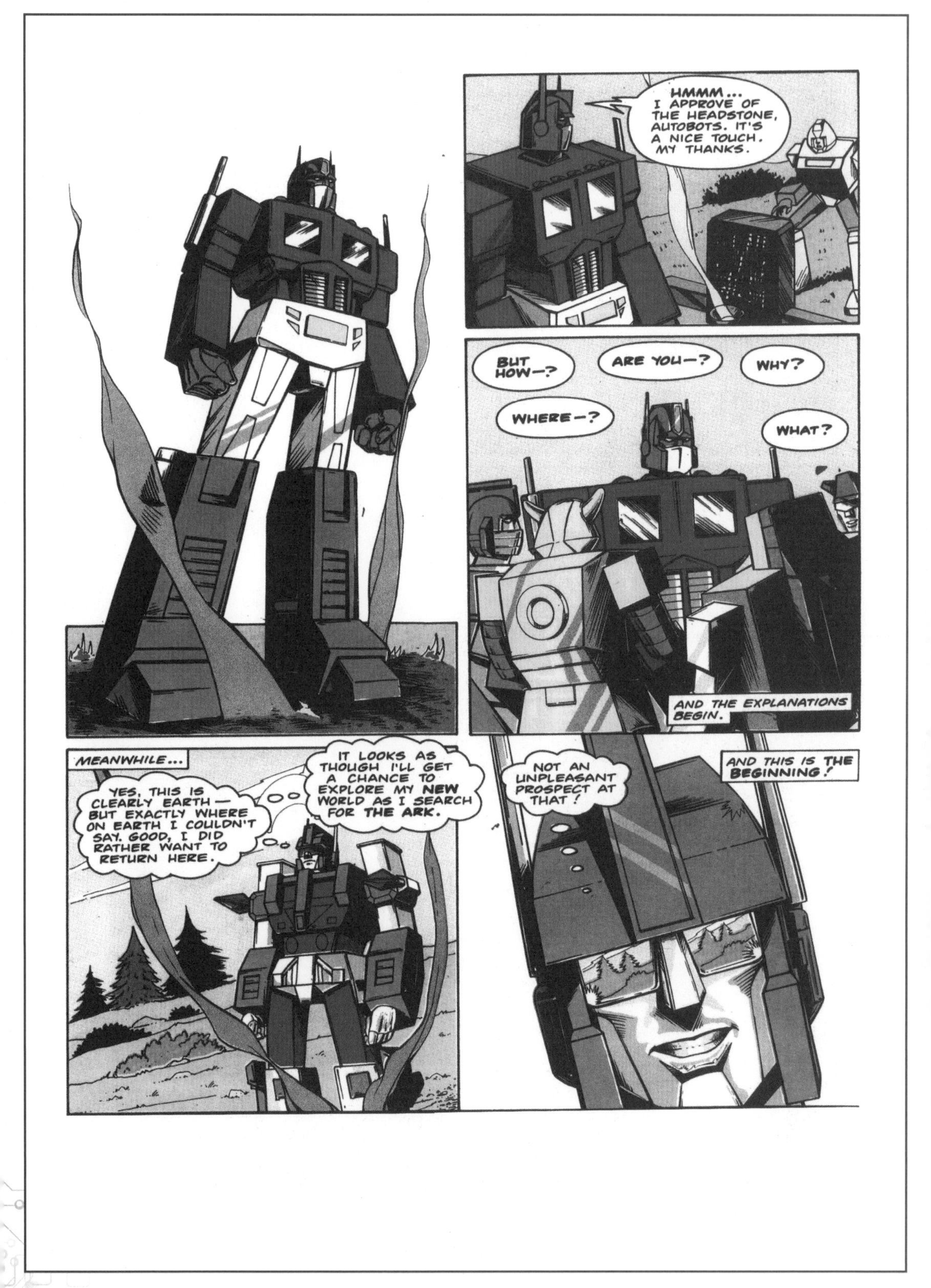
HMMM... I APPROVE OF THE HEADSTONE, AUTOBOTS. IT'S A NICE TOUCH. MY THANKS.
BUT HOW—?
ARE YOU—?
WHY?
WHERE—?
WHAT?
AND THE EXPLANATIONS BEGIN.
MEANWHILE...
YES, THIS IS CLEARLY EARTH— BUT EXACTLY WHERE ON EARTH I COULDN'T SAY. GOOD, I DID RATHER WANT TO RETURN HERE.
IT LOOKS AS THOUGH I'LL GET A CHANCE TO EXPLORE MY NEW WORLD AS I SEARCH FOR THE ARK.
NOT AN UNPLEASANT PROSPECT AT THAT!
AND THIS IS THE BEGINNING!

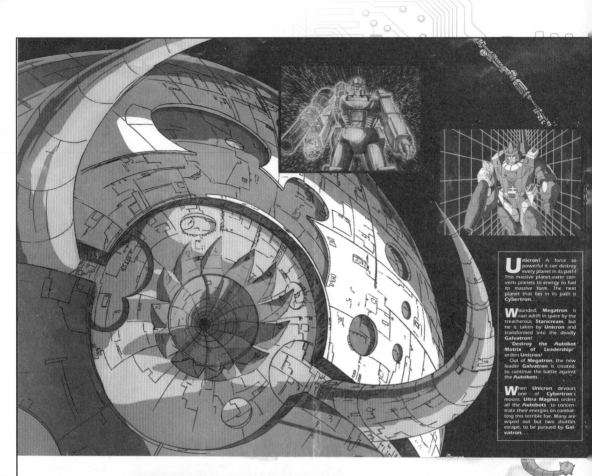

Unicron! A force so powerful it can destroy every planet in its path! This massive planet-eater converts planets to energy to fuel its massive form. The next planet that lies in its path is Cybertron...

Wounded, Megatron is cast adrift in space by the treacherous Starscream, but he is taken by Unicron and transformed into the deadly Galvatron!
'Destroy the Autobot Matrix of Leadership!' orders Unicron!
Out of Megatron, the new leader Galvatron is created, to continue the battle against the Autobots.

When Unicron devours one of Cybertron's moons, Ultra Magnus orders all the Autobots to concentrate their energies on combatting this terrible foe. Many are wiped out but two shuttles escape, to be pursued by Galvatron...

Hot Rod and Kup are brought down in their shuttle by the Quintessons and battle their terrible guardians, the Sharkticons. They are rescued by the Dinobots and Wheelie, who arrive in time to save them.
But Galvatron follows the second shuttle and after a quick and deadly attack, he takes possession of the Autobot Matrix! He returns to Unicron – but attempts to double-cross the giant planet and he and the Matrix are swallowed whole!
Next, Unicron turns to Cybertron...

The Matrix must be redeemed! But only the chosen one can do this. Which Autobot has been chosen?

The Sharkticons are no match for the Dinobots, who, led by Wheelie, put them to flight!

Unicron transforms into a terrifying foe!

Springer, Kup and Hot Rod, with Arcee keeping a protective eye on Daniel, carry on the Autobot fight...

You can read the full story of the movie comic strip in The Transformers: The Movie, available now (A Transformers Winter Special)

Transformers The Movie poster.

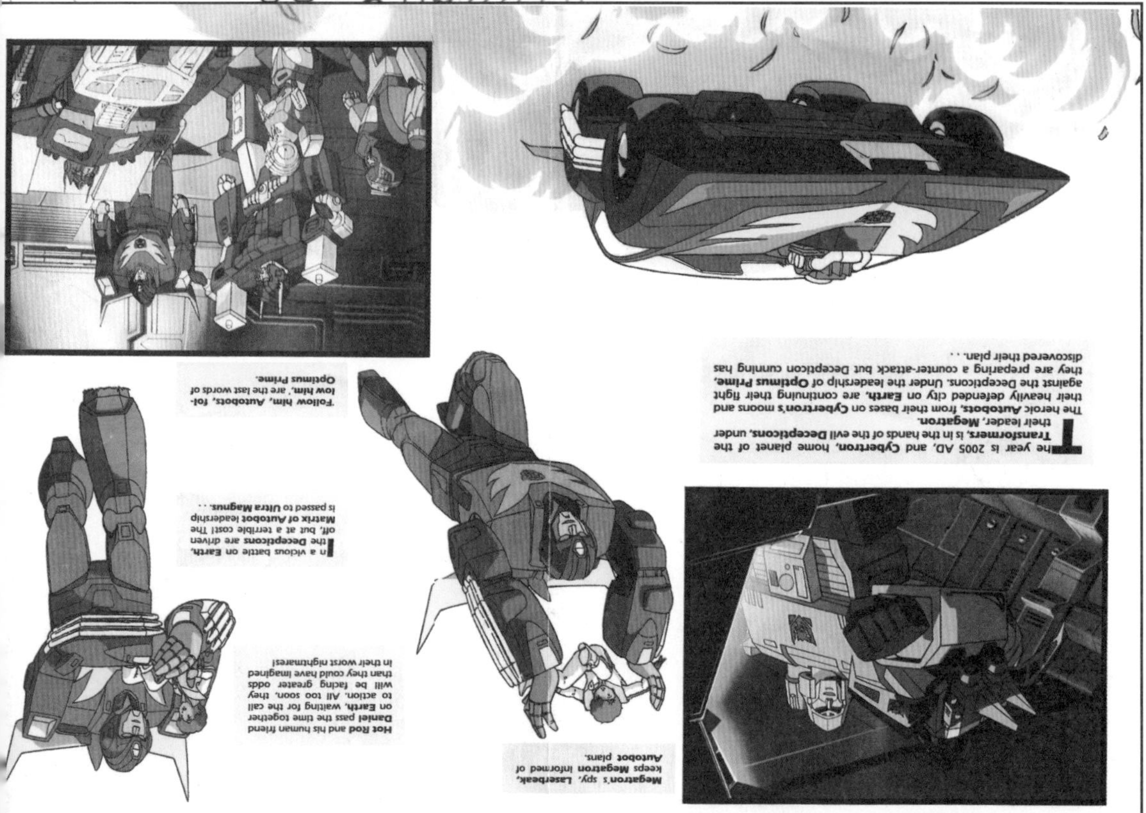

The year is 2005 AD, and Cybertron, home planet of the Transformers, is in the hands of the evil Decepticons, under their leader, Megatron.
The heroic Autobots, from their bases on Cybertron's moons and their heavily defended city on Earth, are continuing their fight against the Decepticons. Under the leadership of Optimus Prime, they are preparing a counter-attack but Decepticon cunning has discovered their plan. . .
Megatron's spy, Laserbeak, keeps Megatron informed of Autobot plans.
Hot Rod and his human friend Daniel pass the time together on Earth, waiting for the call to action. All too soon, they will be facing greater odds than they could have imagined in their worst nightmares!
In a vicious battle on Earth, the Decepticons are driven off, but at a terrible cost! The Matrix of Autobot leadership is passed to Ultra Magnus. . .
'Follow him, Autobots, follow him,' are the last words of Optimus Prime.

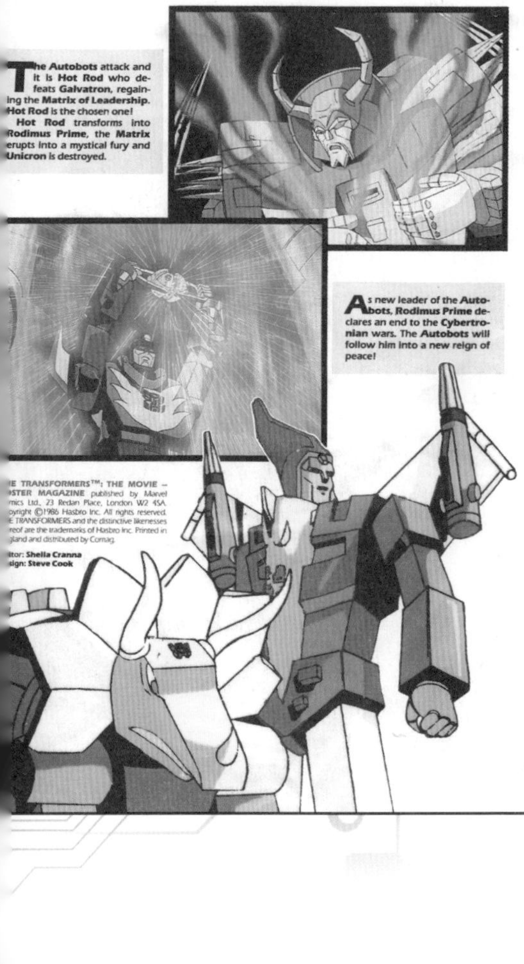

The Autobots attack and it is Hot Rod who defeats Galvatron, regaining the Matrix of Leadership. Hot Rod is the chosen one!
Hot Rod transforms into Rodimus Prime, the Matrix erupts into a mystical fury and Unicron is destroyed.
As new leader of the Autobots, Rodimus Prime declares an end to the Cybertronian wars. The Autobots will follow him into a new reign of peace!
E TRANSFORMERS™: THE MOVIE – STER MAGAZINE published by Marvel mics Ltd., 23 Redan Place, London W2 4SA. pyright ©1986 Hasbro Inc. All rights reserved. E TRANSFORMERS and the distinctive likenesses reof are the trademarks of Hasbro Inc. Printed in gland and distributed by Comag.
itor: Sheila Cranna
sign: Steve Cook

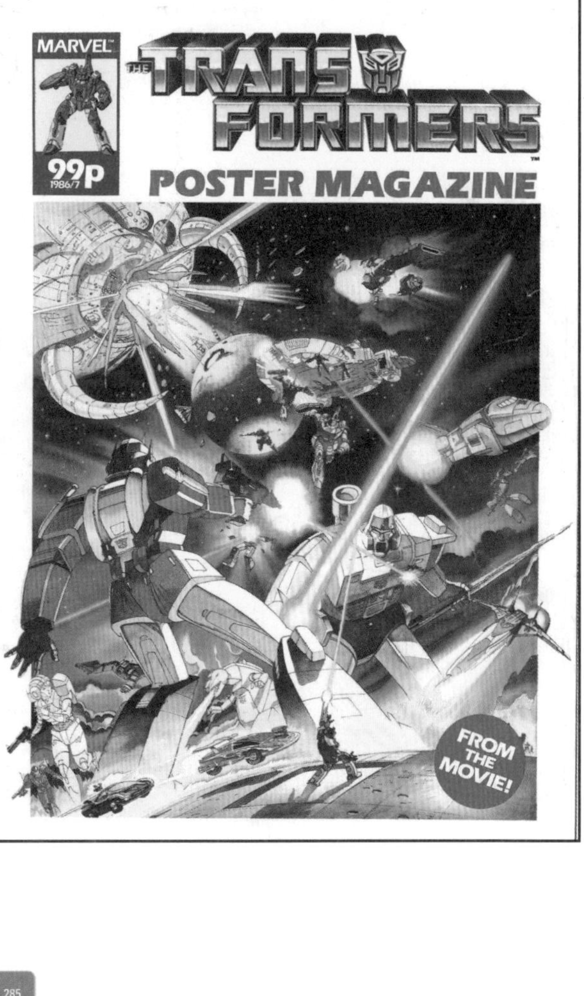

MARVEL
99p
1986/7
THE TRANSFORMERS
POSTER MAGAZINE
FROM THE MOVIE!

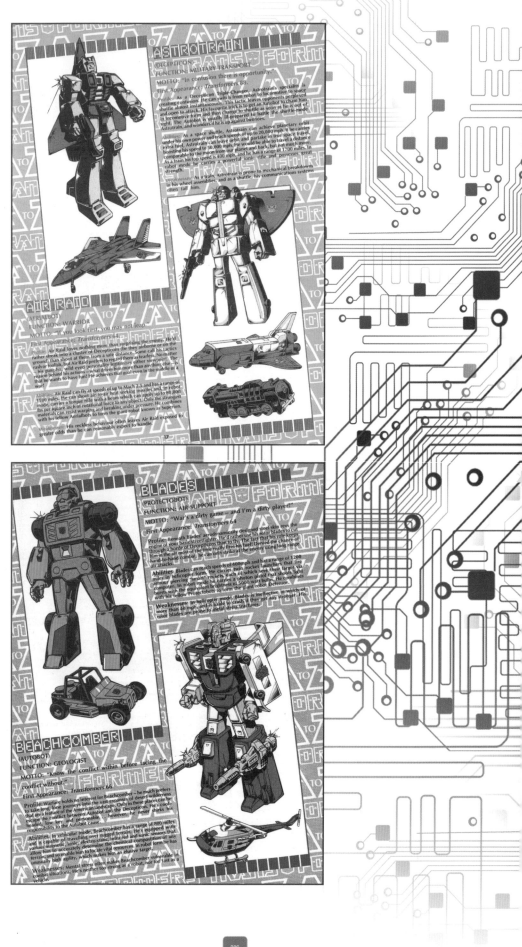

ASTROTRAIN

(DECEPTICON)
FUNCTION: MILITARY TRANSPORT
MOTTO: "In confusion there is opportunity."
First Appearance: *Transformers* 08.

Profile: As a Decepticon Triple-Changer, Astrotrain's speciality is creating confusion. He can switch from robot to locomotive to space shuttle almost instantaneously. This tactic leaves opponents perplexed and open to attack. His favourite trick is to get an Autobot to chase him in locomotive form and then change to shuttle as soon as he's out of sight. The Autobot is usually ill-prepared to battle the shuttle-mode Astrotrain, and wonders if he is up against two foes.

Abilities: As a space shuttle, Astrotrain can achieve planetary orbit under his own power and reach speeds of up to 20,000 mph. If he carries extra fuel, Astrotrain can leave orbit and partake in true space travel, boosting his speed to 50,000 mph. He would be able to travel a distance comparable to the moon from our planet and back, but not much more. As a train his top speed is 400 mph, and he has a range of 1700 miles. In robot mode he carries a powerful ionic rifle and possesses great strength.

Weaknesses: As a train, Astrotrain is prone to mechanical breakdown in his wheel assemblies, and as a shuttle, his communications system often fail him.

AIR RAID

(AERIALBOT)
FUNCTIONS: WARRIOR
MOTTO: "If you look first, you may not leap."
First Appearance: *Transformers* 64.

Profile: Air Raid loves nothing more than surprising the enemy. He'd rather streak into a cluster of Decepticons (be they airborne or on the ground) than shoot at them from a safe distance. Some call his tactics rash or foolish, but Air Raid prefers to regard them as fearless. No matter his gung-ho, wild eyed personality legitimises either viewpoint. The reason behind his actions – what drives him more than anything else – is that he wants to have fun! He achieves that goal even in the middle of a war!

Abilities: Air Raid can fly at speeds of up to Mach 2.5 and has a range of 1500 miles. He can shoot air-to-air heat seeking missiles and, in robot mode, carries a torque rifle with a beam which can apply up to 80,000 lbs per square inch of rotational force to any object. Only the strongest materials can resist warping and breaking under pressure. He combines with his fellow Aerialbots to form the giant robot known as Superion.

Weaknesses: His reckless behaviour often leaves Air Raid exposed to greater odds than he can reasonably expect to handle.

17

BLADES

(PROTECTOBOT)
FUNCTION: AIR SUPPORT
MOTTO: "War's a dirty game – and I'm a dirty player!"
First Appearance: *Transformers* 64.

Profile: Beneath Blades' aerodynamically designed steel skin revs the engine of your basic streetfighter. He'd rather use his rotor blades to cut through a horde of Decepticons than to fly. The fact that his role keeps him in the air most of the time really irks to fuel. Denied the chance of hand-to-hand combat, he can only strike at the enemy using long range air attacks.

Abilities: Blades can reach speeds of 400mph and has a range of 1200 miles in helicopter form. He carries twin rocket launchers that fire armour piercing "smart" rockets, each of which seek their target via a computer. In robot mode he carries a photon pistol that shoots light bursts with the equivalent brightness of 20 watt bulbs. He combines with his fellow Protectobots to form the giant robot Defensor.

Weaknesses: In helicopter mode, Blades is ineffective in winds of more than 40 mph, and is liable to crash if they get any stronger. His rotor blades are prone to metal stress fractures.

BEACHCOMBER

(AUTOBOT)
FUNCTION: GEOLOGIST
MOTTO: "Know the conflict within before facing the conflict without."
First Appearance: *Transformers* 66.

Profile: Warfare holds no interest for Beachcomber – he much prefers to take lone journeys into the vast expanses of desert wilderness that area feature of the American landscape. Only in these places can he escape the conflict between Autobot and the Decepticons. He's cool-headed, low key and personable, however he never shirks his responsibility to the Autobot cause.

Abilities: In vehicular mode, Beachcomber has a range of 800 miles and is capable of travelling over rugged terrain. He's equipped with various magnetic, ionic, electrostatic, infra red and sonic sensors that allow him to accurately determine the chemical composition of any terrain, and so enable him to locate vital resources. In robot form he has unusually high agility, which makes him an elusive target.

Weaknesses: Mental stress often makes Beachcomber vulnerable in combat situations. He's neither too strong as a robot, nor too fast as a vehicle.

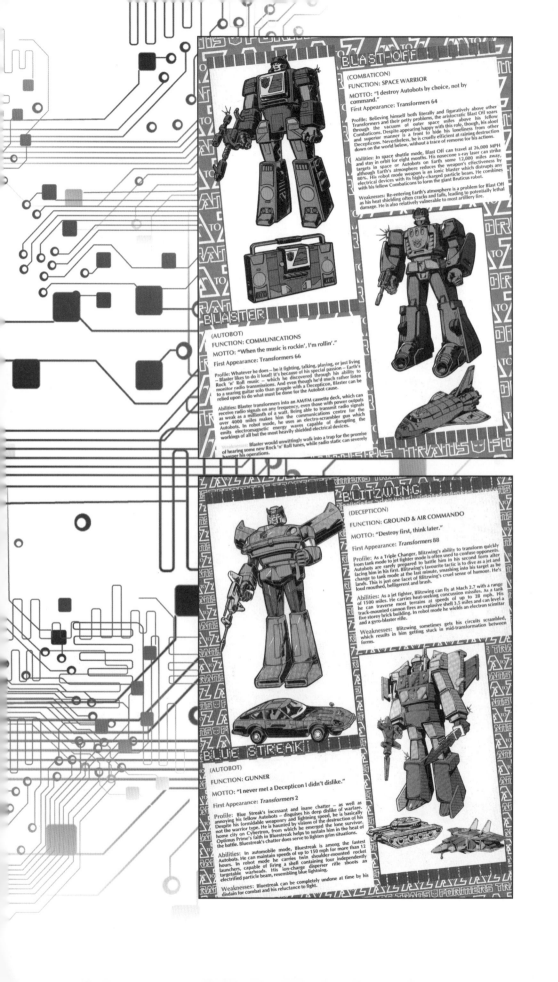

BLAST-OFF

(COMBATICON)

FUNCTION: SPACE WARRIOR

MOTTO: "I destroy Autobots by choice, not by command."

First Appearance: Transformers 64

Profile: Believing himself both literally and figuratively above other Transformers and their petty problems, the aristocratic Blast Off soars through the vacuum of outer space miles above his fellow Combaticons. Despite appearing happy with this role, though, his aloof and superior manner is a front to hide his loneliness from other Decepticons. Nevertheless, he is cruelly efficient at raining destruction down on the world below, without a trace of remorse for his actions.

Abilities: In space shuttle mode, Blast Off can travel at 26,000 MPH and stay in orbit for eight months. His nosecone x-ray laser can strike targets in space or Autobots on Earth some 12,000 miles away, although Earth's atmosphere reduces the weapon's effectiveness by 80%. His robot mode weapon is an ionic blaster which disrupts any electrical devices with its highly-charged particle beam. He combines with his fellow Combaticons to form the giant Bruticus robot.

Weaknesses: Re-entering Earth's atmosphere is a problem for Blast Off as his heat shielding often cracks and fails, leading to potentially lethal damage. He is also relatively vulnerable to most artillery fire.

BLASTER

(AUTOBOT)

FUNCTION: COMMUNICATIONS

MOTTO: "When the music is rockin', I'm rollin'."

First Appearance: Transformers 66

Profile: Whatever he does – be it fighting, talking, playing, or just living – Blaster likes to do it loud! It's because of his special passion – Earth's Rock 'n' Roll music – which he discovered through his ability to monitor radio transmissions. And even though he'd much rather listen to a searing guitar solo than grapple with a Decepticon, Blaster can be relied upon to do what must be done for the Autobot cause.

Abilities: Blaster transforms into an AM/FM cassette deck, which can receive radio signals on any frequency, even those with power outputs as weak as a millionth of a watt. Being able to transmit radio signals over 4000 miles makes him the communications centre for the Autobots. In robot mode, he uses an electro-scrambler gun which emits electromagnetic energy waves capable of disrupting the workings of all but the most heavily shielded electrical devices.

Weaknesses: Blaster would unwittingly walk into a trap for the promise of hearing some new Rock 'n' Roll tunes, while radio static can severely hamper his operations.

BLITZWING

(DECEPTICON)

FUNCTION: GROUND & AIR COMMANDO

MOTTO: "Destroy first, think later."

First Appearance: Transformers 88

Profile: As a Triple Changer, Blitzwing's ability to transform quickly from tank mode to jet fighter mode is often used to confuse opponents. Autobots are rarely prepared to battle him in his second form after facing him in his first. Blitzwing's favourite tactic is to dive as a jet and change to tank mode at the last minute, smashing into his target as he lands. This is just one facet of Blitzwing's cruel sense of humour. He's loud mouthed, belligerent and brash.

Abilities: As a jet fighter, Blitzwing can fly at Mach 2.7 with a range of 1500 miles. He carries heat-seeking concussion missiles. As a tank he can traverse most terrains at speeds of up to 28 mph. His track-mounted cannon fires an explosive shell 3.5 miles and can level a five storey brick building. In robot mode he wields an electron scimitar and a gyro-blaster rifle.

Weaknesses: Blitzwing sometimes gets his circuits scrambled, which results in him getting stuck in mid-transformation between forms.

BLUE STREAK

(AUTOBOT)

FUNCTION: GUNNER

MOTTO: "I never met a Decepticon I didn't dislike."

First Appearance: Transformers 2

Profile: Blue Streak's incessant and inane chatter – as well as annoying his fellow Autobots – disguises his deep dislike of warfare. Despite his formidable weaponry and lightning speed, he is basically not the warrior type. He is haunted by visions of the destruction of his home city on Cybertron, from which he emerged the lone survivor. Optimus Prime's faith in Bluestreak helps to sustain him in the heat of battle. Bluestreak's chatter does serve to lighten grim situations.

Abilities: In automobile mode, Bluestreak is among the fastest Autobots. He can maintain speeds of up to 150 mph for more than 12 hours. In robot mode he carries twin shoulder-mounted rocket launchers, capable of firing a shell containing four independently targetable warheads. His ion-charge disperser rifle shoots an electrified particle beam, resembling blue lightning.

Weaknesses: Bluestreak can be completely undone at time by his disdain for combat and his reluctance to fight.

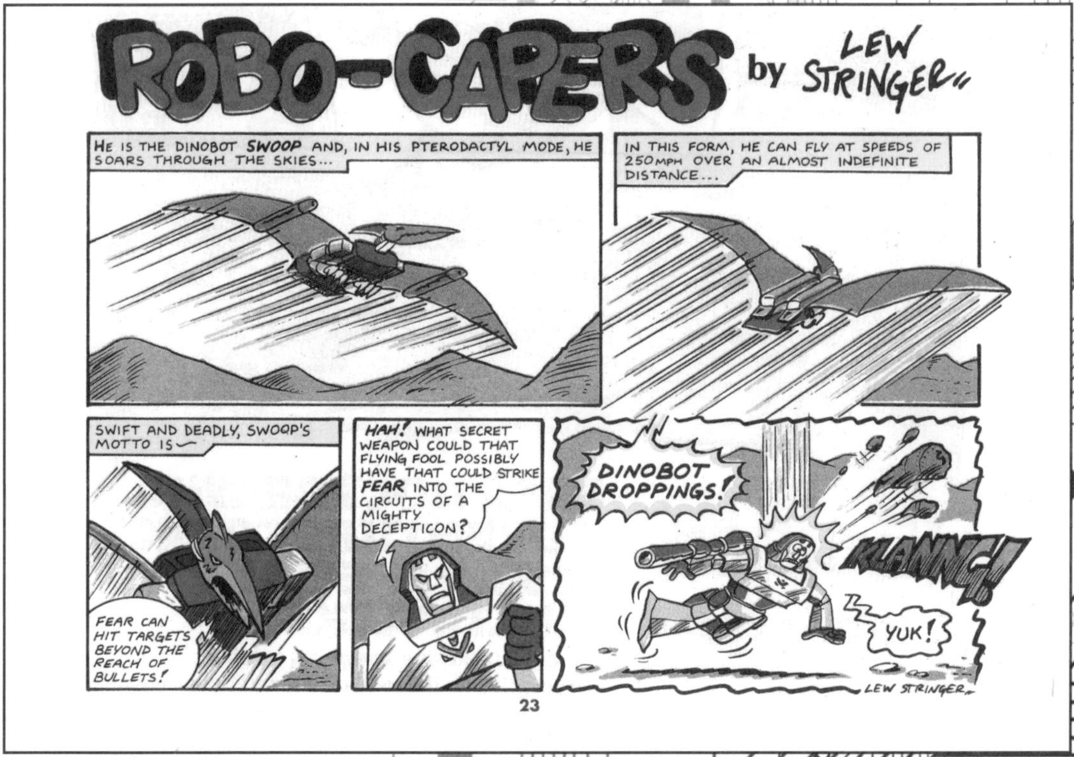

ROBO-CAPERS by LEW STRINGER
HE IS THE DINOBOT SWOOP AND, IN HIS PTERODACTYL MODE, HE SOARS THROUGH THE SKIES...
IN THIS FORM, HE CAN FLY AT SPEEDS OF 250MPH OVER AN ALMOST INDEFINITE DISTANCE...
SWIFT AND DEADLY, SWOOP'S MOTTO IS—
FEAR CAN HIT TARGETS BEYOND THE REACH OF BULLETS!
HAH! WHAT SECRET WEAPON COULD THAT FLYING FOOL POSSIBLY HAVE THAT COULD STRIKE FEAR INTO THE CIRCUITS OF A MIGHTY DECEPTICON?
DINOBOT DROPPINGS!
KLANNG!
YUK!
LEW STRINGER
23

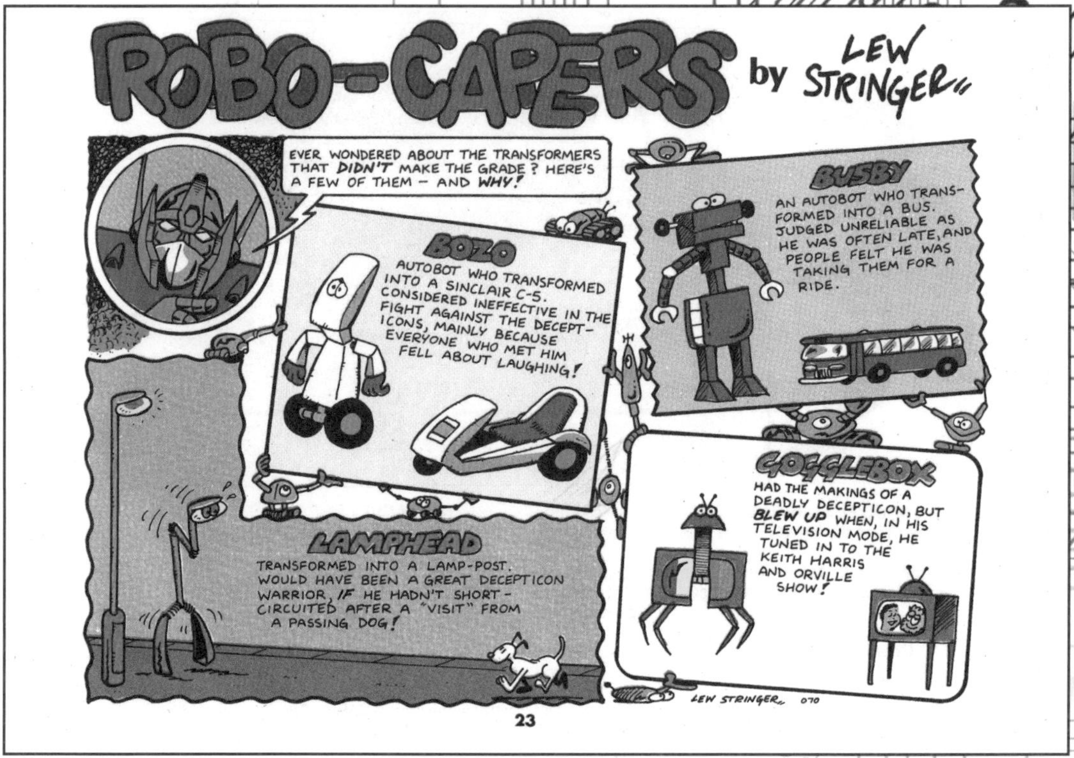

ROBO-CAPERS by LEW STRINGER
EVER WONDERED ABOUT THE TRANSFORMERS THAT DIDN'T MAKE THE GRADE? HERE'S A FEW OF THEM – AND WHY!
BOZO
AUTOBOT WHO TRANSFORMED INTO A SINCLAIR C-5. CONSIDERED INEFFECTIVE IN THE FIGHT AGAINST THE DECEPTICONS, MAINLY BECAUSE EVERYONE WHO MET HIM FELL ABOUT LAUGHING!
BUSBY
AN AUTOBOT WHO TRANSFORMED INTO A BUS. JUDGED UNRELIABLE AS HE WAS OFTEN LATE, AND PEOPLE FELT HE WAS TAKING THEM FOR A RIDE.
LAMPHEAD
TRANSFORMED INTO A LAMP-POST. WOULD HAVE BEEN A GREAT DECEPTICON WARRIOR, IF HE HADN'T SHORT-CIRCUITED AFTER A "VISIT" FROM A PASSING DOG!
GOGGLEBOX
HAD THE MAKINGS OF A DEADLY DECEPTICON, BUT BLEW UP WHEN, IN HIS TELEVISION MODE, HE TUNED IN TO THE KEITH HARRIS AND ORVILLE SHOW!
LEW STRINGER 070
23

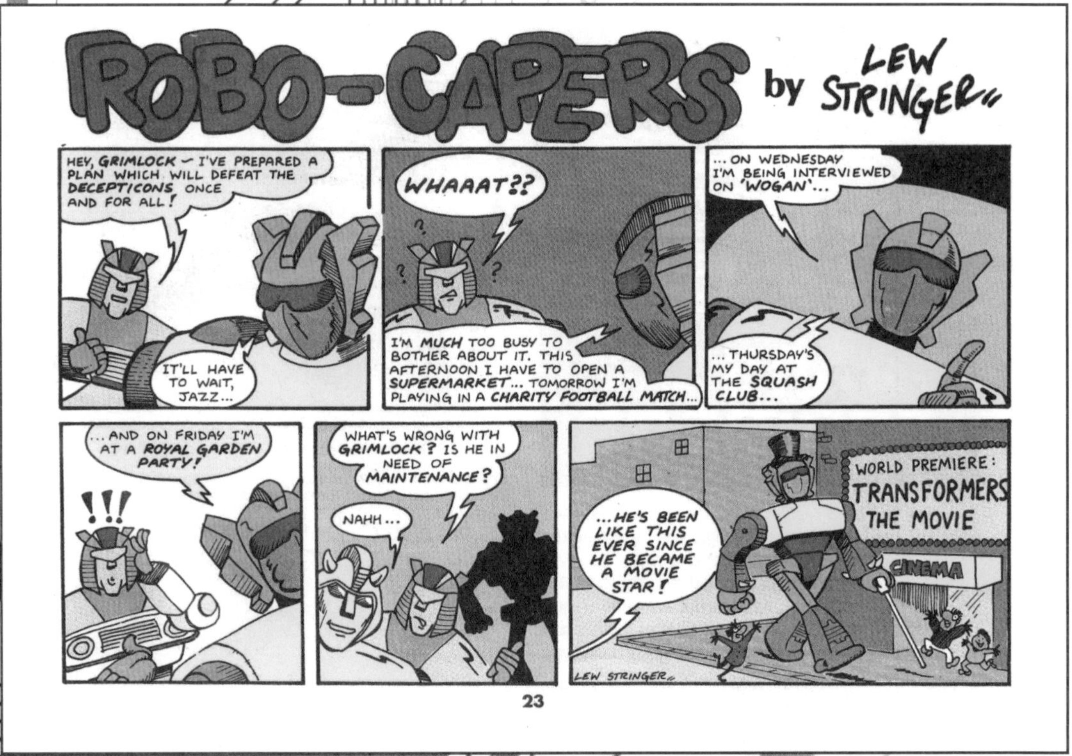
ROBO-CAPERS by LEW STRINGER
HEY, GRIMLOCK – I'VE PREPARED A PLAN WHICH WILL DEFEAT THE DECEPTICONS ONCE AND FOR ALL!
IT'LL HAVE TO WAIT, JAZZ...
WHAAAT??
I'M MUCH TOO BUSY TO BOTHER ABOUT IT. THIS AFTERNOON I HAVE TO OPEN A SUPERMARKET... TOMORROW I'M PLAYING IN A CHARITY FOOTBALL MATCH...
...ON WEDNESDAY I'M BEING INTERVIEWED ON 'WOGAN'...
...THURSDAY'S MY DAY AT THE SQUASH CLUB...
...AND ON FRIDAY I'M AT A ROYAL GARDEN PARTY!
!!!
WHAT'S WRONG WITH GRIMLOCK? IS HE IN NEED OF MAINTENANCE?
NAHH...
...HE'S BEEN LIKE THIS EVER SINCE HE BECAME A MOVIE STAR!
WORLD PREMIERE: TRANSFORMERS THE MOVIE
CINEMA
LEW STRINGER
23

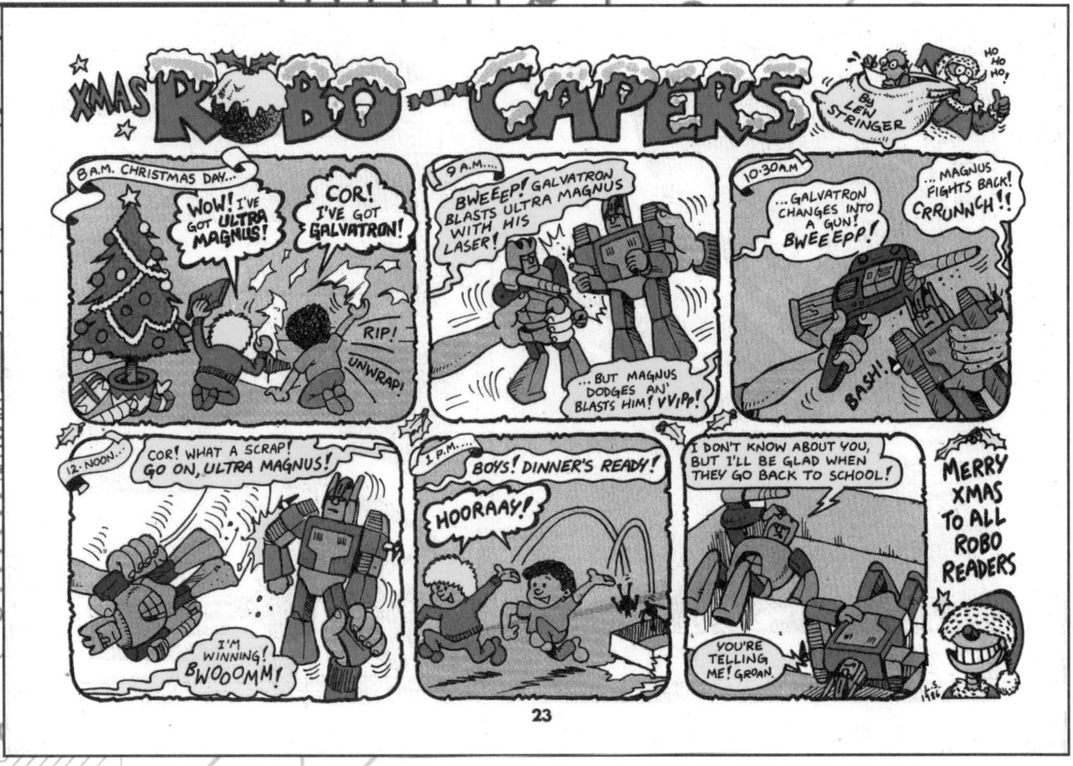
XMAS ROBO-CAPERS
BY LEW STRINGER
HO HO HO!
8 A.M. CHRISTMAS DAY...
WOW! I'VE GOT ULTRA MAGNUS!
COR! I'VE GOT GALVATRON!
RIP!
UNWRAP!
9 A.M....
BWEEEP! GALVATRON BLASTS ULTRA MAGNUS WITH HIS LASER!
...BUT MAGNUS DODGES AN' BLASTS HIM! VVIPP!
10.30 A.M.
...GALVATRON CHANGES INTO A GUN! BWEEEPP!
...MAGNUS FIGHTS BACK! CRRUNNCH!!
BASH!
12 NOON...
COR! WHAT A SCRAP! GO ON, ULTRA MAGNUS!
I'M WINNING! BWOOOMM!
1 P.M....
BOYS! DINNER'S READY!
HOORAAY!
I DON'T KNOW ABOUT YOU, BUT I'LL BE GLAD WHEN THEY GO BACK TO SCHOOL!
YOU'RE TELLING ME! GROAN.
MERRY XMAS TO ALL ROBO READERS
L.S. 1986
23

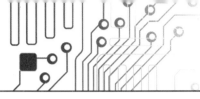

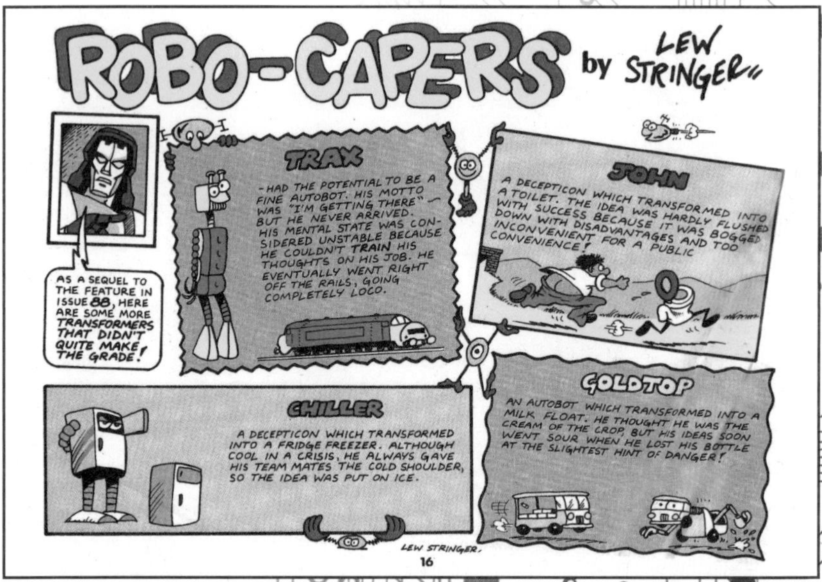
ROBO-CAPERS by LEW STRINGER
AS A SEQUEL TO THE FEATURE IN ISSUE 88, HERE ARE SOME MORE TRANSFORMERS THAT DIDN'T QUITE MAKE THE GRADE!
TRAX
- HAD THE POTENTIAL TO BE A FINE AUTOBOT. HIS MOTTO WAS "I'M GETTING THERE" — BUT HE NEVER ARRIVED. HIS MENTAL STATE WAS CONSIDERED UNSTABLE BECAUSE HE COULDN'T TRAIN HIS THOUGHTS ON HIS JOB. HE EVENTUALLY WENT RIGHT OFF THE RAILS, GOING COMPLETELY LOCO.
J'OHN
A DECEPTICON WHICH TRANSFORMED INTO A TOILET. THE IDEA WAS HARDLY FLUSHED WITH SUCCESS BECAUSE IT WAS BOGGED DOWN WITH DISADVANTAGES AND TOO INCONVENIENT FOR A PUBLIC CONVENIENCE!
CHILLER
A DECEPTICON WHICH TRANSFORMED INTO A FRIDGE FREEZER. ALTHOUGH COOL IN A CRISIS, HE ALWAYS GAVE HIS TEAM MATES THE COLD SHOULDER, SO THE IDEA WAS PUT ON ICE.
GOLDTOP
AN AUTOBOT WHICH TRANSFORMED INTO A MILK FLOAT. HE THOUGHT HE WAS THE CREAM OF THE CROP, BUT HIS IDEAS SOON WENT SOUR WHEN HE LOST HIS BOTTLE AT THE SLIGHTEST HINT OF DANGER!
LEW STRINGER.
16

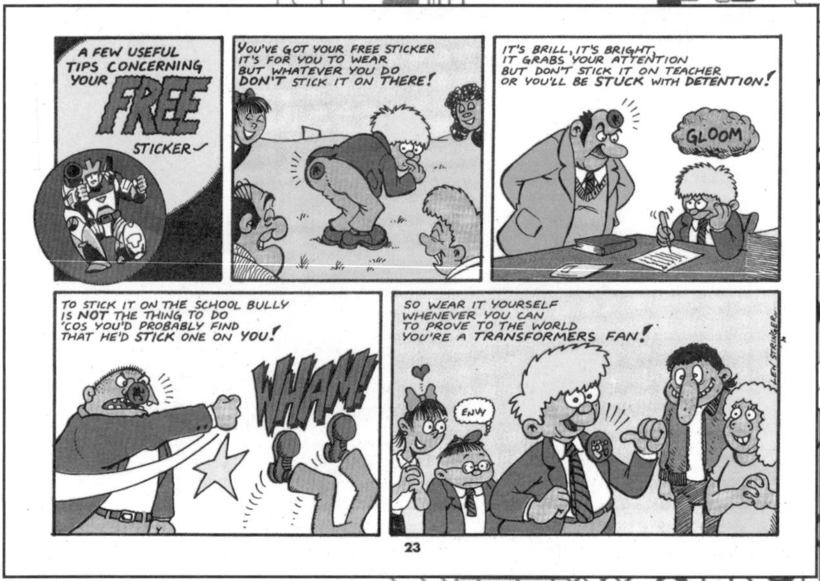
A FEW USEFUL TIPS CONCERNING YOUR FREE STICKER—
YOU'VE GOT YOUR FREE STICKER IT'S FOR YOU TO WEAR BUT WHATEVER YOU DO DON'T STICK IT ON THERE!
IT'S BRILL, IT'S BRIGHT, IT GRABS YOUR ATTENTION BUT DON'T STICK IT ON TEACHER OR YOU'LL BE STUCK WITH DETENTION!
GLOOM
TO STICK IT ON THE SCHOOL BULLY IS NOT THE THING TO DO 'COS YOU'D PROBABLY FIND THAT HE'D STICK ONE ON YOU!
WHAM!
SO WEAR IT YOURSELF WHENEVER YOU CAN TO PROVE TO THE WORLD YOU'RE A TRANSFORMERS FAN!
ENVY
LEW STRINGER
23

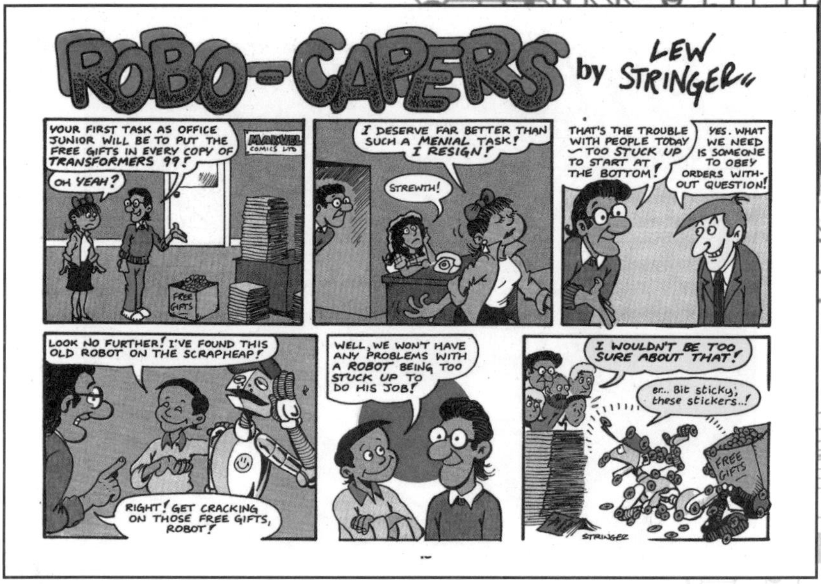
ROBO-CAPERS by LEW STRINGER
YOUR FIRST TASK AS OFFICE JUNIOR WILL BE TO PUT THE FREE GIFTS IN EVERY COPY OF TRANSFORMERS 99!
OH YEAH?
MARVEL COMICS LTD
FREE GIFTS
I DESERVE FAR BETTER THAN SUCH A MENIAL TASK! I RESIGN!
STREWTH!
THAT'S THE TROUBLE WITH PEOPLE TODAY — TOO STUCK UP TO START AT THE BOTTOM!
YES. WHAT WE NEED IS SOMEONE TO OBEY ORDERS WITHOUT QUESTION!
LOOK NO FURTHER! I'VE FOUND THIS OLD ROBOT ON THE SCRAPHEAP!
RIGHT! GET CRACKING ON THOSE FREE GIFTS, ROBOT!
WELL, WE WON'T HAVE ANY PROBLEMS WITH A ROBOT BEING TOO STUCK UP TO DO HIS JOB!
I WOULDN'T BE TOO SURE ABOUT THAT!
er.. Bit sticky, these stickers..!
FREE GIFTS
STRINGER

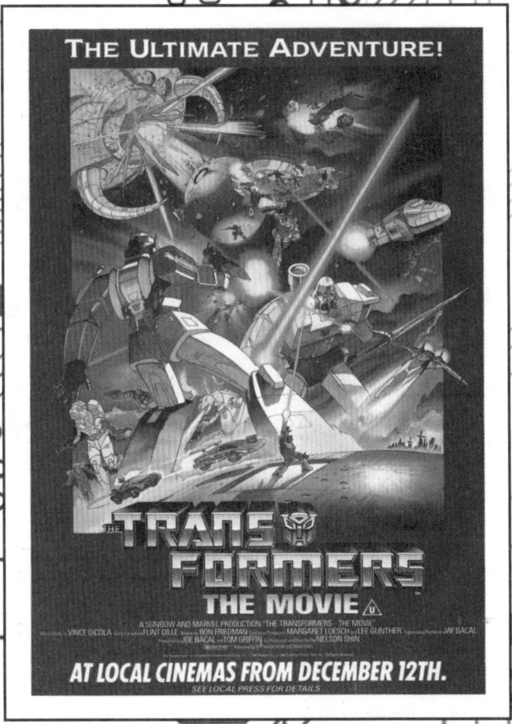
THE ULTIMATE ADVENTURE!
THE TRANSFORMERS
THE MOVIE
A SUNBOW AND MARVEL PRODUCTION "THE TRANSFORMERS – THE MOVIE"
VINCE DiCOLA FLINT DILLE RON FRIEDMAN MARGARET LOESCH LEE GUNTHER JAY BACAL
JOE BACAL TOM GRIFFIN NELSON SHIN
AT LOCAL CINEMAS FROM DECEMBER 12TH.
SEE LOCAL PRESS FOR DETAILS

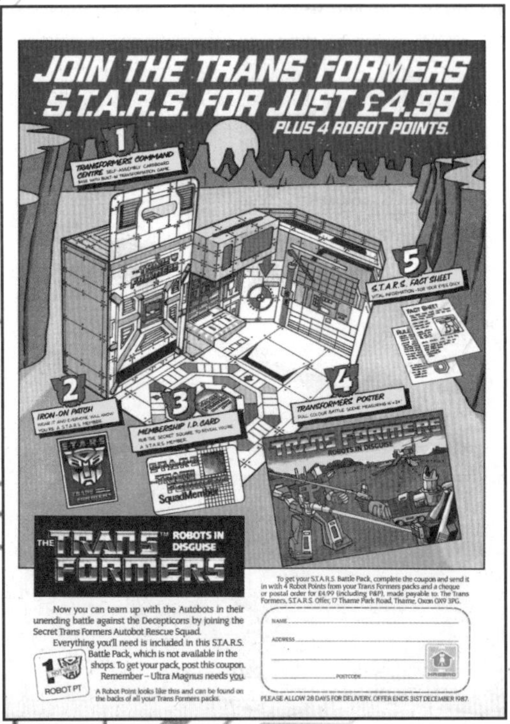
JOIN THE TRANS FORMERS
S.T.A.R.S. FOR JUST £4.99
PLUS 4 ROBOT POINTS.
1
TRANSFORMERS' COMMAND CENTRE
2
IRON-ON PATCH
3
MEMBERSHIP I.D. CARD
SquadMember
4
TRANSFORMERS' POSTER
5
S.T.A.R.S. FACT SHEET
TRANS FORMERS
ROBOTS IN DISGUISE
THE TRANS FORMERS ROBOTS IN DISGUISE
Now you can team up with the Autobots in their unending battle against the Decepticons by joining the Secret Trans Formers Autobot Rescue Squad.
Everything you'll need is included in this S.T.A.R.S. Battle Pack, which is not available in the shops. To get your pack, post this coupon. Remember – Ultra Magnus needs you.
1 ROBOT PT
A Robot Point looks like this and can be found on the backs of all your Trans Formers packs.
To get your S.T.A.R.S. Battle Pack, complete the coupon and send it in with 4 Robot Points from your Trans Formers packs and a cheque or postal order for £4.99 (including P&P), made payable to: The Trans Formers, S.T.A.R.S. Offer, 17 Thame Park Road, Thame, Oxon OX9 3PG.
NAME
ADDRESS
POSTCODE
PLEASE ALLOW 28 DAYS FOR DELIVERY. OFFER ENDS 31ST DECEMBER 1987.

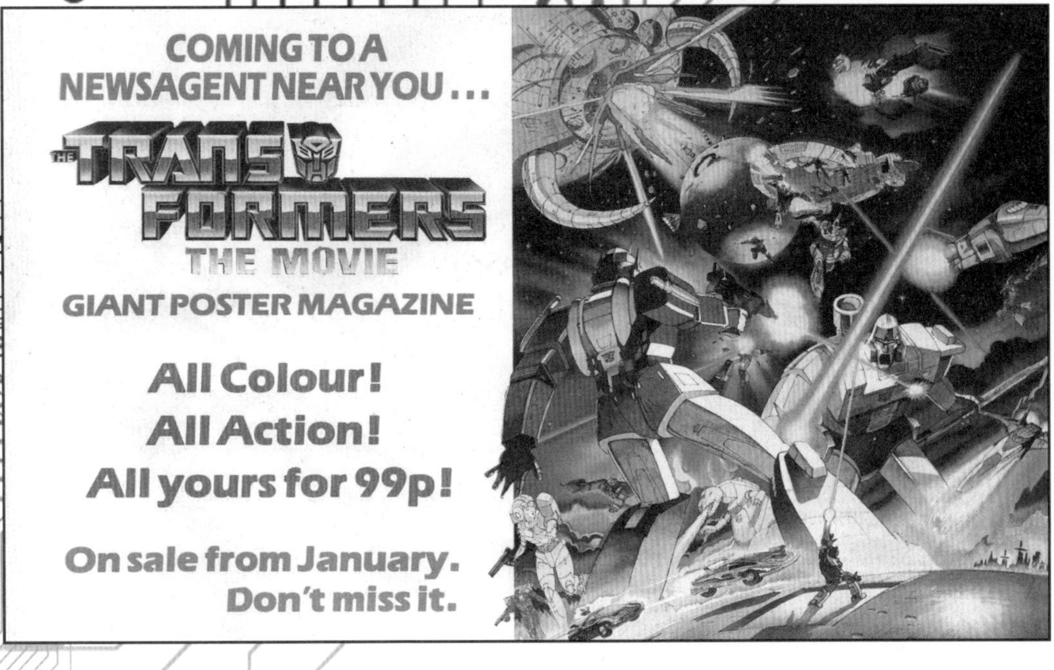
COMING TO A NEWSAGENT NEAR YOU . . .
THE TRANSFORMERS
THE MOVIE
GIANT POSTER MAGAZINE
All Colour!
All Action!
All yours for 99p!
On sale from January.
Don't miss it.

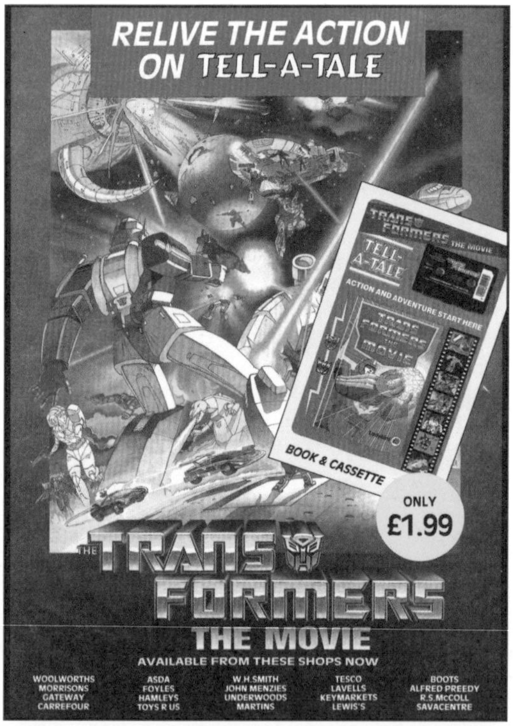
RELIVE THE ACTION
ON TELL-A-TALE
TRANSFORMERS THE MOVIE
TELL-A-TALE
ACTION AND ADVENTURE START HERE
BOOK & CASSETTE
ONLY
£1.99
THE TRANSFORMERS
THE MOVIE
AVAILABLE FROM THESE SHOPS NOW
WOOLWORTHS
MORRISONS
GATEWAY
CARREFOUR
ASDA
FOYLES
HAMLEYS
TOYS R US
W.H.SMITH
JOHN MENZIES
UNDERWOODS
MARTINS
TESCO
LAVELLS
KEYMARKETS
LEWIS'S
BOOTS
ALFRED PREEDY
R.S.McCOLL
SAVACENTRE

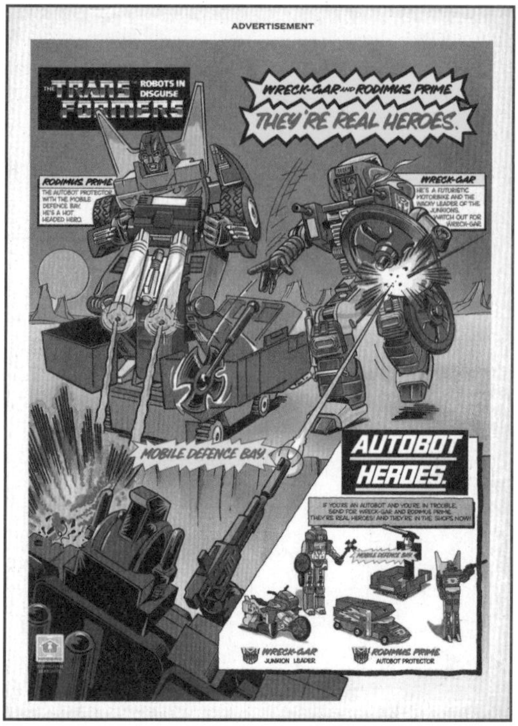
ADVERTISEMENT
THE TRANSFORMERS ROBOTS IN DISGUISE
WRECK-GAR AND RODIMUS PRIME
THEY'RE REAL HEROES.
RODIMUS PRIME
THE AUTOBOT PROTECTOR WITH THE MOBILE DEFENCE BAY. HE'S A HOT HEADED HERO.
WRECK-GAR
HE'S A FUTURISTIC MOTORBIKE AND THE WACKY LEADER OF THE JUNKIONS. WATCH OUT FOR WRECK-GAR.
MOBILE DEFENCE BAY.
AUTOBOT HEROES.
IF YOU'RE AN AUTOBOT AND YOU'RE IN TROUBLE, SEND FOR WRECK-GAR AND RODIMUS PRIME. THEY'RE REAL HEROES! AND THEY'RE IN THE SHOPS NOW!
MOBILE DEFENCE BAY
WRECK-GAR
JUNKION LEADER
RODIMUS PRIME
AUTOBOT PROTECTOR

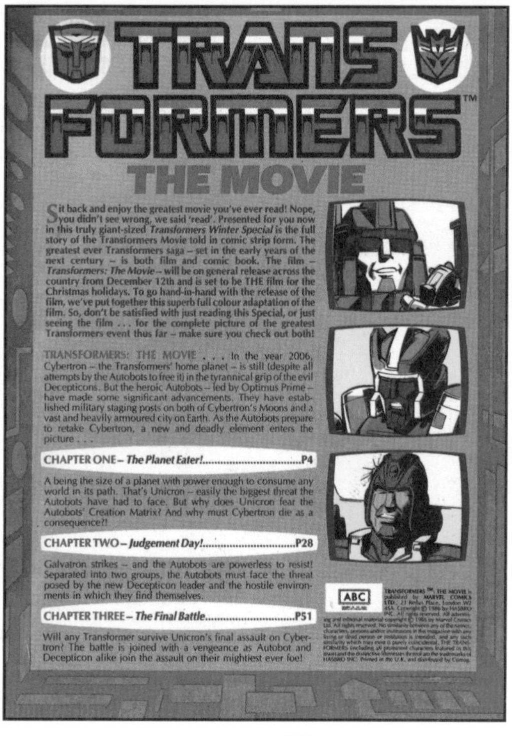

TRANSFORMERS™

THE MOVIE

Sit back and enjoy the greatest movie you've ever read! Nope, you didn't see wrong, we said 'read'. Presented for you now in this truly giant-sized *Transformers Winter Special* is the full story of the Transformers Movie told in comic strip form. The greatest ever Transformers saga – set in the early years of the next century – is both film and comic book. The film – *Transformers: The Movie* – will be on general release across the country from December 12th and is set to be THE film for the Christmas holidays. To go hand-in-hand with the release of the film, we've put together this superb full colour adaptation of the film. So, don't be satisfied with just reading this Special, or just seeing the film . . . for the complete picture of the greatest Transformers event thus far – make sure you check out both!

TRANSFORMERS: THE MOVIE . . . In the year 2006, Cybertron – the Transformers' home planet – is still (despite all attempts by the Autobots to free it) in the tyrannical grip of the evil Decepticons. But the heroic Autobots – led by Optimus Prime – have made some significant advancements. They have established military staging posts on both of Cybertron's Moons and a vast and heavily armoured city on Earth. As the Autobots prepare to retake Cybertron, a new and deadly element enters the picture . . .

CHAPTER ONE – *The Planet Eater!*.................................P4

A being the size of a planet with power enough to consume any world in its path. That's Unicron – easily the biggest threat the Autobots have had to face. But why does Unicron fear the Autobots' Creation Matrix? And why must Cybertron die as a consequence?!

CHAPTER TWO – *Judgement Day!*.................................P28

Galvatron strikes – and the Autobots are powerless to resist! Separated into two groups, the Autobots must face the threat posed by the new Decepticon leader and the hostile environments in which they find themselves.

CHAPTER THREE – *The Final Battle*.................................P51

Will any Transformer survive Unicron's final assault on Cybertron? The battle is joined with a vengeance as Autobot and Decepticon alike join the assault on their mightiest ever foe!

ABC

TRANSFORMERS™: THE MOVIE is published by MARVEL COMICS LTD., 23 Redan Place, London W2 4SA. Copyright © 1986 by HASBRO INC. All rights reserved. All advertising and editorial material copyright © 1986 by Marvel Comics Ltd. All rights reserved. No similarity between any of the names, characters, persons and/or institutions in the magazine with any living or dead person or institution is intended, and any such similarity which may exist is purely coincidental. THE TRANSFORMERS (including all prominent characters featured in this issue and the distinctive likenesses thereof) are the trademarks of HASBRO INC. Printed in the U.K. and distributed by Comag.

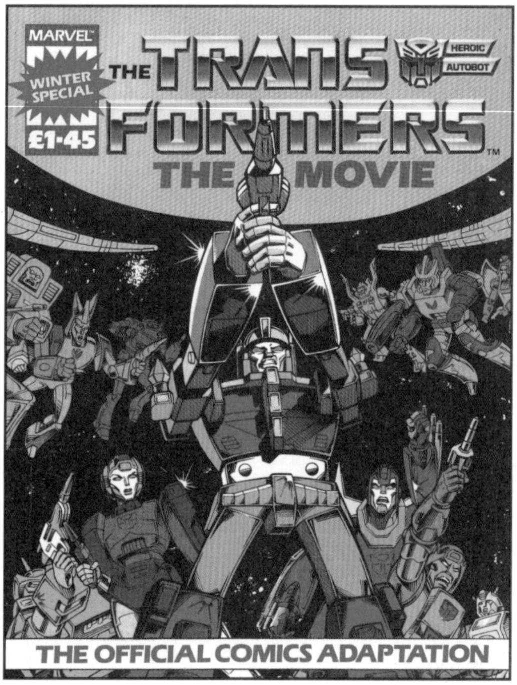
MARVEL™
WINTER SPECIAL
£1·45
THE TRANSFORMERS™
HEROIC AUTOBOT
THE MOVIE
THE OFFICIAL COMICS ADAPTATION